Fifth edition

Teaching Reading in the 21st Century

Motivating All Learners

Michael F. Graves
University of Minnesota

Connie Juel
Stanford University

Bonnie B. Graves
Children's Author

Peter Dewitz
Educational Consultant

Boston   Columbus   Indianapolis   New York   San Francisco   Upper Saddle River
Amsterdam   Cape Town   Dubai   London   Madrid   Milan   Munich   Paris   Montreal   Toronto
Delhi   Mexico City   Sao Paulo   Sydney   Hong Kong   Seoul   Singapore   Taipei   Tokyo

Vice President, Editor-in-Chief: Aurora Martínez Ramos
Editorial Assistant: Amy Foley
Development Editor: Christina Robb
Executive Marketing Manager: Krista Clark
Production Editor: Janet Domingo
Editorial Production Service: Omegatype Typography, Inc.
Manufacturing Buyer: Megan Cochran
Electronic Composition: Omegatype Typography, Inc.
Photo Researcher: Annie Pickert
Cover Administrator: Elena Sidorova

Credits and acknowledgments borrowed from other sources and reproduced, with permission, in this textbook appear on appropriate page within text.

Library of Congress Cataloging-in-Publication Data

Teaching reading in the 21st century : motivating all learners.—5th ed. / Michael F. Graves . . . [et al.].
    p. cm.
  Rev. ed. of: Teaching reading in the 21st century / Michael F. Graves, Connie Juel, Bonnie B. Graves. 4th ed.
  Includes bibliographical references.
  ISBN-13: 978-0-13-209225-8 (hardcover)
  ISBN-10: 0-13-209225-5 (hardcover)
  1. Reading (Elementary) I. Graves, Michael F. II. Graves, Michael F. Teaching reading in the 21st century.
  LB1573.G656 2011
  372.4—dc22

                                                      2010026474

10 9 8 7 6 5   EBM   14 13

www.pearsonhighered.com   ISBN 10: 0-13-209225-5
                                   ISBN 13: 978-0-13-209225-8

As was the case with past editions, this edition is dedicated to Susan Jones, Mike's sister, who in her 35 years of teaching led well over a thousand second-graders toward the high level of literacy they needed to succeed in the 21st century.

It is also dedicated to the more than 3 million other elementary and middle-school teachers who each day nurture over 50 million students toward this same goal.

About the Authors

In writing and revising this book, each of us brought to the task his or her experiences and expertise, and we would like to briefly introduce ourselves.

Michael F. Graves is a professor emeritus of literacy education at the University of Minnesota and a member of the Reading Hall of Fame. Mike taught in the upper grades, and his research and writing focus on vocabulary learning and instruction and comprehension instruction. His current major research effort is an IES-funded research and development project on teaching word-learning strategies.

Connie Juel is a professor of education at Stanford University. Her research centers on literacy acquisition, especially as it is affected by school instruction. She is noted for both her longitudinal research on reading development (often following children across multiple school years) and her work on interventions to help struggling readers. She was awarded the National Reading Conference's 2002 Oscar Causey Award for outstanding contributions to reading research and was elected to the Reading Hall of Fame by the International Reading Association in 2001.

Added to our own experiences are those of the authors of Chapter 4 and Appendix A—Robert Calfee, professor emeritus at Stanford University and a member of the IRA Reading Hall of Fame, and Kathleen Wilson, assistant professor at the University of Nebraska. We also thank Kathleen Clark, assistant professor at Marquette University, for her contributions to Chapters 4 and 7.

Bonnie B. Graves is a full-time education writer and the author of 15 books for children. Bonnie taught in third and fourth grades, and her major interest is making literature enticing and accessible to beginning and middle-grade learners. In addition to writing, Bonnie currently spends time working with children, teachers, and other educators on children's writing.

Peter Dewitz is an educational consultant and researcher who spends most of his time working with teachers and children in public schools. Peter has taught at the University of Toledo and the University of Virginia. He taught in the upper elementary grades and his major research interests are educational materials—specifically the efficacy of basal reading programs—and the development and instruction of reading comprehension.

Together, we have done everything possible to make *Teaching Reading in the 21st Century*, Fifth Edition, the very best book we could create, one that is truly comprehensive and balanced and that addresses the needs of all students, including children of color, students from low-income families, those with disabilities, and those of limited English proficiency.

Brief Contents

Contents

2 Reading Instruction   24

3 Motivation and Engagement 48

4 Classroom Assessment 76

by Kathleen M. Wilson and Robert C. Calfee with contributions by Kathleen Clark

7 Word Recognition   184

with contributions by Kathleen Clark

8 Fluency   222

9 Vocabulary Development   252

10 Scaffolding Students' Comprehension of Text   278

11 **Teaching Comprehension Strategies** **324**

12 Encouraging Independent Reading and Reader Response   350

13 Writing and Reading   372

14 Reading Instruction for English Language Learners   406

Features

In the Classroom

All In the Classroom features reflect what happens when various reading strategies are used in today's classrooms. Those marked with an asterisk (*) on this list provide step-by-step instructional routines that may be transferred directly into their classrooms by new teachers.

Differentiating Instruction for English Language Learners

The Reading Corner

Motivating Struggling Readers

Classroom Portrait

Strengths and Challenges of Diversity

Motivating Children with Technology

Preface

Like its predecessors, *Teaching Reading in the 21st Century*, Fifth Edition, has one goal: to provide you with the knowledge and skills necessary to carry out the most challenging and rewarding task—teaching young children the literacy skills they will need to lead happy, productive, and rewarding lives.

As we crafted the preface to this edition, the most recent reading scores from the National Assessment of Educational Progress (2010) were released and showed that progress of American children is stagnant despite the 6 years of effort under the No Child Left Behind Act of 2001 and the curriculum and assessment practices advanced by Reading First, the 6 billion dollar federal initiative to improve reading achievement in kindergarten through third grade. The actual results of Reading First are complex and ambiguous. Four states—Florida, Utah, Pennsylvania, and Michigan—report robust achievement gains in reading achievement (see Hartman & Florio-Ruane, 2010) but, for the nation as a whole, the Reading First Initiative did not justify the huge expenditure of federal dollars. We, like many of our colleagues (for example, Allington, 2005; NCTE Commission on Reading, 2004; Pressley, 2006), recognize that the Reading First curriculum did not constitute a comprehensive and balanced approach to reading instruction, yet we cannot completely ignore its teachings. So many of the curriculum and instruction guidelines of Reading First are incorporated into this text, but we have put much greater emphasis on motivating children, encouraging independent reading, and giving teachers the tools and knowledge to make strong instructional decisions.

For this reason, our book puts motivation and teacher decision making up front. After the opening chapters that describe the process of reading, the reading proficiency of students in the United States, and reading curriculum (Chapter 1) and basic principles of instruction (Chapter 2), we embark on the two major themes of the book—motivation and teacher decision making. Prompted by both recent research on motivation and recent recognition of the importance of motivation (see, for example, National Research Council, 2004; Pressley, 2006; Wigfield & Eccles, 2002), we consider how to motivate students to read, an increasingly difficult task when most popular entertainment is available electronically and most information is retrieved electronically with video support. Throughout the book we will keep discussing ways to motivate students, especially struggling readers, and we highlight the use of technology as a tool for promoting print reading. In Chapter 12 we provide an in-depth discussion of independent reading and the ways to promote it. Throughout the book we provide extensive and annotated lists of exciting children's literature.

The second theme, teacher decision making, begins in Chapter 4 with its explanation of classroom assessment, where we strongly advocate and illustrate informal classroom assessments over standardized tests. In Chapter 5, we help you use assessment information to differentiate instruction and provide intervention to struggling readers. To help all children to read well, teachers must acknowledge their differences and plan instruction accordingly. In the rest of the chapters we use margin notes to help you make assessment decisions and in Appendix A you will find many useful assessment tools.

The National Reading Panel's *Teaching Children to Read* (2000) and the Reading First initiative stressed five major components of reading, as do we. Chapter 6 considers phonemic awareness and other aspects of emergent literacy; Chapter 7, phonics and word recognition; Chapter 8, reading fluency; Chapter 9, vocabulary development; and Chapters 10 and 11, reading comprehension with a particular emphasis on higher-order thinking skills and deep understanding. These chapters build on what the National Reading Panel suggested and incorporate findings from other equally important research summaries such as the National Research Council's *Preventing Reading Difficulties in Young Children* (Snow, Burns, & Griffin, 1998) and the RAND Reading Study Group's *Reading for Understanding* (2002).

This fifth edition continues a strong focus on English language learners. ELLs are the focus of Chapter 14 and are included in other chapters in the Differentiating Instruction for English Language Learners feature.

In sum, this book presents a multifaceted, comprehensive, and balanced approach to reading instruction designed to help children achieve the high level of literacy essential for the 21st century. It is our hope as well as our very strong belief that *Teaching Reading in the 21st Century,* Fifth Edition, will equip you with the knowledge and skills you need to begin your journey toward becoming the very best teacher of literacy you can be.

New to the Fifth Edition

We have made a number of changes in this edition to ensure that everything you read here is current and accurate.

We have written one new chapter covering an area that is critical to literacy instruction: dealing with individual differences and assisting children who struggle to learn to read. **Chapter 5, Differentiating Instruction and Intervention,** provides teachers with the knowledge and the tools to effectively differentiate reading instruction and provide help for struggling readers. Based on a growing body of research, Chapter 5 will show you how to meet the needs of all students in your classroom and then how to develop an intervention program for those who need additional help. In Chapter 5, we also explain Response to Intervention—a new special education initiative that seeks to prevent reading problems *before* students are placed in special education by improving both general classroom education and intervention.

Chapter 4, Classroom Assessment, has been moved forward, reflecting the importance of assessment to all other topics in literacy. This chapter includes additional information on how to assess emergent literacy and perform an informal reading inventory.

New features in the fifth edition were created so that important themes and topics were continued across all chapters. The important focus on motivation that begins in Chapter 3 continues throughout the book. In nearly every chapter, we have a feature on **Motivating Struggling Readers.** Another feature explores **Motivating Children with Technology.** Because the student body of most schools is becoming more diverse, we attend to the needs of English language learners in a new feature called **Differentiating Instruction for English Language Learners.**

Other major changes include updates to our features. Some of the best and most popular of the newest children's literature have been added to the end-of-chapter Children's Literature lists and **The Reading Corner** boxes. Newer instructional techniques are included in the **In the Classroom** features. Since the last edition, our exemplary Classroom Portrait teachers went back to school and learned some new instructional techniques. A few of the teachers retired and we hired some new fresh talent. Our kindergarten teacher now works in a full-day kindergarten (as do most kindergarten teachers in the United States). Our third and sixth grade teachers now work with more diverse students and must juggle several reading groups, spending less time teaching the whole class.

We've also added additional opportunities for our readers to apply the text concepts. Accompanying the book is an exciting new online resource, **MyEducationLab,** which provides readers with opportunities to apply the text concepts and build their teaching skills.

We have, of course, also updated all the chapters, incorporating the latest information on topics ranging from the findings of the National Assessment of Educational Progress to research-based approaches to fluency, vocabulary, and comprehension instruction.

Special Features

This edition uses a rich variety of special features to emphasize the ways in which reading instruction and learning play out in contemporary classrooms.

Classroom Portraits are in-depth models that show how real teachers—one in a first-grade classroom, another in a third-/fourth-grade classroom, and one in a fifth-/sixth-grade classroom—teach real lessons. These step-by-step, day-in-the-life portraits begin with planning and move through the actual lessons, with illustrations, instructional materials, and instructional notes. We have tried in this unique feature to show you the reality of a lesson from its planning through to its implementation.

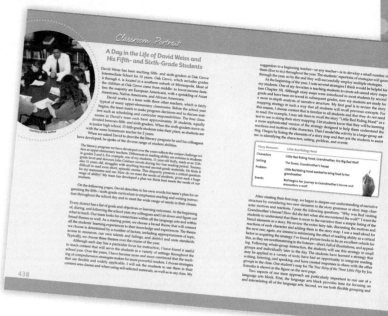

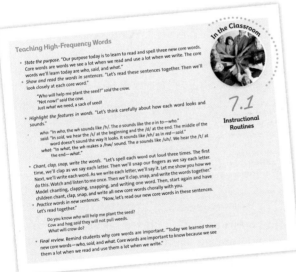

In the Classroom boxes model dialogues, interactions, and vignettes that reflect exemplary literacy instruction. Those marked "Instructional Routines" provide ready-to-use lessons, activities, and graphic organizers that can be transferred directly to your own classroom.

The Reading Corner boxes offer annotated lists of useful and relevant children's literature. An additional list of children's literature appears at the end of every chapter.

Motivating Struggling Readers features provide real-life examples of research-based strategies in action that help make reading exciting for all learners.

New!

Building Awareness of Reading Strategies

Fifth-grade teacher Joe Gonzales motivates his struggling readers as they grow in their strategic proficiency by audiotaping their oral reading and talk about text during small-group instruction and playing it back for them. As the children listen to themselves read and talk, they note the strategies that they hear themselves and others use in the group. The activity helps students become more metacognitive about their reading and more aware of their growth as readers. Before Mr. Gonzales has students do this, he models how to do it for them. To accomplish this, he tells the students that he will audiotape their reading and talk so that they can notice the strategies that they are using. He shares that, when readers notice the way they use strategies, they will become more aware of them and better at using them. He then tapes the day's reading and talk. The next day, he plays the tape for the students. As they listen, Mr. Gonzales notes the strategies that he hears group members using. He makes comments like the following: "David wasn't sure he understood what happened at this point in the story, so he asked a question; Peter answered David's question using his background knowledge. Shyanne noted the sky was getting dark and made an inference that a storm was coming; Jasmine used to live in Kansas. She drew upon her background knowledge to predict that the storm would be a tornado." Mr. Gonzales makes these comments as he hears them

New!

Australian educator Grace Oakley describes electronic talking books as texts "that are backed up with a sound track, graphics, and often animation. Most allow silent reading, although the reader can usually opt to hear the story read out loud by a fluent reader. Indeed, sometimes there is a choice of narrators. The text is often highlighted as it is read by the narrator, allowing the child to follow along. By clicking on a particular word, the child can often access its pronunciation and often a definition, or even a picture." Oakley and her colleague Jenny Jay (2008) have reported a great deal of success with motivating reluctant readers' at-home reading by using electronic talking books. Each week for 10 weeks, they had children ages 8 to 11 select a CD-ROM of electronic talking books to take home from school. At the end of the 10-week project, students reported that they liked the electronic talking books. Moreover, their at-home reading increased by 10

Motivating Children with Technology features provide access to technological resources related to chapter concepts and explain why a technology-based approach can sometimes be more motivating for students than a traditional approach.

New!

Differentiating Instruction for English Language Learners features provide guidance on how to successfully teach English language learners in a classroom of native speakers.

Conferencing

Quiocho and Ulanoff (2009) discuss the importance of conferencing with English language learners (ELLs) as part of an authentic assessment program. They share that during conferences, teachers should ask open-ended questions and include much wait time to allow English language learners to formulate their thoughts. Moreover, Quiocho and Ulanoff encourage teachers to probe students' thinking. They recommend teachers ask students questions such as "Can you tell me more? What else do you remember? What happened next? What do you want me to know the most about what you are writing or reading? How is this connected to . . . [what is being taught]?" Arguably, these kinds of prompts are appropriate for any students who need scaffolding to express themselves, be they English language learners or not. We think it is important, however, to stress the criticality of these supports for children who are just learning to understand, speak, read, and write English.

In discussing ways to provide accommodations to English language learners during content area assessments, Shafer, Willner, Rivera, and Acosta (2009) make the following points: First, make sure you've taught the content the assessment will cover to ELLs. Second, make sure your accommodations address students' linguistic needs. Third, include

To fine-tune your assessment of a student's reading level, use the Sentence Reading and Passage Reading subtests of the Interactive Reading Assessment System (IRAS) or the Graduated Running Record in Appendix A.

Marginal notes offer assessment tips and strategies, as well as cross-references to additional instruments and resources available in the Appendixes.

Assessment

Earlier in the chapter, we suggested that talking to students is a good way to assess their motivation. Observing students, "kid watching" to use the term that Yetta Goodman (1978) coined, is another excellent way of gleaning information about students' attitudes toward themselves and school.

Reflect and Apply questions at the ends of major sections invite you to think critically about what you have read and try out some of the central ideas presented.

Strengths and Challenges of Diversity

All students need and deserve our very best efforts in assisting them to become motivated and engaged readers. Here we deal with two topics that are extremely important for all students but absolutely vital for students who face more challenges than do many of their classmates.

Success

All children need success, but for those children whose preschool experiences have not helped them develop the proficiencies school requires or for those older children who have not met with much success in their first few years of school, fostering success will be both more crucial and more difficult. For these students, success may require more skill instruction and more scaffolding. You may need to meet with the students to teach word recognition skills or develop their sight word knowledge. Older students may require greater attention to vocabulary and

For all these students careful attention to knowledge development and the process of schema building is essential for reading success. Conversely, the youngster who comes to school already reading should not be required to wade through a word study curriculum that she has already mastered or be limited to only very brief and very easy reading materials.

Grouping

Similar considerations for accommodating diversity exist with grouping. One key, as we have already noted, is flexibility—grouping. Thus, if you want to use several different sorts of grouping students who are having particular difficulty understanding the concept of plot so that you can review the concept, it is important to also include each of these students in heterogeneous groups or interest groups to avoid the students' stigmatizing themselves or being stigmatized by others. Simi-

A **Strengths and Challenges of Diversity** section at the ends of most chapters addresses the issues and opportunities in today's diversity-rich classrooms.

Extending Learning activities at the end of each chapter focus on observing classrooms, talking with parents and teachers, or investigating topics further. At least one activity in each chapter encourages you to create an artifact to be included in your teaching portfolio.

Extending Learning

1. One excellent way to better understand and appreciate the nature of good comprehension strategy instruction is to observe a teacher who is doing an excellent job of it. We suggest that you locate an effective strategy instructor, observe her teaching, and afterward talk to her about it. Potential sources for locating teachers are your university instructor, your cooperating teacher, other teachers you know, and your classmates.
2. To really come to understand strategy instruction, it is useful to study quality materials used in teaching strate-

published by the Developmental Studies Center, a nonprofit educational organization in Berkeley, California. Versions of the program are available for kindergarten through grade 6. Get a copy of one of the Making Meaning teacher's manuals, study it carefully, and compare the approach suggested there to the procedure suggested in this chapter. You will find a good deal of similarity but also some important differences. Write a brief description of the Making Meaning approach and its similarities to and differences from the approach suggested here.

Appendix A at the end of the book provides a wide range of ready-to-use assessment instruments developed by assessment experts Robert Calfee and Kathleen Wilson. These assessments evaluate proficiency in areas critical to student success in reading, including emergent literacy, phonics and other word-recognition skills, vocabulary, fluency, and comprehension. **Appendix B** offers detailed lesson plans authored by Michael Graves and Peter Dewitz that show you how to present effective lessons that assist students in understanding and enjoying the books and other materials they read, teach useful vocabulary strategies, and powerful comprehension strategies.

Supplements

MyEducationLab

Teacher educators who are developing pedagogies for the analysis of teaching and learning contend that analyzing teaching artifacts has three advantages: it enables new teachers time for reflection while still using the real materials of practice; it provides new teachers with experience thinking about and approaching the complexity of the classroom; and in some cases, it can help new teachers and teacher educators develop a shared understanding and common language about teaching. . . . *

 As Linda Darling-Hammond and her colleagues point out, grounding teacher education in real classrooms—among real teachers and students and among actual examples of students' and teachers' work—is an important, and perhaps even an essential, part of training teachers for the complexities of teaching in today's classrooms. For this reason, we have created a valuable, time-saving website—MyEducationLab—that provides the context of real classrooms and artifacts that research on teacher education tells us is so important. The authentic in-class video footage, interactive skill-building exercises, and other resources available on MyEducationLab make this site a uniquely valuable teacher education tool.

MyEducationLab is easy to use and integrate into assignments and courses. Whenever the MyEducationLab logo appears in the text, follow the simple instructions to access the interactive assignments, activities, and learning units on MyEducationLab. For each topic covered in the course, you will find most or all of the following resources.

Connection to National Standards

Now it is easier than ever to see how coursework is connected to the International Reading Association (IRA) Standards for Reading Professionals. Each topic on MyEducationLab lists intended learning outcomes connected to the IRA Standards for Reading Professionals. All of the Assignments and Activities and all of the Building Teaching Skills and Dispositions in MyEducationLab are mapped to the IRA Standards for Reading Professionals and learning outcomes as well.

Assignments and Activities

Designed to save instructors preparation time and enhance student understanding, these assignable exercises show concepts in action (through video, cases, and/or student and teacher artifacts). They help students synthesize and apply concepts and strategies they read about in the book.

Building Teaching Skills and Dispositions

These learning units help students practice and strengthen skills that are essential to quality teaching. Students are presented with the core skill or concept and then given an opportunity to practice their understanding of this concept multiple times by watching video footage (or interacting with other media) and then critically analyzing the strategy or skill presented.

IRIS Center Resources

The IRIS Center at Vanderbilt University (funded by the U.S. Department of Education's Office of Special Education Programs, OSEP) develops training enhancement materials for pre-service and in-service teachers. The center works with experts from across the country to create challenge-based interactive modules, case study units, and podcasts that provide research-validated information about working with students in inclusive settings. In your MyEducationLab course, we have integrated this content into appropriate topics.

*Darling-Hammond, L., & Bransford, J., Eds. (2005). *Preparing Teachers for a Changing World*. San Francisco: John Wiley & Sons.

General Resources on Your MyEducationLab Course

The Resources section on MyEducationLab is designed to help students pass their licensure exams; put together effective portfolios and lesson plans; prepare for and navigate the first year of their teaching careers; and understand key educational standards, policies, and laws. This section includes these resources:

- *Licensure Exams.* Contains guidelines for passing the Praxis exam. The *Practice Test Exam* includes practice multiple-choice questions, case study questions, and video case studies with sample questions.
- *Lesson Plan Builder.* Helps students create and share lesson plans.
- *Licensure and Standards.* Provides links to state licensure standards and national standards.
- *Beginning Your Career.* Offers tips, advice, and valuable information on the following:
  - Resume Writing and Interviewing. Expert advice on how to write impressive resumes and prepare for job interviews.
  - Your First Year of Teaching. Practical tips on setting up a classroom, managing student behavior, and planning for instruction and assessment.
  - Law and Public Policies. Includes specific directives and requirements educators need to understand under the No Child Left Behind Act and the Individuals with Disabilities Education Improvement Act of 2004.

Supplements for Instructors

The following supplements are available for instructors to download at www.pearsonhighered.com/educator.

- Instructor's Manual with Test Bank offers teaching suggestions and test items for every chapter.
- PowerPoint Presentations will enhance your teaching of each chapter.

Pearson MyTest

The printed Test Bank is also available through our computerized testing system, MyTest, a powerful assessment generation program that helps instructors easily create and print quizzes and exams. Questions and tests are authored online, allowing ultimate flexibility and the ability to efficiently create and print assessments anytime, anywhere! Instructors can access Pearson MyTest and their test bank files by going to www.pearsonmytest.com to log in, register, or request access. Pearson MyTest gives you the following capabilities:

- Draw from a rich library of assessments that complement your Pearson textbook and your course's learning objectives
- Edit questions or tests to fit your specific teaching needs

Acknowledgments

Clearly, *Teaching Reading in the 21st Century* continues to change and evolve. With each new edition, we have built on the combined expertise of many colleagues throughout the country who are dedicated to literacy education. To you, we extend a special thank-you for your valuable feedback and assistance.

- Our editors, Aurora Martínez Ramos and Christina Robb, who assisted us throughout the revision process; our production editor, Janet Domingo; Annie Pickert, who supplied the excellent photos; and our book packaging and copy-editing experts, Karla Walsh and Omegatype Typography, who finalized and polished the book.

- The many people who granted us permission to cite their work and reproduce their materials in this text.

- The reviewers: Carol L. Butterfield, Central Washington University; Deborah A. Farrer, California University of Pennsylvania; Marie A. Fero, Eastern Illinois University; Kitty Y. Hazler, Morehead State University; Susan Hendricks, University of Nevada, Las Vegas; Kimberlee Sharp, Morehead State University; Maureen Siera, St. Martin's University; Linda Skroback-Heisler, University of Nevada, Las Vegas; and Christina D. Walton, Morehead State University.

- The reviewers of previous editions, who have been so helpful in shaping this text.

- The teachers, researchers, and teacher educators whose names you will see mentioned on nearly every page of this text, especially Jonni Wolskee, Babs Mowry, Alison Montano, Cheri Cooke, Lauren Liang, and Cheryl Peterson, who wrote outstanding lesson plans; Maureen Prenn, who created much of the initial *Instructor's Manual*; Kathleen Clark, who assisted us with the assessment and word recognition chapters; Raymond Philippot, who assisted us with many of the other chapters; as well as Mark Aulls, Ann Beecher, Barbara Brunetti, Jerry Brunetti, David Carberry, Jim Hoffman, Susan Jones, Stephen Koziol, Anita Meinbach, Judy Peacock, Lynn Richards, Randall Ryder, Wayne Slater, Margo Sorenson, Kelly Spies, and Diann Stone. All lent their time and very special talents to this project.

- Our colleagues at the University of Minnesota and Stanford University, with special thanks to Lee Galda, Jay Samuels, Barbara Taylor, and Susan Watts, whose scholarship and dedication to the profession are without equal.

- Kathleen Wilson, of the University of Nebraska, and Robert Calfee, our colleague and Michael's mentor at Stanford, for their outstanding chapter on assessment and their work on Appendix A.

- Our students and teachers from kindergarten through graduate school, who over the years have inspired our thinking and contributed significantly to the ideas you will read about in this text.

- Our friends and family—especially my wife Pamela Dewitz, who listened, encouraged, and sustained me throughout this lengthy revision, and especially our accomplished, supportive children, Julie, Erin (Michael & Bonnie Graves), Rachel, David, and Erica (Peter and Pamela Dewitz).

Teaching Reading
in the 21st Century

1
Reading and Learning to Read

It was the first day of summer vacation, and 10-year-old Carmella couldn't wait to meet up with her best friend Amber at the community pool. Just as she was considering which bathing suit to wear, she heard the patter of rain on the roof and looked out the window. "Daaang," she muttered. "No pool today." She flopped back on her bed and reached for Kate DiCamillo's *Because of Winn-Dixie* on her nightstand. Within minutes, she was deep into India Opal Buloni's new life in Florida, thoughts of the pool temporarily forgotten.

Shutterstock

On the other side of town, when Carmella's friend Amber woke up and saw that rain had spoiled their plans for the community pool, she never thought of picking up a book. Unlike Carmella, she had not mastered the complex process of reading. Reading wasn't much fun for her, and she didn't do it often. Amber will probably spend most of the rainy day watching TV.

For some children, like Carmella, mastering the complex process of reading comes easily, and by fourth grade they are quite accomplished readers. For others, like Amber, this is not the case. As Carmella and Amber progress in school, they both will face increasingly challenging reading tasks, and both will need help in meeting those challenges. Amber—and other students who struggle in reading—will, of course, need more assistance than Carmella and other accomplished readers; but all your students will need the very best instruction and encouragement you can provide if they are to become the sort of readers the 21st century demands.

CLASSROOM vignette

The Reading Process

Why should you care about the reading process? Why is it vital to develop a deep understanding of it? The answer is straightforward. Regardless of what you learn about the specifics of teaching reading from this text, your university courses, in-service sessions, conferences, and discussions with other teachers, much of what you do in the classroom will result from your personal understanding of the reading process. The number of teaching options you have is so great, the needs of different students so diverse, and the specifics of a particular teaching situation so unique that it is impossible to anticipate all of the decisions about literacy instruction that you will make each day. But understanding the mental processes of a reader can prepare you to make wise choices. Reading instruction is regularly buffeted by fads and the only way to resist the current sure cure is to have a solid grounding in the reading process.

Although different authorities view the reading process somewhat differently, over the past 40 years, a widely accepted, balanced, and strongly supported view of the process has emerged. Here, we call this the *cognitive-constructivist view of reading*. This construct forms the foundation of the approach to reading presented in this book. In the next section, we explain several theories that elaborate, complement, and supplement this concept.

The Cognitive-Constructivist View of Reading

The cognitive-constructivist view of reading emphasizes that reading is a process in which the reader actively searches for meaning in what she reads. In fact the reader makes connections between ideas and then integrates these understandings with prior knowledge. This search for meaning depends very heavily on the reader's having an existing store of knowledge. The active contribution of the reader is significant enough to justify the assertion that she actually constructs much of the meaning she arrives at while reading.

For example, as Carmella reads *Because of Winn-Dixie,* she learns that India Opal is sad because her mother recently walked out on her and her father. Later in the book, when Carmella learns that Amanda Wilkinson, a girl India Opal does not at first get along with, is sad because her younger brother recently died, Carmella can construct the inference that Opal and Amanda may become friends. Nothing in the text tells Carmella this; the inference comes from her knowledge that people who have things in common often become friends and from her active processing of the text. Notice in the accompanying classroom example how teacher Martin Cummings highlights this use of background knowledge and encourages active processing with his sixth-graders (In the Classroom 1.1). Mr. Cummings is helping his students realize that readers actively search for meaning in what they read and that the meaning they construct from a text depends on their own knowledge about the world and its conventions.

The Cognitive Orientation

The earliest influence on this view of reading came from cognitive psychology, the orientation that became the main perspective of American psychology beginning in the 1960s (Gardner, 1985). Cognitive psychologists view the learner and her background knowledge as central to learning and the study of learners' thought processes as a fundamental focus of their work. They also view learners as active participants,

In the Classroom

1.1

Using Background Knowledge

Martin Cummings wrote the first paragraph from Sharon Flake's novel *The Skin I'm In* on the board:

> The first time I seen her, I got a bad feeling inside. Not like I was in danger or nothing. Just like she was somebody I should stay clear of. To tell the truth, she was a freak like me. The kind of person folks can't help but tease. That's bad if you're a kid like me. It's worse for a new teacher like her.

He read the paragraph aloud to his sixth-graders and then said, "What does this paragraph tell us? What meaning do you get from it?"

Chris: The narrator's someone young, maybe our age.
Mr. Cummings: What makes you think so?
Chris: 'Cause it says "a kid like me" and sounds like the way kids talk.
Lateisha: Yeah, Black kids, not White kids. I think the person talking is Black.
Mr. Cummings: So you think the narrator's Black. What else do we know about the narrator from this paragraph?
Kyle: She has a low opinion of herself.
Mr. Cummings: How do you know that?
Kyle: 'Cause she calls herself a freak.

who act on, rather than simply respond to, their external environment as they learn. In the cognitive view, reading is very much an active process in which the meaning the reader gleans from a text is heavily influenced by the cognitive work that she puts into the reading process. Both the beginning reader—whom we might observe carefully sounding out words as she reads orally—and the accomplished reader such as Carmella—who appears to be effortlessly absorbing *Because of Winn-Dixie*—are in fact actively engaged in making meaning from the text.

Constructivism

The view of the reading process described here derives from a theory called *constructivism,* a political (Searle, 1993), philosophical (von Glaserfeld, 1984), social (Gergen, 1985), and psychological construct. Here we are using the term in its psychological sense. Constructivism emphasizes the idea that comprehending a text is very much an active process. Constructivism holds that the meaning one constructs from a text is subjective—the result of one particular person's processing of the text. Each reader is influenced by the sum total of her experience as well as by her unique intellectual makeup. Because of this, each reader constructs a somewhat different interpretation of the text, the text as she conceptualizes it (von Glaserfeld, 1984). The three student journal entries listed in Figure 1.1 illustrate this concept. All three students were responding to a prompt for the picture book *Mama Bear* by Chyng Feng Sun. The story tells of a girl who bakes and sells almond cookies in order to earn enough money to buy a large, expensive stuffed

Today's students bring a host of different schemata to today's classrooms.

Steve Skjold/Alamy

Figure 1.1

Kaiya: *Mei-Mei wanted a bear for Christmas.*

Lawrence: *Mei-Mei wanted her mother to be happy.*

Ali: *Mei-Mei wanted to be warm most of all.*

Three Students' Responses to the Same Question About a Story They Read

bear for Christmas because she thinks it will help keep her and her mother warm. The students were asked to respond to this question: "What did Mei-Mei want most for Christmas?" Each answer is, of course, correct yet points up a different perspective on the story.

Having noted that constructivism emphasizes the subjectivity of meaning, we should also note that different texts vary dramatically in how much they constrain it (Stanovich, 1994). An abstract poem may prompt many appropriate interpretations, but a manual on how to install new software should prompt only one. In between these two extremes lies a range of texts that invite various degrees of individual interpretation. However, when reading straightforward stories and a good deal of informational material, most readers will construct quite similar meanings for what they read.

As noted, constructivism is a social construct as well as a psychological one. Most constructivists emphasize that the social world in which we live heavily influences the meaning that we derive from our experiences, including our experiences with text. Thus, constructivism strongly supports the inclusion of a variety of discussion arrangements and group work as part of reading and learning (Calfee & Patrick, 1995).

Word Recognition and Fluency

Before the reader can make connections, before he can bring his knowledge and experience to bear on the text, he has to read the words. Reading is an ongoing, recursive process. Many operations happen at once, but we have decided word recognizing is a good place to start in describing the reading process. For the mature reader word recognition is an effortless process beyond our awareness. Most words we read are recognized automatically, with the reader processing all the letter-sound associations simultaneously or recognizing the word as a whole unit. Only when a new word is encountered, such as *Bangladesh,* is the reader aware that some process must be invoked to identify the word. He may know that he has to break the word into chunks or syllables and then use patterns he knows—*ang, la, esh*—to pronounce the new word. These abilities come to most readers easily but not before moving through several developmental stages. We will outline these developmental stages when we discuss word recognition.

Achieving automatic word recognition is vitally important because automaticity is a prerequisite for fluency, which is the ability to "read a text orally with speed, accuracy, expression and comprehension" (Samuels, 2002b). The component of fluency should also include endurance, because good readers can sustain fluent reading page after page. Reading well for 1 minute, a common test of fluency, might not be the best way to assess it (Deeney, 2010). Fluency is not just an oral phenomenon—it applies to silent reading as well. Because fluent readers can decode a text automatically, they are able to decode and comprehend at the same time, resulting in oral reading that is accurate, smooth, and fairly rapid, with proper expression.

To become fluent readers, students need to do a lot of silent reading in material they find interesting, enjoyable, and relatively easy. To become fluent oral readers, students can engage in a variety of different reading activities such as paired reading, echo reading, and repeated readings (Rasinski, 2003). These and many other tech-

*A*ssessment

Specific approaches to assessing fluency, like 1-minute timed readings, are discussed in the assessment chapter (Chapter 4).

Fostering Fluency

Achieving fluency is often a particular challenge for students learning English as a second language. In addition to going through the processes that native speakers do, nonnative speakers may need to translate English words into their own language in the process of arriving at meaning. Thus, becoming automatic in processing words and fluent in reading texts is extremely important for English language learners. Teacher Marla Roen understands the importance of providing students with plenty of easy reading material to help them gain automaticity.

> I make sure my classroom library is chock-full of books that my third-graders can read with ease. When they select a book for pleasure reading, I tell them that if they can't instantly recognize most of the words in a book, they should choose a simpler one. To help them choose appropriate books, I label the books by difficulty levels and explain the levels to my students. Then I group the books in our classroom library by level. This really helps children select books that fit their comfort zone. Because I have several English learners in my class, I make sure there are plenty of very simply written books for them, books with universal characters, such as Dr. Seuss books, Frog and Toad books by Arnold Lobel, or easy-to-read books that reflect their own culture. Luckily, simple books with multicultural characters are becoming easier and easier to find.
>
> —Marla Roen, Third-Grade Teacher

Differentiating Instruction for English Language Learners

niques for creating fluent readers, as well as the many prerequisite skills that underlie fluent reading (Pikulski & Chard, 2005), are discussed in Chapter 8. The bibliography on page 12 provides examples and information about books beginning readers can use to build automaticity and fluency.

Comprehension: The Construction-Integration Process

While our reader is fluently recognizing the words, she also comprehends the message. We can break the comprehension process into at least three parts—construction, integration, and metacognition. To grasp the process of comprehension we turn to the theory with the greatest clarity—the construction-integration model. Developed by Walter Kintsch (1998) and others, the process begins with construction, in which the reader comprehends sentences and then links ideas from one sentence to another. Integration is the process of using prior knowledge to expand and interpret the meaning the author has put on the pages. Consider these three sentences. *John got a cup of coffee. It was very hot. Now there is a big mess on the rug.* Construction is necessary to link the first sentence to the second. The pronoun *it* links the coffee and its temperature. The first two sentences are integrated with the third when the reader, using her prior knowledge, makes the inference that hot coffee was dropped, perhaps over an expensive rug. In the third phase, metacognition, the reader confirms that this makes sense.

We illustrate the construction-integration process in Figure 1.2. To construct ideas the reader first applies his knowledge of vocabulary and syntax or grammar to understand each sentence, a very similar process to that used in oral language comprehension. Then the reader links one sentence or one idea to another using what he knows about the cohesive ties of language. Understanding the cohesive ties of language, a reader knows that the words *but* and *however* mean that the next idea somehow qualifies the first, that *because* and *since* signal that one idea caused another, and that *some*

Figure 1.2

Construction-Integration Model of Comprehension

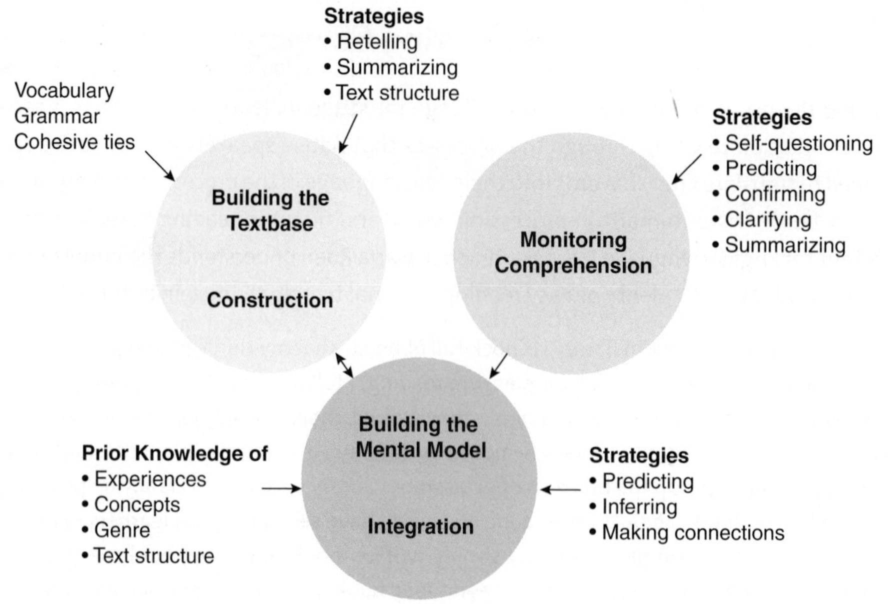

Strategies
- Retelling
- Summarizing
- Text structure

Vocabulary
Grammar
Cohesive ties

Building the Textbase

Construction

Monitoring Comprehension

Strategies
- Self-questioning
- Predicting
- Confirming
- Clarifying
- Summarizing

Building the Mental Model

Integration

Prior Knowledge of
- Experiences
- Concepts
- Genre
- Text structure

Strategies
- Predicting
- Inferring
- Making connections

and *few* refer to a portion of the ideas already mentioned. As the reader integrates ideas using these cohesive ties, he is building a textbase—a relatively literal understanding of the text. A textbase is fleeting and it might be what a reader could immediately recall if you stopped his reading in mid-passage and asked him to retell it.

To preserve this textbase the reader integrates text information and prior knowledge, creating his own mental model. This is the essence of the constructivist process. Reading the text—*Mary looked at the menu trying to find the cheapest entrée, while John gazed lovingly in her eyes*—we know immediately that she is in a restaurant, concerned about money or at least making a good impression, and John is smitten. Each reader will construct a unique understanding of the text, but the writer can limit the variation in responses by the purpose and precision in her words.

Metacognition

The third phase of the construction-integration process is metacognition. Someone has to keep an idea on the whole meaning construction process and ensure that it makes sense. Hence think of your mind's eye, a part of your brain that observes your own cognitive functions, giving frequent thumbs-up when things are progressing well and stopping the whole process when it does not make sense. Active awareness of one's comprehension while reading and the ability to use effective fix-up strategies when comprehension breaks down are absolutely essential tools for becoming an effective reader, and lack of such metacognitive skills is a particularly debilitating characteristic of poor readers.

Metacognitive readers have the ability to mentally step outside of themselves and view their own processing of particular learning tasks. By stepping outside of themselves, they can become self-regulated learners—learners who generate thoughts, feelings, strategies, and behaviors that help them attain their learning goals (Schunk & Zimmerman, 1998). Accomplished readers have metacognitive knowledge about themselves, the reading tasks they face, and the strategies they can employ in completing these tasks. For example, in beginning to read this section, you might have realized that you have no prior knowledge about metacognition (self-knowledge), noticed that the section is brief (task knowledge), and decided that the strategy of reading the section through several times would be fruitful (strategy knowledge). Thus, you exhibited metacognitive knowledge prior to beginning reading.

Strategies

To keep everything on track, the mature reader has at his disposal a set of cognitive tools or strategies. When meaning breaks down a reader can make inferences, ask questions, summarize, search for important ideas, or sound out words (Duke & Pearson, 2002). For example, if a reader comes across an unknown word as she is reading, one very reasonable response would be to read ahead a little to see if the context suggests a meaning. Some strategies help drive the construction of the textbase, others assist the development of the mental model, and still others assist metacognition. A strategy like self-questioning might do all three. When a reader asks himself a question he is checking his understanding. Asking questions while reading, especially inferential questions, can drive the integration of text information and prior knowledge. Summarizing while reading is a good way to check understanding. Figure 1.3 categorizes these research-based comprehension strategies by their function. Some strategies do double duty.

But metacognition and the use of strategies is not just a matter of *skill*; it is very much a matter of *will*. Students need to care whether they comprehend and be motivated to use appropriate fix-up strategies if they do not. The goal is to bring all students to the point where they can and will make the effort to be as metacognitive as possible.

Schema

When psychologists first developed this constructivist view of cognition and reading they wanted to explain how readers use knowledge. Schema theory is concerned with knowledge, particularly with the way knowledge is represented in our minds, how we use that knowledge, and how it expands. According to the theory, knowledge is packaged in organized structures termed *schemata*. David Rumelhart (1980) states that schemata constitute our knowledge about "objects, situations, events, sequences of events, actions, and sequences of actions." We have schemata for objects such as a house; for situations such as being in a class; for events such as going to a football

Assessment

It is vital that you know as much as possible about the background knowledge of both your English language learners and your native English speakers. One of the most practical ways to access that knowledge is to frequently talk to individual students about topics you're dealing with.

Figure 1.3 How Comprehension Strategies Affect the Process of Meaning Construction

Textbase (Strategies that help readers relate ideas to each other)	Mental Model (Strategies that help readers relate text ideas to prior knowledge)	Metacognition (Strategies that help readers monitor and repair comprehension)
Anaphoric relationships	Predicting	Self-questioning
Retelling	Making inferences	Predicting-confirming
Summarizing	Making connections	Clarifying
Narrative structure	Self-questioning	Rereading
Expository text structure		Summarizing

game; and for sequences of events such as getting up, eating, showering, and going to work. We interpret our experiences—whether direct encounters with the world or vicarious experiences gained through reading—by comparing and, in most cases, matching those experiences to existing schemata, which constitute a vast and elaborate network of interrelationships. These networks of *organized* knowledge are virtually endless and constitute much of the intellectual capital that human beings have to work with.

One very important consequence of readers having these rich, internalized networks of schemata is that, once a particular schema is evoked, a huge store of knowledge becomes instantly available. Suppose a student is reading a story and comes across a sentence—*Mark stopped at McDonald's on the way home.* Immediately, her schema for fast-food restaurants provides her with a wealth of information: Mark ordered and picked up his food at the counter; he ordered something like a burger or fries or a soda—not steak or lobster; he had to pay for his food, but not too much; he seated himself in the restaurant or perhaps took his food somewhere else to eat it; and he probably ate it fairly rapidly. Information such as this, and often richer bundles of information, becomes available to us as soon as we evoke a schema for something we are reading or hearing or viewing. The more we know about the subject, the easier it will be to deal with that topic and learn more about it. Schemata assist the reader in initially making sense of what she reads, relating newly acquired information to prior knowledge, determining the relative importance of information in a text, making inferences, and remembering (Anderson & Pearson, 1984).

Good readers simultaneously rely on the text and on their background knowledge as they construct meaning. We as teachers need to provide students with the sorts of texts and tasks that promote this interplay of text and background knowledge. Figure 1.4 depicts situations that encourage too much or too little attention to the text and that should be avoided.

Figure 1.4 **Situations That Encourage Too Much or Too Little Attention to the Text**

Situation	Result
Selection with an unfamiliar topic and difficult vocabulary	The reader will give too much attention to individual words and neglect to use prior knowledge to help in understanding the text.
Too much oral reading with an emphasis on being correct and a penalty for being incorrect	The reader will focus on individual words and letters, rather than on sentences, paragraphs, and ideas.
A less-able student reading orally in front of peers	The reader will focus attention on correctly pronouncing individual words and give little attention to meaning.
Only silent reading with no postreading follow-up discussion	The reader will pay too little attention to the ideas in the text and guess at the meaning with little use of the text to confirm guesses.

In concluding this section on the reading process, it is worth pointing out that although constructivism as a theory was developed nearly 30 years ago, it is fully consistent with the model of reading comprehension developed by the RAND Reading Study Group (2002), a group much more recently commissioned by the U.S. Department of Education to review the research on reading comprehension: "We define reading comprehension as the process of simultaneously extracting and constructing meaning through interaction and involvement with written language." The RAND group goes on to note that comprehension entails three elements:

- The *reader* who is doing the comprehending
- The *text* that is to be comprehended
- The *activity* in which comprehension is a part

Furthermore, the RAND group notes, these three elements operate within and are heavily influenced by a *sociocultural context,* as illustrated in Figure 1.5. The RAND group's orientation, in addition to being consistent with the interactive model, is consistent with the view of the reading process just discussed and with the program of reading instruction we recommend throughout this book.

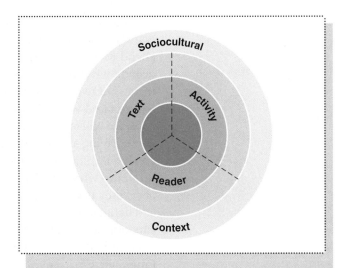

Figure 1.5

RAND Study Heuristic for Thinking About Reading Comprehension

Source: RAND Reading Study Group. (2002). *Reading for Understanding: Toward an R&D Program in Reading Comprehension*, MR-1465-OERI. Santa Monica, CA: RAND Education. Copyright 2002. Reprinted with permission.

Comprehension is an active, constructive process that we will reinforce throughout this book. This means that, if you are to understand and remember the ideas we present, as well as use them in your teaching, you must mentally manipulate them in some way. To help you do this, we include Reflect and Apply sections periodically throughout the text. Ideally, as constructivist and sociocultural principles suggest, you will discuss your responses with others—a study group, your class, or your course instructor.

1. Suppose that one teacher taught the word *relax* by simply saying, "*Relax* means to loosen up," while another taught it by having students view several pictures of people relaxing, having them assume relaxing positions themselves, and then having them talk about situations in which they have felt comfortable and relaxed. Explain how the second teacher is demonstrating a cognitive perspective.
2. Identify a schema that both inner-city students and suburban students are likely to have, one that inner-city students are likely to have but suburban students might lack, and one that suburban students are likely to have but inner-city students might lack. Why do certain groups of students share some schemata but not others? What does sociocultural theory say about the importance of students having different schemata?

Concepts That Elaborate and Complement the Cognitive-Constructivist View

We next consider several concepts that extend the cognitive-constructivist view of the reading process and underlie the instructional procedures we present throughout this book—automaticity, reader-response theory, and sociocultural theory.

Automaticity

The concept of automaticity is both crucial and straightforward. An automatic activity is one that we can perform effortlessly and with very little attention. As David

LaBerge and S. Jay Samuels (1974) pointed out in their pioneering work on automaticity in reading, the mind's attentional capacity is severely limited; in fact, we can attend to only about one thing at a time. Recent research suggests that multitasking, despite what you may believe, is nearly impossible unless one of the tasks is automatic and requires no attention, like listening to music on your iPod (Nass, 2009). If we are faced with a situation in which we are forced to attend to too many things at once, we will fail. For example, a number of people have reached a level of automaticity in driving a stick shift car. They can automatically push in the clutch, let up on the accelerator, shift gears, let out the clutch, and press on the accelerator—and they can do all this while driving in rush hour traffic. Beginning drivers cannot do all of this at once; they have not yet automated the various subprocesses, and it would be foolish and dangerous for them to attempt to drive a stick shift car in an attention-demanding situation such as rush hour traffic.

Reading includes a number of subprocesses that need to take place at the same time—such as recognizing words, assigning meanings to words, constructing the meanings of sentences and larger units, and relating the information gleaned from the text to information we already have. Unless some of these processes are automated, readers simply cannot do all of this at once. Specifically, readers need to perform two processes automatically: They need to recognize words automatically, and they need to assign meanings to words automatically. For example, if a student is reading and comes across the word *imperative,* she needs to automatically recognize the word and automatically—immediately and without conscious attention—know that it means "absolutely necessary." If the student needs to pause often and struggle to recognize and assign meanings to words, reading will be difficult and laborious, and the student will not understand much of what she is reading. At some stage of development comprehension strategies become automatic and readers can generate an inference or monitor comprehension without conscious effort. At this stage we call strategies *comprehension skills* (Afflerbach, Pearson, & Paris, 2008).

Reader-Response Theory

Rosenblatt (1938/1995, 1978) first developed reader-response theory long before our current constructivist view, yet the two are closely aligned. Over the past 30 years, reader-response theory has become a very prominent influence on literature instruction (Beach, 1993; Galda & Graves, 2007; Marshall, 2000). Reader-response theory puts a good deal of emphasis on the reader, stressing that the meaning one gains from text is the result of a transaction between the reader and the text and that readers will have a range of responses to literary works (Rosenblatt, 1938/1995, 1978). When reading complex literary texts, students will derive a variety of interpretations. Many literary texts simply do not have a single correct interpretation, and readers should be allowed and encouraged to construct a variety of interpretations—if they can support them.

One important fact to keep in mind when considering reader-response theory is that it applies primarily to certain types of texts and certain purposes for reading. As part of explaining when and where reader-response theory applies, Rosenblatt (1978) points out that there are two primary types of reading—efferent, or informational, reading and aesthetic reading. In efferent reading, the reader's attention is focused primarily on what she will take from the reading—what information will be learned. Much of the reading of both students and adults is done for the sake of learning new information, answering questions, discovering how to complete a procedure, or gleaning knowledge that can be used in solving a particular problem. Most reading done in such subjects as health, science, math, and geography is informational reading. These texts, unlike many literary texts, often constrain meaning substantially, do not invite a variety of interpretations, and should yield quite similar interpretations for various readers (Stanovich, 1994).

The other sort of reading Rosenblatt considers, aesthetic reading, is quite different. In aesthetic reading, the primary concern is not with what students remember about a text after they have read it but with what happens to them as they are reading. The primary purpose when reading aesthetically is not to gain information but to experience the text. Although the aesthetic reader, like the reader whose goal is gaining information, must understand the text, he must "also pay attention to associations, feelings, attitudes, and ideas" that the text arouses (Rosenblatt, 1978). For the most part, literature is written to provide an aesthetic experience. Most adults read literature for enjoyment; they do not read literature to learn it but often we do learn from it. And students need to be given opportunities to do the same.

Sociocultural Theory

Sociocultural theory extends the influence on the cognitive-constructivist view out from the reader and the text into the larger social realm. Learning is viewed as primarily a social rather than an individual matter. This theory is still very similar to constructivism, in that learning is viewed as an active and constructive task and what is learned is viewed as subjective. As described by its originator, Vygotsky (1978), or by Vygotskian scholars such as James Wertsch (1998), sociocultural theory is complex. However, its implications for the view of reading and learning described here can be succinctly listed.

First, the social and cultural backgrounds of students have a huge and undeniable effect on their learning. Unless we as teachers take students' social backgrounds and modes of learning and thinking into account, little learning is likely to occur. Second, because learning is quintessentially social, much learning—particularly the best and most lasting learning—will take place as groups of learners work together. Dialogue— give-and-take, face-to-face discussion in which students strive to make themselves understood and to understand others—is a mainstay of learning. Third, the classroom, the school, and the various communities of students in a classroom are social contexts that have strong influences on what is or is not learned in the classroom, and each of them must be carefully considered in planning and carrying out instruction.

REFLECT and Apply

3 One excellent way to check your understanding of a concept is to consider its opposite— what it is not. With this idea in mind, develop a list of practices teachers might employ that hinder the development of fluency. Consider the many things that children are asked to do during instruction that interfere with the growth of reading fluency.

4 As noted, a reader can be metacognitive before reading, during reading, or after reading. Now that you have read this section of the chapter, exercise your metacognitive skills by characterizing your understanding of it and noting some of the steps you could take to better understand the concepts presented.

The Reading Proficiency of U.S. Students

Critics of the U.S. educational system have frequently lashed out at what they perceive as the inability of U.S. schools to educate students as well as they once did, the poor performance of U.S. students compared to students in other countries, and the general failure of U.S. schools to effectively teach reading. However, as David Berliner and Bruce Biddle demonstrate in *The Manufactured Crisis* (1995), many of these claims are "myths, half-truths, and . . . outright lies."

Books to Help Build Automaticity and Fluency in Young Readers

As we have stated, to become automatic in reading, students need a lot of practice with easy, understandable, and enjoyable reading. For children who are just beginning to read—typically first-graders—books that include frequently repeated common words (for example, *run* and *book*) and common word parts (for example, phonograms such as *-ick* and *-ake*) are ideal. Consider series books like Junie B. Jones, Nate the Great, or the Magic Treehouse series. Like their predecessors, The Hardy Boys, Nancy Drew, and the Babysitter's Club, the repetitive nature of these books builds fluency. The following list shows specifically designed easy-to-read books from series that help build beginning readers' automaticity and fluency. Also provided are several sources of information on easy-to-read books.

Easy-to-Read Series Books

Norman Bidwell. *Clifford Goes to Dog School.* Scholastic, 2002. Clifford proves to be quite a challenge for dog school. Just one of dozens of books in the Clifford series. 32 pages.

Denys Cazet. *Minnie and Moo: The Attack of the Easter Bunnies* (I Can Read Book 3). HarperCollins, 2005. In this Minnie and Moo adventure, these unconventional cows try to find an Easter bunny for Mr. and Mrs. Farmer's traditional Easter egg hunt. 48 pages.

Lillian Hoban. *Arthur's Birthday Party.* Harper-Trophy, 1999. At his gymnastics birthday party, Arthur the chimp is determined to be the best. 48 pages.

Arnold Lobel. *Frog and Toad Are Friends.* Harper & Row, 1970. The earliest adventures of these two friends. 64 pages.

Cynthia Rylant. *Henry and Mudge and the Tall Tree House.* Simon and Schuster Books for Young Readers, 2002. Henry gets a new tree house but worries that his dog Mudge won't be able to share it with him. One of the newest books in this popular series. 40 pages.

Jean Van Leeuwen. *Oliver and Amanda's Halloween.* Dial Press, 1992. Oliver and Amanda scramble to get just the right costume for Halloween. 48 pages.

Information on Easy-to-Read Books

R. L. Allington. *What Really Matters for Struggling Readers: Designing Research-Based Programs.* Longman, 2001. Chapter 3, "Kids Need Books They Can Read," provides a number of suggestions for choosing books young readers can read.

I. C. Fountas & G. S. Pinnell. *Leveled Books (K–8): Matching Texts to Readers for Effective Teaching.* Heinemann, 2005. Lists thousands of books leveled for grades K to 8.

M. F. Graves & B. B. Graves. *Scaffolding Reading Experiences: Designs for Student Success* (2nd ed.). Christopher Gordon, 2003. Chapter 10, "Assessing Text Difficulty and Accessibility," discusses features that make books easy or difficult.

Here we respond to such criticism and go beyond it to note the sorts of reading skills U.S. students can and must acquire. After presenting solid data to dispel the myth that U.S. students read less well than they used to, we next give evidence to dispel the myth that they read less well than students in most other countries. After that, we briefly characterize U.S. students' reading proficiency and consider the impact of high-stakes testing on reading achievement. Finally, and most importantly, we consider the sorts of reading proficiency required in today's and tomorrow's world. This, of course, is the proficiency you want to help all students to achieve.

A Response to Current Criticisms

Our main purpose in this section is to respond to the frequently heard charge that U.S. students' reading skills are abysmal, that they are far worse than in the past, and that they are pathetic when compared to students in other nations. We base our response primarily on two sources that provide the most reliable large-scale assessment data available—the National Assessment of Educational Progress (NAEP) and the International Association for the Evaluation of Educational Achievement (IEA). The NAEP was established by the federal government 35 years ago to provide a periodic report card on U.S. students' achievement in reading and other academic areas. In other words, it was established to do exactly the job we are trying to do here—communicate about how U.S. students are doing in school. The NAEP tests for long-term trends about every 4 years and reports data for ages 9, 13, and 17. Figure 1.6 shows NAEP results since 1971 (Lee, Grigg, & Donahue, 2007). The trend line for 17-year-olds is basically flat, indicating little or no change in reading performance at the high school level since 1971. The trend line for ages 9 and 13 goes up very slightly from 1971 to 1999 and then just a bit more steeply from 1999 to 2008, indicating a small improvement in reading for this age level. Thus, over the past 35 years, the reading performance of 9- and 13-year-old U.S. students have gone up just a bit, and those of 17-year-olds have remained very much the same. Comparisons with reading levels of earlier times, though difficult to make because comparable data are in short supply, show very similar results (Anderson, Hiebert, Scott, & Wilkinson, 1985).

The IEA was established in the late 1950s to conduct international studies. The most recent IEA study of reading achievement was conducted during the 2006 school year in 40 countries (Mullis, Martin, Kennedy, & Foy, 2007). Figure 1.7 shows the results of this study, which gathered data from over 150,000 fourth-graders. As you can see, the United States ranked 14th among the 40 countries. Although U.S. students did not score quite as well as many students in Europe, they scored 40 points above the international average of 500. This is a very respectable showing indeed.

The best data available indicate that U.S. students' reading proficiency has not declined in recent years and is similar to that of students in other industrialized nations. However, there is still cause for concern. Our interpretation of the NAEP data over the past 35 years suggests a troubling pattern of performance among U.S. students. By fourth grade, the vast majority of students can read easy material and answer simple questions. However, once the texts become slightly more difficult—the sorts of reading middle-grade students are expected to deal with—a large percentage of middle school students cannot read and understand the material and neither can a sizable percentage of high school seniors. And once both texts and questions become

Assessment

Use the NAEP website to find one of the most complete and up-to-date sources of information on how U.S. students are doing in reading.

Assessment

Use the IEA website to find detailed information on the latest IEA study of reading achievement.

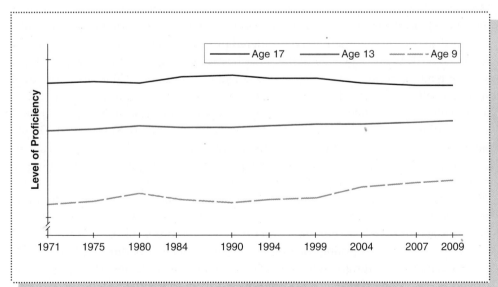

Figure 1.6

U.S. Students' Reading Proficiency 1971–2007

Source: U.S. Department of Education, Institute of Education Sciences, National Center for Education Statistics, National Assessment of Educational Progress (NAEP), various years, 1971–2008 Long-Term Trend Reading Assessments.

Countries	Average Scale Score	Countries	Average Scale Score
Russian Federation	565	Chinese Taipei	535
Hong Kong	564	New Zealand	532
Canada	558	Slovak Republic	531
Singapore	558	France	522
Luxembourg	557	Slovenia	522
Italy	551	Poland	519
Hungary	551	Spain	513
Sweden	549	Israel	512
Germany	548	Iceland	511
Netherlands	547	PIRLS average	500
Belgium	547	Moldova	500
Bulgaria	547	Norway	489
Denmark	546	Romania	489
Latvia	540	Iran	421
United States	540	Indonesia	405
England	539	Kuwait	330
Austria	538	Morocco	323
Lithuania	537	South Africa	302

demanding—the type of material one would need to read to understand political and social issues or enjoy relatively sophisticated literature—very few students, even those about to graduate from high school, can deal with them.

The NAEP results reassure us. However, at the school level NAEP is not an issue. Most schools are focused on their state high-stakes test, which will determine whether the school is accredited or punished at the end of the year. Comparing state test results to NAEP, 40 percent of the students considered proficient on their state test are not proficient on NAEP, and 75 percent of the states have a passing score that is below a basic level of reading on the NAEP (U.S. Department of Education, 2007). The individual states are setting their standards low and may be institutionalizing a set of low expectations. Anthony Applegate and his colleagues compared state tests to NAEP and found startling differences (Applegate, Applegate, McGeehan, Pinto, & Kong, 2009). On the state tests only 22 percent of the questions demanded higher-order thinking, whereas 68 percent of NAEP questions do. Forty-six percent of NAEP questions ask readers to make interpretations and inferences about characterization and plot, but only 24 percent of the questions on state tests assess these skills. If state high-stakes tests continue as the norm and teachers teach students to pass these tests, we may undermine the literacy standards we have embraced, sacrificing higher-order thinking. Some experts believe that high-stakes testing corrupts education (Nichols & Berliner, 2007).

The other continuing literacy concern is the persistent achievement gap in the United States. Many children raised in poverty score lower than their middle-class counterparts. The same is true of many Black, Hispanic, and American Indian students when compared to White students. On the last NAEP assessment the achievement gap between Black and White students had narrowed slightly but was still significantly wide. Far fewer Black students read at a proficient level than do White students, but the gap is decreasing because Black students are making stronger gains. The United States still has a long way to go to ensure that all students become proficient readers.

PEARSON
myeducationlab

Learn about the underlying causes of reading failure and the long-term repercussions of reading difficulty by completing the activity "Understanding the Matthew Effect in Reading." (To find this activity, go to the topic *Struggling Readers* in MyEducationLab and click on Assignments and Activities.)

Literacy for Today's and Tomorrow's World

As important as it is to understand how well U.S. students read, it is even more important to understand present-day literacy requirements and how those requirements are growing. At one time, literacy was defined as the ability to sign your name. At another time, it was defined as the ability to read aloud a simple text with which you were already familiar—typically a passage from the Bible. Today, although there is no single definition of literacy, there is universal agreement that everyone needs a far higher level of literacy than at any time in our past and that this requirement will continue to grow. Irwin Kirsch and Ann Jungeblut (1986) define present-day literacy as "using printed and written information to function in society, to achieve one's goals, and to develop one's knowledge." Lauren Resnick (1987) views present-day literacy as a "higher-order skill" and notes that it requires thinking that is complex, that yields multiple solutions, that involves multiple criteria, and that demands nuanced judgments. David Perkins (1992) notes that contemporary education must go beyond simply presenting students with information and must ensure that students retain important concepts, understand topics deeply, and actively use the knowledge they gain. Finally, the RAND Reading Study Group (2002) notes that the United States today "demands a universally higher level of literacy achievement than at any time in history" and goes on to say that "it is reasonable to believe that the demand for a literate populace will increase in the future."

Present-day literacy requires much more than passively absorbing what is on the printed page. It requires attaining a deep understanding of what is read, remembering important information, linking newly learned information to existing schemata, knowing when and where to use that information, using it appropriately in varied contexts in and out of school, and communicating effectively with others. Literacy for today's world requires that readers be able to *do* something as a result of reading, not merely know something. Moreover, literacy for today's world requires that readers be able to do something with a variety of different texts—not just short stories, novels, poetry, history texts, but also tax forms, computer manuals, complex directions for operating ever more complex machines, and increasingly the text that inform us about the critical issues of our democracy—immigration, health care, national defense, and the economy. More and more literacy means knowing how to use the Internet and making complex decisions about the veracity of information at various websites and blogs. These issues cannot be understood by

Literacy for the 21st century requires much more than passively absorbing what is on the printed page. It requires that readers be able to do something as a result of reading, not merely know something.

Shutterstock

listening to 1-minute sound bites from CNN or MSNBC or reading the latest tweet on your Blackberry. To understand these issues requires reading complex texts, and both the number of complex texts and their level of complexity continue to grow each year.

Literacy is the ability to read critically from a variety of sources, but literacy is also the desire to read for both pleasure and information. Without the inclination to read, without the habit of reading, higher-level reading skills are useless. So in today's world teaching children to read is only half the battle; we must teach them to want to read. When the Wii and the Xbox 360 are more engaging than a novel and cable news sound bites are easier than the *New York Times,* reading is hard to sell. Teaching the love of reading and inspiring children to use print for information may be the most difficult task, one for which we have not yet developed an effective curriculum. The child who can read but does not has no advantage over the child who cannot read.

To be sure, elementary and middle school students do not read all of these types of complex texts, but their early reading experiences should provide a foundation for dealing with complex material in the future. Moreover, given the lower level of reading proficiency demonstrated by many children raised in poverty and many Black, Hispanic, and American Indian students, we need to work especially hard to dramatically improve the reading and the opportunity for these students to read. We particularly need to improve all children's higher-order skills and the desire to seek answers in complex materials. We must nurture and encourage students to become competent readers, who seek to read, in today's increasingly complex and demanding world.

In the Classroom 1.2, which comes from *Standards for the English Language Arts* (National Council of Teachers of English and International Reading Association, 1996), provides a glimpse into a sixth-grade classroom and exemplifies a reading experience that promotes the kind of literacy we are talking about.

*A*ssessment

See the Read-Write Cycle Assessment, an example of an assessment that fosters higher-order thinking, in Appendix A.

REFLECT *and Apply*

5 Suppose you are sitting with a small group of parents at a school open house when one woman abruptly demands to know why today's students read so poorly compared to those in her day. A man picks up her prompt and with similar abruptness wants to know why American kids can't read as well as those in other countries. Compose a response in which you cite data to reassure these parents that U.S. students are certainly holding their own.

6 The concept of present-day literacy is complex. At this point, describe your understanding of the concept in a paragraph or two. Keep your description and add to it as you gain a broader knowledge of present-day literacy in later chapters.

A Literacy Curriculum for Today's and Tomorrow's World

We now turn to a description of program components designed to lead students to the high level of literacy required in the 21st century. Before continuing, we should point out that the focus in this book is reading; therefore, some aspects of a comprehensive literacy curriculum are not discussed, including spelling and handwriting. Also, although we consider writing as it relates to reading, we do not present a comprehensive writing program. Finally, we do not present curricula for specific subjects such as history, science, and the like. However, the reading curriculum we describe in this book is both broad and deep.

In recent years, the federal government has taken an increasingly active role in influencing reading instruction. The federally sponsored report of the National Reading Panel (2000) and the Reading First provisions of the No Child Left Behind Act of 2001 identified five curricular components as having strong support from research and being

Developing Present-Day Literacy in the Sixth Grade

Sometimes visual aids are helpful in fostering high levels of literacy. Here the teacher makes use of a learning web on grizzly bears. A group of sixth-grade students are reading and studying science texts, such as primary sources, magazine articles, textbooks, and essays on scientific and environmental topics. As part of a thematic exploration of large mammals, the students read a number of magazine articles on endangered animals and work in small groups to practice using study strategies, such as underlining, annotation, and summarizing information through visual diagrams. Their teacher models study strategies in explicit class demonstrations.

One day, before reading an article on grizzly bears, the students talk about the specific ways of learning and remembering important ideas and information encountered during reading. The teacher models strategies she uses as she reads, such as underlining and note taking, "thinking aloud" for the class as she sifts through information to highlight and organize important points. She shows students a way to transform key ideas and details that support them into a learning web on grizzly bears that helps show the relationships among key concepts.

The students gather in small groups to read articles about large animals. Working together, they decide which points are important enough to underline or annotate. Each group organizes the information it has found, using a learning web, and then displays its diagram to the class as an overhead transparency, explaining the process used to produce it.

The next day, the students write summaries of the articles they have read and work together to prepare for an oral presentation to the class, using their notes and diagrams to help them plan.

Source: Adapted from IRA and NCTE (1996). *Standards for the English Language Arts.* Newark, DE: International Reading Association; and Urbana, IL: National Council of Teachers of English. Reprinted with permission.

key to effective reading instruction—phonemic awareness, phonics, fluency, vocabulary, and comprehension. Reading First—the massive federal program designed to ensure that the curriculum endorsed by the National Reading Panel (NRP) is implemented in kindergarten through third-grade classrooms throughout the United States—has already had and will continue to have a substantial effect on reading instruction in the primary grades. We believe that the curricular components identified by the NRP and Reading First are vital and should definitely be included in the present-day literacy curriculum. However, like most literacy educators (for example, Allington, 2002; Krashen, 2004; Pressley, 2002; Routman, 2002; Taylor, Pearson, Peterson, & Rodriguez, 2003, 2005), we believe a comprehensive and balanced literacy curriculum that addresses the needs of primary-grade students, upper-elementary students, and middle-grade students includes considerably more than the components endorsed by the NRP and Reading First. The literacy curriculum outlined on the next several pages and elaborated on throughout this book includes all of the components endorsed by the NRP and Reading First, as well as a number of additional components. In this section, we describe eight components that we believe are vital to help all students achieve the sort of literacy required for full participation and success in today's world (see Figure 1.8).

Phonemic Awareness and Other Aspects of Emergent Literacy

As part of learning to read, students need to internalize a substantial body of knowledge about print and the relationship between print and speech. One very important

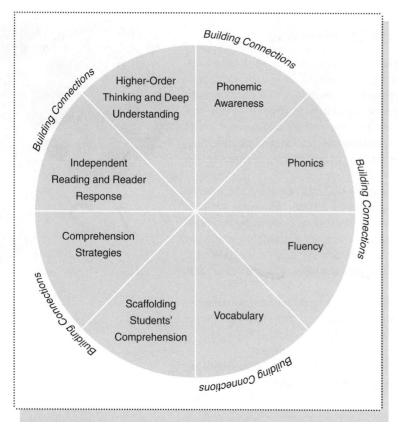

Figure 1.8

Components of the Present-Day Literacy Curriculum

component of such knowledge is phonemic awareness—the insight that spoken words are composed of somewhat separable sounds. But there are many other aspects of emergent literacy. For example, students must recognize that the written language they are just beginning to learn about is in many ways similar to the oral language with which they are already quite proficient. Additionally, as part of emergent literacy, children need to develop positive attitudes about reading and about their ability to learn to read.

Phonics and Other Word Recognition Skills

Phonics is the area of reading instruction that deals with the relationships between letters and sounds. Children use their knowledge of phonics to sound out written words they do not immediately recognize. If an adept reader comes to the word *bike* and doesn't immediately recognize it, she can follow a series of steps to arrive at its pronunciation. Phonic skills help children become independent readers. Other word recognition skills—for example, identifying syllables, blending sounds to form syllables and words, and dealing with word parts such as prefixes and suffixes—also

assist children in becoming independent readers. We deal with phonics and other word recognition skills in Chapter 7.

Fluency and Matching Students with Appropriate Texts

Fluency, as we have already noted, is the ability to "read a text orally with speed, accuracy, expression, and comprehension" (Samuels, 2002b). Additionally, it is important that students become fluent in their silent reading (Pikulski & Chard, 2005). When reading silently, students need to read smoothly, at an appropriate pace, and with good comprehension. There are a number of effective practices for building students' fluency. Additionally, in order to become fluent readers, students need to do a lot of reading in appropriate texts, texts that are not too difficult and that they readily comprehend, learn from, and enjoy.

Vocabulary Learning and Instruction

A huge amount of research has been conducted on students' vocabulary knowledge, and reliable estimates indicate that many students have acquired reading vocabularies of something like 5,000 words by the end of the first grade and approximately 50,000 words by the time they graduate from high school (Graves, 2006). Obviously, vocabulary learning represents a significant task throughout children's years in school, and effectively fostering students' vocabularies requires a multifaceted and long-term program that includes rich and varied language experiences, teaching individual words, teaching word-learning strategies, and fostering word consciousness.

Scaffolding Students' Comprehension of Text and Higher-Order Thinking

Comprehension is both a complex process and the ultimate goal of reading, and as a consequence comprehension instruction needs to be powerful, long-term, and multifaceted. As one facet of comprehension instruction, we need to do everything possible to ensure that students comprehend and learn from each and every text they read—to scaffold their efforts with both narrative texts such as short stories, plays, and novels and expository texts such as the chapters in their science and social studies texts and articles on the Internet. We want students to move beyond comprehension to higher-order thinking. Students should master such complex tasks as analyzing, synthesizing, and evaluating. As students read text we want to promote deep

One hugely important factor in learning to read is reading a lot in material that is understandable and enjoyable.
Paul Conklin/PhotoEdit

and lasting understanding—teaching in such a way that students grasp topics deeply, retain important information, and actively use the knowledge they gain in a variety of tasks in and out of school—which requires a clear conception of the nature of understanding and instructional techniques that lead students to deep understanding.

Teaching Comprehension Strategies

As Pearson, Roehler, Dole, and Duffy noted well over a decade ago (1992), comprehension strategies are "conscious and flexible plans that readers apply and adapt to a variety of texts and tasks." Although many strategies have been identified, a handful of them have been repeatedly singled out as particularly useful, including establishing a purpose for reading, using prior knowledge, asking and answering questions, making inferences, determining what is important, summarizing, dealing with graphic information, imaging and creating graphic representations, and monitoring comprehension (Sales & Graves, 2005).

PEARSON
myeducationlab

Go to the topic *Comprehension* in MyEducationLab to complete related activities.

Encouraging Independent Reading and Reader Response

It is not enough for students to read and comprehend texts they are assigned. Students must become independent readers who voluntarily choose to read for the pleasure, knowledge, and satisfaction that only reading can provide. Additionally, with literary texts, students need to respond to what they read in a variety of different ways. Only by doing a great deal of reading in different types of materials will students really master the skill of reading. Only by doing a lot of reading in material they find interesting and enjoyable will students realize the joy of reading. And only by gaining in-depth knowledge on topics they find particularly important or intriguing will students gain the deep and lasting knowledge needed in today's world. Thus, we strongly advocate truly varied and extensive reading—sensitive and moving fiction such as Patricia Reilly Giff's *A House of Tailors*, revealing nonfiction such as Lori Dolphin's *Our Journey from Tibet*, and light fiction such as Lemony Snicket's *The Carnivorous Carnival*. The whole of this book is devoted to assisting all students in becoming independent and avid readers.

Building Connections and Fostering Higher-Order Thinking

The final component of the critical literacy curriculum cuts across all of the others. Building connections—establishing links among the vast array of schemata that students internalize—is important, whether students are involved in decoding, in higher-order thinking, or in the other components of the curriculum.

Students need to build connections in several directions. First, we want students to realize that what they bring to school—the wealth of out-of-school experiences that they bring when they enter first grade and that are constantly enriched each year—is relevant to what they are learning in school. For example, the pride they felt when they were first allowed to go to the grocery store alone can provide insight into a story character's feelings when she successfully meets a challenge. Second, we want students to realize that the various subjects they study in school are interrelated in many ways. For example, the understanding of the American Revolutionary period they gained in social studies can help them understand the motives of Johnny in Esther Forbes's *Johnny Tremain.* Third, we want students to realize that ideas and concepts learned in school are relevant to their lives outside of school. For example, a character's discovery that persistence paid off in meeting her goal may suggest to a student that similar persistence may lead to success as she tries to help a younger brother develop the habit of putting his toys away neatly. All chapters of this book address the matter of building connections.

Making Instructional Decisions

To develop and implement a critical literacy curriculum, teachers must make instructional decisions and they need the tools to do so. Good teachers make classroom observations, and they employ both informal and formal assessments to understand their students and to gauge their progress. In this book we discuss the range of assessment tools available to teachers and we guide them in their use. Many of these tools are available in Appendix A of this book. After assessments are made, teachers need to use those results to make instructional decisions. We will guide teachers through the process of developing a differentiated curriculum—one that addresses the skills, interests, and motivations of their students.

*A*ssessment

Appendix A contains ready-to-use assessment materials for various components of the present-day literary curriculum.

REFLECT and *Apply*

7. Although almost all schools now make phonics an important part of beginning reading instruction, this was not always the case. Think back to the instruction you received in the primary grades and jot down a statement about how much phonics instruction you received. If possible, compare your experiences of phonics with those of some of your classmates, especially those of different generations.

8. Almost all authorities believe that doing a substantial amount of independent reading is an essential part of becoming a good reader. Consider how much independent reading you have done since you entered first grade or perhaps even before that. Brainstorm some approaches you might use to encourage today's students, many of whom do not do much independent reading, to do more.

An Overview of This Book

We have designed each chapter to facilitate your reading and learning as effectively and efficiently as possible, and most chapters have the same components and the same organization.

Each chapter begins with a photo and an outline of the major sections of the chapter. Next comes a brief scenario in which we capture a problem you are likely to face and that anticipates one or more of the major themes of the chapter. Following the scenario is the body of the chapter, usually consisting of two to four main sections and a number of subsections. Within each chapter we have placed three recurring features. One focuses on differentiating instruction for English language learners. Another provides ways to use technology to motivate and enhance instruction. The third provides ways to motivate and assist struggling readers. After this comes a section titled Strengths and Challenges of Diversity. Here we look back at the chapter and ask whether there is more that can be done to ensure that all students—those whose experiences and schemata differ from those of many of their peers, those who move more quickly than their peers, and those who move less quickly than their peers—achieve in the area covered in the chapter. Finally, we provide Concluding Remarks, a summary and commentary on the chapter.

Each chapter includes a number of additional features. Samples of children's work illustrate their growth toward present-day literacy. Reading Corner boxes provide annotated lists of children's literature useful in teaching particular literacy skills and topics. In the Classroom features offer a variety of examples of classroom interaction—student–teacher dialogues, vignettes, and the like—designed to nurture students toward literacy. Marginal notes on assessment provide important information on this topic and refer you to the Appendix of the book. We will also include features on motivation and differentiation throughout the chapters. To encourage reader involvement, Reflect and Apply sections are embedded at the ends of major sections to give you an opportunity to review and try out some of the central ideas presented.

Chapters end with two standard features. A section titled Extending Learning invites you to apply and elaborate on some of the major ideas presented by observing classrooms, talking with parents and teachers, or investigating a particular topic further. Following this, a section titled Children's Literature provides citations and brief annotations of the selections mentioned in the chapter and occasional citations of other sources of children's literature.

Strengths *and Challenges* of Diversity

In this section of each chapter, we ask whether there is more that can be done to ensure that all students—the diverse groups of children present in almost all classrooms today, those for whom school is easy, and those for whom it's a challenge—achieve at their highest potential.

Different children will arrive at kindergarten, first grade, and every other grade with dramatically different knowledge about the world, about different types of text, about the content of specific subjects, and about school and how it functions. For example, many children who come from the East Coast will have little knowledge of the Southwest desert, children who come from other cultures may lack the American cultural knowledge assumed by some narratives, and children from affluent suburbs may have little understanding of inner-city issues. If all children are to succeed, we must take advantage of the varied schemata that different students have, accommodate students' differing schemata, and do everything possible to make school relevant to the lives of all children.

Because most teachers come from mainstream middle-class backgrounds, recognizing and understanding the differing prior knowledge of students who come from nonmainstream and non-middle-class cultures is particularly problematic and particularly important. Even small differences in background knowledge can sometimes interfere with learning. But many cultural differences are not small. For example, Shirley Brice Heath (1983) compared communication patterns in two working-class communities in the Piedmont Carolinas—an African American community and a White community—to communication patterns in the middle-class school the children attended and found significant differences. One finding was that at home children from both of these working-class communities were used to direct commands such as "Put the book on the shelf." In the middle-class school, on the other hand, children often received indirect commands such as "Is this where the book belongs?" when they left a book unshelved. Because students from working-class communities were not used to such indirect requests, they did not understand the implied command and seemed to be disobeying the teacher by leaving their books where they were. Kathryn Au (1993), Lisa Delpit (1995), and other scholars have documented many cultural differences of this sort. Of course, substantial cultural differences and substantial linguistic differences also exist for many English language learners. To be effective in the diverse classrooms of today's schools, teachers must recognize, understand, and build on the cultural background and practices that children with different backgrounds bring to school.

Concluding *Remarks*

In this chapter, we have emphasized four points. First, we described the concept of the reading process underlying this book—the cognitive-constructivist view. We also described several concepts that elaborate and complement this view—the construction-integration model of comprehension, automaticity, fluency, and metacognition. Second, we briefly characterized U.S. students' proficiency in reading, contrasted their proficiency today to what it was in the past and to the proficiency of students in other industrialized countries, and described the sort of literacy necessary in today's and tomorrow's world. Third, we listed the components of the present-day literacy curriculum that serve as the foundation for the book. Fourth, we gave an overview and explained the common organization that all chapters share.

The topics in this chapter are particularly important to internalize because they underlie the remainder of the book. As we have said several times, reading is enhanced by rich background knowledge. In the case of this book, the more you know about the view of the reading process that informs it, the level of present-day literacy it is designed to help you achieve for your students, the components of the curriculum, and the organization of the book and each chapter, the easier it will be for you to learn, remember, and use the information and procedures presented. We therefore strongly encourage you to review the chapter, take some notes, respond again to some of the prompts in the Reflect and Apply sections, make use of some of our suggestions in the Extending Learning section, and perhaps search out and read some works listed in the references.

Extending *Learning*

Here we suggest several activities that take you beyond this book—to schools, students, teachers, parents, libraries, and others sources of information—to help you more fully understand and appreciate your role in nurturing children toward present-day literacy.

1. One way to increase your understanding of new and complex concepts is to examine several perspectives on them. The concepts about the reading process that we have discussed have all been described in a variety of other texts, and all of them are complex enough to warrant further study. Pick two or three concepts that you would like to further explore, and read more about them either in the references that we have supplied or in a general text on psychology or educational psychology.

2. Go to the NAEP website (http://nces.ed.gov/nations reportcard/reading) and print out a copy of the sample test items. Then go to your state website. If your state does not have a high-stakes test, print one from Texas (www.tea.state.tx.us/index3.aspx?id=3839&menu_id3=793) or Virginia (www.doe.virginia.gov/testing/sol/released_test/index.shtml). Then compare the passages and questions from the national and state test. Which test is the more rigorous assessment of reading? Which test demands higher order thinking?

3. List the components of the present-day literacy curriculum we have outlined and interview some elementary school teachers to find out which components they deal with, which they don't, and the literacy activities they engage in that are not part of the curriculum presented

in this chapter. Try to include teachers from primary, middle-elementary, and upper-elementary grades. Once you have completed your interviews, sum up what you have discovered and comment on (1) the extent to which the teachers you interviewed employ the curriculum we have outlined and (2) any components of the literacy curriculum that are not among the components we consider but that you probably want to include in your classroom.

Children's Literature

DiCamillo, K. (2000). *Because of Winn-Dixie.* Cambridge, MA: Candlewick Press. A poignant and well-told story of a young girl's building a new life after her mother left and she and her father moved to Florida—with, of course, a little help from her dog, Winn-Dixie. 182 pages.

Dolphin, L. (1997). *Our Journey from Tibet.* New York: Dutton. A true story based on interviews with a 9-year-old Tibetan girl, Sonam. Includes dramatic and stunning photos. 40 pages.

Flake, S. G. (1998). *The Skin I'm In.* New York: Jump at the Sun/ Hyperion. Uncomfortable because her skin is extremely dark, 13-year-old Maleeka meets a new teacher with a facial birthmark and makes some discoveries about how to love who she is and what she looks like. 171 pages.

Forbes, E. (1998). *Johnny Tremain.* New York: Houghton Mifflin. Johnny Tremain, apprentice silversmith, takes on the cause of freedom as a message carrier for the Sons of Liberty in pre-Revolution Boston. CD available. 293 pages.

Giff, P. R. (2004). *A House of Tailors.* New York: Wendy Lamb Books. Set in the late 19th century, this novel for intermediate readers tells the story of how 13-year-old Dina adjusts to her new life in the United States after being sent from Germany to live in Brooklyn with her tailor uncle. 149 pages.

Lord, B. B. (1984). *In the Year of the Boar & Jackie Robinson.* New York: Harper and Row. In 1947, a Chinese girl comes to Brooklyn, where she becomes Americanized at school, in her apartment building, and by her love for baseball. Illustrated. 169 pages.

Snicket, L. (2002). *The Carnivorous Carnival: Book the Ninth.* New York: HarperCollins. The continued adventures and misadventures of the Baudelaire orphans in the Series of Unfortunate Events series. 286 pages.

Sun, C. F. (1994). *Mama Bear.* Boston: Houghton Mifflin. Young Mei-Mei bakes and sells cookies in order to earn enough money to buy a large and expensive stuffed bear for Christmas. Illustrated. 28 pages.

PEARSON myeducationlab

Take a look at the topics in the MyEducationLab (www.myeducationlab.com) for your course. In each topic you can:

- Find learning outcomes for the topics covered in this chapter along with the IRA standards that connect to these outcomes.
- Complete assignable activities in the Assignments and Activities section that show concepts in action to help you synthesize and apply strategies.
- Explore IRIS Center Resources—training enhancement materials that provide you with research-validated information and interactive materials to develop your skills in working with students.
- Apply and practice your understanding of the teaching skills identified in the chapter with the Building Teaching Skills and Dispositions exercises.

2

Reading Instruction

It is the beginning of the school year and the principal of Overland Avenue Elementary is meeting with the teachers from each grade level to review the results from last year and discuss possible changes in instruction for the new academic year. During 2008–2009, the school did not meet its Adequate Yearly Progress (AYP) goal, a provision of No Child Left Behind, the federal law designed to insure that all students learn to read. According to the law 81 percent of all students had to pass the state reading test, and that includes 81 percent of African American students, Hispanic students, low-income students, and special education students with only a few exceptions. The fourth-grade teachers assembled at this meeting are not happy. Last year only 74 percent of their students passed the test, and this year 85 percent must pass according to the federal law. The teachers were given a set of reflection questions before the meeting to frame the discussion about improving instruction and learning, including the following two questions:

Bob Daemmrich Photography

1. If your grade level performed well last year what aspects of the curriculum and instruction accounted for that success? How will you sustain those practices?
2. If your grade level performed poorly last year, what aspects of the curriculum and instruction caused the problem? What changes will you make this year?

The teachers had done their homework and came with written answers; they had clearly thought through the questions. In response to the first question they had produced a list of factors that accounted for their success: a fluency program, silent reading time, timed readings, graphic organizers, Accelerated Reader monitoring software, small-group instruction, the school's reading coach, practice books, workstations, websites, the school's reading consultants' model lessons, computer programs, test-taking practice, read-alouds, highlighting while reading, and using data-driven instruction. In response to the second question they added to the list *Weekly Reader*, other workbooks, novels, and increased parent involvement. The explanation for success was a scattershot of materials, instructional routines, and personal assistance from experts. Their suggested changes were additional

Classroom vignette

materials and more parent involvement. Neither of the responses suggested that the teachers understood instruction. Their view of instruction consisted of materials (workbooks), outside assistance (the reading coach), classroom organizational practices (small-group instruction, workstations), and commercial programs (Accelerated Reader). They did not define instruction as a series of explicit teaching moves.

Instruction is the procedures and practices teachers use to help students acquire new knowledge, skills, and attitudes. To do so, teachers explain concepts and skills, show students how to use them, provide assistance as students try out new tasks, and provide ample opportunity to practice. Teachers organize the instruction so that students will use their new knowledge and skills long after they have moved on to another topic or another grade. Good teachers try to make all of this as lively and interesting as possible, because motivated students are more interested and engaged. Good teachers provide the slow students as much help as possible and encouraging those who are surging ahead.

All teachers have a theory of instruction that guides their decisions even if they cannot articulate that theory. In our opening vignette the teachers' theory of instruction was quite primitive. Some teachers believe that teaching is modeling. If you show children how to do everything including silent reading, they will imitate those models. So during sustained silent reading time the teacher kicks back with her latest novel hoping to inspire her students. Other teachers believe that practice makes perfect, and their classroom is a blizzard of workbooks and worksheets where students practice their reading skills. The purpose of this chapter is to help you understand the principles of instruction and by the end of the chapter we hope you will have developed your own theory of instruction, based on what researchers have discovered about effective teaching. We will then apply these principles of instruction to the rest of the chapters as we discuss word recognition, vocabulary, and comprehension.

REFLECT and *Apply*

1. Think about the best teacher or teachers you ever had—elementary, secondary, or higher education. What made the instruction of these teachers particularly strong? Try to ignore for now the personality traits of these teachers.

Instructional Principles

Although providing effective instruction has always been a concern of teachers, researchers, and policy makers, a huge proportion of the most productive research and theorizing on the topic has occurred in the past four decades. Researchers have used two methods to unlock the principles of effective instruction. Many researchers have designed instructional studies and compared one method of instruction to another to determine which is more effective. Through these controlled studies researchers have learned about the importance of clear explanations, modeling, pacing, practice, and feedback (Duffy et al., 1986). Other researchers have taken a second approach and studied effective teachers. They have observed in classrooms, recorded the practices of successful teachers as well as less successful teachers for comparison, and related instructional practices to students' growth in reading. We will first describe the research on effective teachers and take you into successful first- and fourth-grade classrooms. Next we will dissect these classrooms and highlight the instructional principles that underlie their success. We will conclude by looking at the evolution of basal reading programs, which for years have defined the content and methods of reading instruction.

Highly Effective Teachers and Schools

Fortunately, recent research has identified a group of schools and classrooms in which students show particularly strong achievement in reading, achievement well beyond that in average schools and classrooms and well beyond what would be predicted of the students in those classrooms. Six studies stand out, four of which deal with instruction generally (Allington & Johnston, 2002; Pressley, Allington, Wharton-McDonald, Block, & Morrow, 2001; Taylor et al., 2003; Wharton-McDonald, Pressley, & Hampston, 1998) and two of which deal specifically with motivation (Bogner, Raphael, & Pressley, 2002; Dolezal, Welsh, Pressley, & Vincent, 2003). Each of these reports is well worth detailed study, and we encourage you to read them.

Studies of highly effective teachers start with the assumption that by studying experts we can understand the tools of their trade. Thus psychologists have studied expert airplane pilots, radiologists, and teachers and tried to discern the thinking that underlies their expertise. In these studies the researchers, with the assistance of school personnel, identify teachers who achieve superior results as measured by both standardized tests and the professional opinions of their supervisors. These expert teachers along with some more average teachers are observed during the course of school year and their teaching practices are recorded, described, categorized, and then linked to outcomes like students' test performance, reading levels, and the quality of their written work. From these studies we can describe the instructional practices of these highly effective teachers.

In primary classrooms several important practices stand out. First, these highly effective teachers create a stimulating literate environment for their students. The classrooms are filled with print, including books of all kinds for students to read, print created by the students—reports, books, charts, and projects—and print created by the teacher—instructional charts, words and topics being studied, and graphic organizers. Children are constantly busy, with multiple activities and tasks going on at the same time. Teachers instruct the whole class but also work with small groups and confer with individual students. A wide range of texts is employed to teach reading, including basal readers, children's literature, nonfiction books, magazines, and the children's own writing. Because children read many different texts, reading instruction is often integrated with the other content areas, so at times it is hard to tell if the topic is reading, science, or both.

These exemplary teachers demonstrate a rich combination of direct explicit skill instruction (phonemic awareness, phonics, comprehension, and the like) and more holistic activities like reading quality literature, book discussions led by the teacher, and in the upper grades book discussion led by the students. Process writing occurs at all levels; even the youngest students plan, compose, revise, and share what they have written. Exemplary teachers ignore the age-old fight between teaching phonics skills and whole language; they do both. They also ignore the fight between basal readers and literature-based instruction—they employ both. They select a basal story when it is useful to introduce a new concept and skill, and then students read literature to apply what they have learned. As students work with these more difficult texts they meet regularly in small groups and conferences with their teacher for additional help so the teacher can gauge their progress. To orchestrate all of this, the expert teachers

PEARSON
myeducationlab

Explore how a kindergarten teacher creates a print-rich environment by completing the activity "Creating Purposeful Environments for Emergent Readers and Writers." (To find this activity, go to the topic *Emergent Literacy* in MyEducationLab and click on Assignments and Activities.)

Figure 2.1 Characteristics of Teachers Who Produce Outstanding Achievement in Reading

- The best teachers employ a rich combination of skills instruction (phonemic awareness, phonics, comprehension) and more holistic activities (reading quality literature and nonfiction texts, discussing and writing about what they read), focusing on important academic tasks.
- The best teachers teach a lot. They work hard, and their students work hard in turn. They employ a combination of well-planned small-group activities and whole-class instruction.
- The best teachers scaffold students' efforts so that if students put significant effort into learning, they will be successful.
- The best teachers employ higher-order thinking.
- The best teachers integrate reading instruction with language arts and the other content areas.
- The best teachers manage classrooms skillfully.
- The best teachers motivate continually and prominently and repeatedly recognize students' work.

are masterful classroom managers, who use many opportunities to motivate their students. Figure 2.1 summarizes the characteristics of these excellent teachers and In the Classroom 2.1 takes you into an expert's fourth-grade classroom.

In addition to these findings about effective teachers, some of these same studies as well as others have revealed school-level factors that produce superior achievement in high-poverty schools. A summary of these findings reported by Taylor, Pressley, and Pearson (2002) is shown in Figure 2.2. Although these factors are not as directly under your control as are teacher characteristics, they are certainly factors you can look for in schools and work toward as a faculty member.

Traditional Instructional Principles

Mrs. Mowry's class exemplifies many traditional instructional principles that are essential for learning. These principles were developed from about 1960 to about 1980

Motivating Struggling Readers

The Importance of Choice

Life in Mrs. Mowry's classroom illustrates several important principles of motivation, but none more important than choice. Students are given choice about what to read and how to respond to their reading. There is a common text, the basal reader that the teacher uses to introduce concepts and strategies, but beyond that students choose their own reading materials. When they are working in literature circles the teacher allows them to select their own book to study from a small set approved by the teacher. The small-group processes of a literature circle promote motivation and engagement because all students are responsible to the group. When students are reading independently they select their own book after consultation with the teacher. If they can't pick, the teacher will offer suggestions. The classroom itself promotes choice and motivation by having a large well-laid-out classroom library.

A Portrait of Exemplary Fourth-Grade Instruction

In the Classroom

2.1

Mrs. Mowry and her 25 students begin the reading period, in this third week of the school year, discussing the story "Amelia's Road" (Altman, 1995), the selection they read yesterday from their basal reader. Mrs. Mowry wants the students to describe the characters traits of Amelia, a young girl living with her family of migrant workers. Mrs. Mowry first models and describes the concept of a trait. She then lists traits on the board, such as *lonely, imaginative, problem-solver*. She tells the students their task is to take what they have learned about character traits and Amelia and construct a poem about her. A handout helps the students structure their poem, somewhat like a cinquain. When they have finished writing their poem, the students are to return to their independent reading assignment while the teacher confers with individual students.

The teacher conducts short reading conferences with five students a day while the rest of the class works independently or in small groups. During the conferences she discusses what the students are reading, assesses their comprehension and oral reading fluency, and then probes students' critical thinking about their books. The conferences afford her the opportunity to praise and support the students' efforts as readers and guide their reading choices. As the year progresses the conferences continue but the teacher also assesses comprehension by observing the students as they interact in literature circles. She first explains and models literature circles and then lets students choose their books. If students complete their independent reading they are free to explore the literature center that holds activities for genre study, poetry, and writing.

as educators and researchers produced a rich body of basic information about effective instruction. Here we briefly discuss six of the most important traditional principles established during that time:

- Focusing on academically relevant tasks
- Employing active teaching
- Fostering active learning
- Distinguishing between instruction and practice
- Providing sufficient and timely feedback
- Teaching for transfer

We will relate these principles to Mrs. Mowry's classroom and then develop them when we consider new instructional principles that derive from the cognitive-constructive perspective. For more information on these principles, Tom Good and Jere Brophy's *Looking into Classrooms* (2003) is an excellent source.

Figure 2.2 **Characteristics of Schools That Produce High Achievement in High-Poverty Settings**

- Strong focus on student learning
- Strong school instructional leadership
- Strong collaboration among teachers
- Consistent use of data on student performance to guide instruction
- Emphasis on professional development for teachers in the school
- Strong links to parents

Informational Books That Give Students Opportunities to Make Critical Responses

One extremely relevant academic task is making critical responses to informational texts. The books listed here—science and social studies trade books about the world we live in—are interesting and involving and provide extended opportunities for students to make critical responses.

Deborah Chandra & **Madeleine Comora.** Illustrated by Brock Cole. *George Washington's Teeth.* Farrar, Straus and Giroux, 2003. This light-hearted account of the tooth problems that plagued Washington all his adult life provides a unique focus for a detailed timeline of Washington's life and accomplishments. 40 pages.

Rick Chrustowski. *Bright Beetle.* Holt, 2000. This colorful book, illustrated from a bug's eye view, describes the life cycle of a ladybug. The bright colors and accessible text make it a fun read-aloud, share-aloud book. Unnumbered.

Bonnie Graves. *The Whooping Crane.* Perfection Learning, 1997. This informational book begins with a narrative relating a true, potentially fatal incident in 1967 involving a whooping crane chick, then one of 55 remaining of a seriously endangered species; it ends with factual information about the whoopers and efforts to save the species. 54 pages.

Linda Lowery. *Cinco de Mayo.* Carolrhoda Books, 2005. This addition to the On My Own Holidays series, which encourages understanding of diverse cultures, features full-page illustrations by Barbara Knutson and describes the colorful holiday that honors Mexico's victory over the French army at the Battle of Pueblo in 1862. 48 pages.

Sandra Markle. *Outside and Inside Killer Bees.* Walker, 2004. One of the many books in Markle's Outside and Inside series, this addition, with striking photos and accessible text, focuses not only on factual information about bees, such as their anatomy, social behavior, and honey production, but also on the ecological impact of invasive species. 40 pages.

Wendy Pfeffer. *Dolphin Talk: Whistles, Clicks, and Clapping Jaws.* HarperCollins, 2003. From the Let's-Read-and-Find-Out series, this book focuses on dolphin communication while also revealing the basics of dolphin anatomy, behavior, and life cycle. 40 pages.

Laurence Pringle. *Snakes! Strange and Wonderful.* Boyds Mills, 2004. This book, by well-known nonfiction author Laurence Pringle and illustrated in watercolor paintings by Meryl Henderson, presents a wide variety of snakes and explains the unusual behaviors that characterize the various types. 32 pages.

Ken Robbins. *Seeds.* Atheneum, 2005. Through text and photos by the author, this book reveals the basic facts about seeds—their different shapes and sizes and the connections between a seed's structure and function in terms of its transport. 32 pages.

Pamela Turner. *Gorilla Doctors: Saving Endangered Great Apes.* Houghton Mifflin, 2005. This book in the Scientists in the Field series takes a look at mountain gorillas, one of the most endangered species in the world, and reveals through text and photos how veterinarians in Rwanda and Uganda are working to save them.

Carole Boston Weatherford. *Freedom on the Menu: The Greensboro Sit-Ins.* Dial, 2004. As seen through the eyes of a young southern Black girl, this book offers a unique perspective on the 1960 civil rights sit-ins at the Woolworth's lunch counter in Greensboro, North Carolina. Unnumbered.

Focusing on Academically Relevant Tasks

If you are going to get really good at something, you need to do a lot of it. You need to have a lot of what educational researchers have termed "opportunities to learn," chances to learn about and practice whatever it is you are trying to get good at (Berliner, 1979). If students are going to become proficient readers, they need to do a lot of reading. Certainly, plentiful reading is the central academically relevant task in learning to read, but by no means is it the only one.

In addition to reading itself, several subtasks are important. If students are going to become proficient decoders—readers who can use their knowledge of letter-sound correspondences and spelling patterns to decode unfamiliar words—they need to be actively engaged in tasks like reading decodable books. If students are to become proficient at responding to literature orally and in writing, they need many opportunities to discuss and write about what they have read. And if students are to become critical readers and writers of informational prose, they need abundant opportunities to read and write informational material and to make critical responses. These are only some of the reading-related areas in which students must become proficient, but we think we have made our point: Curriculum—what students study—matters! In Mrs. Mowry's classroom students read all the time and respond in writing, in small literature groups, and during individual reading conferences.

Teachers must actively engage students and help them internalize the knowledge and strategies they are learning.
Mark Richards/PhotoEdit

Employing Active Teaching

The term *active teaching* refers to a set of principles and teaching behaviors that research has shown to be particularly effective, especially in teaching basic skills. As noted by Brophy (1986), teachers who engage in active teaching are the instructional leaders of their classrooms; they are fully knowledgeable about the content and purposes of the instruction they present and about the instructional goals they wish to accomplish. Active teachers do a lot of teaching. Although they use discovery learning for some purposes, they do not generally rely on students to discover what it is they are supposed to learn, particularly when the learning deals with basic skills. The concept of active teaching became even more precise when cognitive-constructivists principles defined it in terms of direct explanation and modeling. The active teacher explains concepts and strategies, models strategies, and guides students as they attempt to use the new ideas.

Fostering Active Learning

Just as it is vital that the teacher be actively involved in teaching, it is also crucial that the learner be actively involved in learning (Good & Brophy, 2003). As we explained in our discussion of the cognitive-constructivist orientation in Chapter 1, the learner must do something with the material he is studying if he is to learn much from it. Fourth-grade teacher John Fitzhugh puts it well in the accompanying feature (In the Classroom 2.2).

Distinguishing Between Instruction and Practice

Effective teaching requires both instruction and practice, but the two need to be clearly distinguished. Practice involves asking students to do something they already know how to do. Instruction involves showing or telling students how to do something that they do not yet know how to do. Simply asking students to do something does not constitute teaching them how to do it. Practice is appropriate *after* students have learned whatever it is they are to practice.

Emphasizing this distinction, Gerry Duffy and Laura Roehler (1982) coined the terms *proactive teaching* and *reactive teaching*. Proactive teaching consists of deliberately

In the Classroom

2.2

Actively Engaging Students in Reading and Responding to a Text

Students *must* be actively involved in order for any sort of learning to take place. That's simply a fact. But there are a number of ways this can happen. Say, for instance, a student is reading a trade book on sharks, perhaps Seymour Simon's *Sharks*. As he reads, the student can

- Think about the new things he is learning about sharks.
- Discuss new insights with others.
- Make outlines or sketches that depict his new knowledge.
- Write a brief story about how he might respond if he were in the water and saw a shark fin nearby.
- Draw relationships between the new knowledge and his existing knowledge of sharks.
- Attempt to implement the new knowledge (for example, simulate an underwater environment by making a diorama of sharks and their habitat, as one of my students did).

Or the student can undertake many other activities that cause him to grapple with the new knowledge and integrate it into his existing schema. As we all know, precious little new knowledge will be absorbed passively.

showing students how to do something before expecting them to do it themselves. Reactive teaching consists of first asking students to do something and then showing them how only when they struggle. Proactive teaching sets students up for success, whereas reactive teaching sets them up for failure. Reactive teaching is inefficient because it often leaves the teacher trying to clarify matters after the fact for students who became confused while working at something they did not know how to do; the confusion could have been avoided by providing instructions at the outset. Reactive teaching is especially demoralizing for students who repeatedly fail. Mrs. Mowry illustrated active teaching when she defined and elaborated on the concept of character traits.

Providing Sufficient and Timely Feedback

Feedback is perhaps the most long-standing precept in this section on traditional principles. It's also an integral part of current conceptions of learning (see, for example, Bransford, Brown, & Cocking, 2000). From the dialogues of Socrates to the answers included in programmed instruction, feedback has long been a central component of instruction. In the years before school, young children get a great deal of immediate, positive feedback—fussing brings a bottle; a smile, a lot of attention; saying "ball," a round object to play with. During these same years, young children also receive a good deal of immediate, negative feedback—too much fussing may bring only a closed door, a smile at the television set produces no response, and "bla" spoken in an attempt to get a round object to play with may instead bring a blanket.

Once in school, students continue to get feedback, although with one teacher serving perhaps 30 students, individual feedback is not as readily available as it was at home. But such feedback is every bit as necessary. There is no way for a learner to know whether he is on the right track unless he receives some sort of response. And this rule applies whether the newly learned material is the sound represented by the letter *m,* the pronunciation of the word *rabbit,* or the identification of the central theme in a story. Sometimes feedback can be embedded in the learning situation and does not require a response from another person. For example, when the child reads, "The rabbit really liked the carrots," his understanding of the sentence as a whole is established by his correct pronunciation of *rabbit*; the pronunciation brings the meaning to mind. At other times, peers can provide the feedback; for example, a group of fifth-graders read a novel and agree that the theme is the importance of friendship. But much of the time, such as in learning letter-sound correspondences, the feedback must come from the teacher. Figuring out how to provide timely, telling, and kind feedback for 30 or so students is a major task for a classroom teacher.

Teaching for Transfer

Transfer is the use of knowledge or skills learned in one context to another context. The well-known Chinese proverb "Give a man a fish, and you feed him for a day. Teach a man to fish, and you feed him for a lifetime" emphasizes the tremendous value of transfer. Knowledge and skills that transfer become tools that students can use throughout their lives. In a very real sense, transfer is the central purpose of schooling. Schools are future oriented. Students attend school today so that they can use what they learn tomorrow. We want students to apply what they learn in the early grades to their learning in later grades; even more important, we want them to apply what they learn in school to the world outside of school.

Given the obvious centrality of transfer to schooling, it may shock you to learn that schools have often been unsuccessful in promoting it. Transfer is one of the oldest topics of educational research, and the repeated finding has been that students very frequently fail to use their school learning out of school. The student who adds and subtracts quite competently during math class fails when she tries to calculate how much allowance she has left. The student who writes a competent letter of complaint as a class exercise never thinks of writing the distributor when his magazine fails to arrive two months in a row. As British philosopher Alfred North Whitehead (1929) aptly put it over 70 years ago, the knowledge students have gained in school has all too frequently been "inert"— fragile, tip-of-the-iceberg knowledge that might enable them to choose a correct answer on a multiple-choice test but does not last or serve much purpose in the real world.

Teaching for transfer requires thoughtful and well-planned instruction. The teacher must create learning tasks that facilitate transfer and remind students to use their new skills. Helping a student transfer the decoding strategy modeled by the teacher requires that the teacher use texts where the strategies can be applied and then prompt the student in the use of the strategies when he struggles. In the next section we will introduce the concept of scaffolding or how teachers provide support as students try out new tasks.

2 Think back as far as you can in your schooling—to elementary school, if possible, or to secondary school—and jot down a list of tasks you completed that you think were academically relevant and a list of tasks you completed that you think were not academically relevant. Then write about what does and does not constitute an academically relevant task.

3 Get together with a few classmates, review the descriptions of proactive and reactive teaching we have provided, and create and present two scenarios—one showing proactive teaching and one showing reactive teaching.

4 Think of a teacher you have had who has been particularly effective in using one of the traditional principles we have discussed, and describe what he or she did that was so effective.

Constructivist and Sociocultural Perspectives on Instruction

Our goal in this section is to describe the characteristics of instruction with great clarity. To do so we need to use different terms and consider different concepts, a vocabulary that is closely related to the cognitive-constructivist orientation underlying this book. We view the following concepts as absolutely vital in reading instruction: gradual release of responsibility, direct explanation, cognitive modeling, and scaffolding. These basic concepts can best be seen as an integrated set of principles that teachers should regularly employ. The other terms—zone of proximal development, cooperative learning, and higher-order thinking—expand on the basic concepts.

The Gradual Release of Responsibility Model

The gradual release of responsibility model depicts an entire instructional cycle during which students learn new skills and knowledge and gradually assume increased responsibility for this learning. Within this model are several interrelated concepts— direct explanation, cognitive modeling, scaffolding, and contextualized review and practice. A particularly informative visual representation of the model developed by David Pearson and Margaret Gallagher (1983) is shown in Figure 2.3.

The model depicts a temporal sequence in which students gradually progress from situations in which the teacher takes responsibility for their successful completion of a reading task (in other words, does most of the work for them), to situations in which students assume increasing responsibility for reading tasks, and finally to situations in which students take total or nearly total responsibility for reading tasks—ideally, transfer of learning. This model can play out over a week, a month, or over a full school year. For some skills like decoding in the fourth grade, the students should be fully independent, needing little or no assistance from the teacher. At the same time, they might just be starting to learn how to determine the author purposes, and the teacher will assume full responsibility for explaining and modeling this thinking.

As an example of this model, suppose a teacher decides that students need to learn to summarize. She begins by explaining what a summary is and how to construct one, trying to be as explicit as possible. Next the teacher models the process and lets students observe her thinking as she develops her summary. Then the teacher and students work on one together in a phase called *guided practice*. During guided practice the teacher asks students questions ("Does your summary contain just important

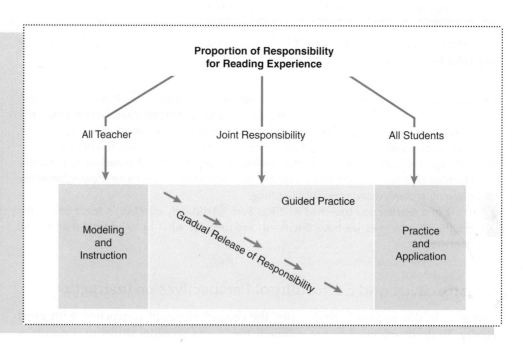

Figure 2.3

The Gradual Release of Responsibility Model

Source: Reprinted from Pearson, P. D., & Gallagher, M. C., "The Instruction of Reading Comprehension," *Contemporary Educational Psychology, 8,* 317–344, Copyright 1983, with permission from Elsevier.

ideas?"); provides hints ("Look for topic sentences"), and models the process again if students need it. After considerable guided practice students are ready to try it out on their own. This instructional cycle may play out over weeks, and the students may be at different stages of the cycle with different skills and strategies. The gradual release of responsibility model always begins with direct explanation, another term for proactive teaching.

Direct Explanation

Direct explanation is an approach to teaching strategies that employs direct instruction, cognitive modeling, and a gradual release of responsibility. Gerald Duffy, Laura Roehler, and colleagues developed it two decades ago (for example, Duffy et al., 1986), and it continues to be highly recommended (Duffy, 2002; Duke & Pearson, 2002; Graves, 2004a). Although direct explanation has most often been used to teach comprehension strategies, it can also be used to teach word recognition strategies, such as using word parts or context to learn word meanings, as well as many other strategies competent readers use.

Reading terminology is often confusing and redundant. We use *direct explanation* to mean the first stage of the gradual release of responsibility model. Nell Duke and David Pearson (2002) use the term *direct explanation* as almost a synonym for the gradual release of responsibility cycle.

When a skill or strategy is first introduced the teacher has to provide

- An explicit description of the strategy—what the students are going to learn to do.
- An explanation of the procedure or process for executing the strategy—how to do it.
- Clear statements about why the strategy is important and when to use it.
- Modeling of the strategy with multiple pieces of text.

PEARSON
myeducationlab

Learn how to explicitly teach students strategies to make meaning from text by completing the activity "Teaching Comprehension Skills and Strategies." (To find this activity, go to the topic *Comprehension* in MyEducationLab and click on Building Teaching Skills and Dispositions.)

Your goal is to illuminate the thinking that underlies the strategy. Being clear and explicit is not easy, because experienced readers are rarely aware of how they infer a word's meaning, find a main idea, or make an inference. Telling students when and why to do something provides motivation and helps the students understand how one particular strategy is related to the larger act of reading. Strategies are used to solve problems when we read, and the teacher needs to point out these problems and how they can be solved through the use of strategies.

Cognitive Modeling

After an explanation, modeling is the next step in the gradual release of responsibility model, but the teacher can and should continue to model a strategy whenever students need greater understanding. When teachers model a task, they actually *do* something, rather than just tell students how to do it. A specific sort of modeling, cognitive modeling, is particularly useful in teaching students difficult concepts and strategies. In cognitive modeling, teachers use explicit instructional talk to reveal their thought processes as they perform the tasks that students will

Cognitive modeling, thinking aloud as you complete a task, has been shown to be a very powerful instructional approach.

iStockPhoto

In the Classroom

Cognitive Modeling

Teacher: Suppose I'm reading along and I come to this sentence: "It was raining heavily and water was standing in the street, so before he left for work Mr. Nelson put on his raincoat, buckled on his galoshes over his shoes, and picked up his umbrella." Let me see—g-a-l-o-s-h-e-s. I don't think I know that word. Let's see. It's raining, and he picks up his raincoat and umbrella and buckles something over his shoes. Galoshes must be some sort of waterproof boots that go over shoes. I can't be certain of that, but it makes sense in the sentence; and I don't think I want to look it up right now.

2.3

Instructional Routines

be asked to perform. For example, a teacher might model the mental process of determining the meaning of an unknown word in context, as shown in the accompanying feature (In the Classroom 2.3).

Cognitive modeling provides a window into the teacher's mind and constitutes one of the most powerful tools for showing children how to reason as they seek to understand a text. As we have stated, cognitive modeling is not easy. Duffy's (2009) *Explaining Reading* provides some strong examples for how to model many reading strategies. After the teacher models the strategy, the students should try it, and the teacher provides help as the students require it.

Scaffolding

As students try out new tasks and new strategies, the teacher provides support by scaffolding the students' efforts. We believe that the term *scaffolding* was first used in its educational sense by David Wood, Jerome Bruner, and Gail Ross (1976), who used it to characterize mothers' verbal interactions when reading to their young children. In these interactions, mothers gently yet supportively guide their children toward successful literacy experiences. Thus, for example, in sharing a picture book and attempting to assist the child in reading the words that label the pictures, a mother might at first simply page through the book, familiarizing the child with the pictures and the general content of the book. Then she might focus on a single picture and ask the child what it is. After this, she might point to the word below the picture, tell the child that the word names the picture, ask the child what the word is, and provide feedback on the correctness of the answer. The important point to note here is that the mother has neither simply told the child the word nor simply asked him to say it. Instead, she has built an instructional structure, a scaffold that assists the child in learning. Scaffolding, as Wood and his colleagues have aptly put it, is "a process that enables a child or novice to solve a problem, carry out a task, or achieve a goal which would be beyond his unassisted efforts."

Teachers scaffold student learning in many different ways. Most frequently the language of the teacher guides the student through the process. If the student is stuck trying to determine the main idea of a passage, the teacher might remind her to re-read the heading and look at the bold print, what we call "moment-to-moment verbal

Scaffolding Small-Group Instruction

Scaffolding student learning is accomplished most easily during small-group instruction. This is especially true for English language learners. We suggest that you bring together fluent speakers of English with students who are just learning English. The students who are stronger in English act as a model for the ELL students and help to support them. Pair up these students; after you ask a question, have them engage in pair-and-share activities. The two students take a moment to discuss the question and formulate an answer. Then one of the students shares the answer with the group. Through this process of pair and share, the ELL student learns how to formulate a response before taking a risk in front of the group.

The key to successful small-group instruction is thinking through how you will assist the students. Much of this assistance comes from moment-to-moment verbal support. Be prepared to ask some of the following questions that scaffold students' use of a main idea strategy. Be sure to have pair-and-share time before students begin responding.

- Can someone retell what we have learned? (Retelling)
- What was difficult to understand in this section? (Clarifying)
- What is the main idea of that section? (Main idea)
- How did you find the main idea?
- How did what you already know help you determine the main idea?
- Which text features helped you determine the main idea?

Differentiating Instruction for **English Language Learners**

support." In another setting the teacher might use a graphic organizer to support or scaffold the student. A story map reminds the reader to look for the critical elements of a narrative—setting, character, problem, and so forth. Even a stack of Post-it notes can remind students to jot down questions while they read—scaffolding a self-questioning strategy. Finally, a teacher might have two students work together on a task, with each student supporting the other. In each of these cases, the teacher is assisting students in doing something that they might not otherwise be able to do. Much of Chapter 10 describes ways to build supportive scaffolds for the many different types of reading students do.

Contextualizing, Reviewing, and Practicing What Is Learned

The release of responsibility model produces deep and lasting learning if students use their newly learned strategies in authentic contexts. Students need many opportunities to practice the strategies and make them their own, with periodic review from the teacher. Although review and practice are traditional instructional activities, the importance of contextualizing students' learning is something we have only recently recognized as absolutely vital to real and lasting learning, and thus we have decided to place all three practices in this section. The concepts are simple, but they must be heeded. If, for example, students learn the strategy of summarizing as part of reading instruction, they must be given opportunities and encouragement to use summarizing when they are working with social studies or science material or when they are gathering information in the library or studying at home. Moreover, students need many opportunities to use the strategy in these authentic contexts.

A literature circle is an excellent example (see Daniels, 2002). As students meet and discuss a novel, they summarize what they have read, clarify difficult vocabulary words, make inferences, and predict what will happen next. The structure of

*A*ssessment

In a weekly newsletter sent home to parents, you can let them know your literacy goals for a certain time period—for example, "Next week we will be working on writing paragraphs. Your child will be learning how to develop a main idea with supporting details."

Working in small groups helps students maximize their own and each other's learning.

Bob Daemmrich Photography

a literature circle reminds and prompts the students to use comprehension strategies, and if the teacher detects problems, she can review the strategies and, if necessary, provide more modeling and scaffolding. As students work in literature circles throughout the year they are regularly reviewing and practicing strategies in a natural context.

Cooperative Learning

David and Roger Johnson define *cooperative learning* as "the instructional use of small groups so that students work together to maximize their own and each other's learning" (Johnson, Johnson, & Holubec, 1994). Robert Slavin defines it as "instructional methods in which students of all performance levels work together toward a group goal" (1987). Cooperative learning is a set of procedures that scaffold student learning. As the Johnsons have repeatedly said, "None of us is as smart as all of us." Groups of students working together have the potential to achieve well beyond what a student working alone can do. Moreover, working in cooperative groups can produce multiple benefits, such as improving students' achievement, effort to succeed, critical thinking, attitudes toward the subjects studied, psychological adjustment, and self-esteem. Cooperative learning can also foster students' interpersonal relationships, improving their ability to work with others and build relationships among diverse racial, ethnic, and social groups. Additionally, as John Seely Brown and his colleagues note (Brown, Collins, & Duguid, 1989), group learning offers learners opportunities for displaying and recognizing the multiple roles that are often required to solve real-world problems and to recognize and confront their own and others' ineffective strategies and misconceptions.

Cooperative learning is consistent with many constructivist and sociocultural principles that we have mentioned. It relies on the belief that the best learning is often social, giving students an opportunity to scaffold one another's work and putting them in a position to respond to and elaborate on one another's thinking. Because of its great potential, throughout this book we frequently suggest group activities for elementary students, and many of the Reflect and Apply sections suggest group work.

The Zone of Proximal Development

Lev Vygotsky (1978), a Russian psychologist, put forth the concept of the zone of proximal development, which emphasizes the social nature of learning and the fact that learning is very much a social phenomenon; in fact, we acquire much of what we learn in our social interchanges with others. According to Vygotsky, at any particular point in time, children have a circumscribed zone of development, a range within which they can learn. At one end of this range are learning tasks that they can complete independently; at the other end are learning tasks that they cannot complete, even with assistance. In between these two extremes is the zone most productive for learning, the range of tasks in which children can achieve *if* they are assisted by a more knowledgeable or more competent other.

If left on their own, for example, many third-graders might learn very little from a *National Geographic World* article on the formation of thunderstorms. Conversely,

*A*ssessment

During the beginning months of the school year, teach students how to evaluate their own work. Gradually, let students do more and more self-evaluation, continually giving them feedback on how well they are doing. By midyear, students will be able to appraise much of their work for themselves.

with your help—getting them interested in the topic, focusing their attention, pre-teaching some of the critical concepts such as the effects of rising heat, arranging small groups to discuss and answer questions on certain parts of the article—these same students may be able to learn a good deal from the article. However, with other topics and other texts—for example, a chapter on gravity from a high school physics text—no amount of outside help, at least no reasonable amount of outside help, will foster much learning for these third-graders. The topic of gravity and its presentation in the high school text are simply outside their zone of proximal development. The zone of proximal development is a useful concept because it helps you think about the difficulty of the text and the task and find ways to adjust them to the abilities of your students.

Teaching for Understanding

As we have noted, over 80 years ago, British philosopher Alfred North Whitehead (1929) railed against schools' fostering what he called "inert knowledge"—fragile, shallow knowledge that is usually soon forgotten and too superficial to be of much use even if remembered. Today, educators are increasingly realizing the value of teaching for understanding—dealing with fewer topics but teaching them in such a way that students not only learn the content itself thoroughly but also appreciate the reasons for learning it and retain it in a form that makes it usable. As Harvard psychologist David Perkins (1992) puts it, teaching for understanding promotes three basic goals of education: understanding of knowledge, retention of knowledge, and active use of knowledge.

We believe that teaching for understanding is terribly important; we address this topic especially in the comprehension chapters. Relying heavily on the work of Perkins and his colleagues (Blythe, 1998; Perkins, 1992; Wiske, 1998), we examine teaching for understanding in detail. Here we will note only that the key to teaching for understanding is teaching fewer topics but teaching them well and that teaching for understanding demands the sort of constructive teaching and learning advocated throughout this section of the chapter.

Teaching skills, strategies, and concepts can be placed on a continuum with more open, student-centered, and indirect approaches at one end and more structured, teacher-centered, and direct approaches at the other. Figure 2.4 places the three most popular methods on this continuum. Guided reading (Fountas & Pinnell, 1996, 2001) is the most indirect approach because skills and strategies are modeled only as students need them. The content of reading is in the foreground and the strategies are in the background. Direct explicit instruction (Carnine, Silbert, & Kame'enui, 1997) stands at the other end. This method calls for a hierarchy of skills, a task analysis of skills, and texts crafted for the specific purpose of teaching the skills. The cognitive-constructivist position, direct explanation and the gradual release of responsibility stand in the middle—the focus of our book. Sometimes, educators endorse one or another of these approaches, largely to the exclusion of others. We believe quite differently. In keeping with current theory and research (for example, Pressley, 2006; Taylor, Pearson, Peterson, & Rodriguez, 2003), we believe that in order to become fully literate, children need to develop a wide array of talents and attitudes and that only a wide array of instructional approaches can help them achieve this goal.

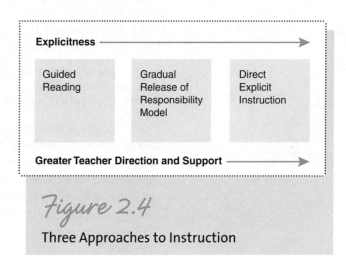

Figure 2.4

Three Approaches to Instruction

5 Each of the instructional concepts in this section is tremendously important. Define each of them in your own words. Next, check your understanding against that of a classmate, and see if you can come up with a common definition of each concept. Finally, team up with this classmate and two others, and together come up with one example of classroom instruction that is in keeping with each of these concepts and one example of a classroom situation in which instruction runs counter to these concepts.

6 Locate the teacher manual from a basal reading program and analyze how comprehension skills are taught. Does the lesson provide for direct explanation, gradual release of responsibility, scaffolding, and contextualized practice?

A Brief History of Reading Instruction in the United States

The history of the United States and its schools reveals cyclical changes in which alternating political and educational stances at first receive widespread support, only to later draw heavy criticism and disapproval (Cremin, 1990; Graves & Dykstra, 1997; Schlesinger, 1986). To understand the development of contemporary approaches to teaching reading, the history of reading instruction in the United States is best studied against the backdrop of tensions between these competing views. In the brief history that follows—parts of which rely heavily on information taken from Nila Banton Smith's *American Reading Instruction* (2002) and David Pearson's "Reading in the Twentieth Century" (2000)—we focus on these tensions.

The Colonial Period and the 19th Century

The period extending roughly from 1600 to 1840 was relatively free of tensions over instructional approaches. The emphasis was on content. The purpose of reading instruction early in the period was clearly religious, as revealed by this excerpt from the Old Deluder Act passed by the General Court of Massachusetts in 1647:

> It being one chief point of that old deluder, Satan, to keep men from the knowledge of the Scriptures. . . . It is therefore ordered that every township in this jurisdiction, after the Lord hath increased them to the number of fifty households, shall then forthwith appoint one within their town to teach all such children as shall resort to him to write and read. (Quoted in Smith, 2002)

Beginning about the time of the American Revolution and continuing until about 1840, the purpose shifted, and reading series reflected what Smith has termed a "nationalistic-moralistic emphasis," as exemplified in these lines from the preface to Lyman Cobb's *The North American Reader* (1835):

> The pieces in this work are chiefly American. The English Reader so largely used in our country does not contain a single piece or paragraph written by an American citizen. Is this good policy? Is it patriotism? (Cobb, 1835)

However, regardless of whether the reading material focused on religious or patriotic content, the method of instruction throughout the period was much the same—the alphabetic-spelling method, a plodding, step-by-step approach in which students first learned the alphabet, next learned to spell a large number of syllables, and then spelled words before they read them. At this point they memorized sections of text (usually religious, moral, or patriotic in content) and read orally (Smith, 2002). Figure 2.5 shows a page from the *New England Primer*, exemplifying the tediousness of the approach.

Not surprisingly, this approach eventually came under fire, most notably by educational reformer Horace Mann, who advocated instead a focus on whole words and letter sounds. In an 1842 report to the Board of Education in Massachusetts, Mann displays his disdain for the alphabetic-spelling approach and foreshadows the controversy that, though modified, continues today:

> Compare the above method [the more meaningful approach Mann favored] with that of calling up a class of abecedarians—or, what is more common, a single child—and while the teacher holds a book or card before him, with a pointer in his hand, says, *a*, and he echoes *a*; then *b*, and he echoes *b*; and so on until the vertical row of lifeless and ill-favored characters is completed, and then of remanding him to his seat, to sit still and look at vacancy. (Mann, 1884/1965)

Basal Readers and Their Impact on Reading Instruction

Beginning in the early 1900s, reading programs and reading instruction began to look more like the approaches you or your parents might have experienced. Teacher's manuals were developed, research on which words appear frequently in English resulted in carefully controlled vocabulary in basal readers, sequences for teaching reading skills were developed, the workbook was introduced, testing was increasingly used, and students were increasingly grouped by ability for reading instruction.

The basal readers themselves consisted of large collections of reading selections, with accompanying worksheets, teacher's manuals, tests, and supplementary material. The books for the earliest grades employed strictly controlled vocabularies and generally contained very brief narratives, relying on pictures to convey much of their meaning. The books in the remainder of the primary grades continued to employ controlled vocabularies and contained largely fiction, which was often quite impoverished. At about the fourth-grade level, selections became longer, vocabulary control eased, the fiction became somewhat stronger, and some expository selections were included. Much of the instruction students received in these programs centered around directed reading lessons—which included preparation for reading, silent reading, and follow-up questions and discussion—on individual selections. These lessons were often punctuated by skills work in decoding, vocabulary, and comprehension, and students spent a good deal of time completing worksheets. Figure 2.6 shows pages from a first-grade reader in a 1950 basal series, typical of the readers of this period.

Although many controversies about reading materials and reading instruction arose during the period, the most persistent and frequent again involved the tensions between more holistic and more segmented instruction, centering on letters, sounds, and words. The alphabetic-spelling method had disappeared, but the whole-word method and various approaches emphasizing phonics continued to be in conflict. This conflict reached a crescendo in 1955 when Rudolf Flesch published his

New England Primer   5

EASY SYLLABLES FOR CHILDREN

Ab	eb	ib	ob	ub
ac	ec	ic	oc	uc
ad	ed	id	od	ud
af	ef	if	of	uf
ag	eg	ig	og	ug
aj	ej	ij	oj	uj
al	el	il	ol	ul
am	em	im	om	um
an	en	in	on	un
ap	ep	ip	op	up
ar	er	ir	or	ur
as	es	is	os	us
at	et	it	ot	ut
av	ev	iv	ov	uv
ax	ex	ix	ox	ux
az	ez	iz	oz	uz

Figure 2.5

A Page from the *New England Primer*

Source: Smith, N. B. (2002). *American Reading Instruction*, special edition. Newark, DE: International Reading Association.

Oh, Jane.
Look and see.
See Baby go.
See Tim go.
See Spot and Puff go.

51

Sally said, "Come, Mother.
Come and see Father.
See Father jump and play.
Oh, oh.
Father is funny."

75

best-selling *Why Johnny Can't Read.* Flesch charged that American children were not learning to read because they were not taught phonics. A decade later, in 1967, Harvard University professor Jeanne Chall published a very influential review of research, *Learning to Read: The Great Debate,* in which she concluded that phonics produced at least somewhat better results than the whole-word method. In that same year, the largest study of beginning reading ever conducted, the First Grade Reading Studies (Bond & Dykstra, 1967/1997), produced findings that tended to support Chall's conclusions.

Although these three publications did change the content of basals, they did not seriously change the influence and prominence of basals in the schools (Pearson, 2000). Contrary to Flesch's charge, most basals had always included some phonics instruction, and basal publishers responded to criticisms by providing somewhat more phonics. As late as 1985, the vast majority of American children continued to be taught with basal readers, and most teachers, if asked, would have said that they used a basal reading approach.

The Challenge to Basal Readers: Whole-Language and Literature-Based Approaches

Advocates of more holistic approaches—whole-language and literature-based instruction—began to challenge basal reading programs. Whole language was first widely popularized in the United States in the writings of Kenneth Goodman (1970) and Frank Smith (1971). The basic charge was that basal approaches break up language and learning to read in a way that is unnatural and artificial and actually makes learning to read more difficult. More specific charges were that basals included too much skills instruction, that instruction in phonics and other subskills of reading was not integrated with actual reading, that vocabulary was much too controlled, that stories were banal and not well constructed, that separating students into ability groups had dire results for less skilled readers, and that teachers were overprogrammed and overscripted. Critics also noted that the selections in basals dealt almost exclusively with White, middle-class characters, themes, and settings and that many of the reading selections were very poor from a literary standpoint. Advocates of literature-based programs had similar criticisms, though they tended not to be as adamantly against basal anthologies and structured programs as their whole-language colleagues. Both groups had a marked effect on basal readers and a huge effect on the reading instruction taking place in U.S. classrooms. In fact, literature-based basals became the most common type of basal in the 1990s.

Having outlined what advocates of whole-language and literature-based approaches were against, we now discuss what they favored. Three very general characteristics stand out: the use of authentic children's literature, a child-centered approach, and a focus on learning to read by reading. Advocates argued that authentic children's literature—books written by professional authors to engage and entertain children—should be the mainstay of reading instruction. Moreover, whole texts should be used; excerpts should be avoided. Students and their needs, desires, and interests need to be the focus of attention, the primary concern. A preset curriculum is suspect. Student-initiated learning is favored over teacher-initiated instruction. Instruction comes when and as needed, while students are actually engaged in reading, and in quite brief minilessons.

The influence of whole-language and literature-based instruction produced a significant change in basal reading programs, especially in first grade. Publishers now picked reading selections by their literary value and not the control and repetition of the vocabulary. Hoffman and his colleagues carefully documented these changes, examining basal programs from 1987 and 1993 (Hoffman, McCarthey, Abbott, Christian, Corman, & Curry, 1994). In the newer programs students had to learn more than twice as many individual words than in the older programs. Each word appeared with far fewer repetitions, and the overall reading level for first grade text was significantly more difficult. On the positive side the material was judged to be more engaging. Educators and publishers were betting that interest and engagement would trump vocabulary and phonics control.

Instruction in skills and strategies still played a prominent part in these new basal reading programs. Phonics instruction was not as robust, but teachers were still directed to explain and model comprehension instruction even if these lessons were not always as explicit as they could be. These basal programs also included a process approach to writing, integration of reading with the other language arts, and the use of book clubs for literature study.

Massive Federal Intervention in Reading and Core Reading Programs

The most recent large-scale movement affecting reading instruction in schools has been massive federal intervention. We will very briefly summarize a lengthy set of events. For some years now, the federal government has sponsored a substantial amount of research on reading through the National Institute of Child Health and Human Development (NICHD), a part of the National Institutes of Health. Most of that research has focused on young children and their beginning skills such as phonemic awareness and phonics and on children who have difficulty learning to read. In 1998, the National Research Council, a prestigious scientific organization, published *Preventing Reading Difficulties in Young Children* (Snow, Burns, & Griffin, 1998), a book that reviewed and brought to prominence much of the research sponsored by the NICHD, as well as other research on early reading.

In 2000, the National Reading Panel (NRP), a group of scholars working at the direction of the U.S. Congress, published the *Report of the National Reading Panel: Teaching*

Children to Read. In this report, the NRP identified five elements of reading instruction that it saw as strongly supported by research: phonemic awareness, phonics, fluency, vocabulary, and comprehension.

The NRP report has had both very strong supporters and very strong opponents, but both supporters and opponents agree that it has had and is very likely to continue to have huge effects on reading instruction. Most notably, a massive federal funding program titled Reading First is specifically designed to promote instruction in each of the five areas endorsed by the report—that is, in phonemic awareness, phonics, fluency, vocabulary, and comprehension. The program has had a substantial effect despite its mixed results (Center for Educational Policy, 2005; see http://ies.ed.gov/ncee). Many schools and districts have endorsed the federal agenda, and most basal readers now reflect the NRP and Reading First priorities.

Basal reading programs responded to the federal initiatives by remaking their programs to reflect the new research priorities. They also changed their identity to become "core reading programs." The change in terminology was significant (Dewitz, Leahy, Jones, & Sullivan, 2010). Whereas *basal* means the base from which students begin reading instruction and then move into ever-wider ranges of literature, *core* conveys the idea that these published programs are the reading curriculum, encompassing the entirety of reading instruction. Core reading programs were marketed as being scientifically based research programs after a number of states and one research lab certified the research base of their instruction. However, subsequent research, especially studies of comprehension instruction, have challenged the research base of these programs (Dewitz, Jones, & Leahy, 2009; McGill-Franzen, Zmach, Solic, & Zeig, 2006).

The newest programs, those published after 2005, have provided a stronger focus on phonemic awareness, phonics, and fluency. They include more decodable books and leveled books. Vocabulary instruction has become more robust, conforming to the suggestions of Beck and her colleagues (Beck, McKeown, & Kucan, 2002). Yet, comprehension instruction still lacks direct explanation and has failed to follow the gradual release of responsibility model (Dewitz et al., 2009). These programs also provide guidelines for teaching small groups of students who have differing skill needs and have moved away from exclusive whole-group instruction that had been the hallmark of core programs in previous decades. Just as publishers responded to literature-based instruction by building the programs around children's literature, now publishers have embraced the suggestions of the large federal initiative. Basal reading programs follow national trends and therefore ensure their prominence in the marketplace.

When you visit schools or talk to other teachers, you are apt to see a variety of approaches to reading instruction, some of them more effective than others. Whole-language and literature-based programs have not disappeared. Some schools and some teachers continue to employ these approaches or at least significant parts of them. Other schools closely adhere to the recommendations of the National Reading Panel and the Reading First legislation. As we noted in Chapter 1, we believe that phonemic awareness, phonics, fluency, vocabulary, and comprehension are vital parts of a reading program. But as we also noted, we and most other reading educators believe firmly that these five elements constitute only part of a comprehensive and balanced reading program that can lead all students to the sophisticated level of literacy necessary in the 21st century. A comprehensive reading program also requires a strong focus on motivation and differentiated instruction fostering higher-order thinking and deep understanding—as well as encouraging independent reading and reader response.

7. How have our expectations for reading changed since the colonial period? Given the high expectations of the current era, can basal programs help us achieve these goals?

8. Describe the program of reading instruction you received in elementary school. Discuss any characteristics of the four historical periods that you saw in your elementary school. You are not likely to identify any characteristics of the colonial period and the 19th century, but you may well identify characteristics of the other periods.

9. Try to identify the best elementary teacher you ever had. Then discuss which characteristics of teachers who produce outstanding achievement he or she did and did not have.

Strengths *and Challenges* of Diversity

As you know, students differ from one another in many ways that we as teachers need to attend to. The instructional principles we discuss in the chapter hold for virtually all students, who must participate in a rich, balanced, and comprehensive literacy curriculum if they are to achieve the level of literacy needed in our society. Still, different students will profit from different experiences. Here we consider differing participation structures as well as high achievement for students of color.

Differing Participation Structures

When working with learners having different cultural and linguistic backgrounds, it is important for the teacher to understand differing participation structures. Participation structures are the tacit arrangements that exist between speakers and listeners as they interact in certain social situations—in this case, classroom conversations. As Shirley Brice Heath (1983) has pointed out, differences in the conversational patterns of middle-class teachers and students who are not from the linguistic mainstream can be very debilitating. For example, Kathryn Au and Jana Mason (1983) explain how the mainstream instructional pattern in which teachers direct questions at individual students clashes with the participation structures familiar to native Hawaiian children. Hawaiian children are used to a participation structure in which several people talk at once. Being singled out to individually answer a question can seem uncomfortable and difficult to understand. Somewhat similarly, some African American students respond well to a performer/audience style of teaching. First-grade teacher Debbie Diller (1999) discovered this in her attempts to more successfully connect with the many African American students in her class:

Assessment

It is important to be candid with students and their parents about both strengths and limitations of students. The final aim of literacy assessment is to provide the ongoing guidance needed to lead students to the highest possible level of literacy.

As I taught students a new concept, I encouraged them to respond chorally or individually at a rather fast, energized pace. "What sounds do you hear at the beginning of *stay*?" I'd ask enthusiastically; "*st st*," the children would respond in rhythm. "Tell your neighbor another word that starts like *stay*," I'd continue. "Tell your neighbor another word that starts with *st*." The children would spontaneously call out words to each other or to me.

—Debbie Diller, first-grade teacher

Of course, other linguistic and cultural groups follow other participation structures, and thus teachers need to learn the cultural and linguistic patterns of interaction followed by their students.

High Achievement for Students of Color

It has now been 50 years since the Supreme Court's landmark *Brown vs. the Board of Education* decision requiring school desegregation. Yet despite a number of strong efforts and the many gains that students of color have made over those 50 years, a large achievement gap continues to exist. By the twelfth grade, average African American and Hispanic students can read only about as well as White eighth-graders. In a recent policy statement on closing this gap (Gordon, 2004), the American Educational Research Association made two recommendations. First, we must "support programs that engage all students in a rigorous, standards-based curriculum. Provide additional time and instruction as needed, but do not lower expectations." Second, we must "create an environment that provides the necessary social support for learning. It is important for students to be surrounded by peers and family members who value and support academic effort." We very strongly support both recommendations, and we add one of our own: Do everything possible to ensure that students are motivated to succeed in school. Motivation is vital for all students, but it is particularly vital for many students of color. We take up the topic of motivation in depth in Chapter 3.

Concluding *Remarks*

In this chapter, we discussed three topics: First, we took you inside successful classrooms and looked at effective teachers. Next, we discussed traditional principles of instruction and newer constructivist and sociocultural perspectives on instruction. Third, we gave a brief history of reading instruction in the United States, including the most recent federal initiatives.

It is worth summarizing several main points. Both traditional instructional principles, such as fostering active learning and providing sufficient and timely feedback, and constructivist and sociocultural principles, such as cognitive modeling and scaffolding, are important. Instruction is not good simply because it represents an idea that has been around a long time or because it represents a new and different idea. Instruction is good because it is motivated by solid theory, backed by research, and able to be used by real teachers in real classrooms.

The history of reading instruction in the United States indicates that various approaches to reading have come and gone, that we have learned a lot and come to much agreement in recent years, but that tensions continue to exist. The most effective approach to instruction, the one most likely to lead the most children to a high level of literacy, is an eclectic, comprehensive, and balanced approach.

It is also important to realize that effective instruction emphasizes different parts of the curriculum, as students become increasingly competent readers. For example, most children will have mastered most of what they need to know about print and most decoding strategies by the end of second grade, and thus these elements constitute a small part of the literacy curriculum after that time. Conversely, all children should receive instruction in vocabulary and various facets of comprehension beginning in kindergarten and continuing throughout their years of school.

Extending *Learning*

As we noted in Chapter 1, in this section we suggest activities that take you beyond this book to observe and work with schools, teachers, and parents and to access various sources of information that can help you more fully understand and appreciate your role in fostering students' literacy.

1. Identify a simple skill that you have mastered but that many of your classmates probably have not. Choose something specific that can be learned relatively easily, such as tying a square knot. Review the traditional and constructivist/sociocultural principles of instruction—active teaching, active learning, scaffolding, gradual release, feedback, and the like—and decide which can be incorporated into your instruction. Next, write out a specific plan for teaching your skill—a lesson plan—noting just what you are going to do and indicating which principles you are following at each point. Rehearse your instruction, with a partner if possible; then teach a small group of your classmates the skill. If possible, have a classmate who is not part of the group observe you. Finally, sit down with your classmates—both the learners and the observer—and critique your instruction, being sure to attend to how well people learned the skill, what did and did not go well, how you might improve the

lesson, what instructional principles you followed, and what additional instructional principles you might incorporate to improve learning.

2. Identify two really excellent elementary teachers. These could be teachers who have been formally recognized as outstanding, teachers you know of from friends or colleagues, teachers you actually had, or teachers recommended by a principal or one of your professors. Make up some observation sheets listing the characteristics of teachers who produce outstanding achievement in reading. Go back to the section Highly Effective Teachers and Schools to develop your characteristics. Then observe the two teachers, and make notes on the extent to which they demonstrate each of the characteristics on the list. Plan on at least three observations, but do more if you can. For each characteristic that the teachers demonstrate, jot down a specific example or two of how they do so. Once you are finished with your observation, write a summary statement on the extent to which the teachers did and did not demonstrate the characteristics and a statement about the extent to which you expect to incorporate the characteristics into your teaching. Finally, discuss your observations and conclusions with a classmate.

Children's Literature

Byars, B. C. (2002). *Keeper of the Doves.* New York: Viking. In this story set in the late 19th century in Kentucky, the precocious Amie McBee searches for her place in the family and discovers a talent of her own, writing poetry. 112 pages.

Inns, C. (2004). *Help!* London: Frances Lincoln. Doctor Hopper (a rabbit) and Nurse Rex Barker (a dog) zoom around to cure sick toys in this witty picture book. 32 pages.

Juster, N. (2005). *The Hello, Goodbye Window.* New York: Hyperion. A little girl visits her grandparents' house and finds a magic gateway in the kitchen window that leads her on a voyage of discovery. 32 pages.

McDonald, A. (2001). *No More Nasty.* New York: Farrar, Straus and Giroux. Fifth grade becomes more than a bit embarrassing and challenging for Simon when his favorite, but eccentric, 74-year-old aunt becomes the substitute teacher in his unruly class. 172 pages.

National Geographic World. Washington, DC: National Geographic Society. This richly illustrated monthly periodical is designed for intermediate-grade students.

Simon, S. (1995). *Sharks.* New York: HarperCollins. With full-color photos and engaging text that describes fascinating details about 350 different kinds of sharks, Simon demystifies this greatly feared predatory fish. Unnumbered.

PEARSON
myeducationlab

Now go to the topics "Emergent Literacy" and "Comprehension" in the MyEducationLab (www.myeducationlab.com) for your course, where you can:

- Find learning outcomes for the topics covered in this chapter along with the IRA standards that connect to these outcomes.

- Complete assignable activities in the Assignments and Activities section that show concepts in action to help you synthesize and apply strategies.

- Explore IRIS Center Resources—training enhancement materials that provide you with research-validated information and interactive materials to develop your skills in working with students.

- Apply and practice your understanding of the teaching skills identified in the chapter with the Building Teaching Skills and Dispositions exercises.

3

Motivation and Engagement

Last year, Cynthia Sanchez, who had spent 5 years working predominantly with inner-city Hispanic students, switched from teaching first grade to fifth grade, and her first year as a fifth-grade teacher was not an easy one. "What a difference four years make," she sometimes sighed to herself. Of course, she had to learn to teach very different aspects of reading than she had taught in first grade. None of her students needed to work on phonemic awareness, only a few needed help with phonics, and many read fluently. She also had to learn to teach fairly sophisticated lessons in social studies, science, math, and other subjects. What turned out to be much more of a challenge than learning how to teach new material, however, was motivating students. Cynthia's first-graders had come to school enthusiastic about their opportunities, excited about learning, confident that they could learn, and ready to put their best efforts into whatever subject they were studying. Some of her fifth-graders displayed very different attitudes. They were not enthusiastic about school or excited about learning. Nor were they confident about learning or prepared to put in their best efforts.

Cynthia soon decided that motivating and engaging students was her number one priority. As the year progressed she talked regularly with her grade-level colleagues, who had many more years of experience in fifth grade. One colleague stressed that the key to motivation was selecting and reading the right books. She felt that her daily read-alouds from authors like Sandra Cisneros and Gary Soto helped to capture her students' imaginations. Another colleague urged her to incorporate Accelerated Reader software into her literacy program. Students like the computer-based assessments and competing for points keeps them motivated. Her final colleague felt that the secret to motivating these students were the projects she developed for her class. Each year they studied the tide pools along the Pacific shore, the Spanish heritage in California, and space science, included a trip to Mt. Wilson observatory. These lengthy reading and writing tasks gave her students concrete goals and a reason to dive into books, articles, and the Internet.

CLASSROOM vignette

Making Motivation a Top Priority

As you will see in this chapter, Cynthia is not alone in realizing that motivation should be a top priority and also not alone in being bombarded with theories of motivation. Other teachers, reading authorities, researchers, and policy makers are increasingly realizing that motivation is essential to learning (Brophy, 2004; National Research Council, 2004; Pressley, 2006). Just as we developed a theory of instruction that should guide your instructional decision making, we will now develop a theory of motivation that should help you shape your students' experience in school. Motivation is complex and not all students are entranced and enticed by the same activities. In order for substantive learning to occur, students must have positive attitudes about themselves as learners, about their ability to succeed in school, and about the instructional goals they, their teachers, and their schools set. Students' reading abilities will grow in direct proportion to the extent to which they see reading as enjoyable, worthwhile, and valuable as a tool for learning. In discussing ways to foster such positive attitudes, we consider the critical importance of success, ways of creating the sort of classroom atmosphere that has come to be called a literate environment, and the importance of positive attributions. We also consider a number of concrete approaches to motivating students, present an extended portrait of a teacher who is a superstar at motivating her students, and discuss ways of grouping students to foster positive attitudes. These building blocks of success are shown in Figure 3.1.

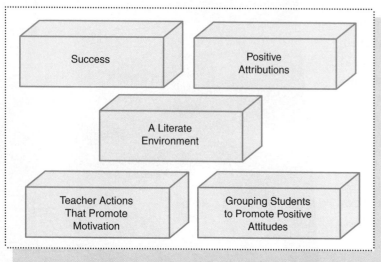

Figure 3.1 **The Building Blocks of Motivation**

The Critical Importance of Success

A dominant thought underlying not just this section of the chapter, but the whole of this book is the overwhelming importance of success. Research has repeatedly verified that if students are going to be motivated and engaged in school and learn from their schoolwork, they need to succeed at the vast majority of tasks they undertake (Brophy, 1986; Pressley, 2006). This, of course, applies to reading just as it does to other schoolwork. Moreover, if students are to become not only proficient readers but also avid readers—children and later adults who voluntarily seek out reading as a path to information, enjoyment, and personal fulfillment—then successful reading experiences are even more important.

A successful reading experience has at least three features. First, and most important, a successful reading experience is one in which the reader understands what she has read. Understanding may take more than one reading, it may require your assistance or that of other students, and it will often require the reader to actively manipulate the ideas in the text. Second, a successful reading experience is one that the reader finds enjoyable, entertaining, informative, or thought provoking. Finally, a successful reading experience is often a means to a larger goal—to learn about galaxies or live in the fantastic world of the Hobbit.

To a great extent, children's success in reading is directly under your control. You can select—and encourage students to select—tasks, materials, and supporting activities that all but guarantee success. Reading assignments that are too long or too challenging for the allotted time will simply lead to frustration. Fifth-grade students who will be reading *Pond & River* by Steve Parker but who have virtually no concept of ecology—they have never even thought about the relationships among organisms and their environment—will find the book impenetrable. Preteaching the concept of *ecology* will greatly increase the likelihood that students will understand the selection and not simply flounder in a sea of new ideas.

Creating a Literate Environment

The term *literate environment* describes the sort of classroom, school, and home environment in which literacy will be fostered and nurtured (Goodman, 1986). In a literate environment people use print to manage and inform their daily lives and also as a source of entertainment and enlightenment. A literate environment includes demonstrations of literacy in action by competent others, time devoted to the practice of literacy, texts that support engagement in literacy, and choice about literate activities. For students who do not come from a literate environment we want to create one in their classroom.

Modeling

Probably the most important component of a literate environment is the modeling done by people children respect and love. In the best possible literate environment, children's teachers, principals, parents, brothers and sisters, and friends read a lot and openly display the pleasure reading gives them. These adults regularly demonstrate the fact that reading opens up a world of information from which they gain knowledge, insight, and power. Unfortunately many children come from homes where little or no reading takes place, and schools must be their literate environment. To be most effective, of course, this modeling should occur not just once but repeatedly—all the time, really. Also, this modeling should include both repeated demonstrations—your reading along with students during a sustained silent reading period, your looking up in a book an answer to a question children have, and your sharing a favorite poem with your class—and direct testimonials—"Wow! What a story." "I never knew what fun river rafting could be till I read this article; I sure wish I'd read it sooner." "Sometimes I think the library is just about my favorite place."

Third-grade teacher Mary Lou Flicker has her own testimonial to the power of modeling.

> I never realized the importance of modeling the kinds of behaviors I would like my students to emulate until one rainy day in March. Normally the kids eat outdoors on picnic tables, but during this unusual California downpour we were forced inside for lunch recess. After the kids finished eating, I told them they could play games together quietly, draw on the chalkboard, read, whatever.
>
> Instead of doing paperwork or watching the kids, I decided to read a book that a young friend had recommended, one of Barbara Park's Junie B. Jones books, *Junie B.,*

First Grader: Shipwrecked. It turned out to be an extremely funny book that I enjoyed immensely. After I finished, I looked around the room. To my amazement, there in the library corner sat Ramon, one of my least-motivated readers, a kid who hardly ever read by choice, fully absorbed in a Junie B. Jones book. Later in the day, when I told Ramon I was so pleased to see him reading, he said, "Well, you looked like you was having such a great time reading that Junie B. Jones book, I just had to find out why!"

—Mary Lou Flicker, third-grade teacher

Several aspects of this experience were motivating to students. First, Ms. Flicker modeled engaged reading. Second, she showed students how much she valued reading by spending class time on reading. Third, she praised her student's good behavior.

Reading aloud to students is another way to demonstrate how much you value reading, and it also becomes an opportunity to teach students about the rewards that reading brings. What you choose to read aloud can serve to entice students to broaden the scope of their reading interests. It allows you to introduce new authors, new genres, and new ideas. All readers need to experience the power of a well-written story, poem, or piece of nonfiction so that they can remember the reward that reading can bring. It creates a communal experience that students can use to understand new texts that they read and new ideas that they consider. Reading aloud sells books and authors. Reading aloud offers you the opportunity to talk about writing in a way that is concrete and engaging; students enjoy learning about how writing works when they are engaged with a text.

Modeling literate behavior is not limited to reading aloud. We model literate behavior when we write a language experience story in first grade, when we record the number of students selecting pizza versus peanut butter and jelly for lunch, when we record what we have learned about snakes on a science chart, and when we write the new words we are learning on the word wall. In many classrooms the first literate activity after the read-aloud is the use of an agenda to record the work and homework for the day. When children observe adults using written language they begin to understand that written language is a powerful tool for recording, remembering, and planning life.

A Print-Rich Classroom

Three kinds of print should fill your classroom—published material, print created by the teacher, and print created by the students. James Hoffman and his colleagues studied literary environments and found that they could link the amount and quality of print in the room to growth in students' reading comprehension (Hoffman, Sailors, Duffy, & Beretvas, 2004). In the best possible literate environment, the classroom is filled with books, books that are readily accessible for students to read in school or take home. Certainly, some books will be in your classroom because they fit within your curriculum. Other materials should be selected so that students have a wide variety of topics, reading levels, and genres to choose from. Still other books should be chosen to reflect the diversity of your classroom—the range of abilities, interests, and cultural, linguistic, and social backgrounds of your students—as well as the diversity of the larger society outside your classroom. Reading well-written texts should become a tool students use to learn more about topics and ideas they are interested in, as well as supplementing their understanding of the required curriculum. This kind of reading gives students a purpose for practicing the craft of reading.

In order to provide all students with appropriate texts and to match individual students with texts, it's important that you assess your students' attitudes toward reading and their reading interests. For some suggestions on doing so, see In the

Assessing Students' Reading Attitudes and Interests

It's important that you get to know your students as readers early in the academic year. You can find out about their reading habits and preferences by having a one-on-one book conference with each of them, and with primary-grade children that's what you need to do. But with older students, a faster and more efficient way to get the information you need is to have them fill out a brief written survey. You can easily create a set of questions that will give you the information you need, such as the following:

- Do you like to read? Why or why not?
- Are you reading anything for fun at this time? What is it? Why do you like it?
- Do you have any favorite authors or titles? Why are these your favorites?
- Is there a certain kind of text that you prefer—books, magazines, fiction, nonfiction, or some other format?
- How do you choose what to read when you go to a library or book store?
- What do you do if what you are reading is too hard or too easy for you?
- What makes a good reader?

Classroom 3.1. In Chapter 6, we give additional information on matching students and texts.

Finding out about your students as readers is vital to being an effective, motivating teacher. You can find books that will appeal to your students by looking at the following annotated lists:

- The Children's Choices list, which appears every October in *The Reading Teacher*
- The Teachers' Choices list, which appears every November in *The Reading Teacher*
- The Notable Children's Trade Books in the Field of Social Studies list, which appears in the May/June issue of *Social Education*
- The Outstanding Science Trade Books for Children list, which appears in the November issue of *Children and Science*

Another effective strategy for identifying books that your students might enjoy is to talk with your school media specialist or the librarians at a local library. They have access to the American Library Association's resources and can give you lists of books that librarians have identified as being of interest to readers of various ages and levels of proficiency. A third way to identify exciting books is to watch the kids. Just like adults, children have their own "bestsellers." Right now second-graders like Junie B. Jones (Park, 2001), third-grade boys are hiding Captain Underpants books (Pilkey, 2001) in their desks, and many fourth-graders are reading the *Diary of a Wimpy Kid* (Kinney, 2007). Although the literary quality of some books may be questionable, teachers must first help students develop the reading habit; then they can refine taste.

As we have noted, the social, linguistic, and cultural backgrounds of your students and of the greater society constitute yet another important factor in selecting books. Readers shape their views of themselves and of the world partly through what they read. Reading about people who are similar to and different from ourselves is important for all students. Recognizing yourself in a book is a powerful affirmation that you are part of the human endeavor—and the world of books. Recognizing the humanity of others who might seem different from ourselves is an important part of becoming a citizen of the world. Good books can act as both a mirror and a window for readers

(Galda & Cullinan, 2009), reflecting their own lives and offering them a chance to understand the lives of others. Perhaps the best books offer an experience that is similar to looking through a window at twilight. At first you can see through the window into another place, but, as the light gradually fades, you end up seeing yourself (Galda, 1998; Galda & Cullinan, 2009). Thinking and talking about experiences like this can help students develop an understanding of themselves and others. And reading books from many cultures exposes students to many wonderful authors. Unfortunately, the number of books by and about people of color published in any given year hovers around 3 or 4 percent—a far cry from the percentage of students of color who attend school. Books that reflect linguistic diversity (bilingual texts) or those that offer international perspectives are even scarcer. Nevertheless, over the past 15 years a number of excellent books have been published that can enrich a classroom collection.

Beyond books, teachers can and should create print for classroom that informs, guides, and reflects learning. The posters, charts, and graphic organizers a teacher creates are far more powerful than the ones bought at the teacher supply store. If students are studying how to determine the main ideas, teachers should create a chart that reflects the rules and procedures that underlie this strategy. Figure 3.2 is an example of such a chart created by the teacher and students in a fourth-grade classroom. This chart is powerful because the students' thoughts and ideas, guided by the teacher, make up the essence of the strategy. The students' thinking is then preserved as a reminder of how to find the main idea and the students can refer to the chart when they are stumped in the midst of a reading task. You and your students should create all sorts of instructional charts—charts that capture the essence of a strategy or charts that reflect what has been learned—such as a time line of the American Revolution—or charts that serve as a model for good writing—the tall tale created by the class. The very act of creating a chart, laminating it, and hanging it on the wall stresses the importance of the strategy or the learning.

Children should create print for the classroom. It is important for teachers to display the stories, reports, and books that students write. You can put their work on a bulletin board; you can bind their stories and add them to the classroom library. These simple acts validate the importance of their writing and encourage others to write. We write well when we have a real audience and the first audience is the other children in the classroom. Therefore it is important to display students' work to provide an audience and to validate the importance of their effort. At least one major bulletin board in your classroom or in the hall should be devoted to students' work and it should change regularly.

Figure 3.2 **Main Idea Anchor Chart Developed by Fourth-Graders**

How to Find the Main Idea

1. Think about the author's purpose. What did he or she want to write about? Why did he or she write it?
2. Look at the title, headings, and bold print words. What is the topic of the passage?
3. Look for a topic sentence—at the beginning, end, or middle of a paragraph.
4. If you can't find a topic sentence, invent your own main idea.
5. Check: Do the other sentences or ideas support the main idea?

Creating a Book Review File

Only a few students might read a book because you, the teacher, told them it was good, but most students will read a book that a peer has recommended. Kathy, a third-grade teacher who has a way of maximizing her efforts, developed a quick and effective book review system. When a student finished reading a book, she went to the file (a small box of 5-by-8-inch index cards) and looked it up by the author's name. If someone else had read it, there was a card on file; if not, the student created a card with the author's last name, the author's first name, and the book title. Then, either on a new card or below the comments of others on an existing card, the student wrote a one- or two-sentence opinion of the book. This file became a favorite aid when students were looking for new books for independent reading and often sparked impromptu conversations between students who had read the same book. It was also an opportunity for students to learn the difference between writing an opinion with a supporting reason and writing a brief summary. Summaries weren't allowed in the file.

The layout of your room influences students' literate behaviors. You need a table to meet with small groups. You need desks, arranged in groups for students to work together, and places to hold the computers and print resources that are essential for inquiry. Probably the most important area is the classroom library. It should be large enough, with comfortable seating, so that several children can relax and get lost in books. The classroom library should have at least six to eight books for every child in the room organized by reading level, by genre, and by topic. Some of the books should be displayed with the cover forward to attract the attention of the students. Posters, puppets, beanbag chairs, and an old pole lamp help to set a mood. Rotate the books regularly so that there are always new books to discover. When you introduce new books or a new author make sure that you call students' attention to these books. Several teachers we know let the students organize the classroom library. This is an excellent way for them to take ownership and as they categorize the books they will learn genre. If you want more ideas about how to merchandize books visit a local Barnes and Noble or Borders bookstore. In the Classroom 3.2 shows an excellent way to create a best sellers list in your classroom.

Time

The careful management of time is essential to creating a literate environment. Teaching reading and writing requires a large uninterrupted block of time, at least 90 to 120 minutes per day. Principals should create schedules that grant teachers considerable flexibility, a schedule where reading and writing is not interrupted with specials, recess, or lunch. This gives the teacher the flexibility to use time to his or her best advantage. As a teacher you will want time to teach the whole class, to meet with groups of students, and to confer with individual students. Whole-group time allows you to read to the class, develop vocabulary knowledge, and teach strategies and skills. During small-group time you can help students apply what they have learned; students can work with each other and they can learn from each other. Providing time in class to read assigned texts also tells students that reading is important. Too often, reading is relegated to homework or serves as filler when there is time left after the "real" work of school is finished. But reading is the "real" work of the classroom! Regularly scheduled time for independent reading such as sustained silent reading tells students that teachers really care about reading. Time devoted to the pleasure of reading tells students that you value reading and want students to do so as well.

Reading independently improves fluency; many children do not do enough of it.

iStockPhoto

We know that reading independently improves reading fluency and reading achievement more generally (Allington, 1984; Knapp et al., 1995; Taylor, Pressley, & Pearson, 2002), but most students do not do enough of it. Most authorities estimate that students spend only about 15 minutes per day doing silent reading in school. It's difficult to become good at something that you do for only 15 minutes a day. These few minutes of in-school reading could, of course, be augmented with independent reading at home, but studies demonstrate that children, unless they are already avid readers, simply do not make the time to read at home. Anderson, Wilson, and Fielding (1988) discovered that among the fifth-grade students they studied, 50 percent read 4 minutes a day or less; 30 percent, 2 minutes a day or less, and 10 percent, not at all. They also found that independent reading time in school and time spent listening to books read aloud by the teacher were important factors in motivating students to read. All in all, we believe that students should do at least 30 minutes of in-school reading a day. This figure includes time spent reading in both language arts classes and other content area classes.

Students also need time to talk about what they read with others. Although we often think of reading as an independent, solitary activity, those of us who are avid readers know the joy of talking about what we have read with others. The social nature of reading in the company of others can become a powerful motivating force, encouraging students to read, to read with understanding, and to share their ideas with others. When students have the opportunity to talk with one another about what they read, they come to realize that there are many ways to understand and respond to a text, and they also have the opportunity to enlarge their understanding and repertoire of responses by listening to the responses of others. Providing time for students to talk about texts with others helps them understand the dynamic nature of engaged reading, even as it motivates them to engage in more reading.

Choice

Students need to have choices about what they read and how they respond to their reading. This does not mean that you never assign selections for students to read or prescribe tasks for students to complete after they have read. It does mean that you structure regular opportunities for students to choose their own reading materials and to also choose their own response mode. Allowing students some choice often helps motivate them to spend time reading. In one classroom we observed, the teacher started a literature circle by giving each group a choice of two or three books. The students considered the three selections and then decided which book they wanted to read. This is minimal choice, but enough for the students to have their say in the curriculum and a feeling of control. Figure 3.3 will help you find culturally diverse books for your students.

Independent reading is one such opportunity where students can choose. Although students, especially those who are struggling readers as well as many English language learners, need support and guidance in selecting books that they can and will want to read, students also ought to be able to choose their own books for independent reading. Some teachers insist that students choose only from the classroom or school library. We suggest that, if reading is the goal, students ought to be able to read all kinds of texts, including newspapers, comic books, and magazines. If we

Figure 3.3 Resources for Finding and Evaluating Culturally Diverse Books

Some basic questions to ask yourself as you are selecting culturally diverse literature:

- Does the book qualify as good literature?
- Is the culture accurately portrayed, demonstrating diversity within as well as across cultures if appropriate and avoiding stereotypes?
- Is the book a positive contribution to an understanding of the culture portrayed? (Galda & Cullinan, 2009)

As you are learning to evaluate literature in terms of literary excellence and cultural authenticity, you may want to rely on published lists of books that have been carefully evaluated by experts in the field. Here are some of the better ones:

- Harris, V. (1997). *Using Multiethnic Literature in the K–8 Classroom.* Norwood, MA: Christopher-Gordon.
- Helbig, A. K., & Perkins, A. R. (2000). *Many Peoples, One Land: A Guide to New Multicultural Literature for Children and Young Adults.* Westport, CT: Greenwood.
- International Board on Books for Young People. (Quarterly). *Bookbird: A Journal of International Children's Literature.* Basil, Switzerland: Author.
- Miller-Lachmann, L. (1992). *Our Family, Our Friends, Our World.* New Providence, NJ: Bowker.
- National Council of Teachers of English. (Multiple editions). *Kaleidoscope: A Multicultural Booklist for Grades K–8.* Urbana, IL: Author.
- Stan, S. (2002). *The World Through Children's Books.* Lanham, MD: Scarecrow.
- Tomlinson, C. M. (1998). *Children's Books from Other Countries.* Lanham, MD: Scarecrow.

You might also consult publication lists from publishers such as Lee and Low, Jump at the Sun/Hyperion, Kane/Miller Book Press, Open Hand, Children's Book Press, Arte Publico, and North-South Books, all of which focus on culturally diverse literature.

And here are some of the major awards given for multicultural books:

- Notable Books for a Global Society (February issue of *The Reading Teacher,* International Reading Association/www.reading.org)
- Coretta Scott King Awards (American Library Association/www.ala.org)
- Pura Belpré Award (ALA)
- Mildred Batchelder Award (ALA)

want students to spend time reading, we must allow them to choose what they read as often as possible. In the Classroom 3.3 offers a suggestion for helping students develop an interest in poetry by making use of these motivating elements—including time for browsing through books, something that often looks unproductive but has been found to be important.

Classroom Climate

A final and equally important component of a literate environment is the atmosphere in which children read. In the best possible literate environment, everything that happens in the classroom sends the message that reading—including learning from what you read, having personal responses to what you read, talking about what you read,

Books About Food and Families in Many Cultures

Alma Flor Ada. *Gathering the Sun: An Alphabet in Spanish and English.* HarperCollins, 2001. Dedicated to Cesar Chavez, this alphabet book recounts stories of family farmworkers during the 1960s. For example, "A is for *arboles*" (trees) shows the fruit trees—plum, pear, peach, and orange—that are so much a part of these families' lives. 40 pages.

Debby Atwell. *The Thanksgiving Door.* Houghton Mifflin, 2003. After burning their Thanksgiving dinner, an elderly couple find themselves the guests of honor at the New World Café, a restaurant owned by welcoming Russian immigrants. 32 pages.

Carmen T. Bernier-Grand. *In the Shade of the Nispero Tree.* Orchard, 1999. Because her mother wants her to be part of the world of high society in their native Puerto Rico, 9-year-old Teresa goes to a private school but loses her best friend. 186 pages.

Nora Dooley. *Everybody Cooks Rice.* Carolrhoda, 1991. Young Carrie gets to sample rice recipes from Barbados, Puerto Rico, Vietnam, India, and more when sent out to fetch her little brother at dinnertime. 32 pages.

Ziporah Hildebrandt. *This Is Our Seder.* Holiday House, 1999. This book provides a simple description of the food and activities at a seder, the ritual meal of Passover, including an explanation of its historical and symbolic significance. 32 pages.

Aylette Jenness. *Families: A Celebration of Diversity, Commitment, and Love.* Houghton Mifflin, 1990. Black-and-white photo essays celebrate the lives of 17 children of many cultures, races, and lifestyles. 48 pages.

Angela Johnson. *The Wedding.* Orchard, 1999. An African American wedding is viewed through the eyes of the bride's younger sister. 32 pages.

Dayal Kaur Khalsa. *How Pizza Came to Queens.* Clarkson N. Potter, 1989. When Mrs. Pellegrino comes to visit May's family, she laments that there is no pizza. So May and her friends, with the help of the librarian who defines the word, buy the ingredients and get Mrs. Pellegrino to make pizza. 24 pages.

Susan Kuklin. *How My Family Lives in America.* Bradbury, 1992. Three young children, an African American, Chinese American, and Hispanic American, describe their families, customs, and favorite recipes. Includes nine recipes for rice. 32 pages.

Patricia McMahon. *Chi-hoom: A Korean Girl.* Boyds Mills, 1993. This photo essay depicting a week in the life of an 8-year-old girl in Seoul gives a sense of an individual's place within a Korean family and culture. 48 pages.

Shulamith Levey Oppenheim. *Ali and the Magic Stew.* Boyds Mills Press, 2002. A beggar helps a young Muslim boy save his seriously ill father by telling him how to get the ingredients for a stew with special healing powers. 32 pages.

Lynn Reiser. *Tortillas and Lullabies/Tortillas y concioncitas.* Greenwillow, 1998. A young girl tells about tortilla making, flower gathering, dress laundering, and lullaby singing—activities her great-grandmother, grandmother, and mother all did and that she does with her doll. The text is in English and Spanish and includes a musical score. 40 pages.

Lisa Shulman. *The Matzo Ball Boy.* Dutton, 2005. In this Jewish version of the "Gingerbread Man," a lonely old *bubbe* makes a matzo ball boy in her chicken soup so he can join her for the Passover seder. 32 pages.

Janet S. Wong. *Apple Pie 4th of July.* Harcourt, 2002. After a young Chinese American girl frets that no one will come to her parents' market to buy Chinese food on the 4th of July, she is happily proven wrong. 32 pages.

Paul Yee. *Roses Sing on New Snow: A Delicious Tale.* Macmillan, 1991. When the governor of South China visits Maylin's home, she creates a new dish in his honor, and her lazy brothers try to take all the credit. However, their attempts to duplicate the recipe only infuriate the emperor, while Maylin triumphs, demonstrating that cooking, like painting, is an art. 32 pages.

and writing about what you read—is fantastic! In such a classroom, students are given plenty of time to read, they are given ample opportunities to share the information they learn and their responses to what they have read with each other, they are taught to listen to and respect the ideas of others, and they learn that others will

Poetry Browsing to Create Interest

Teacher lore has it that it is often difficult to get upper-elementary students engaged in poetry. Whatever the reasons, upper-elementary readers tend to avoid poetry, unless it is humorous verse by authors such as Shel Silverstein and Jack Prelutsky. But this doesn't always have to be the case. Amy McClure and her colleagues (McClure, Harrison, & Reed, 1990) found that, given time and choice, their upper-elementary students came to really enjoy poetry, even selecting books of poetry for independent reading. After assembling a collection of poetry that might interest their students, McClure and her colleagues added it to the classroom library, displaying it so that students were tempted to look at the books. Then they gave students time to browse—to dip in and out of books, finding poems they enjoyed and wanted to read to their buddies and then moving on. Over time, this freedom to simply enjoy and sample a lot of poetry without any task being assigned broke down the negative attitudes that students began with.

listen to and respect their ideas. A literate atmosphere is a thoughtful atmosphere in which values and ideas are respected—values and ideas in texts, one's own values and ideas, and other people's values and ideas.

This kind of climate is developed when teachers, in a positive and supportive manner, help students learn how to engage in discussions and other forms of sharing what they have read. One way students learn to do this is through your modeling how to be positive and supportive as you scaffold students' reading experiences. Modeling and directly teaching students ways to conduct themselves in the classroom, coming up with an agreed-on set of rules for the classroom, and prominently displaying the rules will also help set the right tone. Trust, respect, and responsibility are important ideas in a safe and supportive classroom, and talking about these concepts and how the successful operation of the class rests on them is crucial, especially at the beginning of the year.

REFLECT and *Apply*

1. Describe a successful reading experience you have had in school and an unsuccessful one you have had. What could your teacher have done to make the unsuccessful one more successful?
2. Think about how you choose the books you read as an adult. Do you have favorite authors, topics, genres? Do you follow the recommendations of friends? Do you read book reviews or best-seller lists? How could you incorporate these ideas into your classroom?
3. Identify a grade level, and then list the types of reading materials you would have in your classroom library (books, magazines, etc.), along with two or three specific examples of each type.

The Importance of Positive Attributions

Having considered how the environment you create influences motivation, now we want to consider some of the internal factors that relate to motivation: how students' self-perceptions influence their performance. Educators and psychologists have been studying motivation for many years, and one of the most persistent findings is that the way people view their successes and failures, what has come to be called their *attributions*, has a powerful effect on motivation. A closely related finding is that the

Which of these books would you like to read?

Jeff Greenberg/PhotoEdit

result of repeatedly failing is learned helplessness. Still another finding is the importance of giving students appropriate challenges and engaging in tasks that are worthwhile. In this section, we discuss each of these important concepts.

Attribution Theory

Attribution theory helps to explain and underscore the importance of success to student motivation and engagement. Attribution theory deals with students' perceptions of the causes of their successes and failures in learning. As Merlin Wittrock (1986) explains, in deciding why they succeed or fail in reading tasks, students can attribute their performance to ability, effort, luck, the difficulty of the reading task, or the kindness of teachers. All too often, children who have repeatedly failed in reading attribute their failure to factors that are beyond their control—to an unchangeable factor, such as their innate ability, or to a factor that they can do nothing about, such as luck. Once this happens, children are likely to lose their motivation to learn to read and to doubt their ability to learn. From the children's perspective, there is no reason to try because there is nothing they can do about it. Moreover, as long as they do not try, they cannot fail; you cannot lose a race if you do not enter it.

Learned Helplessness

As Peter Johnston and Peter Winograd (1985) have pointed out, one long-term outcome of children's repeatedly attributing failure in reading to forces beyond their control is the learned helplessness syndrome. Children who exhibit learned helplessness in reading are apt to be nervous, withdrawn, and discouraged when they are faced with reading tasks. They are unlikely to be actively engaged in reading, to have goals and plans when they read, to monitor themselves when they are reading to see if the reading makes sense, or to check themselves after reading to see if they have accomplished their reading goal.

Obviously, we need to avoid this debilitating cycle of negative attributions and learned helplessness. Second-grade teacher Jerry Costello suggests four approaches:

> The first, and almost certainly the most powerful, way I have found to help students understand that they are in control of their learning is something I hear stressed over and over again by my colleagues and read in the literature: Make students' reading experiences successful ones; make them so frequently successful for students that they will be compelled to realize that it is they themselves and not some outside force that is responsible for their success.
>
> Second, I tell students that their efforts *make a difference,* and when they are successful in a reading task, I talk to them about the activities they engaged in to make them successful. Teaching specific strategies is critical. If a student learns to predict and reread and their performance on a test or project improves I can help them attribute their success to these very specific actions. If they understand that their success stemmed from specific strategies they can control then they can alter their attributions. I usually confer with individual students and help them understand how their efforts and their strategies made a difference. This gives them a sense of control.
>
> Third, I avoid competitive situations in which students compare how well they read a selection to how well others read it and instead focus students' attention on what they personally gained from the selection.

Finally, I try to provide a number of reading activities in which the goal is simply to *enjoy reading*, have fun, and experience something interesting and exciting rather than only offering reading activities that are followed by answering questions or some other sort of external accountability.

—Jerry Costello, second-grade teacher

The Importance of Appropriate Challenges

Although we stress the importance of success, providing appropriate challenges for children is equally essential (Pressley, 2006; Taylor et al., 2002). Saying that students should succeed at the reading tasks you ask them to complete and that you should do everything possible to ensure success does not mean spoon-feeding them. Unless readers undertake some challenging tasks, unless they are willing to take some risks and make some attempts they are not certain of, there is little room for learning to take place. In order to develop as readers, children need to be given some challenges. As Mihaly Csikszentmihalyi (1990) has learned from three decades of research on what makes people's lives happier and more meaningful, facing and meeting significant challenges is one of the most self-fulfilling and rewarding experiences we can have. However, when we present students with challenges, we need to be certain that they clearly understand the goals toward which they are working, to give them challenges appropriate for their skills, and to provide them with whatever support they need to meet these challenges. This is, of course, true for all students, but it is particularly true for those students who have often found school difficult. In the Classroom 3.4, which is based on an actual lesson one of the authors observed, shows how one teacher managed this balancing act. About half way through the lesson the teacher and I looked at each other and nodded, acknowledging the fact that the students were so engrossed that there was little for any adult to do.

Can you see how this activity appropriately challenged the students? The anticipation guide provided a task that all of the students could complete. It also created a sense of intrigue or mystery. They students wanted to see if they were right or wrong. They wanted to solve the puzzle. The original book, *All About Snakes*, was at the students' reading level and the initial instruction on text features helped the students navigate the text. The library books provided additional information, and because these books came from a variety of reading levels, all students could find additional books they could read. Even difficult texts could be used because the students knew how to locate information. Finally, the students worked with a partner. This provided additional support; if one could not locate the necessary information the other could.

Concrete Approaches to Motivating Students

There are many teaching techniques that can break the cycle of learned helplessness and encourage our students to become motivated and engaged readers. In this section of the chapter, we list some of the most powerful ways of doing so. Motivation has many roots and the strongest teachers nourish them all. Some students are motivated by the topic—superheroes or NASCAR, for example—and others by the task—perhaps they like to research topics on the Internet. Others look at the final goal—getting an A—and still others are motivated by the social nature of school—they get to work with their friends. As you think about how to motivate your students, make sure your classroom and your teaching include many sources of motivation.

*A*ssessment

Earlier in the chapter, we suggested that talking to students is a good way to assess their motivation. Observing students, "kid watching" to use the term that Yetta Goodman (1978) coined, is another excellent way of gleaning information about students' attitudes toward themselves and school.

3.4

Providing Both Challenges and Supports

Mrs. Montano's goal is to teach her second-graders how to read informational text. For one of her groups she has selected the book *All About Snakes*—an intriguing topic. She starts the lesson by discussing the features of an informational text and their purpose. She points out the title and asks the students why a book has a title. "To tell what it is about." "So you can decide if you want to read it." These ideas are recorded on the chart. Next the students consider the purpose of the table of contents, index, headings, bold print words, charts, graphs, pictures, and captions. Each feature is noted on the chart and its purpose is described. Mrs. Montano explains how we will use these features to help us understand what we are reading and to locate information. She models this briefly with a book about spiders.

Conventions and Purposes Chart for Exploring the Structure of Informational Text

Text Conventions	Purposes
Title	Identifies topic or subject, creates interest
Table of contents	Helps to locate specific topics
Headings	Identify the topic or purpose of a section
Subheadings	Identify the topic or purpose of a paragraph or more
Bold print	Highlights important concepts that demand attention and understanding
Picture	Helps us understand more about the text
Caption	Explains a picture or a chart
Index	Helps to locate specific information

The class then moves to their reading groups and one group of nine students begins to work with the teacher. In addition to *All About Snakes*, the teacher has brought from the library 25 additional books about snakes at various reading levels. Mrs. Montano presents the anticipation guide shown here. The students' task before they read the book is to guess, based on their knowledge, the truth of each statement about snakes. Working independently the students ponder and complete the guide. Then the teacher explains that they are to work with a partner and read *All About Snakes* to determine whether their guess is correct. If they can't find the information in the book, they are free to read in any of the other books from the library.

The students begin to work. They read, they search, they argue. Some answers are found and others are not. They grab other books and turn to the index or the table of contents to locate information about statements they have not yet verified. Note how the Conventions and Purposes chart used at the beginning of the lesson helped the students locate the information they needed. There is a very high level of engagement in the group. Some students begin to argue with each other and point to books to substantiate their claims. The students talk almost exclusively to each other and the teacher is largely ignored. Occasionally Mrs. Montano has to quiet the group, but otherwise they continue to work. The anticipation guide task is completed quickly, but the students continue to read the library books.

Anticipation Guide

Before Reading		Statement	After Reading	
1. True	False	Farmers do not like to have snakes on their farms.	1. True	False
2. True	False	Snakes live where they can locate food.	2. True	False
3. True	False	All snakes are meat eaters.	3. True	False
4. True	False	Snakes cannot see very well.	4. True	False
5. True	False	Snakes stop growing when they are two years old.	5. True	False
6. True	False	Very few snakes have fangs and venom.	6. True	False
7. True	False	Scientists use snakes to help sick people.	7. True	False

Promoting Academic Values and Goals

Ultimately, motivation and engagement are intrapersonal values, and it is the student herself who must become motivated and engaged—with school and schooling. The fact is that a good deal of schoolwork is just that—work—and we need to find ways to help students truly value that work. One approach to doing so is to reinforce students when they demonstrate that they are valuing and "doing" school—for example, complimenting a student who has been getting her homework in daily. Another is to provide students with role models who express a commitment to education. Teachers are certainly important role models. But in some ways, other students are even more important role models. One of the many reasons that it is important for lower-performing students to be grouped with higher-performing students is that the higher performers can serve as academic role models. Another approach is for teachers to directly talk to students about the importance of school and the benefits of doing well in school.

Every school day should start with a very short discussion about what we are going to do and why it is important. Students need to think about school not as a random set of activities that they dutifully complete, but as a set of important tasks chosen by the teacher and the students to build their skill and knowledge. In this short introduction to the day, plant a sense of anticipation, give students something to look forward to—a video from the Internet, a new read-aloud, an experiment in science. Much as the news teases us with a upcoming segment, we can keep the students engaged with less than brilliant activities—we are not always that creative—while they look forward to some exciting event in the afternoon. End every day with a short statement about what the class accomplished and what they learned. At home that night students will have something interesting to tell about school.

Our final suggestion for promoting academic values and goals is to make learning experiences enjoyable. As Nel Noddings eloquently argues in *Happiness and Education* (2003), happiness should be a major goal of education, but frequently is not. We have already said that a good deal of schoolwork is indeed work, and there is no getting around that. But nothing says that work cannot be made as enjoyable as possible. Texts make a difference. As Marilyn Adams wrote: "The cat sat on the mat is not interesting. The cat sat on the dog's mat is interesting" (2009). If, for example, students are learning how to make inferences, teachers can choose texts that students find enjoyable to make the point. For example, "getting" jokes often requires inferences, and reading them is wonderful practice. Stories also often require inferences about, for example, a character's motivation for what he is doing. Speculating about why a compelling character is behaving in a particular way is much more interesting than filling out a worksheet designed to test students' ability to make inferences.

Perhaps students are working on their critical thinking skills, such as learning how to distinguish between fact and opinion or how to differentiate fact, theory, and belief. They can spend time doing uninteresting worksheets, or they can read expository texts about matters they are interested in and then discuss those texts, perhaps distinguishing between facts and opinion. Excellent nonfiction that begs to be analyzed in this way includes *Clouds* by Marion Dane Bauer for primary-grade children, *The Secret of the Sphinx* by James Giblin for intermediate-grade students, and *Are We Alone? Scientists Search for Life in Space* by Gloria Skurzynski for middle-grade students.

Fostering Higher-Order Thinking and Deep Understanding

We believe that fostering higher-order thinking and deep understanding are absolutely crucial to success both in school and outside of school. Lower-order

*A*ssessment

Beginning on the first day of school, be sure to track students' work in and out of class so that you know both how often they do their work and how well they do it. If they are not doing their work or not doing it well, you need to let them know that and then assist them in getting on track.

Cooperative learning not only encourages reading achievement but also supports better interpersonal relationships among children.

iStockPhoto

thinking and shallow understanding are not the cognitive tools students need to succeed, thrive, and contribute in the 21st century. Equally important—and very fortunately—emphasizing higher-order thinking and deep understanding in your classroom also motivates and engages students (Knapp et al., 1995; Taylor et al., 2003). Completing a worksheet that requires a young reader to answer a set of rote questions on the events in Jerry Spinelli's *Loser* simply is not as engaging as trying to figure what it is about Zinkhof that repeatedly gets him in unfortunate situations. Similarly, learning a little bit about a lot of topics is usually not as interesting as studying a few topics in depth. In fact, almost any topic becomes interesting once we begin to understand it deeply. Several years ago, adult author Mark Kurlansky wrote a book titled *Cod: A Biography of the Fish That Changed the World*. In researching that book, he became interested in salt (used, of course, in preserving cod) and wrote another book, this one titled *Salt: A World History*. One of us has read them both and found them fascinating. Even topics like cod and salt—as you learn more about them and discover the impact they have had on civilization—become interesting. That does not mean we should ask elementary students to develop a deep understanding of cod or salt, but it does suggest that some pretty mundane topics can become interesting when we develop a thorough understanding of them.

Ensuring Active Participation, Using Cooperative Activities, and Including Variety

Students are a lot more motivated when actively engaged in learning. This is true for elementary students and for college students; if you are using this book as part of a college class, we hope you are engaged in active learning activities as part of that class. Such activities include constructing models, role-playing teaching situations, doing experiments, creating examples, and observing in classrooms and reporting back to your peers. Students in one study (Boaler, 2002), for example, noted that "you learn more by doing something on your own," "you feel more proud of the projects when you've done them yourself," and "because you had to work out for yourself what was going on, you had to use your own ideas."

Cooperative learning is another form of active learning that has become very widely used, and this is fortunate. Importantly, the advantages of cooperative learning have been found to occur in a variety of domains. Students in cooperative groups showed superior performance in academic achievement, displayed more self-esteem, accommodated better to mainstreamed students, showed more positive attitudes toward school, and generally displayed better overall psychological health. Students in cooperative groups displayed better interpersonal relationships; and these improved interpersonal relationships held regardless of differences in ability, sex, ethnicity, or social class (Johnson & Johnson, 1989). Moreover, cooperative learning has been shown to be successful in teaching students how to resolve conflicts (Johnson & Johnson, 2002). Finally, cooperative learning can create a classroom in which students share the responsibility for each other's learning rather than compete with each other—a very positive situation, particularly for students who often do not do well in school and may become alienated in classrooms where they are too often on their own and do not perform as well as their classmates (Cohen, 1994). For some students the social nature of school—that's where their friends are—is more important than the academic tasks. Working in groups satisfies their social needs while they learn new content and skills.

A number of authors (Aronson & Patnoe, 1997; Cohen, 1994; Johnson et al., 1994; Slavin, 1987) have described approaches to cooperative learning, and using more than one approach can provide variety and accomplish somewhat different purposes. Moreover, as the title of this section suggests, variety itself tends to be motivating and engaging for students. No one likes to do the same thing in the same way all the time, and sometimes adding variety just to add variety makes good sense. Cooperative groups can work as literature circles, book clubs, inquiry groups developing a report, or teams experimenting with a new science concept.

Making Connections to Students' Cultures and Lives Outside of School

It is not at all surprising that students are more engaged and motivated to learn if they feel that what they are learning is related to their out-of-school lives. Although not every topic in the curriculum is going to be connected to students' home lives and cultures, many of them certainly should be. One of the easiest ways to do this is to carefully select the reading material for your classroom so that it reflects the issues, concerns, and cultures of your students, as we discussed earlier in this chapter. At the same time, however, we must admit that assuring cultural matches is easier said than done.

For example, Mr. Augustus had developed a differentiated literature unit around the theme of survival. One group of boys was reading *the Upstairs Room* (Reiss, 1972), two other groups were reading *The Voyage of the Frog* (Paulsen, 1989), and the weaker readers were reading *Baseball Saved Us* (Mochizuki, 1993). Five African American boys were slowly giving up on *The Upstairs Room*, a story about three young Jewish girls hiding in a closet in Holland to escape the Nazis. The boys complained that they just didn't get the book. "Who cares about some girls living 60 years ago." "What does that have to do with me?" Mr. Augustus began to discuss the boys' lives and wondered if they had ever experienced any persecution or discrimination. The boys acknowledged that they had. The teacher led them from their own experience to that of their parents and grandparents under Jim Crow and finally back to life under slavery. With these facts in mind Mr. Augustus helped the boys make connections between discrimination and persecution in different times and places. Rather spontaneously the boys made a connection, and the plight of Annie, Sinni, and Rachel hiding in that closet in Holland immediately became important.

Helping students connect to literature requires selecting the right books and making deliberate efforts to link those books to students' lives. Well-crafted book talks can move that process along. Teachers should regularly give book talks that introduce the genre, theme, and characters to the students. The book talk should make an obvious attempt to relate the book to the students' lives and interests. Although a culturally diverse library is important no matter whom you teach, it's also important to think about the universals that engage all students. Reading fiction that explores topics such as family, friends, and issues of growing up (such as Lindsay Lee Johnson's middle-grade novel *Worlds Apart*), nonfiction about the wonders of the natural world (such as *Penguin Chick* by Betty Tatham), and inspirational biographies (such as *The Sky's the Limit: Discovery by Women and Girls* by Catherine Thimmesh), can draw your students into the world of reading and help them realize that reading, even the reading they do in school, often relates to their lives outside of school.

Class projects can also help students connect home and school. Rather than researching and writing about a topic that has little connection to their community, students can choose to pursue a topic that has relevance to their lives. For example, a group of sixth-grade students in the Pacific Northwest spent a year doing research and writing about how pollution had destroyed the salmon stream that ran by their school. They read, discussed, and wrote while they also cleaned up the stream. The result was a cleaner stream, heightened community awareness of issues of pollution, and a book, *Come Back, Salmon!,* that chronicled their project. Eventually, the salmon even came back. Your students all come from families and communities that have, as Moll (1992) describes it, "funds of knowledge." It's up to you to tap into that knowledge and bring it into your classroom.

Praising Students, Rewarding Them, and Helping Them Set Goals

Praise can be a very effective motivator, and it is certainly a widely used tool. Nevertheless, praise is not without its potential drawbacks. Most importantly, it must be honest, and students must perceive it as honest. According to Guthrie and Wigfield (2000), effective praise is given only in response to students' efforts and achievements, specifies just what students have accomplished to earn the praise, and helps students better appreciate their work. Guthrie and Wigfield also note that effective praise makes it clear to students that they should attribute their success to effort and fosters

Differentiating Instruction

for

English Language Learners

Creating Identity Texts

English language learners experience more success when they can make connections between what they already know and what they are learning to do (Bear, Helman, Templeton, Invernizzi, & Johnston, 2007). One way to do this is to have children create an identity text. An identity text is one that is grounded in and reflective of children's lives. When completed, these texts "hold a mirror up to students in which their identities are reflected back in a positive light" (Cummins, Brown, & Sayers, 2007, p. 219). One way to do this is to have children create memoirs. Memoirs are, by their nature, grounded in and reflective of children's lives. Every child in the classroom can create a memoir. The children who are English language learners can create memoirs that are dual-language texts. On each page, sentences are first written in the child's home language. Then they are written in English, one language on top of the other.

their understanding of the strategies that they used to accomplish the task for which they are being praised.

Before we can praise we have to help students set goals. Students who set goals to learn certain content or processes—such as understanding a difficult concept or being able to self-check as they read—are more motivated to learn than students who do not. Teachers who work with their students to set appropriate learning goals are helping to foster students' long-term engagement and learning (Ames, 1992; Maehr & Midgley, 1996). Once the goals are set we should help students understand how they are progressing in meeting those goals.

Rewards other than praise—points, stars, books, pizzas—can sometimes be effective in the short run. However, one of the most consistent and strongest cautions in the literature on motivation is that extrinsic rewards can undermine motivation in the long run (Guthrie & Wigfield, 2000; National Research Council, 2004; Stipek, 2002). When students become accustomed to getting extrinsic rewards for reading, they may begin reading solely or largely to get the extrinsic reward and actually discontinue reading when the extrinsic rewards are no longer available. Our goal should always be to demonstrate to students that reading is worthwhile for its own sake—for the learning, enjoyment, and satisfaction that it brings. Our greatest tools in accomplishing this goal are giving students good books and other materials to read and scaffolding their efforts so that they can successfully comprehend.

Two computer-based programs, Accelerated Reader (Renaissance Learning) and Reading Counts (Scholastic), are widely used to promote reading and provide motivation. These very similar programs are designed to increase access to books, promote increased time for reading, assess comprehension with computer-based tests, and reward students with points when they have successfully read a book and passed a test. Many teachers and schools believe that these two programs are at the core of their efforts to motivate students. However, the programs have their pitfalls—some students don't like to read for points, and many books are not yet on the system. Yet the largest problem is that points or other extrinsic rewards do not build a long-term love of reading (Krashen, 2003). Students who actively use these programs in school have no increased motivation to read on their own.

Factors That Undermine Motivation

In order to understand just what something is, it is often useful to understand what it is not. Although we certainly do not want to dwell on the negative, we do want to list some factors that undermine motivation. Pressley and his colleagues (Bogner et al., 2002; Dolezal et al., 2003; Pressley et al., 2003) have identified a number of these factors. A few of them are listed in Figure 3.4. Pressley et al. (2003) provide a much longer list. Most unfortunately, when Pressley and his colleagues (2003) observed primary-grade classrooms, they found many of these factors present.

Assessing students' attitudes toward school and your classroom is an important step in building a positive classroom climate. One good way to do so is simply to talk to students from time to time about what they think of school and your classroom.

④ Explain two or three things you might do to help a shy second-grader who tends to lack confidence in her ability develop a more positive attitude toward herself as a learner.

⑤ Now explain two or three things you would not do so that you do not further undermine her attitude toward herself as a learner.

⑥ Suppose you want to convince your fourth-graders that although schoolwork can be challenging, it is worth doing well and doing their schoolwork well will give them a sense of accomplishment and pride. Jot down what you might say to them.

Figure 3.4   Some Factors That Undermine Motivation

Physical Environment

- Few examples of students' work and accomplishments are shown on the walls.
- The room is sparsely decorated, with few posters, pictures, or other elements to make it more attractive and inviting.

Psychological Environment

- The teacher does not have or communicate to students that she has high expectations for their learning.
- The atmosphere fostered by the teacher is not cooperative, and no sense of community and students helping and respecting each other is developed.
- The teacher communicates to students that getting the right answers and high grades are the most important part of school.
- The teacher gives students very little praise.

Classroom Instruction

- The teacher does not check for understanding before moving on.
- The teacher does not use opportunities to connect lessons to other concepts in the curriculum, to previous learning experiences, or to the world outside of school.
- The teacher does not give students time to process questions and think about answers before calling on them.
- The teacher is not fully prepared for the day's lessons.

Classroom Management

- The teacher does not check students' progress as they work and fails to notice students' confusion or off-task behavior.
- The teacher uses negative, punishing techniques to maintain order in the classroom.

Source: Adapted from Pressley et al. (2003, pp. 45–48).

Nancy Masters, a Superstar at Motivating Students

Nancy Masters is a truly outstanding teacher who was observed by Pressley and his colleagues as part of their in-depth studies of motivation in primary-grade classes (Bogner et al., 2002; Pressley et al., 2003). Here is a description of her efforts.*

On a typical day, Nancy Masters used more than 40 different positive motivational mechanisms to inspire and engage her students. Her classroom was filled to overflowing with motivating activities and positive tone. Cooperation was emphasized consistently during both whole-group and small-group instruction. Thus, when students read books with partners, Ms. Masters reminded them that, "The point is, you're supposed to help your partner." She provided reassurance and interesting scaffolding when students took on challenging activities. Thus, before a test requiring

*From "Nancy Masters' Teaching," in *Reading Instruction That Works: The Case for Balanced Teaching* by Michael Pressley. Copyright © 2005 by Guilford Publications, Inc. Reproduced with permission of Guilford Publications, Inc., via Copyright Clearance Center.

application of phonics skills, Ms. Masters reminded her students of the phonics they had been learning and emphasized that they should apply what they knew about phonics on the upcoming test.

Ms. Masters emphasized depth in her teaching, covering mature and interesting ideas. For example, during Black History Month, students not only completed detailed group book reports about five prominent African Americans, she led a discussion about the Jim Crow laws, one in which the students participated enthusiastically, demonstrating they had learned a great deal about discrimination during the month. During this conversation, Ms. Masters talked about different ways that people can affect social change, covering civil disobedience, disobeying unjust laws, and working within the system to change such laws. She and the first-grade students discussed equality and inequality, with student comments reflecting their grasp of some very difficult concepts.

Nancy Masters' teaching connected across the curriculum and community, between school and home. During the first month of the school year, she took her class to visit the kindergarten room. In doing so, she began to become acquainted with her future students while forging connections across grade levels for the kindergarten and grade-1 students. Her students wrote in their journals about this visit. When they wrote stories a few weeks later, Ms. Masters held out as a carrot another visit to the kindergarten room. She told her grade-1 students, "Maybe we'll show the kindergarten [your stories]." Nancy also pointed out times when students' home experience connected with school. Thus, when a student read the word "little" very quickly, Ms. Masters commented, "Have you been working at home with your Mom? I'm so proud of you!" In doing so, she simultaneously emphasized the importance of effort and homework while connecting to the student's home life. Ms. Masters also hosted a career day during which parents talked about and demonstrated their professional skills. After the visits, the students wrote in journals and did an at-home art project about their favorite profession. This special home assignment complemented the regular homework, which consisted of reading 15 minutes a night, doing a short math worksheet, and practicing spelling words.

Nancy Masters gave many opportunistic mini-lessons. In-class assignments seemed appropriately challenging and engaging (i.e., students could not finish them quickly, and they seemed interested in them). Her emphasis on good literature, the writing process, and comprehension were apparent during every class visit. Also, the class constructed many products, which were tangible evidence of accomplishment, including big books that were displayed prominently in the classroom and discussed often. Ms. Masters promised the class that each one of them would be able to take home one class-constructed book at the end of the year. She made many across-curriculum connections for her students (e.g., having students use the Internet and the library to find material about Black History Month, material then used in writing an essay).

Ms. Masters expressively communicated with students. As she read to students, she modeled her interest and enthusiasm and reflected her curiosity about what would happen next in a story, often creating a sense of suspense about the events in a reading. When the class received a new basal reader, she opened it and said, "A brand new book!! It's like a present. I know you want to open it and look inside. Go ahead and look inside. See anything interesting? Anything you've read?"

Ms. Masters provided clear learning objectives and goals. Thus, at the beginning of the school year, she had the students copy stories she had written on the board, explaining they were copying stories so that "You can see what good writing looks like." Similarly, when she taught strategies during writing workshop, Ms. Masters emphasized that use of the strategies would help students write as they needed to write by the end of grade 1.

Nancy Masters emphasized effort attributions. Thus, on the day report cards were distributed to students, she told the students twice that their most important grade was their grade for effort. She and her students often used the term "personal best" to describe how they were doing.

Nancy Masters monitored the students well. She often said, "When I come around, I want to hear you reading or helping your partner or discussing the story." During her walk-arounds, she provided help to students who were struggling.

Of course, Ms. Masters' efforts to motivate her students paid off. There was consistently high engagement in her class. The pace was always quick. The assignments were always interesting. She excited her students about their work. Her students were always engaged in productive work!

Grouping Students for Instruction

One of the most important decisions you make in your classroom, and one that will have a huge effect on motivation and engagement, is how to group students. Students can be grouped in a variety of ways for a variety of purposes, yet in all too many cases grouping has not been used effectively and has had a negative effect on many students, specifically those students placed in the low-ability groups. In this section, we discuss some of the reasons for grouping, some of the problems grouping has produced, and some guidelines for grouping and doing it effectively. We will expand on this topic in Chapter 5 when we discuss differentiation.

A typical class of 25 to 30 students brings with it 25 to 30 different sets of interests, abilities, attention spans, personalities, and reading skills, and it is very difficult to attend to each of these when working with the class as a whole. When teaching the entire class as a single group, teachers tend to teach to an imaginary mean; that is, they gear their instruction to what they perceive to be the middle range of interest, attention span, personality, ability, and so on. Such instruction does not meet the needs of those who are not in this range. Furthermore, in large-group situations, the teacher must work hard to ensure that all students participate.

Dividing students into smaller groups is often helpful for a number of reasons. First, keeping smaller groups of students on task is generally easier than keeping larger groups on task. Smaller groups tend to facilitate direct instructional engagement for more children and for a longer period of time. Second, smaller groups allow you to provide instruction designed to meet the needs of specific students, thus individualizing your reading program. Finally, smaller groups allow more students to be actively involved in instructional activities. In a group of five, for example, it is possible for each student to respond to a question before you either run out of time or test the patience of the other students.

Given these advantages, it is not surprising that students have often been grouped for reading instruc-

Reading with a friend can double reading pleasure.
Bob Ebbesen/Alamy

tion. Especially in the primary grades the amount of time students spend in small groups has been linked to growth in reading achievement (Taylor, Pearson, Clark, & Walpole, 2000). Remember if a teacher spends most of his time working with small groups, students spend most of their time reading and writing independently with minimal supervision. However, grouping—the high, average, and low group—has typically been based on reading ability (Anderson et al., 1985), leading to a number of disadvantages, particularly for students in low-ability groups. As compared to students in other groups, students in low-ability groups are often given less time to read, spend more time on worksheets and less time being actively instructed, and are asked fewer higher-order questions. None of this is ordained. Effective teachers will have her weaker readers read more; she will ask higher-order questions and avoid worksheets. The negative impact of being in the low group—lower self-esteem and lower motivation (Allington, 1983, 1984)—can be mitigated by teaching the skills students need and working hard to bring children from the low group to the middle or high group. Groups should not be permanent; students in the low-ability group in kindergarten and first grade should not stay in that group throughout the elementary school years (Juel, 1990).

Teachers have developed a variety of grouping options, many of which deliberately include heterogeneous groups of students. Using a variety of groups allows you to create appropriate groups for the various goals you have for students. Some of the many useful types of groups include proficiency groups (short-term groups of students who share a common strength or a common instructional need), deliberately heterogeneous groups (groups specifically set up to counteract the potentially negative effect of proficiency or ability groups), formal cooperative groups (heterogeneous groups of students specifically taught how to work together as a team), interest groups (short-term groups of students sharing a common interest), literature circles (a particular sort of interest group in which students read the same selection and meet to discuss and respond to it), and project groups (groups designed to work together on a particular project, such as making a video or preparing a dramatic presentation). The differentiating instruction idea in the next section also illustrates an example of heterogeneous grouping.

In deciding how to group students, there are many factors to consider. Here are some of the most important ones:

- The material your students will be reading
- Your general instructional objectives
- Your specific objectives for individual children or for the group
- Your students' individual strengths and weaknesses
- Students' abilities to work with others in the group
- The number and types of groups you can successfully manage
- The absolute injunction that no student be repeatedly assigned to the low-ability group
- Students' need to learn to work independently, transition from one activity to another, and work cooperatively with their peers

In the Classroom 3.5 illustrates one way for small groups of students to learn about genre.

We do not mean to suggest that there is no place for whole-class instruction. Whole-class instruction is useful when you wish to set the stage for the day, when you need to introduce and model a new reading skill or strategy, when you want to model a writing craft, or when you are reading aloud to develop vocabulary knowledge. Whole-group time may be as brief as 10 minutes and as long as 40 depending on what you need to accomplish. Lengthy whole-class instruction challenges students'

Reflect on how a first-grade teacher prepares her students for successful reading experiences in the activity "Managing Guided Reading Groups."(To find this activity, go to the topic *Organization and Management* in MyEducationLab and click on Assignments and Activities.)

Heterogeneous Small Groups Learn About Genre

Early each year Ms. Weiss sets the goal of helping her second-graders learn to work in groups and, at the same time, discover the books and genres in the classroom library. She begins with a short whole-class lesson and reads to the students a fantasy (*Ralph's Secret Weapon*, Kellogg, 1986), a biography (*Jackie Robinson*, Prince, 2007), a realistic fiction story (*One Morning in Maine*, McCloskey, 1950), and a folk tale (*Ming Lo Moves the Mountain*, Lobel, 1982). She also discusses the characteristics and purpose of each genre and lists them on the board. The results are recorded on a genre chart that the class will maintain for the next few months. The chart will be kept up in the room and new titles added to the chart over the coming weeks and months as new books are read aloud. The accompanying genre chart is in its early stages. More genres and titles will be added as the students read and discuss more books.

Keeping Track of Our Reading

Genre	Purpose	Characteristics	Examples
Realistic fiction	To entertain, to learn about the big ideas in life	Fiction with real characters, real setting, likely problems and solutions	*One Morning in Maine* *The Voyage of the Frog*
Fantasy	To entertain, to amaze through magic	Fiction with strange or otherworldly settings or characters; fiction that invites suspension of reality	*Ralph's Secret Weapon* *Jumanji*
Biography	To entertain, to inform, to inspire	Narrative of a person's life, a true story about a real person	*Jackie Robinson* *Lincoln: A Photobiography*

Students are then assigned heterogeneously to separate tables and each group is handed a stack of 40 to 50 library books and four large cards labeled Fantasy, Information, Realistic Fiction, and Folk Tale. The students must sort the books into genres by reading a bit of each book and noting the kinds of illustrations or photographs. Because the teacher has organized each stack of books to have at least a few of each genre at a variety of reading levels, all of the students in the group will be able to read some of the books. As the students begin the work, the teacher circulates around the room and provides assistance as needed. Sometimes it is difficult to distinguish a folk tale from a fantasy. When the students have finished their sorting, each group must pick one book from each pile and share it with the class. Students learn about some interesting books, they begin to understand genre, and the classroom library gets a necessary clear-up.

attention and must be mixed with pair-and-share activities that ensure widespread discussion before students respond.

REFLECT and *Apply*

7. Reread the description of Nancy Masters's motivational activities in her first-grade class, and pick out five activities that would work just as well with fourth- or fifth-graders. Now look back at the description and see if you can find any activities that would be inappropriate for fourth- or fifth-graders. How many did you find? What does this suggest about the extent to which motivational principles are applicable across grade levels?

8. Because grouping can have such a strong effect on students' learning, it is important that you fully understand its possible effects. Toward this end, get together with a small group of your classmates, generate a list of positive and negative effects of grouping, and brainstorm a list of ways in which you can maximize the positive effects of grouping and minimize the negative ones.

All students need and deserve our very best efforts in assisting them to become motivated and engaged readers. Here we deal with two topics that are extremely important for all students but absolutely vital for students who face more challenges than do many of their classmates.

Success

All children need success, but for those children whose preschool experiences have not helped them develop the proficiencies school requires or for those older children who have not met with much success in their first few years of school, fostering success will be both more crucial and more difficult. For these students, success may require more skill instruction and more scaffolding. You may need to meet with the students to teach word recognition skills or develop their sight word knowledge. Older students may require greater attention to vocabulary and word learning strategies. As this instruction leads to better reading, they must also be brought to realize that success in reading is under their control and that the first step is to read more often.

Other students from diverse cultural and language backgrounds will require that you attend to the language and knowledge gaps they bring into the classroom. Students who are English language learners will need their easiest phonics lessons accompanied with vocabulary instruction. Without vocabulary instruction the simplest words in a decoding lesson—*hog, log,* and *smog*—are just nonsense words. Children in rural America won't get the setting of a story that begins on the stoop of an apartment building and students in Brooklyn, New York, will not understand the lifestyle of a waterman on the Chesapeake Bay.

Assessment

For students who read very little English, translating test directions into their native language is sometimes appropriate and can help them avoid a very frustrating and nonproductive experience. Of course, it is important to let others who make use of the test scores know you've done this so that the scores won't be misinterpreted.

For all these students careful attention to knowledge development and the process of schema building is essential for reading success. Conversely, the youngster who comes to school already reading should not be required to wade through a word study curriculum that she has already mastered or be limited to only very brief and very easy reading materials.

Grouping

Similar considerations for accommodating diversity exist with grouping. One key, as we have already noted, is flexibility—using several different sorts of grouping. Thus, if you want to group students who are having particular difficulty understanding the concept of plot so that you can review the concept, it is important to also include each of these students in heterogeneous groups or interest groups to avoid the students' stigmatizing themselves or being stigmatized by others. Similarly, it's important to see that both low- and high-performing students are sometimes grouped for instruction so that their particular needs are met. Thus, in addition to pulling aside a group that is having problems with plot, it may be useful to pull aside a group of your most proficient writers and give special attention to a concept such as audience.

In summary, we readily admit that making adjustments for differences among students is challenging. There are no perfect answers or solutions; many of the choices you make will be compromises, choices that have both advantages and disadvantages. Still, there are some general rules beyond the specific suggestions we have just made here. Remember that each student is an individual with both emotional strengths and weaknesses and cognitive strengths and weaknesses. Over time, all students need and deserve an abundance of success, appropriate challenges, the opportunity to work with others having similar strengths and weaknesses, and the opportunity to work with others having quite different strengths, weaknesses, interests, and concerns.

Concluding *Remarks*

Creating motivating and engaging classrooms means creating a literate environment—a place, a space, a collection of texts, and an atmosphere—where reading and learning thrive. In motivating and engaging classrooms, students learn to attribute their successes and failures to factors under their control and to avoid learned helplessness. And in motivating and engaging classrooms, teachers employ myriad approaches to

motivating students—including but not limited to ensuring student success, fostering higher-order thinking, employing meaningful tasks, and making connections to students' cultures and lives outside of school.

We close the chapter with two sets of recommendations, found in Figure 3.5, for motivating students. The first is a set that Pressley and his colleagues (2003) gleaned from the work

Figure 3.5 Research-Based Motivational Strategies

Motivational Strategies Gleaned from Brophy

- Model interest in learning. . . . Communicate to students that there is good reason to be enthusiastic about what goes on in school. The message should be that what is presented in school deserves intense attention, with the teacher doing all that is possible to focus students' attention on important academic matters.
- What is being taught, in fact, should be worth learning!
- Keep anxiety down in the classroom. Learning should be emphasized rather than testing.
- Induce curiosity and suspense, for example, by having students make predictions about what they are about to learn.
- Make abstract material more concrete and understandable.
- Let students know the learning objectives so that it is very clear what is to be learned.
- Provide informative feedback, especially praise when students deserve it.
- Give assignments that provide feedback (to your students and to yourself).
- Adapt academic tasks to students' interests and provide novel content as much as possible. [Do not cover material students already know just because it is the mandated curriculum.]

- Give students choices between alternative tasks [for example, selecting one of several books to read].
- Allow students as much autonomy as is possible in doing tasks. Thus, to the extent students can do it on their own, let them do it.
- Design tasks to contain an engaging activity [for example, role playing], product [for example, a class-composed book], or game [for example, riddles].

Motivational Strategies Gleaned from Pressley and His Colleagues

- Demonstrate your deep concern for students.
- Do everything possible to ensure students' success.
- Scaffold students' learning.
- Present appropriate challenges.
- Support risk taking and help students realize that failures will sometimes occur.
- Encourage students to attribute their successes to their efforts and realize that additional effort can help avoid failures.
- Encourage cooperative learning and discourage competition.
- Favor depth of coverage over breadth of coverage.
- Communicate to students that many academic tasks require and deserve intense attention and effort.
- Make tasks moderately challenging.

Sources: Pressley et al. (2003, pp. 27–28), Graves (2004b, p. 448).

of Brophy (1986, 1987), recommendations made nearly 20 years ago. The second is a set that one of us (Graves, 2004b) gleaned from the work of Pressley and his colleagues (Bogner et al., 2002; Dolezal et al., 2003; Pressley, 2006; Pressley et al., 2003). As you read them, we hope that you will notice two points. First, the two sets of recommendations overlap a good deal with each other.

Second, both sets overlap a good deal with the recommendations we make in this chapter. Our point is this: We know how to motivate and engage students; our task is to put this knowledge into action. In the remainder of this book and in our day-to-day teaching in our own classrooms, we keep these recommendations at the center of our thinking. We encourage you to do the same.

Extending *Learning*

1. Spend some time observing a classroom at a grade level you find particularly interesting. Take notes on what you see. What opportunities for engaging in literacy activities are present? How welcoming is the physical setting? What materials are available? Then watch how the teacher and students interact in the classroom. Is the atmosphere safe and supportive? Are students enthusiastic and engaged? Finally, create a list of things to do and

   a list of things to avoid doing in order to best motivate students.
2. The lists that you created in the activity in item 1 represent your judgment based on your observation. There are other sources of information that deserve to be considered. One is the teacher you observed. Talk to the teacher and get his or her perceptions on what motivates students and which specific things he or she does to mo-

tivate them. The other source is, of course, students. Talk to a half dozen or so students and get their perceptions of what is and is not motivating in their classrooms. Once you have the teacher's and some students' perspectives, compare them to your lists and revise or fine-tune your lists as seems appropriate.

Children's *Literature*

Bauer, M. D. (2004). *Clouds.* New York: Aladdin. This delightful kindergarten book presents some basic facts about weather. 32 pages.

Gibbons, G. (2002). *Giant Pandas.* New York: Holiday House. A well illustrated information book about the life and habitat of the giant panda. 32 pages.

Giblin, J. C. (2004). *Secrets of the Sphinx.* New York: Scholastic. The author recounts the history of this monolithic symbol of power and the problems of erosion, air pollution, and tourism that face it today. 48 pages.

Johnson, L. L. (2005). *Worlds Apart.* Ashville, NC: Front Street. Winnie is devastated when her family moves from Chicago to the grounds of a mental institution in small-town Minnesota where her physician father goes to work. 126 pages.

Kellogg, S. (1986). *Ralph's Secret Weapon.* New York: Puffin. Ralph, his aunt, and his bassoon conquer another strange monster. 32 pages.

Kinney, J. (2007). *Diary of a Wimpy Kid.* New York: Amulet Books. The hilarious story of an undersized tween trying to get through life and middle school while surrounded by morons and bullies. 215 pages.

Lobel, B. (1982). *Ming Lo Move the Mountain.* New York: Scholastic. A Chinese fable about a naïve husband and wife, fools who eventually learn from experience. 32 pages.

McCloskey, R. (1950, 1987). *One Morning in May.* New York: Puffin. A young girl loses her tooth while clamming and learns to accept disappointment. 32 pages.

Park, B. (2004). *Junie B., First Grader: Shipwrecked.* New York: Random House. In another exciting adventure, Junie B. wins a starring role as the *Pinta,* the "fastest" of Columbus's ships, in a play to be presented on parents' night. 96 pages.

Parker, S. (2005). *Pond & River* (DK Eyewitness Books). London: Dorling Kindersley. A wonderfully illustrated introduction for the upper elementary student for the plants and animals that live in or near ponds and rivers. 72 pages.

Paulsen, G. (1989). *The Voyage of the Frog.* New York: Doubleday Dell. A boy, grieving for his uncle, inherits his sailboat and learns to survive when caught in a dangerous storm. 160 pages.

Pilkey, D. (2001). *The Adventures of Captain Underpants.* New York: Blue Sky Press. The hilarious and subversive adventures of George and Harold, who are usually responsible for the misdeeds around them. 132 pages.

Reiss, J. (1972). *The Upstairs Room.* New York: HarperCollins. Two sisters must hide in a small room when the Nazis invade Holland during the second world war. 196 pages.

Skurzynski, G. (2004). *Are We Alone? Scientists Search for Life in Space.* Hanover, PA: National Geographic. 92 pages.

Spinelli, J. (2002). *Loser.* New York: Joanna Colter Books. Spinelli explores the cruelty of the student body who pick on a very inept kid who really is a quite lovely boy. 224 pages.

Tatham, B. (2002). *Penguin Chick.* New York: HarperCollins. This information book focuses on one emperor penguin family's survival. 40 pages.

Thimmesh, C. (2002). *The Sky's the Limit: Stories of Discovery by Women and Girls.* Boston: Houghton Mifflin. In this compelling, cleverly illustrated tribute the author recounts the contributions of many curious and brilliant women who have changed the world with their findings. 73 pages.

PEARSON myeducationlab

Now go to the topic "Organization and Management" in the MyEducationLab (www.myeducationlab.com) for your course, where you can:

- Find learning outcomes for the topics covered in this chapter along with the IRA standards that connect to these outcomes.

- Complete assignable activities in the Assignments and Activities section that show concepts in action to help you synthesize and apply strategies.

- Explore IRIS Center Resources—training enhancement materials that provide you with research-validated information and interactive materials to develop your skills in working with students.

- Apply and practice your understanding of the teaching skills identified in the chapter with the Building Teaching Skills and Dispositions exercises.

4

Classroom Assessment

by Kathleen M. Wilson and Robert C. Calfee with contributions by Kathleen Clark

CHAPTER **outline**

The Test: 10:00 A.M., Friday morning, early May. Carol Aiken tinkles a small bell and says, "Put away your books; sharpen your pencils. Time for the reading test. Put your name at the top. Fill every circle. No talking." A few groans, a couple of questions, but by 10:05 A.M. the 32 fifth-graders hunch in silence over test packets, filling in answers. Ms. Aiken roams the classroom, patting a shoulder, cautioning a student with roving eyes, reminding students to recheck their answers, warning when 5 minutes are left. At 11:05 A.M. she says, "Time is up. Pass in your tests—Robert, right now!" The test is finished.

The Project: A month before, in early April. Ms. Aiken's students return from lunch for science. "Today is the A-team report on Mars. Eduardo, you're in charge. Bring up your group to tell us about your project." Eduardo and three classmates tape sheets of butcher paper with the headings *Place in the Solar System, Physical Characteristics,* and *Building a Habitat* on the front wall. Each sheet is a collage of graphics, photos, and notes from websites. For 40 minutes, the group describes the Red Planet. Then they add their sheets to a huge "Planets" display being prepared for Parents' Night. Ms. Aiken prompts each group for accuracy and encourages them to check with the class for understanding. But mostly she watches the class for reactions, interest, and attention. She jots brief notes in the logbook on her lap.

The Report Card: Fast forward to June, with only two more weeks left in the school year. It's mid afternoon, the students are gone, and Ms. Aiken is preparing for the end-of-school-year parent conferences. Phillippa's mother enters the room with her daughter. They greet Ms. Aiken, Phillippa retrieves her portfolio, and the gangly 11-year-old begins her report. "When I started this year, I really wanted to concentrate on history. I don't know why; it just seemed interesting. I'm African American, and there's lots of prejudice, so I wanted to study about civil rights." For ten minutes, Phillippa discusses her year's work, noting strengths and limitations. "I really worked hard this year, and I'm really happy with the paper I did on Coretta Scott King. It's three pages long, and I checked the spelling and punctuation. And I think the computer art work is really great." Ms. Aiken draws the mother into the conversation and then offers her own evaluation. Phillippa is making solid progress. The report card will contain no surprises.

Bob Daemmrich Photography

CLASSROOM
vignette

Our Perspective on Assessment

Assessment

A variety of formative literacy assessments are included in Appendix A.

These three scenarios span the range of methods available to the classroom teacher for appraising student learning. Figure 4.1 shows a comparison of the formative activities that you will use in the classroom to monitor learning to the summative events represented by the externally mandated standardized tests familiar to all of us. Formative assessment refers to focused and ongoing evaluations, like the scores on quizzes or the observations a teacher makes. Summative tests come at the end of a course of study, when students become accountable for their achievement. Formative assessments guide instruction; summative tests evaluate achievement (Bloom, Madaus, & Hastings, 1981). Figure 4.1 shows the extremes of this continuum; there are many variations between these endpoints.

In the chapter, we first describe our perspectives on assessment. Next, we examine teacher-based strategies for classroom assessment, in which your role is to carry out practical research on student learning. Then we look at the place of standardized tests in formal appraisal of student learning. Somewhere between these two poles we will also consider the rising influence of curriculum-based measurements, designed to monitor the learning students are achieving. Teachers design many of these assessments, but many others are commercially created and have had significant influence on classroom practices because of Reading First and a new special education initiative, Response to Intervention, that we will discuss in the next chapter.

Figure 4.1 **Comparison of Assessment for Instruction and Assessment for Accountability**

	Formative Assessment Designed for Instruction	**Summative Assessment Designed for Accountability**
Purpose and Source	Designed by teachers for classroom decisions	Designed by experts for policy makers
	Several sources of information	Stand-alone, single indicator
	Strong link to curriculum and instruction	Independent of curriculum and instruction
Criteria	Valid for guiding instruction	Predictive validity to other tests
	Profile reliability—strengths and weaknesses	Total test reliability—one score
	Sensitive to changes in performance	Stable over time and situations
Pragmatics	Judgmental, quick turnaround, flexible	Objective, cost- and time-efficient, standardized
	Performance-based "real" task	Multiple-choice "school" task
	Continuously, as needed	Once or sometimes twice per year

An Emphasis on Inquiry

We have chosen to emphasize the left-hand side of the spectrum shown in Figure 4.1—teacher-based assessment—for three reasons. First, the teacher's role in standardized testing is often limited to management and reporting. To be sure, teachers do have important responsibilities for managing, interpreting, and applying standardized tests. But administrators select the tests, manuals tell how to give them, and publishers score them and return results and interpretations. Reading programs include end-of-selection tests, multiple kinds of end-of-unit tests, placement tests, portfolio assessment systems, and progress monitoring tests. Teachers must decide which tests to use and how to interpret the results.

The second reason for focusing on teacher-based assessment is that it requires considerable knowledge, skill, and professional judgment. You may know teachers who rely on routine lessons they prepared long ago and stay with the same material year after year. This approach can't prepare today's students for a changing world and is not in accord with our view of reading and writing.

This leads to the third reason for emphasizing teacher-based assessment: Authentic assessment of present-day literacy can never be completely "standardized." Although prepackaged tests provide a rough index of achievement, the teacher can most adequately monitor students' ability to use language to think and communicate. Knowing that a student is at the 50th percentile in reading comprehension doesn't tell you what the student can and can't do. Picking the right answer to a multiple-choice question is less reflective of literacy than being able to explain the shift in the relationship between Charlotte (a spider) and Wilbur (a pig) over the course of E. B. White's *Charlotte's Web*.

Three Themes of Assessment

Three themes of assessment run through this chapter. First is the notion of assessment as inquiry. It is easy to build a test that fails students; it is much more difficult to find ways to discover what students know and can do. Developing this sensitivity requires the teacher to act as a researcher, creating situations that support success and provide a starting point for instruction.

A second theme is development. As an elementary teacher, you may deal with children from kindergarten through sixth grade. You may set your sights on a particular grade or age, but even if you succeed in this endeavor, developmental levels within any class are likely to span two or more years. Students are not identical peas in a pod, and assessment must adapt to individual differences.

The third theme is progress monitoring. Teacher-based assessment builds on a rich array of data sources, including observations, class discussions, and intuitive judgments, as well as more formal assignments and quizzes. As September moves toward June, you must judge both learning and accomplishment. You must come up with a "bottom line"—a number, a score, or a grade. How much has the student grown? How well can the student perform various tasks expected at a particular grade level? Surveys show that elementary teachers don't like to grade students. Their "success" orientation leads them to "accentuate the positive." But parents and other clients need and deserve information about progress and accomplishment. In this case, progress refers to students' growth and learning; accomplishment measures student achievement against a standard. Parents want to know if their child is learning to read and how well he reads compared to other children his age and in his grade. If teachers don't supply the information, then someone else will, probably

PEARSON
myeducationlab

Complete the learning module "Classroom Assessment (Part 2): Evaluating Reading Progress," which outlines how to use progress monitoring data. (To find this activity, go to the topic *Assessment* in MyEducationLab and click on IRIS Center Resources.)

by using standardized tests. We think that teachers can be trusted to assess student learning—indeed, for the kind of assessment described in this book, others must rely on you and your colleagues!

Balanced Assessment

The classroom teacher monitors both progress and accomplishment. Standardized tests are generally limited to accomplishment—and only a small portion at that.

Figure 4.1 laid out the spectrum of assessment strategies: objective or subjective, formal or informal, prepackaged or judgment-based. In your role as a classroom teacher, you confront the practical question of how to achieve a balance that makes effective use of this full range of strategies.

Some educators have questioned whether standardized tests have any place in today's schools (Calkins, Montgomery, Santman, & Falk, 1998; Johnston, 1990; Mitchell, 1992; Wiggins, 1993; Wiggins & McTighe, 1998). Although these tests have limitations, they also have strengths. Problems arise when they are misused or overused. Public information about student achievement frequently depends solely on what students do in an hour or two on multiple-choice items that tap knowledge and skills quite unlike those required for their regular classwork. Imagine the plight of a 7-year-old accustomed to working on "real" problems with adequate time and resources and being able to ask questions when confused. Then comes the day of the test. The teacher calls the class to attention: "Put away your books, sharpen your pencils, be quiet, no questions."

Whether we like standardized tests or not, almost all educators live in a world where state-mandated standardized tests determine the rating of the school, its reputation, and in some cases the job security of the principal and the teachers. Teachers must prepare students for these tests, without letting the tests become the curriculum. When tests become the curriculum, real learning is sacrificed for a narrow set of objectives. Standardized testing measures only some of what students know and are able to do. The curriculum is more than a preplanned scope-and-sequence chart, and instruction is more than transmission of knowledge from teacher to student. Assessment is more than guessing the best answer to a simple question, and performance is complex and interactive. The student's response is important, but the process is also important.

The rest of this chapter explores the broad spectrum of assessment activities, suggesting how to use a variety of methods to explore reading and writing and how to make sound instructional decisions throughout the school year. Genuine balance requires the classroom teacher to move across the spectrum, from portfolios to multiple-choice tests.

Teacher-Based Strategies

In this section, we describe classroom assessments designed to inform teachers' instructional practice, helping them meet the needs of individual students and the class as a whole. The following questions outline several factors central to conducting teacher-based assessment:

- What does the teacher need to know, week by week, and why?
- What about students? What feedback do they need, and when?
- What about parents? How can you connect them with their children's learning?
- What about other teachers? How can you operate as a team to set benchmark assessments?
- What about the principal? When and how can the principal become involved in assessment?

Features of Contemporary Assessment Methods

Classroom assessment is caught between two poles. At one pole educators have become concerned with systematically assessing the growth of discrete reading skills through curriculum-based measures. Spurred on by Reading First and Response to Intervention (RTI), a special education initiative designed to prevent reading problems, classroom teachers are encouraged to regularly assess students' growth on a narrow but important set of skills—letter name knowledge, letter-sound knowledge, phonemic awareness, and oral reading fluency. The other pole reflects a movement described as performance-based assessment, portfolios, or exhibitions (Harp, 1991; Hart, 1994; Herman, Aschbacher, & Winters, 1992; O'Malley & Pierce, 1996; Phye, 1996; Strickland & Strickland, 2000; Wiggins, 1993). We will first consider performance-based assessments and later in the chapter discuss curriculum-based measures. Several features distinguish performance-based assessments.

- Student production is more important than recognition. Students must show that they can do more than pick the right answer. They have to construct something on their own.
- Projects are more important than items. The preference is for depth over breadth, and the emphasis is on validity rather than reliability.
- The teacher's informed opinion is more important than mechanized scoring.

In the Classroom 4.1 on the next page illustrates these concepts.

The Roots Project and Assessment

The linkages among student learning, curriculum, and instruction appear seamless in this example. A conversation with Ms. King offers insights into how the project serves as assessment. Roots was an experiment. She had assigned projects before, but these had been fairly short and prescriptive. She admits that the Roots activity went far beyond what she had originally intended, both in time and in effort. She had expected to stretch her students, but was genuinely surprised by their accomplishments. In planning and carrying out the assessment, she played the role of a researcher: She developed a design, tried some innovative methods, collected data, and reflected on the results. This case conveys several themes.

- *Assessment is integrative.* The Roots project yielded a wealth of information about reading and writing, as well as research skills. Product and process covered the entire curriculum—formal (literacy, literature, social studies, art) and informal (initiative, cooperation, persistence). The casual observer may experience a collage, but Ms. King can identify distinctive elements.

- *Assessment builds on meaningful tasks.* The students weren't taking a test; they were working on a project, solving a problem, doing something that mattered. Motivation and challenge stimulated achievement. It is easy to set up conditions where many students do poorly; creating a situation that promotes success is more difficult.

- *Assessment emphasizes both top-level competence and performance skills.* For Ms. King, the most critical achievements were "top-level"—understanding overall passage structure, an awareness of audience, a sense of thematic coherence. Her notes also covered the "micro-skills" of spelling, grammar, neatness, and even aesthetics. The final products were all polished, but students differed in the guidance they needed

The Roots Project

Ms. King's 30 third- and fourth-graders vary in backgrounds, interests, and achievement levels. Some from poor families receive a free lunch, several have been labeled as learning disabled, and the eight fourth-graders in the class were candidates for retention.

In September and early October, Ms. King organizes each week around "little lessons," based on a short text or a familiar topic. For example, to find out what students know about the concepts of character and plot, she conducts a "movie review," in which students talk about favorite summer movies. To determine what they know about informational text, she arranges a "news report," in which they discuss selected newspaper articles on current events, from which they prepare oral reports. Students also compile personal journals, doing free writing (Monday) and writing on assigned topics (Wednesday and Thursday). Work samples (individual and group) are posted around the room. By mid-October, Ms. King's logbook contains entries about each student's proficiencies, predilections, and problems in reading and writing.

For the post-Halloween parent conferences, Ms. King prepares a one-page synopsis about each student, drawing on her logbook notes and student journals to review the student's status in literature, science, social studies, citizenship, art/music, and physical education. Asked about the place of reading and writing in this mix, Ms. King's response is short and simple: "We work on reading and writing all day long."

Suddenly, it's early April. Ms. King gathers the class. "We don't have much time left," she tells the group. "It's time for our 'big' project. This spring, our project is Roots—your family history, your own book to keep!"

The Roots project is Ms. King's culminating assignment. It lasts almost 6 weeks. The project generates an authentic product but also provides summative assessments of student achievement. The project proceeds in several phases. Students first view selections from the "Roots" television series. Next, they talk about the story line and then, as prologues to their own books, prepare reports on the selections they viewed. For Ms. King, this exercise provides the opportunity to assess students' proficiency in the basic concepts of character, plot, setting, and theme.

In the second phase, students analyze several autobiographies and biographies—from the autobiographical Little House series by Laura Ingalls Wilder to several biographies of Martin Luther King, Jr. They review their family's past, making notes and collecting data. A wall chart serves to display the results—interviews, Bibles and genealogies, letters and photo albums. The tasks are both individual and collaborative; in her logbook, Ms. King records contributions from specific students and group participation.

In the final phase, each student designs and constructs a Roots book. These are lengthy pieces, 20 pages or more; some are handwritten, some computer-assisted. Each book includes a title page, table of contents, dedication, thematic overview (the "Roots" story), research on the student's family, and a "Forward to the Future" piece, where the children imagine themselves at their high school graduation. Each book includes writing, artwork, graphics, and artifacts.

With the Roots project, Ms. King's third- and fourth-grade students demonstrate critical reading and writing skills and strategies they have learned in class. Ms. King has assigned a task that is both relevant and authentic—two factors that can motivate students to do their best work. In the project wrap-up in May, you can see several significant outcomes. First, every student has completed the Roots project with distinction. All have created artistic works of high quality. Second, they don't see these as mere assignments; they are proud of their accomplishments, which they plan to "keep forever." They are eager to explain how they approached the project and what they learned. Third, the students display a strong sense of audience. They see themselves as the primary audience, which is why they plan to keep the books forever, but they also comment on parents' and relatives' reactions. Every classroom visitor becomes an audience member. Finally—and especially important—they express a sense of rich fulfillment.

to make revisions and complete the job. Ms. King noted these variations, which she shared with students and parents.

- *Assessment is purposeful for all involved.* Ms. King described each task, from the year's beginning to its end, in ways that made sense to both students and parents. She explained her September assessments: "I'm going to be checking what each of you can do and where you need help." She connected each lesson with the next job: "We are studying dinosaurs, and you will need to divide long words like *tyrannosaurus* into syllables. The key is to look for vowels." By the time they began the Roots project, students had learned that classroom activities have a purpose, which motivated them to do their best.

- *Assessment emphasizes explanation.* Students must be able to present their work and show their capacity to describe what they are doing and why and how they are doing it. Right answers need right reasons to count. Ms. King encouraged group activities in planning, reviewing, and presenting because they promoted active discussion. She taught students technical vocabularies that helped them communicate with one another. An interesting story requires character development. It needs a problem that is resolved across episodes. In creating stories of their past, present, and future, students used these terms to explain their efforts and to help one another.

- *Assessment is scaffolded.* Just as you can and should support students' reading of individual selections, you can and should undergird their efforts on larger projects. The aim is for every student to produce an exceptional book, but some require more support than others in moving ahead with the project, in their approach to the task, in their ability to sustain the effort, and in their willingness to assist others and to seek out assistance. Ms. King made sure that support was available, from her and from others such as other students, parents, and volunteers. Her logbook captured these facets of student performance.

- *Assessment is guided by developmental standards.* Ms. King's guideposts were as clear in her mind as a scope-and-sequence chart. Her assessments may not have produced numbers, but they referred to growth and to relative strengths and weaknesses. For instance, here are her comments about one of her students, Sam:

> Sam's oral language skills are exceptional, and he works hard on topics that interest him: science, computers, and games. He has made great progress in his writing and spelling but still lacks fluency with mechanics. Unless he is really excited about a project, he is sloppy with the details. He is better with exposition than narrative. Stories bore him, but his "Rockets" report shows that he can do top-flight work. He sometimes behaves immaturely for a fourth-grader and does not listen well. He is impatient with "boring" tasks like documenting or summarizing.
>
> This year, he has learned a lot about the importance of working on assignments that don't have an immediate payoff. He stayed with his Roots biography, even though he became distracted halfway through. At the beginning of the year, he would have dropped it or done a sloppy job. He came to me and explained that he was stuck and wanted to start over. He had lost a page of notes and didn't want to redo them. I asked him to spend a day thinking over his choices and talking about them with his project buddy. The next morning, Sam had written down his choices and explained why he had decided to stay with his first plan. This episode is an important sign of growth.

Ms. King prepared similar comments for each student, which she attached to the district's report card. She found that parents valued these comments as highly as the official grades. They were also excited about the Roots project, because it showed what their children could really do.

*A*ssessment

In the classroom, students may be described in terms of age, grade assignment, or developmental level. In testing and assessment, the focus is on grade-level expectations, or GLEs. In standardized testing, every first-grader is measured against the same standard, regardless of age or developmental level.

Some Answers to Our Opening Questions

Ms. King's Roots project offers answers to the questions posed at the beginning of this section, which we now address one by one.

What Does the Teacher Need to Know, Week by Week, and Why?

Ms. King's answer to the question of what the teacher needs to know changes throughout the school year. At year's beginning, her assessments are formative. They are frequent, focused, and individual. She assigns mini-tasks that inform her about students' skills and interests. By midyear, she switches to larger tasks, giving students more responsibility for their own learning and for self-assessment. By year's end, her assessments become summative. To what degree and in what ways can students demonstrate mastery of external standards mandated by the district and the state? She looks at the quality of the projects but attends to process as well as product, to the way students handle problems as well as the solutions they manage to come up with, and to collaborative contributions as well as individual accomplishments.

What About Students?

What feedback do students need, and when? Ms. King brings students into the feedback loop early and often, explicitly but gently, individually and as a class. She begins the year by telling students what she expects by year's end. She makes it clear that reading and writing are high on her list, along with skills in speaking and in attentive listening. By late fall, she has spent time with individual students, reviewing what she sees as strengths and areas for improvement. She keeps less detailed records than she did earlier, relying more on student work and brief journal notes. At midyear, students are appraising their own work. By the end of the Roots project, they have become their own toughest critics.

What About Parents?

Ms. King relies on three methods to connect parents with their children's achievements. The first is home–school communication. She assigns homework regularly. Weekly newsletters explain assignments and suggest how parents can help their students. She tailors assignments to individual needs. Every student receives the same basic assignment, but she jots down individualized notes on the newsletter for each student's parents. The child who handles basic spelling and punctuation but seldom experiments with unfamiliar words might carry home this note: "For the Dinosaurs report, have Pete think up more interesting words. His vocabulary is rich, but he doesn't use it much in writing. Encourage him to use wild and crazy adjectives and verbs." The second connection is the quarterly conference. Students conduct this event, describing their goals for the quarter, displaying their portfolio of work, discussing successes and shortcomings, and laying out goals for the next quarter. The final home–school connection takes place at the open house night at year's end, where student projects serve as the centerpiece.

What About Other Teachers?

Ms. King collaborates with the other third- and fourth-grade teachers in her school. At the grade-level meeting before the school year starts, the team reviews state and district standards. Woven throughout the plans for instructional activities are benchmark assessments for monitoring student progress. Results from these assessments guide the team's instructional discussions and decisions. The team also decides to carry out an integrated project featuring a different theme for each class as a summative assessment. The projects are an experiment. Although each class may be pursuing different activities, the teachers are convinced that they will be able to determine the degree to which students have met grade-level standards.

What About the Principal?

Ms. King's discussions of student progress with the principal are based on notes from her daily log and student work samples. The plan for multiple formative assessments during the year and the final summative assessment allows Ms. King to demonstrate student learning—to provide the principal with concrete evidence of growth in literacy skills and strategies. The principal must combine this classroom-based information with the standardized test results to build profiles of student progress.

A Final Word on the Roots Project

Ms. King has a substantial impact on her students. She often depends on intuition and experience but can explain her methods if asked. She relies less on standardized tests but prepares her students to deal with them. She understands assessment concepts like reliability and validity and has her own way of interpreting them. Her experience, conviction, and success with students allow her to practice her "art" in a special way. The next section of this chapter describes assessment as inquiry, telling the story behind the story.

By designing a reading-writing assessment, you can see whether your students are able to transfer the skills they have learned when doing projects like the Roots project. You can find a model in Appendix A.

1. Let's say you are looking for a teaching position in a particular district. The personnel director invites you to visit several schools. The district has a reputation for supporting thematic projects and literacy portfolios. You are curious about assessment in the district. What do you look for in classrooms and discuss with colleagues about the potential of projects and portfolios for assessing student achievement?

2. You would like to complement your district's report card with a narrative based on a final project. You have collected several examples, and although the plan will take work, you are convinced of its efficacy. You have 5 minutes to explain your plans to your principal, enough time to make three points. What will they be?

Assessment as Inquiry

Building on the concept of the teacher as a practical researcher, we now describe how the teacher assesses students' development of literacy through a process of professional inquiry. The idea has a long history (Calfee & Hiebert, 1991; Cronbach, 1960; Hiebert & Calfee, 1992; Paris et al., 1992; Stephens & Story, 2000). In 1960, for example, researcher Lee Cronbach recommended assessments based on careful observations, multiple methods and measures, and integrated information, a list found in research textbooks and diagrammed in Figure 4.2. The process begins with framing the question, which then leads to designing a plan of action. Next comes collecting and analyzing data, followed by interpreting, or making sense of, the findings. Finally, action is taken on the results—reporting and making decisions. The process is more a collection of activities than a sequence of stages, more a roller coaster than an elevator, and thus the arrows in the figure are bidirectional. In the following sections, we discuss each element, linking Ms. King's classroom with new cases along the way, to show how assessment becomes an integral part of literacy instruction.

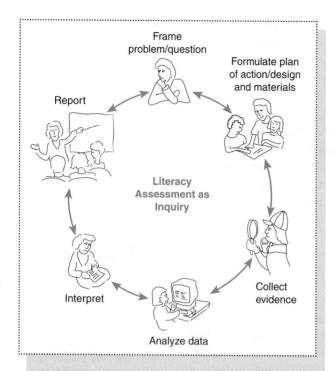

Figure 4.2

Literacy Assessment as a Process of Inquiry

Labels in figure: Frame problem/question · Formulate plan of action/design and materials · Report · **Literacy Assessment as Inquiry** · Interpret · Collect evidence · Analyze data

ssessment

Achievement testing generally measures all students on a single scale. Classroom assessments offer you the opportunity to explore students' strengths and weaknesses more carefully. You can take into account variations in students' interests, between boys and girls, and in language and culture.

Framing the Problem: What Is the Question?

At the beginning of each school year, the primary question for the classroom teacher seems simple enough: What do the students already know? At year's end, the question is similar: What have the students learned? Along the way, questions become more dynamic: How are students responding to various instructional activities? Who is getting it? Who is not? The foundation for these questions is the curriculum. For Ms. King, the curriculum means much more than getting through the textbook. She begins by reviewing goals for the school year. Having taught several grades, she has a good idea of what students need to know and do by the end of the school year. She is familiar with the learning standards the school district has prepared, statements describing student performance at certain mileposts, including the middle elementary grades. Figure 4.3 shows samples from the New Standards program, a national program at the University of Pittsburgh, which has developed curriculum-based assessments used by many states and districts as models. Ms. King is not exactly sure when or how the district decided on these standards, but in her view it is the classroom teacher's responsibility to interpret learning goals. She sees the standards as starting points, minimum achievements, and emphasizes understanding and communication more than the basics. A primary teacher in the same school will be much more focused on basic reading levels, decoding skills, and fluency.

Ms. King's thoughts about summative, bottom-line outcomes shape many of her assessment questions. Her entering third-graders vary considerably in their knowledge and abilities, and so her initial questions center on the students themselves: What will this group of students be like? What are their past experiences? What do they know? What can they do? What do they like? How do they get along together? Some of her questions are linked to curriculum outcomes: Where is each student in relation to year-end standards? Other questions relate to immediate instructional plans: What activities will help this diverse collection of students attain the goals? Finally come questions about program effectiveness: How can I discover what works and what doesn't this year?

Using such questions as a model, you should frame them in your own language. Classroom assessment is applied action research (Calfee, 2000; Hiebert & Calfee, 1992; Patterson, Santa, & Smith, 1993; Shea, Murray, & Harlin, 2005). The strategies and methods for action research are the same as for other research, but as a teacher you don't have the luxuries of unlimited time and resources available to most researchers and so your research questions must be focused and timely.

Consider the tension between developing instruction for individual students and developing instruction for the class as a whole. Suppose that September's activities suggest that some of your sixth-graders can't write and aren't interested. One strategy would be to form a group of low achievers and assign them to practice basic skills, while arranging for the more accomplished students to engage in creative writing exercises. With the average learners, you must manage three groups, but you are pro-

The student reads at least twenty-five books. . . . The quality and complexity of materials to be read are illustrated in the sample reading list . . . [and] should include traditional and contemporary literature. . . .

The student reads and comprehends at least four books . . . about one issue . . . by a single author . . . or in one genre and produces evidence of reading that:

- makes and supports . . . assertions about the text;
- supports assertions with . . . evidence;
- draws texts together to compare and contrast . . . ;
- makes perceptive and well-developed connections;
- evaluates writing strategies and . . . the author's craft.

The student reads aloud, accurately (in the range of 85–90%), familiar material of the quality and complexity illustrated in the sample reading list, and in a way that makes meaning clear to listeners by:

- self-correcting when subsequent reading indicates an earlier miscue;
- using a range of cueing systems, e.g., phonics and context clues . . . ;
- reading with a rhythm, flow, and meter that sound like everyday speech.

The student produces [four types of writing]:

. . . a report [that] engages the reader . . . develops a controlling idea . . . creates an organizing structure. . . .

. . . a response to literature [that] advances and supports a judgment . . . demonstrates an understanding . . . provides closure. . . .

. . . a narrative account [that] . . . establishes a situation, plot, point of view, setting, and conflict . . . creates organizing structure. . . .

. . . a narrative procedure [that] . . . provides a guide to action . . . makes use of appropriate writing strategies. . . .

viding individualized programs based on the assessment results. Or are you? Your attention is divided three ways, students are immersed in different learning paths, and every day individuals must live with their status in the classroom. The year-end standards remain the same for everyone, which means that the low achievers face certain failure.

An alternative strategy starts with a common set of experiences that are tailored and scaffolded around individual differences. For instance, imagine a series of small-scale writing activities throughout the year around holiday topics. These projects will engage students' interest, but will they support skill learning? To make the situation more problematic, suppose three students enter in November, recent arrivals from Cambodia with limited English. How can you meet their needs, while attending to the rest of the class? Helping them learn academic English will take a lot of work. Should you work with them separately or immerse them in the classroom? Their

Differentiating Assessment

Just as instruction must be differentiated, so should assessments. You don't need the same data about all students. When you meet with your new first-grade class, you discover that you have been assigned students whose primary languages include Spanish, Cantonese, Tagalog, Croatian, Farsi, and Hindi. All speak some English, but they are rather shy and withdrawn. How can you find out what they know? Your goal is the same as for the other students—by the time spring arrives, they should be able to handle most elements of the Tile Test that we provide in Appendix A to demonstrate their phonics skills and knowledge. At the beginning of the year, think about situations to engage them in language and literacy activities that will allow you to observe their behavior, including language. You may not understand everything they say, but you can capture glimpses of what they can do and under what conditions they can do it. For everyone in the class, but especially these children, you can create literacy play stations with letter blocks, alphabet and picture books, tape recorders, and perhaps even video playbacks. The idea is to elicit speech by whatever means possible, to model at every opportunity, and to monitor and record the results. Again, the situations are designed for the class as a whole, but support and observations are tailored to the individual.

In a diverse society like ours, teachers need to know more about language and culture than ever before. The assessment task can be quite a challenge if you try to handle the variations by yourself. It helps when school faculty work as a team. You may call on specialists when they are available, but you can also profit by sharing resources and information with colleagues. Ask a fellow teacher to observe one of your lessons, focusing on a particularly puzzling student. Colleagues will include globetrotters who have spent time in other countries and other individuals who are themselves first- or second-generation Americans. These colleagues can provide valuable help in understanding the varied cultural behaviors of your English language learners. Conversations with parents can also provide insights into students' language and literacy abilities.

linguistic heritage offers opportunities to enrich the classroom experiences for the other students. The challenge is to discover ways to connect the new arrivals with the classroom community, despite barriers of language and culture. Sixth-graders are likely to pick up "practical" English fairly quickly, given the chance. How might the holiday theme fit into this picture? Thanksgiving, Christmas, and Valentine's Day might be totally unknown to these youngsters. And their holidays may be equally foreign to you. By Googling "Cambodian celebrations," you learn that the Water Festival is celebrated for three days in November and features processions of brightly decorated boats pulled by costumed oarsmen. The Khmer New Year comes in April, another three-day celebration that combines religious ceremonies, gift giving, and a time for boys and girls to get together for dates. Every culture has holidays—you can move from the casual to the academic by studying differences in music, art, drama, customs, and so on.

Designing a Plan of Action

A design is a refinement of the original question, a plan for arranging conditions and deciding what to assess. You begin with hypotheses, or "hunches," and then create situations to explore these hypotheses, as In the Classroom 4.2 demonstrates. Being

Vocabulary Assessment in the Third Grade

It is the beginning of the school year, and Ms. Furakawa, a second-year teacher, is thinking about ways to assess her third-graders' vocabulary skills. She knows that in order to comprehend and compose, students need to be proficient in using vocabulary strategies—what they need is not a random accumulation of words, but a mastery of concepts, collections of ideas, and words as keys to communication. She has found that students often seem to struggle to find words to express their ideas. Many fall back on informal and commonplace terms. For example, they may say, "What I think about atmosphere is that it's about air and storms and stuff like that."

Ms. Furakawa jots down a "starter" question: What do the students *really* know? Her hunch is that students know only the words that they use, but she decides that this idea is wrong—they surely know more words than they actually use! She asks the other third-grade teacher for advice, and he recommends the vocabulary section of the Iowa Test of Basic Skills (ITBS; Hoover, Hieronymus, Frisbie, & Dunbar, 1996) for a quick vocabulary check. (See Kame'enui, Simmons, & Cornachione, 2001, for an annotated list of published assessment instruments.)

Next, she decides to spend a little time with a few students who appear to have particular problems; they say hardly anything in class discussions. For example, Sam scores at a grade level of 1.2 on the ITBS vocabulary test, two grades below expectation. Sam seldom volunteers during classroom discussions, simply shrugging his shoulders. She decides to explore an alternative hypothesis: Sam actually has a substantial vocabulary (most 9-year-olds do), but his storehouse of words is not tapped in typical school tests and formal talk. What might be the keys to his storehouse?

The design problem in this case calls for Ms. Furakawa to imagine other ways to bring out Sam's vocabulary. He may lack the full range and depth of concepts expected in third grade. He clearly needs to learn how to express himself more effectively. But what is there to build on so that Ms. Furakawa can help him most effectively, assuming that he knows more than he appears to on the surface?

Designing an assessment often means planning mini-experiments for observing performance under different conditions. Ms. Furakawa decides to check out three possibilities: (1) Sam can recognize words that he may not use spontaneously; (2) he may be able to talk about words that he doesn't appear to know; or (3) he may be able to use context to figure out the meanings of unfamiliar words. These and other vocabulary questions are presented in Figure 4.4.

What happens when Sam is asked to make choices about the meanings of more or less familiar words? "Sam, which of these words best describes the pizza we had for lunch today [slight pause between each word and the next]: scrumptious, bedraggled, succulent, delectable, ambrosial, good, yummy?"

What happens when he is asked to explain a word's meaning in different ways? "Sam, what is a diamond? Do you know anyone who has a diamond? What does it look like? Which best describes a diamond—a ring, a jewel, a star? Can you think of another way the word *diamond* is used? What about a diamond in baseball? Is it a catcher's mitt, someone on the team, or the way the playing field is laid out?"

When and how does Sam use context to figure out the meaning of a novel word? Suppose Sam is given these sentences: "The bones from pterosaurs, a giant aerial reptile that terrorized other beasts during the Jurassic Age, have been found throughout the western United States" and "A flying reptile with a body as big as a horse, the pterosaur swooped down on other small beasts and carried them away to his mountain hideaway." What clues can Sam use to understand the meaning of *pterosaur*?

open to alternatives is important; don't deceive yourself by deciding on an answer and then setting up a situation to prove it.

Ms. Furakawa's design, shown in Figure 4.4, begins with easy tasks and moves to tougher ones, adding support as needed. A "clean" assessment investigates student

Depth of Word Knowledge	Characteristics	Meaning Assessment	Strategy Assessment
Can recognize word (listening/reading)	"Has something to do with . . ." (identify picture)	IRAS vocabulary "Does *glad* mean *sad*, or *nervous*, or *happy*?"	"How did you know?" Immediate recall Scaffolded recall
Can define word	"It means . . ."	IRAS vocabulary "What does *scrumptious* mean?"	"I figured it out from the text."
Can understand word in context (listening/reading)	"It is talking about a kind of . . ."	"What does that word mean in this sentence/passage?"	"I know what the parts of the word mean" (dis- = not; like = enjoy; -ed = past tense).
Can use word in appropriate contexts (speaking/writing)	"You have to use *tyrant* here."	Writing samples Oral presentations Fill-in-the-blank exercise "What would be a different word for *sat*?"	
Knows multiple meanings of word	"It can mean _____ or _____."	"Tell me all the meanings of *grow*."	
Can use word in multiple contexts to mean different things (speaking/writing)	"A run earned in baseball; a run in your stockings; to move quickly."	How many different ways can you use the word *run*?"	

Note: See Appendix A.

performance when conditions are optimal. Everyone fails under some circumstances. By finding a way to help Sam show that he knows something about diamonds and reptiles, Ms. Furakawa has a more valid assessment of Sam's capacities and can target instruction that fits his situation.

Sam is only one student. What about the others? The answer is that in-depth assessment allows you to enhance your understanding of student learning by studying particular cases, which you can apply in the classroom turmoil. It is unrealistic that you will have the need or the time do in-depth assessment except for a select number of students who require that attention. You must often collect information on the fly, switching your attention for a few moments to Sam, then to Deborah and a few other students, taking advantage of naturally occurring variations in classroom situations. On occasion, you may ask a specific question of Sam to check out a hunch or assign him a particular task to see how he does. You cannot give huge amounts of individual attention to every student—nor do you need to. But what you learn from studying Sam will help you know how to assess from moment to moment. You are learning to "kid-watch." As you work with groups of students, always keep a pad of paper close at hand. Make notes about words they miss, questions they can and can't answer, and words they do not know.

Planning an assessment design is a matter of making choices. A general assessment, a standardized reading test, or the placement test from your core reading program is

Assessment

Drawing children out can be the greatest challenge for a teacher. The easy answer is to let a shy child blend into the background. But it is important to help a timid student join the conversation in order to access his learning and to improve learning outcomes.

useful for all students at the beginning of the year. It gives you a quick impression of the distribution of skills and abilities in the room. As the year progresses daily activities, as in the Root Project, plus your own observations will tell you which students are progressing and which are not. Keep notes. For those students who struggle with reading and writing, more in-depth assessments are desirable. They give you extra information to guide your instruction. Time is an important consideration in assessment design. How will your assessment plan vary over the months? How will you adjust the plan as you learn more and puzzles emerge?

Time should also capture development. The September focus of a kindergarten teacher will be quite different from that of the teacher with a combined fourth- and fifth-grade class. In kindergarten classes, you can study individual children to discover their interests and find out what they know about letters, sounds, words, sentences, or books. Clay's (1993) concepts-about-print assessment provides a helpful model for teacher-made questions to discover what emergent readers know about print and books. For example, a kindergartner can be asked about directionality with such questions as "Where is the front of the book?" and "Where is the top of the page?" He can also be asked function questions such as "Where do I begin to read on this page?" and questions about boundaries such as "Underline one word. Where does it start? Where does it end?" The focus is not on the "right" answer, but on how the student handles the question. Year-end achievements should be gauged with a greater margin of tolerance in the early grades. Your major task is to move children from the broad spectrum of entry levels toward the academic demands of the next grade.

For a teacher of upper-grade students, choices become more constrained. You must quickly learn how close your students are to handling middle school demands. You can't spend September casually engaging in discussions with students about interests and backgrounds; you are likely to have both a larger class and greater diversity than your kindergarten colleague. Your plan of action requires focus and efficiency. The basic strategy is the same: Explore conditions under which a student succeeds or fails but assume that success is possible. Motivation is especially critical in the later grades. After several years of failure, students may have learned that they cannot learn. Assessment may mean finding ways to convince students that they can succeed. Skill and will are both important, for setting learning conditions and for deciding what evidence best informs you about students' abilities and achievements.

When more precise information is needed, you should also consider running records, informal reading inventories, and assessment of phonological and phonics skills if your students are not yet readers or struggling with basic print skills. In conducting a running record (Clay, 1985), a teacher records on paper an individual student's oral reading behavior as the student reads a short passage, typically between 100 and 200 words (Morrow, 2009). The teacher notes correctly read words, words the reader left out (omissions), the reader's misreadings of words (substitutions), words the reader inserted into the text, repeated words, reversals of words, and self-corrected misreadings of words. Self-corrections are not considered as errors in the scoring of a running record. If a child is able to read the passage with better than 95 percent word recognition accuracy, the text is considered at the child's independent reading level and she can read it without teacher support. If the reading is between 90 and 95 percent accuracy, the text is at the child's instructional reading level and requires instructional support. If the child reads with less than 90 percent accuracy, the text is at the frustration level—that is, too difficult for the child. To conduct this kind of assessment, the teacher needs only the text to be read and a paper and pencil. Running records are typically used for early primary grade readers. They help

Administering one or more subtests of the Interactive Reading Assessment System (found in Appendix A) may help answer reading skills questions that emerge about individual students.

teachers to match text levels to children and yield insights about children's reading processes, specifically the knowledge and strategies a child uses to identify words. This information can guide instruction.

An informal reading inventory (IRI) is a predesigned instrument. Like a running record, it is individually administered. IRIs consist of a series of graded word lists and short passages. The teacher first has a student read the graded word lists. Based on the child's performance on the lists, he is given a passage at a particular reading level to begin. He then reads a series of passages. As he reads each passage, the teacher records his oral reading behaviors as in the running record assessment. The child's oral reading is also timed to provide an assessment of oral reading fluency. Following each passage, the teacher assesses the child's comprehension of the passage either by having the child retell the passage or by asking the child the comprehension questions that come with the assessment. Following the assessment, the teacher can estimate the levels at which the student can read accurately and with good comprehension on his own (independent level), with teacher assistance (instructional level), and without sufficient accuracy or comprehension even with assistance (frustration level). On the Qualitative Reading Inventory-4 (QRI-4; Leslie and Caldwell, 2006), a well-regarded and widely used IRI, the criteria for reading levels are listed as follows: independent reading level—word recognition of 98 percent or better and comprehension at 90 percent or better; instructional reading level—word recognition of 90 to 97 percent and comprehension at 70 to 89 percent; frustration level—word recognition at less than 90 percent and comprehension less than 70 percent. As with a running record, a teacher can analyze students' reading behaviors and answers to comprehension questions (Dewitz & Dewitz, 2003) to identify strengths and weaknesses that can guide instruction.

We provide you with the Interactive Reading Assessment System–Revised (IRAS-R; Calfee & Hoover, 2004) to illustrate the IRI strategy in Appendix A. The IRAS-R includes a set of graded passages and prompts for students' retellings of the passages. You may administer some or all of the components depending on the information you need. The IRAS begins with a selection of letters from the alphabet to measure a student's understanding of sound-symbol relationships. Next are graded word lists, which assess both word recognition skills and vocabulary levels. Lists of synthetic words allow you to diagnose decoding and spelling abilities. Graded sets of related sentences assess students' ability to read connected text where context may be an aid when reading unknown words within a passage. The sentence sets guide you in selecting passages, both stories and reports, to check comprehension skills. Along the way, metalinguistic questions reveal students' thinking processes as they perform different tasks: "Why is *fab* said differently than *fabe?*" As noted, you can use only those parts of the IRAS-R that you need for a particular purpose. You can also use it as a "shell" for developing your own assessments.

Reading assessment experts JoAnne Caldwell and Lauren Leslie (2005) note that if you give a student an informal reading inventory and she does not read at an instructional level on the preprimer or primer level word list and passages, then you should assess the child's phonological awareness. This is the ability to hear, segment, and blend sounds within words (Snow, Burns, & Griffin, 1998). The most fine-grained level of phonological awareness is phonemic awareness—the ability to hear the somewhat separable phonemes in spoken words—which we will discuss in Chapter 6. Research has shown that phonological skills strongly predict reading achievement (National Reading Panel, 2000). Well-regarded phonological assessments are the Phonological Awareness Test or the informal measures in Phonemic Awareness for Young Children (Adams, Foorman, Lundberg, & Beeler, 1998). Another widely used phonemic awareness assessment is the Yopp-Singer Test of Phoneme Segmentation (Yopp, 1995). The assessment is reliable, valid, and quick to administer. Developer Hallie Yopp provides a copy of the assessment in the article in which she describes it [*The Reading Teacher, 49*(1), 20–29].

Collecting Evidence

The collection process entails lots of options. At the outset of the chapter, we discussed the broad continuum of assessment options, from informal tasks to formal methods. Here we focus on midrange methods that provide the most informative strategies for classroom applications: observing, discussing and questioning, interviewing, student work samples, scoring rubrics, and teacher-made tests. At the end we will consider curriculum-based measurements that are being advocated in many schools. These strategies overlap with good teaching practice, and instruction and assessment often intertwine.

Observing

The best information about student learning often comes from looking and listening, or kid watching (Goodman, Goodman, & Hood, 1989). (For more information on observing, see Johnson, Kress, & Pikulski, 1987; Johnston, 1992; and Owocki & Goodman, 2002.) This job is easier said than done. Until you know how to look and listen, it can be hard to both instruct and observe. The classroom may seem a blooming, buzzing confusion. How can you make sense of student responses as you teach? What do you look for? How do you find out what's really happening in students' heads? The following questions offer a framework for looking and listening:

- Who are the students? How many are there? How are groups organized? Which students stand out, and why?
- How do students respond in small-group versus whole-group settings or working individually with you?
- When students are reading are they fluent, do they self-correct, do they use a strategy to identify new words?
- During comprehension discussions, can students summarize what has been read, make inferences, clarify misunderstanding, make predictions and justify those predictions?
- Can students determine the meaning of a new word while reading using context clues or word parts?
- How are the students responding? Are they attentive? Productive? Interested and engaged? What is their level of performance? Of social interaction?
- When students are working independently do they understand the purpose of the task, or do they seek clarification when they do not?

These questions serve as a starting point, but we offer a couple of cautions. First, you can't simultaneously monitor all seven questions for all students, and so for a particular observation you should pick a focus. Select those facets and students that fit a particular situation, and place everything else in the background. A clear purpose allows you to "zoom in," setting the stage for action research. For instance, you might study how a particular student handles different situations with varying amounts of support. How does Sam handle vocabulary in whole-class activities versus small groups? How does he do with and without a helping hand? On topics that are more or less interesting to him? When he is talking or writing? Focusing on Sam and his vocabulary situation makes the job possible. And, as noted earlier, what you learn about Sam can inform you about other students as well.

*A*ssessment

Your first attempts at observing can be frustrating, especially if you work from a complex form—or a blank page! Start simply and jot down miscues while students read. With time, your observational skills will expand, improve, and become automatic.

Second, it's hard to observe while you are teaching. You can remedy this problem in a couple of ways. First, study your class while someone else teaches them—a colleague, a student teacher, the reading specialist. Even brief looks give you a different perspective on students, a chance to see how individuals respond to the classroom ebb and flow. "David never seems to join the discussion. I placed him at the front so that I could watch him."

Another way to find time for observation is to build it into your teaching. You can organize group activities and individual assignments to allow you time to look at learning. It is tempting to use these occasions to work with students having special needs or to respond to questions on homework papers. But sometimes, rather than talk, you might stop, look, and listen. Also, becoming generally more familiar with other classrooms and students will enable you to gain more from your observations.

While observing your class, don't limit your attention to academic work. You can informally assess students' motivation for reading or writing by listening to what they say and watching how they approach a challenging but doable task. For example, when Jim and Nancy begin the task of writing about life in a covered wagon on the Oregon Trail without hesitation, they are demonstrating a high level of self-efficacy for this writing task. Their teacher, Mr. Edwards, has given them multiple opportunities during the year to brainstorm a topic and then organize their ideas in a topical web. They have been taught to use an index to locate additional information for their web in the library books on display in the classroom. When the teacher comments on the quality of their reports, the students attribute success to their decision to work hard this quarter on becoming better writers and improving their report card grades in writing.

When Dave, on the other hand, hears the assignment, he spends the next few minutes in avoidant behaviors. He rummages through his backpack, bothers the student next to him, and so on. Earlier, when the class was asked to read silently about the Westward Movement, he flipped dispiritedly through the history book—he wasn't especially interested in the topic. It seems to Dave that he has always had trouble understanding history. He thinks, "How can I handle the writing assignment when I know nothing about the topic? My writing scores are always low, so what's the point in trying? Mr. Edwards is always asking me to write about things that I can't understand and don't like."

These scenarios challenge Mr. Edwards to analyze his students' confidence and respond to their motivation as well as their performance. When he praises the quality of Jim's and Nancy's reports, their comments lead him to think that they attribute their success on this assignment to their own efforts—just the type of attribution he wants his class to make. Dave's behavior may seem resistant; he "just doesn't care." By checking with him about his perceptions of the situation, Mr. Edwards may find that Dave's attributions emphasize external factors like the difficulty of the task, the irrelevance of the assignment, or other factors that he cannot control. Redirecting the assignment to connect with Dave's interests may open the way to help him understand that his efforts can make a difference. Observing on the fly can capture behaviors that are the starting point for more detailed inquiry.

Discussing and Questioning

New teachers generally anticipate engaging students in active discussions and are then frustrated by the lack of participation. Students either say nothing or go completely wild, leading the teacher to resort to lecturing as a control mechanism. The result is to shut down an important opportunity for assessment. Student talk, when well planned and managed, offers important opportunities to study student thinking.

One way to foster meaningful discussion is the knowledge-as-design approach developed by David Perkins (1994). Perkins suggests that exploration of many topics can be organized around the following questions:

- What is the relevance of the topic?
- What is the structure of the topic?
- What are examples of the topic?
- What are positives and negatives of the topic?

The idea is not to use these questions only in guiding discussion, but to give them away to the students for their personal use. The knowledge-as-design strategy offers students a scaffold for participation and an opportunity, individually and collectively, to think deeply about a topic and voice a variety of opinions while still keeping the discussion on track. In these exchanges, rich dialogues depend on three elements: why the questioner is asking the question, what kind of question is asked, and how the questioner handles the responses (Dillon, 1988).

1. *Why are you asking the question?* In school, most questions attempt to find out if the student knows what the teacher already knows. Outside school, a question is usually a genuine effort by one person to learn something from someone else. Students may be startled when classroom discussion takes this turn and be reluctant to respond. They have learned that school questions have a right answer, and the teacher knows it. "Real" questions seldom have one right answer. Listening to students answer questions reveals much about their thinking.

2. *What kinds of questions lead to rich discussions?* It's useful to think about the kind of answer you have in mind. Questions that lead to yes-no answers do not yield much dialogue unless asking "Why?" is a natural follow-up. The same is true for questions that call for specific answers. Broad questions can be quite simple. While you are reading a story, for instance, a natural question at a critical juncture is "What do you think will happen next?" Starting with broad questions and then exploring the responses can promote rich discussion. We introduce the funnel approach in the following section on interviewing.

3. *How can you extend student responses to more fully reveal their thinking?* Again, keep it simple: "Gee, that sounds interesting—say more." Several boys in a Hawaiian classroom, after reading about volcanoes in their science book, are building a soda-vinegar model. The teacher asks, "Do you think that if you dig really deep you'll find melted rock?" The boys mull it over and decide "No, it can't be!" The teacher continues, "You know, Oahu [their island] was once a volcano." Disbelief registers on their faces, but then one boy mentions that his father told him that the lava rocks in their yard were from old volcanoes. It becomes clear to the teacher that the students "understood" the text at one level but had not connected it with their personal experience. The teacher now questions them about the soda-vinegar activity. This model is a popular activity in elementary classrooms, but misleads students about how volcanoes really operate.

Interviewing

Talking with students can take many forms. Sometimes, you spend time with individual students, not in an on-the-fly conversation or a formal assessment, but in 1- or 2-minute sessions around a particular question with a particular student. In the Classroom 4.3 illustrates the funnel approach, which is an efficient strategy for collecting both broad and focused information during an exchange. The key is to

The Funnel Approach

The funnel approach begins with general queries and moves toward specific questions. Second-grader Martha has problems with story comprehension and can't seem to identify with characters. After reading *Nate the Great* by Marjorie Weinman Sharmat, a simple detective story that tells how Nate finds his friend Annie's lost picture, Martha expresses neither empathy nor interest. The teacher conducts a 1-minute interview using the funnel approach.

> *Teacher:* Martha, what do you remember about *Nate the Great?* What can you tell me about what the characters were feeling?
>
> *Martha:* I dunno. I guess I like the way Nate feels good when he helps Annie find her picture.
>
> *Teacher:* How do you think Nate feels when Annie tells him on the phone about her missing picture?
>
> *Martha:* Happy, because he likes to solve mysteries and call himself "Nate the Great"! And Annie feels sad and mad, 'cause I think she really liked that picture.
>
> *Teacher:* Very nice! What does the story tell you about why Annie likes the picture?

Notice how the teacher starts with a broad question designed to reconnect Martha to an earlier discussion about the story. She focuses Martha's understanding of the characters' feelings. "Why" and "How do you know that" questions delve into students' reasoning and explore their capacity to reflect and make inferences. Whatever Martha answers, the teacher will learn something from this exchange, which she will jot in her logbook.

prepare yourself in advance with a collection of questioning models, such as the funnel approach.

Student Work Samples: Performances and Portfolios

An advantage to using a read-write cycle assessment is that it allows you to see how students write under the best conditions. It merges good instruction with good assessment practices. For descriptions and examples of the read-write cycle model see Appendix A.

During a typical school day, students produce a lot of paperwork. Some products (for example, worksheets) serve for practice, the work of a moment, and are seldom worth keeping. As noted earlier, today's assessment methods are more likely to emphasize authentic performance and showing one's work. Students assemble portfolios for writing and mathematics, science, and social studies (Farr & Tone, 1994; Tierney, Carter, & Desai, 1991). These collections, like Ms. King's Roots project, take shape as major activities representing significant amounts of time, engaging the creative impulse, and reflecting meaningful personal investment.

A writing portfolio can show a student's progression from early ruminations about a task to final publication. The read-write cycle model (the CLAS-Plus assessment model) in Figure 4.5 (Calfee & Wilson, 2004) provides effective support for portfolio projects of students in fourth grade and beyond. The aim is to guide instruction, but the activities also reveal students' abilities to translate prior experiences and topical reading into a well-developed written text, with ongoing support.

Work samples assess both product and process through a series of stages. In the *develop* stage, students brainstorm together, sharing what they know about the topic. They then read stories, articles, books, or Web pages to research the topic further and to study texts that offer models for writing. In the *draft* stage, their ideas coalesce into the beginnings of an essay. During the *review* stage, students conference with peers for feedback and suggestions on their drafts. During the *revision* stage, choices are made about incorporating suggestions and modifying the original draft. The students work on grammar and mechanics in the *polishing* stage. The essays are now ready for the *publication* stage, where their work becomes public. The final result

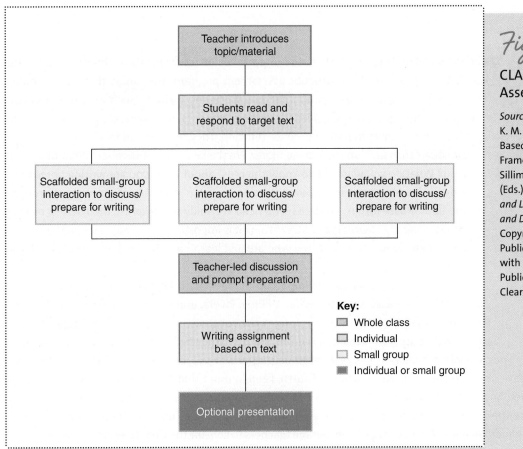

Figure 4.5

CLAS-Plus Model of Assessment

Source: Calfee, R. C., & Wilson, K. M. (2004). "A Classroom-Based Writing Assessment Framework." In C. A. Stone, E. R. Silliman, B. J. Ehren, & K. Apel (Eds.), *Handbook of Language and Literacy: Development and Disorders* (pp. 583–599). Copyright 2004 by Guilford Publications, Inc. Reproduced with permission of Guilford Publications, Inc., via Copyright Clearance Center.

can be judged as a product, but the process reveals student learning and can help inform instruction. The read-write cycle model applies to both narrative and expository text. The flexible framework allows the teacher to employ the model with any genre.

Portfolios often include captions, brief comments by the teacher reflecting on the work and pointing out strengths and areas for improvement. Sticky notes allow the teacher to provide feedback and instructional guidance without marking up the original. Students can add their own sticky note captions, putting themselves into the assessment loop.

Scoring Rubrics

What is the best way to score papers? The answer is the *rubric,* a graduated scoring guide with criteria for each score level, something like a letter grade but without the letters, and with instructions about the meaning of each level on the scale. Figure 4.6 shows a rubric for evaluating primary-grade writing. Later in the chapter, we present a rubric for intermediate-grade reading. Rubric systems include benchmarks, or samples, at each level, along with an explanation of why the work received a particular grade.

Figure 4.7 (pp. 100–101) shows a six-level format for writing in the elementary grades. A rating is provided for five dimensions—length, coherence, grammar/mechanics, vocabulary, and spelling—each of which is important in a well-written composition. A separate score for each dimension allows teachers and students to identify specific strengths and areas that need attention.

*A*ssessment

Portfolios can easily become trash bins if you aren't careful. It is important to have a sorting process in which students select the pieces that reflect their best work and you designate a few critical pieces for inclusion.

Conferencing

Quiocho and Ulanoff (2009) discuss the importance of conferencing with English language learners (ELLs) as part of an authentic assessment program. They share that during conferences, teachers should ask open-ended questions and include much wait time to allow English language learners to formulate their thoughts. Moreover, Quiocho and Ulanoff encourage teachers to probe students' thinking. They recommend teachers ask students questions such as "Can you tell me more? What else do you remember? What happened next? What do you want me to know the most about what you are writing or reading? How is this connected to . . . [what is being taught]?" Arguably, these kinds of prompts are appropriate for any students who need scaffolding to express themselves, be they English language learners or not. We think it is important, however, to stress the criticality of these supports for children who are just learning to understand, speak, read, and write English.

In discussing ways to provide accommodations to English language learners during content area assessments, Shafer, Willner, Rivera, and Acosta (2009) make the following points: First, make sure you've taught the content the assessment will cover to ELLs. Second, make sure your accommodations address students' linguistic needs. Third, include your school's bilingual or ESL teacher in discussions of accommodations. These teachers will have important insights to contribute. Fourth, keep in mind that ELLs are different from one another. An accommodation for one ELL may not be appropriate for another. Fifth, let students experience the accommodations before the assessment so they will get used to the process or the task demands. Shafer and her colleagues encourage teachers to consult the George Washington University Center for Equality and Excellence in Education's database of accommodations for ELL students (http://ells.ceee.gwu.edu).

Figure 4.6   **Rubric for Evaluating Primary-Grade Writing**

Exceptional	Sparkles! Vocabulary uses descriptive words. Creates suspense or surprise. Aware of audience. Strong personal voice. Emotion transmitted. Clincher at end.
Commendable	Clear beginning, middle, and end. Strong story sense. Mostly conventional spelling. Passage flows. Supporting detail.
Adequate	Listing of events. Phonetic spelling. Catalog of facts. Train of thought. Sense of beginning and end, but lost in details.
Some Evidence	Complete thought. Coherent but weak. Inventive spelling.
Little Evidence	Minimal fluency. Off topic. No story line or train of thought. Repetitive.
Minimal Evidence	No meaning in print. Random letters with pictures.

The rubric system also provides information about reading comprehension (see Figure 4.8, p. 102). For example, if a student's book report on Colin Powell is poorly written but shows an understanding of the content, then content and coherence will be high but other dimensions will be low. Doesn't this approach mix reading and writing? The answer is "Yes, but it doesn't matter." Until we develop a mental probe that allows us to tell about a person's internal thoughts, we have to rely on indirect measures. Multiple-choice tests also depend on much more than reading; as we shall see later, they require strategies, motivation, and background knowledge. Asking a student to discuss a passage is probably the most direct method for gauging comprehension but is impractical for a class of 35 students. To assess reading through writing, you look for different features in a composition.

Models for Teacher-Made Tests

Thus far, we have emphasized performance assessments, but you will also need to rely on traditional tests when appropriate. Nitko (1996) and Stiggins (1994) describe procedures for developing various types of teacher-made tests, ranging from multiple-choice to short-answer tests. For children in the early grades, informal reading inventories and running records are a good middle ground between standardized methods and completely open-ended approaches.

Finding ways to adapt these assessment techniques to meet classroom needs is the key. In Appendix A, the Tile Test (Calfee, 1999) and the Graduated Running Record provide models you can use as is or as templates. The Tile Test (see Figure 4.9, p. 102), designed for primary-grade children, uses letter and word tiles in short, engaging activities to quickly assess letter knowledge, sound-symbol relationship, articulation, decoding/spelling abilities, metaphonic understanding, and skill at reading simple sentences. With letter tiles, children who have yet to master paper and pencil can demonstrate what they know about spelling. As shown in Figure 4.9, the student plays a Scrabble-like game, beginning with *pat* and changing one letter at a time to make *sat, sam,* and so on. To assess metalinguistic processes, students are asked along the way to explain their decoding/spelling strategies.

The Graduated Running Record (GRR; see Figure 4.10, p. 103) can be used throughout the elementary grades to measure fluency (reading rate, prosody/phrasing, stress, and intonation). In addition, you can also determine students' understanding of semantic, syntactic, and grapho-phonemic cuing systems by analyzing miscues. In place of leveled books or passages (which can take a significant amount of time to move through), the GRR relies on a single paragraph in which difficulty gradually increases with each sentence. At some point, the student will reach his reading level. The tester then finishes the passage, asking the student to retell the story to determine his comprehension skill.

Progress Monitoring with Curriculum-Based Measurement

In this chapter we have stressed authentic assessment approaches, observing children, collected performance data on classroom tasks, and the use of rubrics, among others. In many schools, however, spurred on by the federal Reading First program and Response to Intervention (Fuchs, Fuchs, & Vaughn, 2008), teachers are being requested to collect progress monitoring data to determine whether a particular reading intervention or reading program is working. Children may be assessed every couple of weeks on their progress in identifying letter names, learning to segment words, or improving their oral reading fluency. Curriculum-based measurement may be designed by teachers or schools can use one of two published assessment systems,

Figure 4.7 Read-Write Cycle Assessment Rubric

Score	Length*	Coherence	Grammar/Mechanics
6	3–5 pages, or 176 or more words	• Writer provides overall links/transitions; examples and descriptions are presented logically. • States main topic and supports it with details and examples. • Shifts topics smoothly; easy to follow and logical.	• Makes few, if any, errors in grammar and punctuation. • Utilizes appropriate variety of sentence structures, including phrases and clauses.
5	1–2 pages, or 86–175 words	• Shows ease and facility in expressing ideas. • Writing flows smoothly and naturally and is understandable. • Generally focused on topic. • Provides description, elaboration, evidence, and/or support. • Writer provides overall links, but transitions may not always be smooth; ideas/reasons are clear and logical.	• Uses some variation in sentence structure, including phrases and clauses. • Minimal errors may be present as complex structures are explored. • Has few run-ons or fragmented sentences.
4	$\frac{3}{4}$ page, or 61–85 words	• Provides descriptions, elaboration, evidence and/or support. • Information or examples may be in a listlike form (no tying together of ideas). • Addresses the topic without wavering. • Writing is generally understandable and coherent, but lacks complete control. • Focus may shift and be somewhat difficult to follow.	• Shows clear sentence sense. • May display variety in sentences. • Makes minimal or no errors in punctuation. • Has few, if any, run-ons or fragmented sentences.
3	4 sentences/ $\frac{1}{2}$ page, or 36–60 words	• Addresses the topic. • Includes little description, elaboration, evidence, or support. • May include rambling sentences or lists with no elaboration. • Vague and/or confusing.	• Uses simple repetitive sentences. • May include fragments and run-ons. • Makes some errors in punctuation and grammar, which do not impede reading.
2	2–3 sentences/ $\frac{1}{4}$ page, or 11–35 words	• Addresses the topic minimally. • May wander off topic. • Fragmented expression of ideas.	• Uses simple sentence structure or phrases with many fragments and/or run-ons. • Makes errors that are highly evident and interfere with reading.
1	1 sentence or less, or 0–10 words	• Generally unintelligible or unrelated. • Copied from the board or another student.	• Unintelligible due to grammar or punctuation. • Copied from the board or another student.

*Grade-level appropriate paper, margins, and penmanship; no skipping of lines.

**Most Anglo-Saxon words can stand alone and be affixed. Affixes are often prepositional: *over-, under-, in-, for-*. Common suffixes include *-ed, -er, -ing, -ly, -hood, -ness*.

Vocabulary	Spelling
• Shows substantial use of complex Romance Language Layer words. • Uses lexical variety. • Uses precision in dealing with topic. • Uses Latin and Greek roots and affixes.	**Complex Conventional** • Shows substantial evidence of attempting complex words with few errors (polysyllabic words, prefixes and suffixes, Latin and Greek roots and affixes). • Shows command of vowels in polysyllabic words. • Shows mastery of conventional spellings for familiar 1- to 2-syllable words.
• Shows some evidence of complex but familiar Romance Language Layer words. • Shows limited variety and reliance on relatively common words (*national*). • Uses Latin (and Greek) roots and affixes. • Uses precise and/or rich language (*no ordinary friend, compassionate*).	**Conventional** • Has command of long/short vowel contrast. • Makes few errors. • Uses polysyllabic words with few or no errors.
• Uses a substantial number of familiar polysyllabic words (*interesting, understand*), including compounds. • Shows noticeably increased precision (*friendly* for *nice*).	**Phonetic Appropriate** • Is beginning to show long/short vowel contrast. • Uses short vowels accurately. • May have other vowel errors (e.g., digraphs). • Reversals may be present (especially in blends and *r/l* patterns). • Polysyllabic words (including compounds), if present, include vowels.
• Uses 1- to 2-syllable words, most frequently with little variety or precision. • May include compounds and Anglo-Saxon** affixation (prepositions, comparatives: *under-, -er, -est*) • May include descriptive words.	**Phonological** • Uses short vowels accurately. • Represents each sound with very few omissions. • Reversals may be present (especially in blends or *r/l* patterns. • Easily readable.
• Frequently uses one-syllable (CVC) and basic sight words. • Uses short, "safe," commonplace words. • Uses simplistic and/or imprecise language.	**Beginning Phonological** • Can identify consonants. • Includes vowels, but frequently the selection is incorrect. • Omits sounds (*sitr = sister*). • Readable with minimal effort.
• Most words are difficult to interpret. • Uses few words and/or limits words to those provided by the teacher. • Uses incorrect and/or ineffective language.	**Alphabetic, Prephonetic** • Uses letters. • Consonants may represent some sounds. • Omits most vowels. • May or may not spell sight words conventionally. • Unreadable or readable with considerable effort.

Figure 4.8   Sample Rubrics for Intermediate-Grade Literacy Standards

| | Level of Proficiency | | |
Standard	Exemplary	Proficient	Developing
Making Sense of a Story	Thoroughly understands complex stories Connects personal experiences to characters and themes Has multiple perspectives across stories	Understands most stories including some complex ones Makes some connections of personal experiences to characters and situations Has different perspectives on a story	Has limited and literal understanding of simple stories Extracts meaning but with little personal connection Describes events, people, and places factually
Using Tools and Strategies in Reading	Masterfully uses several strategies to deepen understanding Makes sophisticated analyses of plot and theme	Uses various strategies to understand story Uses rereading and rethinking to support understanding	Has limited range of strategies Uses some rereading to support understanding

Dynamic Indicators of Basic Early Literacy Skills (DIBELS; Good & Kaminski, 2002) and AimsWeb Pro Reading (Shinn & Shinn, 2002). By 2005 DIBELS was being given to over 2,000,000 children (Afflerbach, 2007). Both of these assessment systems provide 1-minute tests, or probes, of letter-sound knowledge, letter-name knowledge, phonemic segmentation, nonsense word decoding, and oral reading fluency. Following the logic of these assessments, the child has to name as many letters as he can or read as many words as he can in 1 minute. The number of items successfully completed is his score. These tests come with norms and a child is evaluated on his progress in meeting these norms. For example, DIBELS expects the average student to read 90 words correct per minute by the end of second grade. Given these norms teachers can monitor a student's progress in achieving these goals.

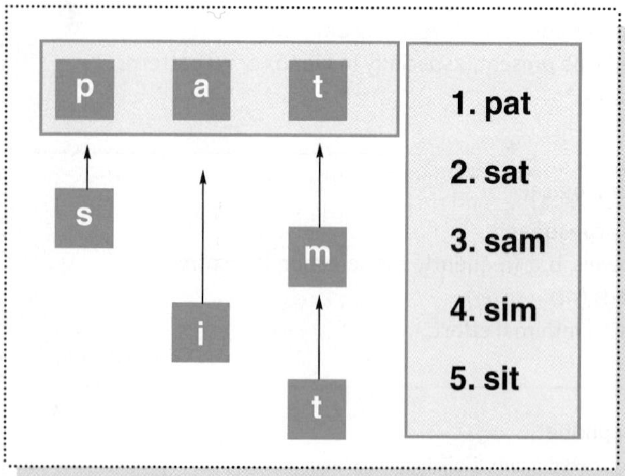

These curriculum-based measures are quick and easily administered assessments of discrete or constrained skills (Paris, 2005). We can measure letter-name knowledge, nonsense word decoding, and oral reading fluency, but DIBELS cannot assess vocabulary growth or reading comprehension. The danger in DIBELS or AimsWeb is confusing the assessment tool with a complete reading curriculum. These curriculum-based measures assess only a small slice of reading and do so well only at the earliest stages of learning to read. Relying on such narrowly conceived assessment tools can cause teachers and administrators to focus reading instruction on the wrong factors and ignore the development of vocabulary, comprehension, and motivation. Although DIBELS and AimsWeb do ask students to retell what they have read, these retelling scores have never been validated. If

Figure 4.9

A Sample from the Tile Test

In a curriculum-based measure (CBM) students complete 1-minute tasks. Afterward, the children can record the number of errors they made and the number of words they read correctly. Each day, following the CBM assessment, children can graph their results in a personal progress file. This is simply a colorful file folder with a bar graph inside. The dates are listed along the bottom of the graph and values representing the number of words read correctly along the left-hand side. Using a colorful marker, children graph only the number of words they read correctly. The bar graphs enable children to see progress and motivate them to improve their performance. Students are eager to graph their performance and the graph gives them a concrete indicator of their improvement as a reader. The desire to improve as a form of self-competition along with concrete measures of efficacy motivate the students to try harder.

Motivating

Struggling *Readers*

you plan to use these assessment tools, have a firm conception of reading in mind and interpret the results with caution.

Analyzing and Summarizing the Data: The Teacher Logbook

It is late September. You probably know a little about your class, partly from discussions with the previous teacher and from spring testing and partly from classroom observations. You will need to organize this information into a coherent portrait for parent conferences and to fine-tune instructional plans for the rest of the fall. You will face similar tasks throughout the year. Students differ, and you must decide how

*A*ssessment

Bridging the home–school gap can contribute greatly to your success with students. Assessment offers opportunities to involve parents, most of whom want to know how their child is doing. Transparency and "early warning" can help greatly in this task.

Figure 4.10 **The Graduated Running Record**

First Home

Mid-First Grade	What made this a good place for a mother, father, and
End of First Grade	children to work and play? Many children who were living
	on this land a very long time ago slept at night in little huts.
Second Grade	These small houses were made with reeds or branches and
	had places carefully made of stones for cooking the food the
Third Grade	family found. Early each morning, the hard-working people
	living together in the tiny village were ready to walk to
Fourth Grade	different places looking for special foods. After gathering a
	variety of edible acorns and seeds using woven reed baskets,
	the women and girls of the settlement mashed the mounds
Fifth Grade	of nuts into meal. Several men traveling by particular routes
	into the wilderness hunted the plentiful small prey such as
	squirrels, rabbits, and birds with nets, curved throwing sticks,
Sixth Grade	or bows and arrows. Other adults rowed large wooden boats
	protected with tar to neighboring island settlements to trade
	for unique and nourishing sources of protein to expand their
	seafood diet.

to meet individual needs, how to organize students, and how to plan activities. You need to think about what you know and how to communicate it to others.

Analyzing and summarizing need not mean a sudden shift in the assessment process. You don't stop collecting evidence to begin analysis; the process is ongoing and interactive. Throughout September, you have formed individual portraits. But now you need to shift your emphasis, thinking about the class as a whole and how to structure the course ahead. It is time to assemble the evidence so that you can decide what it means and how to use it, for your own purposes and for feedback to others.

Teachers use a variety of strategies to handle these tasks. Some rely on basal management systems, and others keep narrative journals. In the Classroom 4.1, about Ms. King and the Roots project, referred on several occasions to her logbook. In this section, we offer a more detailed example of this approach to maintaining assessment records. The teacher logbook, as in the sample shown in Figure 4.11, is a practical method for organizing assessment data (Calfee, 2000; Calfee & Perfumo, 1993).

The logbook is arranged in three segments: a summary of student performance, journal judgments of student achievement, and a curriculum-planning record. You work with the logbook from back to front—that is, from Section III to Section I. Your first task, before school begins, is to review your curriculum plans, especially those for the fall quarter. These plans are laid out at the back of the logbook, much like a road map. Here is where you make notes about how you will start the year, what you know about your class, and your end-of-grade expectations. You need to review your options for materials and activities; a change in the textbook series, a new collection of trade books, or a conference with the librarian may all influence your curriculum plans.

Your main job will be to review and refine a small number of critical curriculum outcomes as your focus for the year. You can't teach everything. With state and local standards as the reference point, what will be your emphasis? What will your students know by year's end? How will you judge the quality of their accomplishments?

The logbook lays out selected curriculum strands such as story comprehension, vocabulary development, and expository skills. Assessments allow you to locate each student on each strand. For example, in Ms. King's combination third and fourth grade, one student is struggling with the task of describing how Wilbur and Charlotte change from the beginning to the end of the story, whereas another can relate these changes to his own personal experience by composing a personal narrative about his emerging friendship with a new stepbrother.

The curriculum-planning section in Section III at the end of the logbook provides the place for you to record your planning activities. It is placed at the back because it is your section; it is for your analysis and reflection, not day by day but long-term, not set in stone but constantly changing. Where is the class headed? Where are they at present? How am I changing in my development as a teacher?

The middle of the logbook, Section II, provides journal space to record evidence about student performance observations, informal assessments of student activities and projects, and questions requiring further thought and action on your part. These notes may comment on students' portfolios, along with more formal assessments. They include brief jottings, notes based on student discussions, pointers to other information, and ponderings about individual students. Before school starts, you will enter preliminary information about the students. During September, a time of ongoing and intense formative assessment, the pages will fill quickly.

Beginning teachers often keep written notes, but seldom do they view these as research. In fact, journal notes offer a valuable record for reflection and action. An empty sheet in Section II warns that the student has slipped from sight. A long list of books read but no evidence of written work is a reminder to encourage the student to put his thoughts on paper. The logbook provides a record and a prompt for genuine differentiation.

Figure 4.11 A Sample from a Teacher Logbook

Teacher: *Ms. King* School: *Lakeview Elementary*

Year: *2005–2006* Grade: *2*

Section I: Student Summary

	Reading/Writing/Language			Math
	Vocab	*Narrative*	*Expos Skills*	*Addition*
Able, J	*+ + +*	*+ +*	*+ + +*	*+ +*
"	"	"	"	"
"	"	"	"	"
Matthews, K	*+ +*	*+ +*	*— —*	*+ + +*
"	"	"	"	"
"	"	"	"	"
Zetter, B	*+ +*	*+ + +*	*+ +*	*+ +*

Karen Matthews is an avid reader as long as a book fits with her interests. She prefers stories and will attempt difficult pieces (The Trolls and Shadows) if they capture her imagination. She seldom selects nonfiction books. Her oral reports are well prepared, and she puts herself into the delivery. She has written only a limited amount; her personal journal contains only brief notes, as do her other reports. She is capable but hesitates to do anything that is not perfect on the first draft. Karen is very capable and has shown growth this year but needs to explore and expand her reading and writing activities.

Section II: Journal Notes

Week of January 15. Worked on nonfiction reading. Students could choose from new selections I laid out in the classroom library with science, geography, and historical events. Jeff Able, who has shown little interest in reading thus far, came to life when he saw the books on space. Now I know how to grab him. Karen Matthews, who has been doing well, asked if she could reread Shadows and described the new collection as "boring."

Section III: Curriculum Plans   *January 20, 2005*

The new state standards emphasize informational reading and writing beginning in third grade, and I want to explore them with my second-graders. They appear to be doing quite well, and I can give them a head start. Story comprehension will stay on my agenda, of course. . . .

I suspect that boys will enjoy informational topics, but girls may be another matter. Check with Thelma (the librarian) on recent acquisitions. Orr's nature books have great graphics—I can bring in more science while dealing with the emphasis on reading.

Finally, Section I includes information about individual students for official analysis and summative assessment. The class list runs down the left-hand column; curriculum strands are along the top. Although this section comes at the end of the process, you open it first for parent conferences, to review student progress, and to discuss students and the class with colleagues and the principal. The entries summarize your judgments of individual student performance for each strand, based on rubrics for each task that describe your interpretation of test scores, observations, and interviews. A question mark indicates uncertainty. For example, suppose Samantha shows little interest in writing; her journal contains a few brief sentences, obtained under duress: "Satrdy we went to Grat Amrica. I went on the Wav." But when you overhear her talk with a friend about the trip to the amusement park, she shares a great deal more information. She clearly has greater command of language than appears in her written work. Analysis leads to action. How can you provide conditions that will elicit the best that she can do? She prefers talking to writing and is impatient with the mechanics. For now, you enter a question mark under expository writing, but plan ways to build her mechanics so that all those ideas can be expressed.

The logbook helps you keep track of students' learning over the school year and pinpoint areas where you need to focus instruction. Analysis means combining information from many sources to create individual portraits and collective images over time. For instance, an example using the format shown in Figure 4.11 combines rubrics and other classroom performance measures with standardized scores. At the individual level, Edward scores at a 4.0 grade level on standardized tests, reads voraciously, and completes assigned writing tasks. His papers are longer than average, and the mechanical details earn a 5 on length and a 6 for grammar/mechanics on the read-write cycle rubric in Figure 4.7. But in both writing and group discussions, he reacts to thematic issues like a first-grader—at a superficial level (a coherence score of 3). He chooses short, simple books for free reading and races through them. He retains the literal information but shows little depth of understanding. Reading seems a retreat into himself. He is small for his age and young for his cohort and has few friends. Perhaps he needs a better audience for sharing his ideas. Participating in a literature circle group may be just what he needs. The other members of the group will model higher-order thinking about the books they read and discuss. He will be given a role and will have to dig deeper than a surface-level understanding of the books to carry out his role. Checking entries in the logbook a few months later, we read that Edward is an eager contributor to his literature circle discussions. His inferences are right on target, showing increased depth of understanding.

Interpreting: Making Sense of the Results

Interpretation gives meaning to evidence and shapes generalizations that lead to action. Interpretation goes beyond concrete data to broader meanings. But inquiry does not travel in a straight line. As noted at the end of the previous section, interpretation is embedded in the questions, the design, and the evidence. You review a student's profile and develop a hunch, which leads you to look again at the data, and so on. Interpretation requires reflection, which means time and occasion to ponder the evidence. Pondering often works best when you also have opportunities to consult with colleagues.

Interpretation faces two challenges—consistency and persuasiveness, which are akin to reliability and validity. Reliability asks "Is the evidence dependable?" while validity asks "Can the evidence answer your question?" Standardized tests, covered later in this chapter, establish reliability and validity through statistics. Teacher-based assessment handles the issues through argument and debate. In the Classroom 4.4 shows a first-year teacher learning how to give meaning to evidence, to shape generalizations that lead to action.

Teachers in the primary grades face similar interpretation problems. When a first-grade student in the middle of the year struggles to read a primer text, the teacher must determine what is underlying those problems. An analysis of oral reading behavior using a running record may reveal that the student has a developing sight vocabulary but few independent word-identification strategies. Further probes with a phonics inventory will help to reveal what the student knows about letter-sound relationships and phonics patterns. It will even be useful to interview the student, stopping while she reads, and ask how she goes about figuring out a new word. This will give you some insight into the student's understanding of the strategies necessary for decoding.

Interpreting Evidence in the Sixth Grade

Jennifer Coombs, a new sixth-grade teacher, is assigned at the last minute to a school in a low-income, urban neighborhood. The previous teacher's notes and the principal's comments suggest that the students have limited experience and poor language skills. Working from Mr. Milton's lesson plans, Ms. Coombs greets her new class. The morning goes fine. After lunch, the students meet to read and discuss their social studies book. After the students read a few pages, they stop to discuss.

> *Ms. Coombs:* Can someone summarize what we have learned? What did the author tell us?
> *Students:* [Silence.]
> *Ms. Coombs:* What was one of the key ideas about the purpose of government?
> *Students:* [Again, silence; clearly, there is a problem.]
> *Ms. Coombs:* Let's start over and first preview the book. Let's look at the title, main heading, and subheadings. What do they tell us about the topic?

What does Ms. Coombs's experience reveal about the students? Several alternatives are consistent with the evidence but call for different courses of action:

- The students are not able to summarize what they have read.
- They feel uneasy with a new teacher and don't want to seem foolish.
- They have little understanding about informational text and don't know how to use text features.
- They really don't know much about the government and have a limited vocabulary.
- They really don't know much about government and don't care very much about the topic.

How can Ms. Coombs further evaluate these interpretations? As we noted earlier, inquiry is not a straight-line process. Validating an interpretation often calls for experimentation—for changing conditions and collecting new data. The teacher may have to model how to read informational text, develop prior knowledge of government, or even switch to a more familiar topic to unravel why these students are having problems discussing what they have read.

4.4

Assessments like these are subjective; they depend on informed judgment. How can teachers assure critics of the trustworthiness of such complex judgments? One approach is to use multiple sources of evidence. You gather one piece of evidence from students' oral reading, another from class discussion, and still another from writing. This is called *triangulation*, and it provides evidence of consistency, the keystone of reliability (Fetterman, 1998). It also ensures validity. Another answer depends on professional interaction. Teachers in Great Britain rely on "moderation" (Harlen, 1994); teacher teams review samples of student work, presenting and defending their interpretations to the group.

Ms. Coombs is still learning about interpretative processes. She is early in her career, with little time to consult colleagues, who are as busy as she is. But she is on the right path—she is inclined to experiment and to persist, not a bad beginning for the first week of school.

Reporting and Decision Making

You have gathered evidence about student achievement and are satisfied with its consistency and substance. What to do next? Inquiry-based assessment serves little purpose unless it leads to action, bringing the inquiry cycle full circle. To guide action, it often helps to gather your thoughts in written form (reports), so that you can see what you think and weigh various alternatives (decisions).

Reports (as in report cards) may bring to mind grades, which are traditionally associated with testing. We will offer a few thoughts about this topic and then look at reports from a different perspective. Grading on the A-to-F scale is familiar to most of us. Some schools now use performance levels, which they link to standards (Marzano, 2000; Nitko, 1996). Whatever the label, reports focus on competition (norm-referenced, grading on the curve) or preset limits (criterion-referenced, 90+ means an A). The goal is to summarize a complex portrait in a single index. Teachers view student achievement as a complex mix of effort and accomplishment. Joan's end-of-year compositions weren't as polished as Susan's, but Joan entered fourth grade barely able to finish a complete sentence whereas Susan was a budding author. No wonder traditional grades frustrate both teachers and students.

Standards-based tests, a newer version of criterion-referenced testing, offer an alternative to grading. Standards lay out what students should be able to do in a particular area at a particular grade level, using descriptions like those in Figure 4.8. Rubrics (see also Figure 4.6) assign students to performance levels by combining information from a collection of work products. You will encounter labels like "Proficient: Meets the Standard," "Accomplished: Exceeds the Standard," and "Fails to Meet the Standard." On the surface, this approach looks different from traditional grading, but for practical purposes the two are much the same. They provide little guidance for instructional decisions; the teacher can place students in achievement groups or tracks, or the school can decide to retain a failing student or place him in a remedial program.

Grades and other summative judgments serve as important indicators at significant mileposts, as students move through the grades. The transition from elementary to middle school marks a major change for a youngster, a time for a clear signal about his level of accomplishment. Even at these points, it makes sense to provide a richer portrait of strengths and areas of need. The logbook provides one model along these lines; other approaches include the portfolios and narrative reports described earlier. All of these techniques call for weaving evidence from student work into an account that lays out a student's progress and accomplishments across the achievement spectrum. The idea is to create a portrait that provides feedback to the student about past efforts but also offers guidance about future choices and decisions, for both student and teacher.

Preparing narratives or case studies for individual students may seem costly in time and effort, and you should probably focus on a small number of students at the outset. Teachers in the United States are driven by an action orientation, and slowing down to reflect on the past and think about the future may seem strange at first. However, this practice is commonplace in other countries, including Great Britain, Australia, and Japan, where students are typically brought into the process. Once you have conducted a few such reviews, the blend of reporting and decision making is likely to "click" for you. Decision making means creating alternatives and making choices. Our recommendation is to use assessment to help you decide when to slow down to solve a problem. Taking time to reflect on student performance can be particularly important at the beginning of the year. Reflection is difficult work; putting your thoughts on paper can help you in this task and makes it possible to compare notes with other teachers.

REFLECT and Apply

This matrix sets the stage for the following questions:

	Grades K–2	Grades 3–4	Grades 5–7
September			
December			
March			
May			

3. As you move through the matrix, how do the six stages of inquiry-based assessment apply? What is their relative importance? What are the special problems? How do you maintain contact with colleagues, students, and parents?

4. You and two other teachers have discussed the inquiry model and are planning for the coming school year. One of the teachers raises concerns. What about students with special needs? He will have two students with learning disabilities in his fourth-grade class. What about combination grades? He is a new teacher and may have a third-/fourth-grade combination class. What about mobility? He may have to deal with midyear entrants. As the experienced team member, how would you handle these issues from an assessment perspective?

5. The other partner, also newer than you, has better news. She will have two computers in her classroom. She will also have an aide because she is three students over the contract limit. She has visited most of the families on her class list and several parents have volunteered to help in the classroom. But she is worried about her class size and the range of individual differences in her third-/fourth-grade combination class. What are your recommendations about how she can take advantage of her resources to handle the assessment tasks throughout the year?

Test-Based Strategies

What kinds of reading tests do students take in classrooms? When do they take them? What do the tests look like? Why do people give them? First, much testing is embedded in core reading programs. These programs provide end-of-selection worksheets, end-of-unit tests, and various methods for formative appraisal of student progress. Also, in May, most school districts give a standardized test of reading achievement for summative assessment. The results are reported in local newspapers. We next describe these types of tests, tell you how to use the information, and suggest how to prepare your students for the task.

Basal Reader Tests

As we noted in Chapter 2, basal readers are planned around the scope-and-sequence chart, a road map of specific objectives laid out in a predefined order (Chambliss & Calfee, 1998). The text is divided into units (several stories lasting a month or so) and lessons (one or two stories that typically last a week). Each lesson includes several objectives, basic building blocks that range from fine-grained tasks ("vowel *a* with silent *e*") to broad goals ("character analysis"). Each objective moves through a sequence of instruction, practice, and testing. Basal lessons follow a fairly standard format across grades and series. The lessons begin with vocabulary instruction, prior knowledge development, and the teaching of key skills and strategies. Students then read the selection and the teacher engages in questioning and discussion. Workbook and little leveled books provide additional practice with the skills and strategies. The most recent programs have specific small-group lessons for students reading above, on, and below grade with accompanying leveled texts.

Assessment is woven throughout these activities, in responses to teacher questions, in demonstrations of oral reading skills, and in worksheet performance. The teacher has many opportunities to judge student performance and understanding. Oral reading fluency and skill in answering questions are key indicators (Cazden, 2001). The student struggling with a new sentence needs attention. So, too, does the student who shrugs his shoulders when asked "What is the cat's name?" Teachers may not record the details, but they keep mental notes.

Basal systems offer many indicators of student performance. Workbooks address practical problems and keep students busy. They also offer practice on testlike activities. Each worksheet covers a single objective and can be scored by a classroom aide or parent. The scores serve mostly to provide feedback to students and parents, but teachers also keep track. Basals also include end-of-selection tests to assess vocabulary retention and story comprehension at the end of the week and end-of-unit tests, given every 4 to 6 weeks, to measure student progress. These tests closely mirror standardized tests but offer both multiple-choice and constructed responses. The results can affect decisions about student placement and progress. Students who are considerably ahead of or behind the middle of the class are assigned to high or low groups. Low-achieving groups read texts at their reading level and spend more time on decoding skills; high-achieving groups work on enrichment exercises. Low groups tend to fall behind in coverage, but all basal programs include intervention programs that are designed to accelerate learning. These intervention programs demand additional instructional time in small groups.

Many types of assessments are provided in core reading programs and the teacher's job is to decide which assessment tools provide useful information about students' progress. The end-of-selection test may tell you whether your students retained the vocabulary words for the week, but the comprehension assessment on the story that was read and discussed all week cannot show who has a comprehension problem or who was simply not engaged in the instruction. The end-of-unit tests may tell you who can independently read, understand, and reflect on a story, but these tests may simply provide the same information that your classroom observations or district-mandated assessments already provide. At all costs avoid redundant assessments, because time for assessments competes with time for instruction. Finally, basal readers provide diagnostic tests which can be used to further your understanding of a struggling reader.

Standardized Tests

Test scores are often used to identify students for special programs such as intervention, retention, or summer school. In all these situations, teacher recommendations are important, especially because you have background information that explains student performance.

You are well educated, and so you know about tests. You have been there—college admissions, teacher certification, driver's license. In our world, the multiple-choice test is a fact of life. These instruments will be around for a while because they are cheap and efficient, offer a simple bottom line, and are "scientific" (Airaisan, 1994; Baumann, 1988; Nitko, 1996; Popham, 1999; Stiggins, 1994). They meet high standards of design and reliability. Test publishers produce technical manuals with detailed information about the standardization procedures, student samples, and lots of statistics.

Standardized tests fall into two broad categories, as shown in Figure 4.12: criterion-referenced and norm-referenced. Criterion-referenced tests include basal tests and tests designed by school districts for local achievement monitoring. The principle guiding these tests is that the student must meet a preset performance level. The class takes a 10-item test on vowels; students who are correct on 9 items have "mastered" the objective and "meet the standard." Students who fall below the criterion are assigned additional practice on the objective until they attain a passing score.

Norm-referenced tests measure individual student standing relative to others—"grading on the curve" (Nitko, 1996). Percentile scores show how many other students rank above or below a particular individual. Someone at the 50th percentile falls right in the middle; a person at the 99th percentile has performed better than 99 percent of those in the norming sample. Stanines sort students much as percentiles do, but in ranges from 1 to 9. Normal-curve equivalents are another variation on percentiles. Scale scores place students on a statistical "growth curve," which lets you know how a student is doing on a developmental learning pathway. The grade-level equivalent, or GLE, also reports growth scores. The third-grader who scores 3.8 at the end of the year is doing about as expected; a score of 3.0, on the other hand, means that the student reads like an entering third-grader and so is in trouble. Assessment experts worry that GLEs can be misinterpreted (Nitko, 1996), but teachers still rely on GLEs because the concept makes sense to them and serves practical purposes. GLEs are most problematic at the extremes. A beginning third-grader with a score of 8.0 can't really handle Dickens's *A Tale of Two Cities*. He may be able to read most of the words in the novel but is unlikely to get much out of it and certainly will not understand the nuances of the narrative. In the middle ranges of a grade, the GLE provides a reasonable indicator of reading achievement.

As a teacher, you will almost certainly receive reports about your students' performance on standardized tests. Whatever the indicator—GLE, percentile, stanine, scale score—the challenge is to use this information along with that from other sources to make informed judgments about student progress. Standardized tests are most accurate for students who know the "school game." Those who are unfamiliar with the cultural and linguistic traditions assumed by test makers may perform poorly, even though they are learning a lot. Later in this section, we discuss two ways in which you can help these students: through the use of test-taking strategies and motivation.

How can you learn to "read" the test reports? Figure 4.13 shows simulated class scores for a standardized test such as Terra Nova—a popular instrument developed by the California Test Bureau (1996). The test report typically appears in your box in

Figure 4.12 **Norm-Referenced and Criterion-Referenced Scoring**

Norm-Referenced Scoring	Criterion-Referenced Scoring
Performance Is Compared with Scores of Others	Performance Is Compared to an Absolute Standard
• Once the test is developed, it is administered to a norm group, and then each student's performance is described by how he ranks in comparison to the group.	• The test is developed with a goal in mind (students must read at a rate of 150 words per minute), or a fixed standard is assigned (80% of the answers must be correct).
Scores Represent a Norm Group	Scores Represent a Standard
• Percentile. The percentile gives the percentage of students whose scores fall below the particular student's score. If a student scores in the 60th percentile, then he outperforms 60% of the students in the norm group.	• Pass-fail. The score either meets or exceeds the preset value.
• Grade-level equivalent (GLE). The average performance of students at a given grade is used to convert a score into a comparative indicator. If a student scores at the average level for all students leaving third grade, he is given a GLE of 3.9, meaning "end of third-grade performance."	• Mastery of learning objective. In this approach, often linked to a curriculum sequence, students, by a given grade level, are expected to achieve a specific outcome. For instance, by the end of kindergarten, students should know all letter names, numbers 1–10, colors, and "common" words.
• Grading on the curve. In this common practice, grades are assigned based on the distribution within a particular class on a particular test. The teacher decides that the top 15% of the scores will receive A, and so on.	• Advanced, proficient, basic. This variation on pass-fail, similar to regular grades but not on a curve, is used by many state and federal assessment programs.

Figure 4.13 Class Scores for a Standardized Test

Teacher Huston
Grade 6

	Student			Class Summary (26 students)	
	Amado, Carlos	Crawford, Michelle	Freeman, Steve		
Reading					
National Percentile	41	55	89	Median National Percentile	60.0
National Stanine	4	5	7	Median National Stanine	6.0
Grade Equivalent	4.9	7.7	11.7	Grade Mean Equivalent	8.8
Normal Curve Equivalent	39	53	77	Mean Normal Curve Equivalent	55.0
Scale Score	702	741	786	Mean Scale Score	750
Language					
National Percentile	36	18	71	Median National Percentile	37.2
National Stanine	4	3	6	Median National Stanine	4.5
Grade Equivalent	4.7	3.3	9.5	Grade Mean Equivalent	5.1
Normal Curve Equivalent	42	31	60	Mean Normal Curve Equivalent	43.8
Scale Score	723	699	758	Mean Scale Score	724
Math					
National Percentile	67	35	75	Median National Percentile	68.2
National Stanine	6	4	6	Median National Stanine	6.8
Grade Equivalent	8.4	5.8	9.6	Grade Mean Equivalent	8.8
Normal Curve Equivalent	60	41	64	Mean Normal Curve Equivalent	60.4
Scale Score	758	738	766	Mean Scale Score	759
Total					
National Percentile	59	40	79	Median National Percentile	52.0
National Stanine	5	5	7	Median National Stanine	5.3
Grade Equivalent	7.7	6.1	10.1	Grade Mean Equivalent	7.3
Normal Curve Equivalent	55	42	67	Mean Normal Curve Equivalent	51.8
Scale Score	748	736	767	Mean Scale Score	742

the fall sometime after school has started. You probably experience number shock, no matter how experienced you may be. Here are a few words of advice:

• Pick one or two indicators to review. Percentiles and grade equivalents often serve as practical starting points, if taken with a grain of salt. The percentile is a national index, which means that your class and students are being compared with students throughout the nation. If you teach in a middle-class neighborhood in the Midwest, you should expect that your class will score around the 50th percentile and perform at grade level. If you work in a more privileged community or an urban ghetto, you should probably consider the setting—not to expect more or less of your students, but to take into account the challenges that you confront.

• Start with summaries, and then look for patterns. The example in the figure presents scores for Reading, Language, and Math. These scores are correlated, which means that performance levels tend to be similar across tests. The Total Score for each student provides an overall achievement index; Carlos is about average, Michelle has some problems, and Steve is excelling. But patterns add important complexity. Reading and Math for the class are substantially above national averages, whereas Language is noticeably below. Carlos did much better on the Math test than on the Reading and Language tests. What might this mean?

- Use other sources of information to develop portraits of student achievement. The report may be six months out of date. The numbers look very precise, but they are actually based on a limited number of multiple-choice questions on a test administered at the end of the previous school year. Test publishers are the first to caution against overreliance on a single indicator.

How can the classroom teacher make the best use of the scores? First, recognize their strengths. They are reliable (Nitko, 1996). The consistency emphasized by testing experts and administrators should be reflected in your classroom assessments. Practically speaking, reliability means that students are ranked much the same across a collection of scores. Suppose you line up a group of students based on their scores on two reading tests. If the rankings are different, which test should you trust? Taking the average doesn't help; if one of your students scored at the top of the class one day and handed in a blank test the next week, should you conclude that he is an "average" student? Probably not. In general, student performance is likely to be about the same on one standardized test as on another standardized test.

Standardized tests are predictive. The question is, what do you do with the prediction? An entering kindergartner's knowledge of the alphabet predicts reading achievement in later grades. Will you improve kindergartners' reading simply by teaching the alphabet? No. Teaching kindergartners the alphabet makes sense for several reasons, but it does not guarantee high levels of reading achievement in the later grades. Here is where information from other sources can be especially critical. Reading means more than picking the right answer on a multiple-choice test. What does the following statement mean: "Martin scored at the 40th percentile at the end of sixth grade"? Here are some possibilities:

1. Martin will score around the 40th percentile on other reading tests.
2. Martin will score at the 40th percentile at the end of seventh grade.
3. Martin will have problems with sixth-grade science textbooks.
4. Martin will have trouble reading the sports section of the newspaper.
5. Martin should be in special education or given remedial tutoring.

Standardized tests do an excellent job when it comes to making predictions like those in the first two entries. They are less trustworthy with respect to the other items on the list. The challenge to you as the classroom teacher is to do something to help Martin begin to move up through the ranks. Other evidence may show that Martin has skills and knowledge not tapped by the standardized test. What if he is helping other students with computer writing assignments? The bottom line is that standardized test scores can fill in one piece of the puzzle, but you shouldn't rely on them too much.

Preparing Students for Standardized Tests

The previous section cautioned against overreliance on standardized tests. This section offers suggestions about how to help students do their best on these instruments, so that you can use the results with confidence. How can you prepare your students for the tests without compromising validity? "Teaching to the test" may improve scores, but scores may no longer mean what they are supposed to mean. When your car runs low on gas, you can fiddle with the gas gauge to make it show "full," but you will eventually run out of gas.

George looked at the test. It said:

Rabbits eat:

○ lettuce

○ dog food

○ sandwiches

He raised his hand.

"Rabbits have to eat carrots, or their teeth will get too long and stick into them," he said.

The teacher nodded and smiled, but she put her finger to her lips. George carefully drew in a carrot so the test people would know.

The first word of advice is to connect the test situation with the best learning in your classroom. Testing can be a shock. *First Grade Takes a Test* by Miriam Cohen (1983) delightfully describes young children's thoughts on their first encounter with a test. The excerpt in Figure 4.14 shows George's thoughtfulness but lack of test-taking savvy. The message is clear: The children are suddenly alone, the task is mysterious, and the activity is disconnected from classroom routines. Students' answers, right or wrong, cannot be trusted to tell you what they know and can do. How can you improve this state of affairs?

The second word of advice is to help students see the test as a problem to be solved strategically and thoughtfully, a process that is consistent with best learning. What does strategic preparation look like? Here are three suggestions for handling the testing game.

The first suggestion centers on the big picture. Why am I taking this test? What will happen if I fail? Who will find out how I did? On your driving test, you had ideas about purpose and audience. You were taking the test so that you could get a driver's license. If you failed, you studied some more and retook the test.

Ask fourth-graders similar questions about school tests, and you likely will find that they don't know why they are being tested. They don't know the rules of the game—"Is it all right to guess?" They worry that they will fail, whatever that means. Test scores may be used to retain students, but publishers caution against this practice. So find out what your students think about tests, and set the record straight. This need not mean generating a cavalier attitude of "These tests don't matter for me," but rather creating an understanding that "These tests matter for all of us!" It means ensuring clarity and honesty about the consequences.

The second suggestion centers on test instructions, which aim to help but can hinder. Standardized tests "script" the teacher: "Read the following instructions." During the test, you can't explain. You can't answer questions. You can't help. But before the students take the test, you can do some things to prepare students. You can teach them to listen carefully and actively. You can tell them the testing vocabulary. You can practice "following instructions," as In the Classroom 4.5 demonstrates.

Most standardized tests provide practice sets. It's generally more helpful to use these practice sets to discuss test-taking strategies rather than for rote practice. Preparing students to deal with test instructions works best when you combine practice with "talking

Using "Simon Says" to Practice Test Taking

The district's benchmark reading tests are scheduled for next week. To prepare his second-graders to follow directions, George Westbelle takes the students through the game of Simon Says. He tells the class that they are going to be taking a test and they will need to listen carefully. He reviews the rules for Simon Says—do it only if "Simon says." He then hands out paper and pencil to each student.

Mr. W: Simon says, "Pick up your pencil." [Students all raise their pencils.]

Mr. W: Simon says, "Write your name on the top of your paper." [Students all fill in their names.]

Mr. W: Write the name on the bottom of your paper. [Several students start to write.]

Mr. W: Whoops! Simon didn't say! [A round of giggles.]

Mr. W: Simon says, "Turn your paper over." [Brief hesitation, and then a rustle of papers.]

Mr. W: Write your name on the back of your paper. [Again, several students start writing.]

Mr. W: Whoops! Gotcha again! Simon didn't say!

Mr. Westbelle keeps the sessions short and snappy, focusing on tasks like those the students will perform during test taking. He offers a word of warning about the technique: "If the game is too close to the test day, students may expect you to say 'Simon says' before each test direction!"

it through." Here is how you can use worksheets to help with both parts of this strategy. First, build a practice test using worksheet material, including directions, a short passage, and test items, as illustrated in Figure 4.15. Choose sample items that allow students to try out particular test-taking strategies. The bracketed entries in the figure are not on the students' sheets but suggest questions to raise during the discussion.

Next, read the instructions, and start the test. Give students a limited amount of time to finish the page (2 minutes is about right for the page in Figure 4.15). Even when there is no preset time limit, students always feel pressed for time, and they need to learn how to deal with this issue. When the time is up, score the test by tallying the answers on an overhead, and discuss the experience. What was easy? What was hard? What was confusing? What did it feel like? Here is where the bracketed questions come in. Such discussions allow students to internalize a variety of test-taking strategies, so that they become more comfortable and competent when facing the real thing.

The third suggestion highlights time and stress. As noted, there is never enough time. Students have only so much energy, and the school day has only so many hours. Most tests do not penalize incorrect choices, so the best advice is "Finish the test!" Advise students that, when uncertain, they should pick the best-looking answer and then move on. Older students may "tick" items about which they are uncertain and return to these if they have time. The main message: Don't skip and don't fret.

Time pressure is part of stress, but, as you know, there is more to it. To manage stress, students must first be aware of it. Imagine a class about 10 minutes into a test: wrinkled brows, fingers tight around pencils, bodies hunched over desks. It looks painful, but the students may not realize the extent of their agony. Learning to monitor stress is the first step in managing it. Here again, talking about the situation gives students permission to think about it and to come up with techniques of their own: "Put your pencil down, relax your shoulders, think nice thoughts."

Ben Franklin wrote, "We must indeed all hang together, or, most assuredly, we shall hang separately!" Competition may be a reasonable goal in high school—who will be valedictorian, receive the highest SAT scores, and so on. In the elementary

Figure 4.15 A Brief Practice Test

THINK ABOUT IT! Taking a reading comprehension test is a tough job. You should always **study the questions** before you try to pick an answer. What do you need to know? Do you need to read the passage? Do the question and the answers raise any alarms? Think about these things while you take this practice test. You will have 2 minutes to complete it. Ready—turn over the page and begin.

Quickly read through these instructions:

> It is easy to make butter. First you need a jar and some heavy cream. Fill the jar partway with cream. Then shake it for about 20 minutes. Soon the cream will start to get lumpy. Stop when most of the cream turns into lumps. You will find that the lumps are butter.
>
> Take the lumps out of the jar, and wash them with cold water. Mix a little salt with the lumps, and pat them together. Leave the butter in a cool place overnight. In the morning, the butter will be hard and ready to eat.

Now answer the questions:

Which word rhymes with *lumps*?

- cream
- leaves
- bumps
- butter

[You don't have to read anything in the passage to answer this question. Why not?]

Which word means the same as *heavy*?

- large
- thick
- strong
- bulky

[Answering this question depends completely on carefully studying the passage. Why?]

What does the passage tell you to do after you have finished making the butter?

- Put the lumps on toast in the morning.
- Throw away the lumps.
- Shake the lumps for 20 minutes.
- Salt the lumps and put them in a cool place.

[You have to read the passage, which tells you exactly what to do.]

If you forget to refrigerate the butter after you have made it, then

- mix it with some more salt.
- eat it as soon as you can.
- it will be soft and not good to eat.
- melt it in a pan and then cool it down.

[The passage doesn't really answer this question but gives you a clue about the right answer. What do you think it is?]

grades, testing can become a community event. Here are fourth-grade teacher William Settlemeyer's thoughts on the matter:

> I try to build team spirit around the test event for my fourth-graders. Seldom do standardized tests mean a lot for individual students in the elementary grades. The better the class does as a whole, the better the school looks! That's what I try to sell.
>
> How do I translate this idea into practice? First of all, I make it clear to students that they are not really competing with one another. I encourage them: "Do your personal best. That's what really counts. That's what you should strive for." Second, I encourage them to support one another before the test—"Hey, good luck! I know you will do great." And

after the test—"I bet you aced that puppy!" Third, I involve parents. I advise them to talk with their children in the days before the test, make sure they get a good night's sleep and a solid breakfast on the day of the test, and talk with them about the test once it is over.

—William Settlemeyer, fourth-grade teacher

What does the advice in this section have to do specifically with reading assessment? Not a whole lot, it might appear. We have mentioned neither content nor skills. Nothing about vowel digraphs, analogies, or main ideas. These objectives are important, but reading tests are only partly about reading. To excel on a sixth-grade science test, students should bone up on electricity, astronomy, geology, and so on. Success on a sixth-grade math test depends on familiarity with fractions. But studying *The Diary of Anne Frank* does not guarantee students will do well on a sixth-grade reading test. Memorizing Latin and Greek prefixes may help a little on a reading test, but don't count on it.

That is why we recommend a strategic approach to reading tests. You can help your students by emphasizing fluent decoding and techniques for searching a passage to find specific information. Students should be alert for key words and concepts like *words, stories,* and *reports.* But the most effective preparation is to back away from the details, carefully study the questions, and strategize about how you will approach the task. Don't spend too much time on test preparation. The evidence suggests that reading widely, building knowledge, learning strategies, and engaging in guided reading are the best test preparation (Guthrie, 2002).

Finally, what should you do when the test is finished? Testing is an important event for students, and you should consider dealing with what can be learned from the event. You can develop your own "after-the-test" plan. Publishers handle scoring and reporting, which means that neither you nor your students will learn the results of the May test until September. But you can deal with the experience as soon as the test is over. Ask students about their reactions. How did they do? How did they feel? What would they have done differently? Celebrate the event! Let students know you're proud of their efforts! Knowing that they all did their best is important in its own right.

6. You are serving on committee to review standardized tests for the district. The committee is looking at six tests, and you can pick one of the following three assignments: teacher manual and instructions, student test materials, or technical manual (reliability, validity, and other technical features). Which assignment would you prefer, and why?

7. Your school places great emphasis on standardized test scores. Students in all grades will be tested in 3 weeks. Your sixth-graders are planning a skit about testing for the first-graders. The principal asks you to explain how the skit will help your students prepare for the tests and how it will help the first-graders. How do you respond?

REFLECT and *Apply*

Strengths *and Challenges* of Diversity

In this chapter we explored the relationship between curriculum, instruction, and assessment. As the cultural diversity of our classrooms expands and as more languages are represented, teachers face new and special challenges, especially when assessing their students. Standardized tests with their fixed protocols are not likely to yield insights in the language skills of many children. Rather it is the informal assessments, assessment as inquiry, that will provide the map to discovering what students know and can do with written language.

The diversity of our classrooms brings to everyone—teachers and students—a broad set of experiences and funds of knowledge. Our assessments must consider this knowledge and assess it. A student's comprehension only makes sense in light of what the student brings to the page. The assessment of reading comprehension must start not with the passage but with the topic and with what the student knows. Before the student reads the passage it is imperative for the teacher to discover what she brings to the text. So it is useful to begin the assessment process with a short interview, perhaps initiated by a discussion of a picture. If the student's knowledge is limited it may be best to try another passage, one that might enable his comprehension. Assessing what the student brings to the passage helps the teacher make a careful distinction between a comprehension problem and the simple lack of prior knowledge.

Assessing the word recognition, vocabulary, and comprehension of an ELL student will require an extended interview and not a standardized test. The ideal procedure stems from the concept of print interviews developed by Marie Clay (2000). In this assessment the teacher and the student engage in a discussion about a storybook and how to read it. Through a series of questions, the teacher asks the student to point out the beginning of the book and where to start reading; identify a sentence, a word, and a letter; and then read. Through this exploration of a book, the teacher learns about the student's concept of print and listens in as the student identifies words, decodes words, and retells what he has learned. The procedure can be adapted to information books and the interview can begin with a survey of the features that structure information in nonfiction texts. These interviews allow the teacher to discover the knowledge and strategies of ELL students in an environment that supports the students' efforts. Just as we stressed the importance of scaffolding students' learning with culturally diverse students, it is necessary to scaffold their efforts during assessment.

Concluding *Remarks*

Assessing reading, writing, and language is a tough job that calls for professional judgment. Effective assessment requires information from a broad range of sources, including standardized tests, classroom portfolios, informal observations, and student conversations. There is no substitute for the teacher's ongoing inquiries into student growth and accomplishment, which are essential for adapting instruction to individual needs.

This chapter has emphasized the interrelatedness of curriculum, instruction, and assessment. The examples have highlighted the academic dimension of schooling, but it's important to keep other dimensions in mind as well, including students' interests, motivation, social interactions, and self-confidence.

Assessment captures the research side of the schooling endeavor, whether you are approaching classroom assessments or preparing for standardized tests. The inquiry approach involves asking the right questions, formulating a clear view of learning goals, determining the current status of the students, and deciding on a course of action. Once the stage is set at the beginning of the school year, the process is continuous, an ongoing series of mini-experiments designed to inform you and your students about progress. Feedback is easy to handle when all is going well, but you also need to be honest with students about both limitations and strengths. The long-term prospects for genuine success are greater for all involved when you are candid with students, their parents, school administrators, and (of course) yourself. The ultimate aim of literacy assessment is to provide the ongoing information you need to guide each student to the highest possible level of present-day literacy.

Extending *Learning*

There is no substitute for involving yourself directly in assessment activities and the inquiry process. The three following exercises are designed to "get you into it."

1. Visit a school or district office, and talk with the people in charge about testing policies and practices. What tests are used? At what grades? Why? What happens to the results? Then study a couple of standardized tests and printouts of the results for a class or two. Think about what you can

learn from these documents. Once you have digested the information, discuss your impressions with a principal, a teacher, and a couple of upper-grade students.

2. Informally assess a student's reading and writing knowledge and skills. You will find several assessment models in the annotated bibliography and Appendix A. The simplest approach, however, may be to find a few short passages, read them yourself to think about what it would mean to understand them, and compose an effective summary of

the material, all as a basis for discussing the passage with the student. Your assessment should cover performance: How well can the student read? Respond? React? Equally important are "think-aloud" questions that ask the student to describe how he is approaching the task and attitudinal questions about motivation and efficacy.

3. Locate two teachers who differ in experiences and assignments and ask them about their assessment policies. In a brief interview, explore their inquiry processes. How do they plan the assessment year? What methods do they use to measure student progress? How do they use standardized test results? How do they communicate with students? Parents? Teachers? How do they handle assessment of special students? Following the interviews, think about what you have learned. If, in a few years, a new teacher asked you about this topic, how would you respond?

Children's Literature

Cohen, M. (1983). *First Grade Takes a Test.* New York: Dell. Not a typical piece of literature, this little book tells a worthwhile story for children and adults about the challenges of standardized tests. Illustrated. 32 pages.

Dahl, R. (1988). *Matilda.* New York: Viking. Matilda uses her mental powers to rid her school of the evil, child-hating Miss Trunchbull and restore her beloved teacher Miss Honey to financial security. 240 pages.

Davis, D. (2004). *The Pig Who Went Home on Sunday.* Atlanta, GA: August House. An Appalachian "three pigs" story. 40 pages.

Finchler, J. (2003). *Testing Miss Malarkey.* New York: Walker Books. A book about a school's preparation for standardized tests. One of many humorous books in the Miss Malarkey series. 32 pages.

Haseley, D. (1991). *Shadows.* New York: Farrar, Straus and Giroux. A *New York Times* review recommends this book as "strong and appealing, tightly written and fast moving, perfect for reluctant readers as well as those who love good books." Illustrated. 74 pages.

Paterson, K. (1977). *Bridge to Terabithia.* New York: Crowell. This tale of an enchanted place, which a boy and girl create from their emerging friendship, ends tragically, but the author's skill in handling this tension earned a Newbery Award. Illustrated. 128 pages.

Perkins, L. R. (2005). *Criss Cross.* New York: Greenwillow Books. This novel explores the universal emotions of adolescence, as teenagers in a small town in the 1960s search for the meaning of life and love. 337 pages.

Scieszka, J. (1989). *The True Story of the Three Little Pigs.* New York: Viking. The wolf gives his version of what really happened in his encounters with the three little pigs. 32 pages.

Sharmat, M. W. (1972). *Nate the Great.* New York: Dell. When Annie's newly painted picture of her dog Fang is missing, she calls on Nate to help her find it. 64 pages.

Sobol, D. J. (2005). *Encyclopedia Brown and the Case of the Jumping Frogs.* New York: Yearling. Encyclopedia Brown solves 10 new mysteries with the help of his partner, Sally Kimball, the prettiest and toughest girl in the fifth grade. 80 pages.

Sperry, A. (1960). *Call It Courage.* New York: Macmillan. This is the story of a young island boy who overcomes his fear of the sea and proves his courage to himself and his tribe. CD and Spanish text available. 95 pages.

White, E. B. (1952). *Charlotte's Web.* New York: Harper. A widely recognized classic of children's literature, this story of an empathic spider and the runt of a pig litter appeals to a wide array of readers. This Newbery Honor story offers many opportunities for assessing students' understanding of thematic issues. 184 pages.

PEARSON myeducationlab

Now go to the topic "Assessment" in the MyEducationLab (www.myeducationlab.com) for your course, where you can:

- Find learning outcomes for the topics covered in this chapter along with the IRA standards that connect to these outcomes.
- Complete assignable activities in the Assignments and Activities section that show concepts in action to help you synthesize and apply strategies.
- Explore IRIS Center Resources—training enhancement materials that provide you with research-validated information and interactive materials to develop your skills in working with students.
- Apply and practice your understanding of the teaching skills identified in the chapter with the Building Teaching Skills and Dispositions exercises.

5

Differentiating Instruction and Intervention

CHAPTER outline

Mrs. Wright is concerned. It is the beginning of her second year as the principal of Pearson Elementary, a small 325-student elementary school in Virginia. Her school is in a rural area where the population is diverse—40 percent are Caucasian, 35 percent are African American, and 24 percent are Hispanic. Twelve percent of the students are in a special education program. Her concerns are triggered by test scores, not the high-stakes scores that schools live and die by in this era of No Child Left Behind, but informal assessments of beginning reading skills that were conducted at the end of first grade and again at the beginning of second grade. This test, the Phonological Awareness Literacy Screening, is used throughout the state to assess skills like letter-name knowledge, letter-sound knowledge, phonemic awareness, spelling, and word and passage reading ability. She has just reviewed the assessments on her entering second-grade students and many of them appear to have word and passage reading skills at or below a first-grade level. That means 25 of her 72 entering second grade students are struggling with reading. Six students are already in special education and another six students are reading as poorly as the special education students. Mrs. Wright has decided that she, the three second-grade teachers, the school's reading teacher, and the special education teacher need to talk about the problem and devise a plan for accelerating the reading growth of their second-grade students.

ThinkStock

Three days later at the second-grade team meeting, the teachers and Mrs. Wright begin to offer ideas and suggestions. It is the district policy to group students heterogeneously into classrooms; so one option—homogeneous classrooms—is off the table. That means each teacher is likely to have students reading from a primer to a fourth-grade level in her room. The teachers offer various suggestions; one suggests purchasing a new phonics program that would help the students catch up. Another suggests a focus on reading fluency, and others think they need more leveled texts. Some want to enlist parent volunteers to work in the classrooms and read with the students. Another suggests that the high school students who must complete community service projects can work a few hours a week with the struggling students. All agree that their current core program offers few ideas for teaching such a wide range of students in a classroom.

*C*LASSROOM **vignette**

Individual Differences in Learning to Read

The problem we have outlined is a real problem, one that is repeated across the country in many, if not most, classrooms. How do you deal with the diversity of abilities and accomplishments in the typical classroom? In any class you will find a range of abilities and interests that make the task of teaching all children to read a challenge. It is especially so given the demands of No Child Left Behind. According to this federal legislation, in 2009 81 percent of students in a school had to pass the state's assessment in reading or its equivalent. In 2010 the passing rate increases to 85 percent, moving inexorably to 100 percent by 2014. To compound the current problem a school cannot achieve the 85 percent pass rate by averaging the results across ability or ethnic groups; 85 percent of African American students, Hispanic students, special education students, and students from poor economic backgrounds in the school must pass the test. This rather egalitarian stance on reading achievement puts even greater pressure on Mrs. Wright and her staff.

Learning Disabilities

Students struggle to learn to read for a variety of reasons. Some students enter school lacking the talent, the cognitive wiring that is necessary to easily unlock the printed code of English (Shaywitz, 2003). A variety of labels have been used to designate these children. They have been called learning disabled and dyslexic. Some suffer from a reading disability or a reading disorder. Others have an attention deficit disorder that prevents them from attending to or processing the print. Whatever the label, a small percentage of students have a basic reading disability that stems from some inner neurological or cognitive problem. For the moment we will avoid the problem of finding the right label, because in each generation the label changes as old labels take on pejorative connotations or as theories of learning evolve. At one time these children were considered to have visual perceptual problems, but that label was dropped when research refuted the idea that problems in visual perception caused reading problems.

Frank Vellutino and his colleagues decided to determine just how many children actually have a learning disability that affects reading (Vellutino et al., 1996). They answered the question by identifying a large number of kindergarten students who appear to be at risk for learning to read and an equal number of kindergarten students who were not at risk. A child was deemed to be at risk because of poor scores on a number of reading measures, like phonological awareness, letter and word identification, and print awareness. Nine percent of the students were judged to be at risk, even though they had average intelligence. The at-risk group was randomly split in half and half of those students received extensive one-on-one tutoring 30 minutes a day for the entire year. The other half received no tutoring but continued in the regular kindergarten curriculum. By the end of kindergarten only 3 percent of the at-risk students were experiencing difficulties learning to read. So that 3 percent is close to the number of students with a true cognitive or neurological impairment. But what of the other children who initially struggled?

Environmental Causes

Other children struggle learning to read because of their home background, the literacy environment in which they live. Our goal is not to cast aspersions on cultural or ethnic groups, but to simply document the differences in literacy experiences among children. Many children come from home backgrounds with little focus on literacy (Delpit, 1995; Heath, 1985). Conversely, many of you grew up in a home that was literacy rich. Your parent read to you on a daily basis, and through this experience you learned how books worked. By the time you entered school you knew how to hold a book, turn the pages, which part told the story, and you developed a love of books. Other experiences in the home, such as the notes and print on the refrigerator and the shopping lists your mother made, deepened your understanding of print and its uses. By learning to spell your own name you discovered some of the principles that underlie our alphabetic language. Heath estimates that children growing up in middle-class professional families will experience 1,500 hours of reading instruction before they start school. This is a tremendous foundation on which to start classroom instruction.

The language skills a child acquires growing up will further affect her acquisition of reading. If you grew up in a middle-class professional home, researchers tell us that you entered school having an oral vocabulary at least twice the size of a classmate being raised by parents at or near the poverty line (Hart & Risley, 1995). How much and how your parents talk to you affects the growth of your vocabulary. Vocabulary then affects reading in several ways. First, it is harder to decode words that are not in your oral vocabulary. Second, having a larger store of words seems to facilitate the acquisition of phonemic awareness (Snow, Burns, & Griffin, 1998). Some research suggests that the number of multisyllabic words in a child's vocabulary attunes the child to the rhythm or breaks in a word—a precursor to phonemic awareness. Third, knowing many words makes it easier to learn even more words. Finally, vocabulary is the basis for comprehension (Graves, 2006). For some children the home language problem is more extreme and they enter school speaking a language other than English. They must traverse two languages while learning to read in one.

The Matthew Effect

The last cause of individual differences in learning to read is the school itself. Not all teachers are equally adept at teaching children to read. If we return to Pearson Elementary School we might want to examine the data on these entering second-graders at the end of their first-grade year. Over 95 percent of the students came from the five first grades in the school. Since these students were heterogeneously assigned to first-grade classrooms, some of the differences in achievement can be attributed to differences in instruction. Some teachers spent more time in small-group instruction and that factor has been linked to higher achievement (Taylor, Pearson, Clark, & Walpole, 2000). Within those small groups, some teachers spent more time on teacher-directed phonics instruction, and that factor has been linked to higher achievement (Connor, Morrison, & Underwood, 2007). Finally, within the small-group instruction, the least experienced of the teachers was not very skillful in coaching students to apply their new word-identification skills. Not knowing how to coach or scaffold learning has been linked to lower student achievement (Piasta, Connor, Fishman, & Morrison, 2009).

Difficulty with reading promotes disinterest, dislike, and avoidance. What happens to these children is called the "Matthew effect" (Stanovich, 1986), or the rich get richer and the poor get poorer. Children who read well tend to read more. Conversely, children who struggle in reading read less and their skill level does not advance. The students who read less may do so because teachers assign less reading to such students. They read less because reading programs make fewer demands on the

*A*ssessment

Start the year by interviewing your students, either individually or as a whole group. Learn about their experiences and what they know. From this knowledge you can plan vocabulary and comprehension instruction.

below-level students than on the above-level students (Dewitz, Leahy, Jones, & Sullivan, 2010). Finally, they read less because the process of reading is not rewarding, like playing golf without talent or practice.

For a variety of reasons, classrooms are not homogeneous assemblies of students. Students vary in ability, in interests, in attention, and in temperament. Yet when the year is done, the teacher's goal is to have them reading well and ready for the next challenge. To create children who are alike—children who all read well—demands that we treat them differently. The goal of this chapter is help you differentiate instruction for all students in your classroom and specifically meet the needs of those who struggle with learning to read, as well as those who excel and the rest in the middle. We will explore differentiation practices in the general education classroom and then examine how classroom teachers, special education teachers, and reading specialists can assist the students experiencing the greatest difficulty learning to read. This last topic will lead us to discuss Response to Intervention (RTI), a model for assisting all students and a process that can be used to identify students for special education.

REFLECT and Apply

We have discussed at least three causes of reading problems, with the obvious possibility that any child's difficulty learning to read can be the result of two or more interacting problems.

1. Considering the different roots of reading problems, which ones do you feel are most easily solved by the general education teacher and which might take the intervention of a specialist?

2. If some of your students struggle with reading because of their lack of background knowledge and vocabulary, how might you address this on a daily basis in your classroom?

3. Think about the expectations in your classroom. How much do you think second-graders, fourth-graders, and sixth-graders should read in a school year? How much of this reading should be guided by the classroom teacher and how much should the student be reading independently?

Differentiating Instruction in the General Education Classroom

Differentiated instruction is not a new concept. Going back 40 or 50 years in educational history, it was called individualized reading. At that time, in the 1950s and 1960s, the term had two meanings. As the term was coined by Jeannette Veatch (1971) it meant the materials, the books, and the method of instruction were tailored to the needs and interests of the students. Students might be reading many different books in a classroom and then having conferences with the teacher. Today, the reading workshop is the modern expression of individualized instruction. We describe the reading workshop approach in Chapter 12 as a process where students spend most of their time reading self-selected books, conferring with the teacher, sharing what they have read, and engaging in mini-lessons that present important skills and strategies. In this classroom routine differentiation takes place because students are reading books geared to their level and interest, and teachers are working with individual or small groups of students to develop their skills as needed.

The other meaning for individualized instruction was associated with a process that tailored reading skills to the needs of the students. This approach, often called individually guided instruction, relied on a skills management approach to individualization or differentiation (Johnson & Pearson, 1975). The reading curriculum was arranged in a hierarchy of decoding, vocabulary, and comprehension skills. Students were tested with criterion-referenced tests and their skills needs were determined. Then each child worked on a particular skill until he passed the next criterion-referenced test. Practicing skills involved completing worksheets and workbooks, and it consumed much more classroom time than did direct instruction from the teacher.

Two Conceptions of Differentiated Instruction

For some educators like Carol Ann Tomlinson (1999) or Irene Fountes and Gay Su Pinnell (1996), differentiation is about matching students with texts and tasks that meet their ability, their interests, and their learning styles. Tomlinson (1999) sets out several criteria for differentiated instruction. First, students learn best when they can connect their interests and knowledge to the curriculum. Students excel when learning tasks are natural. Students learn best when challenged and supported at the same time. So in learning to comprehend informational text the teacher might design a unit on animals, habitats, and adaptation. The teacher would introduce the unit and with the students brainstorm a set of questions. Then after introducing and modeling strategies and explaining graphic organizers the students would be free to choose which animal to study from a range of books in the room. If questions were still left unanswered the students would be encouraged to engage in additional reading.

Sharon Walpole and Michael McKenna (2007) propose a more skill-driven concept of differentiation. A developmental perspective guides much of their thinking on reading. They argue for a sequential instruction of reading skills; developing strong phonemic awareness and phonics should precede work on fluency and comprehension. They believe that assessments should drive instruction. The teacher should organize her instruction by the skill needs of the students and place students in needs-based groups. One group of students with basic decoding problems would work with the teacher on phonemic awareness and phonics. Another group with adequate decoding but weak fluency might focus their efforts on fluency. The better readers would work on vocabulary and comprehension. The teacher meets with each group and delivers instruction that fosters the appropriate growth in skill and in general reading ability. These grouping arrangements are temporary and reorganized based on subsequent assessment data.

The major question about Walpole and McKenna's approach concerns the role of text reading and comprehension in the small-group instruction. Walpole and McKenna imply that small-group instruction of comprehension should take a backseat for students who still struggle with decoding and fluency. Anderson, Wilkerson, and Mason (1991) studied small-group instruction and found that a consistent focus on story meaning produced stronger results for oral reading fluency and comprehension for all students than did a focus on word analysis and oral reading accuracy. When Mathes and her colleagues (Mathes, Denton, Fletcher, Anthony, Francis, & Schatschneider, 2005) studied intervention programs for struggling readers they found no difference between a program that had a strong emphasis on tightly sequenced decoding skills in isolation with minimal text reading and another program that emphasized extensive text reading and taught decoding skills as needed. Taking these two studies together the teacher should be able assist students with the skills they need and still keep the lesson steadily focused on meaning. Teachers should be able to meet the decoding and fluency needs of students and still not lose track of comprehension, because reading always has to make sense. So a small-group reading lesson might start with a review of phonics patterns, a decoding game to practice those patterns, but end with text reading. During and after reading a text students should make predictions, justify those predictions, and discuss the meaning of the text.

Response to Intervention

One factor influencing the whole conception of differentiation is the special education initiative called Response to Intervention (RTI), a process of providing increasingly more explicit and supportive instruction so that all students learn to read. The logic of RTI is quite straightforward. If children are having difficulty learning to read, then the school should provide increasingly more support through carefully crafted small-group instruction delivered within the regular reading time or as a supplemental instruction outside the regular reading time. If after all this extra help the student still has difficulty learning to read educators must conclude that the student has a disability and is therefore eligible for special education. Those students who respond well to extra instruction may not have had a learning disability or at least one that does not respond to instruction; they have just lacked good instruction (Fuchs, Fuchs, & Vaughn, 2008). RTI identifies struggling students early and provides them with help.

RTI also includes a system of assessments to determine who needs this additional instruction and a means of measuring the benefits of this instruction. The first assessments are called universal screening and the latter are called progress monitoring. Universal screening assessments are given to all students in a school to determine who needs additional intervention. Once it has been determined that a student needs additional help, a school can provide various levels of intervention or support, typically called Tier 1, Tier 2, and Tier 3—and sometimes Tier 4. Tier 1 is defined as strong classroom instruction, the instruction that the teacher delivers to the whole class and to small groups. Tier 2 is additional small-group instruction, provided by a reading specialist or a special education teacher typically within the general education classroom. The reading specialist pushes into the general education classroom and provides an additional 30 minutes of small-group instruction. Essentially, the students receive more small-group instruction, but the total amount of time for reading instruction is not extended. At Tier 3 the students not only receive more time for reading instruction, but the instructional groups are smaller, and the work is more focused on the students' needs. The school may create a special intervention time where selected students receive even more instruction. To find this additional time the principal might reduce time in social studies, science, or mathematics instruction.

While intervention is taking place, student progress is monitored using regularly administered curriculum-based measures (CBM) (Deno, 1991). A CBM might be a 1-minute assessment of a student's oral reading fluency, an assessment of letter-name or letter-sound knowledge, or an assessment of short vowel patterns. CBM are typically repeated every week or two and the results are graphed to determine whether the student is making progress. If progress is not apparent, then the teachers meet and revise the intervention plan. Progress monitoring assessments have the same pitfalls as any assessment system. The testing instruments can easily become the curriculum, with teachers teaching to the test and ignoring the transfer of skills. CBM assessments, which are more attuned to lower-level reading skills than higher ones, can become so narrow that educators can lose sight of the larger goal of reading comprehension (Paris, 2010).

If the child continues to experience reading difficulties even with the extra support, then the staff concludes that the student is eligible for special education or Tier 4.

Students who do not succeed at Tiers 2 and 3 and are referred for special education placement are likely to be taught by the same professionals who provided help at Tiers 2 and 3. What limits the effectiveness of the RTI model is the knowledge and skill of the classroom teachers, reading specialists, and special education teachers—all the people charged with assisting the students. It is likely that teachers will use the best instructional knowledge they possess at Tier 2 and may have no new ideas left for more severely disabled readers.

Now that we have considered the levels of assistance within an entire school under the RTI model, we will closely study differentiated instruction in the general education classroom, Tier 1, delivered by the classroom teacher. Then we will turn our attention to interventions for the struggling readers, the kinds of support they would get at Tier 2 and Tier 3.

Differentiating Time, Tasks, and Texts

Several recent large research studies support the concept of differentiating time, tasks, and texts. Teachers should devote more direct instructional time to struggling readers and less time to more advanced students (Connor et al., 2007). Students should read text at their instructional level and texts that match their interests (O'Connor, Bell, Harty, Larkin, Sackor, & Zigmond, 2002). Finally, teachers should differentiate tasks. Strong readers, who decode well, are better served by focusing on vocabulary and comprehension development, whereas struggling readers need to spend more time on decoding tasks. Carol Connor and her colleagues have been systematically studying effective classroom instruction (Connor, Jakobsons, Crowe, & Meadows, 2009). Their method involves observing teachers, recording how they teach reading, and then drawing relationships between their descriptions of classroom instruction and students' growth in reading. Connor, Morrison, Schatschneider, and Underwood (2007) categorize classroom instruction based on a 2 × 2 matrix (see Figure 5.1).

Figure 5.1 **Instructional Activities**

	Teacher Managed	**Student Managed**
Code focused	Phonemic awareness, rhyming, blending, segmenting Letter recognition Letter-sound associations Decoding strategies Spelling	Phonics games Phonics worksheets Writing and sorting spelling words
Meaning focused	Supported oral reading Comprehension strategy instruction Prior knowledge development Oral language development Repeated reading of text Writing compositions	Independent reading Partner reading Completing graphic organizer Independent writing and publishing

Activities are either managed by the teacher or by the students. Student-managed activities take place during small-group time when the students work independently. Students might be reading a book, engaged in partner reading with a friend, or writing a report. Teacher-managed activities can occur during whole-group time or small-group time and include direct instruction in decoding, comprehension, or writing. A teacher might model and explain a strategy or guide students to use the strategy. A code-focused activity helps the student understand the alphabetic principle, develop phonemic awareness, or decode or spell words. A meaning-focused activity engages students in the development of vocabulary, comprehension, or writing of extended text.

Differentiating Time

When Connor and her colleagues studied first-, second-, and third-grade classrooms, they found that small differences in the amount and type of instruction produced large differences in student learning. Students who had weak word recognition skills in first grade benefited from more code-focused teacher-managed instruction and less code-focused student-managed instruction. It was important that students worked directly with the teacher and less important that they independently played word games or copied spelling words. It was particularly important that second-grade teachers continued to work hard on decoding activities, because second grade gave these students another chance to succeed. If teachers added just 5 minutes a day to their decoding instruction, their second-grade students made significant gains in achievement, and almost all were reading at a third-grade level or higher by the end of the school year. Five minutes of instructional time each day is the equivalent of 13 extra hours of instruction over the course of a school year (25 minutes per week × 32 weeks of instruction). Although Connor and her colleagues do not say so explicitly, this additional instructional time can be added to the small-group work.

The other important finding concerns the growth of reading comprehension (Connor, Morrison, & Petrella, 2004). Good readers, those with initial strong oral reading fluency and vocabulary scores, demonstrate the most growth when they are engaged in student-managed meaning-focused activities, whereas students with weaker comprehension skills benefit more from explicit teacher-directed instruction. What this means is that good readers should spend their time reading independently, analyzing and responding to what they read. They do not need a great deal of teacher-managed instruction. Conversely, students with weaker oral reading fluency and vocabulary skills benefit when they are engaged in more teacher-directed comprehension instruction. This instruction should focus on comprehension strategies, vocabulary instruction, text structure, and comprehension monitoring. The work of Connor and her colleagues is a clear demonstration of how teachers should differentiate time and tasks.

Differentiating Tasks

Connor stresses the differentiation of instructional tasks by distinguishing between code-focused and meaning-focused tasks. Within each of these broad categories there are some additional distinctions that should be made. At any level of instruction and for any area of reading some tasks provoke more thought or depth of processing than do others. Some tasks can be completed in a short amount of time whereas others may take days. Consider now the relatively simple task of sorting words to discover or practice phonics patterns addressed by In the Classroom 5.1. These tasks can be made more or less challenging by varying the words that children have to sort.

Assessment

It is useful to time your own small-group instruction and assess your own instructional practices. Purchase a small timer and note how much time you devote to each small group. Also, record how much time your students spend reading text versus working on words and letter-sounds in isolation.

Differentiating Word Study Tasks

A typical child-managed word study task is sorting words. The child is given a set of words that consists of four or five examples of three or four phonics patterns. There may be short *a* words, long *a* words, and short *i* words. Often the teacher includes one or two words that do not fit in any of the patterns; these are the oddballs. The child's task is to sort the words into the three or four phonics patterns. Two completed sorts are depicted.

5.1

Sort A

| CVCe | VCC | CV | |
side	fight	sky	Oddball
side	right	why	wild
sign	might	my	pint
nice	night	fry	
spice	light	dry	
twice			

Sort B

Long *a*	Long *i*	Short *a*	Oddball
play	might	chat	what
rain	write	had	
made	pint	can	
train	sky	plant	
lake			

In Sort A the student can concentrate on just the visual features of a word and perform the sort relatively easily. In fact there is no assurance that the student actually needs to read the words to solve this code-focused task unless the teacher asks her to do so. By looking for *ight*, CVVe, or CV patterns the child can successfully complete the sort. Sort A is probably best used under teacher direction where the teacher can ask the students to pronounce the words after they have completed the task. Sort B cannot be solved by looking at just the visual features of the words. Each word must be pronounced. So the student has to work a bit harder to pronounce the word and isolate the vowel sound. If the student correctly completes Sort B you can be reasonably assured that she can pronounce the words.

Not all comprehension tasks are equal in complexity; not all lead to the same depth of understanding. Ample evidence exists that asking higher-level questions promotes more comprehension than lower-level questions. Questions demanding that readers draw inferences to reach generalizations, justify a conclusion with text evidence, and make judgments promote deeper understanding than do literal questions (Hansen, 1981; Taylor et al., 2000). When students have to explain, justify, and defend answers, they think more deeply than when answering literal questions. Different readers need different levels of comprehension instruction. Students who struggle to understand what they read need more support and guidance from the teacher than students who find the task relatively easy. All students need to employ the same comprehension strategies, but the teacher may vary how they are introduced, demonstrated, and

Differentiating Comprehension Instruction

Mr. Campbell organizes his fourth-grade students into three groups for guided reading, but the groups are not strictly homogeneous. One group has a predominance of students with comprehension problems, but in that group he also places a few students who do comprehend well. Mr. Campbell wants these stronger readers to act as a model for the weaker readers. The other two groups are completely heterogeneous with one caveat—he arranges the groups so that everyone will read texts at their instructional level. All the students will be reading and studying legends as part of a larger unit on Native Americans. The students must discover the problem solved in the legend, who solved the problem, and what this might reveal about one particular Native American culture. Let's consider the group with the weaker readers and then one other group.

Mr. Campbell wants to provide his weaker readers considerable support, so he starts with that group first. Students begin by silently reading a segment of the text and at each stopping point he explicitly focuses on specific reading strategies and the meaning of the legend itself. The students are asked to summarize what they read, consider what needs to be clarified, and look for cause-and-effect relationships—the focus strategy for the next couple of weeks. When students have difficulty he prompts them to say more to expand their summary or to search for words like *because* and *since* that might signal cause-and-effect relationships. If the weaker students still have problems, he might model the task of summarizing himself or begin the task and then ask one of the students to complete the summary.

The stronger readers do not need the support provided to the weaker comprehenders. They are given their legend and told to read it on their own, using a graphic organizer that guides the reading. They are to note the character in the legend, what the legend is trying to explain, and the message or moral in the legend. The students read and work independently. When finished they discuss their findings with the teacher in a small-group discussion. The students start by sharing what they recorded on the graphic organizer. When misunderstandings arise, the teacher may direct the students to reread portions of the text as a way to clarify a problem. The teacher focuses on strategies, summarizing, or cause and effect only when those strategies might clarify their understanding. So if a particular paragraph is not well understood, Mr. Campbell will direct the students to reread it and summarize what they have learned. At times the teacher might simply ask the students what we have to do to clarify an issue. In this stronger group of readers the use of comprehension strategies is assumed and support is provided only as students need it.

practiced, as well as the amount of support provided. In the Classroom 5.2 illustrates two small-group discussions, one with considerable support and another with much less support.

Differentiating Texts

Teachers need to make many important decisions about the texts that students read. One size does not fit all. The texts that students read should be matched to their reading level, their interests, and the skill teachers are seeking to develop. Let's unpack each of these ideas and see what they mean in terms of differentiating texts. It has been the fundamental principle of reading for decades that students should read texts at their instructional level rather than their grade level (Fountas & Pinnell, 1996). Even though these texts lack the vocabulary and more complex structures that would build comprehension, weaker readers make more progress in developing decoding skills and oral reading fluency when they read texts at their instructional level (O'Connor et al., 2002). Graves (2009) provides a clear demonstration of how

reading level and reading ability interact. A fourth-grade student reading at approximately a third-grade level would know 80 percent of the words in fourth-grade text. Not knowing 20 percent of the words would prevent comprehension. In Chapter 8, Fluency, we provide several guidelines for determining the reading level of a text. Developers of core reading programs have recognized the need to have students reading at their instructional level and therefore created three levels of texts for each reading lesson. Core programs provide leveled texts for students reading above grade level, on grade level, and below grade level, and one for English language learners. There is one problem with this system; the texts created for below-level readers are typically shorter and provide less reading practice than do the texts for on-level and above-level readers (Dewitz et al., 2010). Teachers can and should obviously deal with this problem by finding additional texts for students to read at their instructional level.

A special case of instructional-level text is the need to have decodable text for beginning readers. Decodable text provides students the opportunity to practice phonics patterns in connected text that have been previously taught in a teacher-directed lesson. In such texts a majority of the words are phonetically regular. Figure 5.2 shows examples of a decodable text and a text at the same level that is not decodable. Both are samples from a current core reading program. Decodable text offers two advantages to the beginning reader. First, decodable text provides the student with an immediate rationale for all those phonics lessons and activities. By learning those phonics patterns the students can now use what they have learned to read new words. To the first-grader, reading instruction makes sense and the child gains a sense of confidence. Decodable text provides a second benefit. Because the majority of words are phonetically regular, using patterns previously taught, the text schools the child in the left to right progression of reading—carefully decoding and blending letter-sound patterns as she moves across a word (Adams, 2009). When the children read decodable text they use their phonics skills in a more effective and facile manner (Juel & Roper/Schneider, 1985).

Selecting the right text in the upper grades is also an important instructional decision, one that demands careful differentiation. The teacher in the upper grades must ask what kinds of text are most likely to assist students to develop strong reading comprehension skills. In making these decisions the teacher needs to think about the

Figure 5.2 **Decodable and Leveled Text**

Decodable Text	Below-Level Leveled Reader
Pat Can Help	*The Pond*
Pat has a cab.	This is a pond.
Jan has bags.	What animals live in the pond?
Jan has a cat.	Little fish live here.
Jan has a hat.	Ducks live here. They get their food from the pond.
Jan has maps.	This duck looks under the cold water.
Pat can help Jan.	Look! She sees a fish. The duck swims very fast!
Jan can nap.	The fish swims off? The duck will look for more food.

Source: Beck, I., Farr, R. C., & Strickland, D. S. (2009). *Storytown Grade 1, Theme 1.* Orlando, FL: Harcourt, pp. T60, T77.

Differentiating Instruction for English Language Learners

Intervention

One simple truth captures the problem of differentiating instruction for English language learners. What works for most students will work for ELL students. The ELL student must read books at their instructional level. They need to build their background knowledge, especially for American culture. They need clear modeling and well supported guided practice to learn strategies for decoding and comprehension. Above all, they need a steady focus on vocabulary development. The differentiated needs of the ELL student mirror the needs of the English-speaking student. If phonics or fluency is a problem, those issues should be addressed in differentiated instruction. Likewise if vocabulary or comprehension is a problem, the teacher should focus on those components of reading.

What is especially vital for the ELL student is a strong focus on vocabulary. Teachers should focus on words necessary to follow directions, words that describe instructional concepts, and vocabulary terms necessary for text comprehension. Even when teaching basic decoding skills, the teacher should take extra time to focus on meaning of the words used for modeling and practice of phonics patterns. Short CVC or CCVC words (*log, met, wig, fret, chat*) require definitions and discussions of their meaning. In addition, many management techniques specifically for English as a second language proved beneficial for the ELL students (Mathes, Pollard-Durodola, Cárdenas-Hagan, Linan-Thompson, and Vaughn, 2007). Teachers used clear and repetitive language, repetitive routines and gestures, and maintained a high level of student–teacher interactions.

knowledge of the reader and the structure and organization of the text. When students are reading in content areas where their knowledge is just beginning to develop, they benefit most from texts that are well structured, cohesive, with unity, what has been called *considerate text* (Anderson & Armbruster, 1984). If the structure of a text is clear, it is easier for the reader to locate the important ideas. The general principle has an interesting exception. If a teacher seeks to promote the comprehension skills of stronger readers, especially when they are reading in subject areas with which they have some knowledge, she is advised to select a text that has some complexity and presents a challenge (McNamara, Kintsch, Songer, & Kintsch, 1996). Inducing a strong reader to work by presenting a challenge is more likely to produce growth in reading comprehension. We use comprehension strategies to solve problems. Predicting, questioning, inferring, monitoring, and summarizing are all strategies that help develop meaning or resolve misunderstanding. Students, especially good readers, need texts that present some difficulty.

Planning Small-Group Instruction

Effective teachers in the primary grades spend 120 to 135 minutes per day in reading/language arts instruction, with somewhat less time in the upper grades. It is possible to devote too much time to reading/language arts, because if the total school day is not expanded, reading instruction encroaches on mathematics, science, and social studies. Within a reading/language arts block, time should be distributed between whole-group instruction, small-group instruction, and individual projects. During whole-group time teachers read to students, develop vocabulary knowledge, explain and model decoding and comprehension strategies, model writing, and share written products. In the kindergarten and first-grade classrooms, whole-group time often includes a morning message time, where students and teacher engage in interactive writing and explore how the writing process and spelling process work. The morning message is also a useful vehicle for reviewing principles of phonemic awareness, letter identification, and letter-sound associations.

There are some important benefits to whole-group instruction. First, whole-class time allows the teacher to model strategies and develop knowledge. Second, through this whole-class time the teacher can lay out the goals for the day or the week. It makes all students, regardless of ability, feel that they are contributing to an important goal. Some teachers schedule a short whole-group time at the end of the reading/language arts block to review what has been accomplished and allow time for students to share. The teacher might also discuss management problems or set goals for the next day. The third benefit of whole-group time, beyond the direct instruction, is lessening the time spent on superficial or low-level tasks. If too much of the day is devoted to small-group instruction, struggling students, when not engaged with the teacher, tend to spend considerable time in low-level activities—playing phonics games, filling in the blanks on worksheets, or sorting and copying spelling words. If a teacher devotes 60 minutes to small-group instruction, then most students are working individually or with a partner 40 minutes of that time. Expanding small-group time to 90 minutes creates even more time for independent work. Strive for a balance of teacher-directed and independent work.

Teachers should explicitly differentiate instruction when they work with small groups and when they design students' independent work. In fact, differentiation takes place when the teacher is working with groups of students, when she is working with an individual student, or when the students are working independently. First, the research provides ample support for the use of small-group instruction (Taylor et al., 2000). These researchers found that the most effective teachers in the primary grades spent approximately twice as much time in small-group instruction (up to 52 minutes per day) as the least effective teacher. Effectiveness was defined as growth in students' reading ability. Small-group instruction allows the teacher to differentiate in several key ways, as we will discuss.

There is no ideal number of reading groups, but there is an absolute tradeoff between the number of groups and the amount of time that a teacher can work with each group. The total amount of time a teacher can spend on reading is fixed and limited by lunch, recess, specials, and the other major content areas. The research is equally clear that the most effective classroom teachers strike a balance between whole-group and small-group instruction. If a classroom teacher allocates 60 minutes for small-group instruction, three groups gives her 20 minutes to work with each group, four groups provides 15 minutes per group, and five groups provides 12 minutes per group not counting transitions between groups. The more groups you have, the more time will be lost to transition and the less that can be accomplished in that short span of time. Three, perhaps four, groups seem optimal. Furthermore, it is desirable to meet groups for different lengths of time. The needs of the weakest readers require more attention than those of better readers. Recalling the research of Carol Connor and her colleagues discussed earlier in this chapter, we can safely suggest that strong readers can and should read and work independently for longer periods of time.

In the Classroom 5.3 examines how a teacher might plan her small-group instruction for three groups of second-grade students. This example focuses on a typical week and does not break the planning down to daily activities and tasks. Each group is seen for a different length of time, with the below-level readers receiving more instructional time than the on-level or above-level readers. The below-level readers need to spend a larger proportion of their time on decoding while the on-level and above-level readers do not. In fact, the teacher might only touch on a few difficult words with the higher group, focusing instead on vocabulary and comprehension. For those in the middle some decoding work is appropriate because ignoring it leads to slower growth in reading. Remember that some of this decoding work is also covered during the whole-group time.

The texts that the three groups are reading should be related in some way. If the teacher is following a core reading program, then the three or four leveled books are linked to each other and to the main anthology selection by a common topic or theme. If the theme of the main selection is about overcoming one's fears, it is desirable that all students read about the same topic or theme. At the end of the week, students in

In the Classroom

5.3

Planning for Differentiated Small-Group Instruction

Above-Level Readers	On-Level Readers	Below-Level Readers
Vocabulary (2 minutes) • Introduce or review new vocabulary • Apply structural analysis principles as needed	*Decoding + Vocabulary* (5 minutes) • Model decoding strategies • Review decoding strategies with new vocabulary words and review word meanings	*Decoding* (10 minutes) • Segment and blend sounds • Introduce or review phonics patterns • Model decoding strategies • Engage students in one decoding activity
Read Leveled Book for Comprehension (15 minutes) • Introduce new book or chapter and develop prior knowledge • Review reading comprehension strategies • Read text silently and stop to discuss • Use strategies as needed when comprehension breaks down • Introduce or review independent assignment such as a graphic organizer	*Read Leveled Book for Fluency and Comprehension* (15 minutes) • Introduce new book or chapter and develop prior knowledge • Review reading comprehension strategies • Read text with partner or silent read, stopping to apply specific comprehension strategies • Introduce or review independent assignment such as a graphic organizer	*Read Leveled and Decodable Book for Fluency* (15 minutes) • Introduce new book or begin with echo reading • Read with one or more students to coach on word-identification strategies • Use whiteboard to review and model decoding strategies for difficult words • Reread text segments to work on oral reading fluency • Have students retell the story, ask comprehension questions

each group can contribute to the discussion, sharing their story and what they have learned about people and overcoming fears. This drastically reduces the isolation of weaker readers from the ongoing activities in the classroom.

The differentiation of task continues with the reading of the text. The above-level students engage in the application of comprehension strategies only as needed. If students basically comprehend well, it may actually be counterproductive to disrupt their reading by focusing on specific strategies. If readers understand the text, what is gained by asking them to stop and clarify, predict, or make inferences? They should focus on meaning (McKeown, Beck, & Blake, 2009). For the on-level readers, who might not be monitoring their comprehension, placing the strategies more in the forefront may help the readers build greater comprehension. For the below-level students thinking about decoding and comprehension at the same time might be challenging, because cognitive capacity is limited, but students still retell and discuss the story after they finish reading.

Differentiation also demands that when students are working alone or with other students they are engaged in appropriate independent activities. A few findings are clear from the research on independent work and on effective classrooms. First, we would argue that text reading is perhaps the most important task that students can engage in during their independent time. Independent reading is important enough that we devote Chapter 12 to the task of fostering a love of reading. Teachers might ask themselves the following question: "Is what I am asking a child to do more important than reading a book?" Next to independent reading students need to be engaged in projects that are long, lasting more than a day, and demand considerable thought. Writing a reflection on a book, preparing a research report, or developing a creative story are all appropriate independent activities. Longer projects are more meaningful; they evoke more pride of accomplishment and engage students more thoroughly. Few students look with pride on the worksheets they have completed. For students who are still struggling with print skills and fluency, a number of independent activities will sustain their growth in reading. Partner reading builds fluency; phonics games promote decoding. Both hold the students' attention. Using letter dice to make words can be fast paced and engaging, and if students record the words they have made, the teachers can hold them accountable for their practice. However, these activities should be used sparingly.

In the upper-elementary grades differentiation can take on a different look. In the second-grade example we explained how to meet the skill needs of students reading below, on, and above grade level. Each group has a different skill focus but still reads a book that is connected to the theme or topic of the week. This model is closer to the skill-driven model of Walpole and McKenna discussed earlier, but we still keep a focus on comprehension for all three groups. In the upper grades differentiation might be closer to the Tomlinson model, with the teachers working to create instructional units that focus on common themes and knowledge development for all students while differentiating the texts and tasks. In the Classroom 5.4 is a snapshot of such a differentiated unit.

Pink and Say is used to build background about the Civil War and develop interest in the topic while modeling a strategy for reading the novels. Mr. Hernandez will use the book to stimulate interest and have the students brainstorm questions they want to answer. The historical fiction read during language arts and the nonfiction they read during social studies will help them answer their questions. Then he will model the use of a story map that has been adapted to reading a novel. The students will track problems faced by the characters, explore how their characters

A ssessment

The Tile Test in Appendix A can help in determining the skill needs for beginning readers. Use the test to explore their phonemic awareness, letter-sound knowledge, and decoding skills.

A Differentiated Historical Fiction Unit

Mr. Hernandez wants to expose his students to the engaging and instructive qualities of historical fiction. Because the class will soon be studying the Civil War in social studies, he decides to build a reading/language arts unit around historical fiction. He feels that a unit focused on novels about the Civil War will deepen the students' interest in the period, create personal connections to the feelings of common people during the war, and provide an opportunity to teach comprehension strategies in a meaningful context (Guthrie, Van Meter, Hancock, Alao, Anderson, & McCann, 1998). Due to the wide range of reading ability in the class, he selects books that are appropriate to each student's reading level and plans to introduce the unit by reading a historical fiction picture book to the students.

- *Pink and Say* (Polacco, 1994). A picture book about two teenage soldiers, one northern, the other southern, wounded, dazed, and in danger, helping each other to survive after a battle.
- *Civil War on Sunday* (Osborne, 2000). This book, part of the Magic Tree House series, is geared for struggling readers and tells the tale of two children who magically find themselves in Gettysburg and witness and aid people in that famous battle.
- *I Thought My Soul Would Rise and Fly* (Hansen, 1997). The book, selected for the average readers in the class, is set in the immediate aftermath of the Civil War and tells the story of a freed young slave's yearning for an education and struggle with her newly bestowed freedom.
- *Across Five Aprils* (Hunt, 1965, 2002). The book, selected for the stronger readers in the class, tells the story of families and communities living in southern Illinois and caught up in personal, economic, and political upheavals of the Civil War period.

change, and list the important themes in the book. On the story map the students will sort the fictional aspects of the novel from the accurate historical information (see Figure 5.3).

After Mr. Hernandez models the use of the story map, each group will receive its novel and further explanation of the assignment. During reading time over the next two weeks the students will read independently and then work with a partner to complete the story map. The teacher will meet with each group regularly but for varying amounts of time. Mr. Hernandez likes to see his below-level readers daily so that their small-group time can include work on decoding by analogy, a strategy we discuss in Chapter 7. The average readers, because there are many of them, have been split into two groups, and he sees these groups approximately every other day. He also meets with the better readers every other day.

The three or four groups do not work in complete isolation. The teacher holds whole-class meetings where themes common to all three books are discussed. The teacher might ask the students to consider who is brave in their novel and list the number of different ways that characters in the story express their bravery. Mr Hernandez wants the students to understand that bravery is not always a physical act. Later in the unit the class might discuss the concept of loyalty and what people can be loyal to. What happens to loyalty when there is a conflict of beliefs or values within a family? Students keep track of these big themes and write about them at length. At the conclusion of the unit the students consider how reading a novel has expanded their understanding of the social studies content and which reading strategies have helped them understand their novel.

Assessment

When students are engaged with a complex unit of instruction, assess both their reading and writing skills. The Read-Write Cycle Assessments in Appendix A provide a model for assessing what the students have learned and how their skills have developed.

Figure 5.3 Mapping Historical Fiction

Title _____ Author _____

	Historical Elements	Fictional Elements
Setting ❑ Place ❑ Time		
Characters		
Problem ❑ Event ❑ Event ❑ Event ❑ Event ❑ Event		
Resolution		

4 List as many ways as you can to differentiate teaching and learning in the classroom. Decide which would be easiest to implement and which would present the most challenges. As a beginning teacher where would you start?

5 In this chapter we have contrasted a more skills-oriented approach to differentiation to an approach that focuses on interests, abilities, and experiences. Would one of these approaches be more beneficial for upper-grades classrooms? Can you combine a focus on skills and interests and how would you do so?

6 As a beginning teacher what would be your first steps in differentiating instruction? What aspects of differentiation of instruction would be difficult to implement and might have to wait for your experience and knowledge to grow? In short, think about how your instruction might change during the first year of teaching.

REFLECT and *Apply*

Intervention for Struggling Readers

The most effective differentiated general classroom instruction cannot ensure that all students will learn to read. When Juel (1988) studied one set of students from first through fourth grades she found that students who were struggling with reading at the end of first grade still struggled in fourth grade. She concluded that some form

Books for Differentiated Thematic Units

In the upper grades the concept of differentiated novel study has many advantages. Students of different reading levels can read a novel with success. Motivation is enhanced because all students are working on a meaningful project. Finally, a differentiated novel study builds a cooperative spirit in the classroom. The following are some suggested units.

Unit 1: Exploring Friendship

Sharon Creech. *The Wanderer.* HarperTrophy, 2002. (For better readers.) A 13-year-old girl shows her bravery on a dangerous ocean voyage in a small sailboat. 320 pages.

Kate DiCamillo. *Because of Winn-Dixie.* Candlewick Press, 2000. (For average to above-average readers.) Through the help of a goofy dog, Opal learns to listen to the problems of others and in turn begins to feel part of a town where she once felt isolated. 182 pages.

Louis Sachar. *There's a Boy in the Girls' Bathroom.* Yearling, 1987. (For below-average to average readers.) The story of an isolated fifth-grader who through the help of friends learns to restore his self-confidence. 195 pages.

Unit 2: Survival

Ken Mochizuki. *Baseball Saved Us.* Lee and Low Books, 1993. (For below-average readers.) The story of how baseball saved the spirits and hope of Japanese Americans in an internment camp during World War II. 32 pages.

Gary Paulsen. *Voyage of the Frog.* Bantam Doubleday, 1989. (For average readers.) The story of a boy who inherits his beloved uncle's sailboat and then struggles to survive in a storm. 160 pages.

Johanna Reiss. *The Upstairs Room.* HarperCollins, 1972. (For above-average readers.) The story of two Jewish girls who survive the Holocaust hiding in a small room. 196 pages.

Unit 3: A Quest for Personal Identity

Edward Bloor. *Tangerine.* Harcourt Books, 1997. (For above-average readers.) The story of a nearsighted geek who after moving to a new town becomes a hero. 320 pages.

Beverly Cleary. *Dear Mr. Henshaw.* HarperCollins, 1983. (For average readers.) A new kid in town, with recently divorced parents, no dog anymore, and a lunch that gets stolen every day writes in a journal and learns to cope with his feelings and gain confidence. 160 pages.

Jack Gantos. *Joey Pigza Loses Control.* HarperCollins, 2000. (For below-average readers.) The story of a hyperactive boy from a divorced dysfunctional home who learns control and self-acceptance. 196 pages.

of early intervention is needed to prevent future reading problems. Despite the best efforts of classroom teachers, some children need extra help to learn to read. In most schools it takes the combined talents and efforts of many professionals—classroom teachers, reading specialists, special education teachers, the librarian, and occasionally volunteers—to ensure that all children learn to read. Returning to the RTI model we outlined at the beginning of this chapter, all students need effective and differentiated Tier 1 instruction, which has been the subject of this chapter and most of the preceding chapters. Some children will also need additional help at the Tier 2 and Tier 3 levels.

The characteristics of Tier 2 and Tier 3 interventions are determined by how schools use time and human resources to assist struggling readers. Changing the size of the instructional group, the amount of instructional time, and the nature of that instruction can increase reading achievement. Typically, in a Tier 2 intervention the student receives additional small-group instruction focused on the needs of the student. This instruction might be provided by a reading specialist or special education teacher working within the students' classroom and taking this group of students for an extra 20 to 30 minutes per day. A volunteer might also provide the intervention, working with students after school. In either case the goal is to augment the amount of small-group guided instruction. A Tier 3 intervention adds additional time to the students' total time for reading instruction; a reading specialist or special education teacher works with these students in even smaller groups. To accomplish this schools might adjust the entire schedule and create a daily block of time, 30 to 45 minutes, where all students who need it can receive extra intervention while the rest of the students engage in some enrichment. Ultimately, the distinctions between a Tier 2 and Tier 3 intervention are not precise as schools struggle to arrange time and human resources to meet the needs of all students.

The most successful interventions are geared to the youngest students; preventing a reading problem in first grade is easier than assisting a struggling reader in the upper grades (Wanzek & Vaughn, 2007). Yet there are successful models of reading intervention with older elementary students (Lovett, Lacerenza, Borden, Frijters, Steinbach, & De Palma, 2000; O'Connor et al., 2002). The most successful interventions are delivered to small groups of students (three to five) or involve one-on-one tutoring (Wanzek & Vaughn, 2007), but there is no clear understanding whether on-on-one instruction is always superior to small-group instruction. Successful interventions take time, at least half a year or more. Some students may need support in reading for many years. There is evidence that sometimes the underlying reading problem, such as the ability to manage and implement strategies, may be solved in terms of word recognition—I know how to decode a word—only to reoccur when a reader must manage comprehension strategies (Smith, Borkowski, & Whitman, 2008).

The actual instructional design of an intervention can vary widely and still be successful (Mathes et al., 2005), with some interventions having a strong emphasis on text reading and others stressing work on decoding skills in isolation. However, all interventions seem to embrace the following attributes (Coyne, Kame'enui, & Simmons, 2001):

- *Explicit strategy instruction.* Reading requires strategies for identifying words, determining a word's meaning, or understanding a text. In an intervention program the teacher has to clearly explain the strategies and model them explicitly. It is not enough for students to know letter sounds; they must have a strategy or process to use that knowledge, just as they need a process for finding the main idea.
- *Mediated scaffolding.* The student needs support when learning new skills or strategies. Sometimes the support or scaffolding is provided by the sequence of tasks in a curriculum. Easier letters and sounds are introduced before more difficult patterns, or finding an explicit main idea in a paragraph is tackled before dealing with implied main ideas in longer passages. The teacher may also provide scaffolding through the hints, suggestions, or models he provides while students work out a reading task. Several researchers have documented the importance of moment-to-moment teacher scaffolding for

both word recognition and comprehension (Piasta et al., 2009; Taylor et al., 2000).

- *Strategy integration.* Whereas curriculum and instruction break reading down into its constituent elements, students should always understand how the separate skills relate to the ultimate goal—constructing meaning. Phonemic awareness needs to be taught alongside decoding so that students understand that segmenting and blending sounds leads to ease in recognizing words. Decoding and fluency need to be taught along with comprehension of connected text, so that students understand that accuracy and speed are not the only hallmarks of a good reader. It is important for students to understand how the pieces fit together.

- *Priming background knowledge.* Students with reading problems often have memory deficits. What you think they learned on Monday is forgotten by Wednesday. Strong instruction requires that previous knowledge and skills be reviewed daily before new ideas are introduced. To spell, the student has to first segment the sounds in the word. Priming causes the student to think about segmenting before he begins to spell. Asking students to think about a topic before they read should prime the knowledge they need for comprehension.

- *Judicious review.* Students with reading problems need considerable review. Coyne and colleagues (2001) remind us that review needs to be cumulative, varied, and distributed over time. In a sense we cannot assume mastery of a skill. That is one rationale for the use of word walls for decoding. The words on the wall are a running list of the patterns that have been taught and a reminder to the teacher and students that we should use these patterns every day. An effective teacher designs review activities—let's read the wall—so that these words and their phonics patterns are regularly reviewed. Similarly with reading compre-

Changing Students' Attributions

Regular assessments are a positive way to motive struggling readers. All students want to know how well they read—even if, at times, they fear the results. And all students rejoice in small triumphs when they realize their reading is improving. Almost any assessment can be used within a portfolio to track a student's progress. Teachers might record timed repeated readings to build reading fluency or they might regularly have the students note how many sight words they have mastered. The Graduated Running Record in Appendix A can be used to monitor a student's progress. Each time a student reads, his highest level of attainment can be noted.

Recording these results is essential. Equally important is having a short discussion with the student. It is important that teachers work to change students' attributions. If the student is making progress, he reads more quickly or knows more sight words; he should be guided to attribute these results to his own efforts. The teacher should guide the students to notice progress ("Do you think your reading is improving?") and to clarify that progress ("How do you know?"). Then the teacher should ask, "Why do you think you are improving?" If the student does not attribute the progress to his efforts, then the teacher should do so. "You have been reading every night; that is why your fluency is much better." By changing student attributions, we change their motivation.

hension. Teachers don't assume that summarizing has been mastered. Once student have learned a strategy for summarizing they should use it as often as it is necessary.

- *Well-paced instruction.* Strong intervention is well paced. The teacher is organized and plans for several activities within the 30 to 40 minutes available. Each of these activities should be well learned by the students, so that the focus of the instruction is on the content of the activity and not the steps in the procedure. Once students understand how to make words with letter tiles or sort words, only the phonics features change and not the rules of the activity. A well-paced lesson promotes students' interest, engagement, and attention.
- *Motivation.* Students need to be motivated. We can motivate students through the pace of the lesson, the engagement of the activities and text, and through their growing sense of efficacy. If students know they are moving up to harder books, or they are reading faster, they gain a sense of confidence and their self-image as a reader grows. An intervention program should regularly provide students feedback on how they are doing.

Intervention programs can take many forms and there are too many to even attempt a review. Mathes concluded her study of two very different intervention programs by writing "that there is likely not 'one best approach' and not one right philosophy or theory for how best to meet the needs of struggling readers" (Mathes et al., 2005, p. 179). To elaborate on this important point we would like to consider two very different intervention programs, both of which have reported considerable success with struggling readers. Each of these programs has been evaluated by either the What Works Clearinghouse (http://ies.ed.gov/ncee/wwc) or the Florida Center for Reading Research (www.fcrr.org/Interventions/index.htm).

Reading Recovery, which was developed in New Zealand by Marie Clay (1994), is a one-on-one tutoring program for first-graders who are struggling to read. In a typical Reading Recovery session the student reviews letter-sound knowledge using letter tiles, spells words with the same tiles, writes a short story, rereads old books to build fluency, and reads a new book as the teacher assists the student with word recognition strategies. The majority of the time in a session is devoted to reading connected text, and phonics skills are taught as needed. The teacher regularly checks the student's progress by taking a running record. Reading Recovery has been shown to be very effective for the students it serves but some educators have questioned the cost of the program and wondered if Reading Recovery teachers serve students with the most severe reading problems (Hiebert, 1992; Shanahan & Barr, 1995). Reading Recovery teachers go through an extensive training program that can last a year in which they develop strong coaching skills.

In sharp contrast to Reading Recovery is Early Reading Intervention (Simmons & Kame'enui, 2003). Early Reading Intervention (ERI) is a small-group intervention program designed for kindergarten and first-grade students who are struggling with phonemic awareness, letter-sound association, letter-name knowledge, blending, and word reading. A Reading Recovery teacher makes many instructional decisions, whereas ERI is a tightly scripted program and teachers make few decisions. In the span of 30 minutes students will review letter names, isolate initial consonant sounds, write words, read regular words, segment words, and practice spelling words; later in the program the students will read simple sentences. Each of the seven lesson segments are timed and can be completed in 1 to 5 minutes. Whereas reading Reading Recovery emphasizes reading little books, the focus on ERI is letters,

A strong intervention lesson requires preparation, excellent organization, and a quick pace of instruction. Pair up with a colleague and observe each other engaging in intervention instruction. An extra pair of eyes might reveal ways to improve what you do.

Motivating Children with Technology

For students who have struggled with learning to read, computers can provide a motivation boost that can be part of an intervention program. When students are engaged on computers, playing an engaging game, their sense of learned helplessness diminishes. Caught up in the challenge of the game, they think less about the reading skills and more about the challenges of the game. Computer-based reading games are most effective for providing the practice students need to reach automaticity with decoding and sight word recognition. Reading games are most effective when they provide exciting repetitive and challenging practice. The software in the RAVE-O Reading Program (http://ase.tufts.edu/crlr/RAVE-O/Home .html) helps students to develop automaticity in processing orthographic patterns. Students are presented with spelling patterns and are challenged to make as many words as they can in a fixed amount of time. The students can raise the stakes by making more words in the same span of time, or the same number of words in a shorter span of time. Earobic (www .earobics.com) engages students in games to work on skills such as sound and phoneme recognition.

Oral reading fluency programs like QuickReads (Hiebert, 2002) and Read Naturally (Ihnot, 2004) use speech recognition software to track reading performance as the student reads on a computer. The programs report reading rate and accuracy and provide feedback on words that need additional practice. The computer prompts the students to set goals and provides feedback on progress in attaining those goals. Technology is an efficient and motivating way to supplement intervention and provide students with the practice they need. ●

sounds, and words in isolation. ERI yields significant gains in reading because of explicit instruction, knowledge priming, careful saffolding, and very regular review. The lessons are fast paced, challenging the teacher's skill and the students' attention.

The contrast in these two programs illustrates the findings of Mathes and her colleagues (2005) that there may not be one best method for reading intervention. It is also possible that teachers can craft their own intervention programs to provide a balance between developing decoding skills, improving oral reading fluency, and improving comprehension. A school crafting its own intervention plan should be mindful of the criteria laid out by Coyne and his colleagues, which we discussed earlier in this section.

REFLECT and Apply

7 An important criterion of reading intervention is additional instructional time. Talk with a teacher or a principal you know and discuss their school's daily schedule. How do you find time to provide extra instruction in a tightly packed schedule? As part of this discussion consider the problems in establishing an after-school reading program. What are the barriers you would have to overcome to create such a program?

8 Intervention is sometimes provided within the regular classroom and sometimes the students leave to go to the special education teacher or the reading specialist. Spend a day in a school and focus on one student. Bring a stopwatch and record how much time is spent in transition from one activity to another.

9 Discuss with your teacher or another student the merits of scripted programs versus programs that teachers create. Do you believe that scripted programs devalue teachers and reduce their importance?

Strengths *and Challenges* of Diversity

Students from all cultural and linguistic groups encounter problems learning to read and schools must respond. In the preceding sections we outlined the criteria for successful differentiation and intervention. How do these criteria change when working with students who speak Spanish, Urdu, Vietnamese, or Tagalog as their native language? The first answer is that most of what works with native English speakers will work with English language learners (Lovett, De Palma, Frijters, Steinbach, Temple, Benson, & Lacerenza, 2008). These students will need work with letter-name knowledge, letter-sound knowledge, phonemic awareness, and decoding. They benefit from explicit, systematic instruction that is highly interactive, fast paced, and engaging. The same criteria we describe for intervention with students whose first language is English will apply to students who are learning to speak and read English at the same time (Mathes et al., 2007).

Yet the approach with ELL students must be somewhat different. First, the vocabulary learning task for these students is daunting, so our efforts at differentiation and intervention should put a greater focus on vocabulary. Even the mundane task of decoding words must have a strong vocabulary focus. When students decode words, they know

they are successful if the word they pronounce is in their oral or receptive vocabulary. If you are a native speaker of Spanish and you correctly read *hog, log,* and *bog,* you have no feedback system to tell you that your efforts were correct. So all phonemic awareness and phonics lessons should be accompanied with a vocabulary component. Words must be explained as they are being read and pictures help students make a connection between the English word and their native language equivalent.

All intervention efforts with ELL students should have a strong focus on vocabulary and both content words and the function words that reflect the grammar of English. Most reading lessons begin by teaching vocabulary and more words need to be taught to the ELL student. Bilingual students, if there are some in your class, can help to make the transition between English and the student's native language. During comprehension lessons it is important to focus on little words like *some, since, fewer,* and *therefore,* the words that connect one idea with another. Finally, the more students are asked to read and explain the better; they should be encouraged to even use gestures to help them support their comprehension development.

Concluding *Remarks*

In this chapter we discussed the ways schools and teachers can meet the vast array of differences that students bring to school and to the task of learning to read. Many of these needs can be meet within the general education classroom through differentiated instruction. For primary teachers who are concerned about students' development of word recognition ability, teachers can differentiate the skills that each group needs, they can use texts that match the reading levels of their students, and they can vary time, so that struggling readers receive more teacher-directed code-focused instruction and stronger readers spend more time reading and writing independently on important tasks. We also illustrated how upper-elementary teachers can create units of study that take into account the varied reading levels of their students and yet allow all students to study similar content,

work with the same genre, and employ the same comprehension strategies.

Differentiated instruction will not ensure the success of all students. Some struggling readers need additional intervention. Intervention means small-group instruction by well-trained professionals over an extended period of time. Some students will require either more time in small-group instruction in the regular class and/or additional intervention time outside the regular reading block. We demonstrated that there is no single approach to intervention that is preferable, but there are a set of criteria common to strong intervention programs, including explicit strategy instruction, regular review, strategy integration, and pacing and motivation, among others. Even if a school crafts its own intervention program, teachers should stick to a script, by which we mean a regular pattern of instruction with set procedures and time parameters. Consistency is essential. If the students do not improve, then the teachers can modify the instructional plan. If the intervention is haphazard, with capricious instructional decisions, then the teachers do not know what should be changed in the intervention program if the results are disappointing.

As a final thought we believe that experienced classroom teachers or specialists should teach reading intervention programs. Paraprofessionals should not. There is evidence that teachers who lack knowledge of reading instruction, even when using tightly scripted programs, have limited effectiveness. A teacher's knowledge of teaching readers determines how effective she can be in scaffolding a student's learning (Piasta et al., 2009).

Extending *Learning*

There are two important ways you can extend what you have learned in reading this chapter. First, you need to visit classrooms and interview teachers. Second, you need to do some more reading.

1. One means of increasing your understanding of differentiation is to locate schools and classroom where teachers have been successful in differentiating instruction. Observe in these classrooms and then interview the teachers. Find out how they organized their students into groups. Ask how they determine when to move a student to a new group. Study their management system. How do the students know what to do? How effective are the transitions in the classroom? Take notes on how teachers organize the materials in their classroom.

2. When you talk to the teachers, ask how they plan. How do they determine the needs of each group? What skills and activities are essential for weaker readers but unnecessary for stronger students? How do these teachers meet the needs of the best readers in their classrooms?

3. Extend your understanding of differentiation by reading about classroom management. Two books by Fountas and Pinnell are useful: *Guided Reading: Good First Teaching for All Children* (Heinemann, 1996) and *Guiding Readers and Writers: Grades 3–6*. The first book focuses on primary classrooms and the second on upper grades.

Children's *Literature*

Bloor, E. (1997). *Tangerine.* Orlando, FL: Harcourt Books. 320 pages.

Cleary, B. (1983). *Dear Mr. Henshaw.* New York: HarperCollins. 160 pages.

Creech, S. (2000). *The Wanderer.* New York: HarperTrophy. 320 pages.

DiCamillo, K. (2000). *Because of Winn-Dixie.* New York: Candlewick Press. 182 pages.

Gantos, J. (2000). *Joey Pigza Loses Control.* New York: HarperCollins. 196 pages.

Mochizuki, K. (1993). *Baseball Saved Us.* New York: Lee and Low Books. 32 pages.

Paulsen, G. (1989). *Voyage of the Frog.* New York: Bantam Doubleday. 160 pages.

Reiss, J. (1972). *The Upstairs Room.* New York: HarperCollins. 196 pages.

Sachar, L. (1987). *There's a Boy in the Girls' Bathroom.* New York: Dell. 195 pages.

A Day in the Life of Jenna LeBlanc and Her First-Grade Students

iStockPhoto

Jenna LeBlanc is in her first year of teaching in a first-grade class at Edge-brook Elementary School on the outskirts of Washington, DC. Her student teaching had been with older children, so she was not quite prepared for these squirmy 6- and 7-year-olds! Now, in mid-October, however, she believes she would never want to teach another grade. She says, "I have really seen these children emerge as readers and writers. I keep a port-folio on each child, and included in it are samples of their writing since the beginning of the school year. It's exciting to look back at these and see the progress—and to think I had something to do with it."

Jenna teaches 20 children of varied backgrounds and abilities. Most of her students come from working-class families representing a wide range of cultures. Several of her students have parents who recently immigrated to the United States. Among her students, there are eight different languages spoken at home. None of her students have problems communicating in English. But there is a considerable range in their knowledge of English vocabulary. Jenna tells us that, of her 20 students, three were already reading first-grade-level texts when they entered her classroom. Most of the others were not able to read convention-ally and possessed quite a range of knowledge about print. Some children, for example, knew all the alphabet and some initial consonant sounds, whereas others had difficulty naming more than a handful of letters. All were eager to learn.

Jenna's school district uses a basal reading series that includes an anthology of chil-dren's literature and informational texts. Many of the selections are written by well-known children's authors and are grouped by theme. Within a particular theme, such as The World We Share with Animals, there might be a range of genres including predictable texts, narratives, poems, and informational texts. Every child has a copy of the anthology. The basal series also has about 200 "leveled books" (see Chapter 7). These leveled books range from 6 to 20 pages each, and each is a complete text. The 200 leveled books span a continuum of reading difficulty, from books with very predictable texts to some with well-developed stories. These leveled books are leveled readers. Some stress particular phonics patterns and are decodable books. Other leveled readers stress the repetition of sight words, and still others have less vocabulary control but are tied to the theme of the unit. Leveled books provide practice in reading words with the phonics features or sight words under study. Jenna has six copies of each of the 200 leveled books.

In one corner of Jenna's classroom is the library. This inviting place contains an old sofa, pillows, a rug, a few plants, and, most of all, numerous books, magazines, and other reading material. Many books are displayed with their covers showing, as children are drawn more to those than to books with only their spines showing. Jenna frequently displays books related to the theme that is the focus in the basal reading anthology. In choosing books, she tries to include a wide range of reading levels to match the wide range of reading experiences among her students.

"Children do best when they feel secure," Jenna reports. "That's why routines and a daily schedule that become familiar to the children are very important." Jenna's morning schedule looks like this:

8:30–8:50   Book check-in, calendar, morning message
8:50–9:30   Theme-related whole-class activity

9:30–11:00   Centers: Reading, writing, and word study
11:00–11:20   Whole-class sharing of center activities
11:25   Lunch

Let's join Jenna for her morning reading/language arts period.

8:30   Book Check-In, Calendar, Morning Message

As children enter the classroom, they pass a bulletin board that has a chart on it with each of their names printed on an individual library pocket. Each book in the class library has a check-out pocket with a library card in it. When the children leave at the end of the school day, they check out one or two books by putting the library card from the back of the book into the pocket with their name on it on the bulletin board. When they first arrive the next morning, they retrieve the card and place it back into the book they took home before returning the book to the class library.

After checking in their books and putting their personal items in their cubbies, the children gather on a rug in front of the whiteboard and large calendar. Jenna first goes over the calendar and has them locate the date and day. The amount of time spent on this activity varies from day to day. They talk about the season, the weather, birthdays, and other special events.

Every day, Jenna prints a morning news message on chart paper. Jenna asks for volunteers who would like to tell what special things are happening at home, in their lives, or in the world. She writes what is said on the chalkboard under the heading *Morning News*. Since it is relatively early in the school year Jenna does most of the writing, but the children do participate. She asks the children how to spell individual words, what sound a word begins with, or what letter comes next. After the message is finished individual students are asked to come up to circle specific words, find particular sounds, or add a period that might be missing. The morning message allows Jenna to review many of the phonemic awareness, phonics, and writing concepts that have been taught. If there is time, she then has children share information about the books they checked out and read at home.

In addition to a vast selection of interesting reading materials, a classroom library should provide comfortable, inviting places to read.
Thinkstock

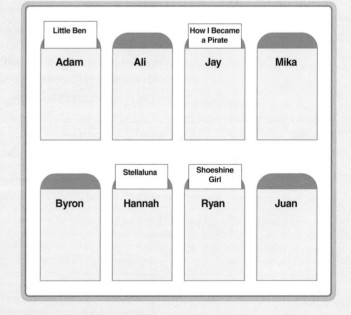

8:50   Theme-Related Whole-Class Activity

The theme for the next few weeks is Animals Who Share the World with Us, and this is the first day of the unit. Jenna likes to start her theme-related work with a whole-class activity that develops the children's knowledge about the theme. In prior conversations with us, she emphasized that she likes "to start with what children know." We see that is the case, as Jenna begins the session today by engaging the children in a discussion about animals they have seen. She makes a language chart on a large sheet of butcher paper. After a child says something, she records the child's name next to what he or she says. As she records their words, she often makes comments—such as why she used a capital letter. Here's part of the language chart:

Jamal	I saw a horse with a policeman on it in DC!
Malt	I have a gerbil at home.
Kara	My dog Nick is black and white.
Tyron	I saw a black-and-white zebra at the zoo.
Cynara	There are lots of deer in the woods and I saw some.

Jenna steers the discussion to where the different animals were seen, and to the environments in which different animals live. She brings out a large piece of butcher paper on which the class will start a wall chart. The paper is divided into sections, with the several headings printed across the top and room to the right to add additional ones, as shown below:

In the Water	On a Farm	In the Woods	In Our Homes	In the Jungle			
fish	horses	deer	dogs	monkeys			
	cows	raccoons	cats	giraffe			
		wolf					
		snake					
		owl					

Jenna starts by asking the children where the animals they have mentioned live, and she records their responses under the appropriate categories. There is some discussion about where zebras might live if they weren't in a zoo and where horses normally would be found.

Next, Jenna brings out a big book version of *Hoot Howl Hiss* by Michelle Koch. She points to the illustrations on the cover. "Michelle Koch is not only the author, she is also the illustrator of the book," she tells the children. "The watercolor illustrations of animals are painted a lot like you paint in our class! Can you name any of the animals you see on the cover and tell where you might find them?" Jenna points to the title words as she asks which animal says *hoot*, which one *howls*, and which one goes *hiss*. They add the words *wolf, snake,* and *owl* to the In the Woods column on the wall chart. Jenna particularly emphasizes the sounds in the word *snake* as she prints the word on the chart. Jenna tells the children that when they are in the writing center, they will draw some of these animals, write about them, and paste their creations on the wall chart.

Jenna asks the children to think about where each animal mentioned in the book lives as she begins to read, "Deep in the woods, owls . . . hoot . . ." She pauses before *hoot,* and several children correctly anticipate it. *Hoot Howl Hiss* is a short book with a very predictable structure. The illustrations help the children identify the animal words. When she finishes reading the book, Jenna asks the children about the sounds various animals make, as well as where they live.

9:30 Centers: Reading, Writing, Science, and Teacher/Word Study

There are four centers in Jenna's classroom: a reading center, a writing center, a science center, and a teacher or word study center where Jenna provides direct instruction. She groups children who need similar word-level instruction there. She randomly divides the rest of her class into groups that rotate through the reading, writing, and science centers. Most days, the children rotate through all four centers. If children finish a center activity before it is time for the next rotation, they are free to return to their desks and read from their anthologies, little books, or books from the library.

The reading center is the classroom library. In that center, the children can either read to a buddy or read independently. Sometimes they have assignments; sometimes they do free reading. During the animal unit, they will find lots of books about animals prominently displayed on the low table in the reading center. Jenna requires some accountability for the students' work at the reading center. At the beginning of the year they complete a simple reading log, recording the title and author of the book and then drawing a picture. As the students grow throughout the year they will write longer responses to their books.

In the writing center, the children draw and write. They can draw a picture of an animal, write its name, and then paste their drawing on the wall chart. Before they paste it, they need to discuss with one other child which environment the animal lives in and whether its name is correctly spelled. The children are encouraged to check the spellings and animal habitats by looking at books in the reading center. Jenna tells us that she encourages the children to use invented spelling in free writing, but when the time comes to make the writing public, she wants the words correctly spelled. She says that she doesn't want the children to reread incorrect spellings on a permanent basis—and she intends to make use of the wall chart throughout the unit.

The science center is used both to promote understanding of science as well as children's reading and writing of expository text. Right now the science center has 20 cups of radish seeds that are

Children use the Internet to find information on animals.
Shutterstock

149

growing in various media—soil, wet towels, sand, and so forth. The children are to observe the growing plants and take notes. They have already practiced drawing growing plans and writing short captions. Also at the science center are many science books—such as *From Seed to Plant* by Gail Gibbons and *The Reason for a Flower* by Ruth Heller. The science center enables the teacher and students to continue a unit of study that began 2 weeks ago even though they have now moved on to the study of animals.

Each group that comes to the teacher/word study center will participate in different types of phonics instruction. The particular focus of the phonics instruction depends on the needs of students. One group of children is working on initial consonants, another on the consonant digraphs *ch* and *wh,* and a third group on short vowels. The basic format for each group, however, is the same. Jenna begins each group by having the children chorally read *Hoot Howl Hiss.* The focus then shifts to a word or two in that story that contains the phonics feature under study. The consonant digraph group, for example, will focus on the words *chirp* and *whistle.*

After locating words with the phonic features in *Hoot Howl Hiss,* Jenna extends the phonics instruction to other words. This extension often involves four activities (described in Chapter 7):

- *Sorting* picture or word cards
- *Blending* and reading new words with new phonics patterns
- *Reading* a leveled book that contains several words with the phonics features
- *Writing* a dictated sentence with words that contain the target spelling pattern

Sorting

To develop phonemic awareness of initial consonant sounds, Jenna has the children do a group picture sort on a pocket chart. She calls out the name of a picture, and they help her place it under one of the word card headings *howl, lion,* and *quack.* She holds up a drawing of a hen and says "Hen, howl—hen, lion—hen, quack." The children agree that the hen picture belongs under *howl.* Then she takes out a drawing of a leg and says, "Hen, leg—lion, leg—quack, leg." The group continues in this manner with pictures of a queen, quilt, horse, and hat as well as pictures representing other words from *Hoot Howl Hiss.*

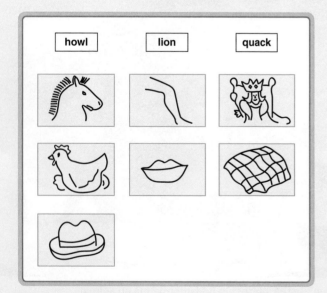

Blending

After the students have sorted words it is important to try out their new letter-sound associations on other words. Sometimes this work is simply practice using the small whiteboard or a hand made flit chart. The teacher writes the word family pattern on the whiteboard—*at,* for example—and then changes the initial sound—*h + at* makes *hat; s + at* makes *sat.* The teacher first models the blending activity and then guides the students through it with a sliding hand gesture. Each group of students will practice making and blending words. Sometimes this will involve the use of letter tiles, other times the students will write the words on their personal whiteboards, and still other times the students will play a blending game.

Reading

To provide reading practice with the newly introduced initial consonant combination *qu*, Jenna uses a leveled book entitled *Quack!* by Matthew Benjamin. She gives each child a copy. "Can you read the word on the cover?" she asks. "The ducks are a good clue!" She has the children point to the letters that say /kw/ in *quack*. She tells the children that *Quack!* is about a mother duck and her three ducklings. Jenna reads the story as the children follow along, finger-pointing to the words as she says them. Then they all read it aloud together. After this rereading, Jenna asks them to go through the book on a word hunt. They are to find all the words that start with *qu* and read them to the child sitting next to them. There are lots of shouts of "Quack!" and "Quick!" and "Quiet!" as they locate these words in the story. Finally, all the students practice reading the story independently.

Jenna LeBlanc always provides time for children to share their favorite books with the class.

Richard Hutchings/PhotoEdit

Writing

To end this word study session, Jenna reads simple sentences and has the children write them. She will later examine what each child has written to see which children might need some extra help. She is particularly interested in their spellings of the initial consonants. She hands out a piece of lined paper and tells them to write as best they can *Ducks quack. Lions roar. I hoot.* Here's what a few children wrote:

Wu	Dks quak. Lins r. I ht.
Kara	Duks quak. Lions rar. I hut.
Dustin	DS QUK LN RR I HT
Jamal	Duks quack. Lions ror. I hoot.

 Whole-Class Sharing of Center Activities

The class gathers back on the rug in front of the calendar. Children bring with them any books they would like to share. Jenna begins by asking them to quack like a duck. Then she turns to the In the Water portion of the wall chart and asks if anyone put a duck up there. Several hands go up, and she has each child go over and point to his or her duck. She then asks for other children who drew animals that live in the water to come up and identify their pictures. There's a sea turtle and a whale among the group. Jenna does the same for the other categories.

With only a few minutes remaining until lunch, not everyone who has a book to share gets a chance to do so. But there's always tomorrow, and Jenna will make sure that any student who didn't get a turn today will get one the next day. Additionally, Jenna looks forward to the afternoon, when she and her students will be able to put their budding literacy skills to use in other curricular areas—science, math, social studies, art, and music.

6

Emergent Literacy

Lee awakened to find her favorite stuffed animal lying next to her—a teddy bear named Pooh after the character in *Winnie the Pooh*. At breakfast, Lee's mother asked her if she could read the letters on her cereal box to Pooh. After breakfast, Lee scurried off to watch "Sesame Street," naming the letters she saw on the screen to Pooh. Later that morning, Lee went to the grocery store with her mom, showing off her letter knowledge by naming print as they wheeled around the store and by helping her mom check off items on the shopping list.

On the way home, Lee was dropped off at an afternoon kindergarten. She put her gear in a cubby with her name above it. She noticed her name, too, on the list of helpers for the day. After settling in, the children gathered around their teacher to hear her read a folktale. Afterward, she asked the children to recall all the characters they could. As they named them, she put a picture of each character on a feltboard. Then she had the children help her retell the story, putting up the characters as they appeared in the story. When necessary, she prompted the children with questions such as "Then who came along?" If they weren't sure, she opened up the book and asked them to check.

At home again, Lee was eager to retell the folk tale. She told it first to her older sister and then to her mom and dad. As she snuggled into bed with Pooh, her dad began reading from James Marshall's retelling of *The Three Little Pigs*. "Once upon a time an old sow sent her three little pigs . . ."

From the time she awoke until the time she was tucked into bed at night, Lee's day was filled with literacy experiences and opportunities to learn about language.

CLASSROOM vignette

Emergent literacy refers to "the reading and writing behaviors that precede and develop into conventional literacy," and when we talk about emergent literacy, we are ascribing legitimacy to "the earliest literacy concepts and behaviors of children and to the varieties of social context in which children become literate" (Sulzby & Teale, 1996). In other words, emergent readers are children who are in the process of learning what reading and writing are for and how to read and write.

For many children these first steps begin at home and are refined in preschool and kindergarten. For some children, those that depend on school to learn to read and write, emergent literacy happens only at school. For all children, emergent literacy is a time of many discoveries about sounds of language, the forms of words, and purposes of books. In the process the child begins to learn how to recognize and spell words while exploring the alphabetic system. The child begins to learn about books and how they are structured and to gain information and enjoy stories. Finally, the child begins a journey of understanding, learning how to comprehend and produce written language.

Children enter school with wide differences both in their exposure to text and in what they know about text. Some kindergartners know the alphabet; some know the sounds the letters make and can reproduce letters or even write a few words. Some have been read to extensively, as Lee has, and understand the basic structure of stories, but many have not. Some children enter first grade as readers, but most do not. Most children in preschool, kindergarten, and first-grade classrooms will need considerable help from you to become competent and independent readers.

In this chapter we will begin by exploring how children's first understandings about reading and writing develop. Next, we will discuss many types of activities that support and encourage the emergence of literacy. Finally, we will take you into one kindergarten classroom and explain how all of these factors are put together. Throughout this chapter we will take a balanced approach. In many cases the children are encouraged to make discoveries about print and language, but often the teacher must directly and explicitly explain things to her students.

Emerging Knowledge About Word Structure

A typical class of entering first-graders, asked what they expect to learn in school that year, will almost always respond that they will learn to read. Despite high motivation and expectations, however, some children will experience considerable difficulty, frustration, and an early loss of self-esteem in the process of learning to read. Why does this happen?

Take a look at the following list of factors that predict children's success as readers (Share, Jorm, Maclean, & Matthews, 1984). Which ones do you think are the most important predictors?

- Phoneme segmentation ability (the ability to tell you the first sound of a spoken word, for example)
- Knowledge of letter names
- Kindergarten teacher's predictions of reading success in first grade
- Performance on the Peabody Picture Vocabulary Test (a measure of oral English vocabulary)

- Parents' occupational status
- Library membership
- Number of books the child owns
- Amount that parents read to the child
- Gender
- Amount that parents read themselves in their spare time
- Whether the child attended preschool

You may be surprised to learn that these factors are listed in the exact order in which they predicted the end-of-year reading ability of more than 500 Australian first-graders. The top two predictors (phonemic segmentation ability and knowledge of letter names) were significantly stronger than the others. No matter how much a child has been read to, then, that child must be able to *independently* identify many printed words in order to read on his own.

First-grade teacher Glenna Schwarze knows that reading independence means making sure her students get instruction in decoding skills:

> I am sure any first-grade teacher will tell you the same thing: At the heart of first-grade reading instruction is ensuring that children learn to decode words. Of course, we want children to be able to instantly recognize as many words as possible, but we also need to be sure they are equipped with strategies and skills to use when they don't instantly know a word. The beginning reader, of course, cannot instantly recognize many words. As teachers, however, we can help children identify words they don't know by helping them recognize the letters in the words and how to translate those letters into the sounds they represent.
>
> —Glenna Schwarze, first-grade teacher

Children need to acquire two insights about language in order to become successful readers: the alphabetic principle and phonemic awareness (Snow, Burns, & Griffin, 1998). The alphabetic principle is the insight that spoken sounds can be represented by written letters. Phonemic awareness is the insight that spoken words are made up of a sequence of somewhat separable sounds, called *phonemes*. Children who have been read to have frequently heard the sounds in spoken words linked to printed words and letters, and this has helped them understand the alphabetic principle and gain phonemic awareness. They may, for example, have attended to the sounds in the rhymes of Dr. Seuss's *There's a Wocket in My Pocket* and laughed at the silly sounds made by a change in the initial phoneme. Children who can take the next step and make this change themselves—transforming *basket* into *wasket*, for example—provide further evidence of phonemic awareness. Alliteration—the repetition of initial consonant sounds used in many nursery rhymes—also focuses attention on phonemes. In the Classroom 6.1 shows how one teacher helps his kindergartners make phonemic connections.

Mr. Felton emphasizes phonemic segmentation and alphabetic awareness in this lesson by reading aloud to his class. He realizes, as research suggests, that the potential for predicting success in reading based on a child's ability in phonemic segmentation and alphabetic awareness is not so straightforward; in fact, these two skills most likely have their origins in having been read to as a young child. So the importance of parents' reading to children, which appears fairly far down the list of predictors, is actually significantly higher than it might seem. In a British study that followed a group of children from ages 3 to 5, researchers found that children's knowledge of nursery rhymes at age 3 was closely related to their ability to perceive and produce rhyme and alliteration as well as to recognize letters and some simple words (Maclean, Bryant, & Bradley, 1988). In other words, children who had experienced a lot of nursery rhymes

Kindergartners and the P Words

Mr. Felton's kindergartners, sitting in a semicircle on the floor, look quizzically at a large chart he has put on a stand. It is a poem that he has printed in large letters with a black felt pen.

"This is a poem, boys and girls," he tells them. "It's from a favorite book of mine called *Whiskers and Rhymes* by Arnold Lobel." He holds up his copy of the book.

"The poem is about a cat named George, who brushes his teeth!"

The children giggle.

"But guess what George uses for toothpaste? Pickle paste!"

The children roar with laughter as they consider toothpaste made from pickles.

Mr. Felton invites the children to come up and take a look at the book and the three pictures that accompany the poem. First, George squeezes a toothpaste tube labeled "Pickle Paste" onto his toothbrush. Second, he brushes his teeth, and green foam emerges from his mouth. Third, George smiles a big green-teeth smile. When the children sit back down, Mr. Felton reads the poem from the chart, pointing to each word as he reads.

Then Mr. Felton asks the children to find the letter *p* in the words. A child comes up and points to the *p* in *pickle*, and another child points to the *p* in *paste*.

Mr. Felton asks, "Which letter in *pickle* makes it say /p/?"

The children respond, "*p*."

He asks, "Which letter in *paste* makes it say /p/?"

The children respond, "*p*."

Mr. Felton says, "The letter *p* says /p/," emphasizing the /p/ as he says "pickle paste."

The children can't help giggling as they say "pickle paste" over and over.

Next, Mr. Felton shows the children a large tube of toothpaste cut out of construction paper—just like the one George had. It has "Pickle Paste" printed on the tube.

Mr. Felton asks the children if they can spot some other *p* words in the room to write on the tube. The children glance around at the books on the chalkboard ledge, most of which Mr. Felton has read to them. They find the *ps* in the title of Dr. Seuss's *Hop on Pop*, James Marshall's *The Three Little Pigs*, and Eve Rice's *Peter's Pockets*.

Mr. Felton carefully prints the following words on the tube as he emphasizes and underlines the letter *p*: *pig, Peter, pocket, hop, pop*. He then tells the children he is going to name some colors, and they should say "pickle" if they hear a /p/. He emphasizes putting his lips together as he pronounces the /p/ in this list of words: *pink, red, green, purple*. Following some discussion, Mr. Felton adds *pink* and *purple* to the tube. He tacks the tube to the wall for future reference and the addition of new words.

at an early age were better equipped with exactly the knowledge and understanding that enhance learning to read in school. It is not just nursery rhymes; children with larger vocabularies and more language experiences acquire phonemic awareness more easily (Snow, Burns, & Griffin, 1998).

Assessment

Marie Clay developed an assessment called the Concepts of Print Test to determine what young children know about words and books. You can find it in M. Clay (1993), *An Observation Study of Early Literacy Achievement* (Portsmouth, NH: Heinemann).

Phonemic Awareness and Alphabet Recognition

Of the two competencies we discuss here, alphabet recognition is the more straightforward: Students need to recognize letters and their distinguishing features in order to work effectively with print. Learning the names of letters is very useful. We discuss alphabet recognition more thoroughly in Chapter 7.

Phonemic awareness is a more complex matter. Although it is a competency that you mastered long ago, you are probably not familiar with the concept. Yet it is astonishingly important to the process of successfully learning to read. In a longitudinal study of learning to read and write in an elementary school in Austin, Texas, one of us found that development of phonemic awareness early in first grade was critical to children's successfully learning to read and write in first grade (Juel, 1988, 1994; Juel, Griffith, & Gough, 1986). As children learn to read, they also grow in phonemic awareness, but they have an easier time of learning to read if they rapidly develop this proficiency (Bruck & Treiman, 1992; Ehri & Robbins, 1992; Vandervelden & Siegel, 1995). That is, children need to perceive words as sequences of phonemes and link those phonemes to letters to begin reading words more efficiently. As Snow and colleagues (1998) note, "The theoretical and practical importance of phonemic awareness for the beginning reader relies not only on logic but also on the results of several decades of empirical research."

What Is Phonemic Awareness?

Phonemic awareness is the insight that spoken words are composed of somewhat separable sounds—sounds that can be played with (*dilly dilly silly Willy*), rearranged (*Connie Juel* becomes *Johnny Cool*), alliterated (*teeny tiny Tina*), and even used to create alternative languages (like pig Latin). Phonemic awareness is not synonymous with phonics; it is not knowledge about which letters represent particular sounds. Rather, it is an insight about speech—an attention to the sounds (phonemes) that reside within words. These sounds correspond to letters, but only roughly. For example, there are three phonemes in *cap*, but there are also three phonemes in *cape* and *shake*. Perceiving words as sequences of phonemes is important in learning to read and write because the link between phonemes and letters is the basis for alphabetic writing systems such as English and Spanish. Keep in mind that a child can be aware of phonemes yet still not recognize a single letter of the alphabet. Phonemic awareness is an awareness of the *sounds* of language; it is not a part of learning to understand or speak oral language.

Understanding phonemes is complicated by the fact that we rarely say them separately; instead, they run together. In speech, we actually begin forming our mouths to pronounce the upcoming phoneme as we are still saying the previous one. For example, in saying *cat*, we begin saying the /ă/ before we finish the /k/. It is almost impossible to say some phonemes in isolation. That is, it is almost impossible to say either the /k/ or /t/ in *cat* without adding a vowel sound, such as /ə/. It is this overlapping, called *coarticulation,* of phonemes that allows our rapid speech. But it is exactly this coarticulation that makes learning to read words so hard. A letter in a printed word does not map onto one clear, distinct sound.

Phonemic awareness does not come naturally. Achieving it demands that a child attend to the form, rather than the meaning, of speech. This is difficult because our natural inclination is to attend to meaning. Thus, even those children who arrive at school with well-developed oral language may not have developed phonemic awareness. Phonemic awareness is not necessary for speaking or for listening, but it is vital to reading. Teaching phonemic awareness is thus sometimes quite difficult. Some children will need a good deal of assistance in gaining this abstract understanding. Fortunately, however, research very strongly indicates that phonemic awareness can be taught (National Reading Panel, 2000). In the Classroom 6.2 lists standards for phonemic awareness for kindergarten children.

In the Classroom

6.2

Phonemic Awareness (Segmenting and Blending Sounds)

In kindergarten, teachers should evaluate whether children are developing phonemic awareness. By the end of kindergarten, children should be able to

- Produce rhyming words and recognize pairs of rhyming words.
- Isolate initial consonants in single-syllable words (for example, /t/ is the first sound in *top*).
- Identify the onset (/c/) and rime (-*at*) and begin to fully separate the sounds (/c/-/a/-/t/) by saying each sound aloud when a single-syllable word is pronounced (for example, *cat*).
- Blend onsets (/c/) and rimes (-*at*) to form words (*cat*) and slowly blend phonemes to make a word (for example, when the teacher says a word slowly, stretching it out as "mmm–ahhh–mmm," children can recognize that the word being stretched out is *mom*).

PEARSON
myeducationlab

Watch the video showing a kindergarten teacher working with a small group on beginning sounds in the activity "Teaching Phonemic Awareness to Young Children." (To find this activity, go to the topic *Phonemic Awareness/Phonics* in MyEducationLab and click on Assignments and Activities.)

Why Do Phonemic Awareness and Alphabet Recognition So Strongly Predict Success in Reading?

Children must unlock the relationships between the sounds they use to say words and the letters they use in reading and writing words. In English, consonants are the easiest phonemes to perceive in spoken words. Children often represent consonants before representing vowels when they begin writing English. A child trying to spell *dog,* for example, tries to connect the phonemes he perceives to the actual letters. Initially, *dog* may be represented by just *D,* since the initial consonant is often the easiest for a child to attend to and attach to a letter. Later, this child may spell it *DG* because he feels these two consonants in his mouth as he says the word. Still later, he may spell it *DAG.* These early spellings are called invented or temporary spelling and are perfectly natural for young children. This type of writing goes hand in hand with development of phonemic awareness (Juel, 2006). In stretching out *dog* (for example, *ddawg, dawguh, dawg),* a child notes changes in the tongue position, the lip movements, and how much the mouth opens as sounds are uttered. This feeling of sounds in the mouth is apparent to anyone watching young children as they write unknown words. Children literally move their mouths and exaggerate sounds as they try to link them to letters. In that parsing of sounds in the mouth, phonemes become more real because they are felt: The tongue pressed on the ridge in the mouth behind the front teeth and the brief holding of air on making the /d/ help children notice the sound of the letter *d.*

At the beginning of first grade, invented spelling plays an important role in Kay Hollenbeck's first-grade classroom, as she explains here:

Having the freedom to use invented spelling is essential for my first-graders. It allows them to be writers from day one. We call it "sound spelling" because they write words the way they think they sound, using the letters they know. This is a big accomplishment for them, and they are proud that they can "write" any word they can say.

For example, yesterday Mara wrote *Tuda iz mi brda i m 6.* When I read the words back to her—"Today is my birthday; I am six"—her face beamed; she was delighted that I could actually read what she had intended to say. I knew what she had written, both because she had chosen letters that approximated the sounds in the words she intended and also because I was able to use context clues. I knew it was her birthday, and the picture she had drawn was a give-away, too—a girl and a birthday cake with six candles! Although Mara was thrilled that I knew her exact words, she also was concerned that she hadn't "spelled the words right." So she asked me to "write them the *right* way." Which I did, of course, in her "word book"—a little booklet of pages stapled together

158

Chapter Six Emergent Literacy

that students keep on hand for me to write words they request. There is one page for each letter of the alphabet.

—Kay Hollenbeck, first-grade teacher

Of course, children like Mara will need to understand the connections between the approximately 44 phonemes of spoken English and the 26 letters that we use to represent them. This is one of the key tasks of learning to read, and it is not easy. As we all know, the English writing system does not reflect a consistent one-to-one relationship between letters and sounds; this is particularly true with vowel sounds. However—and this is a key point—words contain enough predictable correspondences to at least aid in identification or spelling. In identifying the "irregular" word *come*, for example, the letters *c, m,* and the silent *e* reliably represent certain sounds. A child who can figure out which sounds these letters are likely to represent has a powerful tool for recognizing words, whereas the child who cannot figure out letter-sound correspondences will often be stumped when he comes to a word he has not previously learned to read.

REFLECT and *Apply*

1. In her comment about empowering students to become independent readers, first-grade teacher Glenna Schwarze emphasizes that students need both decoding skills and the ability to instantly recognize many words. In your own words, explain why both of these skills are necessary.

2. Suppose you were reading a simple storybook to a kindergarten student and wanted to help him develop phonemic awareness. Describe three things you could do. (You can learn more from this activity if you focus on a particular storybook and give specific examples of what you might point out and questions you might ask.)

Learning to Spell and Identify Words

Children learn to identify words both through their own attempts to map sounds coming out of their mouth to letters in printed words and by receiving assistance and instruction from teachers and other knowledgeable adults. Here we first describe some of children's early understandings and then consider how they learn to connect letters and phonemes.

Some Early Understandings About Print

Children begin to read and write before they can identify or write all the letters of the alphabet and before they have developed phonemic awareness. Often, the first word children learn is their own name. Diane, for example, was 4 years old when her mother, a university student, came to the office of one of the authors. To keep her busy during the meeting, her mom handed Diane her notebook. Diane slowly and laboriously wrote her name and then wrote the message shown in Figure 6.1.

When Diane was finished, her mother asked her to tell what the message said and to also say the letters in her name. She easily told the message. It was about what she and her mom were going to do after they left the office—though she did not look at her paper as she "read" the message. However, Diane was unable to name any but the first letter, the *D*, in her name.

Diane treated her name as a visual unit, without distinguishing and naming individual letters as components. Quite frequently, the first letters children learn are those in their own names. Certainly, writing your name is an important step in declaring your identity (Bloodgood, 1999). Diane does know a lot about print. She knows that it moves left to right across the page, and there were clearly letterlike forms in her

Figure 6.1

Diane's Note

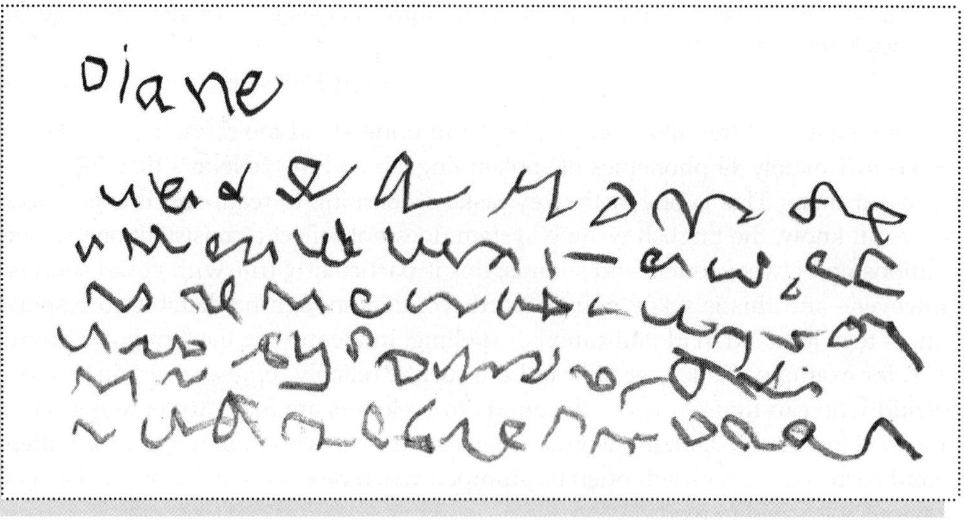

Diane

Figure 6.2 Jake's Drawing

writing. Still, it was real work for her to write her name because she had to remember its visual form without fully understanding that it is composed of individual letters with particular shapes and names. At this point, the letter *d* is not linked to the sound /d/, the letter *i* is not connected to a long *i* sound, and so on.

As children learn letterlike forms, these forms frequently start to creep onto the pages of their drawings. In Figure 6.2 another emergent reader, 5-year-old Jake, has drawn himself doing karate. Even an initial inspection of Jake's drawing makes it evident that he has reached a profound milestone in learning. He understands that the sounds that come out of his mouth as he speaks can be linked to letters, an important discovery about the alphabetic principle. The speech bubble coming out of Jake's mouth contains the letters *a* and *e*, which he says make the sounds he makes as he does a karate chop. This shows some fairly advanced understanding of letters and sounds.

Note that Jake's reversal of letters in his name does not indicate a problem; it simply illustrates that Jake perceives his name as a single visual unit. At this stage of development, Jake does not experience directionality as a relevant characteristic of his world. Until children begin working with print, virtually each thing they experience and learn to name retains the same name, regardless of the way it might be facing. Jake is still Jake whether he stands on his head or his feet. His dog is a dog whether he is coming or going.

Only in writing is this principle violated. Jake will catch on to the importance of directionality in writing as he writes and reads more. Also, once Jake learns the names of the letters, his task will become

Using Letter Puppets to Help Children Understand the Connection Between Phonemes and Letters

In the Classroom

6.3

Instructional Routines

Purpose: To give students practice and feedback in recognizing the initial sound in a word and the letter that represents that sound.

Procedure:

- Purchase or make a set of puppets with alliterative names such as Pink Pig, Red Rooster, Jumping Jerod, Nice Nora, Mad Mike, and so on.
- Put on one of the hand puppets, such as Pink Pig, which has a big letter *P* on it. Introduce the children to it, saying "Pink Pig only likes things that start with a /p/, like her name, Pink Pig." Emphasize the /p/ as you talk, and point out the letter *P*.
- Walk around the room and ask the children what Pink Pig likes as the puppet touches the object. For example, "Does Pink Pig like pencils? Does Pink Pig like Peter? Does Pink Pig like Pasha? Does Pink Pig like red?" and so on.
- After you have touched several objects and the children have responded, ask, "What do you think is Pink Pig's favorite letter of the alphabet?"
- Students can take turns wearing the puppet and asking the same questions, and other puppets can be used to give practice with additional letters.

easier. When he knows that his name is made of the letter sequence *J-a-k-e*, he will find the spelling of his name easier to recall and to write.

In the Classroom 6.3 describes an activity that will help children like Jake further their understanding of letters and sounds.

Connecting Letters and Phonemes: The Alphabetic Principle

The New Standards Primary Literacy Committee (1999) and most state standards today recommend that children segment words into phonemes and know the letters of the alphabet and their corresponding sounds by the time they leave kindergarten. What is important is not so much how many letters and sounds the child knows, but rather the *idea* that letters represent sounds. Yet in many schools, children are expected to know all letter-sounds by the end of kindergarten.

Once children learn letter names and possess some degree of phonemic awareness, they frequently use the names of letters to help them recall and spell words. They may be particularly dependent on the names of initial consonants for word recall. The name of the letter *b* is the sound of the word *bee*, and the name of the letter *j* is part of the sound of the word *Jake*, for example, and this overlap may help children identify these words when they see them in a text (Ehri & Robbins, 1992).

In writing words, children often use letters whose names represent the sounds that they perceive in the words. At first, they may represent only the initial consonant or the most distinctive sound (for example, *b* written for *bee* or *l* for *elephant*). Even this level of processing represents a remarkable advance in understanding. To do this, children need both some phonemic awareness—to perceive the sounds represented by *b* or *l*—and knowledge of the alphabet. When children use this knowledge to spell, the result is invented or temporary spelling. These terms describe young children's attempts to spell words using their limited knowledge about letters and sounds. In the previous section, Diane engaged in invented writing, as do children who write

161

Phonemic Awareness and Alphabet Recognition

Figure 6.3

Jordan's Writing

Im in KinDrGrDin and mi Botr Kirk, is in tthD GrD and mi Botr Tom IS in TTh7 are 8ThT GraD.

byJordan

entirely random strings of letters (for example, *czfdyxsy* for *this is my blue umbrella*). Invented spelling is a more sophisticated accomplishment.

The invented spelling of 5-year-old Jordan, displayed in Figure 6.3, shows how much this emergent reader has already learned about the code of written English. Jordan has encountered some common words frequently enough to have memorized their correct spelling (for example, *Jordan, and, in,* and *is*). He uses the sounds conveyed in the letter names in his spellings (for example, *im*). He more frequently represents consonants than vowels (for example, *kindrgrdin* and *grd*). He is actively working to link the phonemes he perceives to actual letters. For example, on one occasion he writes *grade* as *grd,* whereas on another he writes it as *grod,* adding a letter representing a vowel sound. He will on occasion reverse a letter or number; however, as with Jake, this is not a concern. Jordan is not yet consistently writing silent letters. To do so requires considerable knowledge of within-word spelling patterns (Henderson, 1990). To acquire such knowledge, a child must have engaged in rather extensive reading, and for many children these spelling patterns must be isolated, explained, and discussed. Silent letters must be noticed, and often explained, to be learned. One of the most common within-word spelling patterns is the silent *e* marker, as in *grade.* As Jordan reads more, he will start to notice these patterns. Jordan is likely to progress from *grd* to *grad* to *grade* in writing *grade.* Notice that Jordan spells the last syllable in *kindergarten* with *in.* Jordan is from Texas, where *en* is pronounced /ĭn/. In many regions of the United States, both *em* and *en* receive short *i* pronunciations. That is, words like *pin* and *pen, tin* and *ten,* and *Jim* and *gem* have identical pronunciations. Sensitivity to dialect is important as we evaluate children's speech and invented spellings to plan instruction.

PEARSON
myeducationlab

Analyze two pieces of writing for evidence of emergent understandings about the functions of print in the exercise "Understanding Emergent Literacy Behaviors." (To find this activity, go to the topic *Emergent Literacy* in MyEducationLab and click on Assignments and Activities.)

REFLECT and *Apply*

3 One of us (Juel et al., 1986) once asked some first-grade children to read the word *rain.* Here are the replies of 14 of the children: "ring," "in," "runs," "with," "ride," "art," "are," "on," "reds," "running," "why," "ran," "ran," "ran." We also asked these 14 children to spell the word *rain,* and here are their spellings: *rach, in, yes, uan, ramt, fen, rur, Rambl, wetn, wnishire,* drawing of raindrops, *Rup, ran, ran.* Consider what understandings are suggested by each spelling and reading of *rain.* Also consider what each child needs to learn to progress. Two other first-grade children correctly read the word, but one spelled it *raine* and

another spelled it *rane*. What can you say about these two children's understanding of the code of printed English?

4 Explain the progress in perceiving words as sequences of sounds and connecting those sounds to letters, as well as learning common spelling patterns, that a child is making as his spelling of *rain* moves from *R* to *RAN* to *RANE* to *RAIN*.

Emerging Knowledge About Comprehension and Text Structure

As children learn about words and the alphabetic principle they are also exploring comprehension and the process of constructing meaning. They have much to learn. Children who come from homes where they have been read a variety of books will understand the purpose of print and how books work. They will understand that print conveys information and enjoyment, an escape to the world of stories. They will understand that we read from left to right, that we turn the pages, and that the print conveys the ideas and pictures provide support. Over years of reading the young child may discern the boundaries between words and even begin to recognize a few words and letters. Shirley Brice Heath (1983) has found that children from middle-class homes may have had over 1,000 hours of experiences with print, whereas children from economically disadvantaged homes will have experienced only 50 hours of oral reading experience with a parent or another adult.

Comprehension Acquisition

When children are read to, they acquire some awareness of the process of reading comprehension (Smolkin & Donovan, 2002). Instructive adult readers will reveal the process of text comprehension as they read. Adults will stop to share the pictures, ask questions, point out important ideas, note comprehension problems, and reread to clarify misunderstanding. They will invite the child to enter into the process and encourage questioning and commentary. All of these behaviors during an interactive read-aloud school the child in cognitive actions of a reader. The adult, parent, or teacher is not specifically teaching comprehension, but making the child aware that comprehension is a meaning-seeking process. Consider this interaction between a teacher and a child reading Tomie dePaola's *The Popcorn Book*. In this mixed-genre book, part of the book tells the story of two brothers making popcorn and the other half of the book presents information on the history of popcorn. The underlined portion in the following example is the actual text.

Teacher: <u>In 1612, French explorers saw some Iroquois people popping corn in clay pots. They would fill the pots with hot sand, throw in some popcorn and stir it with a stick. When the corn popped, it came to the top of the sand and made it easy to get.</u>

Child: Look at the bowl!

Teacher (providing an oral commentary on the "story"): Okay, now it's hot enough [for the brothers} to add a few kernels.

Child 1: What's a kernel?

Child 2: Like what you pop.

Child 3: It's a seed.

Interactive Read-Alouds

The interactive read-aloud is an excellent way to build the vocabulary knowledge of English language learners. During the interactive read-aloud, the students and the teacher discuss the story and the words. The pictures provide support for students to learn the words, and the discussion helps the students to pronounce them and clarify the meaning. Pick a book, fiction or nonfiction, that has five to eight important vocabulary words. Make these words the focus on your reading and the discussion. We suggest that you follow a 3-day plan: first focus on vocabulary, then comprehension, and then both.

Day 1. Read the book and stop at particular pages to discuss the particular vocabulary words. Ask follow-up questions after reading the story. Add words to a chart. After you write the words on a chart, adding pictures will help ELL students learn and use these new English words.

Day 2. Read the book without stopping. Afterward, ask questions about target words in the book and refer to pages on which the words appeared. At the end, ask follow-up questions.

Day 3. Do not read the book, but ask targeted questions about the vocabulary words in the book.

Many of the books in the bibliography at the end of the chapter are suitable for an interactive read-aloud.

Child 3: What if you, like, would you think [of] popcorn seed? Like a popcorn seed. Could you grow popcorn?

Teacher: Oh, excellent question. Let's read and we'll see if this [book] answers that question, and if not, we'll talk about it at the end. (Smolkin & Donovan, 2002, pp. 145–146)

In this interaction the child poses a question and the teacher acknowledges the value of the question. The teacher instructs the student in how to answer the question—"Let's read." This construction of meaning, shared by the teacher and the students, helps the students understand the importance of actively asking questions and seeking answers by reading further in the text. This is just one of the several cognitive acts or strategies that teachers can model and students can try out during an interactive read-aloud. In addition to questioning, the reader can activate prior knowledge, monitor comprehension and fix up misunderstandings (although in this example the child was doing the monitoring), generate questions, draw inferences, make connections, create mental images, use knowledge of text structures, and summarize. Although the children are not yet using these strategies independently, the interactive read-aloud is laying the foundation for future direct instruction in comprehension strategies.

Text Structure Knowledge

The interactive read-aloud experience also builds knowledge of the world and of text structure in particular. The more prior knowledge you have about a topic, the easier it is to comprehend a text about it. This is equally true of text structures. When you read a recipe, for example, you anticipate that it will begin with a list of ingredients and that directions will follow in a step-by-step format. You also know that you should probably read the whole recipe before you begin, so that you can estimate the time it will take and be familiar with the ingredients you will need. You have a schema for recipes that allows you not only to comprehend what you are reading but also to write a recipe that others could follow.

Children who have been read to extensively have probably developed a similar schema for how stories like the ones they will encounter in school are put together. They can demonstrate this knowledge if asked. The stories they tell will imitate the stories they have heard; they will generally have a central character who must overcome an obstacle of some sort, and the resolution of that problem will generally develop through a chronological sequence of events. They know, for example, that the wolf is hungry and will blow down the houses of the three little pigs to get food—or, if they have been read a different version, that the pigs will succeed in protecting one or more of their houses from the wolf.

But whether or not children have been read to before they arrive at school, you can provide experiences to help them understand the structures of texts and greatly increase their chances of becoming proficient readers. You can read to them in the classroom, and you can provide opportunities for them to understand story structure at the same time that they grow in vocabulary, ideas, imagination, and love of language and stories. In the Classroom 6.4 shows how one teacher does this in her kindergarten classroom.

Making up stories for wordless picture books helps young children understand the structure of text.

Laima Druskis/Pearson Education

Instruction That Facilitates Children's Growing Literacy

"Mrs. Cooper, you're going to teach us how to read, aren't you?" 6-year-old María asked.

Like María, most youngsters are eager to learn to read. That puts teachers of young children in an enviable position. Fortunately, there are many ways you can assist these eager learners in understanding the organization of text and the structure of words, developing phonemic awareness, and learning to identify words, all the while nurturing their interest, excitement, and desire to become readers.

Creating a Literate Environment

The starting point in fostering children's emerging literacy is to create a language-rich environment as described in Chapter 3—a classroom that abounds with opportunities to read, write, listen, and talk. A language-rich classroom includes

- Walls filled with posters, signs, labels, and student work.
- A reading center with a library chock-full of books, comfortable chairs, pillows, stuffed animals, a rug, and anything else that will make it an enticing and secure spot for young readers.

Using Wordless Picture Books in a Kindergarten Classroom

Seated in a chair with her kindergartners gathered comfortably around her on the carpeted floor, Mrs. Willey displays a copy of the mostly wordless picture book *Have You Seen My Duckling?* by Nancy Tafuri. Mrs. Willey tells the children that they are going to help make up a story about a mother duck who has lost her ducklings.

Mrs. Willey asks the children to close their eyes. "Think about the baby duck, a duckling we call it, that you just saw. Try to imagine what it feels like to be a duckling, to be so new, so small. What do you see? Now, open your eyes. Tell me, what did you see?"

"Grass!"

"Bugs!"

The children take turns suggesting what the world might look like from the perspective of a baby duck.

Next, Mrs. Willey has the children point to the mother duck on the cover illustration and count her ducklings. She opens the book and has them notice what happens on the opening page.

"There are eight ducklings in a nest. But one of them is climbing out!" Tamara volunteers.

Mrs. Willey smiles and turns the page. "Early one morning . . . ," she begins, and then she stops and asks, "What happens?"

Jason replies, "Early one morning, eight baby ducks got up."

"Ducklings!" Tamara corrects him.

"Well, okay, ducklings," Jason says. "They saw a butterfly, and one duckling got into the water and tried to swim after it."

"Then what happens?" asks Mrs. Willey, as she flips the page to uncover new illustrations.

Mrs. Willey continues to call on different children, who add to the story by considering the upcoming illustrations, their own imaginations, and their knowledge of stories, mothers, children, and ducks.

After Mrs. Willey and her kindergartners complete making up a story for *Have You Seen My Duckling?* the children divide into groups, and each group goes to one of three classroom centers. In one center, the children have a few additional copies of the book. Here they each get a chance to retell the story to a buddy.

In the art center, there are some black-and-white drawings of a duck and eight ducklings. The children cut out the drawings, color them in, and paste each one on a tongue depressor to serve as a puppet. Then they retell the story to each other, using their puppets to act it out.

In the library center are several wordless picture books, including *Do Not Disturb* and *Early Morning in the Barn*, two other books by Nancy Tafuri. The children take turns making up stories and telling them to each other as they turn the pages.

myeducationlab

Explore how a kindergarten teacher creates a print-rich environment by completing the activity "Creating Purposeful Environments for Emergent Readers and Writers." (To find this activity, go to the topic *Emergent Literacy* in MyEducationLab and click on Assignments and Activities.)

- A special area designated for writing that contains paper of various sizes, textures, and colors, as well as a variety of pencils, pens, markers, crayons, alphabet strips, and the like.
- A science center where children can explore plants, insects, rocks, and animals, along with short simple books in which children can read about these topics.

In addition to having designated space and materials for reading and writing, children also need time and motivation. The activities you provide to these children on the threshold of literacy will focus on reading for enjoyment as well as reading for meaning; subsequent sections will highlight some of these literacy activities.

Reading Opportunities

Opportunities for children to read in the classroom are almost limitless. Here are some ideas you can try out and expand on in your classroom.

The Morning Meeting

The beginning of each school day is an ideal time to gather your students in a comfortable place and meet with them as a community of learners. The morning meeting can develop and nurture a sense of belonging and purpose, engaging students in a variety of literacy experiences. The amount of time you spend, whether it is 10 minutes or 20, will depend on how long your students are able to focus without becoming restless. This time may be relatively short at the beginning of the year and increase as the year progresses.

During this meeting, many activities can take place. Here are some of the possibilities:

The morning meeting is an excellent opportunity to engage students in a variety of literacy experiences.

Frank Pedrick/The Image Works

- *Attendance count.* Take attendance by showing name cards and having students respond to their names in print. The first word most children learn, because of interest and exposure, is their own name, so students are likely to be successful early on at reading their names.
- *Calendar.* Write the day and date on the board, reminding students of what day came just before and what day will come after (simultaneously teaching and reinforcing children's knowledge of the days of the week and the concepts of *before* and *after*).
- *Weather.* Talk with students about the weather, teaching words such as *rainy, sunny, cold, temperature, cloudy, warm,* and so forth.
- *Current events.* Have students share the events of their lives. This is an excellent way to build oral language skills and expand vocabulary.
- *Morning message.* Have students read your "morning message." This is a short message you write on the board to your class each day so that when they arrive, they know they will be reading a note from you. This message serves two purposes. First, it reinforces the notion that print conveys meaning. Second, it provides children with practice in tracking print as you read aloud. In fact, it is often worthwhile to read the message several times, drawing attention to the letters or words and having students come up to the board and circle the words they recognize. Later in the school year children should help you compose the message, because this allows practice in phonemic segmentation and spelling.
- *The daily schedule.* Going over the day's schedule at the beginning of the day gives students a sense of what the day holds and, equally important, illustrates another use of print. The daily schedule should reflect what students will do in whole-group, small-group, and individual work.

Free "Reading"

Each day, students should have several opportunities to "read" books of their own choosing in any way they like. Some children might wish to share a book with a friend. They might do this by telling a favorite story that they have committed to memory, using the pictures as cues for turning the pages; if you model this activity for them, they will likely find it inviting. Others will silently look at books. Still others will want to be read to or listen to a book on tape or CD. As the year progresses children will want to reread the books they have read with you.

Selecting Books for Specific Purposes

At the beginning of this chapter, we talked about books as the heart and soul of reading. They also serve a host of specific literacy development purposes. Here we consider just three of the many purposes books can serve: motivating students, highlighting sounds, and enabling just-beginning readers to read.

Books That Motivate Children to Enter the World of Print. As a teacher of young children, you will want to select books that develop their vocabularies, expand their knowledge of the world, connect to their lives, add to their knowledge of story structures, and increase their desire to read. Such texts can be well-known children's favorites, such as James Marshall's *The Three Little Pigs* (1989), or newer ones, such as Barbara Joosse's *Nikolai, the Only Bear* (2005).

Books That Highlight the Sounds of Language. Because emergent readers need to attend to the forms of words, it is important to read texts in which the structure of words is particularly transparent, highlighting the sounds of words in order to foster phonemic awareness. You can choose texts with features such as word play, rhyme, and alliteration to accomplish this goal. One example is Jill Bennett's rendition of *Teeny Tiny* (1997). One kindergarten teacher, Jeff Baptista, extends this book to develop phonemic awareness. "After we have enjoyed the story, I will ask them, 'What letter in *teeny* makes it say /t/? What letter in *tiny* makes it say /t/? Can you think of other words that start with /t/, like *teeny tiny*?' Later my students can sort pictures that begin with /t/ and /s/, heightening their awareness of initial consonant sounds. Word-level instruction begins with a focus on meaningful text and then moves to words and letter-sounds. The link between meaning, words, and word parts should always be clear."

Books That Children Can Learn to Read on Their Own. The books with predictable patterns that we described earlier in the chapter are purposely written so that children can remember them after hearing them a few times. The overall structure of the books is repetitive, and the picture clues are rich and informative. All in all, these books can make children "instant readers" after only a few readings by the teacher. The children should reread these books by themselves and with a partner.

Brian Wildsmith's *Cat on the Mat* exemplifies this repetitive structure and strong picture support. In this tale, various animals join a cat on the mat:

> The cat sat on the mat. The dog sat on the mat. The goat sat on the mat.

As the child rereads the text and points to the lines and words after hearing it read several times, he can begin to gain insight into the conventions of print, such as the directionality of print from left to right. After rereading many predictable texts, a child may learn the printed form of some high-frequency words, such as *the,* and some high-interest words, such as *dog;* he may even begin to associate some letters with sounds. The teacher can highlight these connections.

You can encourage such understanding by using big books, which are large enough for the whole class or a group of students to see as you read. They allow you to replicate activities that parents or other caregivers carry out as they read to their children at home: point to the print, track the print as children speak it, and highlight words. Predictable text in big books or on charts can encourage children to follow along, echoing or chorally reading as you point to individual words.

To highlight words, letters, or text, you can frame words in a big book with your hand or cover a page with an acetate sheet on which you underline words, word parts, or letters. You can also ask questions or make comments about specific elements in the text; a few suggestions are listed here:

- Point to where it said *goat*.
- Where does it say *cat?*
- Can you find a word that starts like Devon's name?
- I see some words that end with *at*. What are they?
- Here are some books that we have read before. Can you find *at* in the titles? (The books might include the Berenstains' *Old Hat, New Hat,* Dr. Seuss's *The Cat in the Hat,* and Carle's *Have You Seen My Cat?*)

In the booklists that we include throughout this text, we annotate a number of children's books suitable for reading aloud to emergent readers. A number of these titles are available in both big book and little book format. The following list provides a small sampling of big books.

The Reading Corner

Big Books

Pam Adams. *This Old Man.* Child's Play International, 1999. Ten old men in colorful outfits are featured in this traditional counting song in big book format. 16 pages.

Doreen Cronin. *Click, Clack, Moo: Cows That Type.* Scholastic, 2004. When Farmer Brown's cows learn to type, they send him a note demanding electric blankets. 32 pages.

Lois Ehlert. *Eating the Alphabet.* Harcourt Brace, 1994. Beginning with *apricot* and *artichoke*, this big book takes readers on an alphabetical tour of the world of fruits and vegetables. 32 pages.

Muriel Feelings. *Moja Means One: Swahili Counting Book.* Puffin, 1994. This counting book, which portrays the language and customs of Swahili East Africa, is beautifully illustrated by Tom Feelings. 32 pages.

Lorraine Jean Hopping and Meredith Johnson. *Today's Weather Is . . . : A Book of Experiments.* Mondo Publishing, 2000. Questions suggest various weather experiments students can do, and students can follow instructions to discover the outcomes of these experiments. 32 pages.

Myra Cohn Livingston. *Space Songs.* Scholastic, 1994. This collection of poetry contemplating space is accompanied by bold illustrations. 32 pages.

Bruce McMillan. *Time To . . .* Scholastic, 1996. This story follows a kindergartner through his day as he learns to tell time. 32 pages.

Ann Morris. *Loving.* Scholastic, 1996. This book about families around the world is richly illustrated with color photos. 32 pages.

David Schwartz. *How Much Is a Million?* Morrow/Mulberry, 1994. Marvelosissimo the Magician uses his magic to help explain the concepts of million, billion, and trillion. 32 pages.

Kate Waters and Madeline Slovenz-Low. *Lion Dancer: Ernie Wan's Chinese New Year.* Scholastic, 1995. In this story, 6-year-old Ernie prepares for his first Lion Dance during Chinese New Year. 32 pages.

Audrey Wood. *Silly Sally.* Harcourt, 1994. Sally, a power walker, turns a stroll to the city into a rollicking adventure in this rhyming text. 32 pages.

Developing Phonemic Awareness, Letter Identification, and Word Recognition

Children should receive some of their instruction in flexible small groups. You should have a defined time for small-group instruction. These lessons should be short and fast paced, moving from books to words to sounds, whole to part, or other times from part to whole. Small-group instruction need not focus on just one skill, but may incorporate work on phonemic awareness, phonics, word recognition, and reading little books. Small-group instruction allows you to tailor instruction to the needs of students, as you observe their responses and provide corrective feedback. Membership in the skill groups needs to remain flexible, so as students make progress they can move to another group. While you work with one group, other children can be in the reading corner, creating their own book, engaged in literacy focused play, or—if you are fortunate—working with an instructional assistant.

Students have different needs in kindergarten. Some may have developed the insights about language and words that are necessary for phonemic awareness; others may still struggle. Thus, some students will need more intensive instruction whereas others can move on to work on word recognition and text reading. Students in your class whose first language is not English will have their own set of difficulties. Figure 6.4 suggests how you might allocate time for these activities, depending on the needs of the students.

Phonological Awareness

Phonological awareness can be developed through a wide range of activities. Experts recommend that teachers begin by developing students' awareness of syllables and then move to rhyming (Adams, Foorman, Lundberg, & Beeler, 1998). Next students should develop an awareness of initial and then final sounds, moving eventually to full phonemic awareness and the ability to blend and segment words. The following activities are recommended for developing phonological awareness. They should be structured so that students respond to each task simultaneously. You will want to involve students in every aspect of the activity, with what are called pupil response activities. So if you are working on listening for initial sounds, you can ask students to raise the M card for words like *milk, mother,* or *mat,* and the T card for words like *tiger* and *tepee.*

- Students clap to indicate their awareness of each syllable in a word (*el/e/phant, ti/ger*).

Figure 6.4 Allocating Time for Small-Group Activities

	Below-Level Students	On-Level Students	Above-Level Students
Phonological awareness	5 minutes	3–4 minutes	2–3 minutes
Letter-sound association	10 minutes	5 minutes	5 minutes
Word recognition	3 minutes	5 minutes	5 minutes
Text reading	2 minutes	6–7 minutes	7–8 minutes

- Students indicate with a thumbs up or down whether two words rhyme.
- Students indicate which of three words does not rhyme (*hat, sit, fat*).
- Students sort words or objects by initial sound. Repeat later and sort by the final sound.

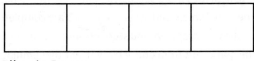

Elkonin Boxes

- Students use Elkonin boxes to represent the sounds in words according to the number of phonemes. They push in two markers for the word *at* and three markers for the word *keep*.
- Students sort pictures into categories by the number of phonemes (sea; dog, run; jump, cat, kite)
- Students blend phonemes into words. (What is /n/ /i/ /s/—*nice*)

Additional ideas for developing phonological awareness can be found in *Phonemic Awareness in Young Children* (Adams et al., 1998), *The Phonological Awareness Handbook for Kindergarten and Primary Teachers* (Ericson & Juliebo, 1998), and *Making Sense of Phonics* (Beck, 2006).

Letter-Sound Associations

While children are developing phonemic awareness they can also learn to identify letters, associate letters and sounds, and even begin to identify words once they are ready for blending. Indeed these three skills reinforce one another. In a small-group lesson the teacher might begin with a phoneme awareness activity, sorting pictures for initial sounds, then move to some letter recognition activities, matching upper- and lowercase letters, and finally associating letters and sounds by having students hold up letter cards when they hear a word that begins with the target sound.

Although there is no perfect sequence for teaching letter names and letter sounds, there are some accepted guidelines. Only a few letters and sounds should be taught at one time. Teach the most common letters first—*m, t, s, r,* and but not *x* or *z*. Teach letters that are least likely to be confused, so *b* and *d* should not be taught together, whereas *t, s,* and *m* are quite distinct. Uppercase letters that do not look like their lowercase equivalents (*aA, eE, qQ*) should be taught later in the sequence; *O, P,* and *S* can be taught earlier. The following activities are suggested for small-group instruction to develop letter-name and letter-sound knowledge.

- Students match pictures to letter cards.
- Students match upper- and lowercase letters.
- Teacher says a word and the students indicate by pointing at small boards with three spaces for beginning, middle, and ending sounds where the designated sound falls in the word. "Listen for /a/. Is /a/ at the beginning, middle, or end of *mat?*"
- Children sing the alphabet song while touching the letters on their individual alphabet strip.
- Students read and discuss alphabet books, focusing on just a few letters and sounds each week.

PEARSON
myeducationlab

Learn how to teach phonics explicitly and then analyze the effectiveness of different teachers' phonics instruction by completing the activity "Effectively Teaching Phonics Skills and Strategies." (To find this activity, go to the topic *Phonemic Awareness/Phonics* in MyEducationLab and click on Building Teaching Skills and Dispositions.)

Motivating Struggling Readers

Kindergarten children rarely have problems of motivation, but sitting and attending can be a real issue. We advocate the use of small-group instruction and learning centers. Careful planning can make both of these activities more successful. Children attend better during small-group instruction when the pace is brisk and several activities are completed within 15 to 20 minutes. Teachers must be well prepared, and students must be familiar with the activities. The rapid pace and the quick shift from one activity to another emulates the fast-paced world in which these students live.

For learning center activities to be successful, the students must practice them thoroughly before trying them out on their own. The teacher must introduce the new letter-sound matching game or word sort during small-group instruction. She must provide several days of practice with feedback to make sure that the students know the procedure for playing the game. She must also coach the students in the accountability piece—after sorting the words the students have to draw pictures of four words in the appropriate letter-sound column. Only after the procedures are well learned are the students ready to use the activity on their own.

Word Recognition

Young children can begin word recognition with a very easy text—a predictable or patterned book. First, the teacher should read the book and then students should echo the teacher, repeating line by line what she reads. Next, the students should attempt to read the book in a choral fashion. After the book has been read and discussed, the teacher should focus on a few words in the text by highlighting or framing these words. The words can then be placed on flashcards and the students with the teacher can study the words. Together they can segment the words into sounds, sort words by beginning or ending letters, and practice reading them. The words can be used in games like Bingo and Concentration.

Writing Opportunities

In order to become increasingly competent readers, children need to become message-makers and authors themselves. For this to happen, you need to create authentic writing opportunities for them. Some tried-and-true approaches are discussed in the following sections.

Journals

When children write, they begin to internalize the notion that ideas can be represented symbolically. We know several kindergarten and first-grade teachers who have students keep journals, beginning on the first day of school. The journal need not be elaborate—several sheets of paper folded over to make a little book would be sufficient. In the journal, students are encouraged to express themselves in whatever way they choose. They can be given ideas to write about or write without prompts. Like most emergent literacy activities, journal writing should be modeled for children, who should be shown many ways to express themselves in writing: drawing pictures, making squiggles, writing letters, and combining several forms of expression. Thus, children can "write" even if they do not yet know the letters of the alphabet. They can then read back what they have written, which is easiest if they can do so right away.

Assessment

Use students' writing journals as tools to assess areas in which students might benefit from individual or whole-class instruction.

Another way for young children to write is to dictate a sentence or two that you or a classroom aide writes down. As children experiment with writing, they should be encouraged to get their ideas down in print even if they do not know some letters or spellings; urge them to use invented spelling.

Kindergarten teacher Sid Burns invites each child to work with a special word each day:

> As children are busy illustrating their "word," I circulate around the room and take down dictations. Each child has his or her own journal. Each student tells me a word that is "on her mind" or special to her that day. (For example, *love* and *heart* were big last week—Valentine's Day fell on Friday.) I write the dictated word in the child's journal. She can then trace or copy it. Sometimes children discuss the word with me or with other children, draw a picture that illustrates the word, and dictate a sentence or two for me to write down regarding the picture. For example, Marta asked me to write, "I love my dog. Her name is Asta." As I wrote the sentences, I used the opportunity to comment on the form of print in a way that was appropriate for Marta. I pointed to the word *dog* and said to her, "dog," emphasizing the initial sound, /d/. "What letter makes that /d/?" Then I asked her to reread the two sentences and point to the words.
>
> —Sid Burns, kindergarten teacher

Language-Experience Activities

Copying down children's dictation and then having them read their own words has been termed the *language-experience approach*. With this approach, the teacher or an assistant writes down the words of a story spoken by a student or group of students, using the students' language. When the story is read, students can easily read along. The vocabulary is familiar because students generated it, and they have prior knowledge related to content because it is based on their experiences. Because this approach is entirely student centered, it is particularly useful for meeting the needs of students who vary in ethnic background, English language competence, or educational needs. In fact, as we point out in Chapter 14, it is an extremely valuable procedure to use with students whose first language is not English.

Shared Reading and Writing Experiences

Another opportunity that encourages writing is the shared reading and writing experience, which we discuss again in Chapters 13 and 14. In the Classroom 6.5 shows first-grade teacher Connie Martinez combining reading instruction with an opportunity for students to compose a rhyme together. Although the children are not *physically* writing the words, they are participating in the act of composing; their teacher provides a sturdy instructional scaffold.

By the end of our week, some of the children on the playground were reciting the poem as they jumped rope. "Silly Willy" made a perfect jumprope jingle. We wouldn't be surprised if the children thought up new verses to add over the days and weeks to come!

Making Books

Children can be encouraged to take their language-experience stories or perhaps write their own stories and

Student-written and -illustrated books provide a wonderful opportunity to involve children actively in writing and reading.

Jeff Greenberg/PhotoEdit

6.5

Reading and Writing Rhymes

Sitting in a large rocking chair, Ms. Martinez holds a big book of Mother Goose nursery rhymes. The children gathered around her can see the words on the first two pages as she begins singing the rhyme:

Lavender's blue, dilly, dilly, lavender's green; when I am King, dilly, dilly, you shall be Queen.

Ms. Martinez has the children take turns pointing to the color words they know. She helps them with *lavender* and has them tell each other what color this is close to (for example, purple). "Is anyone wearing lavender or blue or green today?" she asks.

Next, she asks them which word in the verse rhymes with green.

"Queen!" they chime in unison.

Ms. Martinez stands up and writes *green* and *Queen* directly underneath each other on the portable chalkboard next to her. She asks the children to name the letters in each word and which letters they share.

"E-E-N!" a couple of children answer.

Then Ms. Martinez remarks, "*Dilly* is a silly word!"

So she writes *dilly* on the board, with *silly* right underneath it. She asks them if they can think of some names of boys that sound like *dilly* and *silly*. She helps by saying, "dilly, silly, Billy?"

They shout, "Yes." Then she says, "Dilly, silly, Cassandra?" and they shout, "No."

Ms. Martinez tells the children they are going to write their own rhyme. She puts a large chart pad on a stand. The chart has part of a rhyme already printed on it. The children will suggest words or letters to complete it, and Ms. Martinez will print them on the lines. She begins by asking the children if they want to write about "Silly Billy" or "Silly Willy." They opt for Willy. Ms. Martinez prints *Willy* in the blank on the chart. The children alternate rereading the rhyme, as Ms. Martinez points to each word, and adding a word in the blank. The poem they wrote by filling in the blanks is shown in the accompanying illustration. Every so often during the week, the children recite this rhyme either as a class or in partner reading, always pointing to the words as they say them.

Silly _____

Silly, silly, _____Willy_____ ,

Silly, silly, m_e_ ,

I fell down and scratched my knee.

I stood up and shook my head.

I stood up and this is what I said:

Silly, silly, _____Willy_____ ,

Silly, silly, m_e_ ,

I fell down and hurt my head.

I think I should just go to _____bed_____ .

make them into small books with illustrations. Bookmaking can be as elaborate or as simple as you wish. Books can be laminated and bound with a plastic spiral or hand-sewn binding or simply stapled together. We recommend saving the more elaborate bindings for class books that can be saved and read over and over again.

Mailboxes

A classroom mailbox system in which students can post one letter a day and have pen pals to correspond with reinforces print awareness and gives students motivation for writing and for reading their own writing (because, early on, they will probably be the only ones who can read their messages).

Play Centers

Many kindergarten teachers include play centers in their classrooms. In these centers, children act out real or imagined situations and events. They might act out what happens at a restaurant or events in a story they have just heard. Literacy activities can easily be included in such play centers. In playing restaurant, for example, a simple pad of paper can be provided for a waitress or waiter to write down orders, or a chart of recipes can be printed for the cook to follow. Similarly, in planning to act out a story, you and the children might together block out the sequence of the story, illustrating it with simple pictures and a few words and phrases.

Listening and Speaking Opportunities

Of course, listening and speaking are normal parts of the kindergarten and first-grade school day. Here we briefly mention some specific activities that enhance skills in these areas and, as you know by now, promote skills in reading and writing as well.

Reading Aloud

We cannot overemphasize the importance of reading aloud to all children, but it is especially important for emergent readers and doubly so for students who have not had the benefit of being read to at home. When you read to your class, you give students a chance to hear fluent reading and to develop the critical skill of listening comprehension. You also provide a rich opportunity to develop vocabulary knowledge. Moreover, you give them the pleasure of hearing a good story and sharing enthusiasm for it. You should also read aloud nonfiction books to demonstrate the process of learning from text. The children will be eager to contribute and will actually ask more questions during an information read-aloud than when you read fiction. To create an effective read-aloud experience, it is helpful to keep the following suggestions in mind:

1. Select a story or information book that interests you as well as your students. The book should offer some new words that can be the focus for a follow-up discussion.
2. Practice reading the book, and pick good stopping points for elaborating on the information.
3. When you stop at your stopping point briefly define the new vocabulary and model one or more strategies. You might ask a question, clarify something that is difficult to understand, make a prediction, or solicit questions and comments from the children.
4. Whenever possible, invite students to join in! If a word or a phrase is repeated or if you are reading a story students have heard before, encourage them to read along with you. Also, some stories lend themselves to gestures and simple movement.
5. After you have finished reading, elaborate on the new vocabulary, writing the words on a WOW word chart, where we keep track of new exciting words. Discuss the story or the new ideas learned.

For more ideas on reading aloud and a host of suggestions on specific books to read aloud, we strongly suggest Jim Trelease's *The New Read-Aloud Handbook* (1995).

Recordings

Recording stories yourself or having a classroom aide or older student do so can provide you with an inexpensive and useful resource. Today most of the stories in core reading programs are available on CDs. Of course, commercially prepared tapes and CDs are also available for many popular trade books, and we have indicated those books for which we know recordings are available in the Children's Literature section at the end of each chapter. With recordings, a number of children can listen

The Internet can be used to enhance the experience of an information book read-aloud. Find a website that provides further illustration of the topic you and the children are studying. Suppose as part of a science unit you have chosen to read *From Seed to Plant* by Gail Gibbons (1993). The book provides a detailed explanation of seeds, plants, and how plants grow. After reading this book, use a computer connected to the Internet and an LCD projector to let the children view the process of seed germination and plant growth in time-lapse photography (www.youtube.com/watch?v=d26AhcKeEbE). This experience will make the static picture in the book come alive while also demonstrating how books and the Internet can be used together to gain information and deepen understanding. ●

to stories at any time during the day, and you are freed to give attention to other students.

A Kindergarten Scenario*

To show how a very skillful teacher engages her students in the meaningful literacy experiences we have just described, here we give you a glimpse into a typical day in Jonni Wolskee's full-day kindergarten class. Ms. Wolskee will be the tour guide. The location is small urban school where 75 percent of the students qualify for a free or reduced-price lunch. The class of 26 students consists of 15 African American children, 8 Caucasians, and 3 Hispanics. It is December, and the types of literacy activities you will read about here have been going on all year. We choose to focus on an all-day kindergarten because two-thirds of American children are now enrolled in a full-day kindergarten program (NCES, 2004).

8:20. The students begin their day with a daily morning assignment that reinforces skills—initial sound sorts, rhyming activities, and so on that have previously been taught while also giving the students an opportunity to "warm up" for their day. This morning, my students will complete a phonogram picture sort where they will sort the pictures into columns for the phonograms *-at, -am,* and *-ap.* Once they have finished gluing the pictures into the appropriate columns, they will then write the word next to each of the pictures and circle the phonogram in each word. However, because the students are at different developmental stages, I always have some finish rather quickly, while others are dragging it out to the bitter end. To keep the above- and on-level students from having behavior issues due to boredom, I make sure that in the center of their tables is a book basket that is loaded with previously read books that those students may read.

9:00. After the students have completed their morning assignment, they transition to a rather large carpet in the front of my room where we begin our calendar time, reviewing the days of the week, the month, and the weather. This includes work on math concepts such as pattern, place value, and money. Reading consists of skill instruction, a morning message, and an interactive read-aloud.

*Jonni Wolskee, East Dover Elementary School, Dover, Delaware, describes a typical day in her kindergarten class.

Assessment

The major task of the kindergarten teacher is to move 5-year-olds from a range of entry-level skills and knowledge toward the demands of first grade. To do this, you will need to keep detailed records of each child's growing capabilities.

- *Skill instruction.* I always keep a basket of letters and high frequency words that we are learning. Each and every day the students are drilled on their letters and sounds: /m/ *m,* /s/ *s,* /r/ *r,* and so on. We then read our reading words and segment and blend each word: students say "is," then break it apart into /i/ /z/, and then blend "is." This is meant to be a quick 2- to 3-minute drill.

- *Morning message.* The morning message, *Kindergarten News,* is written on chart paper. The message is usually connected to the book for our read-aloud and provides multiple opportunities to reinforce the structure of words, concept of print, linking letters and phonemes, alphabetic principle, blending, and encoding. The message is already written on the chart paper in a cloze sentence format: *I like to help* _____ *at home.* I give explicit instruction as to where the sentence begins and what it begins with. I also will draw a box around the beginning letter of the sentence. As time goes on, I have the students show me the beginning of the sentence and then they have to put the box around it themselves. The students volunteer to come up and circle high-frequency words that they know, highlight finger spaces, discuss the punctuation used and why, and fill in the blank with a response. When it is time to write the words, we stretch the words as we write them. Again, I start off with a lot of modeling, but with scaffolded instruction, over time, the students will begin to take this job over from me until they are independent.

- *Read-aloud.* This morning we are reading *Swimmy* (Lionni, 1973). I begin with reading and tracking the title of the text. I tell the students that the title is the name that the author has given the book and often can give a clue as to what the book is about. I begin my think-aloud by saying, "I see quite a few red fish swimming in the sea. I also see just one black fish swimming alone. I think that Swimmy is the name of one of the fish. I wonder why the black fish is swimming alone?" I then ask the students about a time that they have ever been alone and how they felt when they were alone. One of my students said that he felt sad and lonely. I then say, "I think that the black fish feels lonely and sad. Let's read on to find out."

During reading we soon come to the part of the story where Swimmy feels sad and alone because the big tuna had eaten up all of his brothers and sisters. I remind the students of the prediction we made about Swimmy feeling lonely. I ask them to give me a thumbs up if our prediction was correct or a thumbs down if our prediction was incorrect. Most of my class gives me a thumbs up. However, I had a few put a thumb down, so I take the opportunity to explain why our prediction was correct. I try to maintain eye contact with those who misunderstood our prediction during my explanation.

During a fictional story such as *Swimmy,* we come across key vocabulary words that I have highlighted in highlighter tape. The words I selected for this story are *creatures, marvel,* and *school.* When I encounter the word in context I give a brief explanation of what the word means and move on: "'Then, hidden in the dark shade of rocks and weeds, he saw a school of little fish, just like his own.' A school is a large group of fish." When reading a nonfiction story to the students, I always preteach the key vocabulary words using explicit instruction, but again give a quick explanation when we come to the word in the text without breaking stride. The vocabulary cards are used throughout the week in simple and quick reinforcement activities to enhance their understanding of the word so that they own it for future use.

When reading narrative text, I save my vocabulary focus for the end of the text. I go back into the text and find the word *creatures* in the story. I explain how it is being used in the text. I never ask the students what they think it means because it reinforces the wrong concept to everyone if they are incorrect. "It says that the sea is full of creatures. The creatures are the jellyfish, lobster, anemones, and all of the different fish that he saw." I then show the word *creatures* on an index card with a picture of living things on it and explain that the word *creature* means any living thing that is not a plant. This means that the jellyfish, lobster, anemones, and fish are all living things. I give examples of other living things and nonexamples such as chairs, rocks, plants, and so on.

I ask my students to describe how Swimmy and all of the red fish felt at the end of the story. Many of my students said, "Happy because they were able to scare away the bad fish who tried to eat them."

9:45. During this time I teach three ability-based reading groups. Each rotation lasts approximately 20 minutes, but I do try to squeeze in an extra 5 minutes with my struggling students whenever possible. The rotations include instruction with a teacher, instruction with a paraprofessional, and independent practice at a differenti-ated literacy center. My groups are ability based, which means that my students are grouped based on teacher observations and informal assessments. The groups are fluid, which means students will be moved in or out of their groups based on growth or needed reinforcement.

- *Small-group instruction.* During the 20 minutes, the students are allotted time for phonemic awareness activities, phonics activities, word recognition, and reading little books. However, students are not given the same amount of time to practice each skill. Struggling students are going to need more instruction in phonemic awareness and phonics activities whereas above-level students spend more time with word rec-ognition and text reading. As my students grow in reading ability their instruction will change.

The students from my below-level group come and sit on their assigned spot on the carpet. We are working on two- and three-phoneme words. I show them an Elkonin box and three chips and tell them that we are going to count the sounds in some words. When I model the activity, I say, "My turn." Then I say the word "sit." I break the word apart—/s/ /i/ /t/—and move a chip into a box for each sound in the word. I tell them that we are going to do this together. The students each have an Elkonin board with three boxes on it. They also have three chips. I say, "Our Turn," and I say the word "sit" and they repeat the word "sit." Then, together we move the chips. I watch for any confusion and make the corrections now. Then I say, "Your Turn," and watch the students complete this independently. The students now com-plete this activity independently with the following words: *am, was, dug, be, done, chair, flew, is, thumb, bird.*

Next, we move to our phonics activity. I hold up a flip chart of letters. The con-sonants are on the ends with the vowels in the middle. This is my real/nonsense flip chart. I begin by making the last two letters *a* and *t* for the -*at* word family. These letters will not be changed. I begin by flipping the first letter to *c* and make the word *cat*. The students read the word *cat* together. I then change the *c* to *p* to make the word *pat* and the students read the word *pat*. I run through all the letters in the al-phabet for the beginning sound and the students read them together. If they make any mistakes, I offer them corrective feedback and we move on. As the year goes on and they master this skill, I will then keep the beginning the same and only change the final letter: *cat, cap, caj, cab, cag,* and so on. When they master the final letter, they will then manipulate the middle vowel sound. We always discuss real versus nonsense words and often this affords me an opportunity to teach the meanings of new words.

For our book reading I pass out the story "The Mat." I read the story to the students the first time around. Then the students echo read the story with me. The next day the students will read it chorally and then independently. I use many kinds of texts—leveled readers, patterned text, and many nonfiction expository books. The lessons for the other groups will emphasize more decoding and text reading and focus less on phonemic awareness and letter-sound knowledge. The Tile Test, the first test in Appendix A, is designed to assess emergent and early reading skills.

- *Literacy Centers.* These centers are meant to reinforce the skills that have been taught in small-group instruction and provide opportunities for students to read and write. There are two rules for centers: (1) There should always be an accountability piece to show that the student has spent his or her time meaningfully. For example, if the students are sorting words by letters they draw two pictures for a letter and write the word next to the picture. (2) The students need to be able to complete this work independently. This means that the work needs to be at the student's ability level. There are five literacy centers that I use in my classroom:

  1. Word center: Students play word games, sort pictures and words, and make words using cards and dice.
  2. Reading center: Students read individually or with a partner leveled books, nonfiction books, and pattern books. They draw and write about what they read.
  3. Listening center: Students listen to previously read and new stories. Then they draw pictures about the stories and write about what they have heard.
  4. Writing center: Students write about pictures, complete simple story frames, or complete cloze activities from books they have heard.
  5. Computer center: My students use various commercial computer reading programs.

When students have completed each of their center accountability pieces, they will put them back at their tables for me to correct.

11:00. Lunch.

11:30. Math. I use a math series that utilizes a lot of manipulatives and hands-on learning. This provides an excellent opportunity for students to write and express how they come to a particular answer or concept. I have the students use a strategy called Picture, Answer, Word. My students always draw a picture to show what the problem is, then they compute the answer, and finally, they write how they came to the answer.

12:10. Recess.

12:40. Special classes.

1:30. Writing. My students write in their journals every day. Sometimes I pick the topic and other times they choose. I regularly model writing and present mini-lessons on some aspect of writing. My students learn to use word walls and to stretch words to aid spelling. In the mini-lessons we talk about how to develop ideas, how to organize

Ms. Wolskee leads her kindergarten students in a word recognition activity.

Courtesy of Peter Dewitz

sentences, and how to spell words. When our writing time is up, each of my students shares what they have written and we all discuss some of the wonderful ideas and details their peers came up with in their writing. We also talk about common mistakes that we observed in their writing as well. By the end of the year, they are so meticulous about their writing, many do not want to misspell anything and completely embrace the word wall.

2:30. Social studies/science. The students are learning about pumpkins so I am reading the nonfiction text *A Day at the Pumpkin Patch* (Faulker & Krewesky, 2006). I begin with a KWL chart and the students tell me what they know about pumpkins: "They are orange. Pumpkins are round. You make them into jack-o'-lanterns." Then I ask my students what they would want to know about pumpkins and they reply with questions. "Do pumpkins grow?" "Where do pumpkins come from?" "What is in a pumpkin?" When I write their responses on the chart, I am always stretching the word out loud for my students to hear as I write it. I tell the students that we will read and look for the answers to their questions and hopefully learn some new interesting facts about pumpkins.

I will preteach the key vocabulary words to the students before I read the text. The words we are learning are *stem, ribs,* and *pulp.* I show the students vocabulary cards with the pictures and words on them. I hold up a picture of ribs and tell the students that the ribs of the pumpkins are the deep lines or ridges that run from the top of the pumpkin to the bottom. I ask the students whether our classroom pumpkin has ribs or not. They all give me a thumbs up. I continue in the same way with the other vocabulary words.

I read the text to the students and briefly discuss the vocabulary words as they come up in the text. I also make sure to briefly stop and discuss the questions from the KWL chart as we find the answers to them in the text. When I finish reading the text I ask my students what they have learned about pumpkins from our book. They gave responses such as "Some pumpkins have ribs. There are seeds inside of pumpkins. Little pumpkins are green. Pumpkins grow in a pumpkin patch. Pumpkins seeds are planted in the spring and summer. Pumpkins have stems. Pumpkin blossoms are yellow." The next day we will read a fictional book about jack-o'-lanterns.

3:10 Dismissal.

REFLECT and *Apply*

⑤ Jonni Wolskee is an outstanding teacher, and she does a terrific job developing her kindergartners' literacy skills. She engages her children in reading and writing experiences where their understanding of books and print can be nurtured. She also provides direct explicit instruction in print concepts, phonemic awareness, and vocabulary. How important is exposure versus direct explicit instruction? Which children need which type of instruction?

Strengths *and Challenges* of Diversity

Some children enter school with considerable experience with print, message-making, books, and exposure to the different places and creatures of our world. Others have few of these experiences. These children will almost certainly need a good deal of help in learning the forms of words and the content in books (Burns, Griffin, & Snow, 1999; Torgesen, 1998). For children who come to school with less exposure to print and books or having used primarily a language other than English, one-to-one assistance from an adult or older students can be particularly helpful. The task that is easiest to orchestrate is simply having the adults read appropriate books to or with the younger students—predictable books, concept books, alphabet books, and others that foster emergent literacy. As the older students read, they can answer questions the younger students have and talk to the younger students about what they liked in the book, what they would like to read next, and other matters related to fostering their interest in reading. These assistants can also take dictation from children, print out the dictation, and let children read back their own stories.

Additionally, as we emphasize in Chapter 14 for children whose primary language is not English, bilingual volunteers who speak the children's first language as well as English can be of tremendous help. The many English language learners in today's classrooms must, of course, learn to read in English. But they also need to have their own languages recognized and validated. There are a number of ways in which you can contribute to this validation. You can learn a few words in each of your students' languages and introduce them to the class as a whole. You can also sometimes find books that cleverly incorporate several languages. Charlotte Pomerantz's *If I Had a Paka: Poems in Eleven Languages* is a collection of 12 poems that incorporate languages including Dutch, Samoan, Swahili, Vietnamese, and Yiddish. But if you have a class in which students speak a number of languages, you're going to need some help in reading to students in their own languages. This is where volunteers who speak students' first languages can really help. Hearing books read in their native languages in your classroom can be an extremely positive experience for English language learners as they strive to become literate in English.

All children need different kinds and amounts of instruction to nurture their growing literacy. In Ms. Wolskee's classroom, there were ample opportunities for children who were reading at different levels to select appropriate books to take home. Similarly, all children were involved in writing, but the writing was quite varied, allowing each child to be successful with the knowledge of print conventions he had achieved. Those children who needed more explicit instruction in letters, sounds, or phonemic awareness received it during small-group instruction.

Some children will come to your classroom needing considerable help in the area of phonemic awareness; others won't. There is little point in spending valuable class time "teaching" children something they already know. That is why Ms. Wolskee provides small-group instruction geared to the needs of the students. However, whatever the levels of your students, it is vitally important to remember that the pieces of language and print, such as alphabet knowledge and phonemic awareness, are only building blocks to reading and writing. So as you plan instruction, you will want to provide activities that have meaning, importance, and relevance to your young students, who are eager to learn the skills that will make them successful communicators.

Concluding *Remarks*

In this chapter on emergent literacy, we talked about the progression most children follow as they learn to read and the many and varied learning experiences they need in order to become readers and writers. In learning to read, at first children may rely on distinctive visual cues such as word length, initial or distinctive letters, and illustrations as the primary ways to access printed meaning. As children gain phonemic awareness and letter knowledge, they use their understand-

ing that letters correspond to speech sounds as a means to recognize words. Using letter-sound knowledge is often difficult because reading requires an understanding of the rather abstract concept of phonemes. In fact, learning to read is much harder than learning to speak because reading requires a *conscious* awareness of phonemes that is not needed in speaking. The knowledge and competencies that children need to gain as developing readers include knowledge of stories, phonemic awareness, alphabet knowledge, and a beginning understanding of how letters and sounds relate to make printed words.

The latter part of this chapter described instructional ideas for facilitating and nurturing children's growing literacy in the four modes of language—reading, writing, listening, and speaking. These included creating a literate classroom environment and providing a multitude of reading, writing, listening, and speaking experiences. Some of these literacy activities can revolve around the classroom morning meeting, morning message, and daily schedule. Other important experiences suggested were free reading and engaging students with a variety of books while providing activities that foster knowledge of how printed language works. Writing opportunities, also stressed in this chapter, are crucial to help children learn about the form and function of written language. Some ways to provide these opportunities include student jour-

nals, language-experience activities, the shared reading and writing experience, bookmaking, classroom mailboxes, and play centers. Finally, listening and speaking opportunities for emergent readers were discussed. These included reading aloud, choral reading, audio recordings, and sing-alongs. The chapter concluded with a kindergarten scenario that described the many and varied literacy activities Ms. Wolskee provides for her kindergartners.

Besides the many practical and concrete ideas we hope you have gleaned from this chapter, what we also hope you will take away is the underlying message that our job as teachers of young children is to provide the kinds of literacy experiences that ensure for all children the strongest possible literacy footing on which to build lifelong reading and writing skills and a lifelong love of reading.

Extending *Learning*

1. Find an adult who reads to a young child at home or in a day care center. Carefully watch and listen to their storybook interactions. How does the adult keep the child's attention? What appears to interest the child? What does the child wonder about in the story? What does the child ask about? What is the child learning about the form or content of books and print in this interaction?

2. Observe a preschool or kindergarten classroom. Make a list of the kinds of literacy activities you see. Then explain how each of these activities helps children learn about books and print. Alternatively or in addition, observe a preschool or kindergarten child outside of school, and make a list of the literacy activities the child is involved in.

3. In the latter part of the chapter, we mentioned using books with children for three different purposes—to motivate children to expand their knowledge of the world and their imaginations by reading, to highlight the sounds of language in words, and to engage students in reading

right from the start by using books with predictable text and helpful illustrations. Go to a library, perhaps a public library, that has a good collection of children's books. Begin an annotated list of books that you think will motivate children to read and to expand their knowledge of the world, books that highlight the sounds of language in words, and books that contain predictable text and helpful illustrations that allow reading right from the start. Include five to ten books in each of these three categories.

4. Go to a kindergarten class to observe children's writing activities. Jot down the different kinds of activities you see them engaged in. Write a paragraph or so describing which of the writing opportunities presented in this chapter you would most like to try in your own classroom, and why.

5. Record samples of children's writing. Examine their spelling and see what their spelling reveals about children's knowledge of phonology and orthography.

Children's *Literature*

Bennett, J. (1997). *Teeny Tiny*. New York: Putnam. In this reprint illustrated by Tomi de Paola, a very small woman finds a very small bone and puts it away in her cupboard before she goes to bed. Illustrated. Also available in Spanish. 32 pages.

Berenstain, S., & Berenstain, J. (1970). *Old Hat, New Hat*. New York: Random House. Rhyming text poses the question of whether a new hat can really replace a perfect old one. 32 pages.

Carle, E. (1996). *Have You Seen My Cat?* New York: Simon & Schuster. A boy encounters cats of all sorts while searching for his own lost cat. 24 pages.

Cowley, J. (1990). *Dan the Flying Man.* Bothell, WA: The Wright Group. This book about a flying man is designed for group reading. 16 pages.

dePaolo, T. (1978). *The Popcorn Book.* New York: Holiday House. Two boys are at home making popcorn for a light snack. Interspersed into the narrative is the history of popcorn and the Native Americans who developed it. 32 pages.

Faulkner, M., & Krawesky, A. (2006). *A Day at the Pumpkin Patch.* Toronto: Scholastic. A nonfiction book that describes pumpkins and how they grow and gives instructions on how to carve a jack-o'-lantern. 32 pages.

Gibbons, G. (1993). *From Seed to Plant.* New York: Holiday House. A simple introduction to plants, discussing reproduction, pollination, seed dispersal, and growth from seeds. 32 pages.

Hall, J. (2000). *What Does Rabbit Say?* New York: Doubleday. Rhyming text follows a boy and girl as they ask what sound their pet rabbit makes. 32 pages.

Hoban, T. (1988). *Look, Look, Look.* New York: Greenwillow. In this colorful book, photographs of familiar objects are first viewed through a cut-out peephole, then revealed in their entirety. 42 pages.

Hoban, T. (1973). *Over, Under, and Through and Other Spatial Concepts.* New York: Macmillan. Spatial concepts are illustrated with text and photos. 32 pages.

Jenkins, E. (2005). *That New Animal.* New York: Farrar, Straus and Giroux. The arrival of a new baby is told from two dogs' point of view. 32 pages.

Joosse, B. (2005). *Nikolai, the Only Bear.* New York: Philomel. Nikolai, the only bear of the 100 orphans at the Russian orphanage, finds the perfect family at last. 32 pages.

Keats, E. J. (1998). *The Snowy Day.* New York: Viking. This 1963 Caldecott Medal classic, about a young city boy enjoying adventures in the snow, is now in board book format. Spanish text and CD available. 32 pages.

Lionni, L. (1973). *Swimmy.* New York: Dragonfly Books.

Lobel, A. (1985). *Whiskers & Rhymes.* New York: Scholastic. This collection contains short, humorous rhymes in the nursery rhyme tradition. 48 pages.

Marshall, J. (1989). *The Three Little Pigs.* New York: Dial. In this version of the familiar tale, one of the three pigs survives the wolf by using its head. 32 pages.

Pomerantz, C. (1993). *If I Had a Paka: Poems in Eleven Languages.* New York: Mulberry Books. A collection of 12 poems incorporating words from 11 languages, including Swahili, Samoan, Yiddish, Indonesian, Vietnamese, and Dutch. Unnumbered.

Rice, E. (1989). *Peter's Pockets.* New York: Greenwillow. Peter's new pants don't have any pockets, so Uncle Nick lets Peter use his until Peter's mother solves the problem in a clever way. 32 pages.

Seuss, Dr. (1957). *The Cat in the Hat.* New York: Random House. Two children sitting at home on a rainy day are visited by a cat that shows them some tricks and games. CD available. 61 pages.

Seuss, Dr. (1963). *Hop on Pop.* New York: Random House. Pairs of rhyming words are introduced and used in simple sentences. CD available. 64 pages.

Seuss, Dr. (1974). *There's a Wocket in My Pocket!* This is a good book for developing phonemic awareness. New York: Random House. CD available. 24 pages.

Tafuri, N. (1987). *Do Not Disturb.* New York: Greenwillow. On the first day of summer, the forest creatures scurry about and make noise in this wordless picture book. 32 pages

Tafuri, N. (1983). *Early in the Morning in the Barn.* New York: Greenwillow. This almost-wordless picture book depicts farm animals along with some text showing the sounds they make. 32 pages.

Tafuri, N. (1996). *Have You Seen My Duckling?* New York: Greenwillow. This 1985 Caldecott Honor book, in which a mother duck leads her brood around the pond as she searches for one missing duckling, is now in board book format. 32 pages.

Wildsmith, B. (1982). *Cat on the Mat.* Oxford, UK: Oxford University Press. The cat liked to sit on the mat until the other animals wanted to sit on it too. 16 pages.

7

Word Recognition

with contributions by Kathleen Clark

CHAPTER outline

Six-year-old Anthony tries to read a page from the popular children's book *Rosie's Walk,* by Pat Hutchins. He sits in a circle with other children around his first-grade teacher, Ms. Sullivan. Yesterday, Ms. Sullivan and the children read the story aloud together. The story is about a hen named Rosie, who takes a walk around a farmyard, blissfully ignorant of the fox that follows her. Along her way, Rosie walks

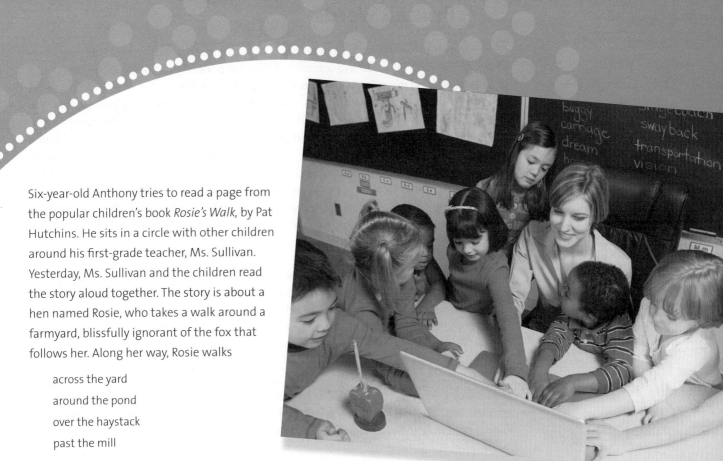

> across the yard
> around the pond
> over the haystack
> past the mill

Ms. Sullivan has all the children point to the words as they read. Some children are better at this than others. Ms. Sullivan either has the entire class read a line aloud, calls on a few children to read, or calls on one child to read. She has just called on Anthony. He points to *around* and slowly says, "around the . . . ," stops, and looks up. Ms. Sullivan suggests that he look at the picture.

Anthony looks at the page and asks, "Tree?"

"Well," says Ms. Sullivan, "it does look as if she might walk around that tree, but what is the tree in front of? What is all this?" (as she points to the pond).

Anthony smiles and says, "Water."

"Yes," agrees Ms. Sullivan. "It is water. Remember, though, it is a special kind of water. Look at the word. What letter does it start with?"

"*P,*" replies Anthony.

"*P,* puh—does *water* start with a puh?" asks Ms. Sullivan. "No. So it can't be *water.* Look at the letters. *P,* puh, and the *on* and *d.* You know the letter *d.*"

"*D,* duh," volunteers Indigo.

"Yes." Pointing to the letters, Ms. Sullivan slowly says, "It's a puhond."

"*Pond,*" declares Anthony.

CLASSROOM *vignette*

The Importance of Recognizing Printed Words

For young children like Anthony, learning to recognize printed words is *the* big challenge on the way to becoming a reader. There are a lot of places Rosie the hen could walk around, and guessing words rarely works. Rather the reader, like Anthony, must confront the print itself. Anthony is a typical 6-year-old native English speaker. He entered first grade with a command of spoken English that is nearly complete in terms of its underlying grammar and phonological development. He already has a vocabulary that would be the envy of any nonnative English speaker who, as an adult, is trying to learn English. And his emerging literacy skills are evident in his responses to Ms. Sullivan. Nonetheless, Anthony, like most first-grade children, will work hard at learning to recognize words and acquiring a basic reading vocabulary. Also, like most young children, Anthony will depend on his classroom teacher to help him acquire these reading skills.

Clearly, both spoken and printed English involve the same language. But the reason Anthony can't read, although he is already quite competent at speaking and understanding oral English, is that he does not yet know how to translate the printed word into the spoken word. The printed word is a barrier between him and the meaning of the text. He needs to learn how to get meaning from this printed form of language. To do this, he must, in a sense, get his eyes to do what his ears currently do for him.

The goal of both listening and reading is the same—to construct meaning, to understand. But it is easier to understand when listening than when reading for several reasons. We will briefly look at six of these reasons and why Anthony's task as a reader is harder than his task as a listener.

Why Listening Is Easier Than Reading

Spoken language is characterized by a number of features that help speakers to communicate. These features are much less present in written language, as we will discuss.

Shared Background Knowledge

Conversational partners typically share background knowledge about topics. When talking with a friend, you most likely share a history of the people, places, and events the two of you discuss. You probably know which words, concepts, and topics your friend will easily understand and which will require more elaboration. This knowledge of your friend enables you to adjust your language as needed. There is typically much less shared background knowledge between an author and readers. For example, Pat Hutchins, who wrote *Rosie's Walk*, does not know if Anthony has ever seen a pond.

Immediate Feedback

When you are listening to what a friend is saying and don't understand what she says, you can simply tell her so—"Wait a minute. What do you mean when you say to 'caramelize' the onions before I put them in the stew? How do I caramelize them?" In contrast, when you don't understand something you are reading in a book, you cannot ask the author what she meant.

Visual Cues from the Speaker

A listener can see the speaker's features. Lips move as they shape sounds. The movement provides visual clues to the speech sounds being produced. In a noisy environment, these clues are especially useful. Additionally, speakers can enhance their message by exaggerating or adding intonation, facial expressions, vocal emphasis, tone of voice, repetition, and gesture. Body language can even override the speaker's words and send a different message than the words do.

More Common Words

Words used in spoken English are typically more common than those used in written English. For instance, in a conversation with a friend you might say, "Last night, I just talked on and on about . . ." In penning your autobiography, however, you might write, "All evening, I chattered incessantly about . . ." Someone reading your autobiography will need to know what the words *chattered* and *incessantly* mean. If they do not, they will not understand your message. The more unfamiliar readers are with the words on a page, the more difficult the reading will be.

Contextualized Meaning

In a conversation, the listener benefits from the context created by the shared background knowledge, immediate feedback, visual cues, and more common vocabulary that are characteristic of spoken language. Conversely, when a reader reads, he must construct meaning without many of these supports. Without such supports, meaning is *decontextualized* (Purcell-Gates, 1989).

No Translation Needed

Most important, the input modality in listening is primarily aural. A listener hears the words and immediately understands the message. In contrast, the input modality in reading is visual. To access meaning in printed language, a reader must essentially translate the printed words into their spoken forms. Thus, a child's basic problem in learning to read is learning to translate printed words into the spoken language she already understands.

Skilled Readers Automatically Recognize Words

Skilled readers recognize words automatically. They can identify words so quickly that they don't need to consider the meaning of the surrounding context (Adams, 1990; McConkie & Zola, 1981; Stanovich, 1991a, 1991b, 1992). For example, if you are reading "Kevin was walking his . . ." and then come to the word *dog*, you automatically—instantaneously and without conscious attention—process the letters in *dog*, even though in this case the word is fairly predictable. This seemingly obsessive processing of the letters in words actually makes word recognition faster than trying to predict upcoming words based on context, such as guessing the kind of animal Kevin might be walking.

Because young children cannot read many printed words automatically, we encourage them to use the context, any illustrations, and what they already know about language and the world to support their fledgling word recognition. However, as a child is taught specific ways in which letters relate to sounds, these letter-sound cues to word identification must take precedence over contextual and picture cues. Ultimately, letter-sound cues provide much more reliable information and a more efficient means to word recognition than do contextual cues or illustrations.

Your ability to reflect on, enjoy, and learn from a text depends on your thinking about the content as you read. Automatic word recognition enables a reader to think about content when reading. Still, automatic word recognition does not ensure good comprehension. It's what is called a necessary but insufficient condition. Even with it, a reader may lack the prior knowledge, conceptual background, interest, analytic skill, wit, and other factors required to understand a particular text.

The challenge you will face as a teacher of young children is to help them learn to recognize words without losing sight of the goal of reading—getting meaning. Children must learn how to rapidly pronounce *pond*, but they must also know the meaning. Accurate and automatic word recognition is the quickest route to a text's meaning. Explicit instruction in letter-sound patterns and relationships will be helpful for the vast majority of children.

In this chapter, we help you to build your understanding of the structure of spoken and printed words and of instructional procedures for teaching beginning readers how to recognize words. Without instruction in how to recognize words, most children will struggle with learning to read in first grade. And studies in several countries with different curricula and languages (Clay, 1979; Juel, 1994; Lundberg, 1984) have found that children who flounder with reading at this tender age have great difficulty catching up. Hence, it is critical for teachers of young children to be thoroughly competent in teaching beginning reading. Word recognition is a considerable focus of reading instruction in the early primary grades.

The Structure of Spoken and Printed Words

Say your name out loud. You just created speech. You used your vocal system to modify the flow of air as you exhaled from your lungs. There are a limited number of ways you can affect this exhalation in your throat. You can modify it with your tongue and with your lips. You can change the direction in which the outgoing breaths are channeled and the length of time it takes the air to pass through the vocal system. Making a speech sound requires several simultaneous manipulations. You can build a puff of air behind your closed lips and let it suddenly burst out to make a /p/ sound; or, as you let out the burst, you can move your tongue up to touch the ridge behind your upper front teeth and make it a /t/ sound.

The Makeup of Spoken and Written English

The speech sounds that are used to distinguish one word from another in a particular language are called *phonemes*. In English, /s/ and /e/ are phonemes. Phonemes are a rather abstract level of language analysis, and what is perceived as a phoneme differs from one language to another. In English there are approximately 44 phonemes.

Phonemes: Vowels and Consonants

Phonemes are divided into vowel sounds and consonant sounds. *Vowel* sounds are made when the air leaving your lungs is vibrated in the larynx but then has a clear passage from the larynx to outside your mouth. How you hold your tongue as the air passes by determines which vowel sounds you make. *Consonants* are speech sounds that are made when the airflow is obstructed in some way in your mouth. For example, the consonant sound /p/ is made by letting air build behind the lips before it is released from your mouth.

Syllables, Onsets, and Rimes

In all languages, the basic phonological unit of speech is the *syllable.* At a minimum, a syllable contains a vowel. Most basic syllables contain an onset and a rime. The *onset* is the initial consonant or consonants, and the *rime* is the vowel and any consonants that follow it. In *sat,* the onset is *s* and the rime is *at.* In *smack,* the onset is *sm* and the rime is *ack.* In the two-syllable word *something,* *s* is the onset in the first syllable and *ome* is the rime; *th* is the onset in the second syllable and *ing* is the rime.

In speech, the syllable is the most noticeable unit. It is no coincidence that nursery rhymes and Dr. Seuss books are filled with wordplay involving the onsets and rimes of syllables. Onsets and rimes are naturally compelling sound units, and playing with them typically delights young children. They are likely to repeat lines such as "Jack and Jill went up the hill" literally hundreds of times, just for the fun of it.

Different languages have different rules about what sounds can precede and follow the vowel in a syllable. In English, an onset can be made up of a single consonant (such as *b* in *back* or *s* in *sit*) or a cluster of up to three consonants (*bl* in *black* or *str* in *strike*). Although most English syllables have an onset, they do not have to. Consider the word *about.* The first syllable is *a.* It has no onset. It has only the rime. A rime in English must contain a vowel, and a rime usually ends with a consonant or a consonant cluster. The *it* in *sit* and *ack* in *back* are examples. In English, the most common syllable structure is consonant-vowel-consonant (or CVC), as in *dog, cat,* or *pig.* CVC syllable units can be strung together to create multisyllabic words, such as *market* or *napkin.* English also allows several modifications of this CVC unit. For instance, two or three consonant sounds can occur together, as in *flat, split, blast,* or *splash.*

There are six common spelling patterns for syllables in English, as shown in Figure 7.1. These are the consonant and vowel spelling patterns that readers usually encounter in words. As you look at Figure 7.1, remember that there can be up to three consonants on either side of a vowel in a syllable.

Figure 7.1 Six Common Spelling Patterns in English Syllables

1. Syllable that ends with a consonant: **CVC** (*sat, splat, napkin*), **VC** (*at, up*); the vowel is usually short.
2. Syllable that ends with a vowel: **CV** (*me, spider*), **V** (*a, halo, baby*); the vowel is often long.
3. Final *e:* **CVCe** (*take, home, cupcake*); the vowel is often long while the final *e* is silent.
4. Vowel team (for example, *ai, ee, ea, oa*), as in *team, green, lean, toad, peanut;* in these particular pairs, the first vowel is often long and the second one silent, but that does not apply to many vowel teams.
5. Vowel plus *r:* *ar, ur, ir, or, er* (for example, *far, fur, fir, for, her*)
6. Consonant plus *le,* as in *little, purple, turtle, treble*

Note: C stands for consonant, V stands for vowel.

Word Families and Phonograms

Unfortunately, quite a few terms are used in discussing word study, and they are not always used consistently. Many current instructional materials are likely to refer to onsets and rimes. Some materials refer to *phonograms*. Phonograms are rimes that share the same spellings. You will sometimes see the terms *rime* and *phonogram* used interchangeably. Words that share phonograms are called a *word family*. Thus *cat, bat, hat, flat,* and *mat* share the *at* phonogram (or rime) and belong to the *at* word family. Similarly, *same, game, tame, blame, fame,* and *flame* share the *ame* phonogram (or rime) and belong to the *ame* word family.

Morphemes

All languages use *morphemes* to represent the meaning level of speech. Morphemes are the smallest meaning units into which a word can be divided. Both words and parts of words can be morphemes. *Dog* is a morpheme, and the *-s* in *dogs* is also a morpheme; the *-s* has meaning by indicating that the word is plural. Figure 7.2 shows various ways of segmenting words.

Any word can be described at both the morphemic level and the phonological level. *Dog* is a one-syllable word with one morpheme. Its phonological structure is the common CVC syllable pattern: *d* is the onset and *og* is the rime. *Dog* is also called a *root word*, or *root*, because it can both stand alone and be combined with other roots to form new words. *Doghouse* is a *compound word* containing two root words, *dog* and *house*. *House* consists of the onset *h* and the rime *ouse*.

Figure 7.2

Various Ways of Segmenting Words

	PLANET	CATS
Morphemes	planet	cat s
Syllables	plan et	cats
Onsets and rimes	/pl-an-ət/	/k-ats/
Phonemes	/p-l-a-n-ət/	/k-a-t-s/

Affixes: Prefixes and Suffixes

Morphemes that cannot stand alone to form words are called *affixes*. There are two types of affixes. A *prefix* is placed before a root to form a word with a meaning different from that of the root. White, Sowell, and Yanagihara (1989) have produced a list of the most frequently occurring prefixes, shown in Figure 7.3. A *suffix* is placed after a root to form a word with a different meaning or a different grammatical function. There are two kinds of suffixes: inflectional and derivational. *Inflectional suffixes* make a word plural or indicate tense, as do the *-s* in *dogs* and the *-ed* in *snowed*. There are only a few inflectional suffixes, but they occur frequently. Figure 7.4 shows a complete list of inflectional suffixes taken from Rinsky (1993). *Derivational suffixes* alter a word's meaning and its grammatical function. Common suffixes include *-ly* as in *lively*, *-ive* as in *selective*, and *-ment* as in *excitement*. There are a relatively large number of derivational suffixes, and most of them occur relatively infrequently. Figure 7.5, also taken from Rinsky (1993), shows a few derivational suffixes and illustrates their effects when attached to root words.

In sum, the structure of spoken and printed words is complex. To provide effective word recognition instruction, you need to be familiar with the structure of words and the ways that they can be analyzed.

The Alphabetic Principle

The basic principle underlying English writing is the *alphabetic principle*—phonemes are represented by letters. The three letters in *mad*, for example, correspond to the

Figure 7.3 Most Frequently Occurring Prefixes

Prefix	Words with the Prefix	Prefix	Words with the Prefix
un-	782	inter-	77
re-	401	fore-	76
in-, im-, ir-, il- ("not")	313	de-	71
dis-	216	trans-	47
en-, em-	132	super-	43
non-	126	semi-	39
in-, im- ("in" or "into")	105	anti-	33
over- ("too much")	98	mid-	33
mis-	83	under- ("too little")	25
sub-	80	All others	100 (estimated)
pre-	79	Total	2,959

Source: White, Thomas G., Sowell, Joanne, & Yanagihara, Alice. (1989, January). "Teaching Elementary Students to Use Word-Part Clues." *The Reading Teacher, 42*(4), 302–308. Copyright © 1989 by the International Reading Association (www.reading.org). Reproduced with permission of the International Reading Association via Copyright Clearance Center.

three phonemes /m/, /a/, /d/. The four letters in *dash* correspond to the three phonemes /d/, /a/, /sh/. The correspondence between letters and sounds in English is not perfect. There are only 26 letters to represent the approximately 44 phonemes. Many letters represent more than one sound. For example, *e* represents the sound you hear in *pet* and also the sound in *Pete*. Two or more letters sometime represent a single sound. For example, *ea* represents the sound you hear in *head* and also the sound in

Figure 7.4

A Complete List of English Inflectional Suffixes

s (es)	plural	boys, brushes
's, (s')	possessive apostrophe	boy's, boys'
s	third-person singular	sings
ed	past tense	grabbed
ing	present participle	singing
en	past participle	has/have eaten
er	comparative	taller
est	superlative	tallest

Source: Rinsky, Lee Ann, *Teaching Word Recognition Skills* (5th ed.), © 1993. Reprinted by permission of Pearson Education, Inc., Upper Saddle River, NJ.

Figure 7.5 A Few Derivational Suffixes

Root Word	Part of Speech	Suffix	Affixed Word	Part of Speech
base	n.	-ic	basic	adj.
correct	adj.	-ly	correctly	adv.
fool	n.	-ish	foolish	adj.
allow	v.	-ance	allowance	n.
person	n.	-al	personal	adj.
attract	v.	-ive	attractive	adj.
clever	adj.	-ness	cleverness	n.
agree	v.	-ment	agreement	n.

Source: Rinsky, Lee Ann, *Teaching Word Recognition Skills* (5th ed.), © 1993. Reprinted by permission of Pearson Education, Inc., Upper Saddle River, NJ.

meat. And many sounds can be represented by more than one letter. For example, *booth, threw,* and *blue* all have the same vowel sound. Vowels are the most troublesome in this regard, but some consonants also represent more than one sound. For example, *c* can represent both /s/ and /k/.

Another difficulty with alphabetic writing systems is that phonemes don't exist as nice, neat, cleanly divisible units. They are only somewhat separable in words. For example, as you say the word *mad,* you actually begin forming your mouth to say the *a* while you are still saying the *m;* likewise, you begin to pronounce the *d* while finishing the *a.* As we shared in Chapter 6, this is called *coarticulation,* and it allows rapid and seamless speech. However, it also makes phonemes harder to hear. Moreover, some phonemes are even impossible to say in isolation without adding a vowel sound. For example, if you were to tell a child the sounds the letters *d* and *p* make, you would probably say something like "duh" and "puh." But there is no *duh* in *dad* and no *puh* in *pat.* Yet adding the schwa vowel to the consonants *d* and *b* makes the sound a bit easier for children to hear and aids blending (Murray, Brabham, Villaume, & Veal, 2008).

Devising a writing system to link letters and sounds required considerable insight and abstraction. Only relatively recently in human history were alphabetic writing systems invented—sometime between 1000 and 700 B.C. These systems are often considered to be among the most important human inventions. Their abstract nature is part of the reason that children have difficulty learning them: Being able to attend to a less-than-concrete phoneme in a spoken word, isolate it from the other sounds in the word, and attach it to a letter is quite a mental feat.

The Structure of Printed Words: The Good News

We are thus faced with the fact that the English writing system presents considerable challenges to children learning to read. The good news, though, is that many of the words with the strangest spellings tend to be the ones we see most frequently in print (e.g., *said, was, what, their, where, through*). Because of this, we have many opportunities to memorize them. The even better news is that despite glaring exceptions, there is a lot of regularity in English spelling. Even words with strange spellings include some letters that provide useful sound cues to their identity. Usually, the most reliable letters are the consonants.

Through years of reading, you have learned a lot about the structure of printed words even though you may not be able to articulate what you know. You also know intuitively that some letter sequences are much more likely to occur than others. For instance, you know that words are more likely to start with *pr* or *br* than with *rb* or *rp*—but just the opposite is true at the ends of words. You have this tacit knowledge because for years you have carefully looked at individual words as you read.

Even multisyllabic words, though they can be admittedly difficult, yield to analysis. Multisyllabic words are simply strings of syllables, and these syllables are composed of onsets and rimes. Though not perfectly consistent, there is a tendency in English to "chunk" words into syllables by placing at a syllabic division letter sequences that are less likely to occur next to each other within a syllable. For example, in the word *haystack* we have several clues as to where to divide the word. First, there are two morphemes, *hay* and *stack.* Second, each syllable is a common variant of CVC units and contains common onsets (*h* and *st*) and common rimes (*ay* and *ack*). Third, the letter combination *ys* is not likely to begin a syllable. Double consonants are also a common signal of a syllabic division. Only one consonant is actually pronounced, as you can see in *dinner* or *rabbit.*

A big part of what makes you an efficient recognizer of words is having read a lot. There is a lesson in this: *Wide reading is important for children to develop word recognition proficiency.* Most young readers will need instruction to develop their ability to recognize words, and all children need to read a lot to develop reading proficiency.

1 Identify the onsets and rimes in *hen, past, back, mill,* and *time.* Then make a list of other words that share one of these rimes and thus belong to the same word family.

2 What are the morphemes, roots, and affixes in the words *haystack, dinner,* and *beehives*? What are some clues as to how to divide the words into syllables?

3 Skilled adults can read nonsense words almost as quickly as they can read their own names. See how quickly you can read these nonsense words: *zat, mig, unplick, kip, cleef, fand,* and *bufwixable.* The extent to which you read them quickly offers proof of the incredible sophistication skilled readers have in analyzing words and generating their pronunciations.

Our Position on Phonics Instruction and Related Matters

Phonics is an umbrella term for instruction about letter-sound correspondences. Acquiring phonics knowledge is critical to becoming an accomplished reader. Although a small percentage of children acquire phonics knowledge on their own, most children need direct teaching. This position is consistent with the findings of Jeanne Chall, a Harvard professor who reviewed the research on beginning reading instruction in a landmark book titled *Learning to Read: The Great Debate* (1967), and with most interpretations of Guy Bond and Robert Dykstra's first grade study (1967/1997), the most ambitious study of beginning reading conducted in this country. This position is also consistent with a host of research reports, syntheses of research, and position statements published over the past decade or so. These include special issues of the *American Educator* published in 1995 and 1998; the International Reading Association's position paper on phonics, *The Role of Phonics in Reading Instruction* (1997b); Elfrieda Hiebert and her colleagues' *Every Child a Reader* (Hiebert, Pearson, Taylor, Richardson, & Paris, 1998); Snow and her colleagues' *Preventing Reading Difficulties in Young Children* (1998); Burns and her colleagues' *Starting Out Right* (Burns et al., 1999); the American Federation of Teachers' *Teaching Reading Is Rocket Science* (1999); and the *Report of the National Reading Panel: Teaching Children to Read* (National Reading Panel, 2000). This position finally is consistent with the majority of research on beginning reading and with common sense. We are the enormously fortunate inheritors of an alphabetic writing system; we need to teach our children how to take advantage of that system.

Some children need less phonics instruction than others, and phonics instruction must always be kept in proper perspective—as a means to an end. Comprehension is the goal of reading, and reading, writing, speaking, listening, and being read to must form the heart of the literacy curriculum. But for readers who have not yet mastered the code of written English, learning to read words—which includes phonics—plays an absolutely essential role.

Learning to Read Words

Research suggests that children move through a series of overlapping developmental phases as they learn to read words. In these phases, children read words in different ways. We first will summarize the phases, and then describe the more general cognitive processes in which readers engage as they read words.

Developmental Phases in Learning to Read Words

Ehri (Ehri, 1998; Ehri & Snowling, 2004) has articulated a developmental theory of word reading that is grounded in two decades of research. According to Ehri, as children learn to read words, they form connections between the features of printed words and the sounds they represent. Children look at a printed word, pronounce it, and then analyze how the print represents the sounds in the word. This analysis helps children to store the word in memory. When children encounter a word in print, they draw on the connections they have formed for the word. Children form different kinds of connections as they move through four developmental phases: pre-alphabetic, partial alphabetic, full alphabetic, and consolidated alphabetic.

Pre-Alphabetic Phase

Very young children read words based on visual but nonalphabetic features. For example, children might read the word *look* by remembering that the *os* in the word look like "two round eyes" (Ehri, 1998, p. 19) or the word *camel* by remembering the two humps in the word (Gough, Juel, & Roper/Schneider, 1983). This kind of word reading is also known as visual cue reading (Gough, Juel, & Roper/Schneider, 1983) and logographic reading (Frith, 1985).

Partial Alphabetic Phase

In this stage, children are learning letter-sound correspondences and use what they know to form partial connections between letters and sounds in words and word meanings. Initial and final letters are often the letters used to remember and read words. For example, a child might use the *s* and *n* to remember and read the word *spoon* (Ehri, 1998). A problem for children in this phase is misidentifications that result when words have similar letters. For example, a child would identify *kitten* and *kitchen* as the same word (Gaskins, Ehri, Cress, O'Hara, & Donnelly, 1997). Similarly, a child would have difficulty distinguishing between *drop, drip,* and *damp* (Ehri, 1998).

Full Alphabetic Phase

In the next phase, children have well developed knowledge of letter-sound correspondences. They have formed what Ehri (1998) calls complete connections between letters and sounds in words and word meanings. For example, Ehri explains that a child in this phase would have formed connections between the *s, p, oo,* and *n* in the word *spoon* and would use them all to read the word. This kind of reading has been referred to as *alphabetic reading* (Frith, 1985) and sequential *decoding* (Marsh et al., 1981). Chall (1996) has described children who read words in this manner as "glued to print."

Consolidated Alphabetic Phase

In the last phase, children consolidate the letter patterns that they see across words into larger units (Ehri, 1998). They connect these larger units to the spoken forms of words and their meanings. For example, Ehri explains, as children encounter words such as *nest, pest, rest, best,* and *test,* they consolidate the *e, s,* and *t* into the unit *est* (a rime). This consolidation enables children to read words more easily. As Ehri describes, a child in this phase would read the word *chest* using two units—*ch* and *est*—rather than the four letter-sound correspondences a child in the full alphabetic phase would require—*ch, e, s, t.* This kind of reading has been called *orthographic reading* (Frith, 1985) and ungluing from print (Chall, 1996).

Processes Involved in Reading Words

Ehri (1998) has emphatically stated "teachers need to understand the processes that their instruction is aimed at teaching and the behaviors that indicate whether students are progressing along the lines expected in learning to read. Teachers need this knowledge to evaluate and improve the effectiveness of their instructional efforts" (p. 4). We agree. Before we discuss particular instructional techniques, we summarize the cognitive processes at which word recognition instruction is directed. We draw on Ehri's (1998) and Thompson's (1999) articulations of these processes. Clear and succinct, they provide a useful framework within which to understand related instruction.

Ehri has identified four processes readers use to recognize words. These are *sight word reading, decoding, analogizing,* and *contextual guessing.* Thompson (1999) has described these processes as *recall* (sight word reading) and *generation* (decoding, analogizing, using context). When a child encounters a known printed word in text, he reads it as a whole unit from sight. That is, he recalls it from memory. When he encounters an unknown printed word, he needs to generate a pronunciation for it. This is accomplished through decoding, analogizing to known words, or using contextual information.

Decoding is the process of identifying letter-sound correspondences as well as larger units in a word and blending them to form a word. For example, a child who encounters the unknown word *drop* might map the letters onto individual letter-sound correspondences to generate a pronunciation (i.e., /d/ /r/ /o/ /p/) or might use the onset and rime to decode the word (i.e., /dr/ /op/).

Analogizing is the process of comparing an unknown word to a similarly spelled known word. For example, a child who is reading Peter McCarty's *Little Bunny on the Move* might read the word *bunny* by analogizing to the known word *sunny.* To identify *bunny,* the child has recalled from memory the known word *sunny,* identified the analogous word part *unny,* and replaced the *s* with *b.* Analogizing is probably the process that adults use when encountering a new and complex word.

When readers use contextual information, they draw on *semantic* cues (meaning cues) and *syntactic* cues (grammatical cues) to identify a word. For example, a child who doesn't know the word *bird* in a sentence could use an illustration of a bird on the page to correctly guess the word's identity. Similarly, a child reading the sentence "Sam was walking his dog" who didn't know the word *dog* would stand a good chance of correctly guessing the word from the sentence context. There are very few words that would make sense in the sentence and fit the grammatical structure.

A caution as you consider teaching children to use contextual information to support word recognition—research has shown that most words are not very predictable from contextual information (Gough & Walsh, 1991; Stanovich, 1980). Those that are tend to be *function* words—words that primarily express grammatical relationships, such as articles (e.g., *a, an, the*), prepositions (e.g., *of, to, in*), and conjunctions (e.g., *and, for, but*). *Content* words carry most of the meaning in a sentence. They aren't very predictable. We want very beginning readers to use all of what they know to identify words, but we don't want to overemphasize the use of context. Research has shown that relying on contextual information to identify unknown words is a process that very beginning readers and older weak readers rely on, which can easily become a bad habit (Nicholson, 1991; Stanovich, 1986). Skillful readers recognize most of the words they read at sight; when they don't know a word, they generate a pronunciation for the word using their extensive letter-sound and orthographic (spelling)

*A*ssessment

The Tile Test found in Appendix A provides a strong measure of students' understanding of letters, sounds, words, and sentences.

knowledge (Adams, 1990; McConkie & Zola, 1981; Stanovich, 1991a, 1991b, 1992; Thompson, 1999).

Word Study Instruction

Word study refers to instruction about words. Remember, any sort of word study instruction is a means to an end—comprehension of text. We want to empower children with the knowledge and skills to unlock the meanings of printed words. Word study instruction can include a focus on high-frequency words, letter-sound correspondences, the larger units in words, and attention to the meaning elements in words (e.g., affixes and root words). You need to tailor your instruction to students, and research that one of us conducted suggests that different learners will need different emphases (Juel & Minden-Cupp, 2000). You want to keep word study instruction active as well, as in the following examples of active teaching and learning in word study:

- Children sort picture cards on the basis of the phonemes in pictured words.
- Teachers provide explicit instruction about which letters represent which sounds.
- Teachers explain and demonstrate how to blend individual phonemes to form words.
- Children sort word cards on the basis of letter-sound correspondences and other units in words.
- Children read text with repetitions of high-frequency words and common spelling patterns.
- Children write words that share common features (e.g., phonemes, rimes, affixes, roots).
- Children write dictated words and sentences with target spelling patterns or high-frequency words.

Six General Principles of Word Study Instruction

The word study instruction we recommend follows six basic principles:

1. Start where the child is.
2. Make word study an active process of classification.
3. Base word study on contrasting words with different sounds or spellings.
4. Help children understand how the writing system works.
5. Teach students how to develop a strategy for unlocking the pronunciations of unknown words.
6. Keep comprehension as the goal.

1. *Start where the child is.* Begin with concepts about words the child already understands and words the child can read. For example, if the child writes words primarily as initial consonants—*pig* as *p, dig* as *d,* and *big* as *b*—but stops there, then it is time to teach rimes such as *ig* and to help the child perceive and manipulate the letter sounds in *ig.*

2. *Learning occurs as an active process of classification.* Word study is based on this premise. Children learn about words by analyzing and classifying them on the basis of whether or not they share certain features, for example, a phoneme, onset, rime, affix, or root word.

PEARSON
myeducationlab

Watch the video showing a first-grade teacher administering an assessment of phonemic awareness in the activity "Assessing Student Phonemic Awareness." (To find this activity, go to the topic *Phonemic Awareness/Phonics* in MyEducationLab and click on Assignments and Activities.)

3. *Word study instruction is based on contrasts.* That is, children learn to perceive short *i* by contrasting short *i* words with words that have another vowel. By contrasting *sit* with *sat*, *bit* with *bat*, *pit* with *pat*, and *slip* with *slap*, the child can begin to perceive which letters represent which sounds. By comparing words that have contrasting patterns, a child can focus on which features make which differences in words, but only if he pronounces the words while sorting them.

Words can be contrasted in different ways. Sorting picture cards is one effective way to highlight contrasts in phonemes. A picture card is simply a card with a picture on it, such as a pig, rug, wig, or hug. Picture sorting for particular phonemes or rimes develops children's phonemic awareness—the ability to hear the somewhat separable sounds in spoken words. For example, children must determine whether the picture of a hug goes under the picture of a pig or under the picture of a rug (*hug–pig* or *hug–rug*). Does the word *hug* fit better with the sound /ug/ or the sound /ig/? To make these categorical judgments, children must engage in critical thinking rather than drill or memorization (Bear, Invernizzi, Templeton, & Johnston, 2007). However, these sorts can easily become mindless drill unless children are challenged to pronounce and justify their decisions.

4. *Children need to understand how the writing system works.* In learning to read and write, children need to understand how speech is written down. They need to perceive units of speech, such as phonemes and rimes. They need to learn which speech units are represented by which letters. Teachers of emergent readers will need to model how to segment spoken words into speech units and then how to connect these units to letters. They will need to help students perceive the units of speech that are represented in writing—words, syllables, and phonemes. And finally, they will need to help children learn how to represent these units in their own writing.

5. *Children need strategies to determine pronunciations of unknown words.* It is not enough to learn the patterns within a word; the students need a process to help them employ that knowledge. For example, a student might successively blend sound to pronounce the word *splat,* but use an analogy process to pronounce *banter.* (If I know *can* I know *ban,* and if I know *her* I know *ter.*) Ultimately, the reader has to use these strategies and know when to use them.

6. *Keep comprehension as the goal.* Children are learning to recognize words so that they can read stories, informational books, poems, and other texts.

4 A child reads the word *clothes* as *color* in one part of a passage and a few sentences later reads it as *cold.* At what stage of word recognition is the child? How can you move this reader to a higher level of word recognition?

5 Explain two major reasons why the alphabetic principle is difficult for some children to learn. How is the English alphabetic system less than perfect?

Getting Started with Word Study: Building a Basic Reading Vocabulary

So where do you begin? Picture a kindergarten or first-grade classroom. The door opens, and suddenly the room fills with bright-eyed children eager to learn. However, these hopeful, energetic children may or may not be able to recognize or produce the letters of the alphabet, may or may not accurately track speech to print by finger-pointing to memorized text, may only be able to scribble letters or intersperse letters and scribbles in their writing, and may not be able to read any words. In other words,

Differentiating Instruction for English Language Learners

Proximal Partners

- Bear, Helman, Templeton, Invernizzi, and Johnston (2007) remind us that English language learners must have opportunities to practice and ask questions when working on tasks. They suggest teachers assign "proximal partners" to English language learners—someone to pair up with as they engage in learning tasks. Bear and his colleagues note that it is helpful when possible to pair an outgoing English language learner with a more reserved but more proficient native English speaker. This creates a balance of skills between partners. Such pairings can be used in a picture sort for short vowel sounds. Both children have their own cards to sort. As the children sort the cards, they say the name of the picture. Then they place the card with other cards representing the same vowel sound. Afterward, they explain their sorts to their partners. This allows the English language learner to practice using spoken English and to have an opportunity to ask questions and receive feedback.

- A major task of second language acquisition is learning the vocabulary. Bear and his colleagues note that concept sorts are a good way of helping English language learners with this task. Let's say that children are studying the weather as part of the science curriculum. During word study instruction, your English language learners can engage in a picture sort of cards that represent weather-related terms (e.g., the sun, rain, snow, clouds, thermometer). Bear and his colleagues provide a set of such cards in their text *Words Their Way with English Learners*, but you can also make your own. Pair English language learners with native English speakers and have them engage in and talk about their sorts.

children with a wide range of proficiencies enter your classroom. One of your first tasks is to identify what individual children do and do not know and can and cannot do. Following this, your job will be to help every child become a competent reader and writer.

We start by sharing how to help children develop a basic reading vocabulary. Then we discuss teaching children letter-sound correspondences and the larger units in words. Afterword, we discuss the importance of contextual reading to word recognition development. We conclude with our thoughts on the importance of wide reading to children's word learning.

Assessing Sight Vocabulary

Skilled readers have substantial sight vocabularies. Very likely, you have not needed to decode or otherwise generate a pronunciation for a single word that you have read in this text. You read the words automatically. Beginning readers have very limited sight vocabularies. A good way to develop children's sight vocabularies is to start with words they already know. Most children entering first grade can read their names and a few words, such as color words, names of family members, and kinds of household pets.

A quick individual assessment of the words each child knows will help you to plan instruction. Your school may provide the assessment, or one may come with the set of published materials in use at your school. You can also use the word list shown in Figure 7.6, which includes both high-frequency function words and common content words. You can modify it by adding words that you are planning to have children read in books, on charts, around your room, or at home. To create a quick assessment

Assessment

Graded word lists, part of the Interactive Reading Assessment System that is found in Appendix A, can be used to assess students' sight vocabulary.

if you don't have one, clearly print a set of words on a list with space between them. Make as many copies as you need to assess children in your class. Individually, have children read the list. On your copy, note (1) whether the child reads a word correctly and (2) the nature of any misreadings—write the word or word part the child says in response to the word on the list. This will give you information on how the child approaches reading words. You can build on the child's existing knowledge to further word learning.

Word Banks

A word bank is a child's personal collection of words. Children work with these words regularly in class to cement them in memory. To create a child's word bank, print words on small cards. It is important that you—rather than the child—print the words because emergent readers are still learning how to form letters. The child keeps the cards in a small plastic bag or some other container.

The first word in a word bank can be a child's first name. Then add words the child already can read. Next, personalize the word bank by asking the child what other words she can read and adding them to the collection. You might also add a few words that the child volunteers she would like to learn. These might include a favorite food, the name of a pet, the name of a favorite friend, or a favorite activity. Add new words to the word bank each day. Both you and the child may select words to add. Good words to choose are those that the child will see a lot in print and use in daily writing. High-interest words are good choices as well. A child's word bank should grow until it has about 100 words. At that point, it becomes unwieldy. Figure 7.7 shows the word bank of a beginning first-grader.

Reviewing words and seeing them frequently in books and poems will help children continue to recognize them as new ones are added. Remember that young readers typically have incomplete knowledge of the letters in a word. They might recognize a word by its initial consonant or by its length. As new words are added to the word bank, old words can be "forgotten." For example, a child who "knows" the word *cat* in her word bank because the first two letters are *ca* may fail to recognize it when the word *can* is added to the bank. The more times children look at their word bank words and compare them, the more likely they are to form connections between all the letters in the word and the sounds they make. This is what enables them to fully learn the words. First-grade teacher Gordon Scholander describes how he uses word banks with his emergent readers:

My young scholars frequently enjoy sharing their word banks. They will sometimes read their word bank cards to each other, or, with a buddy, they'll sort their cards into categories—such as animals or words that start or end with a particular letter. Sometimes I'll have them spread out ten or so of their individual word bank cards on their desks or work with a buddy to try variants of a "pick-up" game. Here are some prompts I give them for the game:

- Pick up all your animal words. Read your words to a buddy. Do you and your buddy have any of the same animals?
- Pick up all your color words. Hold up the card with your favorite color on it.
- Pick up all your words that start with /sssss/. Read them to a buddy.
- Pick up all your words that start with the letter *b*. Read your *b* words to a buddy.
- Pick up words that rhyme with *cat*. What do you have?
- Pick up all your words that have three letters. Read them to a buddy.
- Pick up your longest word and share it with a buddy.

—Gordon Scholander, first-grade teacher

Figure 7.6

A List to Use for a Quick Check on Words Children Know

the	dog	big	cat	run	is
at	like	see	can	to	dog
he	my	yellow	and	red	get
up	go	she	girl	bus	was

Figure 7.7

Marcos's Beginning First-Grade Word Bank

Marcos

cat	soccer
the	pizza
and	Luis
red	

High-Frequency Words

High-frequency words are the most common words in printed English. Children will encounter them over and over when they read, including function words like *as, the, and,* and *of,* and content words such as *girl, blue,* and *little.* Some high-frequency words are very regular in their letter-sound correspondences. That is, they sound the way they look (e.g., *then, it, she*). Some are not very regular (e.g., *was, there, said*). It is difficult to read very much without knowing high-frequency words well. Along with letter-sound (phonics) instruction, high-frequency word practice will be helpful in getting beginning readers started. Many lists of high-frequency words are available, and most published reading series identify the high-frequency words that appear in their materials.

Teacher educator and former teacher Linda Allen (1998) has shared an effective instructional routine for teaching high-frequency words. Allen calls high-frequency words "core" words. In the instructional routine, rhythm and movement support learning. The routine is an enjoyable one that children find very motivating. Allen advocates grounding word study—core word and otherwise—in stories, informational books, or poems. We share Allen's instructional routine here.

A core word lesson typically involves about three new words. The teacher first presents the core words in a series of sentences from a text that children have read or will read with the teacher. If the sentences in the book are too long or not quite right for this step in the lesson, the teacher can modify them. The target core words in the sentences are highlighted in some way, for example, underlined or written in a contrasting color. Then each core word is analyzed apart from the sentences. The teacher points out the sound and visual features of each word. This helps children to notice the letters and sounds in the word and form connections between them. Next, children chant the spelling of each core word as they clap, snap their fingers, and write the words on a sheet of paper, on a small white board, or in a word study journal. Children then read new sentences containing the core words. Following the lesson, the words are placed on what is known as a word wall for future reinforcement and reference, as we will discuss shortly.

In the Classroom 7.1 shows a core word lesson. The book around which the lesson is built is Joanne Oppenheim's *"Not Now!" Said the Cow.* The book is a predictable text in which a crow finds a sack of corn seed on the ground. For each step in the planting and growing process, he asks various barnyard animals to help him. The language the crow uses to ask and that which the animals use to respond (in the negative) is a repetitive pattern. At the end of the book, the crow makes popcorn. All the animals wish to help him eat the popcorn, but the crow replies that he will eat it "all by myself."

Word Walls

Primary-grade teachers often have word walls. They typically set aside a bulletin board or a wall for this purpose. Word walls can be organized in two ways. Most teachers organize their words alphabetically by the word's first letter. Along the top of the word wall are the letters of the alphabet. Teachers place words under the letter with which they begin as children learn them. Generally, teachers add a handful of words to the word wall each week. Cunningham (2009) notes that first-grade teachers typically begin word walls with children's names and then focus on high-frequency words. A word wall organized alphabetically assists students as they spell. A student who can't remember how to spell *friend* segments the word and isolates the initial sound. Then he searches under the *f*s to find the word.

Teaching High-Frequency Words

- *State the purpose.* "Our purpose today is to learn to read and spell three new core words. Core words are words we see a lot when we read and use a lot when we write. The core words we'll learn today are *who*, *said*, and *what*."
- *Show and read the words in sentences.* "Let's read these sentences together. Then we'll look closely at each core word."

> *"Who* will help me plant the seed?" *said* the crow.
> "Not now!" *said* the cow.
> Just *what* we need, a sack of seed!

- *Highlight the features in words.* "Let's think carefully about how each word looks and sounds."

> *who:* "In *who*, the *wh* sounds like /h/. The *o* sounds like the *o* in *to—who.*"
> *said:* "In *said*, we hear the /s/ at the beginning and the /d/ at the end. The middle of the word doesn't sound the way it looks. It sounds like /eh/ as in *red—said.*"
> *what:* "In *what*, the *wh* makes a /hw/ sound. The *a* sounds like /uh/. We hear the /t/ at the end—*what.*"

- *Chant, clap, snap, write the words.* "Let's spell each word out loud three times. The first time, we'll clap as we say each letter. Then we'll snap our fingers as we say each letter. Next, we'll write each word. As we write each letter, we'll say it. Let me show you how we do this. Watch and listen to me once. Then we'll clap, snap, and write the words together." Model chanting, clapping, snapping, and writing one word. Then, start again and have children chant, clap, snap, and write all new core words chorally with you.
- *Practice words in new sentences.* "Now, let's read our new core words in these sentences. Let's read together."

> Do you know *who* will help me plant the seed?
> Cow and hog *said* they will not pull weeds.
> *What* will crow do?

- *Final review.* Remind students why core words are important. "Today we learned three new core words—*who*, *said*, and *what*. Core words are important to know because we see them a lot when we read and use them a lot when we write."

Word walls can also be organized a second way—by the rime or spelling pattern. These word walls have six sections for rimes beginning with *a, e, i, o, u,* and *y.* Thus, *cat, made,* and *rain* are all organized under *a.* This word wall facilitates the process of decoding by analogy. If the child encounters the word *remain* she can look at the word wall and find the word *rain* and the spelling pattern *ain* to help her read the word. If you teach analogy strategies, this type of word wall will be very useful.

Cunningham cautions that it is not enough for teachers to have a word wall; they must *do* word walls with children. This involves chanting and writing selected words and other reinforcement activities. Cunningham describes a favorite reinforcement activity, a game called *Be a Mind Reader.* A teacher thinks of a word on the word wall but keeps the word to himself. Children write down the numbers 1 through 5 as a list on their papers. Then the teacher gives the children five clues to the word that move from broad to narrow. As the teacher says each clue, children list the word they think the teacher has in mind. When the clues have all been given, the teacher reveals the word. By clue 5 most of the children have the word. The teacher then has the children share when they knew the word—after clue 4, 3, 2 or 1. A set of clues for the high-frequency word *every* might be as follows: (1) It's on the word wall. (2) It has five letters. (3) It begins with the short *e* sound. (4) It's a two beat (i.e., syllable) word. (5) In the word the *y* sounds like a long *e*. The high-frequency word *outside* might be given the following clues: (1) It's on the word wall. (2) It has seven letters. (3) It's a compound word. (4) It ends with a silent *e*. (5) It's the opposite of *inside*.

Teaching Letter-Sound Correspondences

Learning to read requires learning to understand the code of written language. In English, this is very much a matter of acquiring phonics knowledge—which sounds are represented by which letter(s). First-grade teacher Glenna Schwarze knows that reading independence means making sure her students get instruction in decoding skills:

> I am sure any first-grade teacher will tell you the same thing: At the heart of first-grade reading instruction is ensuring that children learn to decode words. Of course, we want children to be able to instantly recognize as many words as possible, but we also need to be sure they are equipped with strategies and skills to use when they don't instantly know a word. The beginning reader, of course, cannot instantly recognize many words. As teachers, however, we can help children identify words they don't know by helping them recognize the letters in the words and how to translate those letters into the sounds they represent.

> —Glenna Schwarze, first-grade teacher

Research has shown that phonics instruction most benefits beginning readers when it is explicit and systematic (National Reading Panel, 2000). This means that letter-sound correspondences are specifically taught to children with instruction that follows a predetermined order (Beck, 2006). You will often see the following sequence recommended for teaching phonics elements: consonants, short vowels, long vowels, and vowels with other sounds. This order is likely because there is less variation in sounds that consonants make (Beck, 2006) and in the ways that short vowel sounds are represented in many primary-grade words. As Beck (2006) emphasizes, however, while we don't want to begin word study with complex vowel patterns, we also don't want to wait to teach some vowel sounds until all the consonants have been taught; vowels are needed to form words, and we want children forming and reading words right from the start.

In the Classroom 7.2 describes the major kinds of phonics elements for your reference. One difficulty in learning to teach beginning reading is developing an explicit knowledge of the units in words. At the end of the feature, we note the phonics elements that the New Standards Primary Literacy Committee (2004) states first-graders should know.

Next, we share a number of instructional routines for developing phonics knowledge that involve manipulating letters, phonograms, or other word parts. Beginning readers find the hands-on nature of these activities engaging and motivating.

Teaching Consonants

Teaching consonants involves teaching individual consonants (e.g., *s, n, d*), consonant blends (e.g., *st, cr, spr*), and consonant digraphs (e.g., *sh, ch, th, ph*). Researcher and former elementary school teacher Isabel Beck (2006) has developed a set of instructional routines for teaching letter-sound correspondences that we think makes pretty good sense, leading students through a series of steps to learn particular correspondences. First, the teacher directs children's attention to the

Assessment

A decoding test is provided in Appendix A as part of the Interactive Reading Assessment System. When you score students be sure to note the phonics patterns that present difficulty and those that do not.

Common Letter-Sound Correspondences

Consonants

- Consonants are all the letters but the vowels (*a, e, i, o, u,* and sometimes *y*); *y* is a consonant when it is at the beginning of a syllable (e.g., *yes, yelp, yellow*).
- The following consonants have two sounds:
    - *c* ("hard sound" as in *coat* and *cake*; "soft sound" as in *city* and *cereal*)
    - *g* ("hard sound" as in *girl* and *gap*; "soft sound" as in *giant* and *gentle*)
    - *x* (can sound like /ks/ as in *text* and *x-ray* or /z/ as in *xylophone* and *Xerox*)
- Consonant blends are two or three contiguous consonants in which each consonant is heard.
    - Common two-letter blends: *bl, br, cr, cl, dr, fl, fr, gl, gr, pl, pr, tr, sc, sk, sl, sm, sn, sp, st, tr, tw, sw*
    - Common three-letter blends: *scr, spr, squ, str, phr, sch, thr*
- Consonant digraphs are two contiguous consonants that together form a new sound.
    - Common consonant digraphs: *sh* (*she*), *ch* (*chain, chef, chorus*), *th* (*these, think*), *wh* (*white, which*), *gh* (*laugh, ghost*), *ph* (*phone*), *ng* (*ring*)

Short and Long Vowels (*a, e, i, o, u,* and sometimes *y*)

- Short vowels are the sounds the vowels make in the words *bat, pet, sit, hot,* and *bug*.
- Long vowels are the sounds the vowels make in *cake, see, ride, so,* and *cube*. The letter *y* also serves as a vowel, representing the long *i* sound (*shy, crying*) or the long *e* sound (*baby, bumpy*).

Vowel Digraphs

- For digraphs with two contiguous vowels, you may have been taught the expression, *When two vowels go walking, the first does the talking*. This speaks to words in which the first vowel in the digraph is long and the second one is silent (e.g., *meat, boat, rain, cue*). However, there are so many exceptions (e.g., *eight, they, break, ready, again, laugh, eye*) that it's best not to teach it as a phonics rule.

Diphthongs

- Words with two contiguous vowels are pronounced with a gliding sound as one sound moves into the other. Common diphthongs include *oi* and *oy* (*coin, boy*), *ou* (*shout*), and *ow* (*how*).

R-Controlled Vowels

- Vowels change their sound when they are followed by the letter *r* (*car, her, sir, for, fur*).

Common grammatical endings

- Plural *-s* can sound like /s/ as in *cats* and *banks* or /z/ as in *dogs* and *cars*.
- The past-tense ending *-ed* can make three sounds: /ed/ as in *waited*, /d/ as in *yelled*, or /t/ as in *asked*.

Note. According to the New Standards Primary Literacy Committee (2004), first-graders should know the following letter-sound correspondences: beginning and ending consonants; two-consonant beginning blends; consonant digraphs *ch, sh,* and *th*; short vowels; long vowels that follow the CVC*e* pattern (e.g., *cake*); and the vowel digraphs *ai, ee, oa,* and *ea*.

target correspondence. Then the teacher connects the letter with the sound it makes. Next, the children discriminate among words that have and do not have the correspondence or that have the correspondence in different positions in the word (e.g., di*p*, *p*ad). Beck's instructional routines most often involve a pocket chart for demonstration purposes and small word pockets for children to use. A word pocket is simply a one-pocket pocket chart, easily created from construction paper or tag board. Simply fold the bottom inch or so of the paper or tag board up and tape or staple the sides together. The paper fold serves as a pocket in which letter cards sit and can be seen. The teacher will need large letter and word cards. Children will need small ones. In her book *Making Sense of Phonics*, Beck (2006) provides letter cards that teachers can reproduce. Another good source for letter cards (and much else) is Cunningham, Hall, and Heggie's (2001) *Making Words: Multilevel, Hands-On Phonics and Spelling Activities.*

In the Classroom 7.3 shows a lesson that employs Beck's instructional routine and suggested language for teaching a single-letter consonant correspondence, in this case the correspondence *b* = /b/. We ground the lesson in Jim Aylesworth's text *Old Black Fly*. Grounding a phonics lesson in a text selection is not absolutely necessary, and at times it is not possible. However, like Linda Allen and many other educators, whenever possible we advocate connecting word study lessons to enjoyable experiences with books—the kinds of experiences that will motivate children to learn to read. Note that the same routine could be used for a consonant digraph. The only difference in the procedure is in the letter cards. When teaching a consonant digraph, the two letters that make up the correspondence (e.g., *sh*) should go on the same card. This provides children with an extra visual support for connecting the two letters with the single sound that they make.

In the Classroom

7.3

Teaching Single-Letter Consonants and Consonant Digraphs

- Say: "Yesterday, we listened to the book *Old Black Fly*. Old Black Fly had a very busy bad day. *Busy* and *bad* begin with the same sound: the /b/ sound. Watch my mouth /b/. [Children watch.] You say /b/." [Children respond.]
- Show children the large letter *b* card. Say: "This is the letter *b*. The letter *b* stands for the /b/ sound in *busy* and *bad*. Say /b/. [Children respond.] Each time I touch the letter *b*, say /b/." Touch the letter *b* card several times.
- Give each child a letter *b* card. Say, "If the word I say begins with the /b/ sound, hold up your card and say /b/. If it does not begin with the /b/ sound, shake your head no." Example words: *bit, bank, tack, buckle, something, bunny, table, bought, beautiful, room*.
- Say: "Old Black Fly might have gotten caught in something a spider spins. What is this?" When children have identified *web*, have them repeat it a few times. Then say: "The word *web* ends with the letter *b* that stands for the /b/ sound. I'm going to say some words that end with the letter *b*. Say them after me." Example words: *jab, tub, crib, bob, cab, grab*.
- Say: "I'm going to say some more words. If a word ends with the /b/ sound, hold up your *b* card. If it doesn't end with the /b/ sound, put your *b* card behind your back." Example words: *jab, come, sob, grab, ground, crib, track, crab*.
- Give each child a word pocket. Say: "I'm going to say some words that begin with /b/ and some that end with /b/. When a word begins with /b/, put your letter *b* at the beginning of your word pocket, like this [show children]. When a word ends with /b/, put your letter *b* at the end of your word pocket, like this [show children]." Example words: *batter, bump, tab, bottle, drab, banana, butter, mob, washtub*.

Reviewing Consonants: Ms. Campbell's Class

At the center, Ms. Campbell gives a copy of the read-aloud text *What Do You Like?* to each child. Ms. Campbell has them chorally read the text together. They point to each word as they read it. Then Ms. Campbell passes out a set of small word cards to each child showing *rainbow, like, love,* and *play.* Three of these words are high-frequency words, and *rainbow* is one that Ms. Campbell knows the children would like to learn. Ms. Campbell tells the children to find the page in their book that has *rainbow* on it, which they easily do. Ms. Campbell then says, "Find the word card that says *rainbow.* Check it to see if it is a match by putting it under the word *rainbow.*" She asks the children how they know the word is *rainbow.* Most say because it is long and starts with the letter *r.* Sara mentions that she can also hear an *a* in it. Because they have already learned the letter-sound correspondence for *b,* Ms. Campbell also has them put their fingers on the letter *b* at the beginning of *bow* and say the sound it makes (/b/).

Ms. Campbell next has the children put *rainbow* on their desk and search their word banks for other *r* words, which they line up under *rainbow.* Ms. Campbell asks them to read their list to the person sitting next to them. Ms. Campbell repeats this procedure with the words *like, love,* and *play.*

The final word center activity is called Writing for Sounds. Ms. Campbell gives the children pencils and blank sheets of paper, on which they write their names. Ms. Campbell has them write the letters *p, l,* and *r* across the top of the paper. Then she calls out words that start with one of these letters. When she calls out "play," she expects children to write it under the letter *p.* She doesn't expect them to necessarily write all of the word's letters, but she encourages them to write as many as they can. She tells them to write the sounds they hear. She emphasizes the initial consonant as she says the word, as this is the phonics element the group has been working on. Ms. Campbell will look at these papers later to check on how each child is progressing. Right now, she simply collects them because it is time for the children to rotate to another center in the room.

You'll want to continually review letter-sound correspondences until children have learned them, as In the Classroom 7.4 demonstrates. We share how first-grade teacher Ms. Campbell helps a group of students review initial consonant sounds. The class has just listened to and discussed Michael Grejniec's *What Do You Like?* Now during center time, Ms. Campbell tells each student which center to go to, reminding them that they will spend 20 minutes rotating through each center. One group goes to the classroom library, where they can read with a buddy or read alone. Ms. Campbell has added a copy of *What Do You Like?* to the center. Another group goes to the writing center to write and illustrate "I Like" books. Another group of children will work with Ms. Campbell reviewing initial consonant sounds and reading leveled books that stress these sounds. They bring their word bank to the center.

Teaching Vowels

Early literacy expert Leslie Mandel Morrow (2009) explains that vowels are challenging for children because they make so many different sounds. Often, short vowels are taught before long vowels. To review, short vowels are the sounds the letters *a, e, i, o,* and *u* make in the words *hat, let, bit, pot,* and *cup,* the CVC pattern. Long vowel sounds are easier for children to hear in words but have multiple spellings for the same sounds. This can be confusing for children. The long vowel spelling pattern that likely comes immediately to your mind is the CVCe (or CCVCe) pattern, as in the words *make, ride, mole, tube, shame, phone,* and *whine.* In this pattern, the *e* at the end of the word is silent and makes the first vowel sound long. The letter *y* acts as a vowel as well as a consonant. It can sound like a long *e* (*lovely, happy*) or a long *i* (e.g., *fry, my*). Other long vowel patterns include *vowel digraphs* and *diphthongs*. A vowel digraph is a single vowel sound represented by two letters. For example, the two vowels in *meat, pain, sheep,* and *day* are vowel digraphs. Diphthongs are also represented by two letters that have a glided pronunciation as one sound moves into the other (Venezky, 1999). The vowels in *boy* and *noise* are diphthongs. Beck (2006) notes that it isn't important for children to be able to label vowel digraphs and diphthongs as such. Rather, they need to learn the sounds that are associated with two-letter vowel patterns. *R*-controlled vowels are another kind of vowel. They are not short or long vowels but rather have their own *r*-influenced sounds. The *r* changes the sound the vowel makes. Read the following words to yourself. As you read, note how the vowel sound changes when *r* is added: *cat, car, put, purr, fit, fir, not, nor*.

As Morrow (2009) notes, there are many phonics rules but only three are consistent and thus worth teaching. Drawing on her work, we share these here. First, in a consonant-vowel-consonant word (CVC) (e.g., *sun, man, pet*), the vowel sound is typically short. Second, in a consonant-vowel-consonant-silent *e* word (CVCe), the final *e* is silent and the first vowel is typically long (*same, hope, bike*). Third, a vowel that follows a consonant (CV) is typically long (*me, so, became*).

We highlight a number of instructional routines for teaching vowels. In the Classroom 7.5 summarizes Isabel Beck's (2006) instructional routine for teaching short vowels. We also describe how word sorting can be used to foster knowledge of vowel sounds. Word sorting activities are an integral part of word study instruction in many classrooms. According to Bear, Invernizzi, Templeton, and Johnston (2007), sorting words according to a particular feature requires children to closely examine the letters and larger units in words and thus fosters word learning and the development of spelling knowledge. Word sorts work better when the child has to pronounce the words before sorting them. The average child will sort *cat, rat, sat, chat, can, ran, fan,* and *span* without ever actually reading the words. Sorting *play, rain, made, make, day, slay,* and *gain* into a long vowel category and *pant, thank,* and *stand* into short vowels demands that the words must be read.

Sorting Words: Short Vowel Sounds

We are pattern seekers and sorting words helps children to develop their knowledge of spelling patterns in words. For example, Johnston, Bear, Invernizzi, and Templeton (2009) recommend a pattern sort for words with contrasting short vowel sounds. For the purpose of illustration, we'll focus on short *e* and short *u*. A teacher selects a set of one-syllable words with these short vowel sounds and writes them on word cards. Then she places the cards in random order in the lower pockets of a pocket chart. For a short *u* and short *e* sort, these words might include *sub, bet, fed, hum, men, nut, led, cup, bus, den, let, tub, pen, but, cut, shut, hen, tug,* and *sled*. Then the teacher has the children read the words together while focusing their attention on the vowel sounds in the words. Next she places the cards for *bug* and *red* in two top pockets of the pocket chart. Johnston and her colleagues explain that these serve as "header" cards for the sort. The teacher models reading *sub* and comparing it to the header word *bug*. As she models, she stretches the vowel sound: "suuuub, buuuug." Then she tells the children that the words have the same sound in the middle and so she places the word *sub* beneath *bug* in the pocket chart. She and the children engage in the same procedures for the word *bet*, and *bet* is placed underneath *red* in the pocket chart. The teacher next calls on individual children to identify where to place the other word cards. When all the word cards are placed, the teacher has the children read each list with her. She tells the chil-

Teaching Short Vowels

- *Lesson introduction.* "We're going to read Nancy Antle's book *The Good Bad Cat* together today. Before we start, we're going to learn the short vowel sound for the letter *a*." Point to the words *Bad* and *Cat* in the title. "The words *Bad* and *Cat* have the short *a* sound." Stretch the short *a* sound as you say the words, so children have an easier time hearing it [Baaaaaad . . . Caaaaaat]. "Say the words with me."

- *Focus attention on the sound the short vowel makes at the beginning of the word.* "Let's look at these words. They begin with the short *a* sound." Have the following words in a pocket chart or on the board: *ant, apple.* "I'm going to say each word. Repeat it after me." Point to each word as you say it; children repeat it. "Say the short *a* sound /a/."

- *Connect the letter with the short vowel sound it makes.* Show children the large letter *a* card. "This is the letter *a*. The letter *a* stands for the /a/ sound in *ant* and *apple*. Say /a/. Each time I touch the letter *a*, say /a/." Touch the letter *a* card several times.

- *Discriminate between words that have the short vowel sound at the beginning of the word and words that do not.* Give each child a letter *a* card. "If the word I say begins with /a/, hold up your card and say /a/. If it doesn't begin with /a/, shake your head no." Say the following words: *at, am, bone, pickle, apple, bird, animal.*

- *Focus attention on the sound short a makes when it is in the middle of a spoken word.* "I'm going to say some words that have short *a* in the middle. Listen for the short *a* sound. I'm going to stretch it out so you can hear it. Then say each word after me. We'll stretch the sounds out together." Say and have children repeat the following words, making sure to stretch the short *a* sounds: *caaat, paaan, flaaag, jaaam.* "Now, we're going to say some more words. But this time we won't stretch the short *a* sounds. We'll have to listen carefully for the short *a*. I'll say each word first. Then you say it after me." Say the following words, without stretching the short *a* sound: *rat, tan, slap, glad, sat.*

- *Discriminate between words that have the short a sound in the middle of a word and those that do not.* "I'm going to say some more words. If a word has the /a/ sound in the middle, hold up your *a* card. If it does not have the /a/ sound in the middle, close your eyes. I'm going to stretch the sounds so you can hear them." Say the following words as children respond: *jab* [jaaab], *come* [cooome], *sob* [sooob], *grab* [graaab], *grip* [griiip], *crib* [criiib], *track* [traaack], *crab* [craaab]. "Now, I'll say some more words. This time, I'm not going to stretch the sounds. Listen carefully to the middle of the words. Hold up your *a* card when you hear the short *a* sound. Close your eyes when you don't." Say the following words without stretching the sounds: *hat, lamp, slip, shop, jam, chomp, past.*

- *Discriminate between words that have the short a at the beginning of the word and those that have it in the middle.* Give each child a word pocket. "I'm going to say some words that begin with short *a* and some that have short *a* in the middle. When a word begins with /a/, put your letter *a* at the beginning of your word pocket, like this [show children]. When a word has /a/ in the middle, put your letter *a* in the middle of the word pocket, like this [show children]." Examples words: *apple, tap, ant, bad, sand, ask, rat, ash, man, last.*

dren that, as they read, they are to think about how the words on each list are the same. When children have read the lists, the teacher explains that the words on the first list all have the short *u* sound and that the words on the second list all have the short *e* sound. Finally, Johnston and her colleagues explain, the word cards are removed from the chart, shuffled, and resorted.

In the Classroom 7.6 shares Beck's (2006) instructional routines for teaching long vowel patterns, diphthongs, and *r*-controlled vowels, following which we describe word sorting with these patterns. Word sorts for these patterns are particularly helpful to children as there are so many visual patterns that represent the long vowel sounds.

Teaching Vowel Patterns

The CVCe Pattern

- *Show children how adding an e to short vowel words they already know will change the vowel sound from short to long.* Put the letter cards for *c, a,* and *n* in a word pocket or pocket chart. Say: "Here is a word we know—*can.* In *can* we hear the short *a* sound. Read the word with me. [Children read.] Now, I'm going to add the letter *e* to the end of *can.* When I do, it changes the short *a* sound to the long *a* sound. The *a* now says its name. The new word is *cane.* Read the word with me. [Children read.] If I take away the *e,* we have the word *can* again."

| c | a | n | | c | a | n | e | | c | a | n |

- Say: "Let's do another word." Put the letter cards *c, a,* and *p* in the pocket chart or word pocket. Say: "Read this word with me." Now, add the *e.* Say: "Remember, when we add the *e,* the vowel changes from short to long. It now says its name. Say the long *a* sound for me. [Children respond.] Now, let's read this word (*cape*) together. [Children read.] Now, I'm going to take the *e* away. Read our short vowel word with me (*cap*)."

| c | a | p | | c | a | p | e | | c | a | p |

- Give children the following letter cards: *a, e, d, m, n, r, t.* Say "Line your cards up in front of you. Together we're going to spell and read some words. Follow my directions. The first word we're going to spell and read is *man.* Use three of your letter cards and make the word. Let's read it together—*man.* Now add your letter *e* to the word to change the vowel sound from short to long. Read the word with me—*mane.* [Children read.] Now, take away the *e* and read the word—*man.* [Children read.] Let's do some more." Lead children through the same steps for the following words: *rat, rate, rat; mat, mate, mat; mad, made, mad.*

Vowel Digraphs, Diphthongs, and r-Controlled Vowels

- *Connect the first two-letter vowel pattern with the sound it represents.* Say: "On our shelf today is a book I know you'll enjoy. It's called *Sail Away* by the author Donald Crews." Use your large letter cards to make the word *sail* in the demonstration word pocket. "This is the word *sail.* Read it with me." Children read. Pointing to the *ai,* say, "When we see an *a* and an *i* together in a word, they make the long *a* sound. This is the sound we hear in the middle of *sail.*" Now take the *s* and *l* away. Say: "When I touch the *ai,* say the long *a* sound." Put the *s* and *l* back. Say: "Read the word with me: *sail.*" Children read. Repeat this procedure a few times.

| s | ai | l | | ai | | s | ai | l |

- *Connect the second two-letter vowel pattern with the sound it represents.* Say: "Two other letters can make the long *a* sound." Make the word *say* in the demonstration word pocket. Say, "This is the word *say.* Read it with me." Children read. Pointing to the *ay,* say, "When there is an *a* and a *y* together in a word, the sound we hear is also long *a.*" Now, take the *s* away. Say: "When I touch the *ay,* say the long *a* sound." Put the *s* back. Say: "Read the word with me: *say.*" Repeat this procedure a few times.

| s | ay | | ay | | s | ay |

- *Connect the two two-letter vowel patterns with the sound they represent.* Put *sail* and *say* one on top of the other in the word pocket. Say, "As I point to each word, read it with me." Have children read each word a number of times. Each time you point to a word, underscore with your finger the two letters that make the long *a* sound.

| s | ai | l | | | s | ay |

- *Discriminate words that may compete with target two-letter vowel patterns.* Write the following words on chart paper or the board: *pay, nail, man, may, tan, tail, play, main, ran, ray, pan, stray.* Say: "Read these words. Pay careful attention to the vowels in the words."

Sorting Words: Long Vowel Patterns

As we've discussed, word sorting is very useful for helping children learn the visual patterns in words. One kind of sort that Invernizzi, Johnston, Bear, and Templeton (2009) recommend for developing long vowel knowledge is a pattern sort. Children analyze and sort words by both their sounds and spelling patterns. The "header" cards are words that represent the spelling pattern the teacher wants children to notice and learn. For example, a teacher may want children to notice different spelling patterns that represent the long *a* sound. A sort might focus on consonant-vowel-consonant-silent *e* (CVCe) words and consonant-vowel-vowel-consonant (CVVC) words, for example, with header cards *race* and *main*. The teacher would then present children with a set of words to sort, such as *rain, cake, plane, train, plate, sail, cape, jail, grape, nail, vase, snail, gate, tail, skate, blaze, hail, pain, snake,* and *cane.* Children read each word, notice its spelling pattern, and place it under the appropriate header card. When the children have sorted the words, the teacher and children read each list and confirm that the words fit the pattern.

PEARSON myeducationlab

Watch a primary-grade teacher instruct a small group about two spelling patterns for the /oy/ sound in the activity "Teaching Students Word Identification Strategies." (To find this activity, go to the topic *Phonemic Awareness/Phonics* in MyEducationLab and click on Assignments and Activities.)

Teaching Blending

In order to read, children must learn how to blend the sounds they're learning to form words. As Beck (2006) notes, many beginning readers find learning this very challenging. You'll need to model it many, many times and to engage children in many experiences with blending activities. In the Classroom 7.7 shows two variations of blending activities. In the first activity, initial blending, the teacher models how to blend the beginning consonant (the onset) with the rime *at.* She then models how the rime *at* can be analyzed into its component phonemes and blended. The second activity is Beck's (2006) successive blending routine, with phonemes blended serially. You may use this following initial blending or begin blending instruction with it. Beck explains successive blending as follows: "In successive blending, students say the first two sounds in a word and immediately blend those two sounds together. Then they say the third sound and immediately blend that sound with the first two blended sounds. If it is a four-phoneme word, then they say the fourth phoneme and immediately blend that sound with the first three blended sounds" (p. 50). Beck explains that successive blending reduces the memory demands on children. With each successive blend, children must only hold in memory two sounds, and only two sounds are blended.

Body Coda Blending

Bruce Murray and his colleagues have discovered that stressing the blending of the final sound onto the two initial sounds can be a great help to young readers (Murray et al., 2008). As we already discussed, a single syllable word can be divided into onset and rime (*m + op*). The word can also be divided into the body and the coda (*mo + p*) where *mo* is the body and the *p* is the coda. Blending activities should include practice changing just the final sound in the word. "Let's read *ba*; it's /ba/. Now let's add the letter *t*; what is the word? [Children respond.] Now let's change the ending letter." *bat* becomes *ban, bad, bam, bass, back,* and *bath.* Changing the final letter promotes flexibility in decoding and avoids the rhyming response children acquire when the teacher just changes the initial sound.

Word Building Activities

Skillful readers see and use nearly all the letters as they read words (Adams, 1990). Thus, as teachers we must provide children with learning activities that foster close analysis of the letters in words. We share two techniques for word building, one designed by Beck (2006) and the other by Cunningham and Cunningham (1992). Both techniques involve students in building words while following the teacher's serial

Blending Activities

Initial Blending

Say: "If I don't know what a word is right away, here's how I figure it out. First, I look at the word, and I find any parts I know. So let's pretend I don't know this word—*mat*." Write the word *mat* on the board. As you point to the *m*, say, "I know it starts with an /mmmm/ sound. Then I see the *at*." Point to the *at*. "I already know *at*. So I say /mmm/ /aaaaatttttt/—*mat*. That makes sense. I can also say /mmmm/ /aaaa/ /tttt/—*mat*. Move your finger from *m* to *a* to *t* as you blend the sounds.

Successive Blending

- Place letters for the word you will blend in a pocket chart with spaces between (*r e d*). Then give each child a set of letter cards. Have children set their cards up in front of them with spaces between them.
- *Model.* Point to the *r* and *e* one at a time. Say: "/r/ [Pause] /e/."
- *With children.* Say: "Point to your letters as I point to mine. We'll say the sounds together." Children respond.
- *Model.* Slide the letter *e* over to the letter *r* (*re d*). Run your finger under the *re* and say, "/re/ /re/." Then separate the cards again.
- *With children.* Say: "Let's do it together. Slide your *e* over to your *r*. As we say the sounds, slide your finger under the *re*." Children respond.
- *Model.* Slide your finger under the *re*. Say: "/re/." Hold the sound until you point to the *d* and say, "/d/."
- *With children.* Say: "Together now. Slide your finger under your *re* and say /re/. Hold the sound until you point to your *d*." Children respond.
- *Model.* Move the *d* over to the *re* (*red*). Slide your finger under *red* and say, "/red/. This is the word *red*." Then separate the *d* from *red* again.
- *With children.* Say: "Together now. Move your *d* over to the *re* and read the word—*red*." Children respond.

direction. Also, in both activities, each word the children create is different from the previous word by only one letter. What differentiates Beck's technique from that of Cunningham and Cunningham is the nature of the teacher's serial direction. In Beck's technique, the teacher identifies the letter children change to form the next word. In Cunningham and Cunningham's technique, called "making words," children must listen and decide for themselves which letter to change. Additionally, the children work toward making a "mystery word," a word that uses all the letters provided. In the Classroom 7.8 shows examples of each procedure.

*A*ssessment

The decoding and vocabulary test part of the Interactive Reading Assessment System found in Appendix A can be used to assess the strategies students use to decode larger units in words.

Teaching Larger Units in Words

To help children read words using the larger units in words—as opposed to individual letter-sound correspondences—we need to develop their knowledge of these larger units and their ability to recognize them in the printed words they encounter. Once children know some initial consonants (onsets), we can expand their word knowledge by teaching rimes and other units. Children then can use these units to decode by analogy.

Teaching Rimes

Recall that a rime is the first vowel in a syllable and all the letters that follow it. In the one-syllable word *mat*, *at* is the rime. In the two-syllable word *backbone*, *ack* and

Word Building Activities

Beck's Word Building Routine

- *Demonstrate word building.* Place the letter cards for *h*, *a*, and *m* in a pocket chart to make the word *ham*. Say: "This is the word *ham*. Read the word with me. [Children respond.] Now, watch what I do. I'm going to change the letter *a* to *i* and make a different word. Read the new word. [Children respond.] Now, it's your turn to build some words. I will tell you which letters to use. After we build each word, we're going to read the word together."

- *Lead students in word building.* Give each child a set of letter cards (*a, d, d, h, i, m, t*). Sequentially have the children build the words as directed. After children have built each word, write the word on the board in a list. Direct the children in the following way:

  "Put the letter *i* after the *h*. Put the letter *t* at the end. What's the word?" (*hit*)
  "Change the *t* to a *d*. What's the word?" (*hid*)
  "Change *i* to *a*. What's the word?" (*had*)
  "Change the *d* to *m*. What's the word?" (*ham*)
  "Change the *a* to *i*. What's the word?" (*him*)
  "Change the *h* to *d*. What's the word?" (*dim*)
  "Change the *m* to *d*. What's the word?" (*did*)
  "Change the *i* to *a*. What's the word? (*dad*)

- *Read the words.* Say, "Read each word as I point to it." Have children read the listed words.

Making Words

Give the children letter cards for *n, t, r, s, p,* and *i*. Give them the following directions:

"Take three letters and make the word *tin*."
"Change one letter to make the word *tip*."
"Change the letters around to make the word *pit*."
"Change one letter to make the word *pin*."
"Add a letter to make *spin*."
"Change a letter to make the word *spit*."
"Take away two letters and add a letter to make the word *rip*."
"Add one letter to make the word *rips*."
"Add another letter to make the word *trips*."
"Now use all your letters to make the mystery word (*prints*)."

one are the rimes. Remember, too, that rimes are also referred to as phonograms and spelling patterns. Sometimes you hear them called chunks, although the term *chunks* tends to apply to various kinds of larger units in words. There are many common rimes whose pronunciations are quite regular. Figure 7.8 lists 37 rimes that occur in nearly 500 primary-grade words (Wylie & Durrell, 1970). Just by knowing a few rimes, children can use them to read and write many words that have them. For example, a child who knows the rime *ot* can use it to read *not, hot, rot,* and *dot*. The New Standards Primary Literacy Committee (2004) has noted that by the end of first grade, children should know word families ending in common rimes (e.g., *in, at, ent, ill, or, un, op, ing*).

One way of explicitly and systematically developing children's knowledge of rimes is to teach them key words. A key word is a one-syllable word that has a common rime. Children are taught to use the key words to analogize to unknown words that share the rimes. In this way, the key words help children to "unlock" the

Children develop automaticity of word recognition with practice. Children who are motivated by technology may enjoy and benefit from the following word study practice activities.

- Read Naturally (Ihnot, 2008) is a commercially available program. The primary focus is developing children's fluency, of which automatic word recognition is, of course, a part. The company has produced a series of word study activities—Word Warm-Ups—that children complete in about 10 minutes with the support of audio CDs. There are three levels of Word Warm-Ups. The first focuses on developing automaticity reading one-syllable, phonetically regular words (e.g., *sad*, *big*). The second level of Word Warm-Ups primarily develops automaticity reading words with two syllables and with common affixes. The third level focuses primarily on multisyllabic words.

- The Starfall website (www.starfall.com) has numerous activities to help early primary-grade children develop their word recognition skills. In the Learning to Read section of the site, a voice prompts children to build words using onsets and rimes. For example, given the rime *an*, the voice says "Make a word with /a/ /n/ /an/ to match the picture *fan*." As the voice pronounces each phoneme, and then the rime, the associated print is highlighted on the screen. The picture that represents the word then appears. Afterward, children build multiple words by dragging various onsets over to the rime. The computer voice provides support in this process. This website also provides opportunities for children to practice reading words in sentences and simple texts. Under Fiction and Nonfiction in the I'm Reading section of the site, children can put together sentence puzzles. The computer voice supports puzzle completion and children's sentence reading. The same section offers texts of multiple kinds—plays, fiction, nonfiction, comic books, folktales, and myths. No voice accompanies children as they read these texts, but there is an engaging sound when each page in the online text turns.

- The International Reading Association's website (www.readwritethink.org) has a number of engaging online word study activities for children (as well as many resources for teachers). In Construct a Word, children build words using onsets and rimes (www.readwritethink.org/files/resources/interactives/construct). In another activity, children sort words according to rime (www.readwritethink.org/files/resources/interactives/wordfamily).

pronunciation of the unknown words. For example, with the key word *cat* a child can figure out *sat*, *mat*, *rat*, *flat*, and *splat*. This strategy is also called *decoding by analogy*. A number of studies have demonstrated the effectiveness of this strategy for helping children learn to recognize words (Gaskins et al., 1997; Leslie & Allen, 1999; White, 2005). Linda Allen (1998) has provided a lesson sequence for teaching key words. She refers to rimes as spelling patterns. In the Classroom 7.9 shows how a teacher might use Allen's lesson sequence. As you review the routine, note how the teacher cognitively

Figure 7.8 **Thirty-Seven Rimes That Occur in Nearly 500 Primary-Level Words**

ack	ail	ain	ake	ale	ame	an
ank	ap	ash	at	ate	aw	ay
eat	ell	est	ice	ick	ide	ight
ill	in	ine	ing	ink	ip	ir
ock	oke	op	or	ore	uck	ug
ump	unk					

Teaching Key Words

- *State the purpose.* Say: "Our purpose today is to learn to read and spell the key word *back*. Key words are words that have spelling patterns we can use to read and spell other words. The spelling pattern is the first vowel and all the letters that follow it."

- *Word building.* Give each child a set of cards as follows: *back, ack, b, r, l, t, bl, qu.* Children will build each word using the onsets (*b, r, l, t, bl, qu*) and the rime (*ack*). Serially, give the children the clues below. As they build each word, copy it onto a blank card. Put the card in the pocket chart for later in the lesson. Or write it on the board or chart paper.

> "Spell the word that is the opposite of front." (*back*)
> "Spell the word that is something on which you'd hang your coat." (*rack*)
> "Spell the word *lack*. This word means you haven't got something." (*lack*)
> "Spell the word that would hurt if you sat on it." (*tack*)
> "Spell the word that is a color." (*black*)
> "Spell the word that is the sound a duck makes." (*quack*)

- *Cognitive modeling.*

Example 1: Put the following sentence on the board.

> Crow said, "Just what we need—a *sack* of seed!"

Say: "Let's say I'm reading this sentence, and I don't know this word (*sack*). First, I look at the spelling pattern in the word. Then I think of a key word I know that has the same spelling pattern (*back*). I tell myself, if this word is *back,* then this word is *sack.* Then I reread the sentence to make sure it makes sense: 'Just what we need—a *sack* of seed.' Yes, that makes sense."

Example 2: Say: "Let me show you another example."

> I will *pack* my suitcase.

Say: "I see this word (*pack*) has the *ack* spelling pattern. I know the key word *back* has the *ack* spelling pattern. So I'll use it to help me read this word. I say to myself, if this is *back,* then this is *pack.* Now I read it again to see if it makes sense—'I will *pack* my suitcase.' Yes, it makes sense."

- *Reading and transfer.* Present new sentences for students to chorally read. They can be on chart paper, the board, or sentence strips.

> The train was coming down the track.
> I had a snack after school today.
> Mom told me not to smack my lips.
> I put my books in a stack.
> Don't step on the *crack.*

- *Onset/rime practice.* Using the pocket chart with word cards from earlier in the lesson (or from the words listed on the board), lead students through the following routine. For each word on the list, point to the onset and say, "First say—." Have the children say the sound the onset makes. Then point to the rime and say, "Then say—." Have children say the rime. When children have said the rime, say, "Put it together and you get—." Children then say the word. As they say the word, underscore the word from left to right with your finger. An example for the first word is below. Have children engage in the routine for the words *rack, lack, tack, black,* and *quack.*

> *Teacher:* "First say—"
> *Children:* "/b/"
> *Teacher:* "Then say—"
> *Children:* "/ack/"
> *Teacher:* "Put it together and you get—"
> *Children:* "back"

- *Final review.* Remind students why key words are important. Say: "Today we learned a number of words using the key word *back.* Key words are important to know because they help us read lots of words that have the same spelling pattern."

models the thinking involved in the strategy. Following key word lessons, the key words are placed on the word wall for children's future use and reference.

One caution—as you make decisions about instructional techniques to use with students, keep in mind the following. Research strongly suggests that working with rimes is useful only after children can analyze them into their component sounds (Ehri & Robbins, 1992; Gaskins et al., 1997; Vandervelden & Siegel, 1995). Because many poor readers cannot do this without explicit instruction (Juel & Minden-Cupp, 2000), you want to make sure to still attend to individual letter-sound correspondences as you teach children to work with the larger units in words.

Decoding Multisyllabic Words

As we've shared, the basic unit in speech is the syllable. All words have one or more syllables. As children become more advanced readers, they encounter increasing numbers of multisyllabic words, which can be intimidating for them. As teachers, we want to help children realize that multisyllabic words are simply strings of syllables comprising spelling patterns that they already know. Children need to examine long words and find familiar "chunks." These chunks can be onsets, rimes, affixes, or root words.

In the Classroom 7.10 shows two similar approaches to decoding multisyllabic words. Both focus children's attention on chunks in words. In the first approach, the teacher focuses on locating and using multiple rimes to decode a multisyllabic word. The lesson is grounded in Bill Cosby's *One Dark and Scary Night,* a leveled text for younger readers. Teachers-in-training have regularly used this approach and lesson sequence with much success for many years in a university-based literacy center (Leslie & Allen, 1999). The second approach features an activity called "word detectives." In this approach, readers notice and use different kinds of chunks to recognize multisyllabic words. With either approach, you'll want to provide students with multiple examples when they are first learning the techniques and then with scaffolding across time as needed. And when working with children on learning to recognize multisyllabic words, it's critical to emphasize that children are locating and using chunks in words as a strategy for figuring out how to pronounce large words. Without an explicit emphasis on the strategic nature of the technique, many children may not transfer it to other reading situations when they encounter unfamiliar multisyllabic words.

Teaching Meaning Units in Words: Prefixes and Suffixes

Many multisyllabic words contain prefixes and suffixes. Teaching students to be on the lookout for these can really help them with decoding. We discussed prefixes and suffixes previously in this chapter and listed possible prefixes and suffixes to teach in Figures 7.3, 7.4, and 7.5. In the Classroom 7.11 (p. 216) describes a simple and straightforward routine to teach them. Note that there are many more prefixes and suffixes than you need to or *should* teach. Teach only those that are fairly frequent in the material your students read.

The Importance of Contextual Reading

Read, Read, Read

In this chapter, we looked at specific instructional ideas for increasing children's knowledge about how words are constructed and how to read them. We emphasized teaching high-frequency words, letter-sound knowledge (phonics), and larger

Decoding by Analogy

Using Multiple Rimes to Decode

Ms. Sampson has written the following sentence on the board: *I <u>tightened</u> every muscle in my body so I couldn't move.* She thinks aloud as she cognitively models how to decode *tightened*.

In the Classroom

7.10

Ms. Sampson: "Let's say I don't know this word (*tightened*). First, I look at all the parts of the word to see if there are rimes that I know. I see *ight* as in the key word *night*. And, I see *en* as in the key word hen. I also see the ending *ed*. I'm going to write the key words I know with those rimes above the parts of the big word that share those rimes."

> night hen
> I t*ight*en*ed* every muscle in my body so I couldn't move.

Ms. Sampson: "Now, I tell myself, if this is *night*, this is *tight*. If this is *hen*, this is *ten*. I put the two chunks together and get *tighten*. Next I add the *ed* and put the three chunks together—/tight/ /en/ /d/. Now I read the sentence again to make sure it makes sense."

> I t*ight*en*ed* every muscle in my body so I couldn't move.

Ms. Sampson: "Here's another big word we'll read in the story (*tomorrow*). I see two rimes I know. The key words for them are *for* and *show*. So I say to myself, if this is *for*, this is *mor*. If this is *show*, this is *row*. I get *morrow*. I know the little word *to* that this big word begins with. Next I put the chunks together. I get *tomorrow*. Then, I read it again to see if it makes sense."

> for show
> Think about tomorrow, playing and having fun.

Word Detectives

Each day, Ms. Kenney writes a multisyllabic word on the board, talks about any clues to its identity that she can find, and lists these clues on the board. Then she writes another multisyllabic word on the board and asks the children to find clues to its identity. The following words and clues show some of the ways children have tried to figure out the words:

- *chipmunk*

  Karl noticed the rime *ip*.
  Marty said she got *unk* because she knew the word *skunk*.
  Tasha volunteered the pronunciation of the consonant digraph *ch*.

- *shameful*

  Katy said she instantly saw the affix *ful*.
  Ming said he knew the *ame* rime by heart.
  Tasha volunteered the pronunciation of the consonant digraph *sh*.

- *transit*

  Lily said she knew how to chunk it because she saw the familiar *an* and *it* rimes.
  Kyle added that that the letter combination *ns* doesn't start a syllable.
  Mike volunteered the pronunciation of the consonant blend *tr*.

units in words. However, we recognize that it is not possible to teach every phonic element and spelling pattern that children will encounter. They will acquire a lot of knowledge about words from wide reading. Moreover, we want to emphasize again how important it is for children to apply their developing word recognition skills during contextual reading (Juel & Roper/Schneider, 1985). Many teachers rely on core reading programs to teach reading and the most recent research suggests that there is not enough text in a core reading program for a child to become a fluent reader

Teaching Affixes

- Write two familiar words containing the affix you want to teach on the board. Ask students to define the words. Suppose you wanted to teach the prefix *un*. Most students know what *unhappy* and *unkind* mean, so these would be appropriate words to use for instruction.
- Underline the affix, and note its spelling. Then, if the affix is a prefix with a concrete meaning, either elicit the meaning from students—if you think they know it—or give them the meaning. *Un*, of course, means "not." (If the affix is a suffix, it is usually best not to define it. The abstract definitions of suffixes are often confusing.)
- On the board, write a word that contains the affix but that students probably don't know. With *un*, you might use the word *unreal*. Ask students to use their knowledge of *un* and the root word (in this case, *real*) to figure out the pronunciation and meaning of the new word: *un* means "not," and *real* means "real." So *unreal* means "not real." (If the word part is a suffix, they will only need to figure out the pronunciation of the new word.)
- Tell students that they are likely to see the affix fairly frequently, and that often, if they cover it up, they'll recognize or be able to decode the root word. Then, if they add the affix back, they will probably be able to pronounce the complete word and understand its meaning.

(Brenner & Hiebert, 2010). For most teachers we know, this is routine knowledge. Georgia Woods talks about how she has children read following instruction in the long *a* vowel sound.

> I like to begin and follow up activities on spelling patterns for long *a* with reading books such as *Who Has a Tail?* (Level G) by Fay Robinson. This text has actual photographs of animals, and many of the words show spelling patterns for long *a*. For example, here are the lines from pages 3 and 4:
>
> Who has a tail that shakes like a rattle?
>
> The snake does. When this snake shakes its tail, the tail rattles. That way, other animals hear it. They stay away.
>
> As you can see, this book gives students much practice reading long *a* spelling patterns in words such as *tail, shake, stay,* and *away.*
>
> —Georgia Woods, first-grade teacher

Assessment

Use the passages of the Interactive Reading Assessment System found in Appendix A, to observe and assess contextual reading.

Coaching Word Recognition

Coaching children to apply their developing word recognition skills during contextual reading is important and it helps them become more metacognitive and strategic readers (Taylor, Peterson, Rodriguez, & Pearson, 2002). They develop what Marie Clay (2001) has called a "self-extending" system: a system for recognizing words and understanding text that children will continually expand and refine over time. Accomplished teachers provide students with general and specific word recognition cues (Clark, 2004). General cues are nonspecific in nature. For example, when a child encounters an unknown word, the teachers say something like "How are you going to figure that out?" or "Look at the word and think about what you need to do." Specific cues focus children's attention on salient features of words. For example, the teachers offer suggestions like "Cover up the ending," "Use what you know about *r*-controlled vowels," or "Look for a chunk you know." To craft specific cues, the teachers consider such factors as the sounds the consonants make in the unknown word, particularly those that could represent more than one sound, like *c* (*cat, city*), *s* (*says*), and *g* (*grand, giraffe*); the sounds the vowels make; the presence of blends, digraphs, or silent letters; and any rimes and affixes in the word.

Next we share a few excerpts from one of the teachers' small-group reading lessons. Elizabeth Fry, a veteran first-grade teacher, was among the most accomplished teachers in a nationally focused large-scale study of teachers that "beat the odds" in teaching children to read (Taylor, Pearson, Clark, & Walpole, 2000). In the first excerpt, Ms. Fry coaches a student as the group reads Kathy Dubowski's *Cave Boy*. Peter is having difficulty recognizing the word *always*. When he becomes stuck, Ms. Fry prompts him to consider his strategies. When he identifies a well-learned strategy, Ms. Fry positively reinforces his thinking. Peter then identifies the first two letters in the word. Ms. Fry knows that the *al* looks unfamiliar to her first-graders, so shares the pronunciation of the word part. Then she cues Peter to examine the vowel pattern in the word. He identifies it, and Ms. Fry prompts him to put the word parts together. Peter does, and he independently adds the *s*. Ms. Fry then has him reread to make sure it makes sense.

> *Peter:* "Stop all that . . . banging. Stop all that noise. That is Chief Grump. He is a . . . a . . ."
> *Ms. Fry:* What can you do if you're stuck?
> *Peter:* Cover up the *s*.
> *Ms. Fry:* Cover up the *s*. That's a good start.
> *Peter:* There's an *al*.
> *Ms. Fry:* Yes. The *al* sounds like the *al* sound in *ball*.
> *Peter:* " . . . al . . ."
> *Ms. Fry:* Now look at the vowel pattern.
> *Peter:* *ay* . . . long *a*
> *Ms. Fry:* Now, put the two parts together.
> *Peter:* " . . . always . . . always . . ."
> *Ms. Fry:* Exactly. Start again to see if it makes sense.
> *Peter:* "He is always mad about something."

During the school year, Ms. Fry teaches students to coach one another (with her support), as the following two excerpts show. Children are reading Linda Hayward's *All Stuck Up*. In the first excerpt, Brady is stuck on the word *caught*, and Ms. Fry invites the others in the group to provide him with clues. Jake tells him to "throw the *g-h* away," a procedure that Ms. Fry has taught, modeled, and encouraged throughout the year. Jacinda focuses Brady's attention on the vowel pattern *au*, a pattern that students have studied and practiced in isolation and in context. Brady needs more help, so Ms. Fry has him think about the context. With these supports, Brady is able to recognize the word. Ms. Fry confirms his word recognition and affirms his effort.

> *Brady:* "Brer rabbit is always thinking of ways to not get . . . kuh . . . kuh . . ."
> *Ms. Fry:* Can we give him some clues?
> *Jake:* Throw the *g-h* away.
> *Jacinda:* The double vowel.
> *Ms. Fry:* Think about the story and ask yourself what makes sense: "He's thinking of ways to not get . . ."
> *Brady:* "kuh . . . caught!"
> *Ms. Fry:* *Caught*, that's right. You worked hard to figure that out.

Next, Carrie is trying to figure out *pretty*. Betta offers a clue about the sound the *y* makes. Marcus focuses her attention on the consonant blend. These are helpful clues, and Carrie is able to decode the sounds in the word. However, she accents the wrong word part. So Ms. Fry has the students read the word with her.

*A*ssessment

Tape record your interactions with students while they are reading aloud and note how you coach their use of word identification strategies. You may need to model more strategies and help the students use them.

Carrie: puh . . . er . . .
Betta: There's a *y* acting like an *e*.
Marcus: There's a *p-r*.
Carrie: pre-TUH-y
Ms. Fry: Let's read it together.
All: pretty
Carrie: "Pretty soon."

Coaching fosters children's knowledge of letters and patterns in words within the context of real reading. This makes the connection for children that learning letter-sound correspondences and the larger patterns in words is a means to an end—reading and understanding a text—and not an end in itself. These coaching exchanges also illustrate some important concepts that we have discussed. First, they show learning in children's zone of proximal development. The words were not too easy but not so hard that children could not be successful with support. Second, the coaching exchanges demonstrate supportive structures, or scaffolds, that teachers create to help children solve particular problems—in this case decoding words. Third, the exchanges show how children can serve as supports to one another given instruction and practice in specific techniques. Finally, we have talked about how important motivation, engagement, and a positive environment are to learning. Ms. Fry's practice of having her first-graders give clues about unfamiliar words to one another has resulted in high levels of motivation and engagement among children and created a supportive learning environment in the reading groups. Children readily participate both when it is their turn to read aloud and their turn to "whisper read" when a peer reads. Children all track the print as they read and are anxious to help one another with unknown words. When a reader stumbles on a word, everyone in the group works to think of clues to give. And because everyone in the group readily and positively provides support, children feel free to take risks and grow as readers.

We hope that the ideas we have presented for word study instruction will give you a good foundation on which to begin planning instruction for beginning readers. Remember to base word study instruction on the six principles we discussed at the outset of this chapter. Use your imagination, summon up your creativity, and have fun. Your enthusiasm will be contagious.

REFLECT and *Apply*

6 Much word study instruction begins with sorting picture cards for sounds and follows that activity with sorting word cards based on their spelling patterns. Explain the rationale for this basic two-step process.

7 Let's say you are listening to a first-grader read the following line from a leveled text: *"Hello," said the firefighter.* The child struggles to read the word *firefighter*. Together with a partner, generate three to five coaching clues you could give the child. Base your clues on phonics elements and larger units in words.

About Reading a Lot

Primary-grade children must do a lot of reading to develop accurate and automatic word recognition. Leveled books are short books that use high-frequency words and words that repeat the phonics features that children are learning. These books provide children with contextual reading practice. Many reading series include leveled books as part of their materials. Another excellent resource is Irene Fountas and Gay Su Pinnell's *The Fountas & Pinnell Leveled Book List, K–8+* (2009). At a nominal cost for a classroom of children, teachers can also access downloadable and printable leveled texts online at the Reading A to Z website (www.readinga-z.com/index.php). To give you a flavor for texts at different levels, the following excerpts are taken from leveled books.

Robin Bloksberg's *The Hole in Harry's Pocket* is a Level I text. At the end of first grade, children are expected to be able to read most of the words in a Level I text.

> Harry liked to walk to the store. He liked to hop on the curb. He liked to look in all the windows and count cracks in the sidewalk.
> Harry got the milk. But when he looked for his money, it was gone! What could he do?

By the end of second grade, we expect children to accurately read most of the words in a Level L text, such as the popular Cam Jansen mystery series by David A. Adler (text from *Cam Jansen and the Mystery of the Stolen Diamonds*).

> Eric opened his eyes. "It's no use," he said, "I'll never have a memory like yours."
> "You have to keep practicing," Cam told him. "Now try me."
> Cam looked straight ahead. She said, "Click," and then closed her eyes. Cam always said, "Click" when she wanted to remember something. She said it was the sound her mental camera made when it took a picture.

By the end of third grade, we expect children to accurately read most of the words in a Level O text, such as the popular Ramona series by Beverly Cleary (text from *Ramona Quimby, Age 8*).

> Ramona had reached the age of demanding accuracy from everyone, even herself. All summer, whenever a grown-up asked what grade she was in, she felt as if she were fibbing when she answered, "third," because she had not actually started third grade. Still, she could not say she was in second grade, since she had finished that grade last June. Grown-ups did not understand that summers were free from grades.

Book levels are not perfect, of course. But the levels can give you a feel for benchmarks in word recognition at the end of grades 1 through 3. Teachers need to have a large selection of leveled books available. These books should be linked to word study instruction, and read and reread until children can accurately read them at appropriate rates. Plastic tubs full of leveled books are staples in most K through grade 3 classrooms. The movement is from predictable texts in kindergarten to chapter books by the end of second grade.

Strengths *and Challenges* of Diversity

Many children readily succeed at word study and become accomplished readers quite quickly. Others struggle and will need additional instruction, support, and encouragement. Research has shown that children with insufficient phonemic awareness will likely struggle with learning to read. The problem is that they cannot hear the somewhat separable phonemes in spoken words very well. If they can't hear the phonemes, they will have a terrible time trying to map them to print—something necessary in learning to recognize words.

One way to see if children can hear phonemes in spoken words is to have them sort picture cards. Start with a sort based on initial consonants (onsets). For example, you can have children sort picture cards that represent *s* words, *b* words, and *m* words. A more difficult sort would involve picture cards that represent one-syllable words that have either the short *a* sound or the short *i* sound in the middle. To help children hear onsets and rimes, you can read nursery rhymes and stories that employ alliteration. It would also be useful to give these students a short phonemic awareness inventory. The Phonological Awareness Test (Robertson & Salter, 2007) or the assessments inside *Phonemic Awareness in Young Children* (Adams, Foorman, Lundburg, & Beeler, 1998) provide very useful information.

You can gain insight into how children hear sounds in words and link those sounds to letters by examining their spelling. A child who consistently and accurately uses initial (or other) consonants in her writing—spelling *rain* as *r* or *dog* as *dg*—signals a readiness to learn specific word families or rimes. A child who spells *rain* as *b* and *dog* as *x* will likely need instruction in initial consonants. A child who spells *rain* as *rane* will benefit from sorting words with *ain, ane,* and other long *a* patterns.

Additionally, you can determine your students' needs by looking at what they do when they don't instantly recognize a word in print. Bear in mind that if children are stumbling over many words, the text is probably too difficult. Children need to be able to decode most of the words in the texts they read (about 98%). At this level of accuracy, they can understand the text and enjoy reading. Children's attempts at words they cannot identify provides you with information for planning instruction. Do they guess randomly or focus on pictures for cues to the word? Do they look at initial letters? Do they look for patterns they recognize within words? Our job is to identify what our students know and plan appropriate activities to extend that knowledge.

For children who are really struggling in first grade, there are a number of special programs available. The best known is a one-to-one tutoring program called Reading Recovery, which Marie Clay (1979, 1994) developed in New Zealand some years ago. Gay Su Pinnell and her colleagues (Pinnell, Fried, & Eustice, 1990) adapted it for use in the United States. A small-group approach that is proving very successful is Early Reading Intervention (Kame'enui & Simmons, 2005), a scripted program for building phonemic awareness, letter-sound association, and early reading skills. Another option is to have community members provide supplemental support for beginning readers. Johnson, Invernizzi, and Juel's *Book Buddies: Guidelines for Volunteer Tutors of Emergent and Early Readers* (1998) provides very explicit instruction for word study with struggling readers.

To provide supplemental support to older children who struggle with word recognition, you might consult Patricia Cunningham and Richard Allington's *Classrooms That Work: They Can All Learn to Read and Write* (2006). It is filled with practical ideas to help all students become good readers. If you are seeking supplemental programs for struggling readers, you can consider several options. Elfrieda Hiebert (1996) has developed a program for third-grade students. Taylor, Hanson, Justice-Swanson, and Watts (1997) created a cross-age tutoring program for second- and fourth-grade children. Lynn and Douglas Fuchs (2000) developed an ingenious peer-tutoring program for children in grades 2 through 5. Another option would be to draw on the approach described in the *Howard Street Tutoring Manual: Teaching At-Risk Readers in the Primary Grades* (Morris, 2005).

Although most children do not have many reading skills when they enter school, some children do. Among your responsibilities will be to provide these children with books that will challenge them and expand their knowledge. In a typical first- or second-grade classroom, you might need to stock books that extend to the upper-grade levels.

Concluding *Remarks*

This chapter has emphasized the importance of word recognition in learning to read. We began by discussing why it is so important for children to learn to recognize words early on. Then we discussed the structure of spoken and written words and how children come to recognize words. In the remainder of the chapter, we described specific instructional techniques to develop children's word recognition ability.

The topics in this chapter are particularly important to understand thoroughly because without the ability to read words, children will have difficulty with nearly everything else at school. Learning to recognize words may just be a piece of literacy instruction, but it is foundational to further literacy development. Without word recognition competence, attaining present-day literacy is extremely unlikely.

Extending *Learning*

1. Observe a first-grade classroom or, better yet, several first-grade classrooms at different times during the year. What kind of word study instruction do you see? What kinds of texts are the children reading? How are the children progressing?

2. Meet individually with several kindergarten and first-grade children. Have them spell some words for you, such as *cat, run, jump, name, goat, van, arm, stripe, little, coat, rope, back, smash,* and *light.* What can you tell from the child's spelling about what he or she knows about words? What might you plan for word study instruction to help the child grow?

3. Individually, have several first-grade children read to you. Notice what happens as each child reads. Does the child look at the words? What happens when the child forgets a word? What can you infer the child knows about words from how he or she reads? What might you do to build on children's current knowledge?

Children's *Literature*

Adler, D. (Many titles in Cam Jansen series by this author). New York: Puffin Books. This is a staple for second grade.

Antle, N. (1996). *The Good Bad Cat.* Grand Haven, MI: School Zone. A rhyming story about cats. 32 pages.

Aylesworth, J. (1995). *Old Black Fly.* New York: Henry Holt. A fly annoys and meets his end. Audiocassette available. 32 pages.

Bloksberg, R. (1995). *The Hole in Harry's Pocket.* New York: Hyperion.

Cleary, B. (Many titles in the Ramona series by this author). New York: Avon Books. This is a staple for third grade.

Cosby, B. (2005). *One Dark and Scary Night.* New York: Scholastic. A boy searches for comfort during a thunderstorm. 40 pages.

Crews, D. (2000). *Sail Away.* New York: HarperCollins. A family's adventure on a sailing trip during a storm. 40 pages.

Dubowski, K. E. (1988). *Cave Boy.* New York: Random House. This Step into Reading book provides easy language and illustrations for a young reader. 30 pages.

Grejniec, M. (1992). *What Do You Like?* New York: North-South Books. Children discover they can like the same things and still be different. 32 pages.

Hayward, L. (1990). *All Stuck Up.* New York: Random House. A Step into Reading book about Brer Rabbit and Fox. 32 pages.

Hutchins, P. (1968). *Rosie's Walk.* New York: Macmillan. A hen unwittingly leads a fox into one disaster after another before arriving safely home from her walk. 32 pages.

Martin, B., Jr. (1992). *Happy Hippopotami.* San Diego: Harcourt Brace. In a lively rhyming story about a rollicking day at the seashore (with alliteration galore), hippos "board a beach-bound bus" and enjoy "swimming, sunning, and snacking." 32 pages.

McCarty, P. (2003). *Little Bunny on the Move.* New York: Henry Holt. An engaging little bunny has an important place to go. 32 pages.

Oppenheim, J. (1989). *"Not Now!" Said the Cow.* New York: Bantam, Doubleday, Dell. A beginning reading book based on the little red hen. Unnumbered.

Pikulski, R., et al. (eds.). Houghton Mifflin's Guided Reading collection. New York: Houghton Mifflin. This reading series has leveled books.

Robinson, F. (1996). *Who Has a Tail?* Boston: Pearson. This predictable text repeats *ay, ai,* and *a* consonant *e* patterns. It is one of many leveled readers in the Ready Readers series. 16 pages.

Zimmerman, A., & Clemesha, D. (1999). *Trashy Town.* New York: HarperCollins. This delightful tale of a trash man's job provides plentiful opportunities for pointing out alliterations, onsets, and rimes. 28 pages.

PEARSON myeducationlab

Now go to the topic "Phonemic Awareness/Phonics" in the MyEducationLab (www.myeducationlab.com) for your course, where you can:

- Find learning outcomes for the topics covered in this chapter along with the IRA standards that connect to these outcomes.

- Complete assignable activities in the Assignments and Activities section that show concepts in action to help you synthesize and apply strategies.

- Explore IRIS Center Resources—training enhancement materials that provide you with research-validated information and interactive materials to develop your skills in working with students.

- Apply and practice your understanding of the teaching skills identified in the chapter with the Building Teaching Skills and Dispositions exercises.

8

Fluency

His name was Jimmy Parker, and one of us went through eight years of grade school with him. It was a small school with only one classroom for each grade level, and, therefore, the same students stayed together over the years and got to know each other really well. Jimmy had blond hair, blue eyes, and a lot of freckles. He was a popular boy and did well on the playground, originally with games like dodge ball and tetherball, and later with football and basketball. But he was not good at reading. In fact, he was terrible at it. Round-robin reading was an almost daily activity in the school, and day after day, year after year, Jimmy would stand up and stumble with excruciating slowness through a passage in the basal reader. It was a terrible experience for Jimmy, for all of us listening, and probably for the teachers too. But concepts like automaticity, fluency, and using appropriate texts were unknown to our teachers, and so Jimmy's pain and embarrassment continued year after year.

Jimmy had not learned to read well by the time we finished grade school, and it is unlikely that he ever became a fluent reader. It is even more unlikely that he became an avid reader, a person who made reading a significant and major part of his life. It is too late to change the experiences Jimmy had, but appropriate attention to fluency can change the reading experience for many other children.

CLASSROOM vignette

Fluency and Its Importance

Fluency is the ability to read rapidly, smoothly, without many errors, and with appropriate expression. Fluency is often thought of as an oral phenomenon, and we assess fluency by asking students to read orally. But there is also such a thing as silent reading fluency (Pikulski & Chard, 2005). When reading silently, a fluent reader reads rapidly, without stumbling over words, and with good comprehension. You cannot, of course, hear fluent silent reading, but you can recognize it because the child reads relatively rapidly, without seeming to struggle, and with good understanding of what he has read. In assisting readers to become fully competent, our goal for them is fluency in both oral and silent reading with comprehension.

As Melanie Kuhn and Steven Stahl (2003) explain, when considering fluency and its importance, it is useful to think in terms of children progressing through several stages of reading development, a process described by Jeanne Chall (1996). The first stage, the emergent literacy stage, occurs before formal reading instruction begins and is a period in which children begin to understand some very basic facts about reading: that print represents spoken language, that we read from left to right and from top to bottom, that words are separated by white space, that words are made up of somewhat separable sounds, and the like. In the second stage, children begin formal reading instruction, with the emphasis on decoding. In the third stage, children move from concentrating on decoding and slowly reading word by word to becoming automatic in their reading and thereby reading smoothly, accurately, and with expression. Many children enter this stage of fluency building in the early primary grades and continue to build fluency over time. It is important that their fluency increase steadily because, in the third and fourth grade, they are expected to read and learn from longer and increasingly difficult text. Other children, however, do not enter the fluency stage in the early primary grades, and these children need special help in becoming fluent readers.

Fluency is so important because of the limited processing capacity of our brains and the consequent importance of learning to automatically process words. As David LaBerge and Jay Samuels (1974) noted in their pioneering work on automaticity, the mind's capacity to process information is limited. Basically, we can attend to only one thing at a time. Reading, however, demands that we attend to at least two operations. On the one hand, we need to decode the individual words; on the other hand, we need to engage in a number of cognitive processes to comprehend what we are reading. If too much of our limited processing capacity is taken up with decoding individual words, we are left with no resources to comprehend what we are reading. The solution is for readers to become automatic in processing words. As defined by LaBerge and Samuels, an automatic activity is one that we can perform without conscious attention. If children can decode most of the words they encounter automatically, they will have the mental resources to comprehend what they are reading.

As LaBerge and Samuels (1974) also explain, the road to automaticity is quite straightforward. We become automatic at an activity by doing it repeatedly in nontaxing conditions. One of the best examples of an activity at which many of you reading this have attained an appropriate level of automaticity is driving a stick-shift car. Driving a stick-shift car requires that you push in the clutch, let up on the accelerator, shift gears, let out the clutch, and press on the accelerator—all in a very brief period of time. Moreover, it requires that you do this while simultaneously watching the traffic, noticing brake lights, looking for debris on the road, and being alert to the possibility that someone will cut in front of you or engage in some other unpredictable behavior. If you are not automatic at the various steps involved in shifting, you will not have the mental capacity to monitor the traffic and respond to what might literally be a life-or-death situation. And how do you get to be automatic at driving a stick-shift car? You do so by repeatedly practicing driving and shifting in situations in which you don't have to worry a lot about traffic—perhaps in a parking lot or on side streets. You do it again and again, and eventually it becomes second nature, requiring almost none of your mental resources.

Fluency is more than just automatic word recognition; it requires the ability to read with proper phrasing, intonation and stress. Taken together these features are the attributes of prosody, a characteristic of fluency that is linked to comprehension (Kuhn, Schwanenflugel & Meisinger, 2010). As the child develops, she moves away from a staccato word-by-word method of reading to one that sounds more like natural oral language. Measurements of prosody predict reading comprehension beyond the predictions explained by measures of oral reading rate or word reading efficiency. At the moment we do not know if reading with prosody leads to increased comprehension, if gains in reading comprehension lead to increased prosody, or if the relationship is reciprocal. We do know enough to stress that singular focus on reading rate without a equal focus on prosody will not result in better comprehension.

The road to becoming automatic, fluent, and expressive in reading is based on a lot of reading in nontaxing situations. Fortunately, current research and theory allow us to make much more specific recommendations. For a number of years, fluency was a largely neglected area of reading instruction. However, that changed when the National Reading Panel (National Institute of Child Health and Human Development, 2000) identified fluency as one of the five cornerstones of reading instruction. It changed even more when fluency became one of the five components of Reading First, the federal program that has strongly influenced primary-grade reading instruction. Today, fluency is a strongly recommended part of a comprehensive reading program and the subject of current research in several recent books, including Jean Osborn and her colleagues' *A Focus on Fluency* (Osborn, Lehr, & Hiebert, 2003), Timothy Rasinski's *The Fluent Reader* (2003), Rasinski and his colleagues' *Fluency Instruction: Research-Based Best Practices* (Rasinski, Blachowicz, & Lems, 2006), and Samuels and Farstrup's *What Research Has to Say About Fluency Instruction* (2006). In this chapter, we describe a number of approaches to building fluency, discuss ways of assessing fluency, consider the sorts of fluency instruction different readers need, and identify ways of matching readers with texts.

1. We have just given an example of an activity that some people do automatically—driving a stick-shift car. Think of an activity you do automatically, and consider how you achieved this automaticity. Talk to some classmates about automaticity, the activity that you do automatically, and how you became automatic at it. Then ask your classmates about some activities they do automatically and how they achieved automaticity.

2. Think back to your elementary schooling and remember students who were not fluent in reading—students like Jimmy Parker, mentioned in the opening scenario. Journal your opinions about those students' attitudes toward reading, their attitudes toward school more generally, and whether they ever became real readers. If you cannot remember any actual students, journal about some imaginary ones.

REFLECT *and* Apply

Individual Approaches to Building Fluency

In this longest section of the chapter, we describe a number of methods for helping students become more fluent. We begin with some generalizations about fluency instruction. Then we discuss several methods of one-to-one instruction, powerful instruction to be sure but very costly in terms of teachers' time. Next, we present several methods of promoting fluency for small groups or even the entire class. Finally, we discuss the approach to fluency that is most appropriate for more able readers and that ought to be a part of all readers' activities—wide reading in interesting and enjoyable texts.

Some Generalizations About Fluency Instruction

There are a number of validated approaches to fluency instruction. Before discussing them, however, we want to list several characteristics of the most successful approaches:

- Teachers model fluent reading when they read aloud to their students.
- Students need a specific and concrete goal. At times they might read to increase their reading rate, and other times they might read to learn their part for readers theater. Teachers chart progress and frequently show students (privately) this concrete evidence of their progress.
- Students do a substantial amount of reading. In order to become more fluent, students need to actually read; they can't just pretend to read. This means that you need to build some accountability into whatever approach you use.
- Students read in comfortable and nontaxing situations, in which they are not likely to receive harsh corrections from the teacher or be embarrassed by reading poorly in front of their peers. This means avoiding round-robin reading.
- There is evidence that students are generally capable of picking appropriate texts for repeated reading, neither too easy nor too difficult. Still, as we note later in Matching Students and Texts, ensuring that students have appropriate texts is crucial to successful fluency instruction—and to all other instruction.
- When monitoring oral reading, teachers should correct fewer miscues and allow students to read without too many interruptions, seeking smooth and fairly rapid reading rather than perfection. Overemphasis on making no errors is likely to cause too much concentration on accuracy.
- In most approaches, students read orally, and they read the same material several times, often three to five times. However, in some approaches, students read more material but only once. As we stress later in Wide Reading in Appropriate Texts, for students whose fluency is progressing normally, silent reading may be the most appropriate road to fluency.
- At least when repeated reading is involved, students need material that presents at least a slight challenge, particularly by presenting some words that are not already automatic for students. At the same time, it is important not to make the material too challenging, as automaticity is achieved by multiple successes in nontaxing situations.

The Original Method of Repeated Reading

Having developed the theory of automaticity, Samuels (1979, 2002b, 2006) decided to search for a practical application of the theory and found one in the method of *repeated reading.* Samuels began by suggesting that in learning to efficiently recognize words, children go through three stages, much like those of Chall (1996) described earlier in the chapter:

- *The nonaccurate stage.* At the beginning, students have considerable difficulty in recognizing words, do so only with considerable time and effort, and are not always accurate. If you listen to these children read aloud, you will find that they misread a number of words, stumble and read slowly, do not use appropriate expression, and do not sound as though they are understanding much of what they read—as indeed they do not understand much of what they read.
- *The accuracy stage.* At this stage, students are able to recognize words accurately, but doing so requires a good deal of attention, effort, and time. If you listen to these children read aloud, you will find that although they read accurately, they read slowly, haltingly, and without appropriate expression. They do not sound as though they understand what they are reading, and, in fact, many times they do not understand what they are reading.
- *The automatic stage.* Finally, students are able to recognize words accurately and instantaneously, and doing so does not require much attention, effort, or time. If you listen to children at this stage read aloud, you will find that they read accurately, at a good pace, and with appropriate expression. They sound as though they understand what they are reading, and indeed they usually do.

Samuels next wondered about other tasks involving slow, inaccurate, and stumbling efforts in the beginning before eventually becoming fluent and automatic. He thought of two—sports and music. In football, for example, a would-be offensive center may at first hike the ball over the quarterback's head, on the ground, or to his left or right. Eventually, however, the center learns to consistently hike the ball just where it needs to be, into the quarterback's outstretched hands. Moreover, the center then learns to accurately hike the ball while preparing to block the oncoming defensive center and carry out any other defensive assignments. Similarly, a beginning saxophone player may initially be unable to make any sound on the instrument before moving to a level at which she sometimes plays the right notes and sometimes the wrong ones. Only then can she progress to a level at which she accurately plays all the notes but without expression and feeling, before finally achieving the goal of playing with feeling and grace, captivating an audience with her skill. In both cases, the route to fluency is similar. The aspiring athlete or musician repeatedly practices the tasks to be mastered in nontaxing situations, gets feedback on his performance, and eventually becomes automatic and therefore fluent.

These examples provided Samuels with the inspiration for repeated reading. He noticed that many less skilled readers did not practice the same way that beginning musicians or athletes did. Instead of repeatedly reading a single passage until they got it right, most less skilled readers instead faced a new and difficult passage each day, stumbling through it without success and were often embarrassed by reading poorly in front of their classmates. Samuels reasoned that if students who were relatively accurate but nonfluent in their reading could repeatedly practice reading the same passage, with each successive reading they should become more automatic and therefore fluent. Moreover, just as musicians repeatedly practice a single piece with the goal of achieving greater skill with that piece and greater skill generally as musicians, students who repeatedly read the same passage should become more automatic and fluent in reading that passage as well as with other passages generally.

Samuels (1979) initially tested his hypothesis by providing individual repeated reading sessions for a class of students with intellectual disabilities. The results of this

8.1

Instructional Routines

The Original Method of Repeated Reading

Like other methods of repeated reading, the original method is used with students who are relatively accurate in their reading but not yet automatic. This original approach involves one-to-one instruction.

- Have the student select a book that she finds interesting and enjoyable. If you think the selection is either too hard or too easy, help her find a more appropriate text. The text should be at her instructional level.
- Mark off a half dozen or so 50- to 200-word segments in the selected book. Begin with 50-word segments and gradually lengthen them as the student becomes increasingly able to deal with longer texts.
- Explain the nature and purpose of repeated reading to the student. She is going to read the same passage several times, trying to read it more smoothly and a bit faster each time. Note that she should not ignore comprehension but that her main goal is to read smoothly and fairly rapidly. It is important to explain the role of practice and make comparisons to music and athletics.
- Have the student read the passage aloud and chart both her speed and the number of word recognition errors she makes.
- At this point the student returns to her seat and repeatedly practices reading the passage until she feels ready to read to you again. She should keep rereading the passage, sometimes to herself at her seat and sometimes to you, until she reaches a rate of 85 words per minute. Although accuracy of word recognition is a goal, do not press the student too much for accuracy, and do not demand complete accuracy before moving on to another passage. Experience shows that too much stress on accuracy will make the student anxious and reduce her chances of meeting the rate goal.
- Once the student reaches the target rate of 85 words per minute, show her the graph of her progress, and prepare to move to another passage, probably on another day.

Assessment

The assessment process is built into many fluency activities. Each time a student reads, you should record his accuracy and oral reading rate. These records can be used to determine the success of the activities.

initial testing were very positive. In the Classroom 8.1 shows the original repeated reading procedure.

With each reading of a passage, reading speed increased, the number of word recognition errors decreased, and students read with more expression. Moreover, when the students went on to a new section of a book, their beginning reading speed for that section was faster than their beginning reading speed for the previous section. That is, students' performance increased on both the texts they reread and the texts they were reading for the first time.

Figure 8.1 shows one student's progress in rate and word recognition using the original method of repeated reading on five passages. The student began the new passages with Tests 1, 8, 15, 21, and 25. The figure shows how, as the student repeatedly read each passage, speed increased and word recognition errors decreased. Moreover, the student's first reading of each successive passage was faster than the first reading of the previous passages, with fewer word recognition errors in the first reading of each successive passage.

The original method of repeated reading clearly does what it is supposed to—increase students' oral reading fluency. At the same time, it is costly in its requirement of one-to-one instruction. In some situations, however, parents, aides, and other students may be able to monitor the procedure, making it more feasible in the classroom.

Simultaneous Repeated Reading and Echo Reading

Simultaneous repeated reading is another one-to-one approach that has been used successfully (Heckelman, 1969). Its main difference from the original method of repeated

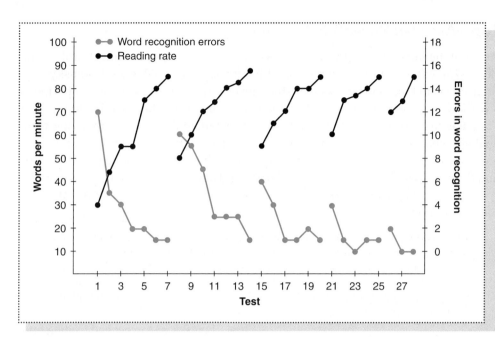

Figure 8.1

Progress in Reading Rate and Word Recognition for a Student Using the Original Method of Repeated Reading with Five Passages

Source: Samuels, S. Jay. (1979, January). "The Method of Repeated Readings." *The Reading Teacher, 32*(4), pp. 403–408. Copyright © 1979 by the International Reading Association (www.reading.org). Reproduced with permission of the International Reading Association via Copyright Clearance Center.

reading is that the teacher or other competent reader and the student repeatedly read the passage together. The teacher (or other competent reader) at first takes the lead, reading in a strong voice, and then gradually reads more and more softly as the student takes primary responsibility. Like the original method of repeated reading, the teacher helps the student choose a book that is interesting and just a bit challenging, marks off passages of 50 to 200 words to read, explains the procedure and purpose to the student, charts progress in rate and perhaps word recognition, and shares the chart with the student to give concrete evidence of progress. As noted, simultaneous repeated reading calls for the teacher to read along with the student on each reading of the passage. The advantage of simultaneous repeated reading is that the student gets repeated models of fluent oral reading and receives sturdier scaffolding than when reading alone. The disadvantage is that it is labor intensive, requiring the teacher or some other adult to participate in every reading the student does. In a variation called *echo reading,* the student reads after the teacher, repeating what the teacher read. Although these individual techniques for developing fluency are labor intensive, with a classroom aide or a parent volunteer they become more possible.

Small-Group and Whole-Class Approaches to Fluency Development

The approaches described thus far have been shown to be effective and viable options. However, as one-to-one approaches, they have the disadvantage of taking a good deal of a teacher's or some other adult's time for each student. The approaches described next are group or whole-class approaches, making them feasible for teachers who do not have the time for one-to-one instruction.

Repeated reading sessions help students increase their reading speed.

Monkey Business/Fotolia

Tape-Assisted Repeated Reading

At about the same time that Samuels was developing repeated reading, Carol Chomsky (1978) was developing a somewhat different approach to fluency. Chomsky's approach was to tape short books that students repeatedly listened to over a period of a week while also repeatedly reading them and comparing their reading to the tape. They then worked in a small group with her on game-like activities involving word analysis, vocabulary, writing, and discussion. The children were third-graders with adequate decoding skills but poor fluency and with negative experiences in reading and therefore negative attitudes toward reading. They were also from homes in which books and reading were not prominent. Chomsky described their skills and attitudes toward reading.

> They hated reading, avoided it whenever possible, and consistently met the many opportunities for meaningful reading, adequately provided for in a lively classroom, with a total lack of response.... [They] couldn't so much as read a page of simple material to me. The attempt to do so was almost painful, a word-by-word struggle, long silences, eyes eventually drifting around the room in an attempt to escape the humiliation and frustration of the all too familiar hated situation.
>
> —Carol Chomsky, researcher and reading tutor

Chomsky decided that students needed an opportunity to learn that reading was accessible to them in nonthreatening, nontaxing, and nonembarrassing situations. And she realized that having children repeatedly listen to tapes until they had virtually memorized them and then work with her on the passage they had already mastered could provide this opportunity. She therefore got the five children she was working with tape recorders, made tapes of some short and easy books, had them read the books repeatedly over a period of a week, and then met weekly with them as a small group to work on skills, discuss what they had read, and do some writing. The program, which extended over a period of four months, produced positive results for

Motivating Struggling Readers

Goals Are Important

A key aspect of developing reading fluency is motivation. Some students thrive on knowing that their reading rate is increasing, and plotting their oral reading scores during repeated reading gives them a great sense of accomplishment. Tape-assisted reading can also be very motivating with the right hook. We believe that students should use the tape-assisted method to learn a book well that they plan to read to kindergarten or first-grade students. Set up the activity in the following way. Tell third- or fourth-grade students how important it is for kindergarten students to listen to good children's stories. The class project this year will be to read to the kindergarten students. To read well we need to practice the book several times before we go to the kindergarten class. This sets an important goal for the oral reading or fluency practice. Help the students select a good book to read to the kindergartens and show them how to use the audio or tape recorder to practice. If recording equipment is not available, students might practice with each other until they are ready to read to the kindergarten students. Reading to kindergarten students is authentic, and students feel that they are accomplishing an important task. A reading comprehension element can be included in this activity. After reading the story, students can ask the kindergartners questions, and the act of developing the questions will boost their own comprehension.

Tape-Assisted Repeated Reading

Tape-assisted repeated reading can be set up in a number of ways. The following is one approach.

- Select some books that are a bit of a challenge for the students you will be working with and for which recordings are available or which you can record yourself. Most laptop computers can record using the QuickTime program.
- Tell students that they will be reading the books several times in order to improve their reading and that they should choose books that are interesting and present a bit of a challenge. Have students choose their own books, but monitor their choices and suggest other books if any are too easy or too difficult.
- Have them listen to the book or a part of it repeatedly while silently or orally reading along with the tape. Tell students they should continue listening and reading until they can read smoothly and feel they are ready to read the text to you.
- Have students read the book or passage aloud to you. Record reading rate and number of word recognition errors. Have them talk a bit about the book and also discuss it with them, both as an informal check on comprehension and as a reminder that comprehension is the goal of reading. Make charts showing each student's rate and number of word recognition errors over time to show students their progress.

all five students. Both their overall reading scores and their word recognition scores went up. They read much more fluently. Equally important, their attitude toward reading became much more positive.

In a later investigation that involved taped reading, Michal Shany and Andrew Biemiller (1995) found that both repeated reading with teacher assistance and a tape-assisted repeated reading approach significantly improved the reading rates and comprehension of at-risk third- and fourth-grade children. Shany and Biemiller further found that with tape-assisted reading, students read twice as much as in the repeated reading approach.

In the Classroom 8.2 shows an approach to tape-assisted repeated reading based on the work of Chomsky (1978), Shany and Biemiller (1995), and Osborn and her colleagues (2003).

Tape-assisted repeated reading is certainly an alternative to teacher-assisted repeated reading, and it requires less time on the part of the teacher or an aide. Moreover, the availability of commercial programs that employ tape-assisted repeated reading, which we discuss later in this chapter, makes doing this type of reading very convenient.

Partner Reading

Partner reading, or buddy reading, is another approach that is less demanding on teacher time. In partner reading, more capable readers pair up with less capable peers and take turns reading to each other, with the stronger partner reading each passage first and the less strong reader following. It is important that partner reading be done on a regular basis, two or three times a week. Like all skill development, regular practice is essential. Like virtually all fluency approaches, partner reading can take place in different ways. In the Classroom 8.3 shows a slightly modified version of the procedures suggested by Osborn and her colleagues (2003).

8.3

Instructional Routines

Partner Reading

Partner Selection Procedure

- The teacher uses fluency scores to rank-order the class from top to bottom.
- The teacher splits the class into two groups of equal size.
  Group 1: top to middle readers
  Group 2: middle to bottom readers
- The top reader in Group 1 is paired with the top reader in Group 2, and so on down the lists.

Partner Reading Procedure

- The Group 1 reader always reads first to set the pace and ensure accuracy.
- The Group 2 reader reads, attempting to match the partner's pace and fluency.
- The teacher closely monitors fluency, moving around the room to listen to each set of partners, keeping partners on track, and providing feedback as needed.

Assessment

The use of use of choral and partner reading and readers theater requires periodic assessment. After a few weeks using any of these activities, conduct a fluency check on the weaker reader and evaluate the impact of the activities.

Choral Reading

Choral reading is a frequent activity in many classrooms, and it is a great way to get the whole class or a small group involved at the same time. With choral reading, the teacher chooses a selection that will lend itself particularly well to oral reading—perhaps a humorous poem from Jack Prelutsky's *It's Raining Pigs and Noodles*—and explains the importance of reading the passage smoothly, with expression, at a good rate, and accurately. Next he reads a passage aloud as a model and then has students read it aloud in unison several times. In this way, less fluent readers first have the scaffold of hearing the teacher read the passage and then can read the passage a few times rather quietly and perhaps lagging just a bit behind their more skilled classmates, before finally reading louder and more smoothly with their more skilled classmates. This is just the sort of nontaxing situation students need to develop automaticity and fluency. Primary-grade teachers often use choral reading quite a bit, but it is also appropriate for older students who need to improve their fluency, and it is likely to be an enjoyable experience for all students. Choral reading, like all fluency practices, requires a goal for students, such as learning a piece to later read on their own to the class or to their reading group. The proof of the activity is the wonderful reading they deliver to their peers.

Readers Theater

Readers theater refers to the well-rehearsed reading of scripts, with feeling and expression, in front of an audience (usually the class), but without the memorizing of lines, costumes, prompts, scenery, make-up, and other time-consuming and sometimes expensive features of a full-blown play performance (Martinez, Roser, & Strecker, 1998). As an approach to building fluency, readers theater has several positive characteristics. For one thing, motivation is likely to be strong because the repeated reading that students do in order to master their parts takes place under the guise of preparing for the upcoming presentation and not as a fluency exercise. For another, both more skilled and less skilled readers can participate, thus avoiding any stigma that might be associated with being in a fluency group. The more skilled readers can be given longer and more difficult parts, with the less skilled readers assigned shorter parts, thus allowing all students to work at their own levels. Strive for parts in which all

Schedule for a Week of Readers Theater

Readers theater is the sort of activity that is best done occasionally, and a week is often an appropriate amount of time for a readers theater segment.

Select a script or several scripts, and make copies for each reader. If you are working with an entire class, you will have several different groups, so you can differentiate the reading levels. Each group of students can then read a script at their instructional level.

Monday

Introduce or review the procedure, stressing the importance of students' practicing their parts so that they can do really fluent presentations. Assign parts, taking special care to assign each student only as much as she can handle.

Tuesday–Thursday

Have students practice their parts, both at home and at school. They can practice independently some of the time, but it is also important that they practice with a partner, with a group, and with you as their audience so that they get some assistance and feedback and are prepared for their class presentation on Friday. Of course, if students do not need 3 days of practice or their attention begins to wane, you can shorten the practice.

Friday

Have students perform their scripts for an audience, probably the class, but others should certainly be welcome. Be encouraging and supportive, and make this a festive occasion.

students read as much as possible. In the Classroom 8.4 shows an outline for a week-long readers theater exercise.

Radio Reading

Radio reading, originally developed by Frank Greene (1979), can be thought of as a variation of readers theater, with the same goal to motivate students and give them an opportunity to repeatedly practice a passage so they can read it fluently to an audience. The main difference is that with radio reading the students are motivated to practice the passage by assuming the role of professional announcers preparing to read the passage to a national audience, and it is fun to add in an announcer's desk and a microphone. Stress the importance of reading fluently, accurately, and expressively. Another difference is that because this isn't "theater," a variety of types of texts can be used. The procedure lends itself particularly well to expository texts, news stories, public service announcements, and other sorts of informational broadcasts you might hear on the radio or television. A third difference is that with radio reading, in addition to practicing before reading to the class, each student creates one factual question and one inferential question about the reading, thus giving direct attention to comprehension. As with all fluency practice, students need to begin by observing you model fluent reading and then spend time practicing their piece for the broadcast at the end of the week. As we have noted in earlier chapters, students generally lack experience reading expository texts, so opportunities to read exposition are particularly welcome.

Wide Reading in Appropriate Texts

As we have noted several times in describing the components of a comprehensive reading program and will continue to note throughout this book, wide reading is a very important part of reading instruction—for all students. Wide reading builds automaticity, vocabulary, world knowledge, and the desire to read more. One of the ways you get good at reading—in fact, one of the ways you get good at anything—is to do a lot of it. If students are to make reading a habit, something that is a frequent and vital part of their lives, they must read and read and read. Wide reading both at home and at school is also an important part of fluency instruction.

Wide reading is essential for becoming fluent. Remember that the road to automaticity and hence to fluency is to practice repeatedly in situations that are interesting, enjoyable, and nontaxing; wide reading certainly fits that description. In fact, for many children—those reading at grade level and those at or near the fluency norms for their grades—wide reading in interesting and enjoyable books is the primary road to fluency. We will say more about which students should do wide reading as their primary fluency activity and which should engage in a more direct approach to fluency instruction, as well as do wide reading, later in Choosing Among Approaches to Fluency. Jack Detmar is one teacher who recognizes the importance of both wide reading and other approaches to building fluency.

> I always hate to be part of a bandwagon, but I'm afraid that these days that's just what I am. I have always been a huge supporter of the position that students need to read a lot if they are to read well, and hence wide reading has always played a big part in my classroom. However, after I began reading about the National Reading Panel's emphasis on fluency instruction, read some articles about fluency, and went to an inservice of the topic, I have come to realize that some students need more direct help with fluency than wide reading provides. We currently do as much independent silent reading in my class as we ever did, and all my students have plenty of opportunities for wide reading, but I also use more direct approaches such as repeated reading for those students who struggle with fluency.

> —Jack Detmar, second-grade teacher

One particular type of book may be particularly powerful for developing fluency—the series book. These books first appeared early in the 20th century with the Bobbsey Twins starting in 1904 followed by Tom Swift in 1910. For many years the best-known series were the Hardy Boys starting in 1927 and Nancy Drew in 1930. There are many contemporary versions of the series book, including the Baby-Sitters Club (Martin, 1986) and all its variations, Goosebumps (Stein, 2003), and the currently popular Diary of a Wimpy Kid (Kinney, 2007) and Captain Underpants (Pilkey, 1997) series. Each generation of American children seem to thrive on the series book and they develop fluency in a number of ways (Mackey, 1990). The series book is addictive and after reading one book many children are eager to read more. The books provide extensive practice that is not taxing, and the structure of the books makes reading relatively easy. According to Mackey (1990), the characters, setting, and problems are repetitive so the reader only has to concentrate on the developing plot. Many authors of series books include literary devices that school children in how to read a novel. Often the author will speak directly to the reader, pointing out important clues and ideas and foreshadowing new plot developments. All of this makes reading easy and builds fluency as students continue through the series.

The impact of the series book can be seen in one case study of a young fifth-grade girl, Megan, whose score on an oral reading fluency test given at the beginning of the year was 70 words correct per minute, a score below the 25th percentile. About that time she went to New York City with her family and visited the American Girl store. Megan bought the Julie doll and the book about a girl living the counterculture life in the 1970s. She read the book, and then ordered another and another. By March she had read 15 American Girl books and other related works of historical fiction, also discovering the American Girl mysteries. Her fluency scores soared to 156 WCPM while she gained a growing knowledge of American history and its various cultural periods.

Fluency-Oriented Reading Instruction—Putting It All Together

Fluency-oriented reading instruction (FORI) is a whole-class program designed to build oral reading fluency (Stahl & Huebach, 2005). In FORI the basal reading program is restructured to emphasize fluency, using a variety of techniques incorporating much of what we have already discussed. First, the reading selections in the basal are introduced and discussed with a strong emphasis on comprehension, because a focus on meaning builds word identification and comprehension skills (Anderson, Wilkinson, & Mason, 1990). Second, students read material at their instructional level when possible, although sometimes students will read more difficult material but reread it often. Third, students reread material often because research suggests that children do not read enough in school at an appropriate level (Gambrell, Wilson, & Gantt, 1981). They echo read their basal materials, they reread their basal stories with a partner, they read their stories at home to their parents, and they reread the stories to themselves. Fourth, a specific time is set aside each week for partner reading, in which peers support one another in a format that provides more practice time than round-robin reading. Finally, students must read widely outside the basal reading program both within the classroom and at home. Because evidence shows that basal reading programs do not provide enough text for students to become fluent readers (Brenner & Hiebert, 2010), students must read extensively from trade books, including non-fiction, chapter books, and novels. The research on FORI indicates that all children make significant gains. The child who enters second grade reading at a primer level is likely to make 2 years progress and a child who reads at a third-grade level is likely to progress 3 years in reading ability. In the Classroom 8.5 provides an illustrated plan for implementing FORI in the classroom.

Kuhn did a small study comparing fluency-oriented oral reading to wide reading, listening, and a no-treatment condition, and found that the fluency-oriented oral reading group outperformed the listening and no-treatment groups on tests of identifying words in isolation, number of words read per minute, and quality of oral reading. However, the wide reading group outperformed the fluency-oriented oral reading group on a comprehension measure. As we have noted, we recommend wide reading for all students, regardless of whether they are engaging in other fluency-building activities.

3 Choose one of the three one-to-one approaches to building fluency (the original method of repeated reading, simultaneous repeated reading, or echo reading), and describe a student with whom you would use it. Indicate the number of sessions that might be necessary, how long each might take and over what time period. Then justify the benefit of the one-to-one approach for that student.

4 Choose one of the group approaches to fluency instruction (tape-assisted repeated reading, partner reading, choral reading, readers theater, or radio reading), and describe a group of students for whom it seems appropriate. Note how often you would use it and over what time period, and explain why a group method is preferable to a one-to-one approach with these students.

5 Describe several students for whom independent reading will be the primary path to fluency. How often might you engage these students in fluency activities like choral reading, readers theater, and radio reading? Briefly describe your rationale for the amount of time you will spend on these activities.

REFLECT and *Apply*

Fluency-Oriented Reading Instruction (FORI)

FORI requires the use of several fluency techniques during the week, including echo reading, partner reading, repeated readings, and wide reading at home and in school. This reading requires using a core reading program in a new and creative way. Following is the plan for the week.

	Day 1	Day 2	Day 3	Day 4	Day 5
Whole Group	Read main basal anthology story to the class modeling fluent reading	Discuss the reading selection focusing on story mapping or another comprehension strategy	Vocabulary instruction, journal writing, or other whole-class activities	Review comprehension strategies for the week	Vocabulary instruction, journal writing, or other whole-class activities
Small Group	Echo read the story and apply comprehension strategies	Introduce a second selection, model fluent reading, and echo read the book	Read and discuss the second selection, applying comprehension strategies	Introduce a third selection, model fluent reading, and echo read the book	Read and discuss the third selection, applying comprehension strategies
Independent Work	Partner read the basal anthology selection or readers theater for the selection	Independent reading of stories or informational books at school and at home	Partner read the basal anthology selection or readers theater for the selection	Independent reading of stories or informational books at school and at home	Perform readers theater or share a passage that students can read well.

Assessing Readers' Fluency

Good readers begin their road to becoming fluent in the first grade. By the end of the second grade, they can read grade-level materials orally at something like 90 words per minute and are well on their way to becoming successful readers. Poor readers, on the other hand, may still struggle with fluency in the upper-elementary grades and beyond. For example, sixth-graders who are at the 10th percentile in fluency still read orally at something like 90 words per minute (Hasbrouck & Tindal, 2005). Because it is so important and because different students need different sorts of instruction and practice with fluency, assessment is vital for all students in the primary grades and all students whom you suspect may not be fluent readers in the upper-elementary and middle grades.

Although fluency is a straightforward concept, it has several components; if possible, each of these ought to be assessed. The components to consider are rate, accuracy, expression, and comprehension. Time may not always allow you to assess all the components of fluency. Because assessing only some of them is definitely worthwhile, rate and accuracy are the first components to consider. Fortunately,

Technology and fluency instruction are natural partners and each provides its own form of motivation. Children are intrigued with computers and their fascination grows with their expertise. Using a computer-based program the students can select passages, reread them to build fluency, and receive a record of progress. Voice-activated fluency programs with recognition software can listen to children read, note errors, and provide a steady record of progress. A computer-based fluency program can do much of what a teacher can do and with a great deal of patience. These programs provide the motivation and the practice, plus they free up the teacher to work with other students.

Motivated by the same factors that gave rise to small-group and whole-class fluency instruction—the need to find instruction that did not require a great deal of teacher time or the assistance of aides—several companies have developed prepackaged fluency programs. Fluency training is a rather straightforward matter, based primarily on modeling, repeated reading, and feedback; both taped programs and computer programs lend themselves well to providing instruction and practice incorporating these features. Several programs are currently available, and with the recent emphasis on fluency, more are undoubtedly coming. Here we describe two representative programs.

Read Naturally Masters Edition

Read Naturally was one of the first companies to produce a fluency program. In fact, the company was founded specifically to provide fluency instruction. It published its first program in the early 1990s. The current basic Read Naturally program is titled Read Naturally Masters Edition (Ihnot, 2001). The program is available in eight levels—1.0 to 8.0—each including the following components:

- 24 high-interest nonfiction stories on blackline masters
- 12 cassettes or 12 CDs of the stories
- Four multiple-choice questions and one open-ended question for each story
- Graphs on blackline masters where students chart their progress
- Activities, including reading, rereading, timing, answering questions, and graphing

The basic Read Naturally approach, the method used in a lot of fluency instruction, is shown here.

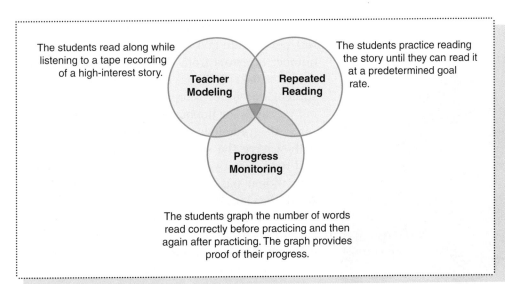

The students read along while listening to a tape recording of a high-interest story.

The students practice reading the story until they can read it at a predetermined goal rate.

Teacher Modeling

Repeated Reading

Progress Monitoring

The students graph the number of words read correctly before practicing and then again after practicing. The graph provides proof of their progress.

Read Naturally Approach to Fluency Instruction

Source: Read Naturally Rationale and Research. St. Paul, MN: Read Naturally. Copyright Read Naturally, Inc. 2005. All rights reserved.

In addition to its Masters Edition, Read Naturally offers a number of other programs, including a multicultural series, a Spanish series, assessment material, and, probably most notably, the Read Naturally Software Edition (Ihnot, 2004). The software edition parallels the taped edition in many ways but also takes advantage of some of the functions computers make possible, such as letting students click on unknown words to get definitions, allowing teachers to set rate criteria, and automatically graphing student progress.

QuickReads

Pearson Learning's QuickReads is a fluency program developed by Elfrieda Hiebert based on her oral reading fluency research that stresses limiting the number of rare multisyllable words when students work to improve reading fluency (Hiebert, 2005). The QuickReads program comes in both a paper-and-pencil and an electronic version. Expository passages are organized in sets of five short passages around a common topic. The program includes science and social studies passages leveled for second, third, fourth, fifth, and sixth grades. At each grade level 90 passages are organized into specific topics—dinosaurs, plants, American heroes, and celebrations. In the paper-and-pencil version, the students read a short passage several times, working to raise their reading rate. The teacher or a peer times each reading and the results are recorded. To keep a focus on comprehension students complete a short graphic organizer and answer a few comprehension questions. In the electronic version students read passages into a computer equipped with voice-activation software. The computer notes oral reading errors and records the time. The students then reread the passage, trying to improve their reading times. The computer gives feedback on growth in reading fluency and identifies words that need additional attention. Both versions of QuickReads have been shown to increase students' reading ability (Hiebert, 2005).

Given the expense of many fluency programs, teachers must question whether commercial programs provide a benefit over and above many of the fluency practices discussed in this chapter. In one study Melanie Kuhn (2004/2005) followed students engaged in repeated reading, echo reading, and partner reading, with positive feedback from the teachers. She also observed another group engaged in wide reading. Both groups made gains, with the wide reading group making gains in both fluency and comprehension. Both of these methods avoided the expense of a commercial fluency program. ●

there is a well-established, easy, and quick procedure for doing so. Called curriculum-based measurement (CBM), it was originally developed by Stanley Deno (1985). In using CBM, you simply select a grade-appropriate passage, have the student read orally for 1 minute, keep track of errors, and arrive at a words correct per minute (WCPM) score by subtracting the number of errors from the total number of words read. Rasinski (2003) has added a step of tallying the student's accuracy score, a useful addition. Selecting passages for fluency assessment requires some care. All grade-level passages are not alike, even if they have the same readability level. Students will read narrative passages more rapidly than informational passages (Dewitz, Mann, & Murray, 2009); the clarity and coherence of the writing also makes a difference. If you start monitoring fluency growth with narrative passages stick to narrative passages throughout the year. In the Classroom 8.6 shows a version of CBM that incorporates Rasinski's addition.

Once you have determined the student's rate and accuracy, you can compare them to the nationally accepted norms. Oral reading rate norms taken from the work of Jan Hasbrouck and Gerald Tindal (2005) are

Some older readers still need fluency activities.

Shutterstock

Procedures for Measuring Rate and Accuracy

- Identify a 100- to 200-word passage at the student's grade placement.
- Ask the student to read the passage aloud in a normal way at a normal rate for 1 minute. If the student hesitates on a word for 2 to 3 seconds, pronounce it aloud. Audio record the reading, and mark the point in the text reached in 1 minute.
- Mark any uncorrected errors the student makes. Mispronunciations, substitutions, reversals, omissions, and words that you pronounce for the student after a hesitation of 2 to 3 seconds are counted as errors.
- Determine rate by counting the total number of words read correctly during the minute. For example, a student might correctly read 47 words in a minute.
- Determine accuracy by dividing the number of words read correctly by the total number of words read. For example, a student might read 50 words in a minute and make 3 errors, leaving 47 words read correctly. Dividing 47 by 50 yields an accuracy score of 94 percent.

8.6

Instructional Routines

shown in Figure 8.2. Reading accuracy is typically categorized into three levels—independent, instructional and frustration (Rasinski, 2003). If a student reads a text with 98 to 100 percent accuracy, that text is considered to be at the student's independent level and can be read with no assistance. A text at the instructional level (the level at which she can read with some assistance) is typically read with 90 to 95 percent accuracy. The level indicating a student's frustration level (the level at which she is likely to find text too challenging) is 90 percent accuracy and below.

Students who are 20 percent or more below the reading rate norm for their grade level but at the independent or instructional level with respect to accuracy are likely to profit from instruction and practice on fluency. Students at the frustration level may need assessment of basic decoding skills. We discuss a variety of assessments and provide assessment tools in Appendix A.

As we noted, expression, sometimes called *prosody* in the current literature, is another component of fluency that deserves assessment. You assess expression by listening to students read orally and making a subjective judgment about their performance. The rubric shown in Figure 8.3, which was developed and tested by the National Assessment of Educational Progress (U.S. Department of Education, 1995), has proven to be an effective and easily used tool for rating expression. Simply have the child read grade-level material orally, and then rate the reading as Level 1, 2, 3, or 4. Students rated at Levels 3 or 4 are considered fluent in expression, whereas students at Levels 1 and 2 are not.

The final step in assessing fluency is to consider comprehension. If you assessed fluency with a 1-minute read, return the passage to the student and have them finish reading it. Then ask the student to retell the passage. A story map offers a simple system for scoring retelling of a narrative passage (Marshall, 1983). During retelling note whether the student names the characters, setting, goal, and problem, as well as the events and resolution.

*A*ssessment

Having students read for 1 minute is the typical method of assessing fluency. Yet you might also assess fluency for 3 or 4 minutes to test endurance and see whether students can sustain their rate over a longer passage.

Figure 8.2

Mean Oral Fluency Rates, 2005

Grade	Fall WCPM	Winter WCPM	Spring WCPM
1	—	23	53
2	51	72	89
3	71	92	107
4	94	112	123
5	110	127	139
6	127	140	150
7	128	136	150
8	133	146	151

Source: Hasbrouck, J., & Tindal, G. (2005). "Oral Reading Fluency: 90 Years of Measurement" (Tech. Rep. No. 33). Eugene: University of Oregon, College of Education, Behavioral Research & Teaching. Used with permission.

Figure 8.3   Oral Reading Fluency Scale

Level 4   Reads primarily in larger, meaningful phrase groups. Although some regressions, repetitions, and deviations from text may be present, these do not appear to detract from the overall structure of the story. Preservation of the author's syntax is consistent. Some or most of the story is read with expressive interpretation.

Level 3   Reads primarily in three- or four-word phrase groups. Some smaller groupings may be present. However, the majority of phrasing seems appropriate and preserves the syntax of the author. Little or no expressive interpretation is present.

Level 2   Reads primarily in two-word phrases with some three- or four-word groupings. Some word-by-word reading may be present. Word groupings may seem awkward and unrelated to larger context of sentence or passage.

Level 1   Reads primarily word-by-word. Occasional two-word or three-word phrases may occur, but these are infrequent and/or they do not preserve meaningful syntax.

Source: U.S. Department of Education, National Center for Education Statistics. (1995). *Listening to Children Read Aloud, 15.* Washington, DC: GPO.

You might assign a point for each story element and then compute a percentage score. For an expository selection, look for main ideas and details. Information on other assessments is provided in Appendix A.

Once you have assessed a student's fluency, it needs to be recorded so that you can monitor progress. It is generally recommended that you gather data at least three times a year. Figure 8.4 shows a form for describing all four aspects of fluency, with data entered for four second-graders' fall scores. Students with more severe fluency problems might be assessed more frequently.

Each of the four students presents a different profile and will require different sorts of attention. Malcolm is doing just fine. His rate, accuracy, expression score, and retelling score are all solid. He does not appear to need any special work in fluency. Jimmy, on the other hand, is doing poorly on all measures. He reads slowly, makes quite a few errors, reads without expression, and does not demonstrate good comprehension of what he reads. He appears to need special assistance in several areas, not just fluency. Mari presents a less even profile. Her rate is satisfactory, but her accuracy is low; her expression is good, but her comprehension is a bit low. She will need further assessment but will probably profit from work on word recognition and vocabulary as well as fluency. Hector presents yet another profile. His rate, accuracy, and expression are all satisfactory, but his comprehension appears to be quite low. Further assessment is definitely in order for Hector. In the next section of this chapter, we will consider what sorts of fluency instruction these and other students should receive.

PEARSON
myeducationlab

Watch a video of a second-grade teacher administering a fluency assessment and answer the following questions in the activity "Assessing Students' Reading Fluency." (To find this activity, go to the topic *Fluency* in MyEducationLab and click on Assignments and Activities.)

Choosing Among Approaches to Fluency

Thus far in the chapter, we have defined fluency and explained its importance, described a number of approaches to promoting fluency, and discussed ways of assess-

Figure 8.4 **Class Fluency Record**

Student	Rate			Accuracy			Expression			Comprehension		
	F	W	S	F	W	S	F	W	S	F	W	S
Malcolm C.	50			94%			3			30		
Jimmy V.	30			77%			1			10		
Mari R.	50			86%			3			22		
Hector A.	45			94%			3			15		

Teacher _____ Grade ___2___ Year_____

ing it. Next we consider which approaches are likely to be appropriate for various sorts of students. To do so, it will be convenient to group the different methods under three categories. The first category contains only one approach—wide reading. For many students, those who are making good progress in fluency and are near or above the fluency norms shown in Figure 8.2, wide reading in material they find interesting, enjoyable, and occasionally a bit challenging is *the* major road

Using Joke Books to Develop Intonation, Inflection, and Phrasing

Motivating Struggling *Readers*

Molly Ness (2009) suggests using joke books to help struggling readers develop appropriate intonation, inflection, and phrasing as they read. Ness observes that to tell a joke successfully, tellers must pay attention to punctuation, intonation, and phrasing—some of the very aspects with which disfluent readers struggle. Not only do jokes require readers to attend to important components of fluency, Ness remarks, they are fun for children, who are motivated to read them over and over. Ness offers tips for teachers interested in using jokes for fluency practice. Work with a disfluent reader one-on-one. Have the child read the joke orally. Note with the child what makes the joke funny. Help the child identify which words or phrases require emphasis, how to parse the joke into meaningful phrases for delivery, and where and for how long to pause to preserve and communicate the humor. Then model how to tell the joke. Afterward, chorally read the joke together, telling the child to make her reading sound like yours. After a few readings, record the child's reading of the joke, play it back, and note the progress made. Ness explains that students can practice telling jokes with one another or on their own over a number of days. Then students can perform them during a classroom "Comedy Hour." Three joke books for students are Marco Maestro's *What Do You Hear When Cows Sing?: And Other Silly Riddles*, Michael Dahl's *The Everything Kids' Joke Book: Side-Splitting, Rib-Tickling Fun*, and Bob Phillips and Steve Russo's *Fabulous and Funny Clean Jokes for Kids*. •

Books to Build Fluency in Developing Readers

The following list includes books that Melanie Kuhn (2004/2005) used in investigating fluency-oriented oral reading, a few newer books similar to those she used, and some Spanish-English dual-language books, which may be particularly useful with Latino English language learners.

Barbara Bottner. *Pish and Posh* (I Can Read Book 2). HarperCollins, 2005. Wacky surprises occur when best friends Pish and Posh discover a book of fairy magic. 48 pages.

Betsy Byars. *The Golly Sisters Go West* (I Can Read Book 3). HarperTrophy, 1989. The singing, dancing Golly sisters, May-May and Rose, travel west by covered wagon, entertaining people along the way. 64 pages.

Betsy Byars. *Hooray for the Golly Sisters!* (I Can Read Book 3). HarperCollins, 1992. In these five amusing stories, May-May and Rose "cross the big river" and entertain folks with their zany variety shows. 64 pages.

Jack Gantos. *Rotten Ralph Feels Rotten.* Farrar, Straus and Giroux, 2004. When mischievous cat Ralph becomes ill after raiding garbage cans and is taken to the vet, he becomes lonesome for Sarah and makes his way home. 48 pages.

Lillian Hoban. *Arthur's Funny Money* (I Can Read Book 2). HarperTrophy, 1984. In this story, one of Hoban's many delightful tales of Arthur, his little sister Violet has a problem with math and Arthur is penniless, so they go into business and solve both problems. 64 pages.

Russell Hoban. *Bedtime for Frances.* HarperCollins, 1995. The endearing little badger Frances comes up with all sorts of delaying tactics to postpone her bedtime. 32 pages.

Jeff Kinney. *Diary of a Wimpy Kid.* Amulet Books, 2007. Part of a continuing first-person story of a middle school student who can't seem to get many things right but has a humorous view of the world around him.

Arnold Lobel. *Frog and Toad Together* (I Can Read Book 2). HarperTrophy, 1979. A collection of five tales about friends Frog and Toad, each a masterpiece of humor and sensitivity. 64 pages.

Herman Parish and Lynn Sweat. *Amelia Bedelia, Bookworm* (I Can Read Book 2). Greenwillow, 2005. When Amelia Bedelia helps out at her local library, she does everything by "the book," which, of course, gets her into a whole lot of trouble! 64 pages.

Shelley Moore Thomas. *Get Well, Good Knight* (Puffin Easy-to-Read). Puffin, 2004. When little knight's three dragon friends come down with awful colds, he sets off to find a healing potion. 48 pages.

Dual-Language Books in English and Spanish

Catherine Bruzzone. *Pupagesy Finds a Friend/Cachorrito encuentra un amigo.* Barron's Educational Series, bilingual edition, 2000. Pupagesy can't find anyone to play with until he meets a white mouse. 28 pages.

Susan Lowell. *The Three Little Pigs/Los tres pequeños jabalies.* Rising Moon Books, bilingual edition, 2004. In this southwestern retelling of The Three Little Pigs, three wild boars try to outsmart a hungry coyote. 32 pages.

Pat Mora. *Listen to the Desert/Oye al desierto.* Clarion, 2001. A brightly illustrated picture book that introduces readers to some of the desert sounds. 32 pages.

Pat Mora. *Uno, dos, tres/One, Two, Three.* Clarion, 2000. In this simple counting book, two little girls buy presents for their mother in a Mexican market. 48 pages.

Spanish Translations

Crockett Johnson (translated by **Teresa Mlawer**). *Harold y el lapiz color morado.* Rayo, 1995. In this children's classic, *Harold and the Purple Crayon,* he draws the world with a purple crayon. 64 pages.

Arnold Lobel (translated by **Pablo Lizcano**). *Sapo y Sepo son amigos.* Alfaguara, 2003. *Frog and Toad Are Friends* is a collection of five short stories about the friendship of a frog and a toad, another children's classic. 66 pages.

to fluency. This is the primary method to use with Malcolm. The second category contains three approaches—choral reading, radio reading, and readers theater. All three can be used from time to time to celebrate, motivate, and improve oral reading. All students—including Malcolm, Jimmy, Mari, and Hector—will profit from using these approaches from time to time. Remember, though, that students who are struggling will need to take smaller, less demanding parts. The third category includes all the other approaches: the original method of repeated reading, simultaneous reading, echo reading, tape-assisted repeated reading, partner reading, and the use of commercial programs. Students who are not making adequate progress in fluency—those who are 20 percent or so below the rate norms for their grade or those who show an uneven profile across the four components of fluency we have described—are candidates for these other approaches. Mari, who seems to do well on everything but rate, clearly needs to use one or more of these approaches. Jimmy undoubtedly needs one of these approaches, but he needs other special work too. And Hector probably needs one of these approaches and may need other special work as well. Remember if you adopt FORI, fluency-oriented reading instruction, many of these approaches will be incorporated into the students' daily work. However, there's no reason to limit your selection to one approach; using more than one approach provides variety and gives students some different opportunities.

Assessment

Observe students as they work at partner reading or readers theater to determine their level of motivation. If they are not engaged in the task, either change the goal or switch to a new fluency task.

Matching Students and Texts

Matching students and texts is vital in planning fluency instruction as well as in choosing selections for all other purposes—including reading to students, doing shared reading, scaffolding reading experiences for the whole class or small groups,

Resources for Developing Fluency

In this chapter we have highlighted many techniques for helping children develop fluency as well as emphasizing the importance of wide reading in appropriate texts. To build fluency children need texts they can read on their own or with just a little support. The following sources list books that reflect the families, communities, and cultures of English language learners.

- Bebop Books is an imprint of Lee & Low specializing in books that reflect cultural diversity. The texts are leveled to help teachers match texts to students (www.leeandlow.com/p/overview_bebop.mhtml).
- Scholastic has a series called New Connections to English that includes fiction and nonfiction texts leveled using a variety of systems (e.g., Lexile, Guided Reading). (http://teacher.scholastic.com/products/classroombooks/newconnections.htm).
- National Geographic School Publishing (www.ngsp.com) has a couple of book series for English language learners. A series called Into English! focuses on building content area knowledge while developing English language reading. Another, Rise and Shine, is composed of leveled readers.

Differentiating Instruction

for

English Language Learners

fostering independent reading, and planning and assigning homework. The various methods of matching students and texts all rely on three considerations: (1) the students' reading proficiency and motivation, (2) text difficulty and accessibility, and (3) your personal and professional knowledge about your students, the books and other reading materials in your classroom, and the various purposes for which students are reading.

Assessing Students' Reading Proficiency and Motivation

Approaches to assessing students' reading proficiency and motivation can range from informal teacher-based approaches to more formal text-based approaches. At the informal end of the continuum are your observations of students and their reading. It is important to be constantly alert to how students are doing in reading and their attitudes toward reading, and one way of doing so is to repeatedly ask questions such as these: Do students read voluntarily? Do they read when they are asked to do so? Do they seem to enjoy reading, or is it a real task for them? What sorts of books do they choose? Do they generally finish the books they choose? Do they talk about books, bring books to school, and share books with their friends? As part of these informal observations, it is useful to listen to students read, ask them a few questions, and make brief notes on their comprehension, reading rate, fluency, and attitudes. These sorts of informal observations are necessary and particularly useful for assessing attitudes and motivation, but they are only one of several approaches that should be used in concert.

Next on the informal–formal continuum is the informal reading inventory (IRI). IRIs consist of passages that a student reads orally to a teacher. They can be used to assess the appropriateness of specific texts or levels of texts for individual students as well as to investigate areas of strength and weakness for individual students. IRIs allow you to check a student's rate and fluency as well as consider decoding strategies, miscues, vocabulary, and reading comprehension.

You can construct an IRI yourself, or you can select an already constructed IRI from several sources. In the Classroom 8.7 shows one way to construct an IRI yourself.

The assessment of fluency also requires an assessment of comprehension.

Elizabeth Crews/PhotoEdit

Obviously, an IRI can provide a great deal of useful information, and you will learn a lot from going through the process of constructing one. Equally obviously, constructing an IRI is time-consuming. Fortunately, the Interactive Reading Assessment System–Revised (Calfee & Hoover, 2004), which is described in Chapter 4 and included in Appendix A, includes a set of graded passages and prompts for students' retellings of the passages. Alternatively, the commercially published Qualitative Reading Inventory-5 (Leslie & Caldwell, 2010) contains an extensive set of graded passages. Beginning with either assessment tool is an excellent way to become knowledgeable about IRIs and incorporate them into your classroom.

The more formal end of the assessment continuum includes commercially produced standardized reading tests such as the Stanford Achievement Test Series (Harcourt Educational Measurement, 2001) and TerraNova, the Second Edition (CTB/McGraw-Hill, 2001). Tests such as these have the advantage of being group administered and thus take much less time than individual observations and IRIs. They yield a number of indices of performance for each student tested, including grade-level

Constructing an Informal Reading Inventory

- Select a set of texts of increasing difficulty representative of the material you plan to use for fluency instruction, perhaps half a dozen texts in all.
- Select two passages that seem representative of the book as a whole in terms of sentence length, vocabulary, prior knowledge required, and so on. A 100- to 125-word passage is generally sufficient for beginning readers, and a 200- to 250-word passage is appropriate for higher ability levels.
- Make sure the student feels at ease. Then introduce the passage by saying, "I'm going to have you read this paragraph to me, and then I'd like you to tell me about what you read."
- As the student is reading, follow along with a duplicate copy. Circle words that the student has difficulty with or omits during reading, noting in the margin any mispronunciations or substitutions of one word for another. In addition, note any significant behaviors exhibited by the reader, such as lack of expression during reading, finger-pointing, holding the text close to the eyes, or a markedly slow or rapid rate.
- Afterward, check comprehension by asking the student to retell what he has read. Initially, ask the student to respond without looking back at the passage. However, if he needs to look back in order to give a satisfactory retelling, let him do so. Characterize the retelling using simple descriptions, such as "complete, coherent, and shows good understanding," "somewhat sketchy but showing basic understanding," or "sketchy and not showing much understanding." You might also want to ask a question or two, perhaps an inferential question and an application question, and record the student's success with those. Additionally, your notes should indicate whether the student looked back to retell the passage.
- If you are uncertain about the student's competency based on one text, you can repeat the IRI with a second passage that is harder or easier, assessing until you determine the instructional level.

equivalents, an important score for matching students and texts. For example, a standardized test score might indicate that a particular student had a grade-level equivalent of 2.5, indicating that he scored somewhere between the average second-grader and the average third-grader on the test. For such a score, a second- or third-grade book *may* be appropriate for fluency work. But standardized tests have both strengths and weaknesses, and precisely indicating the level of text that a certain student should read for a certain purpose is not one of their strengths. Lacking other information, begin fluency instruction with a text at a student's tested grade level, and then carefully monitor the student's reading to see whether that text is indeed appropriate. Use other information gained from your observations, an IRI, or some other source combined with the standardized test score in choosing a text for the student. Always monitor the student's reading and be prepared to change texts if need be.

Assessing Text Difficulty and Accessibility

As with reading proficiency and motivation, there are various approaches to assessing text difficulty and accessibility. We will describe traditional readability formulas, such as the Fry Readability Formula, the Lexile system for rating books, and a system of book "leveling" developed by Fountas and Pinnell (1999).

Readability formulas are based on objective measures that take into account certain characteristics of a text and yield a grade-level equivalent for it. This traditional approach to assessing text difficulty generally considers two factors—measures of both vocabulary difficulty and syntactic complexity. When applied to a text, the formula indicates that the text is written at such and such a grade level. The Fry formula (Fry, 1977) is one widely used measure. It assesses word difficulty by considering the average number of syllables in the words of a text, and it assesses syntactic complexity by considering the average number of words per sentence. For example, when applied to Marion Ripley's *Private and Confidential: A Story About Braille*, the Fry formula indicates that the book is written at approximately the second-grade level. It would therefore appear to be appropriate for students reading at the second-grade level. However, both estimates of text difficulty and the reading levels resulting from testing students are approximations. As we have noted, efforts to match students and texts must always be undertaken with the realization that the initial matches should be considered tentative and that you need to continually monitor students and be prepared to offer another book if the first one isn't working. Nevertheless, as long as you understand that such matches are approximations, readability formulas and other approaches to assessing text difficulty can be quite useful. In the Classroom 8.8 shows the procedures for the Fry formula and a graph used in applying the formula.

The second text difficulty tool we consider, the Lexile Framework for Reading, is a multipart system that uses a complex formula of word difficulty and sentence complexity to determine the reading level of short texts and books. The Lexile website (www.lexile.com) has a database that list the levels for tens of thousands of books and an online tool for calculating the Lexile levels for text you input. Like the Fry formula, the Lexile formula considers word difficulty and sentence complexity in a sophisticated way to determine text difficulty. Unlike the Fry formula and most traditional formulas, the Lexile formula yields a Lexile level, a score ranging from 200 to 1700, instead of a grade-level equivalent. Lexile levels can then be compared to students' scores on standardized tests, many of which yield Lexile levels, or they can be roughly equated with grade levels using the conversion chart shown in Figure 8.5.

A third approach to assessing text difficulty, the leveled books approach, was developed as a way of ranking books for difficulty and accessibility by considering a number of factors beyond those taken into account by traditional readability formulas or by computer-based formulas such as the Lexile Framework. Irene Fountas and Gay Su Pinnell (2006) and their colleagues have examined a large number of books and categorized them in levels ranging from Levels A and B (for children just beginning to read) to Level Z (for students reading at the seventh- and eighth-grade level). Among the many factors considered in Fountas and Pinnell's leveling process are the number of ideas in the book, size of the print, layout, correspondence between text and pictures, and sophistication and familiarity of the topics. The following excerpts are parts of their descriptions of Levels A and B books, such as Syd Hoff's *Barney's Horse*, and of Level M books, such as Jan Brett's *The Mitten*.

Figure 8.5 **Chart for Converting Lexile Levels to Grade-Level Equivalents**

Lexile Levels	Grade-Level Equivalents
200L to 400L	1
300L to 500L	2
500L to 700L	3
650L to 850L	4
750L to 950L	5
850L to 1050L	6
950L to 1075L	7
1000L to 1100L	8
1050L to 1150L	9
1100L to 1200L	10
1100L to 1300L	11 and 12

Levels A and B Books

Levels A and B books are very easy for young children to begin to read. Many of these books focus on a single idea or have a single story line. There is a direct correspondence between the text and the pictures, and children can easily relate the topics to

Using the Fry Readability Formula

1. Randomly select three 100-word samples from the book, short story, chapter, or article that you want to assess, one each from the beginning, middle, and near the end of the selection. For longer selections, you may want to take additional samples. In counting the 100-word samples, do count proper nouns, initials, and numerals. Count hyphenated words as one word.

2. Count the number of sentences in each 100-word sample, estimating to the nearest tenth of a sentence, and average that count.

3. Count the number of syllables in each 100-word sample, and average that count. Syllables are based on sounds, not necessarily letters. There are as many syllables in a word as there are vowel sounds. Thus, *want* has one syllable, *stopped* has one, and *wanted* has two. When counting syllables for numerals, initials, and symbols, count one syllable for each symbol. Thus, *1945* has four syllables; *IRA*, three syllables; and *&*, one syllable.

4. Find on the Fry graph the lines corresponding to the average sentence length and the average number of syllables. Go to the intersection of these two lines to get the approximate grade level of the selection. An example is given below the graph.

Graph for Estimating Readability—Extended
by Edward Fry, Rutgers University Reading Center, New Brunswick, NJ 08904

Average number of syllables per 100 words

108 112 116 120 124 128 132 136 140 144 148 152 156 160 164 168 172 176 180 182

Average number of sentences per 100 words

APPROXIMATE GRADE LEVEL

1 2 3 4 5 6 7 8 9 10 11 12 13 14 15 16 17+

Example	Example	Example
First 100 Words	118	5.4
Second 100 Words	123	5.0
Third 100 Words	113	5.2
Average	118	5.2

Estimated Grade Level: 6th

Source: Fry, E. B., Polk, J. K., & Fountoukidis, D. (2000). *The Reading Teacher's Book of Lists*. Paramus, NJ: Prentice Hall.

their personal experience. The language, while not exactly duplicating oral language, includes naturally occurring syntactic structures. Teachers can use books at these levels to introduce children to word-by-word matching and locating known words.

Level M Books

Books in Level M are long, with lots of text per page, smaller print, and narrower word spacing. There is a wide variety of texts, but they all have complex language structures and sophisticated vocabulary. They are highly detailed and descriptive and present more abstract concepts and themes. The subtleties of these texts require more background knowledge. Many characters are involved in more complex and expanded plots; character development is a prominent feature. (Fountas & Pinnell, 2006, pp. 136, 142).

The newest list of leveled books (Fountas & Pinnell, 2006) shows approximately 16,000 titles.

Another subjective approach to assessing text difficulty is to consider the array of factors affecting difficulty discovered in recent psychological and linguistic research (Graves & Graves, 2003). Although this approach does not yield a single answer, such as a grade-level equivalent, Lexile score, or Fountas and Pinnell level, it does suggest the factors to look for as you consider the appropriateness of various reading selections for your students.

- Vocabulary
- Sentence structure
- Length
- Elaboration
- Coherence and unity
- Text structure
- Familiarity of content and background knowledge required
- Audience appropriateness
- Quality and verve of the writing
- Interestingness

Not all of these factors are weighted equally; they are weighted differently from one book to another, and as we have noted, they do not yield a numerical score. However, considering them does help you think deeply about the match between a student or group of students and a text.

Your Personal and Professional Knowledge

At this point, we have already discussed assessing students and assessing reading materials, but in completing our consideration of matching students and texts, we want to say a bit more about each of these topics and also make some comments about purposes. In considering students, it is important to go beyond the information gleaned from IRIs and standardized tests and think of each student as a person with strengths and weaknesses, likes and dislikes, favorite topics and boring ones, and varying tolerance for challenges.

In considering reading materials, it is important to go beyond the grade level provided by a readability formula, the Lexile level provided by the Lexile Framework, the level assigned by the Fountas and Pinnell system, and the factors influencing text difficulty and consider the content of each book and how individual students are going to respond to that content. Is the book about salamanders you're considering for Teddy too difficult according to a readability formula but probably a great choice for Teddy because anything as slimy and snakelike as a salamander is sure to enthrall him? Is the coming of age novel you're considering for both Tammy and Ramon far too mature for almost all the other students in the class but a perfect fit for these two very mature students? Will a simple narrative set in the desert be particularly difficult for your Hmong students because they are unfamiliar with desert environments?

In addition to considering the students and text, it is important to consider the purpose for which students are reading. When your purpose is to improve fluency

PEARSON
myeducationlab

Practice identifying the components of effective fluency instruction in different teachers' classrooms by completing the activity "Fostering Reading Fluency." (To find this activity, go to the topic *Fluency* in MyEducationLab and click on Building Teaching Skills and Dispositions.)

and you are using an approach in which students repeatedly read the same text, the text needs to be slightly challenging so that there is room for improvement across the repeated readings. Similarly, when you are working with the class or a small group, scaffolding their reading of a particular text, you will generally want to use texts that are a little challenging, ones that your students can succeed at because you are assisting them. Conversely, when students are doing independent reading and do not have your assistance, they should frequently read in texts that are not a challenge, ones that they find interesting and enjoyable but not taxing. Similarly, when you are teaching a comprehension strategy, you want to use a text that is sophisticated enough to require the use of the strategy but not one where decoding is a problem; students can hardly be expected to use a comprehension strategy if they cannot decode the text. Matching students and texts is important for all of the reading activities students undertake. Fluency instruction and practice are no exception.

REFLECT *and Apply*

6. Make a copy of the Class Fluency Record shown in Figure 8.4, and make up rate, accuracy, expression, and comprehension scores for two students who show quite different profiles. Jot down the fluency activities you might provide for each of these students, and briefly justify the activities you suggest.

7. Your observations are particularly important in assessing students' motivation to read and the extent to which they need to be challenged in the fluency activities you give them. You use them, of course, in choosing activities that will be at just the right level of difficulty for particular students. Make up a brief observation form that includes half a dozen or so types of behavior you want to consider, and briefly note why each is important.

8. Identify one widely used book you estimate to be at about the second-grade level and one you estimate to be at about the fourth-grade level. Look up each book in the Lexile Book Database at www.lexile.com, and convert the Lexile level into a grade-level equivalent using the conversion chart shown in Figure 8.5. Compare your estimates to those you got using the Lexile Book Database and the conversion chart, and jot down a comment on the agreement or disagreement between the estimates.

Strengths *and Challenges* of Diversity

Several sorts of diversity are particularly important in considering fluency instruction—diversity in language, background knowledge, reading proficiency, and motivation and tolerance for challenge. Each type of diversity will have its own influence on your approach.

Diversity in Language

For English language learners who are still struggling to learn oral English, achieving fluency in English may be a real struggle. If such students are in true bilingual reading programs, it would almost certainly be best if they could become fluent in their first language initially and then work on attaining fluency in English. However, bilingual reading programs are rare and not the situation most students face. The alternative is to give English language learners as much support as possible and ensure that students have sufficiently easy English texts. Model fluent reading of text several times, allow students enough repetitions to truly master one passage before moving on to another, and be sure that students are not forced to read haltingly in front of other students.

Diversity in Background Knowledge

Many English language learners, minority students, and children of poverty come to school with experiences and, therefore, background knowledge very different from those of middle-class students. It is particularly important to provide these students with texts for fluency instruction and practice that deal with topics they know something about and have some interest in. Talk to children about their experiences and interests, talk to their parents or other caregivers, and work with your school librarian and other professionals to get all students books that they will find interesting, enjoyable, and appropriate, given their experiences.

Diversity in Reading Proficiency

As noted at the beginning of this chapter, more skilled readers move easily through Chall's (1996) stages of reading development. They learn to read easily, quickly acquire decoding skills, and soon achieve a significant degree of automaticity, reading smoothly and accurately, with expression and comprehension. For these students, wide reading is the key to fluency, although exercises like readers theater and radio reading can be interesting alternatives. Unfortunately, less skilled readers find learning to read difficult. These students will learn to read smoothly, accurately, expressively, and with comprehension only with a good deal of direct attention to fluency instruction. These students, too, need to do wide reading in accessible and interesting texts; they should have opportunities to engage in choral reading, readers theater, and radio reading. But they also need a lot of work with more direct approaches to building fluency—repeated reading, tape-assisted repeated reading, and the like.

Diversity in Motivation and Tolerance for Challenges

The more success students have experienced with reading, the more motivated they are to read and the more willing they are to accept challenges. Conversely, the less success students have had with reading, the less likely they are to be motivated to read and the fewer challenges they are likely to accept. And the more reading problems students have experienced, the more we have to work extremely hard to make fluency instruction a pleasant, nonthreatening, and nonembarrassing activity. This means providing less successful readers with texts that are not too challenging, giving them plenty of opportunities to practice in private before they read orally for you, and not putting them in situations in which they are likely to stumble through a text in front of other students. It also means that less successful readers need to compare their current fluency achievement with their previous achievement and not with norms or with the achievement of other students in the class. With less successful readers as with more successful ones, one of our major tasks as teachers is to continually stretch them to reach higher levels of achievement.

Concluding Remarks

In this chapter, we have defined fluency and described many different procedures for assisting students in becoming fluent—the original method of repeated reading, simultaneous repeated reading, echo reading, tape-assisted repeated reading, partner reading, choral reading, readers theater, radio reading, fluency-oriented reading instruction (FORI), commercial fluency programs, and wide reading. We have also discussed ways of assessing fluency, suggested criteria for choosing among the many approaches so that students get the types of fluency instruction they need, and described several tools for assessing students and assessing texts in order to match students with appropriate texts.

In recent years, fluency instruction has been identified as a critical component of a comprehensive and effective reading program. All students must reach the goal of reading fluently if they are to progress from novices just learning to read to actual readers who can and do read—children and later adults who read for enjoyment, for learning, to become informed citizens, to investigate topics as diverse as health and hobbies, and for the myriad of other benefits one can gain from reading. You will need to select approaches to fluency that fit your students, your teaching style, and the overall context in which you teach. But one thing is certain: Fluency instruction should be a definite part of your curriculum.

Extending Learning

1. One excellent way to understand a phenomenon is to engage in a process in which you experience it. This works particularly well with the process of becoming automatic in reading because there is a very simple way of experiencing it. Find a fairly lengthy and complex sentence, and write it backwards. Here is an example with a very short sentence: "Bob had a cow" becomes "Woc a dah boB." Once you have written out your backward sentence—and remember that it needs to be a good deal longer and more complex than the example we have given—repeatedly

read it aloud from back to front (right to left) until you can read it fluently. Time each reading, and make a note of how rapidly you move toward automaticity with the reversed sentence. This is a much simpler task than the one beginning readers face, so don't think their progress toward automaticity will be nearly as rapid. Still, the task will give you a good sense of what it means to move from consciously having to think about each letter as you read to becoming automatic in processing words.

2. Get together with a teacher who is working with some students on fluency (probably a second- or third-grade teacher or possibly a teacher in a higher grade with struggling readers), and volunteer to help with fluency activities for 2 to 4 weeks. Describe the fluency activity or activities you use. Keep a log book in which you chart student progress and keep a record of how each ses-

sion goes, for you and for your students. Once you have completed your tutoring, write a brief summary of the experience. In the summary, explain what you did, how the fluency work was similar to or different from that described in this chapter, what your students gained from the activities, what you learned from them, and what you plan to do about fluency instruction in your classes.

3. Identify a widely used children's book such as Sid Fleischman's *The Whipping Boy* and use three of the four approaches listed in this chapter to assess text difficulty and accessibility—the Fry formula, the Lexile Book Database, the levels provided by Fountas and Pinnell (2006), and the subjective approach that two of us have described (Graves & Graves, 2003). After you have used the approaches, write a fairly detailed critique of the information each yielded and its advantages and disadvantages.

Children's Literature

Brett, J. (1989). *The Mitten: A Ukranian Folktale.* New York: Putnam. A variety of animals are sleeping very snugly in Nicki's lost mitten—up until the bear sneezes, that is. 32 pages.

Dahl, M. (2002). *The Everything Kids' Joke Book: Side-Splitting, Rib-Tickling Fun.* Avon, MA: Adams Media. Offers jokes that upper-grade students will find hilarious and provides tips on how to tell jokes. 144 pages.

Fleischman, S. (2003). *The Whipping Boy.* New York: Harper-Trophy. Prince Brat's whipping boy, the orphan Jemmy, teaches the royal heir about life and friendship when the spoiled prince flees the castle. 96 pages.

Hoff, S. (1987). *Barney's Horse.* New York: Harper & Row. Barney's horse becomes frightened by the new overhead trains he encounters in the city. 32 pages.

Kinney, J. (2007). *Diary of a Wimpy Kid.* New York: Amulet Books. This series tells the tale of an undersized weakling coping with middle school. 217 pages.

Maestro, M. (1997). *What Do You Hear When Cows Sing? And Other Silly Riddles.* New York: HarperCollins. A joke book to tickle primary-grade readers' funny bones. 48 pages.

Phillips, B., & Russo, S. (2004). *Fabulous and Fun Clean Jokes for Kids.* Eugene, OR: Harvest House. Just what the title promises, jokes that will please both students and the adults in their lives. 132 pages.

Pikley, Dav. (1997). *The Adventures of Captain Underpants.* New York: Scholastic. A tale of an elementary school superhero with a large bag of tricks. 121 pages.

Prelutsky, J. (2005). *It's Raining Pigs and Noodles.* New York: HarperTrophy. This wonderful read-aloud collection of humorous poems with "impeccable rhythms and rhymes" appeals to a child's sense of humor. 160 pages.

Ripley, M. (2003). *Private and Confidential: A Story About Braille.* New York: Dial Books for Young Readers. Laura finds out that her new pen pal is nearly blind and learns to use a braille machine to write to him. 28 pages.

PEARSON
myeducationlab

Now go to the topic "Fluency" in the MyEducationLab (www.myeducationlab.com) for your course, where you can:

- Find learning outcomes for the topics covered in this chapter along with the IRA standards that connect to these outcomes.

- Complete assignable activities in the Assignments and Activities section that show concepts in action to help you synthesize and apply strategies.

- Explore IRIS Center Resources—training enhancement materials that provide you with research-validated information and interactive materials to develop your skills in working with students.

- Apply and practice your understanding of the teaching skills identified in the chapter with the Building Teaching Skills and Dispositions exercises.

9

Vocabulary Development

CHAPTER outline

At 9 months, Julie spoke her first word. "Ba," she said with great gusto while pointing to the ball in her picture book. Over the next 5 months, Julie added another 50 words or so to her repertoire. After that, her vocabulary grew by leaps and bounds. Everyone in her family was an avid reader, everyone read to her a lot, and everyone talked to her a lot. By the time she started school, she had an oral vocabulary of several thousand words. Was Julie an unusual 5-year-old wordsmith? Not really. Julie's vocabulary development is typical of many children, but not all children by any means.

After she began school, Julie, like many of her counterparts, began rapidly acquiring a reading vocabulary. Soon, both her reading and oral vocabulary grew impressively. Aided by her teachers—and, of course, by the reading she did and her growing understanding of the power of words—Julie acquired the vocabulary she needed to succeed in and out of school.

As noted, Julie's vocabulary development is not unique. But neither is it typical of all children. Children who grow up in homes where they are seldom read to, where they are not talked to a lot, or where English is rarely or never spoken are likely to have small English vocabularies when they enter school. And having a small English vocabulary is likely to adversely affect their success in school.

Fortunately, teachers are in an enviable position. You have the unique opportunity to exert a powerful effect on the vocabularies of the students you teach. Teaching vocabulary can improve students' reading comprehension, their writing, their speaking, their success in school, and their success beyond school.

CLASSROOM vignette

The Vocabulary Learning Task

Fortunately, because vocabulary is tremendously important to students' success, we currently know a great deal about how to create an effective vocabulary program (Baumann, Kame'enui, & Ash, 2003; Graves, 2006). Several considerations are particularly important to keep in mind as you begin planning a comprehensive and effective program. To begin, the vocabulary learning task is enormous! Estimates of vocabulary size vary greatly, but a reasonable estimate based on a substantial body of rigorous work (Anderson & Nagy, 1992; Anglin, 1993; Hiebert, 2005; Nagy & Anderson, 1984; White, Graves, & Slater, 1990) suggests that the books and other reading materials used by schoolchildren include well over 100,000 different words. The average child enters school with a very small reading vocabulary, typically consisting largely of environmental print. Once in school, however, a child's reading vocabulary is likely to soar at a rate of 3,000 to 4,000 words a year, leading to a reading vocabulary of something like 25,000 words by the time she is in the eighth grade and maybe well over 50,000 words by the end of high school (Graves, 2006).

Quite obviously, each year students learn many more words than we can teach directly. This represents a tremendous learning achievement, yet it is partially explained by the fact that students lack deep and rich meanings for many of the words they know. Instead, their partial and incomplete meanings often hinder full comprehension of reading materials containing the words and lessen their confidence in using them in speaking or writing. Isabel Beck and her colleagues (Beck, McKeown, & Omanson, 1987) have distinguished three levels of word knowledge—unknown, acquainted, and established. Unknown words are, as the name indicates, completely unfamiliar. The word *repel* is likely to be unknown to most third-graders. A word at the acquainted level is one whose basic meaning is recognized, but only after the student gives it some deliberate attention. *Resident* would probably be understood by most fifth-graders but would require a moment's thought. At the established level, words are easily, rapidly, and automatically recognized. For most second-graders, the word *house* is at the established level.

Of course, students do not need to know *all* the words they encounter in reading at the established level—just most of them. As we noted in Chapter 1, words that are not recognized automatically—not established—will thwart the process of comprehending text. Moreover, as just suggested, unless words are understood at the established level, students are not likely to use them in speaking and writing.

There is increasing evidence that the vocabularies of many children of poverty entering school are much smaller than those of their middle-class counterparts. There is also evidence that having a small vocabulary is a very serious detriment to success in reading. These two facts make it especially important to find ways to bolster the oral and reading vocabularies of students who enter school with limited word knowledge (Becker, 1977; Biemiller, 2010; Hart & Risley, 2003; National Reading Panel, 2000; RAND Reading Study Group, 2002; White et al., 1990). For similar reasons, bolstering the oral and reading English vocabularies of English language learners is critically important (August, Carlo, Dressler, & Snow, 2005; Helman, 2008).

A comprehensive and effective vocabulary program must respect these facts about children's word knowledge and how it grows, and the program we describe here does so. The program has four major emphases. First, it provides children with frequent, extensive, and varied language experiences. Second, it includes instruction in individual words. Third, it provides students with instruction in learning words independently. Finally, it fosters word consciousness; that is, it builds students' interest in words, teaches them to value words, and gets them actively involved in building and honing their vocabularies.

Frequent, Extensive, and Varied Language Experiences

A variety of language experiences—listening, speaking, reading, and writing—are important for children's growth in learning. For example, shared storybook reading, an interactive oral reading approach, has been shown to be very productive, as we will discuss. Listening is a child's earliest language experience; children begin to perceive speech sounds well before the end of their first year. Speaking comes next; most children utter their first word at about age 1. The most general statement that can be made about listening and speaking in the preschool years and beyond is that children need as much of both as possible. They particularly need to engage in real discussions—give-and-take conversations in which first caretakers and later teachers give young learners the opportunity to think and discuss topics of interest in an open, positive, and supportive climate. In summing up the major message of their longitudinal study showing the huge and ever-widening gap between the vocabularies of middle-class children and of many children reared in poverty, Betty Hart and Todd Risley (1995) note that "the most important difference among families was in the amount of talking that went on." Anything that we can do to promote real discussions in school and out of school is very worthwhile.

Of course, reading to children is also very valuable and extremely important (Cunningham, 2005). As teachers, we should frequently read to children, model our enthusiasm for reading, and do everything we can to get parents and other caregivers involved in reading to and with their children. Reading to children has been found to be effective in promoting vocabulary growth.

Reading to children is enhanced in an approach called *interactive oral reading*, in which an adult and a small group of children focus on and discuss words that come up in the reading. Shown to be particularly effective (Beck & McKeown, 2004; Biemiller, 2003; De Temple & Snow, 2003; Zevenbergen & Whitehurst, 2004), interactive oral reading is designed for primary-grade students. It is particularly useful for students who come to school with relatively small vocabularies or who are English language learners and therefore need special assistance to catch up with their peers. The following characteristics of effective interactive oral reading are taken from De Temple and Snow (2003), our own experiences, and reading of the literature:

Reading to children is especially effective when coupled with discussion and when students are actively involved and responding to the book being shared.

Frank Pedrick/The Image Works

- Both the reader and the children play active roles.
- The book (or other reading selection) is read several times.

- The adult reader focuses the children's attention directly on words.
- The adult reads fluently, using an animated and lively reading style.
- The books are interesting and enjoyable and stretch children's thinking a bit.
- The books contain somewhat challenging words that children are likely to encounter in the future.

In the Classroom 9.1 shows the steps of the interactive oral reading approach developed by Andrew Biemiller (2003).

One point about interactive oral reading deserves special emphasis. It is, as we just noted, particularly appropriate for students who come to school with limited vocabularies. These students have a lot of catching up to do, and only sustained efforts can have the sort of effect needed. Ideally, such efforts would begin in kindergarten and continue throughout the primary grades.

Of course, once students can read, they should be reading as much as possible in a variety of materials. Wide reading is important for a host of reasons, but it is particularly important to vocabulary growth. If students learn to read something like 3,000 to 4,000 words each year, it is clear that most of the words they learn are not taught directly. With a 180-day school year, teaching 3,000 to 4,000 words would require teaching approximately 20 words each and every school day. Obviously, this does not happen. Instead, students learn many of the words that make up their vocabularies from their reading (Anderson, 1996). Thus, if we can substantially increase the amount of reading students do, we can markedly increase their vocabularies. Moreover, wide reading will foster automaticity, provide knowledge about a variety

In the Classroom

9.1

Instructional Routines

Interactive Oral Reading as Described by Biemiller

Day 1

Read the book through once, including some comprehension questions after reading it but not interrupting the reading with vocabulary instruction. (Experience has shown that children may object to interrupting the first reading of the book with vocabulary instruction.)

Day 2

Reread the book, teaching about eight words. When you come to a sentence containing a target word, stop and reread the sentence.

After rereading the word, give a brief explanation. For example, after reading the sentence "It seemed like a good *solution*" in a second-grade book, pose the question, "What does *solution* mean?" Then answer your question with something like "A *solution* is an answer to a problem." Remember to keep the definitions simple, direct, and focused on the meaning of the word as it was used in the story.

At the end of the day's instruction, review the words taught by rereading the sentences in which they appeared and the definitions you gave. Write those words on a vocabulary chart.

Days 3 and 4

Reread the story two more times, teaching about eight new words each time. As on Day 2, briefly define the words as you come to them, and review all of them at the end of the reading.

At the End of the Week

Review all of the words taught during the week, this time using new sentences to provide some variety but giving the same definition.

Researchers Linda Labbo, Mary Love, and Tammy Ryan (2007) describe a *vocabulary flood,* a technique they designed for at-risk readers. During read-alouds, teachers help students to "notice" interesting words that an author uses. This helps children develop the sense of word consciousness we discussed in this chapter. The teacher records the interesting words on a chart. The next day, the teacher and students revisit the read-aloud book, and the teacher has students make connections to the words—children note what visual images the words inspire, how the words relate to other words they know, and how the words connect to themselves. The next day, the teacher creates a set of true/false sentences that use two to three of the words. Students answer the questions using a thumbs up or down to indicate their responses to the questions. On the fourth day, students reenact the read-aloud story using the interesting words from the chart. The teacher takes digital photographs of the reenactments. The photographs are printed out and children label the pictures. They use the interesting words in their label descriptions. These activities help children to see and use the interesting words multiple times in meaningful contexts. When children see and use words over and over, they come to learn them.

Motivating **Struggling** *Readers*

of topics and literary forms, and leave students with a habit that will make them lifelong readers.

Unfortunately, many students do very little reading, and some do almost none (Anderson, Wilson, & Fielding, 1988). Richard Allington (1977) summed up the situation nicely in his memorable plea for students to do more reading—"If they don't read much, how they ever gonna get good?" The answer is clearly that they are not. Moreover, as Allington (2001) and a number of others have noted, a substantial amount of the reading students do needs to be easy enough that they can understand and enjoy what they are reading rather than struggle to decode it.

Finally, as we now know but somehow did not know a few years ago, writing is a powerful ally and aid to reading. From the very beginning, students need to engage frequently in activities in which reading and writing are paired, and some of these paired activities should focus on words.

1. Based on the growth rates we suggest, give some estimates of the size of students' reading vocabularies at the end of grades 2, 3, 4, 5, and 6. Note that because we give a range for vocabulary size at the end of first grade and a range of growth rates, a range of answers will be correct.
2. Suppose that two concerned parents, fluent in both English and Spanish, come to you and say that they really want to help their daughter build her reading vocabulary but don't know just how to do that. Assuming that you do not want to suggest they do direct teaching of words, what might you suggest they do to help their daughter build her English and Spanish vocabulary?

REFLECT *and Apply*

Teaching Individual Words

It is important to understand the various word learning tasks students face and ways of identifying words to teach. We will consider teaching procedures for each of these word learning tasks.

Word Learning Tasks

All word learning tasks are not the same, differing on matters such as how much students already know about the words to be taught, how well you want them to learn the words, and what you want them to be able to do with the words afterward. Students face five tasks in learning words, involving different levels of difficulty and types of learning required.

Learning a Basic Vocabulary

Many children arrive at school with substantial oral vocabularies, perhaps numbering 5,000 words. Some children raised in poverty, however, come to school with meager oral vocabularies, and, of course, some English language learners come to school with almost no English vocabularies. For such children, building a basic oral vocabulary of the most frequent English words and learning to read the 1,000 or so most frequent words automatically are of utmost importance.

Learning to Read Known Words

Learning to read words that are already in their oral vocabularies is the major word learning task of beginning readers. Words such as *surprise, stretch,* and *amaze* are ones that students might be taught to read during their first 3 years of school. By third or fourth grade, good readers will have learned to read virtually all the words in their oral vocabularies. However, this task will remain incomplete for many less able readers and for some English language learners.

An effective way to identify potentially difficult words is to list them on the board, point to them one by one, and have students raise their hands if they don't know a word.

Michael Newman/PhotoEdit

Learning New Words That Represent Known Concepts

The next word learning task students face is learning to read words that are in neither their oral nor reading vocabularies but for which they have an available concept. For example, the word *pant* would be unknown to a number of third-graders, but almost all students have seen dogs panting and know what it is like to be out of breath. All students continue to learn words of this sort throughout their years in school, and this is one of the major word learning tasks for intermediate-grade students. It is also a major learning task for English language learners, who, of course, have a great number of concepts for which they do not have English words.

Learning New Words That Represent New Concepts

Another word learning task students face, and a very demanding one, is learning to read words that are in neither their oral nor reading vocabulary and for which they do not have an available concept. Learning the full meanings of words such as *equation, impeach,* and *mammal* is likely to require most elementary students to develop new concepts. All students continue to learn words of this sort throughout their years in school and beyond. Once again, learning new concepts will be particularly important for English language learners. Also, students whose backgrounds differ from that of the majority culture will have probably internalized a set of concepts somewhat different from concepts of students in the majority culture. Thus, words that represent known concepts for some groups of students will represent unknown concepts for other groups.

Clarifying and Enriching the Meanings of Known Words

The last word learning task is that of clarifying and enriching the meanings of already known words. The meanings students originally attach to words are often imprecise and become fully specified only over time (Carey, 1978). For example, students initially might not recognize any difference between *brief* and *concise,* what distinguishes *cabin* from *shed,* or that the term *virtuoso* is most frequently applied to musicians. Although students will expand and enrich the meanings of the words they know as they repeatedly meet them in new and slightly different contexts, direct approaches to teaching meanings are definitely warranted.

Identifying Vocabulary to Teach

Once you have considered the word learning tasks students face, you still must select specific words to teach. We recommend a two-step process in which you first get some idea of words likely to be unknown to your students and then follow several criteria for selecting the words to actually teach.

Three sources are useful for identifying words to teach: word lists, selections your students are reading or listening to, and the students themselves. Word lists are particularly useful for identifying a basic oral vocabulary to teach students who have not already developed such a vocabulary. The most readily available list is Graves and Sales's First 4,000 Words, available at www.thefirst4000words.com. These roughly 4,000 English words occur so frequently that they are crucial for students to master. Two other useful lists are Biemiller's Words Worth Teaching in Grades K–2 and Words Worth Teaching in Grades 3–6, both of which are available in Biemiller (2010).

The second source of words to teach is the text students are reading or listening to. English, like all natural languages, consists of a small number of frequent words and a very large number of infrequent words. Once students acquire a basic vocabulary of 1,000 to 2,000 words, the number of different words you might teach is so large that frequency does not provide much of a basis for choosing which ones to teach. At this point, using your best judgment to select vocabulary from the material students are reading and listening to becomes a better approach.

In most reading selections, you are likely to find more potentially useful vocabulary to teach than you have time for. In winnowing the number of words to teach, the answers to the following four questions can be helpful.

- "Is understanding the word important to understanding the selection in which it appears?" If the answer is no, then other words are probably more important to teach.
- "Are students able to use context or structural analysis skills to discover the word's meaning?" If they can use these skills, they should be allowed to practice them. Doing so will both help them consolidate these skills and reduce the number of words you need to teach.
- "Can working with this word be useful in furthering students' context, structural analysis, or dictionary skills?" If the answer here is yes, then working with the word

*A*ssessment

Observing students in a variety of situations—conversations, discussions, and writing—will give you a good understanding of what words your students know and how well they know them. Fortunately, much of the assessment information you collect on students' vocabularies can be acquired "on the fly."

*A*ssessment

The Interactive Reading Assessment System in Appendix A contains word lists representing the vocabulary students are likely to encounter in grades 1 through 7.

can serve two purposes. It can aid students in learning the word, and it can help them acquire a strategy they can use in learning other words. You might, for example, decide to teach the word *regenerate* because students need to master the prefix *re-*.

- "How useful is this word outside of the reading selection being currently taught?" The more frequently a word appears in material students read, the more important it is for them to know the word. Additionally, the more frequent a word is, the greater the chances that students will retain the word once you teach it.

Finally, the ultimate source of information about the words to teach is students themselves. You can identify words on word lists or in upcoming selections that you think will be difficult for your students and build simple tests to find out whether they are difficult (see Graves, 2009b, for sample items). Of course, constructing tests is time-consuming and certainly not something you need to do for every selection. However, several experiences of identifying words that you think will be difficult and then checking students' performance against your expectations will sharpen your general perceptions of which words are and are not likely to cause problems.

In addition to testing students on potentially difficult words using traditional types of tests, you can take the opportunity to ask students which words they know. One easy way of doing this is to simply dictate words or to list words on the board and have students raise their hands if they do not know a word. This approach is quick, easy, and risk-free for students; it also gives students some responsibility for their word learning. Moreover, research (White, Slater, & Graves, 1989) indicates that students can be quite accurate in identifying words that they do and do not know.

Methods of Teaching Individual Words

How might you go about providing instruction for each of the five word learning tasks described? As you will see, the instruction needed for some word learning tasks is much more complex than for others. Note too that some of these instructional methods will promote deeper levels of word knowledge than others.

Learning a Basic Vocabulary

As we have noted, building a basic vocabulary of very frequent words is crucial so that students don't repeatedly stumble over words they don't know. The first 100 words on the First 4,000 Words list account for about 50 percent of the words students encounter as they are reading; the first 300 words, about 60 percent of the words they will encounter; and the first 1,000 words, about 70 percent of the words encountered. As we have also noted, many students already have these words in their oral vocabularies, but many children of poverty and many English language learners do not. We need to ensure that all students have these words in both their oral and reading vocabularies. Interactive oral reading, discussed earlier in this chapter (see In the Classroom 9.1), is the major approach we suggest for building a basic oral vocabulary. For building a basic reading vocabulary, we suggest that you identify 10 or so words for instruction each week, define the words (unless they are function words like *the, and, of,* and the like), use them in context, and give students opportunities to contribute what they know about the words. Keep a list of words that have been taught and display them prominently in the room, perhaps pasting them to the classroom wall. After the words are initially taught, help students review and rehearse them in a variety of ways, including but not limited to the following:

- Point out the words and (if they are not function words) briefly define them as you are reading to students.

- Have students rapidly read the words on the wall. This can be done individually or in groups, and it is a good idea to make it a game-like activity when possible.
- Have students "cheer" the words—"about, A-B-O-U-T, about"—an idea suggested by Patricia Cunningham (2005).
- Students can "walk the wall"—circle the room in pairs, quizzing each other on the words as they walk, an idea suggested by Peter Dewitz (personal communication, May 2005).
- Students can listen to the words and their definitions on audio.
- Students can work in pairs or larger groups teaching and testing each other on the words.
- Students can draw pictures illustrating the words and share their pictures with the class.
- Students can write the new words on cards and build constantly growing individual word banks.
- Students can play games and complete puzzles with the words.
- Students can categorize the new words and relate them to other words.
- Students can engage in a number of other activities that give them opportunities to hear the words and associate them with their meanings.

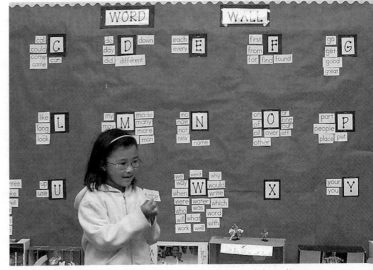

Word walls are useful for building vocabulary and decoding skills.

Cindy Charles/PhotoEdit

Brief on-the-spot assessments, along with the immediate feedback they enable you to offer students, are one of your most useful assessment tools.

Additionally, quiz students on sets of the words from time to time, give them feedback on how they are doing, remind them of the importance of learning these words, and talk to them about their perceptions of their progress.

Learning to Read Known Words

In learning to read known words, the basic task for the student is to associate what is unknown, the written word, with what is already known, the spoken word. To establish the association between the written and spoken forms of a word, the student needs to see the word at the same time that it is pronounced. Once this association is established, it needs to be rehearsed and strengthened so that the relationship becomes automatic. We have listed these steps to emphasize just how straightforward the process is:

Step 1. Look at the word.

Step 2. Listen to the word while looking at it.

Step 3. Rehearse and repeat that association again and again.

Each of these three steps can be accomplished in a number of ways. Students can see the word on the board, on a computer screen, or in a book they are reading or that you are reading to them. They can hear the word when you say it, when another student says it, or when a voice simulator on a computer says it. And they can rehearse the association by seeing the word and pronouncing it a number of times, writing it, and playing games that require them to recognize printed versions of it. However, wide reading in enjoyable and easily read materials that contain many repetitions of vocabulary words is by far the best way to empower students to automatically and effortlessly recognize these words whenever they see them.

Introducing New Words Representing Known Concepts

Purpose

- To provide students with a basic understanding of a word's meaning and give them practice in using the dictionary.

Procedure

- In a handout, on a computer file, or on the chalkboard, give students a word in context—for example, use this sentence for the word *excel*:

    To get into the Olympics, a person must really *excel* at an Olympic sport.

- Have students read the word and the context-rich sentence and then look up the meaning of the word in a dictionary.
- Discuss the word and its meaning.
- Elaborate on the word, citing other examples of excelling and discuss what it means to excel.
- Ask students to use the word in context.

9.2

Instructional Routines

Finally, one very important point to remember when teaching these words is that there is no need to teach their meanings. By definition, these are words students already know and understand when they hear them; they simply cannot read them. Time spent "teaching" students the meanings of words they already know is time wasted.

Learning New Words That Represent Known Concepts

In the Classroom 9.2 shows a simple and straightforward approach to teaching new words representing known concepts.

Learning New Words That Represent New Concepts

As we have noted, learning new words that represent new concepts is often a challenging task. In the Classroom 9.3, based on a method developed by Dorothy Frayer (Frayer, Frederick, & Klausmeier, 1969), illustrates one very effective method to help students gain knowledge of new words that represent new concepts. Although the example is for primary-grade students, the procedure is appropriate for all grade levels.

Teaching concepts using the Frayer method will take a good deal of your and your students' time. The method also will require considerable thought from the students and you. However, for important concepts, the fruits of the labor will be well worth the effort, because with this method students can gain a new idea, another lens through which they can interpret the world.

Clarifying and Enriching the Meanings of Known Words

Semantic mapping and semantic feature analysis are two methods of clarifying and enriching the meanings of known words (see In the Classroom 9.4, pp. 264–265). These methods, both developed by Dale Johnson (Heimlich & Pittelman, 1986; Johnson & Pearson, 1984; Pittelman, Heimlich, Berglund, & French, 1991), are also useful in preteaching unknown words to improve students' comprehension of a selection, one of the most important purposes of vocabulary instruction. They work particularly well because they focus not only on the word being taught but also on related words and on the part the word plays in the selection. These two methods can also be used to teach new concepts—if the concepts are not too difficult and if students already have at least some information related to them.

Introducing New Words Representing New Concepts

Purpose

- To introduce second-grade students to the new word *globe* and the concept of globe.

Procedure

- Define the new concept, giving its specific attributes. For example,

    A *globe* is a spherical (ball-like) representation of a planet.

    When possible, show a model or a picture illustrating the concept.
- Distinguish between the new concept and similar but different concepts with which it might be confused. It may be appropriate to identify accidental attributes that might falsely be considered definitive attributes of the new concept. For example,

    A globe is different from a map because a map is flat. A globe is different from a contour map, a map in which mountains and other high points are raised above the general level of the map, because a contour map is not spherical.

- Give examples of the concept, and explain what makes them good examples:

    The most common globe is a globe of the earth. Globes of the earth are spherical [display a sphere or spheres such as a ball or an orange] and come in various sizes and colors. A much less common globe is a globe of another planet. A museum might have a spherical representation of Saturn.

- Give nonexamples of the concept, such as a map of California or a map of how to get to a friend's house, and explain why they are not examples of the concept at hand.
- Present students with examples and nonexamples of the concept, and ask them to distinguish between the two. You might include an aerial photograph of New York (nonexample), a red sphere representing Mars (example), a walking map of St. Louis (nonexample), and a ball-shaped model of the moon (example).
- Have students present examples and nonexamples of the concept, and explain what makes them examples and nonexamples. Give them feedback on their presentations.

We have listed six approaches for teaching individual words, and five of the approaches—all of them except the approach for teaching students to read known words—go well beyond simply providing students with the definition of the new word. As Steven Stahl (1998) points out, what we know about teaching individual words suggests using vocabulary instruction that "(a) includes both definitional and contextual information about each word's meaning, (b) involves children more actively in word learning, and (c) provides multiple exposures to meaningful information about the word." Although the six approaches described here are certainly

myeducationlab

Watch a video of a second-grade teacher teaching multiple meanings of the word *draw* in the activity "Teaching Multiple Meanings of Words." (To find this activity, go to the topic *Vocabulary* in MyEducationLab and click on Assignments and Activities.)

Motivating Children with Technology

Kathy Schrock is administrator for technology for the Nauset Public Schools in Massachusetts. Her website is a rich resource for teachers (http://school.discoveryeducation.com/schrockguide). Schrock highlights two software programs that help students create concept maps or semantic maps—Kidspiration and Inspiration (http://kathyschrock.net/creativeclassroom/concept mapping.htm). Shrock notes these programs enable students to focus on the content of their maps rather than on drawing the maps by hand, something that is challenging for many students. Moreover, Schrock relates, an advantage of these programs is that they allow students to alter the content of their maps over time as their thinking develops and knowledge changes.

Semantic Mapping and Semantic Feature Analysis

Semantic Mapping

Sometimes called semantic webbing, semantic mapping makes use of a graphic organizer that looks something like a spider web. Lines connect a central concept to a variety of related ideas and events. The illustration shows a semantic map for the word *tenement*. You and your students might create a map such as this before or after reading a social studies chapter on urban housing.

9.4

Instructional Routines

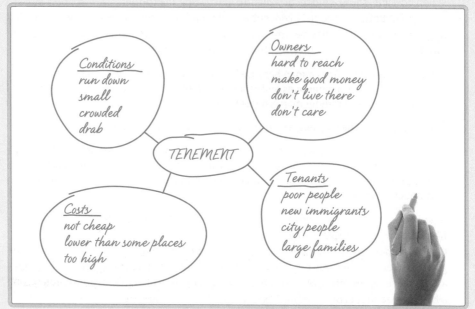

Purpose

- To enrich and clarify students' existing knowledge of a concept by having them identify categories of ideas and events related to that concept.

Procedure

- Put a word representing a central concept, such as *tenement,* on the chalkboard.
- Have students form groups, brainstorming as many words as they can think of related to the central concept.
- Write students' words on the chalkboard, grouped in broad categories.
- Have students name the categories and perhaps suggest additional ones.
- Discuss with students the central concept, the other words, the categories, and their interrelationships.

Semantic Feature Analysis

This procedure employs a grid, such as the following sample grid on *vehicles,* which is modeled on one provided by Pittelman and her colleagues (Pittelman et al., 1991).

Purpose

- To enrich and clarify students' existing knowledge of a concept by having them identify words that belong to a category, list the features of the words they have identified, and compare and contrast them using a grid.

Vehicles						
	two wheels	four wheels	more than four wheels	motor	diesel fuel	gasoline
car	−	+	−	+	−	+
bicycle	+	−	−	−	−	−
motorcycle	+	−	−	+	−	+
truck	−	+	+	+	+	−
train	−	−	+	+	+	−
skateboard	−	+	−	−	−	−
sailboat	−	−	−	−	−	−
iceboat	−	−	−	−	−	−

Procedure

- Select a category—for example, *vehicles*.
- With students' help, list words that fall into this category.
- With students' help, list the features of the items you have identified. For example, some of the features of vehicles might be two wheels, four wheels, motor, and gasoline.
- Use plus and minus signs to indicate which items possess and do not possess each feature. Discuss these distinctions with students.
- Add more words and features. Work with students to extend the grid, particularly when making distinctions that require adding features. For example, a feature such as "operates on water" would be needed to distinguish rowboats from iceboats.
- Have students complete the grid. They can do this independently, in groups, or with your help.
- Examine and discuss the completed grid. This discussion is often the most interesting and revealing activity. For example, you would want to acknowledge that a few cars do use diesel fuel and many small trucks use gasoline.

As with many instructional activities, follow the gradual release of responsibility model (described in Chapter 2) in working with semantic feature analysis. Initially, you may need to do much of the work. Later, students can be given grids with some terms and attributes and asked to add to both the list of related words and the list of attributes and then to fill in the pluses and minuses. Still later, after becoming proficient in working with partially completed grids that you supply, students can create grids for sets of related words that they themselves suggest.

Another level of challenge and interest can be added by including the designator *S*, meaning "sometimes," in addition to the pluses and minuses. For example, *S* might be used in the vehicle grid in the "car" row under the headings "diesel fuel" and "gasoline" because some cars do use diesel fuel. In all cases—whether or not *S* is used—there should be a good deal of discussion, for the essence of semantic feature analysis lies in the discussion.

Differentiating Instruction

for

English Language Learners

Building Knowledge of Target Words and Word Analysis

A recent instructional intervention that addressed English language learners' vocabulary development (Carlo, August, Snow, Dressler, Lippman, Lively, & White, 2004) showed extremely positive results in 9 fifth-grade classrooms. The 15-week intervention was organized around the theme of immigration, and each week's instruction focused on a single text. On Monday, teachers provided the English language learners with both written and recorded versions of the text in Spanish, the children's first language, to preview. On Tuesday, the teachers introduced the text and 10 to 12 target words to students in English. The students practiced using the context to infer the words' meanings. On Wednesday, English language learners and native English speakers worked together in small groups to complete cloze activities. (In the cloze technique, students are presented with sentences, or a paragraph, in which every *n*th word has been deleted. Students must use the context to fill in the missing words.) On Thursday, students engaged in word association activities, synonym/antonym tasks, and semantic feature analysis. On Fridays, they worked with cognates, root words, and multiple meanings of words. The study's results showed that the English language learners—as well as native English-speaking students—increased their knowledge of target words while enhancing their word analysis skills.

enough to begin your efforts in teaching individual words, you may eventually want to add others, such as those described in *Bringing Words to Life* (Beck, McKeown, & Kucan, 2002), *The Vocabulary Book* (Graves, 2006*), Teaching Individual Words* (Graves, 2009b), and *Essential Readings on Vocabulary Instruction* (Graves, 2009a).

REFLECT and Apply

3 Consider each of the five word learning tasks we have listed, and explain how each of them requires a different sort of learning. It would be useful to work with a classmate in doing this, but after you have discussed your response, write it out. Writing your response will force you to really think it through, and it will give you a response on paper that you can examine and evaluate.

4 Identify a group of students. Select one word that is likely to be in their oral vocabularies but that they probably don't recognize in print, one that is a new label for a known concept, one that represents a new concept, and one that they probably know but for which you would like to give them a fuller understanding. Choose an instructional procedure described in the chapter for teaching each word, create the materials you would need, and then explain how you would go about teaching each of them. If you have a few classmates available who could serve as "students," role-playing the teaching rather than explaining how you would do it is an excellent alternative.

Teaching Word Learning Strategies

As we noted at the beginning of the chapter, students learn something like 3,000 to 4,000 words each year, many more than could be directly taught. Thus, even when instruction in individual words is as frequent and rich as possible, students still need to learn much of their vocabulary independently. In this section of the chapter, we consider three strategies that students need to become independent word learners: using context clues, using word parts, and using the dictionary.

Using Context Clues

It is almost certainly the case that we learn most of the words we know from meeting them in context (Anderson & Nagy, 1992; Sternberg, 1987). No other explanation can account for students' learning 3,000 to 4,000 words each year. At the same time, gleaning a word's meaning from most contexts is not an easy task. However, wide reading exposes students to a huge number of unknown words. Given a typical amount of reading over a year's time, students with average skills in learning words from context might acquire over 1,000 words from meeting them in the context of their reading. Additionally, students learn a large number of words from oral contexts— conversations, lectures, films, and even television. Of course, students who have better-than-average skills in learning words from context will acquire more words this way than students with only average skills.

In this section of the chapter, we discuss teaching students to use context clues— the words, phrases, and sentences that surround an unknown word and provide clues to its meaning—to learn word meanings. Teaching students to use context clues requires a significant effort both for teacher and students, but research shows that it can be done (Fukkink & de Glopper, 1998), and several effective models of instruction have been described (for example, Baumann, Font, Edwards, & Boland, 2005; Graves, 2006). The method we describe here, which we call *balanced strategies instruction,* is our recommended approach for teaching students to use context clues, word parts, and the dictionary. In the Classroom 9.5 describes the basic components of balanced strategies instruction.

Balanced strategies instruction can be used at a variety of grade levels to teach students to use context clues. However, the ideal grades for in-depth instruction are the upper-elementary grades. In earlier grades, we would use less formal instruction. In the Classroom 9.6 (p. 268) describes a unit designed for fourth grade. A more detailed description of the approach is given in Appendix B.

Balanced Strategies Instruction

1. *Make motivation a prime concern.* Stress how learning and using the strategy will help students with their reading and learning in school and outside of school.
2. *Use prominent visual displays.* Before teaching the strategy, as you are teaching it, and after you have taught it, use posters and the like to create interest in the upcoming instruction, highlight major features of the strategy, and remind students to continue to use it after the initial instruction.
3. *Follow the direct explanation model for the initial instruction.*
   - An explicit description of the strategy and when and how it should be used
   - Teacher and/or student modeling of the strategy in action
   - Collaborative use of the strategy in action
   - Guided practice using the strategy with gradual release of responsibility
   - Independent use of the strategy (Duke & Pearson, 2002, pp. 208–210)
4. *Provide substantial and long-term follow-up after the initial instruction.* Prompt students to use the strategy, review it periodically, and do everything possible to help students internalize and use it over time.

In the Classroom

9.5

Instructional Routines

Teaching Context Clues

Day 1: Introduction of Unit/Motivation

Because learning to use context clues is a demanding and challenging task, introduce the unit with a substantial motivational activity. For example, show a film that includes a lot of clues to the setting but does not directly identify it, and ask students to use clues in the film to infer where the film takes place. Next, suggest that figuring out word meanings from context is a lot like using clues in a film to infer where it takes place.

Day 2: Introduction to Using Context Clues and the Four-Step Strategy

Review the major points made on the first day and then introduce a strategy for figuring out the meanings of unknown words students come across as they read. The strategy entails four steps: (1) reading carefully and stopping when you come to an unknown word, (2) reading slowly from that point forward, looking for clues to the word's meaning, (3) going back and rereading the sentences preceding the term if necessary, and (4) selecting a word or phrase that seems to capture the meaning of the term and substituting it for the unknown word to see if it works. After explaining the strategy, model the technique, explain when and where students are likely to use it, and let students try it out with some texts containing difficult words and particularly informative context clues. As students are working with the strategy, scaffold their efforts—provide additional clues as necessary, let them work in pairs if that is helpful, and answer any questions they have. At the end of the day, put up a large and colorful poster listing the steps of the strategy, and leave the poster up throughout the unit and for some time after the unit is concluded. We elaborate on this strategy in Appendix B.

Days 3–10: Additional Instruction, Practice, Encouragement, Increased Responsibility, and Transition to Increasingly Challenging Texts and Tasks

Over the next eight days, provide more detailed instruction on the four-step strategy, interrupt the hard work from time to time for games that employ the strategy, engage students in guided practice in both narrative and expository texts, have them use the strategy with a variety of authentic texts, and assist them in making plans for how they'll internalize the strategy and use it in the future. Increasingly, the students talk more and you talk less. They take more responsibility for the strategy and do more of the work, and they increasingly self-monitor and self-regulate their use of the strategy. At the same time, always be there to support students' efforts—providing encouragement, scaffolding, and feedback as needed.

Using Word Parts

Although context clues provide the most important word learning strategy, use of word parts is a close second. As Jeremy Anglin's (1993) study of elementary students' vocabularies indicates, about half of the "new" words that students meet in their reading are related to familiar words. Once students can break words into parts, they can use their knowledge of word parts to attempt to deduce their meanings—if, of course, they understand word parts and how they function. The three types of word parts to consider are prefixes, suffixes, and non-English roots.

We have already discussed prefixes and suffixes as elements that students need to deal with as they decode words, and we provided a brief procedure for teaching them when we discussed word recognition. Here we consider prefixes, suffixes, and non-English roots as elements students can use in gleaning word meanings. Among these three, prefixes are the most powerful elements to teach as an aid to deducing word meanings (see Figure 9.1).

Figure 9.1 Why Prefixes Are Particularly Worth Teaching

- There are relatively few prefixes to teach.
- They are used in a large number of words.
- They are consistently spelled.
- They appear at the beginnings of words, where they are easy for students to spot.
- They generally have a clear lexical meaning that can be attached to the root word to yield a new meaning. For example, *predawn* means "before dawn."

Suffixes are more complex than prefixes and present a different learning task for native English speakers than for English language learners. As noted in Chapter 7, there are two types of suffixes: inflectional and derivational. Inflectional suffixes, the most common type, have grammatical meanings (for example, *-ed,* indicating the past tense) that are difficult to explain. Native English speakers already have a tacit understanding of the function of inflectional suffixes, and attempts to teach their meanings may cause confusion. English language learners, on the other hand, do need to be taught their meanings, and we recommend using the procedure described in Chapter 7 for doing so. Derivational suffixes, most of which are less common, have abstract meanings (for example, *-ence,* indicating a state of being), and these too are often difficult to explain. Because they are uncommon and difficult to explain, we recommend leaving instruction in derivational suffixes for the secondary grades.

Non-English roots (for example, *anthro,* meaning "man" and appearing in such words as *anthropology, misanthrope,* and *philanthropy*) present teaching and learning problems not found with prefixes and suffixes. There are a larger number of non-English roots, each used in relatively few words compared to common prefixes and suffixes. They have a variety of spellings that often make them difficult to identify, and the relationship between the original meaning of the root and the current meaning of the English words is often vague. For these reasons, we do not recommend systematic instruction in non-English roots at the elementary level.

A list of the prefixes sufficiently frequent to warrant teaching is shown in Figure 7.3 of Chapter 7, and In the Classroom 9.7 describes the use of balanced strategies instruction for teaching them. More details on that instruction are given in Appendix B.

Using the Dictionary

As George Miller and Patricia Gildea (1987) have convincingly demonstrated, elementary students frequently have difficulty using the dictionary to find definitions of unknown words. For example, after finding the phrase "eat out" in the definition of *erode,* one student showed her confusion in using the definition by composing the sentence *Our family erodes a lot.* Many students need help in using the dictionary effectively, and balanced strategies instruction can provide that help.

Begin by telling students that you are going to work on using the dictionary to define words, and tell them that the activity is worthwhile because using the dictionary sometimes isn't as simple as it seems. Then put some guidelines, such as those shown in Figure 9.2, on a bulletin board, and leave them up over the coming weeks.

Don't ask students to memorize these guidelines, but talk through them, amplifying as necessary. For example, you should probably add to the third guideline

PEARSON
myeducationlab

In the video clip shown in the activity "Fostering Independent Word Learning," a literacy coach teaches her students strategies to learn new words. Watch the video and answer the following questions. (To find this activity, go to the topic *Vocabulary* in MyEducationLab and click on Assignments and Activities.)

Teaching Prefixes

Day 1: Introduction and Motivation

Introduce the concept of prefixes and the strategy of using prefixes to unlock the meanings of unknown words. Motivate students by stressing the value of using prefixes, and give students an overview of the unit. During the 4-day unit, you will teach six of the most frequent prefixes.

Day 2: Introduction to the First Three Prefixes and the Prefix Strategy

Introduce the first three prefixes to be taught (*re-*, *in-*, and *un-*), and give their meanings. Describe the prefix strategy, which consists of (1) identifying and removing the prefix from the new word, (2) noting the meaning of the prefix and the meaning of the root word, and (3) combining the meanings of the prefix and the root word to infer the meaning of the new word. Model the strategy yourself, let students try it out with your help and each other's help as needed, and have them practice using the strategy with a number of words containing the three prefixes. Put up a poster that shows the prefixes you have taught and the prefix strategy.

Day 3: Reviewing the Prefix Strategy and Teaching the Remaining Three Prefixes

Review the prefix strategy, model it yourself, let several students model it, and answer any questions students have. Teach the meanings of the next three prefixes (*dis-*, *en-*, and *non-*), and have students practice using the strategy with a number of words containing these three new prefixes. Add the three new prefixes to the poster.

Day 4: Reviewing the Information About Prefixes, the Prefix Strategy, and the Six Prefixes Taught in the Unit

Review everything you have done so far, take any questions students have, and have them practice using the prefix strategy with all six prefixes you have taught.

Beyond Day 4: Reviewing, Prompting, Guiding Students to Independence, and Teaching Additional Prefixes

From time to time, point out the prefixes you have taught when they appear in the selections students are reading, remind students of the value of using prefixes to infer word meanings, and briefly review the prefix strategy. Later in the year, teach a second set of six or so prefixes from the list in Figure 7.3 (page 192), and later still teach another six or so.

Figure 9.2 Guidelines for Looking Up Definitions in the Dictionary

- When reading a definition, be sure to read it all, not just part of it.
- Remember that many words have more than one meaning.
- Be sure to check all the definitions the dictionary gives for a word, not just one of them.
- Decide which definition makes sense in the context in which the word is used.
- Often, the dictionary works best when you already have some idea of a word's meaning. This makes the dictionary particularly useful for checking on a word you want to use in your writing.

by telling students that if they find that they still know nothing about an important word after considering context, looking for word parts, and checking the dictionary, they will probably want to ask someone about its meaning.

The remainder of the procedure continues to follow the balanced strategies instruction model. Do some modeling; demonstrate how you would look up the meaning of an unknown word. Think aloud, sharing your thinking with students as you come across the unknown word in a text. Show students how you look through a dictionary and find the word, locate the definition that seems to fit, consider all of that definition, and then mentally check to see if the meaning you chose makes sense in context. Then, gradually let students take over the procedure and model it for you and for each other. Finally, encourage students to use the procedure when they come across unknown or vaguely known words in context, and from time to time give them opportunities to model their thinking as they use the dictionary so that you can check their proficiency and give them feedback and further instruction as needed.

A dictionary is a handy tool for readers of all ages.
Bob Daemmrich/The Image Works

In addition to learning this general approach to using a dictionary, students need to learn about the particular dictionary they use—what the entries for individual words contain and how they are arranged, what aids to its use the dictionary provides, and what features beyond the basic word list the dictionary includes. Much important information appears in the front matter of the dictionaries themselves, but it is very seldom read, and simply asking students to read it is hardly sufficient instruction. Thus, explicit instruction in how to use specific dictionaries is usually beneficial.

5 In order to get a feeling for the extent to which context reveals word meanings, team up with a classmate. Each of you should independently select and photocopy a few passages of college-level material. Next, read, identify, and "white out" some difficult words in each passage. Then get together and discuss how and to what extent you can infer the deleted words' meanings from context.

6 Stop by the curriculum materials library at your university or a local public library, and examine the different levels of dictionaries found there. Note, for example, how dictionaries for younger students have fewer words, define words more simply, and are generally easier to use and therefore more appropriate for younger readers.

REFLECT
and *Apply*

Fostering Word Consciousness

The fourth part of a comprehensive vocabulary program involves fostering word consciousness. Word consciousness is a disposition toward words that is both cognitive and affective. The word conscious student knows a lot of words, and she knows them well. Equally important, she is interested in words, and she gains enjoyment and satisfaction from using them well and from seeing or hearing them used well by others. She finds words intriguing, recognizes adroit word usage when she encounters it, uses words skill-fully herself, is on the lookout for new and precise words, and is responsive to the nuances of word meanings. She is also well aware of the power of words and realizes that they can be used to foster clarity and understanding or to obscure and obfuscate matters.

Fostering such attitudes is a worthy goal across the elementary school years—and, of course, in the years beyond the elementary grades—and there are myriad ways to develop and nurture such positive attitudes. These include modeling and encouraging adept diction, promoting wordplay such as rhymes and puns, using wordplay books and playing word games, and providing intensive and expressive instruction in vocabulary. In the Reading Corner, we list a few word books and word games. In the remainder of this section, we consider some ways of modeling and encouraging adept diction and discuss approaches to intensive and expressive instruction. For additional suggestions on developing word consciousness, see Graves (2006), Graves and Susan Watts-Taffe (2008), and Judith Scott and William Nagy (2004); for a detailed discussion of some cognitive aspects of word consciousness, see Nagy and Scott (2000).

Modeling and Encouraging Adept Diction

The starting point, we believe, in encouraging and nurturing word consciousness lies in our own attitude toward words and how we project it to students. We want children to feel that adept diction—the skillful use of words in speech and writing—is worth striving for. We want them to see that by using the right word themselves and recognizing the adept word choices authors make, they can both communicate more effectively and appreciate more fully an author's message. Various conscious efforts can promote skillful diction. One is to model adept word usage in your classroom

---

The Reading Corner

Books About Words and Word Games

Ann Rand (author) and **Paul Rand (illustrator).** *Sparkle and Spin: A Book About Words.* Chronicle Books, 2006. In this classic, recently reissued, Ann Rand uses rich rhythms, resonance, and pitch to entice readers to appreciate the power and music of the words they hear every day. This rich language, coupled with the colorful artwork of her husband, makes this a book to be read and enjoyed again and again. 40 pages.

Catherine Falwell. *Word Wizard.* Clarion, 1998. In this picture book, a magic spoon helps a young girl realize she can rearrange the letters in words to form new ones. She helps a lost boy get home by changing *ocean* to *canoe*, *shore* to *horse*, and so on. 32 pages.

Fred Gwynne. *A Little Pigeon Toed.* Simon & Schuster, 1988. A marvelous collection of ambiguous phrases and amusing illustrations depicting the wrong interpretations of those phrases. Other similar books by Fred Gwynne include *Chocolate Moose for Dinner* (Windmill Books, 1976) and *The King Who Rained* (Simon & Schuster, 1970). 48 pages.

Richard Lederer (author) and **Dave Morice (illustrator).** *The Circus of Words.* Chicago Review Press, 2001. Anagrams, palindromes, spoonerisms, and more from one of the leading wordplay artists. Lederer's *Pun and Games: Jokes, Riddles, Daffynitions, Tairy Fales, Rhymes, and More Word Play for Kids* (Chicago Review Press, 1996) is another choice young readers will enjoy. 144 pages.

Jack Prelutsky (author) and **Peter Sis (illustrator).** *Scranimals.* Greenwillow, 2002. In this adventure, children set sail for Scranimal Island, where poet Prelutsky and artist Sis create a memorable cast of scranimals including Parroters, Potatods, and Ostricheetahs. Other books that show off Prelutsky's inventive wordplay include *It's Raining Pigs and Noodles* (Scholastic, 2001) and *An Ogre's Awful Day* (Scholastic, 2002). 48 pages.

talk, deliberately using and perhaps explaining words that at least some of your students might not yet know. Thus, in describing how you were startled by a low-flying jet on the way to school, you might tell your fourth-graders that the jet made a *thunderous* noise and point out that *thunderous* is an excellent word for describing a really loud noise because it reminds us of the great booming sound of thunder.

A simple, widely used, and very effective way of focusing students' attention on words is to include a word-of-the-day activity in daily plans. Appropriate for all ages, word-of-the-day activities can take a number of forms. In a first-grade classroom, word meaning can be linked to word recognition and general language facility by sharing with students a particular word of interest and paying special attention to the way it sounds, the way it looks, and what it means. The words of the day can be added to a bulletin board each day until, at the end of the month, the entire board is filled. Words of the day can also be acted out, used in a game of charades, or illustrated. In addition, they can be made part of a song, riddle, pun, poem, or some other form of artistic expression. Fifth-grade special education teacher Bette Rochman explains how she uses word-of-the-day activities in her class:

> I teach fifth-grade youngsters with learning disabilities, and one vocabulary activity I have found to be quite successful is to pair up students to be responsible for coming up with a word of the day. After our morning announcements, the student pair responsible for that day's word writes it on the board and explains to the class what it means, why they selected it, and how to use it in a sentence. Sometimes the pair selects words they aren't too sure about and says something like, "We're not sure exactly how you use this word, but when we find out, we'll let you know!" I let the students know that such partial knowledge of the word is certainly okay, as long as students set their sights on gaining fuller knowledge. Of course, students always enjoy stumping me by presenting words that are new to me as well as to their fellow students!
>
> —Bette Rochman, fifth-grade special education teacher

Students can select words from any number of sources—books, newspapers, another classroom, their parents, and teachers, to name a few. Teachers can also suggest that students find their special words in particular sources in order to complement certain classroom activities. For example, during a unit on newspapers, the teacher might suggest that students find words in a newspaper; during a unit on weather, she might suggest that students choose "weather words." More often, however, it is worthwhile to let students find their words wherever they wish. Then they tend to view the words as their own, take greater pride in sharing them, and more readily see learning new words as an enjoyable experience.

Another occasion for focusing attention on words comes when children are reading, as sixth-grade teacher Terry Cronemeyer suggests:

> I personally love words and take every opportunity I can to point out wonderful word choices. This opportunity most often arises in conjunction with the literature children are reading. Because good authors employ appropriate and often colorful words, I will often point out to my sixth-graders particularly felicitous or interesting word choices. For example, I was sitting in on a literature circle with a group of students who were reading and discussing Russell Freedman's *Eleanor Roosevelt: A Life of Discovery* when one of the students chose to read these lines aloud, "Franklin remembered Eleanor as a skinny girl in a hopeless party dress. Now she was wearing a stylish outfit from Paris." I decided I could not resist butting in. "How could a party dress be *hopeless?*" I asked. A lively discussion then ensued that uncovered the ripples of meaning that Freedman was able to achieve by using that particular word.
>
> —Terry Cronemeyer, sixth-grade teacher

Still another opportunity for recognizing and promoting adroit word usage comes from children's own writing. Thus, you might compliment a third-grader for describing banana slugs as *gigantic* and give a little recognition to a sixth-grader who noted that the odds of winning the lottery are *astronomically small*. During writing conferences, you might also encourage students to rethink word choices in an effort to make their writing more colorful and precise.

Providing Intensive and Expressive Instruction

Some very interesting and highly effective activities that can foster word consciousness have been developed and carefully researched by Isabel Beck and Margaret McKeown (1983) and by Ann Duin (Duin & Graves, 1988). The activities are quite similar, and both seek full and deep understanding of words; however, Duin's goal also involves children in using the words in writing. Developing and presenting these activities involves several steps, the first of which is to select a small set of words that are semantically related. For example, a set used by Beck and McKeown—*rival, hermit, novice, virtuoso, accomplice, miser, tyrant*, and *philanthropist*—contains words that refer to people; a set used by Duin—*advocate, capability, configuration, criteria, disarray, envision, feasible, habitable, module, quest, retrieve*, and *tether*—contains words that can be used in talking about space exploration.

The next step, the central part of the instruction, is for students to work extensively and intensively with the words, spending perhaps half an hour a day over a period of a week engaging in a dozen or so diverse activities—really getting to know the words, discovering their shades of meaning and the various ways in which they can be used, and realizing what interesting companions words can be. Beck and McKeown's activities, for example, include defining the words, asking students to use them in sentences, and asking students to respond to words such as *virtuoso* and *miser* with thumbs up or thumbs down to signify approval or disapproval. Their activities also include asking which of three actions an *accomplice* would most likely engage in—robbing a bank alone, stealing some candy, or driving a getaway car—and asking questions—"Could a *virtuoso* be a *rival*?" "Could a *virtuoso* be a *novice*?" and "Could a *philanthropist* be a *miser*?"

Duin begins with defining the words and asking students to use them in sentences. Her other activities include asking students to discuss how *feasible* space travel might soon be, asking them how a space station could *accommodate* persons with disabilities, and asking them to write brief essays called "Space Shorts" in which they used the words in dealing with topics such as the foods that might be available in space. Reports from teachers on these activities indicate that students really get involved in them and do indeed become more word conscious (Duin & Graves, 1988).

The third step, only used when students are to use the words in their writing, is for students to write more extensive essays—using as many of the taught words as possible, playing with them and exploring their possibilities. Students appear to really enjoy this activity. As one teacher observed, "Students who were asked to write often and to use the words in written classwork showed great involvement in their writing."

Finally, we conclude with a fourth step—directly discussing with students the word choices they make, why they make those choices, and how adroit use of words makes speech and writing more precise, more memorable, and more interesting.

Duin found that students were very successful using the words in their writing, as this seventh-grader's essay—with the taught words italicized—demonstrates:

> I think the space program would be more *feasible* if we sent more than just astronauts and satellites into space. We need to send tourists and change the whole *configuration* of the space shuttle so that it could *accommodate* more people. While the tourists are in space, they could fly some of the manned-maneuvering units and *retrieve* stuff from space. They could maybe even see if our planets are *habitable* now. When the tourists would come back, they would have the *capability* of doing anything in space. They truly

would be *advocates* of space. But, in order to make these special missions happen, we will need to add more *modules* onto our space station, so that we can store more equipment, supplies, food, and people!

After about ten years or so we would perhaps go back to the same old thing with astronauts and satellites until we found another new idea for the space program.

My *quest*, someday, is to reach the stars. I hope to be not just an engineer, but a space engineer. We have to get more people interested since the crash. We have to try harder than ever.

—Seventh-grade space exploration fan (Duin & Graves, 1988, p. 209)

Obviously, this student enjoyed the instruction, learned from it, and tried to do her best—managing to get 9 of the 13 unit vocabulary words into her essay. To be sure, some of the usage is a bit forced, but at this point in the student's writing career that is probably just fine. She is interested in words and in using new and different words in her writing. With practice, feedback, and encouragement from thoughtful respondents to her writing—her teachers and her peers, for the most part—we expect her to become a skilled and precise word user.

To learn more about how to effectively teach vocabulary, complete the activity "Teaching Academic Vocabulary." The activity outlines an instruction sequence that will help students to not only learn the definitions of target words, but also to be able to use and understand the new vocabulary in reading, writing, speaking, and listening. (To find this activity, go to the topic *Vocabulary* in MyEducationLab and click on Building Teaching Skills and Dispositions.)

7 Review a recent paper you wrote, looking at your word choices and asking yourself if you used appropriate, powerful, and perhaps even colorful words. If you did, consider how these helped make the paper strong and effective. If you didn't, try going through the paper and changing some of the vocabulary to make it more appropriate, powerful, and perhaps colorful. Then look at your changes and consider how they affect the paper.

8 Get together with a classmate, identify a group of students, and brainstorm a set of brief and upbeat activities you might employ over a semester to foster their word consciousness.

REFLECT and *Apply*

Strengths and Challenges of Diversity

Teachers also need to consider the particular needs in vocabulary instruction for four groups—gifted learners, special students, children who had little exposure to books and reading before they came to school, and students who speak English as a second language.

With gifted students, be leery of teaching a new vocabulary learning strategy when the student already has a perfectly good one. If a student already has a strategy for learning words from context that works well for him, there is no reason to teach him a new strategy.

With special students, be patient, making sure they get the opportunity to work with higher-level tasks as well as less challenging ones. You're likely to find that teaching special students vocabulary learning strategies will take time and effort, and it may be tempting to avoid or minimize such attempts and simply teach them individual words. But don't give in to these temptations. Special students need vocabulary learning strategies more than students who are more able.

Students who have not had rich experiences with language, books, and reading outside of school also deserve special consideration. As the in-depth studies of Betty Hart and Todd Risley (1995, 2003) make all too clear, some students, often those raised in poverty, do not begin school with the same vocabulary knowledge and language skills that many children with richer out-of-school literacy experiences do. These students need time, nurturing, and instruction. Like special students, they need and deserve to be taught strategies, and they need opportunities to have fun with words and to develop word awareness. They will also profit from being taught individual words, including perhaps a basic vocabulary; they may well profit from instruction and experiences designed to build their oral language skills.

Students who have not had rich experiences with language, books, and reading outside of school particularly need the frequent experiences of reading appropriate books that we have discussed earlier. The various booklists in this text and the annotated bibliographies at the ends of chapters will of course be useful in locating appropriate books.

Finally, there is the special case of building the vocabularies of English language learners, particularly those who know few English words. We have four suggestions. First, pair each English language learner with a native English speaker. Have each pair frequently read together, do writing and other school-work together, and perhaps even work on homework together. Also encourage out-of-class activities among the pairs.

Second, get some reading materials specifically for your English language learners, including short and simple selections containing mainly vocabulary students already know, selections that include some challenging vocabulary, and selections in native languages. If available, bilingual materials that include both English and native language versions are very valuable. Michele Salas's *A de alfabeto/A Is for Alphabet* (Spanish), Max Velthuijs's *Rah was Rah/Frog Is Frog* (Somali), and Truong Tran's *Going Home, Coming Home/Ve nha, tham que huong* (Vietnamese) are three examples of this growing genre.

Third, contact parents and enlist their aid. In many cases, parents' assistance will be largely in encouraging their children, ensuring that they have a time and place to do homework and seeing that they do it. Let parents know about books or homework you send home, and keep in touch with them on their children's progress. Not surprisingly, research shows that effective schools make concerted efforts to reach out to parents (Taylor, Pearson, Clark, & Walpole, 2000).

Fourth, consider some sort of systematic word study that takes place both in and out of school. Interactive oral reading—which we described on pages 255–256—can be particularly useful for English language learners with small English vocabularies.

Concluding Remarks

In this chapter, we have described the vocabulary learning tasks students face, noted the importance of wide reading, described five word learning tasks and ways of selecting vocabulary to teach, and presented teaching procedures appropriate for each of the five word learning tasks. We have also suggested approaches for teaching students to use context and prefixes to unlock word meanings and ways of teaching them to use the dictionary. Finally, we have described methods of promoting word consciousness.

Summed up this way, the task of teaching vocabulary appears to be a large one. However, no single teacher is expected to accomplish all of the various tasks of vocabulary instruction. You can choose which word learning task is most important at a particular point in your class, which level of word knowledge you expect students to achieve with particular words, which teaching plan will be most appropriate for the words in a particular selection your students are reading, and what

specific words you wish to teach. Moreover, as we suggested earlier, not every teacher needs to take major responsibility for teaching students to use context, word parts, and the like. You and the other teachers in your school can work together to decide who will be responsible for these various tasks. We believe that the discussion and teaching procedures presented here will enable you to make appropriate decisions that will help your students gain rich and powerful vocabularies.

Rich and powerful vocabularies are, of course, an important part of present-day literacy. Students who have achieved the level of literacy necessary in today's world have vocabularies that enable them to use precise and even colorful language in their own speech and writing, to recognize and appreciate the skillful use of words in the literary selections they read, and to understand the sometimes subtle and often crucial meanings of words in the informational reading they do.

Extending Learning

1. Throughout the chapter, we have emphasized the importance of wide reading for developing vocabulary. Your ability to promote wide reading among your students will depend heavily on getting the right books into children's hands. As one step toward becoming more skilled in selecting books for children, imagine a particular grade level and group of students, and brainstorm possible topics that would interest this group. Then, using bibliographies, library card catalogs, electronic databases, or the advice of a librarian, select half a dozen books on this topic that are likely to be of interest to your students. If the students you are considering include less skilled

readers or English language learners, be sure to include some books appropriate for these children.

2. Identify a grade level and group of students to whom you might teach vocabulary. If at all possible, this should be an actual group of students whom you can really teach. If you are able to work with elementary students, talk to their teacher and ask her to select half a dozen or so words that she would like her students to learn. If not, select a set of words yourself. Next, identify one of the procedures presented in the chapter appropriate for teaching these words, develop whatever materials you need, and prepare to do the teaching. If you haven't taught much

before, it would be a good idea to rehearse with a class-mate. Finally, teach the vocabulary, and then talk to students afterward to get their reaction to your instruction.

If it isn't possible to work with a real class, simulate this experience using your classmates as students.

Children's Literature

Books

Freedman, R. (1993). *Eleanor Roosevelt: A Life of Discovery.* New York: Scholastic. In this rich and insightful photobiography of an admirable and courageous woman, photos appear on almost every page and fill some pages. 198 pages.

Salas, M. (2003). *A de alfabeto/A Is for Alphabet.* Leon, Spain: Everest. In this Spanish/English book, each letter is presented first in Spanish and then in English. 32 pages.

Tran, T. (2003). *Going Home, Coming Home/Ve nha, tham que huong.* San Francisco: Children's Book Press. In this English/Vietnamese book, a young girl from the United States visits her grandmother in Vietnam and learns that she has a home in both countries. 31 pages.

Velthuijs, M. (2000). *Rah was Rah/Frog Is Frog.* London: Millet. In this Somali/English book, Frog at first wants to be like the other animals but then decides he is happy being himself. 28 pages.

Bibliographies

Book Links (bimonthly from the American Library Association, 50 E. Huron St., Chicago, IL 60611). This glossy magazine features annotated bibliographies, essays, reviews, and recommendations for using literature with children from preschool through eighth grade.

CCBC Choices (annually, in Spring). This annotated list of recommended children's trade books is produced by a committee of the Cooperative Children's Book Center, P.O. Box 5288, Madison, WI 53705-0288.

Children's Choices (annually, in October). *The Reading Teacher.* Fiction and nonfiction books that elementary and middle-school children have identified as some of their favorites are listed.

New Books for Young Readers (annually, in May). Edited by Lee Galda, College of Education, University of Minnesota. This annotated list gives new trade books that have been selected for their appeal and appropriateness for children from preschool to young adult. Department of Curriculum and Instruction, 159 Pillsbury Drive S.E., Minneapolis, MN 55455.

Notable Children's Books (annually, in March). *School Library Journal* and *Booklist.* This nonannotated list of recommended children's trade books is compiled during the American Library Association's winter meeting. Copies are available from ALA.

Notable Children's Trade Books in the Field of Social Studies (annually, in April/May). *Social Education.* Short reviews cover notable social studies trade books for kindergarten through eighth grade.

Outstanding Science Trade Books for Children (annually, in March). *Children and Science.* Short reviews cover outstanding science trade books for prekindergarten through eighth grade.

Teacher's Choices (annually, in November). *The Reading Teacher.* Fiction and nonfiction books teachers have identified as among their favorites for kindergarten and elementary-age students are listed.

Trelease, J. (2006). *The read-aloud handbook* (6th ed.). New York: Penguin Books. This rich source provides information on predictable books, wordless books, reference resources, picture books, short novels, novels, poetry, and anthologies.

PEARSON myeducationlab

Now go to the topic "Vocabulary" in the MyEducationLab (www.myeducationlab.com) for your course, where you can:

- Find learning outcomes for the topics covered in this chapter along with the IRA standards that connect to these outcomes.

- Complete assignable activities in the Assignments and Activities section that show concepts in action to help you synthesize and apply strategies.

- Explore IRIS Center Resources—training enhancement materials that provide you with research-validated information and interactive materials to develop your skills in working with students.

- Apply and practice your understanding of the teaching skills identified in the chapter with the Building Teaching Skills and Dispositions exercises.

10
Scaffolding Students' Comprehension of Text

CHAPTER outline

"I love to read!" Ethan exclaims. Those four words are music to any teacher's ears. If only we could hear every child we teach saying them! So how do we get that to happen?

Part of the answer lies in making reading a purposeful, successful experience for every child. Easily said, but not so easily done, given the complexities of the reading process and of our modern world, where students arrive in your classroom from vastly different backgrounds and with diverse interests, abilities, and needs. Despite the complications, however, there are things you can do, such as implementing in your classroom instructional frameworks and procedures that have been evolving over the years to provide students with the support they need to develop as readers. In this chapter, we describe some of these frameworks and procedures.

As you read this chapter, imagine a class full of students, *your* students. Think about how these frameworks and procedures will help ensure the success of your students, continually learning and relearning that reading is purposeful and enjoyable. If virtually every reading experience students have in your classroom is successful and fulfilling, they will almost certainly become skillful and avid readers. And you may well have the pleasure of hearing them utter that gratifying statement, "I love to read!"

CLASSROOM *vignette*

Instructional Frameworks and Procedures

How do you motivate, guide, and support students in the texts they read? In this chapter, we look at four frameworks and several individual procedures designed to scaffold students' efforts in their reading and understanding of various texts, thus helping them develop literacy skills, boosting higher order thinking, while nurturing positive attitudes about reading. Three of the frameworks—the directed reading activity (DRA), the directed reading-thinking activity (DR-TA), and the scaffolded reading experience (SRE)—can be implemented with students at all grade levels. The fourth, guided reading, is designed primarily for beginning readers in grades 1 through 3. In addition to these four frameworks, we describe several individual procedures to help students better comprehend and learn from the texts they read: story grammars or story maps, K-W-L, reading guides, discussion webs, and semantic webbing and weaving. All these techniques promote higher-order thinking.

The Roles of Reader, Selection, and Purpose in Planning a Successful Reading Experience

When we look carefully at what it means to comprehend text, three factors are always involved: the reader (who is reading), the selection (what is being read), and the purpose or purposes for reading (why reading is being done). We cannot overstate the importance and interconnectedness of these three components in planning any classroom reading experience. These critical factors should be at the forefront of your thinking whenever your students are about to read.

Assessment

To fine-tune your assessment of a student's reading level, use the Sentence Reading and Passage Reading subtests of the Interactive Reading Assessment System (IRAS) or the Graduated Running Record in Appendix A.

Reader

The readers will obviously be the focal point of your planning when you think about reading instruction. This means considering the readers' needs and concerns, interests, background knowledge, and strengths and weaknesses as learners. When you begin planning reading instruction, you will want to take all of these factors into account. However, your students' background knowledge—what they know and have experienced—is probably the most crucial variable in their successfully making meaning with the text.

Effective teachers, as Linda Gambrell and Susan Mazzoni (1999) remind us, assess what students already know and "*link* new ideas, skills, and competencies to prior understandings." Lamont Franklin is one such teacher. He reflects on the importance of background knowledge as it relates to a selection his fifth-graders are about to read:

> I teach fifth-graders who are average-to-poor readers living in a Midwestern city. Our social studies curriculum includes a unit on Australia, and one of the reading selections is an informational piece on the Great Barrier Reef. Although most of my students have heard of Australia and seen pictures of it in the media, they haven't been there. In fact, most have never even seen an ocean. To read this article successfully, these students will need prereading experiences that provide background information to help fill the gaps in their repertoire of concepts about Australia and about oceans, reefs, and other

topics central to this piece. Also, because the reading level of the article is sixth grade, and many of my students read below sixth-grade level, I'll have to do something extra to make sure they understand it. This may include preteaching potentially difficult vocabulary and providing them with a graphic organizer that shows what topics are included and how they are organized.

—Lamont Franklin, fifth-grade teacher

On the other hand, if the class reading the selection on the Great Barrier Reef lives in Hawaii and does have adequate background knowledge to successfully comprehend the text, the issue becomes one of activating those schemata (McMahon & McCormack, 1998). In this case, the activities will serve to activate already existing schemata. These may include having students discuss what they know about the topic before reading it, perhaps even writing down what they know about Australia and reefs, as well as their experiences and knowledge of the ocean. After reading the article, the students might discuss new information or ideas they discovered from the reading, questions that arose while they read, and where they might find the answers to those questions.

Selection

As you plan reading instruction your next consideration is the texts or the reading selections. Ideally, your students will be reading a wide range of materials that reflect a variety of cultures, including easy selections as well as some that are more challenging and that deal with topics that reflect the array of diverse interests your students have. In today's classrooms, it is particularly important to have materials that reflect our multicultural society. Figure 10.1 provides a short list of authors who create books that illuminate a variety of cultures.

In addition to providing students with material reflecting different cultures, levels of difficulty, and interests, it is vital to give students opportunities to read a variety of genres. Students should become familiar with narratives, informational texts, and poetry, as well as the many genres within these broad categories. By the time students leave middle school they should have had experiences with realistic fiction, historical

Figure 10.1 **Authors Who Create Books Illuminating a Variety of Cultures**

Alma Flor Ada	Virginia Hamilton	Jerry Pinkney
Joseph Bruchac	Minfong Ho	Faith Ringgold
Ashley Bryan	Angela Johnson	Allen Say
Floyd Cooper	Barbara Knutson	Virginia Driving Hawk Sneve
David Diaz	Jeanne M. Lee	Gary Soto
Leo and Diane Dillon	Julius Lester	Mildred Taylor
Arthur Dorros	Patricia McKissack	Joyce Carol Thomas
Tom Feelings	Walter Dean Myers	Yoshiko Uchida
Jean Craighead George	Lensey Namioka	Mildred Pitts Walters
Paul Goble	Ifeoma Onyefulu	Lawrence Yep
Eloise Greenfield	Brian Pinkney	Ed Young

Struggling readers often do not like to read. Hence, in addition to helping struggling readers develop their reading ability, we need to help them to enjoy reading. If struggling students enjoy reading more, they are likely to do more of it and get better at it. Finding high-interest books that students can read is therefore important. Teacher Mandy Gregory has a website with many useful resources for teachers (www.mandygregory.com) where she lists a number of series books that her struggling readers have enjoyed. She also notes that teachers can become members of Titlewave (http://titlewave.com), where they can access *School Library Journal* booklists, organized by grade level and nature of text (e.g., fiction, non-fiction, graphic). Another source for high-interest/low-readability books is High Noon Books (www.highnoonbooks.com). High Noon's texts are organized by readability, genre, and subject. For example, High Adventures Set 1 includes titles at third-grade readability but that will appeal to students ages 11 and up. The stories in the set include one about a tornado, a fire at a circus, and a crash at sea. Texts written for students in the same age range but with a fourth- to fifth-grade readability include the titles *Great Disasters in History* and *Great Medical Milestones.*

fiction, fantasy, folk tales, biography, autobiography, and other expository text. We recommend making a chart of the genres to hang in your classroom, using it as a point of discussion when new texts are introduced. Ask students to classify each selection under its appropriate genre.

As you think about what your students will read, think in terms of units of instruction, not individual selections. A unit might be organized to learn about a particular genre (e.g., fantasy), study a particular author (e.g., Roald Dahl), examine a particular topic (e.g., whales and dolphins), or explore a particular theme (e.g., justice). Some units might focus on just one genre whereas others might incorporate several different genres. If you are using a core reading program, these units have already been planned for you. Some units in core reading programs are well constructed and lead children to important understandings. Many, however, are just loose assemblies of text with only vague titles to hold them together. The units you plan should reflect the purposes you set for your students. The units you create need to be differentiated—one size does not fit all. All students might be studying fantasy, but the text for students with weaker print and fluency skills needs to be selected for their reading level. In all cases we believe that you need to create units that will lead to higher-order thinking, units that will take students beyond the literal into a deep understanding of topics or themes.

Generative topics are one way to build higher-order thinking (Perkins, 1992, 2004; Perkins & Blythe, 1994). Generative topics can be concepts, themes, procedures, historical periods, theories, ideas, and the like. For example, in the field of literature, plot is a generative topic. Generative topics are central to the subject area students are studying, accessible to students, and connectable to many other topics in the same subject and in other areas. Plot is central to the study of literature, a critical element in many types of literature and many individual pieces of writing, and exists outside of literature as well. Historical episodes—for example, the Civil War period—basically follow a plot, as do our lives. As another example, consider cause and effect. Cause and effect is a concept central to much of history, and, like the generative concept of plot, cause and effect also exists in areas outside of history. In fact, many, if not most, fields of study—science, humanities, and art, for example—deal with cause and effect.

Your students have probably already thought about many generative topics. Consider the idea of beauty. Beauty is a central concept in art and literature, of course, but beauty also plays an important role in our lives and even in science. Frank Press (1984), former president of the National Academy of Sciences, once spoke of the discovery of the double helix that broke the genetic code as not only rational, but beautiful as well. Finally, consider the topic of health. Health can be considered a part of science, but it is also a subtopic of social science; there is psychological health as well as physical health. Of course, health can also be related to government, when legislatures set school lunch rules and regulations. Some examples of generative topics and ideas generated from them for first-graders and fifth-graders are shown in Figure 10.2.

Public libraries, bookstores, and children's literature websites can lead you to literature on the topics you are exploring in the classroom. For example, a quick search of the Hennepin County libraries' website (www.hclib.org), a Minneapolis-area library system that two of us use a lot, yielded 44 children's titles on the subject "seasons of the year." At the Barnes & Noble website (www.barnesandnoble.com), we searched books for children using the key word *seasons* and found 2,180 possibilities. The Barnes & Noble site also showed book covers and listed book reviews from sources such as the *School Library Journal* and the *Horn Book.*

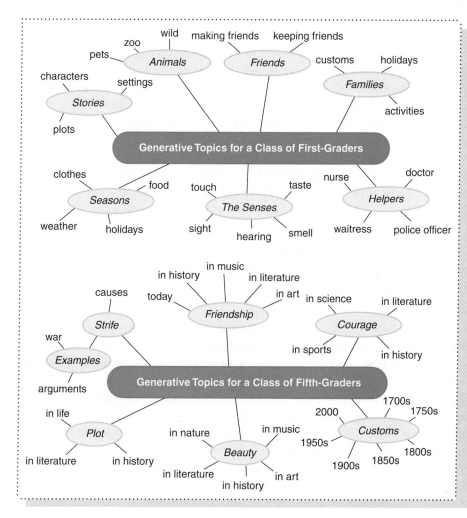

Figure 10.2

Some Generative Topics for First-Graders and Fifth-Graders

No two readers are the same. Each will bring a unique set of experiences, expectations, and abilities to the texts he or she reads.

James Shaffer/PhotoEdit

Purpose

Can you imagine reading something without motivation, without a purpose? As John Guthrie (Guthrie & Anderson, 1999) reminds us, "Reading is a conscious, deliberate act prompted by a plausible purpose." Purpose is what motivates us, helps focus our attention, and gives us something tangible to work toward (a goal). We read because somewhere in those combinations of symbols is something we need or want—information, escape, excitement, or knowledge, for example. This is the message we want students to internalize from day one.

The Function of Purposes

Purposes serve a variety of functions in reading. First, purposes motivate or give a reason for reading. Such motivation is missing when a teacher merely states, "Open your science text and read Chapter 5." "Why?" a student might ask—and rightfully so. In order to motivate with a purpose for reading, the teacher might say, "What are three things you'd like to find out about earthquakes? Write those down, and then read Chapter 5 to see if the author answers those questions for you. Later, we will talk about what you learned."

In addition to motivating a person to read, purposes also determine *how* a selection is read—quickly, in order to get the gist of the text, or slowly, in order to really understand the material. Your students might give a photosynthesis experiment a quick read if their purpose is to see what materials they will need, but fully absorbing the steps in photosynthesis will take a slow and careful reading.

Having clear purposes also aids comprehension. Such purposes can serve as a cue for activating a reader's background knowledge before reading a text, suggest a plan for the reader to use while reading, and help him sort out relevant from irrelevant information.

Matching Reading Purposes with the Text and the Reader

The following guidelines can help you align reading purposes with the text being read and the students who are reading.

- *Select text-appropriate purposes.* For example, after studying the concept of theme, an appropriate purpose for a group of second-graders reading the stories in Arnold Lobel's *Days with Frog and Toad* might be to discover each story's theme. On the other hand, it would be inappropriate to read the stories of these anthropomorphic characters to find out the attributes of amphibians.
- *Select reader-appropriate purposes.* You wouldn't ask a group of beginning readers who had no experience with theme to read *Days with Frog and Toad* to discover the book's themes. You could, however, ask that same group of students to find out the problem in each story and how it is resolved.
- *Select purposes with significance and value that are important to the reader.* For example, if students needed to update their knowledge about fire safety, an appropriate purpose for reading an article on the subject would be to add new information

to what they already know. They could make a chart that reflected both their old and new knowledge, which they could then share with a wider audience.

- *Choose a single purpose more often than multiple purposes.* As teachers, we don't want to overload our students with so many reading purposes that they either fail at some or are only somewhat successful at each. We'd rather they were really successful with just a few.
- *Encourage students to develop their own reading purposes.* Students need to be continually nudged and encouraged to take responsibility for their own learning, to realize what it is they need to know and how to achieve their personal goals.

Purpose is something we take for granted as adults, something so internalized we don't consciously think about it as we read. However, it is an all-important factor to consider if we want students to succeed in the reading they do in our classrooms.

1. Suppose you are teaching second grade and your students are going to read nonfiction books about different occupations. When you go to the library or school media center to select "occupation" books for your class, what questions will you ask as you look through the books to make your selections? (For example, How difficult is the vocabulary?)

2. Suppose you are teaching fourth-graders who come from a variety of backgrounds. Your literature curriculum includes *Number the Stars* by Lois Lowry, an award-winning middle-grade novel set in Nazi-occupied Denmark. The story revolves around 10-year-old Annemarie, who, with the help of her family, helps her best friend's family escape to Sweden. Are all of your students likely to succeed in reading this selection without help from you? Why or why not?

Four Frameworks for Scaffolding Students' Reading

In this section, we describe four frameworks that organize classroom reading instruction with the purpose of guiding students into, through, and beyond the texts they read: directed reading activity (DRA), direct reading-thinking activity (DR-TA), scaffolded reading experience (SRE), and guided reading. Guided reading is more suitable to the primary grades, but can be applied in all grades, whereas the others are suitable for all grades.

Directed Reading Activity

For decades, the directed reading activity (DRA) has served as the basic lesson format for the basal reader. First described by Emmett Betts in 1946, the procedure has five steps to guide students through a reading selection. First, the students are prepared for the selection, which the teacher does by creating interest, establishing purposes, and introducing new vocabulary. During the second step, students read silently. In the third step, the teacher checks students' comprehension in a discussion and also sometimes develops word recognition skills when necessary. In the fourth step, students read parts of the selection again, this time aloud, to focus on writing craft or to develop fluency. The fifth step involves postreading follow-up activities. The following list summarizes the five steps in DRA:

1. Readiness
2. Directed silent reading

3. Comprehension check and discussion
4. Oral reading
5. Follow-up activities

Although the procedure has been justly criticized as inviting a rigid, one-size-fits-all reading instruction approach and as being too teacher dominated, it is worth considering because it has served as the basis of so much reading instruction, quite possibly the instruction you or your parents received. Additionally, it is the precursor of the more flexible scaffolded reading experience, which we describe later in this chapter, and the directed reading-thinking activity, which we describe next. If you want to know more about the DRA itself, *Reading Strategies and Practices* (Tierney & Readence, 2005) includes both a description and an evaluation.

Directed Reading-Thinking Activity

In Phase 1 of the DR-TA, Susan Jones asks her students to make predictions about the story told in *The Best Worst Day*.

Courtesy of the author

The directed reading-thinking activity (DR-TA), developed by Russell Stauffer (1969), is a procedure that focuses on student-generated purposes. The importance of having students generate their own purposes is based on the premise that reading is a thinking process that involves the reader in using his own experiences to reconstruct the author's ideas. The teacher's role in the DR-TA is to create a situation in which this thinking process will occur.

Implementing the DR-TA for a group of students in any grade has two phases: teacher direction of the reading-thinking process and a skill-training phase. During the directed-thinking phase of the DR-TA, the teacher involves the reader in three steps: predicting (setting purposes), reading, and proving. The teacher encourages students to make their own predictions concerning what they are about to read, to read to discover the accuracy of their predictions, and to verify their predictions by orally rereading the passage that yields the answer. (See In the Classroom 10.1 for an illustration of this procedure.)

The second phase of the DR-TA—the skill-training phase—occurs after students have read a selection and completed the directed-thinking phase. Here students reexamine the story, which might involve analyzing teacher-selected words or phrases, pictures, or diagrams. The purpose of revisiting the story is to develop students' reading-thinking abilities and other reading-related skills. This skill training might include vocabulary work, creating semantic webs or weaves, summarizing, and other postreading activities.

Scaffolded Reading Experience

The scaffolded reading experience (SRE) is similar to the DRA and DR-TA in that it takes students through the prereading, during-reading, and postreading phases of a text reading, yet it is markedly more flexible. Its simple design can easily be implemented in any reading situation at any grade level. The SRE is based on the notion of scaffolding, which, you will recall, is "a process that enables a child or novice to solve a problem, carry out a task, or achieve a goal [that] would be beyond his unassisted efforts" (Wood, Bruner, & Ross, 1976). The scaffolded reading experience (Avery & Graves, 1997; Clark & Graves, 2005; Graves & Graves, 2003; Graves, Graves, & Braaten, 1996; Watts & Graves, 1997) is designed to do just that—to ensure a student's reading success in whatever she is reading, for whatever purpose.

Phase 1 of the DR-TA

The following is an example of how to implement phase 1 of the DR-TA with second-graders who are reading the short chapter book *The Best Worst Day* by Bonnie Graves:

- Give each student a copy of *The Best Worst Day*.
- Direct students' attention to the title and the picture on the cover and ask, "What do you think the story might be about?" Some possible answers: "I think something good *and* bad will happen." "I think the girl hanging on the bar is going to get hurt."
- After several students give their predictions, ask, "Which of these predictions do you agree with?" Encourage students to make several different suggestions.
- Tell students to read a segment of the story silently to see whether their predictions are correct.
- Have students read passages aloud that prove or disprove their predictions.
- Proceed through the story; students make new predictions, read silently to see whether their predictions are accurate, and then read aloud the relevant passages and evaluate and revise their predictions as necessary.

The SRE framework takes into consideration the three all-important factors discussed at the beginning of the chapter: purpose, selection, and reader. After carefully considering a purpose, a selection, and a group of readers, the teacher develops a set of prereading, during-reading, and postreading activities that supports students in achieving their reading goals. The SRE has two phases: a planning phase and an implementation phase. In the planning phase, the teacher considers the following:

- *The reader.* Her needs, concerns, interests, strengths, weaknesses, background knowledge—anything that might influence her success (or failure) in reading a particular selection
- *The selection.* Its topics and themes, the background knowledge required, its organization, difficult vocabulary or other stumbling blocks, and the opportunities it presents for instruction
- *The purpose or purposes for reading.* What the reader is to gain from the reading experience. For what purposes is she reading?

As we have previously emphasized, these three factors are interrelated, and decisions made about one factor will influence and constrain the decisions made about the other two. In other words, purpose is linked to text and the students who are reading it, and students' skills and interests will largely determine which selections and purposes are appropriate for them.

In the next three sections, we discuss the three facets of the implementation phase: prereading, during-reading, and postreading activities of SREs. Then we discuss comprehensive SREs that include prereading, during-reading, and postreading activities.

Prereading Activities

Prereading activities get students ready both cognitively and affectively to read a selection. Taking time to prepare students before they read can pay big dividends in terms of their understanding and enjoyment of what they read. Here we describe six categories of prereading experiences.

Motivating and Setting Purposes for Reading. Motivational activities incite enthusiasm, an eagerness to discover what the written word has to offer. As Kathryn Au

Assessment

Your assessment of students' reading abilities will be most accurate when they are doing something that matters to them. Therefore, you will want to design reading situations in which students can and will do their best. In a journal, jot down the kinds of topics and activities that motivate your students.

(1999) notes, "It is students' interest that must serve as the starting point." In other words, motivational activities will draw on the interests and concerns of the particular group doing the reading.

Activating Background Knowledge. Having appropriate background knowledge is absolutely crucial to understanding text. When activating background knowledge, you help students draw on information they already have about a particular subject; when *building* background knowledge, you provide students with information they need to understand the text. For example, let's say a group of third-graders is going to read an expository piece on wildfires. To activate their prior knowledge, you might have them talk or write about what they know about fire. To build their background knowledge, you might draw an illustration of the fire triangle, explaining the three elements necessary for making fire, or show a video about wildfires.

By activating background knowledge you seek to draw students into the text by helping them recall situations in their lives that are similar to those found in the selection. In the Classroom 10.2 shows a prereading activity that relates a reading to students' lives. It is designed to help students make connections with text through a prereading journal activity.

Building Text-Specific Knowledge. In contrast to activities concerning background knowledge, some activities should build text-specific knowledge that students need for comprehension. Outlines and graphic organizers work well to build text-specific knowledge for expository texts. For example, before students read a chapter on waves in their science text, you might provide them with a graphic organizer as shown in Figure 10.3.

Previews are another way of building text-specific knowledge. Previews are something like a movie trailer, providing a bit of information about the text. For in-

In the Classroom

10.2

Instructional Routines

Prereading Activity Relating the Reading to Students' Lives

- *Selection:* Various biographies of Martin Luther King, Jr.
- *Readers:* Fourth-grade students, several of whom have parents who emigrated to the United States and four of whom recently moved to the United States from Somalia. All of these fourth-graders have experienced firsthand the concept of discrimination, owing to events that occurred in their community as a result of a large influx of Somalians.
- *Reading purpose:* To learn more about the life of Martin Luther King, Jr., and to understand and appreciate the purpose and results of his efforts to promote civil rights.
- *Goal of the activity:* To make connections with the topics and themes found in the biographies.
- *Rationale:* Having students write about times they felt discriminated against and later talk about them will help them better understand the concept of discrimination, a central theme in the biographies of King and a topic that has become an issue in their community. This writing will also help build an immediacy and relevancy for the biographies students will read.
- *Procedure:* Before students begin reading biographies, ask them to write in their journals about a time in their lives when they felt that they were not treated as well as others, when they felt they were mistreated or treated unfairly. After students write, encourage them to read aloud or to discuss what they have written.

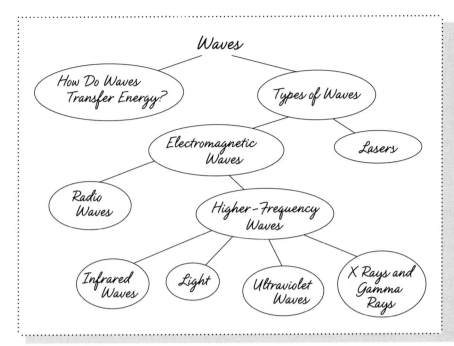

Figure 10.3

Graphic Organizer of Topics in Chapter on Waves

formational texts, a preview might discuss topics, events, people, or places covered in the selection. For narratives, a preview might introduce the setting, characters, and perhaps a bit of the plot. Previews have been shown to be effective in facilitating comprehension with students of all ages and abilities and for English language learners as well as native speakers (Chen & Graves, 1996; Dole, Valencia, Greer, & Wardrop, 1991; Graves, Prenn, & Cooke, 1985).

Preteaching Vocabulary and Concepts. Teaching selected vocabulary and concepts before students read a selection can help them better understand and appreciate a text. Chapter 9 discussed the various sorts of word learning tasks and instruction needed to facilitate that learning.

Melanie Kuhn and Lesley Mandel Morrow (2003) have discussed how the Internet can provide a rich and motivating resource for building background knowledge prior to reading a selection and for extension activities following reading. As an example, Kuhn and Morrow describe how websites can support and extend children's experience of E. L. Konigsberg's *From the Mixed-Up Files of Mrs. Basil E. Frankweiler.* They suggest that teachers have children explore the Metropolitan Museum of Art, where the story is set, via the museum's website (www.metmuseum.org/explore/index.asp). Additionally, they direct interested teachers and students to a website that a teacher and her students created to go along with the story (http://litplans.com/authors/E_L_Konigsberg.html). Another popular book for upper-elementary readers is Avi's ghost story *Something Upstairs.* Avi's website provides an intriguing introduction to the book (www.avi-writer.com/books/books/something.html). The website EyeWitness to History is a valuable resource for information to support both fiction and nonfiction reading. For example, upper-elementary and middle-grade students often read the "twin texts" *Fever 1793* by Laurie Halse Anderson and *An American Plague: The True and Terrifying Story of the Yellow Fever Epidemic of 1793* by Jim Murphy. At www.eyewitnesstohistory.com/yellowfever.htm students can read about the Philadelphia yellow fever epidemic in 1793. ●

Prequestioning, Predicting, and Direction Setting. Attention-focusing activities have the similar purpose of highlighting what readers should look for as they read and directing them to a particular aspect or several aspects of the text. With prequestioning activities, you and your students pose questions about the upcoming text that they would like to find answers to. Predicting activities involve students in making predictions about the text and then reading to find out whether their predictions are accurate. Direction setting reminds students about what to attend to while they read. You might say, "Read the story to find out if your predictions are correct." Other times, you might write instructions on the chalkboard, a chart, or a handout so that students can refer to them.

Suggesting Comprehension Strategies. In the past several years, a number of reading strategies have been identified as valuable for understanding, remembering, and enjoying text (Pressley, 2000). In this chapter, we discuss how to teach these strategies. Once your students learn how to use these strategies, you can provide a valuable aid to their comprehension by, as part of your prereading scaffold, suggesting strategies for students to employ while reading.

Prereading Activities: A Summary. By now, you are probably aware that the possibilities for prereading activities are almost limitless. But there is a common thread to all of them—each builds a bridge from the students to the selection, connecting what students already know to what they will learn or meet in the text. Sometimes just one brief prereading activity will be sufficient. At other times, you may want to support students' efforts by using several activities. Your prereading plans will be determined by the purposes for reading, the selection itself, and those who are reading it. Don't overteach. You can undermine the pleasure of discovery and kill the anticipation by doing too much to get the students ready.

REFLECT
and **Apply**

③ In what kinds of reading situations are prereading activities likely to be unnecessary? In what situations are prereading activities essential? Why do you think relating the reading to students' lives is a useful prereading activity?

④ Do any of your college instructors engage their classes in prereading activities? If so, what activities? Do they help you better understand the assigned reading material? Explain.

⑤ What functions do prereading activities serve? Jot down as many as you can, and briefly explain how each prepares readers to comprehend and enjoy the selection they will read.

During-Reading Activities

During-reading activities include both tasks that students do themselves as they are reading and actions that you do to assist them—activities that facilitate or enhance the actual reading process. You have two major considerations when planning during-reading activities. First, you need to consider how the students will read the text—orally taking turns, orally with partners, silently by themselves, or some combination of these. The second consideration is how you will assist or scaffold their understanding. What questions will you ask? What support will you provide?

Reading the Text. Beyond the primary grades, most reading is carried out most efficiently through silent reading. Silent reading will be the most frequent during-reading activity done by middle- and upper-elementary students. But not all students have the endurance to read a long text silently, so you may need to break it into chunks. The goal for these students is to move them from some form of supported reading to independent silent reading.

Oral reading provides support for younger readers and older students who are not yet confident of their silent reading skills. Three popular read-aloud activities are choral reading, readers theater, and buddy reading. In choral reading—by using contrasts such as high and low voices, different voice combinations, sound effects, movements, gestures, or increasing and decreasing tempo— students together convey and interpret the meaning of a text. Choral reading builds confidence, fluency, and automaticity as students respond creatively to a text. Readers theater, in which students take turns or assume roles in reading portions of text aloud, can be used effectively to interpret poetry, narratives, and even expository materials (Young & Vardell, 1993). In buddy reading, two people read the same passage aloud together or take turns reading. This kind of oral reading is particularly useful for younger students, English language learners, and those who need extra support. It also does much to boost the reading skills and self-esteem of the older child who reads with his younger buddy (Brozo, 2002; Cunningham & Allington, 1999; Friedland & Truesdell, 2004). Buddies can be two peers, a parent and a student, an aide and a student, or a teacher and a student.

Although students will generally read silently, sometimes it is appropriate for students to have material read to them. Reading aloud to your students can

Reading aloud to students is a powerful way to engage them in text and demonstrate the beauty and power of language.

Thinkstock

- Make certain texts and passages accessible and, through intonation, stress, pauses, and inflection, give to a text meaning that their own silent reading might not (Horowitz & Freeman, 1995).
- Convey your enthusiasm for information, ideas, and language and provide a model for expressive reading.
- Demonstrate the beauty and power of language, especially for students who struggle with reading on their own or have had little exposure to books.

Supported Reading. While students are reading, many will need help with the ideas in the text. Supported reading activities focus students' attention on certain ideas as they read, help them clarify what they do not understand, record main ideas, draw critical inferences, attend to graphic information, and summarize what they are learning. Particularly with exposition, it is appropriate to support students' reading, to help them focus on, understand, and learn from certain aspects of the text. Supporting students' reading should lead them to higher levels of understanding. The following two options for supporting students' reading each include a style of questioning as well as a framework for discussion that help students comprehend what they are reading. While students are reading is a prime time to help them grapple with the text.

- *Guided comprehension.* This uses a series of questions and probes that will help students improve their understanding of a text. In guided comprehension the students read a portion of the text and then stop to discuss it. At each stopping point the teacher works to guide their understanding by focusing on a few critical ways of thinking. Students should engage in three activities each time they stop to discuss: paraphrase what was read, clarify misunderstandings, and make inferences. Paraphrasing gives you insight into what students understand and it is a process that helps them integrate text ideas. Clarifying makes students aware of comprehension problems and causes them to work to fix them. Inferences are essential for connecting one idea to another and connecting text ideas to prior knowledge. Figure 10.4 outlines the process of guided comprehension.

Figure 10.4 The Process of Guiding Comprehension

The students will read a portion of the text and then stop to discuss it. Use the following questions to guide the discussion.

SUMMARIZE OR PARAPHASE what has been read up to the first stopping point. You might say:

> What is the author trying to tell us? What is the story or passage about?
> What is the author talking about?
> Who can retell the story to us?
>> Probe: What else can you tell us about the story?
>> Probe: Who can add on to what _____ told us?

MONITOR COMPREHENSION to focus on text or comprehension problems.

> What problems did you encounter reading this section?
> Does that make sense? Is that said in a clear way?
> What questions do you think we need to ask?
> What words or phrases might be difficult for someone to understand?
> If none of the students encountered a problem, discuss one piece of the text that does present some difficulty. Think aloud about the difficulty you had and how you resolved it.

MAKE INFERENCES necessary to understanding the selection. You might use any of the following probes or queries.

> How does the character feel?
> What is the character's goal?
> How can we use what we know about _____ to understand the text?
> How does what the author said about _____ connect to what the author already told us?
> What clues led us to the author's main message?
> Can you visualize the character or the setting the author is trying to describe?
> What did you feel, smell, or see while reading?

PROBING DEEPER: Ultimately you want the students to think deeply about the text, search for information, and justify their answers. When the students answer your questions, ask one of these follow-up questions:

- How did you come up with that answer?
- Where in the text did you find your answer?
- What clues in the text led you to that answer?
- What strategy did you use?

QtA

The QtA procedure includes several steps. First, the teacher explains to children that texts are in fact written by ordinary people who are not perfect and who create texts that are not perfect. Consequently, readers need to continually work hard to figure out what the authors are trying to say. Once students understand this reality, the class reads a text together, with the teacher stopping at critical points to pose queries that invite students to explore and grapple with the meaning of what is written. The queries include initiating prompts such as "What's the author trying to say?" to get students started grappling with the text, follow-ups such as "What does the author mean by that?" to encourage them to dig for deeper meaning, and follow-ups such as "How does that connect with what the author told you?" to encourage them to integrate the information in the text. Importantly, queries are not scripted, and teachers are encouraged to modify those suggested and make up their own queries to fit the students and texts they are working with. A detailed description of the QtA procedure is included in Appendix B.

- *Questioning the Author.* QtA is a large-group questioning and discussion technique developed by Beck and McKeown (Beck, McKeown, Hamilton, & Kucan, 1997; Beck, McKeown, Worthy, Sandora, & Kucan, 1996). QtA is designed for upper-elementary-age students. It is, as Beck and McKeown explain, "an approach to text-based instruction that was designed to facilitate building understanding of text" (Beck et al., 1997). In the Classroom 10.3 describes the QtA procedure and more examples are provided in Appendix B.

Modifying the Text. Sometimes, because of curriculum requirements especially in content areas, students will be reading selections whose length or difficulty presents too much of a challenge. In these cases, modifying—altering the original text—is a practical and powerful option. For example, if you know that a selection presents too much of a challenge to your readers, you could read parts of the text aloud as students read silently along. Another option is to have students read only selected portions of the text—those you think are most critical. This makes an otherwise impossible task feasible for your less competent readers. A successful reading experience is always the goal, and for some students, such as those learning English, modifying the text to create a doable reading task is one more way to ensure that success.

During-Reading Activities: A Summary. To plan during-reading activities you need to ask three questions. How will the students read the text—orally or silently? When will we stop to discuss? What discussion questions and procedures will I follow? Your goal is to develop the deepest level of understanding.

6 Briefly discuss, in writing or with a classmate, the purpose and function of supported reading activities. Discuss your personal philosophy about supported reading activities, including when they might be appropriate and when they might be inappropriate.

7 Identify a narrative or expository text you might use in the classroom. Design the support a group of average readers would need. Where would you stop to discuss? What questions would you ask to guide their thinking?

REFLECT and *Apply*

Postreading Activities

Generally, postreading activities encourage students to *do* something with the material they have just read, to think—critically, logically, and creatively—about the information and ideas that emerge from their reading, to respond to what they have read, and sometimes to transform their thinking into actions. These responses can take a variety of forms—speaking, writing, drama, creative arts, or application and outreach. Their joy and excitement should come from the reading itself. If you have to dress every text with an amazing artistic and dramatic activity, then you may communicate the message that it is not the reading that is motivating but what comes after.

Questioning. By encouraging students to think about and respond to the information and ideas in the material they have read, either orally or in writing, postreading questioning activities can promote thinking on a number of levels. They might help readers recall what they have read, show that readers understand what they read, or give readers an opportunity to apply, analyze, synthesize, evaluate, or elaborate on information and ideas. Questions might also encourage creative, interpretive, or metacognitive thinking and illustrate the various perspectives among readers. Questions can be of various kinds, but it is important that at least some of them give students the opportunity to engage in higher-level thinking (Beck & McKeown, 2001; Pearson & Duke, 2002). In the Classroom 10.4 gives some sample postreading questions for the various types of thinking.

Discussion. A large number of classroom reading experiences include discussion—exchanging ideas out loud. The intent of discussion is to freely explore ideas, to learn something new, or to gain a different perspective by pooling the information or insights that more than one person can give. Research studies show that positive effects accrue when children engage in small-group discussions about text. These discussions enhance text recall, aesthetic response to text, and reading comprehension (Gambrell, 1996).

To become proficient in discussion, students need explicit instruction, modeling, and many opportunities for practice. Students also need feedback from you and their

In the Classroom

10.4

Sample Postreading Questions for Various Types of Thinking

Here are some questions that teachers might ask students after they read *Shh! We're Writing the Constitution* by Jean Fritz.

- *Recalling:* How many delegates were supposed to attend the grand convention in 1787?
- *Understanding:* How did the delegates keep the proceedings secret?
- *Applying:* What are some things you might do to keep a meeting secret?
- *Analyzing:* Why did the delegates decide to keep the proceedings secret?
- *Synthesizing:* What do you think might have happened if the public had found out what was going on in the meetings?
- *Evaluating:* Do you think it was a good idea to keep the meetings secret? Why or why not?
- *Elaborating:* What do you think were the most effective features of the delegates' plan to keep the proceedings secret?
- *Creating:* What if the delegates had decided there should be three presidents presiding over the nation instead of one? What might have happened?
- *Interpreting*: How do you think Benjamin Franklin felt, being the oldest delegate at the convention?
- *Thinking metacognitively:* Did you understand the author's description of the three branches of government on page 14? If you didn't, what might you do to make this explanation clearer to you?

peers on what has been learned in a discussion and on the process of the discussion itself. Literature circles, which we will explore in Chapter 12, are a structured way for students to learn the art of discussion and to develop comprehension.

Writing. Writing has been called the twin sister of reading—a powerful way to integrate what students know with the information presented in a text, as well as to find out what they really do and don't understand. Writing is powerful because it requires a reader to actively manipulate information and ideas. As a postreading activity, writing can serve to connect information and ideas in a logical way. Writing also provides opportunities for students to extend ideas and to explore new ways of thinking, doing, and seeing—to invent, evaluate, create, and ponder. Writing is discussed at length in Chapter 12, which includes many examples that can be used as postreading activities. Figure 10.5 outlines three postreading activities that relate appropriately to the readers, selection, and purpose of reading.

Student-led discussions encourage students to be responsible for their own learning.

Thinkstock

Drama. As a postreading activity, drama, like writing, encourages students to extend existing meanings they have constructed with a text and to generate new ones. In the hands of a skillful, sensitive teacher, drama can become an enjoyable and highly motivating way to involve students in all of the cognitive tasks we listed at the beginning of this section—recalling, applying, analyzing, synthesizing, evaluating, and creating—through plays, skits, retelling of stories, pantomimes, and readers theater. In the Classroom 10.5 shows a list by multigrade teacher Harold Bulinski with several instances of how he uses dramatization as a postreading activity. These examples illustrate only a few of the great variety of possibilities for dramatizing text.

Artistic and Nonverbal Activities. As the work of Howard Gardner (1993) has shown, people have multiple intelligences—a variety of ways to learn, express, and transform

*A*ssessment

After students have read part or all of a story, asking them to retell or pantomime what they have read can help you assess whether or not they have understood the story.

Figure 10.5 Matching Postreading Writing Activity to Readers, Selection, and Purpose

Readers	Selection	Purpose	Appropriate Postreading Writing Activity
Primary-grade students	Poem about feelings	To respond personally to the poem	Write a poem describing similar feelings that students have had.
Fourth-grade students	Numerous books on animals	To learn about the characteristics of a variety of animals and to synthesize that information	Create alphabet picture books reflecting an animal or animals of their choice.
Fifth-grade students	Chapter on electricity	To understand and remember the information presented in the text	Write summaries for each of the sections of the chapter.

Students' Postreading Dramatizations

- Second-graders pantomime Indian tigers while listening to Ted Lewin's informational picture book *Tiger Trek* read aloud.
- Small groups of first- through third-graders prepare a dramatization of their favorite poem in Jack Prelutsky's *Tyrannosaurus Was a Beast*.
- Two fifth-graders play the parts of Gilly and Miss Ellis, Gilly's caseworker, and dramatize the opening scene in Katherine Paterson's *The Great Gilly Hopkins*.
- Two fifth-graders, after reading a chapter on the 1960s in their social studies text, portray Martin Luther King, Jr., and Lyndon B. Johnson. They carry on a conversation posing as these two historical figures. Later, their conversation is recorded on a video that is aired on a community cable station.

10.5

what they know. These categories take into account modes of expression that are not predominantly verbal, including the visual arts, music, and dance. We also include response activities that involve the creation of media productions, visual displays, and representations.

Artistic and nonverbal activities, such as creating models and visual displays, provide students with the opportunity to share what they've learned as well as reinforce newly acquired knowledge.

Ariel Skelley/Corbis

Art, music, and dance each represent a specialized language that can be used in response to printed and spoken communication. Numerous children's books can help connect students with the arts—for example, in *To Be an Artist* by Maya Ajmera (2004), photos and text reveal how children around the world express themselves through art. In her article "Music and Children's Books," Kathleen Jacobi-Karna (1996) gives an extensive list of children's books that suggest musical possibilities. In the Reading Corner, we list 11 titles, many of which are recommended by Cheri Estes (1995) in her article "Musical Links, Part I."

In addition to responding to a selection through art, music, and dance, students can engage in other types of artistic and nonverbal activities. These include media productions, such as making audiotapes, videos, or PowerPoint presentations. Or students might enjoy creating visual displays, using bulletin boards, artifacts, models, and specimens.

Application and Outreach. Each of the previously mentioned categories in one way or another reflects the idea of going beyond the text to explore other realms and other applications of information and ideas. In application and outreach endeavors, readers take the ideas and information from a text and deliberately test, use, or explore them further. Students might read a story about making ice cream or an article describing several science experiments, but it's not quite as much fun as actually following the steps and eating the ice cream or doing the

Books That Invite Musical Connections

Anna Harwell Celenza. *Bach's Goldberg Variations.* Charlesbridge, 2005. This tale tells of how Bach helps out a talented young musician. CD included. 32 pages.

Claude Clement. *Musician from Darkness.* Little, Brown, 1990. In lyrical prose, Clement tells the story of an outsider from a primitive society who discovers the power and magic of music. 26 pages.

James Lincoln Collier. *The Jazz Kid.* Holt, 1994. In this story, set in Chicago in the 1920s, 12-year-old Paulie wants to become a jazz cornetist and play the Black jazz music of Louis Armstrong, King Oliver, and the New Orleans Rhythm Kings. But his prejudiced parents are against it. 224 pages.

Jane Cutler. *The Cello of Mr. O.* Dutton, 1999. In wartime, a man's music helps sustain a town's spirit. 32 pages.

Tony Johnston. *The Harmonica.* Charlesbridge, 2004. The harmonica given to him by his father helps a Polish boy survive Nazi brutality. 32 pages.

Robert Kraus. *Musical Max.* Simon & Schuster, 1990. Max the musical hippo drives his father and neighbors crazy with his daily practicing on every sort of instrument. One day, he loses interest and stops. But the effect is not what the complainers thought it would be. 32 pages.

Bill Martin, Jr. *The Maestro Plays.* Holt, 1994. The subtleties of music are introduced with rhyming text as Martin describes the way a maestro plays the music. 32 pages.

Metropolitan Museum of Art. *Go In and Out the Window: An Illustrated Songbook for Young People.* Holt, 1987. Art and music are brought together in this handsome volume of 61 familiar songs illustrated with works from the Metropolitan Museum of Art. 48 pages.

Brian Pinkney. *Max Found Two Sticks.* Simon & Schuster, 1994. A would-be drummer, Max beats on different surfaces, echoing the sounds around him. He imagines church bells, a marching band, a train. Then a real band marches by and a drummer tosses Max a pair of sticks. 40 pages.

Pam Munoz Ryan. *When Marian Sang: The True Recital of Marian Anderson, the Voice of the Century.* Scholastic, 2002. This book provides an introduction to the life of Marian Anderson, the first African American to perform at the Metropolitan Opera and a civil rights activist whose life and career encouraged social change. 40 pages.

Mildred Pitts Walter. *Ty's One-Man Band.* Four Winds, 1987. A young African American child, while playing by the pond, meets a one-legged, one-man band who brings music to the community. 32 pages.

experiments. The logical next step after reading about something is to try it out in the real world.

Fiction, nonfiction, and poetry can also spark many different kinds of personal and social action. For example, after reading Chris Van Allsburg's *Just a Dream*—in which a child dreams about a future wasted because of poor management of the environment—students might decide to write letters to state and local representatives encouraging them to support legislation that protects the environment, or they might develop an environment-related ad campaign for their school or their neighborhood.

Another kind of outreach activity is for students to share their enthusiasm for books and reading outside the school doors in the form of book clubs. One such book club takes place between sixth-graders and senior citizens in Winchester, Massachusetts. The club is called the Literary Lunch Bunch; students and seniors meet to share a midday meal and discuss books (Abramson, 2002). Alternatively fourth- and fifth-graders might prepare a picture book to read to kindergarten students and in so doing work on their oral reading fluency by dramatizing the reading and then questioning. This activity is best suited for children who need to improve their fluency.

Reteaching. The six types of activities that we have just discussed encourage students to make logical connections between ideas and to explore new ways of thinking and of expressing themselves. Our seventh category, reteaching, is the safety net in the reading scaffold, a way to make sure students leave a reading selection with a sense of accomplishment, of a job well done. Reteaching is often necessary when students, after reading a selection and engaging in various activities of an SRE, have not reached their reading goals. Robert Dickenson, a fifth-grade teacher, discusses his reteaching approaches:

> I sometimes find it necessary to include reteaching activities in the scaffold I build to support my students' reading experience. This happens when my students have not reached their reading goals. These reteaching activities usually consist of a retracing of the steps of a specific activity *with* students, to see what went wrong and where—for example, if students had difficulty completing a reading guide or answering postreading questions. In these cases, my reteaching might include discussing with students the problems they had and why they had them, and then reviewing the purposes and steps involved in completing the guide or answering the questions.
>
> Alternatively, reteaching sometimes involves creating a totally different activity. I do this when the original activity was a disaster—something that happens more times than I'd like to admit, even though I'm a seasoned teacher.
>
> —Robert Dickenson, fifth-grade teacher

Postreading Activities: A Summary. Postreading activities help students go beyond the text and do something with the material they have read in order to help them see the relevance of reading, how it relates to their own lives and to the wider world around them. These types of activities will also help students better remember what they have read, provide them with opportunities to express themselves in a variety of ways, encourage the development of multiple intelligences, and give them opportunities to see how others interpret selections and additional opportunities to succeed. In the previous three sections, we have focused on individual prereading, during-reading, and postreading activities. These activities are interrelated—linked, one to the other, in response to the students, the selection, and the overall purpose for

Using the Scaffolded Reading Experience Framework

Differentiating Instruction for English Language Learners

The scaffolded reading experience lesson framework is well suited to supporting English language learners during reading lessons and content area lessons that involve texts. Fitzgerald and Graves (2004) note that reading in a second language involves more processes than reading in a first language, and that a significant additional process is that of translation. To support English language learners with this additional process, Fitzgerald and Graves recommend the following activities. During the prereading part of a scaffolded reading experience, preview the selection in English language learners' first language. To scaffold English language learners during reading, provide them with a list of major events or headings in their first language. To further support these students, Fitzgerald and Graves suggest, have them listen to an audio of the selection as they read. For postreading, have English language learners work in small groups with native English speakers to review the major events or outline important points depending on the nature of the selection (i.e., fiction/nonfiction). Then discuss the text as a whole class. Allow English language learners to use their first language to support their thinking and to express their ideas as needed during the discussion.

reading. Additionally, Appendix B includes a very detailed SRE for Kate DiCamillo's *Because of Winn-Dixie.*

Finally, we want to reemphasize that the purpose of an SRE is not to fill up precious reading time with a lot of activities, no matter how engaging or purposeful they might be in their own right, but rather to provide a scaffold for students to successfully build meaning from the texts that they read and then do something with their newly gained knowledge and insights.

Assessment

A detailed SRE lesson plan is available in Appendix B.

8 What purposes do postreading activities serve? Do you think you will engage your students in postreading activities for most of the reading they do in your class? Why or why not?

9 Suppose you are teaching fifth-graders who have just finished reading biographies of prominent figures in U.S. history. What sorts of postreading activities might these students engage in and why? Now, suppose you are teaching first-graders who have just read a beginning chapter book on the theme of friendship. What sorts of postreading activities might these students engage in and why?

REFLECT and *Apply*

Guided Reading

Guided reading, first developed by Irene Fountas and Gay Su Pinnell (1996), is a framework for reading instruction used primarily in grades 1 through 3; however, it can be adapted to use with older students (Tierney & Readence, 2000). In guided reading, the teacher guides small groups of students in their reading of texts that offer a bit, but not too much, of a challenge for them.

In the first step of guided reading, the teacher selects appropriate materials for students to read. A good rule of thumb is that with teacher support, students should be able to read 90 percent of the words accurately. Once the text has been selected, the students are given individual copies. The teacher briefly introduces the selection to the students, clarifying concepts or vocabulary that might prove difficult, prompting students to engage in certain reading strategies, and generally preparing the students for the reading. Next, the students read either quietly or silently while the teacher observes them, guiding when necessary and encouraging the use of strategies to unlock meaning.

After the students have finished with the reading, they talk about what they have read, either recalling details of the selection or offering personal responses. This is a time, too, to discuss any problem solving they did during the reading, focusing on vocabulary and decoding strategies. The teacher may also recommend that students revisit the text at this time to increase their fluency or may use the text to teach a skill or concept. Extending the text through postreading activities, such as those discussed with the SRE, can also take place during this portion of guided reading.

Another important aspect of guided reading is teacher assessment and follow-up. While students are reading and after, the teacher makes notes and keeps a record of students' progress in areas such as strategy use, fluency, self-monitoring, and correcting. As with the SRE framework, guided reading is not meant to be the sole element of a literacy program. In contrast to the SRE, which can be implemented with any size group—whole class or small group, heterogeneous or homogeneous—guided reading is usually done in small homogeneous groups.

During guided reading, all students read from the same text quietly or silently while the teacher observes, guiding them to use strategies to unlock meaning. After reading, students talk about what they have read.

Michael Newman/PhotoEdit

Individual Procedures for Fostering Comprehension of Text

In this section, we describe a number of additional teacher-guided procedures that differ from the four instructional frameworks we just described in that they were designed to achieve very specific instructional goals or to focus on a particular part of reading. Some are used prior to reading, some during reading, some after reading, and some at several points in the reading process. All of them encourage active and reflective thinking and can be modified for any elementary classroom. We have divided the procedures described here into three categories:

- Procedures for narratives
- Procedures for expository texts
- Procedures appropriate for all types of texts

For a complete list and descriptions of procedures for fostering comprehension and other aspects of reading, we recommend *Reading Strategies and Practices* (Tierney & Readence, 2005).

Procedures for Narratives

As we have already noted and as Rosenblatt (1978) explains at length, narratives are written primarily to entertain. Most well-written stories, whether simple or complex, have a fairly similar structure, and most children have a basic schema for this structure. Teachers can help students make this understanding explicit and give them a language for talking about stories. When teachers build on this schema, students' comprehension and enjoyment of narrative literature will be enhanced, as will their writing in this genre. Story grammars and story maps provide two ways to help students enhance their schema for stories.

Story Grammars and Story Maps

To identify the common elements that make up a well-developed story, several variations of story grammar have been developed (Mandler & Johnson, 1977; Thorndyke, 1977). Story grammar is similar to sentence grammar in that it attempts to explain the various components in a story and how they function. The story grammar we have found most helpful is a synthesis of those that both educational researchers and fiction writers have identified as consistent across stories. This grammar includes a setting with a character who has a problem to solve or a goal to achieve, the character's attempts to solve the problem or achieve the goal, the results of these attempts, and a conclusion. This conclusion illuminates the story's theme. Story grammars find their instructional application through both guided questioning and the use of graphic organizers generally called story maps.

A story map is a listing of the major ideas and events in a story, beginning at the starting point and moving through the story in sequential order. Beck and McKeown (1981) recommend that teachers create a story map to help identify the major structural elements, both explicit and implicit, in a story that students will be reading in class. Based on the map, the teacher then generates a question for the students to answer related to each major event. In the story map illustrated in Figure 10.6, based on the story *The Bear's Toothache* (McPhail, 1972), you will see that the left column gives the story event and the right column the corresponding question for students to answer. These questions, when answered, constitute the essence of the story and elicit information that is central to understanding it.

Figure 10.6 **Story Map and Questions for** *A Bear's Toothache*

The Story Map	Questions
Character: A boy lying in bed hears a loud moaning outside his window.	Who are the characters in our story?
Setting: A house, bedroom.	Where does it take place?
Problem: A bear with a bad tooth.	What did the boy hear outside his window?
Goal: Remove the tooth and alleviate the pain.	What did the boy try to do for the bear? Why do you think the boy wanted to help?
Event 1: Boy tries to pull the tooth.	
Event 2: Boy gives bear steak to eat to loosen the tooth.	What are some of the ways the boy and the bear tried to get rid of the painful tooth?
Event 3: Boy tries to hit the tooth with his pillow.	
Event 4: Boy ties a rope around the tooth and bear jumps out of the window.	How did they ultimately get the tooth out?
Resolution: The tooth popped out and the bear gave it to the boy to put under his pillow.	How do you know that the bear was pleased at the end of the story?

To create a story map, decide what the starting point for the story is, list briefly the major events in chronological order, and then write a question for each event. Students should discuss the major elements of a story before they read and use them as they read to record their understanding of the story. Research by Dreher and Singer (1980) indicates that story maps are most useful for primary children or older students who do not have a decent concept of narrative structure.

As a postreading activity, teachers often have students complete a graphic organizer such as the story map depicted in Figure 10.7. Introduce the story map by reading a very well-structured narrative, like *The Bear's Toothache,* to the students and discuss

Figure 10.7 **A Sample Story Map**

Characters _____

Setting _____

Time _____

Problem _____

_____

Goal _____

    Event 1 _____

    Event 2 _____

    Event 3 _____

    Event 4 _____

Resolution _____

its story elements. As you discuss the story, enter character names, setting, problems, events, and resolution into the story map. After completing a few story maps with the students, they will be ready to complete one on their own or with a partner. Story map and questions driven by story maps can improve students' existing schema for a story and improve their story comprehension. As Beck and McKeown note, however, story map questions are not the only questions to ask concerning reading selections. Once students understand the essence of the story, then interpretive, analytical, and creative questions are appropriate and important.

Procedures for Expository Texts

As we mentioned earlier, in contrast to narratives, which are written primarily to entertain, expository texts are generally written to impart information or knowledge. We typically read them to make that information and knowledge part of our own schemata, either to use or to store for future application. That purpose alone makes reading these texts a different sort of endeavor than reading a story in which places, characters, and events unfold in our imagination. As Rosenblatt (1978) has suggested, readers take two different stances when reading—an aesthetic stance for narratives and an efferent stance for expository text. The primary purpose when reading aesthetically is not to gain information, but to experience the text. In reading efferently, however, your purpose is to locate or remember information. Therefore, with most expository texts, your attention will be focused primarily on what you will take from the reading—what information you will learn.

Successful comprehension of exposition requires skills and schemata not demanded for story reading, offering a special challenge to both teacher and student. Here we describe two procedures that are particularly useful for helping students comprehend expository material—the K-W-L procedure and reading or study guides.

K-W-L

K-W-L stands for what you <u>K</u>now, what you <u>W</u>ant to know, and what you <u>L</u>earned. The K-W-L procedure, developed by Donna Ogle (1986), is a three-part process designed to motivate and guide readers in acquiring information from expository texts; it is perhaps the best-known and most frequently used procedure for delving into expository texts. In the Classroom 10.6 illustrates how this procedure is put into practice in a California classroom with a group of fourth-graders who are reading the trade book *Earthquakes* by Seymour Simon.

Reading Guides

Reading guides are "teacher-developed devices for helping students understand instructional reading material" (Wood, Lapp, & Flood, 1992). Although reading guides, also called study guides, are sometimes useful in working with narratives, they are most often designed to help students understand and learn from expository material. These guides consist of questions and activities related to the specific texts students are reading and their purposes for reading them. Students respond to the questions or engage in the activities as they read the text. Reading guides provide a learning scaffold for students, while at the same time giving them control over their learning.

Using the K-W-L procedure with students can help motivate and guide their reading of non-fiction texts.

Stephen Shepherd/Getty Images

10.6

Using K-W-L

After motivating students by relating the topic to their lives, fourth-grade teacher David Scott writes the title *Earthquakes* on the chalkboard. Underneath that title and to the left, he writes the heading *What Do You Know?* He then asks students to tell what they know about earthquakes and jots down their responses under the heading, as shown here.

Not all of the students' responses are accurate, despite Mr. Scott's questions during the brainstorming session to help them consider the correctness of their statements, such as "How did you learn that?" or "How could you prove that?" Later, during the postreading discussion, he and his students will clear up the remaining misconceptions. After Mr. Scott's students give a variety of responses, he shows them the cover illustration of *Earthquakes* and asks them to think about the kinds of information that might be included in the book. He then writes their suggestions underneath their initial responses.

Next, Mr. Scott reminds his students that informational books such as *Earthquakes* are written to provide knowledge that we might need or want. He then asks students to think about what they would like to know about earthquakes—things they don't already know or aren't quite sure of. He records these responses in the middle column—*What Do You Want to Know?* Mr. Scott has his own questions prepared in case students do not zero in on the important purposes for reading the book. He will add his questions to the students' questions.

On the chalkboard to the right of the previous two headings, Mr. Scott writes *What Did You Learn?* He explains to students that this is the last part of the K-W-L procedure. He says, "You have already completed the first two steps—thinking about and writing down what you know about earthquakes and what you would like to know. The last step is to record what information you do learn as you read."

At this point, Mr. Scott gives students their own K-W-L charts and tells them, "In the first column, record what you *know* about earthquakes; in the second column, what you *want* to know. Then, as you read, write what you *learned* in the third column." He also reminds students that not all of their questions will be answered in the text. Later, they will talk about where they might find answers to those questions.

The K-W-L procedure is very useful for dealing with informational material, both in hard copy and websites (Pritchard & Cartwright, 2004). The three phases of the procedure—brainstorming, establishing purposes through questioning, and finding answers to those questions—virtually guarantee that students will be actively involved in their learning. The procedure itself provides a scaffold to support students' own interests and inquiries.

EARTHQUAKES

What Do You Know?	What Do You Want to Know?	What Did You Learn?
Can cause damage	What causes earthquakes	
Are unpredictable	How earthquakes are measured	
Are scary	What places have earthquakes	
Happen in California	What was the worst earthquake	
Not all are the same	When most earthquakes happen	
Shake the earth	What we can do about earthquakes	
Don't happen at night		
Are getting worse		

Categories of information that might be included:

How earthquakes happen · When they happen · What we can do about them · How much damage they do · Why they happen · Descriptions of some of the worst earthquakes

K-W-L

Source: Heimlich, Joan E., & Pittelman, Susan D. (1986). *Semantic Mapping: Classroom Applications.* Copyright © 1986 by the International Reading Association (www.reading.org). Reproduced with permission of the International Reading Association via Copyright Clearance Center.

Figure 10.8 Time Line for *A Dream of Freedom: The Civil Rights Movement from 1954 to 1968* by Diane McWhorter

Date	Important event or events	Why was this event important?
1954		
1955		
1957		
1960		
1961		
1962		
1963		
1964		
1965		
1966		
1968		

As Karen Wood and John Mateja (1983) have noted, a reading guide serves as a "tutor in print form." One such tutor in print form is a time line such as Figure 10.8. Time lines can serve as valuable reading guides for texts that deal with events occurring over a specific period of time, such as Diane McWhorter's *A Dream of Freedom: The Civil Rights Movement from 1954 to 1968*. A time line can list dates and then ask students to name the significant event for each date and explain the reason or reasons for the event's significance. Completing such a guide as they read helps students both in developing a schema for the historic events in order of occurrence as well as in practicing their critical thinking skills.

This, of course, is only one of many types of reading guides. One teacher we know provides students with questions that encourage them to make connections between themselves and the text, similar to the Reflect and Apply questions you find throughout this text. Another teacher frequently distributes a handout that lists the main headings of the selection students are reading and provides space for their notes following each heading. Wood and her colleagues (1992) describe many other types of reading guides.

Procedures Appropriate for All Types of Text

We want to again note that the primary purpose for engaging students in any of the procedures we describe is to enhance their reading enjoyment, to foster understanding and learning, and to increase their competence and confidence in making meaning with texts. Some procedures are appropriate for any type of text, if adapted to reflect the specific selection, readers, and purposes involved. Here we present a few of them; we believe the discussion web and semantic webbing and weaving activities meet the criteria for engaging students with the text while developing their literacy.

Discussion Web

The discussion web (Alvermann, 1991) uses a graphic aid to help students look at both sides of an issue raised in a text before they draw conclusions. Using this graphic aid as a guide, students meet in pairs and then in groups of four to reach consensus about the issue. They complete a discussion web that shows positive factors and ideas in the *Yes* column, with contradictory factors and ideas in the *No* column.

The discussion web can be used any time students read material that raises a question that might evoke dissenting viewpoints. For example, in *Soul Moon Soup* by Lindsay Lee Johnson, Phoebe Rose decides to leave her first "real" home with her grandmother and go back to the city to live with her mother. Students might use the discussion web to decide the answer to this question: Should Phoebe Rose have left her grandmother and friend Ruby to make a new start with her mother in the city? The discussion web can be used to present both sides of the discussion and then students can reach a conclusion. Suppose students have read a selection on the Civil War that discusses Stephen A. Douglas, Abraham Lincoln, and their opposing views on slavery. As a postreading activity, you might substitute the names *Douglas* and *Lincoln* for the *Yes* and *No* columns of the discussion web, write *Slavery* in the box where the question usually goes, and then initiate a student discussion of the two men's differing views on the issue.

Semantic Webbing and Weaving

Semantic webbing and weaving are procedures that students can use on their own or with your help to organize ideas and graphically show their interrelatedness. Semantic webbing, or semantic mapping, has been described as a vocabulary technique. Its name comes from its use of a graphic organizer that looks like a spider web. The web connects a central topic to a variety of related ideas and events, as shown in the web on sea otters in Figure 10.9 (Heimlich & Pittelman, 1986).

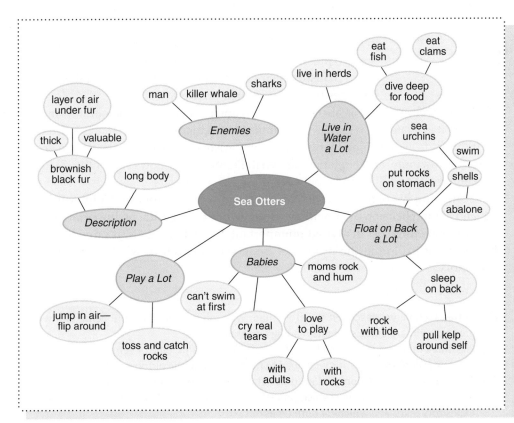

Figure 10.9

Sample Semantic Web on Sea Otters

Source: Heimlich, Joan E., & Pittelman, Susan D. (1986). *Semantic Mapping: Classroom Applications.* Copyright © 1986 by the International Reading Association (www.reading.org). Reproduced with permission of the International Reading Association via Copyright Clearance Center.

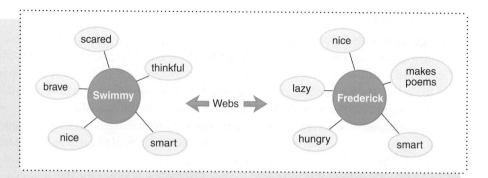

Figure 10.10

Sample Semantic Webs Comparing the Characters Swimmy and Frederick

Figure 10.11

Sample Weave Comparing Swimmy and Frederick

	Swimmy	Frederick
scared	yes	no
brave	yes	sort of
nice	yes	yes
smart	yes	yes
thinkful	yes	sort of
lazy	never	sometimes
hungry	no	yes
poet	no	yes

Source: Calfee, R. C., & Patrick, C. L. (1995). *Teach Our Children Well.* Stanford: Stanford Alumni Association.

myeducationlab

Learn how to deliberately teach readers to use comprehension strategies and skills over a period of time by completing the activity "Scaffolding Reading Comprehension." (To find this activity, go to the topic *Comprehension* in MyEducationLab and click on Building Teaching Skills and Dispositions.)

Webbing can be used with students of any age before reading to develop and connect a key concept in the selection to their prior knowledge. The thought processes involved in organizing concepts by making connections between them prepare the reader to make similar connections when meeting the ideas in the text. This web, or visual display, illustrates graphically the interconnectedness of ideas that are centrally important to the text.

This webbing activity can be used before, during, and after reading. The students and the teacher might brainstorm a primitive web before they read, copy it down, and then add to it as they read. The items in bold on the sea otter web were organized before the students read. The students added more information as they read about the sea otter. Webbing can be done as a teacher-led postreading activity as well. For example, after reading the stories *Swimmy* and *Frederick the Mouse,* both by Leo Lionni, a second-grade teacher used semantic webs as in Figure 10.10 to do a character study of the main characters in the two picture books (Calfee & Patrick, 1995). Students can be asked to justify their choices and note the page numbers of the passages that support their answers.

Like a web, a weave is also a graphic organizer, a visual display of information and how it is related. A weave is very similar to a semantic feature analysis (Chapter 9). It differs from a web by highlighting comparisons. Notice how the weave on the characters Swimmy and Frederick, shown in Figure 10.11, allows students to focus on the similarities and differences between these two characters.

Using graphic organizers such as webs and weaves supports high-level thinking and comprehension by providing a framework for focusing on important points, rather than getting lost in myriad unimportant, unrelated details. It provides a public forum for exploring the process of understanding a text, whether narrative or expository.

REFLECT and *Apply*

10. In this section, we described the story map. Why might this procedure be helpful with a group of primary-grade students reading a folktale?
11. Pick three different expository texts. Can you use the same type of semantic web for each text? Why does the semantic web need to fit the text and the purpose of the activity?
12. Skim through this section, and jot down the various procedures that are described. Draw a semantic web that shows which procedures are recommended for narratives, which for expository texts, and which for both types of text.

Strengths and Challenges of Diversity

We hope by now we have made the point that successful reading experiences are created by taking into account the varying needs and talents of the individual readers in your classroom. In this section, we give some suggestions for further addressing the needs of your students with diverse strengths and needs.

Virtually all of the activities described in the chapter will scaffold students' reading, and thus all are appropriate for readers who might experience difficulties. Here we highlight some that are particularly appropriate for readers who are challenged and note also a few additional techniques to use with these students.

- Have students who listen to a selection on tape tell about the selection in their own words. Type up their recollections in a booklet for them to read independently. This is particularly useful for English language learners who do not yet automatically recognize common words. It is also an opportunity for more accomplished students to pitch in and do some of the typing.
- Have students read the material with a partner who is a more accomplished reader—a classmate, an aide, an older student, or a classroom volunteer parent or grandparent. The reading "buddies" can take turns reading from the text or read the text in unison.
- Encourage students to read books at their reading level or below. Frequent reading of this kind of material will improve automaticity and confidence.
- For upper-elementary or middle school students who read several grades below their grade level, consider using high-interest easy-reading books, books specifically written for students reading below grade level. One of the authors and a colleague (Graves & Philippot, 2001) have described this genre.

- Show by your attitude and actions your total confidence that students can successfully read a selection and that you will support them in their efforts.

Your classroom will also have its share of competent readers who read above grade level. You will want to provide for their needs, challenging and inspiring them to go further in their thinking. Here are a few suggestions:

- Have additional reading material available that relates to the selection being read. For example, if the class is reading *Lincoln: A Photobiography* by Russell Freedman, make available other biographies of Lincoln or other biographies by Freedman.
- Let students select their own additional reading materials related to a selection's theme, genre, or author.
- Invite students to engage in long-term, in-depth projects that relate to the material being read. For example, upper-grade students could research and read periodical and Internet literature dealing with the topics in their science text. This would provide them (and the rest of the class) with information more current than that provided in the text.

As we have cautioned many times, all students, regardless of their particular needs or talents, need to explore ideas and express themselves in a variety of ways—through writing, speaking, and artistic and dramatic endeavors. We need to take care to be inclusive, not exclusive, in providing a wide variety of opportunities for students. Sometimes students who struggle with the basics or lack traditional literacy skills have been left out of enrichment activities and the growth that they can provide. We believe that all students deserve and will benefit from a range of activities and should explore as many as possible. In this way, they will make connections between what they know and what they discover in texts and will apply that new knowledge to make their lives more enjoyable, productive, and meaningful.

Concluding Remarks

This chapter has focused on teacher-led approaches and procedures that foster students' comprehension and enjoyment of the texts they read in the classroom, highlighting the possibility of offering a wide range of approaches and customizing activities in order to accommodate individual differences. The four frameworks—directed reading activity (DRA), directed reading-thinking activity (DR-TA), the scaffolded reading experience (SRE), and guided reading—provide ways to ensure that students are successful with the texts they read and to nurture their competence and confidence as readers. And the time-tested procedures that we discussed in the latter half of this chapter—such as K-W-L, story maps, discussion webs, and semantic webbing and weaving—provide additional strategies for engaging students with the narratives and exposition they read, thereby increasing their comprehension and enjoyment of those texts.

Extending *Learning*

1. Visit an elementary school classroom, and take notes on the kinds of supports the teacher provides for students as they read a selection. Using the same selection for the same group of students, design your own plan for helping them understand and enjoy the selection. Try out your lesson on your target students, or share it with your classmates.

2. From the children's section of your library, select an expository text that you think would interest students at the age level you would like to teach. Create a scaffolded reading experience especially for those students and that text. Give your plan to a classmate to get his or her feedback. We recommend the following four books to help you select appropriate titles: *From Biography to History,* edited by Catherine Barr (1998); *Kaleidoscope: A Multicultural Booklist for Grades K–8* (4th ed.), edited by Nancy Hansen-Krening, Elaine M. Aoki, and Donald T. Mizokawa (2003); *Books Kids Will Sit Still For: 3,* by Judy Freeman (2006); and *Adventuring with Books: A Booklist for Pre-K–Grade 6* (13th ed.), edited by Amy A. McClure and Janice V. Kristo (2002).

Children's *Literature*

Ajmera, M. (2005). *To Be an Artist.* Watertown, MA: Charlesbridge. Photos and text reveal how children around the world express themselves creatively through various art forms. Unnumbered.

Brown, M. (1998). *Arthur's Mystery Envelope.* Boston: Little, Brown. Arthur thinks he's in trouble when the principal asks him to take home a large envelope marked CONFIDENTIAL. Audio CD available. 58 pages.

Compestine, Y. C. (2001). *The Runaway Rice Cake.* New York: Simon & Schuster. The Chang family learns about the power of sharing during this Chinese New Year celebration. 32 pages.

DiCamillo, K. (2000). *Because of Winn-Dixie.* Cambridge, MA: Candlewick Press. This is a poignant and well-told story of a young girl who must build a new life after her mother leaves and she and her father move to Florida—with, of course, a little help from her dog, Winn-Dixie. 182 pages.

Duncan, A. F. (1995). *Willie Jerome.* New York: Macmillan. No one but Willie's sister appreciates his jazz trumpet playing until she finally gets their Mama to really listen to Willie play and let the music speak to her. Unnumbered.

Freedman, R. (1987). *Lincoln: A Photobiography.* New York: Clarion. In photographs and text, this Newbery Medal–winning book traces the life of the Civil War president. 150 pages.

Fritz, J. (1987). *Shh! We're Writing the Constitution.* New York: Scholastic. The author gives a humorous behind-the-scenes account of how the Constitution came to be written and ratified. 64 pages.

Graves, B. (1996). *The Best Worst Day.* New York: Hyperion. In this chapter book, second-grader Lucy struggles to prove herself "best" in order to win the friendship of Maya, the new girl in class. 64 pages.

Hallworth, G. (1996). *Down by the River.* New York: Scholastic Cartwheel. This is a collection of Afro-Caribbean rhymes, games, and songs. 32 pages.

Houston, J. (1977). *Frozen Fire: A Tale of Courage.* New York: Atheneum. Determined to find his father, who has been lost in a storm, a young boy and his Eskimo friend brave windstorms, starvation, and wild animals on their trek through the Canadian Arctic. 149 pages.

Johnson, L. L. (2002). *Soul Moon Soup.* Ashville, NC: Front Street. Written in free verse, this poetic chapter book tells the story of the homeless Phoebe Rose, who, after being banished by her mother to live in the country with her grandmother, learns family secrets and hopes for her mother's return. 134 pages.

Lewin, T. (1990). *Tiger Trek.* New York: Macmillan. Informative narrative tells of the preying habits of the Indian tiger and the numerous animals that live on a hunting preserve in central India. Unnumbered.

Lionni, L. (1984). *Swimmy*. New York: Pantheon Books. Through teamwork and cooperation, Swimmy the fish and his friends triumph over the "big" fish. Videocassette available. 32 pages.

Lionni, L. (1985). *Frederick*. New York: Pantheon Books. Frederick, an apparently lazy mouse, has a special surprise for the mice who thought he should have been storing up supplies for the winter. 32 pages.

Lobel, A. (1970). *Frog and Toad Are Friends*. New York: Harper & Row. The five stories are about the friendship of Frog and Toad and their adventures in the woods. 64 pages.

Lobel, A. (1979). *Days with Frog and Toad*. New York: Harper & Row. This classic beginning chapter book with five humorous stories stars best friends Frog and Toad and dramatizes universal truths about life and friendship. 64 pages.

Lowry, L. (1989). *Number the Stars*. Boston: Houghton Mifflin. In 1943 during the German occupation of Denmark, 10-year-old Annemarie learns about courage when her family shelters a Jewish family from the Nazis. 137 pages.

McPhail, D. (1972). *The Bear's Toothache*. Boston: Little, Brown and Co. The story of a little boy's attempt to help a bear in distress. The perfect book for introducing the concept of narrative structure to young children. 20 pages.

McWhorter, D. (2004). *A Dream of Freedom: The Civil Rights Movement from 1954 to 1968*. New York: Scholastic. In this history of the modern Civil Rights movement, the author focuses on the monumental events that occurred between 1954 (the year of *Brown v. the Board of Education*) and 1968 (the year that Dr. Martin Luther King, Jr., was assassinated). 160 pages.

Paterson, K. (1978). *The Great Gilly Hopkins*. New York: Crowell. This novel portrays feisty 11-year-old Gilly, a foster child who, in her longing to be reunited with her birth mother, schemes against all who try to befriend her. Spanish text available. 152 pages.

Prelutsky, J. (1988). *Tyrannosaurus Was a Beast: Dinosaur Poems*. New York: Greenwillow. Poems celebrate 14 dinosaurs in rollicking rhyme and illustration. 32 pages.

Simon, S. (1991). *Earthquakes*. New York: Morrow. This text, illustrated with colorful photos, describes how and where earthquakes occur, how they can be predicted, and the damage they cause. Unnumbered.

Van Allsburg, C. (1990). *Just a Dream*. Boston: Houghton Mifflin. A young boy has a dream about the environment that causes him to wake up to his indifference. Unnumbered.

PEARSON myeducationlab

Now go to the topic "Comprehension" in the MyEducationLab (www.myeducationlab.com) for your course, where you can:

- Find learning outcomes for the topics covered in this chapter along with the IRA standards that connect to these outcomes.

- Complete assignable activities in the Assignments and Activities section that show concepts in action to help you synthesize and apply strategies.

- Explore IRIS Center Resources—training enhancement materials that provide you with research-validated information and interactive materials to develop your skills in working with students.

- Apply and practice your understanding of the teaching skills identified in the chapter with the Building Teaching Skills and Dispositions exercises.

A Day in the Life of Dolores Puente and Her Third- and Fourth-Grade Students

Dolores Puente has been teaching for 8 years at Lincoln Elementary School, a K–6 school in a suburb of Los Angeles. Lincoln's students are primarily from middle- to lower-income families. About half of the students in Ms. Puente's combination third/fourth grade are of European American descent; the other half are of Hispanic, Asian, and African American descent. When we asked how she would describe her reading program, Ms. Puente thought for a moment. "You know, based on workshops the district has had on the Report of the National Reading Panel and the impact of No Child Left Behind, I've changed it somewhat in the past several years. I'm more conscious of ensuring that all of my students learn crucial skills and strategies than I once was. So far our school has always made Annual Yearly Progress (AYP) but with decreased funding that may not always be the case."

She continues, "I still plan to do a lot with literature—I always have, and I plan to continue. I have an overall plan for teaching the literacy skills that appear in our curriculum, and I make a big effort to teach certain skills when my students find they need them in order to reach a particular goal. For example, if they are involved in projects that involve library research, I'll create lessons to help them with note taking and summarizing. But I can tell you this, no matter what we're involved in—social studies, science, mathematics, or art—reading and writing instruction is an integral part of our day, beginning with the morning meeting and continuing to the afternoon wrap-up."

Dolores Puente realizes that teaching reading and writing cannot and should not be limited to one specified time slot in the day. Although Ms. Puente does set aside a specific amount of time each day for what she officially designates as reading—a time in which students are actively engaged in reading activities aimed directly at improving reading skills, strategies, and behaviors—this is only part of literacy learning in her classroom. Because she and her students use language throughout the school day, there are literacy opportunities from the moment students step into the classroom to the moment they leave.

Let's join Ms. Puente for a day with her third- and fourth-graders. The day is Monday, January 11. She has the following schedule posted on the wall.

Thinkstock

8:30	Unpack, silent reading, journal writing	12:25	Read-aloud time
8:45	Morning meeting, news reports	12:40	Mathematics
9:00	Reading and language arts	1:35	Specials: art, music, physical education, library
11:00	Recess	2:20	Science or social studies
11:15	Intervention/enrichment	3:05	Wrap-up
11:50	Lunch	3:15	Dismissal

Much thought and planning occurred well before this day arrived. The idea for building activities around the central concept of courage had sprouted many months earlier. In fact, she had written it on her yearly planner back in August. Shortly after the winter holiday, Ms. Puente formulated a general goal for her literacy activities:

> To learn more about the concept of courage as displayed in the lives of people past and present from a variety of cultures as it is expressed in literature, art, history, science, and in our local community, school, and families.

After formulating a general goal, she started to do some brainstorming as the second step in planning the unit's activities. She thought about her curriculum and how she could incorporate literacy activities and the theme of courage in a variety of subject areas, taking into account the curriculum standards for the state of California. Here is what she jotted down in her brainstorming:

Reading, Language Arts

Read and write biographies. Biography as a literary form or genre. Discuss various genres. Present opportunities for listening and viewing, also tapes and films, possible guest speakers. Readers theater and dramatics? Graphic displays to chart what parts of the world courageous people have come from. Work on strategies of summarizing and determining what is important. Figurative language—simile and metaphor.

Social Studies

We need to study early California history, both pre-Columbian times and the influence of the Spanish. Our study of biography will help us study explorers like Captain Cook, Juan Cabrillo, and Junipero Serra; early settlers like John Sutter, Mariano Vallejo; women like Biddy Mason who influenced the lives of African Americans; and Cesar Chavez, who worked to improve the lives of migrant workers. All of these people displayed courage in a variety of ways.

Science

We will be reading about the plant and animal kingdoms. Think about where courage might come in here. Animals? (Food for thought!) Link the study of plant life and habitat to the landforms found in California—mountains, desert, and rainforest. This ties to our social studies unit. Present some biographies of courageous scientists, particularly those representing diverse cultures. George Washington Carver. Work on strategies for gleaning information from informational books.

Art

Talk to Julie, the art teacher. She has her students work to learn and emulate the style of famous artists. Have her suggest some biographies the students could read about courageous artists. Create a classroom mural about our most courageous heroes. Are artists courageous heroes? What about the Hopi potter Al Qoyawayma, who switched from being a successful engineer to pursue his culture's ancient art, or Maya Lin, who designed the Vietnam War Memorial. Does it take courage to pursue your artistic dreams?

After her initial brainstorming, Ms. Puente plotted her ideas on her monthly calendars, outlining her general plans for the weeks to come. Once she had her general plans outlined, she then focused on the individual weeks and days, making more detailed plans, finding books, looking at websites for video and other research information, and lining up field trips and guest speakers. Her overall plan is shown in Figure 1.

	WEEK 1	WEEK 2
Morning Meeting	Intro concept of courage, courage unit, news reports on courage	Review goals and projects for the week, discuss courage, news reports
Reading and Language Arts	Review skimming	Practice determining importance with biographies
	Begin lessons on determining importance strategy	Discuss vocabulary work, dictionary skills
	Discuss biographies (culturally diverse)	Meet with groups to refine use of determining importance strategy
	Silent and oral reading—small-group instruction & individual reading	Response journals
	Response journals	
Intervention / Enrichment	Enrichment—introduce literature circles—historical fiction	Enrichment—continue literature circles—historical fiction
Reading Aloud	Biddy Mason biography	Biddy Mason biography
Mathematics	Simple fractions and decimals	Continue work on simple fractions and decimals
	Reading strategies for word problems	Reading strategies for word problems
Science & Social Studies	Social Studies	Social Studies
	Reading about early California explorations—apply determining importance strategy	Make time lines for people in biographies
Wrap-Up	Concerns and highlights of the day	Concerns and highlights of the day

Figure 1 Four-Week Plan for a Unit on Courage

She had more ideas than it would be possible for her to implement. However, the activities that best fit her students and their mutual goals will come into focus as the days progress and her plan becomes more precise and detailed. Also, the ongoing needs and interests of her students will influence her choices of which activities to implement—plans for Tuesday will need to be altered to reflect what occurred on Monday. Ms. Puente's plans are guidelines that she knows will be shaped and reshaped day by day, minute by minute.

Ms. Puente does not integrate all her curricula. The concepts and skills that underlie mathematical reasoning may be undermined by trying too hard to fit them into the reading and language arts curriculum. When her students are at specials—art, music, physical education, and the library—she has a planning period when she can meet with her colleagues. A change this year is the addition of an intervention/enrichment period. This is part of the school's Response to Intervention (RTI) initiative. During this 30-minute period some students leave the room for extra help in reading, mathematics, and speech. The rest remain with Ms. Puente, who extends her reading/language arts instruction.

Let's return now to January 11 and see how Ms. Puente incorporates reading activities into every aspect of her students' day.

WEEK 3	WEEK 4
Review projects for the week, discuss courage, reports on courage by presidents	Review projects for the week, discuss courage, reports on courage by presidents
Finish reading biographies	Students continue to write rough drafts of biographies
Motivate, explain, and model biography writing using think sheet	Critique groups; revise biographies
Writing strategy (writing creative leads)	Individual writing conferences
Students do prewriting for biographies	Students begin to share biographies with the class
Guest speaker whom students interview	
Enrichment—plan mural for early California leaders	Enrichment—use time to finish other projects
Cesar Chavez biography	Cesar Chavez biography
Solve problems with numeric equations	Solve problems with numeric equations
Write and edit own word problems	Bio of Albert Einstein
Social Studies	Social Studies
Reading about early settlers in California—note taking and summarizing	Make time lines for early Californian settlers
Concerns and highlights of the day	Concerns and highlights of the day

8:30 Unpack, Silent Reading, Journal Writing

As students arrive, they take out their journals and write their entry for the day. Students who did their writing at home take out a book and read. Ms. Puente greets every student and chats about what he or she is reading and what they found to write about. Since Ms. Puente believes in modeling the behavior she expects of her students, today she writes in her journal as well. Here is her entry for January 11:

> Today we begin our unit on courage. I've been excited about this unit ever since I wrote the idea on my school calendar back in August. And I'm even more excited now because of the successful unit we had in the fall that revolved around the concept of thankfulness. What I had written on the yearly calendar was "courage"— the unifying theme for January–February. Courage to my way of thinking is a concept worth spending some time on, and January–February seems the perfect time to do it—because Martin Luther King Jr.'s birthday is in January, and February is both Black history month and a month to remember and honor presidents. I'm looking forward to seeing how the kids respond to this idea and what we will learn together.

As you can see from Ms. Puente's journal entry and from our discussion of her planning, she has done a lot of preparation.

After students finish their journal responses, they begin silent reading. Ms. Puente joins them in silent reading. This morning, she is reading an article from *The Reading Teacher.*

8:45 Morning Meeting

The morning meeting is a time to talk about daily concerns and to read and discuss the schedule for the day. Today, before the schedule is even discussed, Ms. Puente puts the outline for a courage map in a chart on the SmartBoard and asks students to brainstorm examples of three related concepts—courageous people, courageous deeds, and other words for *courage.* She organizes these as a semantic map. The SmartBoard images can be preserved and expanded as the books and topics in the unit are discussed.

After students have given their responses, Ms. Puente explains that they will be focusing on the concept of courage for the next several weeks, thinking about how courage relates to many things they learn about and do, in school and out. In previous weeks, Ms. Puente's class has been working on giving news reports, which involve answering these questions: Who? What? When? Where? Why? How? Today Ms. Puente would focus students' attention on a larger theme. She begins by saying

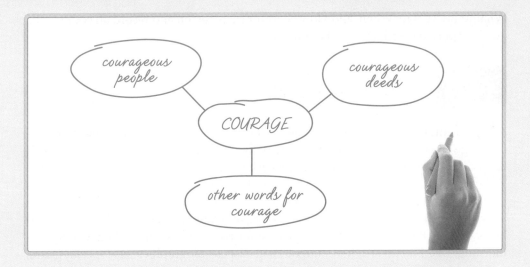

she is going to read a newspaper article that she thinks illustrates the concept of courage and asks students to listen to see whether they agree with her. The article focuses on a single mother of five who is getting her college degree. After reading the article, Ms. Puente tells students why *she* thinks the woman shows courage and then encourages students to give their opinions.

Next, Ms. Puente displays the news report chart and shows students how she would complete it, sharing with them her thought processes as she does so.

News Report Chart

What is the report about? A woman getting her college degree.

Who is the report about? Janet Crow, single mother of five.

Where did the event take place? State University, Middletown, U.S.A.

When did the event take place? December 23.

How does this event show courage? I think it takes courage to go back to school when you're older because there may not be many people your age at school and it's probably been a long time since you've had to study and take tests. Also, Janet had to give up some things for herself and her kids. She was taking a chance that getting a college education would allow her to get a better job so her kids might have more opportunities. I think that takes courage.

Ms. Puente explains to students that their news reports for the next several weeks are to focus on courage. They can select articles from newspapers or magazines to read to the class, or they can write up a short report from TV or radio news. They can also report courageous events that take place in school or at home. As a class, they will do two things to help remember the people and events students report—complete a

What, Who, Where, When, and How chart for each person and record all courageous events reported on a large sheet of butcher paper.

After the morning meeting and news reports, Ms. Puente begins the reading/ language arts block of activities, which usually runs from 9:00 to 11:00 and ends with recess, but sometimes she pushes recess earlier when the students are getting antsy. Today, though, Ms. Puente is not following her usual time schedule. The activities for the morning meeting and news reports demanded extra time. Also, because the activities Ms. Puente has planned for reading and language arts require a sustained block of time, the students will have to wait for recess. For their reading activity this morning, Ms. Puente and her students will discuss biographies as a special genre, review skimming as a reading strategy for selecting a biography to read in depth, and read silently for 15 minutes. Beginning tomorrow, Ms. Puente will also work with a selected group of students who need help with various skills, especially the skill of determining importance. Language arts endeavors revolve around journal writing, with the students eventually selecting a historical figure to study and write about. The biography project provides tools students can use to read and study biographies of famous Californians during social studies.

To motivate her students, Ms. Puente has spent some time selecting biographies (with the help of librarians and media specialists as well as several bibliographies) that reflect her students' linguistic and cultural backgrounds, interests, and abilities while also meeting the social studies standards for California. Her selection of biographies also reflects her goal to expose students to individuals of many different cultures.

On the chalkboard ledge and table, she has displayed numerous biographies of culturally diverse individuals. These range from picture books to lengthy chapter books.

Ms. Puente begins by telling students that all the books on display have one thing in common—each of them focuses on the life and deeds of a single individual and many are individuals important in the early history of our state. After that, she has students think about and discuss why a book might have been written about these people and writes students' suggestions on the board.

Next, she reads a paragraph or two from several preselected biographies that she knows will pique her students' interests. After reading, she reminds students that these books are called biographies—written accounts of a person's life. She writes *biography* on the board and talks about how biographies differ from other types of books. She asks students to tell about biographies they have read, note if they liked them, and explain why.

Ms. Puente explains that during the next 4 weeks students will be reading and writing biographies and will get to choose which biographies they want to read and whom they want to write a biography about. She discusses with them what they might expect to gain from biographies, why biographies are interesting and informative, and how the ideas revealed in biographies might be useful in their own lives. To help students decide which biography they want to read, Ms. Puente suggests that a good strategy to use is skimming. She models the strategy with several of the biographies—reading the title and the table of contents, scanning the chapters from beginning to end, commenting on illustrations and photographs, and maybe reading a few passages aloud. Then she models her thinking in trying to decide whether *Bridget "Biddy" Mason: From Slaver to Businesswoman* by Jean K. Williams is the biography she wants to read:

> Hmm. This might be an interesting book. I like reading about heroic women. But I see that Biddy lived in the 19th century and began her life as a slave and then influenced the early development of Los Angeles. Also, it's kind of long and has a lot of words I don't know. I like learning new words, but it may take me too long to read if I have to stop and look up a lot of words in the dictionary, and I wouldn't want to skip too many words. I think this is a book Tara would like—and I'm going to recommend it to her—but I think I'll see what some of the other books are like.

Ms. Puente then models skimming and considers a few more books before letting students choose their own books to skim. Finally, she tells students to skim at least three books and then choose one of those to read. She gives them 20 minutes to skim and get started on their reading.

At this point Ms. Puente introduces the graphic organizer for biography. The students will be using this when she reads to them, when they read their own biographies, and later in the unit when they compose a biography. The graphic organizer is designed so that students can capture the important events in a life and at the same time grapple with the significance of those events. As Ms. Puente reads the biography of Biddy Mason the students will record the major events of her life and then discuss why these events were important. Next week, when students compose their biographies, they will use the same document to plan their writing.

Examining a Biography

The famous person is _____

What were his or her major accomplishments?	

	What were the important events in this person's life?	Why were these events so important?
Childhood		
Education		
Adulthood		
Death		

What can we learn from this person's life?	

Writing personal responses in journals requires that students think about the ideas in a text and express their ideas in writing.

Shutterstock

The next activity, writing in and sharing response journals—which Ms. Puente has labeled in her plans under the subject language arts—is a continuation of the previous reading activity and one the students are familiar with, having kept reading journals of various sorts since the beginning of the school year. It is also an activity students will be involved in daily until they finish reading their selected biographies. Ms. Puente's students have made dual entries in their journals before, but because they will be doing something slightly different in these journals, she spends a little time motivating, explaining, and modeling the procedure.

"You know," Ms. Puente tells her students, "when I was reading through biographies to bring to class, I kept reading things that made me stop and think, 'Wow, that's neat,' or 'I know how she feels. I felt that way myself.' Things like that. I'll show you what I mean."

After that, Ms. Puente reads a sentence or two from a biography about mathematician and computer genius An Wang to illustrate her point, and then writes the following on the board:

RESPONSE JOURNAL

Idea from Biography

Page 8. Wang's new word processor made it easy to see your words and to correct your mistakes

My Response

Thank you, Wang!

As Ms. Puente explains to her students, "When I read that Wang had invented the word processor, it really hit me how this man had made my job so much easier and more enjoyable. I really feel grateful to him."

Ms. Puente proceeds to describe several other types of responses she had—questions brought to mind, ideas that prompted her to make connections with her own experiences, strong feelings she had in response to certain events or ideas—and writes these on the board. After sufficient explanation and modeling, Ms. Puente tells students she wants them to use their journals similarly while reading in their biographies—to write, for example, a quotation, idea, or word on the left side of the journal page and their response to it on the right side. This kind of activity encourages the generative learning we discuss in Chapter 10.

Next, Ms. Puente distributes the journals, but before students begin reading and writing in them, she makes certain that they are clear on the purpose and procedure for this activity. She assigns reading buddies to students who might need extra help with reading and writing. Buddies go to special locations designated to be conference areas—places where students are free to interact with each other without disturbing other students.

While students are reading silently and writing in their journals, Ms. Puente is reading a biography and writing in her journal. Her classroom aide (who is available every day from 10:30 to 12:00) circulates among students to offer advice and encourage students to keep on task. Before students leave for lunch each day at 11:50, Ms. Puente asks if any of them have something they would like to share from their journals. If so, a few students read from their journals; if not, Ms. Puente shares something from hers.

Intervention/Enrichment

Ms. Puente has four students who leave the class for extra help in reading and one who is seen by the speech therapist. These intervention lessons are scheduled so they do not disrupt learning for these students. While these students are gone, Ms. Puente has decided to start a literature circle project with the rest of the class. Today she will be introducing literature circles and modeling the various roles that the students will take during the discussion. She hopes that as the four students with reading difficulties catch up they can join the literature circle process. Although she recognizes that these students need extra help, she regrets what they will be missing in her classroom.

Teachers can make a number of books avvailable and invite students to skim these to select one to read in depth.

Digital Vision/Getty Images

Read-Aloud Time

This routine fosters quiet and rest after an active play period. It also provides students with an opportunity to hear good literature skillfully read. Today, Ms. Puente begins reading aloud from *Bridget "Biddy" Mason: From Slaver to Businesswoman* by Jean K. Williams. To preserve the atmosphere of calm that prevails at this time of day, she begins reading with only a brief introduction in which she talks about courage and how students will see many examples of courage as they listen to the biography. Before she begins reading the first chapter, she encourages them to think about and remember one example of Mason's courage that is illustrated in the chapter.

12:40 Mathematics

Before students begin independent work and small-group instruction on a specific math skill, Ms. Puente conducts a 15-minute whole-class lesson on two topics: reviewing how to solve story problems and presenting the new "mystery" math word for the week. At the beginning of the lesson, Ms. Puente writes this problem on the board: The gym floor is 100 × 50 feet. How far did Matt run if he ran 10 lengths of the gym?

"Does this problem sound familiar?" she asks her students.

The students are well aware of what Ms. Puente is talking about. The week before, they had been keeping track of how many times they ran across the gym but didn't calculate how *far* they had run. Ms. Puente refers her class to the questions for solving word problems shown in their math book.

Questions to Ask When Solving Story Problems

What situation is described?

Can I describe the situation with a drawing, diagram, or mathematical sentence?

What am I trying to find out?

Do I need to combine, separate, or compare?

Are all the data given necessary?

Are the data complete?

Do I know what to do to determine the answer?

How will I know if the answer I get is reasonable?

Together they come up with this equation: 100' × 10 = 1,000'.

Ms. Puente challenges students with these questions: "Did Matt run more than a mile or less than a mile? How much more than a mile or less than a mile? Try and find out, and we'll discuss the answers tomorrow."

Before they begin their independent and small-group sessions, Ms. Puente shows students the first clue for the "mystery" math word for the week. The clue is *A* × *B* = *C*. Students are not to say the word out loud but to put their written guesses with their name and the date on them in the mystery word box. Each day, Ms. Puente reports how many have correctly guessed the word and gives a new clue. At the end of the week, she reveals the mystery word, and if 90 percent of the class has guessed it, the class gets a special reward. The mystery word this week is *product*.

 Specials: Art, Music, Physical Education, Library

As her students march off to art, Ms. Puente uses the 45-minute planning time to organize ideas and materials for the next day. Once or twice a week she meets with her colleagues who teach third and fourth grade to coordinate math, science, and social studies instruction. This year her individual planning time is interrupted by RTI meetings to consider the progress of individual students, discuss intervention strategies, and review data. Ms. Puente is not sure what to make of this new world and the increasing time that it requires.

Last week, Ms. Puente began motivating students for their unit on early explorers of California and the Spanish who eventually settled in Alta California. She decided that reading and research on these topics would best be accomplished through both group and individual work. When planning goals and activities for the unit, she also made provisions for those with special needs and interests. Additionally, the books Ms. Puente selected for the unit reflect the varied reading abilities of her students to ensure that all students succeed with the reading they do.

To begin, Ms. Puente reviews the special features of informational books, reminding students that informational books are written and organized differently from picture books and chapter books because their main purpose is to provide the reader with information, whereas stories are primarily meant to entertain. To illustrate what she means about communicating information as the main goal of informational books, she reads a few book titles aloud and asks students to tell what sort of information they think each book will disclose. Next, she explains that informational books often have a number of special features. These include a table of contents, headings and subheadings, introductory paragraphs and summaries, graphs, illustrations, labels, charts, maps, indexes, and glossaries. Ms. Puente points out these features in several books she has preselected for this purpose. After Ms. Puente has reviewed these features, she asks students why the author might have included them. She also discusses how informational books differ from biographies. While both convey information, each takes a very different form. To capture these differences she share a passage about Columbus from a biography and from an informational book.

Next, Ms. Puente divides the class into two groups—those who want to learn more about early explorers Captain James Cook, Vitus Bering, and Juan Cabrillo, and those who want to learn more about early Spanish colonizers Juan Crespi, Junipero Serra, and Gaspar de Portola. Each student is to select three books to skim, including the social studies textbook on California history. Paying attention to the various features of the books—table of contents, headings and subheadings, introductory paragraphs and summaries, graphs, illustrations, labels, charts, maps, indexes, glossaries—students are to record in their informational books journal one piece of information they find interesting about each book. The next day they will meet again with their groups to share what they found. To tie in the courage theme, Ms. Puente also asks students to think about the courage it took to explore and settle new lands. They will discuss this idea in greater depth as they get further into their study groups.

Ms. Puente always makes sure her classroom has comfortable places for independent reading.

Elizabeth Crews/PhotoEdit

Students gather with their groups and select and skim their books, recording the title and one piece of information from each in their journals. Because students have differing interests and abilities and work at varying rates, Ms. Puente has provided for individual needs:

- Students who need special assistance—for example, English language learners or students with reading difficulties—will be assigned reading partners.
- Additional activities will challenge students who are particularly talented in various areas. Students can create a graph, either on graph paper or on the computer, indicating the number and kind of features found in the various books on their selected topic; write glossaries for those books without them and include student glossary pages in the books for other readers to use; or draw additional illustrations, charts, or maps for the various books.
- These projects are optional and ongoing, with students working on them at their own pace. Ms. Puente will meet with students interested in pursuing these projects to explain how to do them. Any student in the class has the option of working on these projects. Students can work on them individually or in groups. Also, students might choose to work on these projects at other times of the day when their other work is completed.

3:05 Wrap-Up

About 10 or 15 minutes before the end of the day, one of Ms. Puente's students plays the class theme song on the boom box. This tune gives students a sense of order and belonging—they expect it, they know what it means, and it is *their* class song. By the time the song is completed, students are in their seats and ready to review the schedule for the day, which is written on the chalkboard. Together they read and briefly talk about each subject or activity, with a student in charge of leading the discussion. During this time, students ask questions, share something they enjoyed or learned, or bring up problems they had. Problems that can't be resolved easily are tabled until there is a better time for resolution, perhaps at the next day's morning meeting time.

3:15 Dismissal

After the students have gone and while the day's events are still fresh in her mind, Ms. Puente begins planning for the next day. She knows this planning can't take place without first reviewing the day's activities and reflecting on what worked, what didn't work, and why. Quickly, she makes a few entries in her teacher's logbook. On Jenny's page, she writes "Used context cues to figure out several unknown words she ran across in her reading," and on Terrell's page, "Pleased to see Terrell become extremely absorbed in Margo Sorenson's *Fight in the Fields*, a hi-lo adventure biography about Cesar Chavez. Ask him about it." She jots down comments for a few other students and glances briefly at some of her yearly goals.

Next, as she looks at what she had planned for Tuesday, she realizes she will have to make some changes. In math, some students had a difficult time solving the word problem. Instead of taking whole-group time for another problem, she decides she will group the students who need a bit more instruction for a mini-lesson. Other students then will have more time to work independently and to tutor other students. Because her parent volunteer comes on Tuesdays from 12:25 to 1:25, the volunteer can monitor these students while Ms. Puente works with the group that needs more assistance on word problems. She jots down her plans, makes a few additional comments in her logbook, and walks to the teachers' lounge to get a well-deserved cup of coffee.

11

Teaching Comprehension Strategies

CHAPTER **outline**

As an accomplished reader with years of experience reading various types of text for a variety of purposes, you have internalized a wealth of reading strategies. Suppose, for example, you are reading an ERIC report on the Web, and you come across a mention of previewing as a prereading activity, something that rings a bell but not a loud one. In this case, perhaps you search ERIC itself for "previewing," and if that doesn't work perhaps you try searching using Google.

Or, suppose it is Saturday, and you have two tests coming up on Monday. You need to read a novel, three textbook chapters, and four journal articles. What do you do? You know you won't have time to read and study each in depth, so you must use some efficient approaches to understand and remember what you read. The novel you read quickly, skipping over lengthy descriptions and dialogue and concentrating on the basics of setting, plot, and characters. As you read, you look for recurring themes. When you finish, you might ask questions like "Why was the protagonist so driven?" and "What were the main themes?" Before you read the chapters and articles, you might think about points your instructor emphasized. While you read, you might take notes or underline material relevant to these points; after your first reading, you might reread the sections that are most relevant to the course.

What you have done in each of these cases is to use reading strategies—deliberate plans to help you understand and recall what you read. Learning to use reading strategies is one of the most important parts of becoming an accomplished reader.

Jacek Chabraszewski/Fotolia

CLASSROOM vignette

What Are Comprehension Strategies?

As defined by David Pearson and his colleagues (Pearson, Roehler, Dole, & Duffy, 1992), reading comprehension strategies are "conscious and flexible plans that readers apply and adopt to a variety of texts and tasks." Accomplished readers use them in order to better understand, learn from, and remember what they read. One strategy, for example, is determining what is important—that is, deciding which of the numerous concepts in any text deserve special attention. Particularly when reading informational material to gain specific knowledge on a topic, readers must determine just what it is they need to learn. In the opening scenario of the chapter, we suggested one way to identify the important information in a textbook is to consider which points in the chapter the instructor has emphasized. Another way would be to read the chapter introduction and summary, and still another way would be to skim through the chapter, noting what is highlighted in the headings and subheadings.

As Michael Pressley (2000) has noted, and as his research with Peter Afflerbach (Pressley & Afflerbach, 1995) very clearly demonstrates, mature readers have a wide repertoire of reading strategies available, and they flexibly employ whichever strategies best fit each reading situation they encounter. This is something that all readers need to learn to do, including English language learners and students with special educational needs. Unfortunately, research indicates that comprehension strategies instruction is not as frequent an activity as it should be (Pressley, 2006).

Characteristics of Comprehension Strategies

Michael Pressley (2000) asked the purposely awkward question, "What should comprehension instruction be the instruction of?" We have already discussed how word recognition, fluency, and vocabulary are key to comprehension. Now we want to consider comprehension strategies, and their twin comprehension skills. In any core reading program, in most state curricula, and in your own school, educators will speak and write about comprehension strategies and skills. The difference is subtle. We want all of our students to be skillful readers, but also strategic readers. A strategy that is performed effortlessly and with minimal conscious attention is a skill, and a skill performed with deliberate thought and intention is a strategy (Afflerbach, Pearson, & Paris, 2008). Most of what readers do to determine main ideas, summarize, and make inferences can be considered both skills and strategies, and in core reading programs they frequently carry both labels. Some skills, like determining the author's purpose, discerning fact from opinion, or sequencing events seem to carry just the label of a skill. In this chapter we will focus on strategies.

Strategies Are Conscious Efforts

At least when they are initially taught, the strategies discussed here are conscious efforts that you ask students to deliberately engage in. For example, after teaching students how to make inferences while reading, you will sometimes ask them to make inferences about specific aspects of material they are reading, and they will sometimes deliberately pause as they are reading and realize that they need to make an inference. With practice and experience, however, some strategies are likely to become increasingly habitual and automatic; for example, readers will frequently make inferences without realizing they are doing so. Nevertheless, even well-learned strategies can be brought to consciousness and placed under the control of the reader.

Strategies Are Flexible

Flexibility and adaptability are hallmarks of strategies. The very essence of teaching students to be strategic is teaching them that they need to use strategies in ways that are appropriate for particular situations. For example, the strategy of summarizing can be used in a variety of ways. Some students might compose a written summary at the end of a textbook chapter as a way of retaining the information. Other readers might stop in the middle of their reading and briefly summarize what they have read as a means of checking their understanding. Ultimately, strategies should be used when necessary and appropriate, and teachers should refrain from insisting on deliberate use of strategies when students understand what they read.

Strategies Are Widely Applicable

Many strategies can be used across a wide range of ages, abilities, and reading material. For example, it is appropriate for a first-grader to orally summarize a book like Elissa Haden Guest's *Iris and Walker and the Substitute Teacher* or David McPhail's *The Teddy Bear*. It is appropriate for a fifth-grader to summarize the major events in the life of the 12th-century Muslim warrior Saladin in Diane Stanley's *Saladin: Noble Prince of Islam* or those in the life of the suffragist Esther Morris in *When Esther Morris Headed West: Women, Wyoming, and the Right to Vote* by Connie Nordhielm Woolridge. It is appropriate for a graduate student to summarize the major tenets of the reader-response approach to literature as they appear in a text like Louise Rosenblatt's *The Reader, the Text, the Poem*.

Strategies Can Be Overt or Covert

Some strategies involve readers in creating some sort of observable product, whereas others involve mental operations that cannot be directly observed. Summarizing, for example, is a strategy that often results in a written record of what was read. Determining what is important, on the other hand, is a strategy that frequently does not result in the reader's writing down anything. When you are initially teaching a strategy, you may want students to produce an observable record of their use of the strategy so that you know that they are able to use it. However, much of the time, the strategies students use will be solely mental processes.

Strategies Lead to Higher-Level Thinking

The use of comprehension strategies takes the reader beyond the literal meaning of the text into deeper interpretation leading to the doorstep of judgments. When readers make inferences, determine importance, create graphic images, and monitor their comprehension, they are engaging in higher-order thinking. Strategic reading and higher-order thinking have much in common (Resnick, 1987). Each can be effortful and complex. Both involve self-regulation of thinking, the construction of meaning, and the search for structure in a text.

① For each of the five characteristics of comprehension strategies we just described, come up with a situation in which you used a comprehension strategy having that characteristic. Understanding these characteristics fully is important, so we suggest you write out your responses.

Key Comprehension Strategies

Mature readers use a wide repertoire of comprehension strategies. Fortunately, however, there is substantial agreement on the key strategies that students need to master (National Reading Panel, 2000; Pressley, 2006; RAND Reading Study Group, 2002; Sales & Graves, 2005). The key strategies we recommend are shown in the following list and discussed in the remainder of this section:

- Establishing a purpose for reading
- Using prior knowledge
- Asking and answering questions
- Making inferences
- Determining what is important
- Summarizing
- Dealing with graphic information
- Imaging and creating graphic representations
- Being metacognitive

Assessment

The article "Assessing Students' Metacognitive Awareness of Reading Strategies" (Mokhtari & Reichard, 2002) contains a tool for surveying the class and determining what they know about comprehension strategies.

Each of these strategies involves readers in actively constructing meaning as they read. Additionally, many of these strategies cause readers to transform ideas from one form to another or generate relationships among ideas. For example, when readers summarize, they must transform the author's text into something more concise, and when they make inferences, they must relate information in the text to information they already know. These strategies are not distinct entities. To summarize you must be able to determine importance, and making inferences is impossible without using prior knowledge. When readers ask questions they are establishing a purpose for their reading. As students are introduced to and use strategies, they should understand that these strategies share common goals and facilitate each other.

Establishing a Purpose for Reading

One of the first things a good reader does as she approaches a text is to establish a purpose for reading. That purpose will depend on the text, the reader, and what she needs from the text. How the reader reads—whether, for example, she takes notes, reads slowly or quickly, or rereads—will, in turn, depend on this purpose.

Sometimes the reader's purpose is to find a specific piece of information, perhaps the score of a soccer match, a critic's opinion on a current movie, or certain facts about the brain in a trade book such as *Phineas Gage: A Gruesome But True Story About Brain Science* by John Fleischman. Sometimes the purpose is to learn everything possible from the text, perhaps in preparation for a test. Sometimes it's to simply enjoy the reading, as is often the case with a novel or short story. And sometimes it's simply to fall asleep. All of these and many other purposes are totally legitimate and have their place. The goal is for the reader to identify the appropriate purpose for a particular situation and read in a way to accomplish that purpose.

Using Prior Knowledge

When readers purposely bring to consciousness what they already know relating that knowledge to the text, they put a set of schemata into place, establishing a framework for the new information they will encounter. Let's say, for instance, that a fifth-grader is perusing the library shelf and picks up a book titled *ER Vets: Life in an Animal Emergency Room* by Donna M. Jackson. Before the student begins reading the book, she thinks about what she knows about hospital emergency rooms and veterinarians. As she thinks and reads, she recalls times she accompanied her own dog to the vet and the time she was taken to the ER when she fell off her bike and broke her arm. Thus, she reads the book with the realization that animals sometimes have life-threatening emergencies as people do, but this book is going to present something different, something she really hasn't considered before. The student is using her prior knowledge to set up expectations of what she might encounter in the text. When she reads about one of the emergency situations, she will be able to contrast it with her own emergency room experience, and making that contrast will help her both understand and remember the material.

Asking and Answering Questions

When the reader poses questions prior to reading a selection or as he is reading the selection and then attempts to answer the questions while reading, he virtually guarantees that reading will be an active process. It also serves to focus the reader's attention. A reader who has asked a particular set of questions will be particularly attentive to the information that answers those questions.

Consider a sixth-grader preparing to read a chapter on nutrition in a health text. As the first step, he might survey the chapter and find these headings: Nutrients and the U.S. RDA, The Seven Dietary Guidelines, Shopping for Groceries, and Preventing Disease Through Proper Diet. Then he might pose one or two questions about each heading: What are nutrients? What is the U.S. RDA? What are the seven dietary guidelines? Do I follow them in my diet? Should I follow them? How is shopping for groceries related to nutrition? Can a proper diet prevent all disease? As he reads, the student will get answers to some of his questions, find that others are not answered in the chapter, and pose and answer additional questions.

Making Inferences

Readers can infer meanings by using information from the text and their existing knowledge of the world to fill in bits of information that are not explicitly stated in the text. No text is ever fully explicit, and thus readers must constantly make inferences to understand what they are reading. By teaching students to make inferences, you are helping them learn to use their existing knowledge along with the information in the text to build meaning.

Suppose that a fifth-grader is reading a science text and learns that woodchucks build deep burrows and huddle in them in large groups during the winter. Knowing that a fair number of animals hibernate, she might infer that woodchucks hibernate in their burrows. Then, remembering that last week her teacher explained that ground temperature remains stable and fairly warm at depths greater than three or four feet, she might further infer that woodchucks make their burrows deep in order to take advantage of this warmth. Making inferences is subtle and complex. In the Classroom 11.1 lets us look in as one teacher introduces making inferences to a fourth-grade class.

11.1

**Instructional
Routines**

An Introduction to Making Inferences for Fourth-Graders

An inference is hard to define, but somewhat easier to illustrate. Mr. Hernandez introduces the process of making inference by writing the following sentence on the whiteboard: *Mary looked at her menu carefully, trying to find the cheapest entrée, while John gazed lovingly in her eyes.* He then tells his students that they just made three inferences and they are not even aware that they made them. He further explains that an inference is something that the author did not tell us, but we can figure it out. He then explores the three inferences.

- Mr. Hernandez explains that the author didn't tell the students where John and Mary are, but they can probably figure it out—they can make an inference. Students immediately raise their hands and offer that John and Mary are in a restaurant. Mr. Hernandez asks, "What told you that they are in a restaurant?"

  Robert responds, "They are looking at menus and you don't have menus at home."

  Sarah says, "The word *entrée*; we don't talk about food at home like that, but a menu might have that word."

  Mr. Hernandez explains that to make such an inference we use clues from the text, the words *menu* and *entrée,* plus what we know, that restaurants have menus, to figure out what the author did not tell us. Mr. Hernandez quickly sketches a chart on the whiteboard.

Clues from the Text	Prior Knowledge	Inference
Menu, entrée	Restaurants have menus so you can select your food.	John and Mary are in a restaurant.
Cheapest	When I don't have a lot of money I go for the grilled cheese.	Mary thinks John does not have much money.

- Mr. Hernandez continues to explore the next inferences by asking what else did the author fail to tell us, but we can figure out. "What do we know about Mary? What are some important clues in the text?" The students talk about the words *cheapest* and *entrée* make inferences that Mary is being cautious, this is a first date, and John is poor.
- Mr. Hernandez then draws the students' attention to the next inference, asking, "What do we know about John? What didn't the author tell us?" With some giggling, the students state that John likes or is in love with Mary. Mr. Hernandez wants to know how they made those inferences—what text clues were important. The students easily identify the word *lovingly,* but *gaze* takes some clarification. He also has the students consider what they know by asking how people behave when they are out on a date.
- Mr. Hernandez will expand this lesson to larger pieces of text and then to full stories. Students will continue to ask themselves what the author did not say that we can nevertheless infer. What clues did the author leave and what knowledge and experiences do I have that help me make these inferences?

Determining What Is Important

Because most texts contain much more information than a reader can focus on and learn, determining what is important is a crucial and frequently required strategy. Using this strategy requires that readers understand what they have read and make judgments about what is and is not important. Sometimes, texts include direct cues to what is important—overviews, headings, summaries, and the like. As seventh-grade science teacher Victor Hammel notes, it is well worth teaching students to use these aids.

Drawing on Cultural Beliefs and Knowledge

Quiocho and Ulanoff (2009) emphasize the importance of connecting reading activities to English language learners' lives. This is particularly important when children are learning to draw inferences. Quiocho and Ulanoff note that English language learners benefit when teachers explicitly teach them to use their cultural beliefs and knowledge, along with information in text and their general world knowledge, to support their inferential thinking. That is why the pre-reading discussions are so critical. As the discussion develops, the teacher can informally assess what the students know, and then broaden and deepen their knowledge by presenting new concepts and facts while drawing upon the experiences of others in the class. Knowledge is the foundation for making inferences.

Differentiating Instruction
for
English Language Learners

At the beginning of each year, I make it a point to go through the textbooks we will be using and talk with my students about whatever learning aids the books contain. At this time, I also model how I would use these aids. Although some students would make good use of the aids even if I didn't discuss them and model how I use them, a lot of students wouldn't. The benefit to them, as well as the time I save by helping students learn to use the aids independently, is really substantial.

In addition, I check the books to see how well the aids work. For example, I look at the headings to be sure they accurately reflect the content that follows them. Sometimes textbooks aren't that well constructed, and when that's the case, I tell students. I think this is an important part of becoming a critical reader—knowing that you have to use your brain as you read and that even textbooks aren't perfect.

—Victor Hammel, seventh-grade teacher

Efficiently learning from informational text requires well-honed strategies.
Mary Kate Denny/PhotoEdit

We certainly agree with Mr. Hammel that such aids can be useful. In many cases, however, the text does not contain obvious clues to what is important, and students need to rely on their prior knowledge to infer what is important in a particular selection. Without specific text aids the students will have to be shown how to make judgments about what is important and what is trivial.

Summarizing

Summarizing requires students to first determine what is important and then condense it in their own words. Some years ago, Ann Brown and Jeanne Day (1983) developed and researched some very effective rules for summarizing. Slightly modified, they include the following steps:

- Delete trivial or irrelevant information.
- Delete redundant information.
- Provide a superordinate term for members of a category.
- Find and use generalizations the author has made.
- Create your own generalizations when the author has not provided them.

Dealing with Graphic Information

PEARSON
myeducationlab

Examine the three artifacts presented in the activity "Teaching Visual Literacy" and consider the types of text the students needed to be exposed to in order to demonstrate such visual literacy capacities. (To find this activity, go to the topic *Media/Visual Literacy* in MyEducationLab and click on Assignments and Activities.)

Readers can often improve comprehension by giving conscious attention to the visual information supplied by the author. Before youngsters learn to read, they are drawn to and fascinated by the visual material books offer. Teaching them when, how, and why to examine the illustrations, graphs, maps, diagrams, and other visuals that accompany selections will enable them to make optimal use of the visual aids texts often provide. History texts, for example, almost always contain maps that include a legend to the symbols they employ. Students need to learn that maps usually have legends, the kind of information legends normally contain, where legends are typically placed, and how to interpret them. Specifically, students need to know how visual information expands on what the text says and how the text can help explain the purpose of a graph or a chart.

Imaging and Creating Graphic Representations

Some readers can improve their comprehension by creating visual representations of text, either in their minds or on paper. One kind of image occurs when readers visualize people, events, and places, usually with narrative material. Another kind of imaging consists of visually organizing key ideas in a text to graphically display their relationship, used most frequently with expository text. One particular form of graphic representation students enjoy creating and that has proved very useful for them is semantic mapping. As you will recall from our discussion of semantic maps or webs in the chapters on vocabulary and scaffolding instruction, we emphasized the use of maps by students or by teachers and students working together. Here we are concerned with students learning to create their own semantic maps. This works best if you give the students a partially completed map and then ask them to fill in the rest of it. Over time they are responsible for more and more of the map until they can create them on their own as an independent comprehension strategy.

Being Metacognitive

Good readers are metacognitive. They understand themselves as readers, the reading tasks they face, and the strategies they can employ in completing these tasks. Before reading, they consider such matters as their purpose in reading, the difficulty of the text, how much they already know about the topic of the text, and how long they have to complete the reading. During reading, they monitor their comprehension, employ fix-up strategies like rereading if they do not understand something, and use the comprehension strategies we have just described when needed. After reading, they self-check to see if they have what they want and need from the text and again use fix-up and comprehension strategies as needed. For example, realizing that the history chapter she has just read is crucial to the report she is writing, a sixth-grader might write a summary of it.

Being metacognitive is a more general strategy than the others we have discussed; but the other strategies help to develop metacognitive thinking. When children ask questions or summarize, they are reflecting on what they have comprehended and they are being metacognitive. In an approach called reciprocal teaching students continually use four strategies—predicting, clarifying, questioning, and summarizing. These strategies help readers become more metacognitive (Palincsar & Brown, 1984). Readers who are being metacognitive are asking themselves questions like these: Am I understanding what the author is saying? What do I do if I don't understand what I am reading? What could I be doing to better understand what the author is saying? Can I do something to help me remember the material better? Which of the strategies I know should I employ here?

In helping students to be metacognitive, teachers are teaching them to be active learners who monitor their reading and take appropriate steps when they are not getting what they want and need from texts. Teachers are also encouraging them to think about the comprehension strategies they have learned and to use them when needed. It is extremely important that students thoroughly learn a small repertory of comprehension strategies like the nine strategies just described and employ them where appropriate (Cummins, Stewart, & Block, 2005). After initially teaching strategies, teachers need to encourage, foster, and prompt students to use them over a considerable period of time, as sixth-grade teacher Ron Novack does in the scenario captured by In the Classroom 11.2.

The strategies described here—establishing a purpose for reading, using prior knowledge, asking and answering questions, making inferences, determining what is important, summarizing, dealing with graphic information, imaging and creating graphic representations, and being metacognitive—will help students reach the goal of understanding and learning from what they read. These strategies will also promote deeper understanding of the stories and books that students read. In learning these strategies, students are internalizing an approach to reading and thinking that is active and reflective, an approach vital to literacy in the 21st century. Having learned this mode of reading and thinking, students will be both able and inclined to engage in a variety of reading and learning strategies in order to understand, appreciate, and learn from what they read. It should be noted that students will differ in the rate at which they learn the strategies that have been described. It is vital that all students be given sufficient time and scaffolding to thoroughly learn and internalize the strategies you teach.

It is also vital that students get a real sense of what it means to be strategic. One way to help students understand the concept of being strategic is to use children's literature that illustrates children using strategies, like those selections listed in the Reading Corner on page 335.

Assessment

Find out the conditions under which a student uses or fails to use comprehension strategies, with the assumption that success is eventually possible, of course. One part of assessment is convincing students that they can achieve.

Fostering Metacognition

To foster students' metacognition and help them thoroughly internalize and fluently use the strategies you have taught, it is important to repeatedly remind them of the importance of being metacognitive and employing the repertoire of strategies they have learned, which Mr. Novack is doing as he questions his students.

Mr. Novack: What does it mean to be metacognitive?

Felicity: To monitor your reading and do something when what you are reading doesn't make sense.

Doug: To think before you read something and have a good idea of why you are reading it and what you want to get out of it.

Artrell: To decide which of the comprehension strategies we know we should use in a particular situation.

Mr. Novack: What do you do when you are reading along and suddenly realize you don't understand what you're reading?

Amad: When that happens to me, I go back and read the same words again.

Mr. Novack: You mean you reread. That's a good strategy.

Ted: If I'm reading science or social studies, or something like that, and there are words I don't know, I'll look them up or ask somebody.

Mr. Novack: You consult another source. That's a good strategy, too.

April: Sometimes it helps me to look at the pictures or maps, if there are any.

Mr. Novack: You consider any graphic information. Good.

Doug: If something isn't making sense, I'll think about something I already know and see how it fits what I'm reading.

Mr. Novack: You connect what you already know with what you're reading. Excellent strategy.

Felicity: I try to picture in my mind what I'm reading, what the author's describing. I guess I'm always drawing pictures in my mind when I read.

Mr. Novack: You're imaging, and that's another very effective comprehension strategy.

Clearly, Mr. Novack encourages his students to do whatever is necessary to arrive at a satisfactory understanding of what they are reading. This, of course, is precisely what we want to prepare students to do.

Summarizing, as we have discussed in this chapter, is a powerful strategy. Ms. Lloyd, a teacher known to one of us, has used the bio-cube activity to help students to synthesize and summarize their learning after reading biographies. She found the activity on the ReadWriteThink website (www.readwritethink.org/files/resources/interactives/bio_cube). After students go to the bio-cube link, they complete an interactive online planning sheet. They are presented with six buttons, one for each slide. As they click on each button the corresponding slide appears. The computer prompts them to fill in specific information. On slide one students note the name of the person whose biography they read, the time period in which the person lived or the biography took place, and the place where the person lived. On slide two, students summarize the subject's personal background. On slide three, students record the individual's personality traits. On slide four, the student notes the significance of the person's life. On slide five, the biggest obstacle the individual faced is recorded, and on slide six an important quotation from the biography is included. When the information is recorded, students print the bio-cube and then they cut the shape out and fold and glue the sides to construct the cube. Ms. Lloyd's students printed their cubes on cardstock for durability. Then she had students summarize the lives of the people about whom they read in small groups, using the bio-cubes to prompt their summaries. Although bio-cubes can, of course, be made without accessing the computer activity, the electronic format is a motivator for many students. •

Books That Illustrate Strategic Behavior

Children's literature abounds with characters (real and imaginary) who strategically go about trying to achieve their goals or solve problems. These characters, who exhibit deliberately planned behavior that takes into account their unique situations, are among children's favorites in literature. Here is a small sampling.

Alma Flor Ada. *My Name Is Maria Isabel.* Atheneum, 1993. Renamed Mary by her teacher, Maria Isabel, recently arrived in the United States from Puerto Rico, finds a way to get back her own name *and* to fit in with her classmates. 57 pages.

Nan Willard Cappo. *Cheating Lessons.* Atheneum, 2002. After Bernadette suspects someone of cheating to get their high school quiz team into the state quiz bowl competition, she seeks out the cheater. 240 pages.

Louise Erdrich. *Grandmother's Pigeon.* Hyperion, 1996. After three eggs in Grandmother's bird nest collection miraculously hatch a breed of passenger pigeons long thought to be extinct, Grandmother's family takes matters into their own hands when visiting scientists threaten the hatchlings' freedom. 32 pages.

Dennis Brindell Fradin. *My Family Shall Be Free: The Life of Peter Still.* HarperCollins, 2001. After buying his own freedom from slavery, Peter Still heads north to earn the money to free his wife and children. 176 pages.

Rosa Guy. *The Disappearance.* Delacorte, 1979. After leaving an alcoholic mother behind in Harlem, Imamu Jones finds hope for a better life with a middle-class family in Brooklyn. Once there, he becomes involved in locating his missing sister. 246 pages.

Patricia Hermes. *Mama, Let's Dance.* Little, Brown, 1991. Eleven-year-old Mary Belle learns to cope with being in charge of her brothers and sisters when her mother leaves home. 168 pages.

Barbara Knutson. *Love and Roast Chicken: A Trickster Tale from the Andes Mountains.* Carolrhoda, 2004. In this Peruvian tale, Cuy the guinea pig uses his smarts to outwit a hungry fox and powerful farmer. 40 pages.

Gary Paulsen. *Hatchet.* Bradbury, 1987. This gripping adventure story is about Brian Robeson's surviving 54 days alone in the northern Canadian wilderness. 195 pages.

Eileen Ross. *Nellie and the Bandit.* Farrar, Straus and Giroux, 2005. Plucky Nellie uses her brains to repeatedly outwit the bad guys. 32 pages.

Louis Sachar. *Holes.* Farrar, Straus and Giroux, 1998. In this Newbery Medal–winning book, the ever-unlucky Stanley Yelnats, after being sent to a detention camp for a crime he didn't commit, manages to turn around four generations of family bad luck through his own resourcefulness and tenacity. 233 pages.

Marjorie Weinman Sharmat. *Nate the Great and His Mother's Monsters.* Delacorte, 1999. When his mother's treasured recipe for monster cookies disappears, Nate uses his sleuthing talents to recover it. 48 pages.

Cynthia Voight. *Homecoming.* Atheneum, 1983. After their mother abandons them in a shopping mall parking lot, 13-year-old Dicey keeps her three younger siblings fed and out of harm's way as they journey in search of a home. 312 pages.

Nancy Willard. *Shadow Story.* Harcourt, Brace & Company, 1999. Holly Go Lolly, who has played with shadows all her life, saves herself from the evil ogre Ooboo by luring him into a forest she creates with hand shadows. 32 pages.

2 Identify one of the nine strategies that you use or that is similar to one you use. Then describe, preferably in writing, two or three situations in which you have used it and why it was appropriate in those situations.

3 Consider the nine strategies we have discussed, and identify those that are likely to be particularly useful for second-graders, for fourth-graders, and for sixth-graders. Then compare your assessments to those of a classmate.

4 One approach good readers learn is to coordinate their use of the various strategies they know. That is, in reading a text they often use several strategies, not just one. Find a short informational text that you would like to learn from and read it fairly carefully. Then consider the nine strategies we have discussed, and jot down a list of those you used as you read the passage.

REFLECT and *Apply*

A Powerful Approach to Teaching Strategies

The past two decades have produced a very substantial body of research and theory on teaching comprehension strategies (see, for example, Block & Pressley, 2002; Brown, Pressley, Van Meter, & Schuder, 1996; Deshler & Schumaker, 1993; Dewitz, Carr, & Patberg, 1987; Dole, Brown, & Trathen, 1996; Duffy et al., 1987; Pearson & Duke, 2002; Pressley, 2006; Reutzel, Fawson, & Smith, 2003). This research has demonstrated some very positive results. As Michael Pressley has pointed out, "The evidence is overwhelming that upper-grade elementary students can be taught to use comprehension strategies, with substantial improvements in student comprehension following such instruction" (2002). Actually, Pressley need not have limited his claim to upper-grade students because one of the best studies—by Brown and her colleagues (1996)—clearly shows that children as young as second-graders can profit from strategy instruction. However, not all younger students are ready to profit from strategy instruction. They need to attain a certain level of oral reading fluency to have the attention and cognitive resources to try out and monitor the use of strategies (Smolkin & Donovan, 2002; Willingham, 2006).

The extensive body of theory and research on comprehension strategies instruction has shown two approaches for teaching strategies to be extremely effective: direct explanation of strategies (Duffy, 2002; Duffy et al., 1987; Duke & Pearson, 2002) and multiple strategy instruction (Pressley, 2002; Pressley, El-Dinary, Wharton-McDonald, & Brown, 1998; Reutzel et al., 2003). Direct explanation is, as the name indicates, the more direct and explicit of the two and typically the teacher and students work with one strategy at a time, gradually phasing in new strategies. Multiple strategy instruction, with reciprocal teaching (Palincsar & Brown, 1984) and transactional strategy instruction (Brown, Pressley, van Meter, & Schuder, 1996) as the two prominent brands, embeds strategy instruction in the ongoing discussion of the texts. Here we describe a synthesis of these two methods designed by one of us (Sales & Graves, 2005). Later we will examine reciprocal teaching.

To illustrate the approach, we describe the first 2 days of instruction in a fourth-grade class working with the strategy of determining what is important. Next, we note how instruction proceeds and changes over the course of a 3- or 4-week unit. After that, we discuss the ways in which good strategy instruction must be constructive in nature. Finally, we note the types of transfer, review, and integrating activities that are needed to make a strategy a tool that students will really use. Although instruction will vary somewhat with different strategies, different students, and different age groups, the general plan being presented is widely applicable. In Appendix B we present a 3-day sequence for making inferences.

The First Day's Instruction on Determining What Is Important

The activities described in this section are those used on the first day of instruction on a new strategy. In this illustration, the students are fourth-graders, and the strategy to be taught is determining what is im-

Reading strategies help students understand and learn from the texts they read.

iStockPhoto

portant. The students have had some experience with the strategy in previous grades, but this is the first time it has been formally taught. The first day's instruction includes four different general components.

Motivation and Interest Building (about 5 minutes)

To capture students' attention and build interest, strategy instruction must be embedded in a meaningful area of study (Guthrie et al., 1998). Students do not have a natural passion to find the main idea or make an inference, but they do like to learn about violent weather, snakes, and volcanoes. If strategy instruction is a tool that will take them to deeper understandings, they will work with you. Ask students about the reading they have been doing in science and social studies, and discuss some of the challenges they face. One of the challenges likely to come up is that these books cover a lot of information, and it is hard to remember all of it. Explain that the strategy they will learn—determining what is important—will help them to better understand and remember what they read.

Teacher Explanation (about 5 minutes)

Introduce the strategy by having students guess the categories represented by various sets of words you write on the board. Choose categories and words of interest to the particular group of students being taught. We have chosen fast-food restaurants, sports that use balls, and sports that don't use balls. Write the word sets on the board underneath unlabeled umbrellas—an idea suggested by James Baumann (1986) and illustrated in Figure 11.1. Tell students that these words are examples of more general ideas. Have them guess what those more general ideas are and write them in the umbrellas above the sets of examples. Explain that determining a general idea or label for words and phrases is just the beginning; next they will determine important ideas in paragraphs and longer selections.

Next, explain that when using this strategy, they should focus on the most important information and let less important details fade into the background. Tell students that knowing how to determine what is important can make understanding and remembering what they read much easier. Sometime the author provides clear clues as to what is important and sometimes he does not. Then it is up to us, the reader, to invent the main idea.

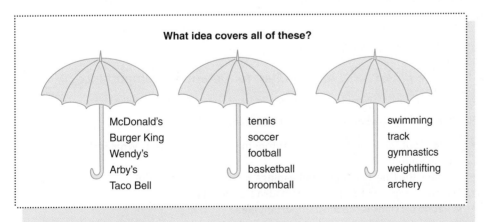

What idea covers all of these?

McDonald's	tennis	swimming
Burger King	soccer	track
Wendy's	football	gymnastics
Arby's	basketball	weightlifting
Taco Bell	broomball	archery

Figure 11.1 Word Sets for Motivation and Interest Building

Teacher Modeling (about 5 minutes)

Reveal more about how the strategy works by writing on the board a sentence such as *Matthew Blaine, a fourth-grade student at Ridgeview Elementary School, won first prize in the Rotary Speech Contest with his essay titled "What Freedom Means to Me."* Read the sentence aloud, and model the thought processes you might go through in identifying the most important information in the sentence:

> Let's see, what is the main idea the author is communicating in this sentence? The topic seems to be Matthew Blaine. And what is the most important information about Matthew? Winning first prize sounds pretty important. [Circle the phrases *Matthew Blaine* and *won first prize in the Rotary Speech Contest* on the board.] The other information—that he's a fourth-grade student at Ridgeview Elementary School and the title of his essay—is interesting, but not as important. [Cross out *a fourth-grade student at Ridgeview Elementary School* and *with his essay titled "What Freedom Means to Me"* on the board.]

The board work used to illustrate the most important information in the sentence is shown here:

Matthew Blaine, a fourth grade student at Ridgeview Elementary School, won first prize in the Rotary Speech Contest with his essay titled "What Freedom Means to Me."

Once you have explained the strategy and modeled it, check to see whether students understand by asking a few students to explain the strategy and tell why it is worth knowing. As you work through this example and others, develop an anchor chart with the students. An anchor chart is a list of the rules and routines that are part of the overall strategy. Figure 11.2 is an example of such an anchor chart.

Large-Group Student Participation and Teacher Mediation (about 10 minutes)

Put a paragraph from one of the students' social studies or science texts on the overhead, and read it aloud. The paragraph should be one in which the important information stands out. The sample paragraph used here is taken from *Scaly Babies: Reptiles Growing Up* by Ginny Johnson and Judy Cutchins (p. 24):

> For many people, the word *reptile* describes an ugly, slippery, and sometimes dangerous animal. But reptiles are not slimy, and most are not dangerous. There are nearly six thousand different kinds of these scaly-skinned animals in the world today. It is true that some are large and scary-looking and a few are venomous, but most reptiles are harmless to humans. Like many wild animals, reptiles may strike or bite to defend themselves. But they rarely bother a person who has not disturbed or startled them.

PEARSON
myeducationlab

Watch the video included in the activity "Using Think-Aloud to Model Effective Reading Comprehension" to see a teacher modeling the reading of informational text. Reflect on the lesson by answering the questions following the video. (To find this activity, go to the topic *Comprehension* in MyEducationLab and click on Assignments and Activities.)

Figure 11.2 **Anchor Chart for Determining Importance**

How we determine what is important while reading

- Think about the topic. What is the author mainly writing about? What is the author's purpose?
- Examine the title, headings, subheadings, pictures, and bold print.
- Search for topic sentences and main idea statements.
- What do we think is the most important idea?
- If we can't find a clear main idea statement in the text, we need to invent one.
- Let's check. Do the other ideas, the details, support the main idea we found or invented?

Ask students what the paragraph is mainly about (reptiles). Next, ask them how they determined this (everything in the paragraph is about reptiles). Have students supply the details about reptiles that are given in the paragraph and write these on the board, as shown in Figure 11.3.

After you have written the details students have suggested on the board, ask them which information in the paragraph is the most important. Explain that all of these details say something about reptiles, but that one is the most general and important idea, probably the idea that the author really wants to get across. Help students determine the most important idea by asking questions such as these about each of the details: Is this the most important idea in the paragraph? Do the other ideas support this one? Do you think this is the main concept the author is trying to tell you?

After students have agreed on the most important idea (something like "Although many people think reptiles are dangerous, most are not"), rewrite the chart on the board to show the most important idea with supporting details underneath it, as shown in Figure 11.4. After 30 to 45 minutes of instruction move on to something else and resume the lesson the next day.

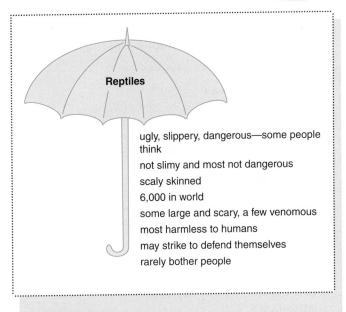

Figure 11.3

Details About Reptiles Suggested by Students

The Second Day's Instruction on Determining What Is Important

Very briefly review the first day's lesson, again discussing what strategies in general are and what the specific strategy of determining importance is. Motivate students by reminding them how helpful the strategy will be for understanding and remembering what they read, and model your thought processes as you determine what is important in a short text—probably the paragraph with which you ended yesterday's lesson.

More Large-Group Student Participation and Teacher Mediation (10 to 20 minutes)

Work together with students to determine the most important ideas in several additional paragraphs from the same book. Remind them of the anchor chart and review the essentials of the strategy. Call on students to determine what is most important in each paragraph and to explain how they determined that their selection shows the most important information. On the board, create a visual display similar to the first paragraph example if the students need it. If students seem to understand the strategy, move to the next step. If not, do some further explaining and modeling.

Cooperative Group Work (about 10 minutes)

Once large-group questioning indicates that students have a basic understanding of the strategy, they need a chance to practice it. Initially, they can practice in pairs because students

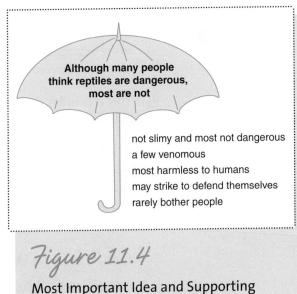

Figure 11.4

Most Important Idea and Supporting Details

Figure 11.5 Graphic Organizer for Previewing, Questioning, and Determining Importance

Reading for Information

Title of Book / Article ____________________ Author ____________

PREVIEW: Look at title, headings, charts, bold print, pictures.	What will I learn about?	
MY QUESTIONS:	What questions do I have?	
DETERMINE IMPORTANCE	Key Facts	Main Ideas

working together support each other. You want to ensure that students achieve and feel successful at this point. Because they have worked only with paragraphs thus far, they should continue with paragraph-length selections in this practice session. Also, because the selections used thus far have been examples in which the important information stood out clearly, the practice paragraphs should also clearly reveal the important information. Two or three such paragraphs might be appropriate for this part of the lesson. A simple graphic organizer, as shown in Figure 11.5, can help students implement the strategy.

Sharing Group Work and Teacher Response and Mediation (about 10 minutes)

Once students have had an opportunity to use the strategy in pairs, they should share their work with the class. Call on pairs to present the important information they found in the passages, and discuss how they determined that this was the crucial information. Monitor their responses carefully, and provide feedback and clarification as necessary.

This concludes the first 2 days of instruction and practice with the strategy. The remainder of the unit is discussed in the next section. First, however, we do want to remind you that teacher explanation, modeling, and mediation need to be carried out in a way that engages students and keeps them attentive. It is difficult to capture the flexibility and fluidity of good strategy instruction in a written text. Also, we want to note that the instructional periods will vary greatly according to the age and maturity of the students. All of the time estimates we give are suggestions. You need to spend whatever time is necessary for your students to learn.

Overview of a Unit

A typical unit might last for 3 or 4 weeks, embedded as part of the study of a social studies or science topic. Although instruction should continue to include a number of the features of the first day's instruction, it should gradually change in the following ways as students become increasingly competent with the strategy.

- Strategies are used on authentic tasks.
- Instruction becomes less concentrated each week.
- Texts become longer and more challenging.
- Students do more of the work.
- Students are encouraged to use the strategies independently.

As students become more adept at determining importance, the strategy will be used alongside the other strategies students have learned. A colorful bulletin board such as that shown in Figure 11.6, or the anchor chart, can serve as a reminder for

Figure 11.6

Strategy Bulletin Board

In the Classroom

11.3

Determining Importance to Learn About Mountain Gorillas

Ms. Fravel's fourth-grade class is studying primates. Each pair of students has selected a specific topic, and when their studying is complete, they will report back to the whole class. After deciding to study the mountain gorilla, Tayjaun and Justin have collected a number of books. Right now they are reading *Mountain Gorillas in Danger* by Rita Ritchie and using a graphic organizer to record the most important ideas in the book. The graphic organizer presented in Figure 11.5 guides them to use several comprehension strategies.

Tayjaun and Justin begin by previewing the book and noting the chapter titles, bold print, and pictures. They realize the book will be about threats to gorillas and how people can help. Next they write down a few of their questions, much like the K-W-L procedure we discussed in the previous chapter. Then as they read they note important information and formulate statements about what is important. Tayjaun and Justin are using three strategies. They are establishing a purpose for reading by previewing the text, asking questions, and searching for the main idea.

Twice a week Tayjaun, Justin, and the other students in the group meet with Ms. Fravel and share what they have accomplished. At this time she assesses their use of the strategy and helps refine their thinking. These mini-lessons provide more scaffolding and review. At the end of the unit the students will be reporting on what they have learned. This unit is also an example of the jigsaw technique that puts students in the position of becoming experts. The jigsaw form of cooperative learning (Johnson, Johnson, & Holubec, 1994; Slavin, 1987) was developed by Elliot Aronson and his colleagues. In this example each pair of students becomes an expert on one class of animals, thus building their knowledge, interpersonal skills, and sense of academic competence.

students to use the strategies they've learned or reviewed during the year and as a refresher on how to use them.

Strategy Use While Reading

Good strategy instruction is neither rigid nor teacher centered. Rather it is flexible, interactive, and constructivist. After the initial 2 or 3 days of instruction the students' goals will be to read and learn about snakes, the solar system, or the westward expansion and the strategy of determining importance will be a tool they use to broaden and deepen their knowledge. As the students work on their science unit they will use the strategy as part of independent and partner work. They will also meet with the teacher two or three times a week to discuss what they are reading, what they are learning, and how the strategy of determining importance is helping them. These small-group lessons will allow the teacher to review the strategy, conduct mini-lessons, provide feedback, and motivate the students to use the strategy. In the Classroom 11.3 lets us look in as Tayjaun and Justin work on their project about mountain gorillas.

*A*ssessment

The ultimate test of the effectiveness of strategy instruction is whether students spontaneously use the strategies. Plan observations and interviews from time to time to check for and promote spontaneous strategy use.

Multiple Strategy Instruction— Reciprocal Teaching

Reciprocal teaching, developed by Annemarie Palincsar and Ann Brown (1984), is a procedure in which students and a teacher work together to improve students' understanding of complex informational texts and at the same time improve students' general ability to monitor their comprehension and learn from such texts. The extensively researched procedure has produced very positive results with first-graders (Palincsar & David, 1991), sixth- and seventh-graders (Palincsar & Brown, 1984), and even college students (Fillenworth, 1995). Studies show that students who work with reciprocal teaching increase their group participation and use of the strategies taught while learning from the passages studied and increasing their learning when reading independently. The studies also demonstrate that the procedure can be used in various settings and that students maintain the gains they achieve.

Frequently observe students to see how well they are internalizing the strategies that you teach.

Michael Newman/PhotoEdit

The procedure employs four carefully selected strategies: generating questions, clarifying issues, summarizing, and making predictions. Each of these strategies serves one or more definite purposes. Questioning focuses students' attention on main ideas and provides a check on their current understanding of what they are reading. Clarifying ensures that students are actively engaged as they are reading and helps avoid confusion. Summarizing requires students to attend to the major content of the selection and determine what is and is not important. And predicting requires students to rehearse what they have learned thus far and approach the next section of the text with some expectations of what is to come.

Initially, reciprocal teaching is teacher directed. At first, the teacher serves as the leader of the group, taking the primary role in carrying out the strategies and modeling them for others in the group. The leader's task includes modeling the strategies he wants the children to learn, monitoring students' learning and understanding, scaffolding their efforts, providing students with feedback, and tailoring the session to the students' existing level of competence. One central purpose of reciprocal teaching, however, is to get students actively involved in using the strategies—that is, in doing the questioning, clarifying, summarizing, and predicting themselves. Thus, from the beginning, the teacher increasingly hands over responsibility to the students in the group. As soon as possible, the teacher steps out of the leadership role, and each student in the group takes her turn as group leader. It is, in fact, when students have the leadership role that they do some of their best learning. The teacher, however, continues to monitor the group as much as possible and intervenes when necessary to keep students on track and to facilitate the discussion.

In the Classroom 11.4 shows the four steps of the procedure and very briefly illustrates the responses they might prompt for fifth-graders reading Bradley Cruxton's *Discovering the Amazon Rainforest.*

In formal studies of reciprocal teaching, students have usually worked with reciprocal teaching for a 20-day period, which has been sufficient to produce the gains described earlier. To give you a more concrete indication of what those gains look like, we present a transcript of a seventh-grader's work with the procedure. In the Classroom 11.5 (pp. 345–346) presents the student's discussion of several texts (taken

Reciprocal Teaching

The session begins with reading a short segment of text, typically a paragraph or so. The leader reads it aloud or students read silently. The four steps of reciprocal teaching then follow.

Questioning

Once the segment has been read, the leader or other group members generate several questions prompted by the passage, and members of the group answer the questions. For example, after reading the opening paragraph of Cruxton's *Discovering the Amazon Rainforest*, a student might ask, "What does a rainforest look like?" Another student might respond, "Very tall trees, lots of plants and animals, not much light under the tall tree branches."

Clarifying

If the passage or questions produce any problems or misunderstandings, the leader and other group members clarify matters. For example, in continuing with *Discovering the Amazon Rainforest*, a student might point out that the only plants that can grow in the rainforest are those that can grow upward toward the light, because the branches of the giant trees act like a sun umbrella and block the light. Other members of the group might agree but then point out that some plants, such as mushrooms, don't need light.

Summarizing

After all the questions have been answered and any misunderstandings have been clarified, the leader or other group members summarize the segment: "A rainforest is a place of giant trees, lots of rain, many different kinds of plants and animals, with little change in temperature, day to night, season to season."

Predicting

Based on the segment just read, segments that have preceded it, and the discussion thus far, the leader or other group members make predictions about the contents of the upcoming section: "I think in the next section we will learn about some of the different kinds of living things—plants, animals, and people—that reside in the rainforests."

The sequence of reading, questioning, clarifying, summarizing, and predicting is then repeated with subsequent sections but now the students take the lead in using the strategies and the teacher provides support. Eventually the students should be able to sustain the discussion on their own.

---

myeducation**lab**

Learn how to explicitly teach students strategies to make meaning from text by completing the activity "Teaching Comprehension Skills and Strategies." (To find this activity, go to the topic *Comprehension* in MyEducationLab and click on Building Teaching Skills and Dispositions.)

from the work of Brown & Palincsar, 1989) and illustrates the student's progress by showing her performance on five different days.

As the transcript illustrates, the student progressed from being unable to phrase an appropriate question to phrasing a very clear and concise one. As the student became increasingly competent, the teacher gradually turned over responsibility for generating questions to her. On day 1, the teacher had to phrase the question for the student. On day 4, he provided substantial scaffolding to assist the student in phrasing a question. On day 7, he needed to use much less scaffolding. On day 11, when the student produced two good questions, he reminded her that the procedure called for only one. And on day 15, he simply praised the student, as she was able to produce a clear, concise, and appropriate question without the teacher's assistance.

As the transcript further shows, the leader's role is crucial. Skilled leaders can keep the discussion on track, constantly assess students' strengths and weaknesses, and provide just enough scaffolding to challenge students while ensuring that they succeed. No one, of course, is better able to do this than a skilled teacher.

Increasing the Questioning Ability of a Seventh-Grade Student

Day 1

- **Text:** The water moccasin, somewhat longer than the copperhead, is found in the south-eastern states. It lives in swampy regions. It belongs, as do also the copperhead and the rattlesnake, to a group of poisonous snakes called pit vipers. They have pits between their eyes and their nostrils which, because they are sensitive to heat, help the snakes tell when they are near a warm-blooded animal. Another name for the water moccasin is "cotton-mouth." This name comes from the white lining of the snake's mouth.

Student: What is found in the southeastern snakes, also the copperhead, rattlesnakes, vipers—they have. I'm not doing this right.

Teacher: All right. Do you want to know about the pit vipers?

Student: Yeah.

Teacher: What would be a good question about the pit vipers that starts with the word *why*?

Student: (No response)

Teacher: How about, "Why are the snakes called pit vipers?"

Student: Why do they want to know that they are called pit vipers?

Teacher: Try it again.

Student: Why do they, pit vipers in a pit?

Teacher: How about, "Why do they call the snakes pit vipers?"

Student: Why do they call the snakes pit vipers?

Teacher: There you go! Good for you.

DAY 4

- **Text:** Spinner's mate is much smaller than she, and his body is dull brown. He spends most of his time sitting at one side of her web.

Student: (No question)

Teacher: What's this paragraph about?

Student: Spinner's mate, How do Spinner's mate . . .

Teacher: That's good. Keep going.

Student: How do Spinner's mate is smaller than . . . How am I going to say that?

Teacher: Take your time with it. You want to ask a question about Spinner's mate and what he does, beginning with the word *how*.

Student: How do they spend most of his time sitting?

Teacher: You're very close. The question would be, "How does Spinner's mate spend most of his time?" Now, you ask it.

Student: How does Spinner's mate spend most of his time?

DAY 7

- **Text:** Perhaps you are wondering where the lava and other volcanic products come from. Deep within our earth there are pockets of molten rock called magma. Forced upward in part by gas pressure, this molten rock continually tries to reach the surface. Eventually—by means of cracks in the crustal rocks or some similar zone of weakness—the magma may break out of the ground. It then flows from the vent as lava, or spews skyward as dense clouds of lava particles.

Student: How does the pressure from below push the mass of hot rock against the open-ing? Is that it?

Teacher: Not quite. Start your question with, "What happens when?"

Student: What happens when the pressure from below pushes the mass of hot rock against the opening?

Teacher: Good for you! Good job.

(continued)

DAY 11

- **Text:** One of the most interesting of the insect-eating plants is the Venus's flytrap. This plant lives in only one small area of the world—the coastal marshes of North and South Carolina. The Venus's flytrap doesn't look unusual. Its habits, however, make it truly a plant wonder.

  Student: What is the most interesting of the insect-eating plants, and where do the plants live?

  Teacher: Two excellent questions! They are both clear and important questions. Ask us one at a time now.

DAY 15

- **Text:** Scientists also come to the South Pole to study the strange lights that glow overhead during the Antarctic night. (It's a cold and lonely world for the few hardy people who "winter over" the polar night.) These "southern lights" are caused by the Earth acting like a magnet on electrical particles in the air. They are clues that may help us understand the Earth's core and the upper edges of its blanket of air.

  Student: Why do scientists come to the South Pole to study?

  Teacher: Excellent question! That is what this paragraph is all about.

Source: Brown, Ann L., & Palincsar, Annemarie. (1984). "Reciprocal Teaching of Comprehension-Fostering and Comprehension-Monitoring Activities," *Cognition and Instruction, 1*(2), pp. 138–139. Reprinted by permission of the publisher (Taylor & Francis Group, www.informaworld.com).

Because reciprocal teaching is consistent with the principles of effective teaching, is strongly supported by research, and assists students in understanding and learning from challenging expository material, we recommend using it in your classroom as yet another procedure for fostering your students' increasingly sophisticated literacy.

REFLECT and *Apply*

5 Get together with half a dozen of your classmates, pick a strategy and a grade level, and design the first 2 days of instruction on the strategy, with each of you creating one segment of the instruction—for example, the motivation and interest-building segment. Then, actually present the instruction to another group of your classmates.

6 Consider our description of the ways in which strategy instruction changes as you progress through a unit, and see if you can come up with some other ways in which it might change as students become more and more competent and comfortable with a strategy.

Organizing Your Strategy Curriculum

Assessment

Meet individually with students to discuss their strengths and the areas that need improvement. Use student work samples and your journal notes to identify their strengths and weaknesses in using comprehension strategies.

We have outlined nine important strategies that good readers use and we have provided a thorough description of how to teach students to determine importance. In Appendix B we give similar treatment for a lesson on making inferences. As we conclude the chapter, we need to consider how these strategies might be organized into a curriculum. In some cases, the curriculum will consist of teaching one strategy a week and covering 20 or more during the school year (Dewitz, Jones, & Leahy, 2009). Strategy instruction should be cumulative, building an expanding repertoire of strategies that the students can use. Thus, at the beginning of the school year, you should begin with establishing a purpose for reading and using prior knowledge. Once students are reasonably adept at these two strategies, you can add on asking and answering ques-

Fifth-grade teacher Joe Gonzales motivates his struggling readers as they grow in their strategic proficiency by audiotaping their oral reading and talk about text during small-group instruction and playing it back for them. As the children listen to themselves read and talk, they note the strategies that they hear themselves and others use in the group. The activity helps students become more metacognitive about their reading and more aware of their growth as readers. Before Mr. Gonzales has students do this, he models how to do it for them. To accomplish this, he tells the students that he will audiotape their reading and talk so that they can notice the strategies that they are using. He shares that, when readers notice the way they use strategies, they will become more aware of them and better at using them. He then tapes the day's reading and talk. The next day, he plays the tape for the students. As they listen, Mr. Gonzales notes the strategies that he hears group members using. He makes comments like the following: "David wasn't sure he understood what happened at this point in the story, so he asked a question; Peter answered David's question using his background knowledge. Shyanne noted the sky was getting dark and made an inference that a storm was coming; Jasmine used to live in Kansas. She drew upon her background knowledge to predict that the storm would be a tornado." Mr. Gonzales makes these comments as he hears them on the tape, rather than waiting until the end of the tape. On a subsequent day, he engages students in the activity again. They do this at various points in the school year so that they can see their progress.

tions using the Question–Answer Relationship (QAR) procedure (Raphael, 1986). At this point, the students should be able to use three different strategies during teacher guided small-group work, when they work with partners, or when they read alone. To this set of three strategies, we would finally add summarizing and being metacognitive. Thus we have introduced the same set of strategies used in reciprocal teaching.

At this point, the further introduction and use of strategies should be determined by the texts that the students are reading. If you plan to use fiction or your core reading program mandates extensive work with fiction, then it is important to add in story mapping for its own sake and as a structure of summarizing fiction. Fiction also demands that the process of making inference be included. The reader is often called on to infer a character's feelings, motives, and traits. Finally, when reading fiction it is useful for students to create their own mental images of settings, characters, and events.

Expository material calls for a different set of strategies and these should be taught during social studies and science study. In these content areas, determining importance is critical and it is essential for summarizing. Graphic information predominates in content materials and students need to know how to read and interpret it. Finally, students should be able create their own graphic representations of what they read. Expository material demands different inferences than does narrative and students must learn to infer cause-and-effect relationship, search for problems and solutions, and infer the main idea. When students are reading in the content areas they are still responsible for establishing a purpose, using prior knowledge, and asking and answering questions. Whereas some strategies, like setting a purpose, are relatively easy and demand little work, learning to make inferences may require months of study.

During the course of a school year in the upper elementary grades you should be able to focus on the five basic strategies and then consider at least one additional strategy for narrative and expository text. The remaining strategies can be introduced the following year. It would be very useful for all the grade-level teachers to meet and decide which strategies, beyond the basic five, should be introduced each academic year.

Assessment

As Michael Pressley and others have noted, active comprehension develops over months and years, not days and weeks. This means that the observations you use to assess students' use of the strategies you teach needs to extend throughout the year and, if possible, be continued by the students' teachers in the years following initial instruction.

Strengths *and Challenges* of Diversity

As we have repeatedly noted, a balanced literacy curriculum is for all students—more accomplished readers, less accomplished readers, students who come less prepared to school, and students who do not speak English as their native language. This is as true for comprehension strategies as it is for other parts of the curriculum; however, adjustments for individual needs will be important here as well.

One danger is that capable readers who have already learned comprehension strategies might be both unreceptive to learning new ones and actually confused by attempts to replace an already functional strategy with a new one. The solution here is to know your students and their capabilities well, find out what strategies they already have, check periodically to see if they view the new ones as useful, and avoid imposing new strategies when they comprehend well.

With less proficient students, on the other hand, comprehension strategies are likely to be particularly welcome—if, that is, students see them as helpful, and the strategies truly are. You need to be especially careful to introduce them at a rate slow enough to prevent frustration yet rapid enough to avoid boredom, to give students plenty of time to apply them in class, and to deliberately structure students' work and the assessment system you use to reward their use of strategies. Over the past two decades, Donald Deshler and Jean Schumaker (1993; Schumaker & Deshler, 2003) have conducted more than a dozen studies clearly indicating that at-risk students can successfully learn to use comprehension strategies—if they are properly instructed. English language learners can be introduced to comprehension strategies but they will require considerably more support than native speakers (Gutierrez, 2005).

For students from certain cultures, the group work involved in learning strategies may be particularly facilitative and comfortable. With these students, you might let the group work continue for some time, gradually building in independent assignments and explaining to students that they will often need to use strategies in situations in which their classmates are not available, such as with work done at home.

Concluding *Remarks*

In this chapter, we focused on teaching reading comprehension strategies. Up to this point, we have

- Defined comprehension strategies
- Identified nine key strategies
- Described well-researched procedures for teaching strategies
- Described a strategy curriculum

One very important task remains—making your decision on which strategies to teach. These strategies will, in many cases, be determined by your state or district curriculum or your core reading program. If you are working with a core reading program, plan to spend more time on each strategy than the program prescribes and teach fewer strategies than it suggests. In many cases, a core program will teach the same strategy under two or more different labels or will needlessly separate one strategy into parts. Making inferences, drawing conclusions, and making generalizations all demand the same inferential thinking. Noting details and determining the main idea are part and parcel of the same strategy: determining what is important. You should teach a few strategies well, rather than many strategies less well. Comprehension strategies are complex procedures, and they need to be learned well if they are to be of real use to students.

The other important consideration is your district or state standards. In almost all schools students will be assessed on these standards starting in third grade. The five basic strategies—setting a purpose, using prior knowledge, asking and answering questions, summarizing, and metacognition—are essential and should be stressed from the beginning of the school year. Then, while continuing to work with these strategies, turn your attention to the district or state standards. Many of these standards will overlap with our list of nine comprehension strategies. In most states, students are expected to determine the author's purpose, which overlaps with determining the main idea; similarly, cause and effect is related to making inferences. You would be remiss in ignoring your state standards.

Whatever strategy or strategies you teach, remember that learning the strategy itself is not the primary goal. Comprehension strategies are a means to an end—students' understanding of, learning from, and enjoyment of reading materials. Strategies are one of the key means of fostering higher-order thinking. When students make inferences, search for importance, summarize, and monitor, they will reach a deep understanding of what they read.

Extending Learning

1. One excellent way to better understand and appreciate the nature of good comprehension strategy instruction is to observe a teacher who is doing an excellent job of it. We suggest that you locate an effective strategy instructor, observe her teaching, and afterward talk to her about it. Potential sources for locating teachers are your university instructor, your cooperating teacher, other teachers you know, and your classmates.

2. To really come to understand strategy instruction, it is useful to study quality materials used in teaching strategies. One very solid set of materials, Making Meaning, is published by the Developmental Studies Center, a non-profit educational organization in Berkeley, California. Versions of the program are available for kindergarten through grade 6. Get a copy of one of the Making Meaning teacher's manuals, study it carefully, and compare the approach suggested there to the procedure suggested in this chapter. You will find a good deal of similarity but also some important differences. Write a brief description of the Making Meaning approach and its similarities to and differences from the approach suggested here.

Children's Literature

Cruxton, B. J. (1998). *Discovering the Amazon Rainforest.* New York: Oxford University Press. This book in the Discovery series describes the tropical rainforest of Brazil and examines plans for saving the rainforest. 64 pages.

Fleischman, J. (2002). *Phineas Gage: A Gruesome but True Story About Brain Science.* Boston: Houghton Mifflin. This fascinating and admittedly gruesome book tells about Phineas Gage, who, having survived a hideous brain accident in the mid 19th century, provided doctors with valuable information about how the brain functions. 85 pages.

Guest, E. H. (2004). *Iris and Walter and the Substitute Teacher.* San Diego, CA: Gulliver/Harcourt. When Iris's beloved teacher becomes ill, her grandfather steps in as substitute, with mixed results. 44 pages.

Jackson, D. M. (2005). *ER Vets: Life in an Animal Emergency Room.* Boston: Houghton Mifflin. A behind-the-scenes look at the animal-saving drama of a veterinary ER room. 96 pages.

Johnson, G., & Cutchins, J. (1988). *Scaly Babies: Reptiles Growing Up.* New York: Morrow. This informational book has four chapters of descriptive text and color photographs highlighting snakes, lizards, crocodiles, turtles, and their young. 40 pages.

McPhail, D. M. (2002). *The Teddy Bear.* New York: St. Martin's Press. A young boy's lost teddy bear ends up being found by a homeless old man who learns to love it as much as the boy did. 32 pages.

Ritchie, R. (1999). *Mountain Gorillas in Danger.* Boston: Houghton Mifflin. This is a short book that features classic photographs of mountain gorillas while the text presents the threat they face. 32 pages.

Sendak, M. (1963). *Where the Wild Things Are.* New York: Harper & Row. When Max is sent to bed without his supper, he imagines a world where he is king of the "wild things." 32 pages.

Stanley, D. (2002). *Saladin: Noble Prince of Islam.* New York: Morrow. This picture book relates the life story of Saladin, a 12th-century Muslim hero who held off the crusaders and united his people. 48 pages.

Woolridge, C. N. (2001). *When Esther Morris Headed West: Women, Wyoming, and the Right to Vote.* New York: Holiday House. This inspiring nonfiction picture book tells about the life of Esther Morris, a trailblazer for women's rights. 32 pages.

PEARSON myeducationlab

Now go to the topics "Media/Visual Literacy" and "Comprehension" in the MyEducationLab (www.myeducationlab.com) for your course, where you can:

- Find learning outcomes for the topics covered in this chapter along with the IRA standards that connect to these outcomes.

- Complete assignable activities in the Assignments and Activities section that show concepts in action to help you synthesize and apply strategies.

- Explore IRIS Center Resources—training enhancement materials that provide you with research-validated information and interactive materials to develop your skills in working with students.

- Apply and practice your understanding of the teaching skills identified in the chapter with the Building Teaching Skills and Dispositions exercises.

12

Encouraging Independent Reading and Reader Response

CHAPTER outline

"Hey, I read that book. It's cool!" Michael said.

"We're reading it now . . . for literature circle," Ian told him.

"Really? We read it in book club."

"Book club? What's that?"

"It's what we do in school . . . for reading. Everybody reads the same book, then we get together and talk about it. It's fun to hear what other people think about the same book. Sometimes they have the same ideas about a book, and sometimes they don't. It's kind of weird how people can read the same book and come up with lots of different ways to talk about it. Our teacher says it's because we have different experiences and those experiences make us see things differently."

"Your book club sounds a lot like our literature circle. We have some really cool discussions."

This conversation tells us a lot about these boys *and* their teachers—they very strongly value reading and responding to literature, something not all students do. How can we as educators make sure that all of our students very strongly value reading and responding to what they read? We can create classrooms that nurture independent reading and provide the time and space for students to respond to literature—two topics we discuss in this chapter.

Bob Daemmrich/PhotoEdit

CLASSROOM
vignette

Independent Reading

Independent reading, as we define it here, means students' selecting their own material to read for their own purposes. These purposes may include pleasure, information, insight—whatever motivates those who love reading to pick up a book. If students are to become fluent and engaged readers who constantly choose to read for knowledge and pleasure, it is crucial that they be given many opportunities to do so. Some years ago, Dixie Lee Spiegel (1981) suggested several benefits of independent reading. These are still true today. Independent reading

- Develops positive attitudes toward reading.
- Gives students a chance to expand their knowledge.
- Provides practice in decoding and comprehension strategies.
- Helps develop automaticity.
- Develops and expands students' vocabularies.

PEARSON
myeducationlab

Watch videos of five second graders reading independently and with others in the Literacy Portraits section of MyEducationLab. (For just one example, look at Rakie's February video clip, where she is buddy reading with Audri.)

More recently, Richard Anderson (1996) and Anne Cunningham and Keith Stanovich (2003) have summarized research that clearly demonstrates the rich cognitive gains that come from wide reading, including substantial growth in vocabulary and knowledge (A. Cunningham, 2005). However, two central questions remain. How much time should we provide for independent reading? How do we motivate students to engage in it?

Providing Time to Read

Common sense tells us that we get better at just about anything by doing more of it. Reading is no exception, and, as we just noted, research confirms this notion. In one study, for example, Anderson and his colleagues (Anderson, Wilson, & Fielding, 1988) investigated fifth-graders' activities outside of school and the relationship of those activities to reading proficiency. Not surprisingly, they found that students who spent time reading books made greater strides in reading than those who spent their time on other activities. Independent reading, therefore, has to be scheduled along with all the other activities we advocate—scaffolded reading, vocabulary development, word study, and comprehension strategy instruction.

How much time should be set aside each school day for students to read independently for pleasure? When Michael Pressley and his colleagues looked at effective teachers they reached the conclusion that about two-thirds of a child's day should be spent reading and writing real texts. This means that students should be reading somewhere between 30 to 40 minutes a day, with some of this time reserved for independent reading instead of guided reading. Other research recommends at least 10 to 15 minutes a day of independent reading (Fielding, Wilson, & Anderson, 1986). The amount of time spent in independent reading each day will depend on a number of factors—how often you schedule independent pleasure reading; what other opportunities for sustained reading students have in your classroom; the likelihood that students will read outside of school; and the age, interests, and maturity of students. As a rule of thumb, we recommend beginning with 5- to 10-minute periods for primary-grade children and 15- to 20-minute periods for older students. These times can, of course, be increased if your curriculum and students' interest and involvement allow it. All in all, the exact amount of time is not as important as making certain that there *is* a time set aside for pleasure reading on a consistent basis. Perhaps the easiest way to include independent reading is to make it part of the small-group rotations. So every day students read with the teacher, they work on projects independently and with others, and they read independently.

Providing a Rich Array of Reading Material, the Incentive to Read, and a Place to Read

Motivating students to read requires attention and planning, but the secrets to motivating students are often found within your own experiences as a reader. Avid readers have patterns to their reading. Many enjoy the same author, so when James Patterson or Jodi Picoult publishes a new novel they rush to read it. Other avid readers peruse the bestseller lists in bookstores and newspapers. Oprah Winfrey sets the reading tastes for many adults. Still others have interests or topics that they read about in great depth. Finally, many readers exchange information at work, at parties, and over email about what they are reading and how they are enjoying it. The secret to motivating independent reading is providing students with a steady source of information about good books and interesting authors. This is true for all students, but particularly for those who do not gravitate to reading and those whose home environment does not prompt and nurture reading. Students' reading material can come from a variety of sources—including their homes, their friends, the classroom library, classroom book clubs, the school library, and the public library. Types of selections can and should run the gamut from fiction to nonfiction, trade books, magazines, even textbooks—the choice is up to the student.

Although what children choose to read will vary considerably and come from a variety of sources, we have found it extremely important for the classroom teacher to make reading materials readily available—in fact, to make them virtually unavoidable. The classroom teacher needs to regularly talk about and share books. One week he might feature the works of a well-known author, such as Richard Peck, and if the students conduct an author study, reading the works of that author over several weeks, we can guarantee that library check-out rates for that author will increase, spurred on by the interests of the students in the class and what they tell their friends in other classes. In many classrooms teachers and students maintain a list of classroom and grade best-sellers. In some classrooms students keep a large chart of their best-loved books and each student may rate a book by adding a gold star after the title on the chart. In other classrooms the bestseller list is kept in a folder. In many of these classrooms students regularly give book talks.

One absolute essential for stimulating independent reading is a well-stocked classroom library, a feature lacking in all too many schools (Allington, Guice, Michelson, Baker, & Li, 1996). A stimulating classroom library should do what a good bookstore does, entice you to browse, sit, and read. Your classroom library should have the following characteristics:

- A semiprivate focal area that is attractive and that communicates the importance of the library in the classroom
- Comfortable seating for four to six children
- At least five to six books per child in your classroom
- Books that include a variety of genres, topics, and reading levels, as well as magazines, newspapers, manuals, and electronic text
- Shelving that holds books for display, preferably with the covers facing out
- Literature-oriented displays and props: posters, puppets, bulletin boards about the latest books, or book jackets

- To further student ownership of the classroom library, bulletin boards maintained by students to recommend specific books to classmates

Commercial book clubs, such as the Scholastic Book Clubs, Inc. (800-724-2424), make it very easy for you and your students to order books, and the extra points your students earn will help you stock your classroom library. We also suggest that you visit garage sales and used bookstores. You will also want to become thoroughly acquainted with your school library and local public library and the media specialists and librarians there, and you will want to introduce your students to these resources. Regular class visits to the school library and occasional field trips to the local public library are time well spent. For a young child the first important legal document in his life is a library card.

In the Classroom 12.1 provides some guidelines for choosing books.

Assisting Students in Selecting Material

Helping students select the right material—material that they can read, will read, will enjoy, and will profit from—is tremendously important. Moreover, this task is particularly important and particularly difficult with less able and less avid readers, students who do not read much and are therefore less familiar with what's available and less skilled at selecting appropriate material. As you are thinking about matching students and texts—particularly matching less proficient readers with texts they can and will read—be sure to consider the information on text difficulty we presented in Chapter 8. In the Classroom 12.2 offers some guidelines for assisting students in selecting reading material they will enjoy.

Establishing and Maintaining an Independent Reading Program

There are two ways to schedule independent reading time in your literacy program. One is to establish a designated time for everyone to read—for example, the last 15 minutes before lunch or after returning from recess. The problem with this approach is that the demands of instruction, working on strategies, vocabulary study, and scaffolded reading tend to swamp this designated time and often it is sacrificed for other pieces of instruction. This is especially true in schools that live and die by their test scores.

In the Classroom

12.1

Guidelines on Choosing Books for Your Classroom Library

- Find out your students' interests. The first few weeks of the year, ask students what interests them. Jot their responses in a teacher logbook. Then, throughout the year, record the likes and dislikes of each student and the books and other material they have enjoyed reading. Watch what the students read; they will tell you what is hot.
- Get recommendations from your colleagues and the school media specialist. Ask your students' former teachers what reading material has been successful with these students and your school media specialist about what is available and what she recommends for your particular group of students.
- Become familiar with the many guides to selecting reading material for children, such as the *Horn Book Guide to Children's and Young Adult Books* (2002) and *Best Books for Children: Preschool Through Grade 6* (Gillespie, 2002).

Guidelines for Helping Students Select Reading Material

- Give book and author talks. Occasionally, introduce students to new authors by telling a little about them, giving previews of their works, and reading excerpts from their books.
- Read from a "big book" and then make multiple copies of the "little" books available.
- Read a chapter from a novel or chapter book and then make that book available.
- Suggest that students use the "Goldilocks Principle"—choose a book that's not too hard, not too easy, but "just right."
- Invite students to give book and author talks in which they recommend books and authors they have enjoyed.
- Invite students to write previews, reviews, and testimonials and display them around the room.
- Invite your school media specialists or public librarians to talk about their favorite books and authors as well as give information on the public library's resources and how to locate materials.
- Invite other adults—parents, the principal, secretary, custodian, coach, nurse—to talk about their favorite books.

The second approach is to require independent reading but make it part of the students' rotations or personal everyday activities. So during a typical day a student might work with the teacher, read in a literature circle, complete a reading or writing assignment with a partner, and read independently. Independent reading is part of the daily activities all students complete but when they do so is up to each individual student. By incorporating an uninterrupted reading time into your daily routine, you will be not only contributing to students' growth in reading fluency but also sending several powerful messages. Among these are that reading books is important, that reading is something everyone can do, that reading is important to you, that children are capable of sustained thought, and that you believe they can and do comprehend what they read (McCracken & McCracken, 1978).

Encouraging Out-of-School Reading

Thus far, we have stressed the importance of in-school reading because it is the reading that you as a teacher have the most control over. However, anything you can do to encourage and support out-of-school reading is likely to be well worth your efforts. As we have said repeatedly, students need to read a lot if they are to get really good at it *and* enjoy all the cognitive benefits reading provides. Students spend only about 14 percent of their time in school, with the rest of their time either sleeping (33%) or doing something (sports, eating, video games, TV, hanging out) at home or in the community (53%) (Donovan, Bransford, & Pellegrino, 1999). This being the case, out-of-school reading can, and if at all possible *must*, contribute hugely to the amount of practice students get.

Getting parents involved can greatly enhance students' out-of-school reading time. One way to do this is with book bags and home/school reading logs.

An inviting, well-stocked classroom library goes a long way in nurturing lifelong readers.

Richard Hutchings/PhotoEdit

Australian educator Grace Oakley describes electronic talking books as texts "that are backed up with a sound track, graphics, and often animation. Most allow silent reading, although the reader can usually opt to hear the story read out loud by a fluent reader. Indeed, sometimes there is a choice of narrators. The text is often highlighted as it is read by the narrator, allowing the child to follow along. By clicking on a particular word, the child can often access its pronunciation and often a definition, or even a picture." Oakley and her colleague Jenny Jay (2008) have reported a great deal of success with motivating reluctant readers' at-home reading by using electronic talking books. Each week for 10 weeks, they had children ages 8 to 11 select a CD-ROM of electronic talking books to take home from school. At the end of the 10-week project, students reported that they liked the electronic talking books. Moreover, their at-home reading increased by 10 percent. Most of the parents reported that the electronic talking books positively influenced their child's reading ability and attitude toward reading and that their child enjoyed reading the books more than traditional books. For students who are motivated by technology, electronic talking books can be a good option for use during school hours or at home. An inexpensive online resource for electronic talking books is the Raz-Kids site (www.raz-kids.com). Raz-Kids is a sister website to Reading A–Z, a popular online resource for guided reading texts. Like Reading A–Z, Raz-Kids provides fiction and nonfiction leveled texts. The texts on the Raz-Kids site are supported with oral readings and animated pictures, however, and another feature allows children to record their own reading. ●

Book bags are simply bags made of sturdy material, such as corduroy or canvas. And book logs are small journals that fit into the bags. Students carry books to and from school in these bags. Parents and students use the logs to make comments about the books they read.

Here's how one teacher orchestrated an out-of-school reading program. Students and their parents in Roslyn Breslouer's first grade participated in a program called "We Love to Read Beary Much" (International Reading Association, 1997a):

As part of the "We Love to Read Beary Much" program, my first-graders carry books home for their parents to read with them. Their parents sign a comment sheet, and many include notes about their reading experience. I think something as simple as sending home a book or letter on a regular basis makes a big difference. I think parents just need that personal communication.

As part of the bear theme, all students have their own bear symbol on a bear bulletin board, and they get a bear sticker for every book that a parent has signed a card for. We have a big bear named Love-a-Lot that sits on a chair in the front of the classroom. Sometimes children read to Love-a-Lot or to Ted, the troll who sits on the bear's lap.

One of the keys to the success of this program is a classroom library well stocked with paperbacks. Another important factor is keeping parents involved. To do this, I hold "We Love to Read Beary Much" parties in December, March, and June each year. These parties often draw 15 to 20 parents, who sometimes bring along grandparents, aunts and uncles, and students' younger siblings. Students recite poetry to the group of parents, who then spread out and read to their own children (and sometimes others as well). They like the idea that they can read with the children and hear the children read and recite. I also hold after-school workshops twice a year to give parents advice on how to read to children.

It's especially enjoyable to me that the program gets the parents to spend quality time with their children to read and discuss books. By the end of the year, the kids love books. Books are an integral part of their lives.

—Roslyn Breslouer, first-grade teacher

One of the keys to a successful independent reading program is accountability. As a teacher you want to make sure that students are reading appropriate books and reading with meaning. When the National Reading Panel (NICHD, 2000) studied programs that encourage independent reading, like sustained silent reading, they could find little experimental research to support such practices. Yet others have found a strong relationship between extensive reading and increased reading achievement (Anderson et al., 1988). Some have suspected that independent reading without some accompanying instruction or accountability may not be very beneficial (Kamil, 2008). Therefore we turn to two projects that have added some accountability to independent reading with considerable success.

Thomas White and James Kim (2008) developed a program to motivate children to read over the summer. At the end of the school year the students are assessed to determine their reading levels and interests. Then each student is given a book to take home and read. After reading the book the student completes a response card and reflects on fluency and comprehension practices (see Figure 12.1). When the card is mailed to the school district, the student is mailed another book. This process is repeated throughout the summer, with the student receiving up to eight books. The response card provides a good way for students to reflect on their reading and a way for the teacher to maintain accountability, although it

*A*ssessment

Occasionally collect students' home/school reading logs, tally the number of books students have taken home to read, and note the types of books students have chosen. This will give you an idea of not only how much and how often students read at home, but also what their interests are and what level of books they choose to read.

Figure 12.1 **Responding to Books with Oral Reading and Comprehension Scaffolding**

1. What is the title of the book you read?

   _____

2. Did you finish reading this book? ❏ Yes ❏ No, I stopped on page _____

3. How many times did you read this book? ❏ 1 time ❏ 2 times ❏ 3 times or more

4. What did you do to better understand this book? (check all that apply)

   ❏ I reread parts of this book.

   ❏ I made predictions about this book.

   ❏ I made connections (text-to-text, text-to-self).

   ❏ I summarized parts of this book.

5. After you read this book, tell someone what the book was about. Pick a part of the book to read aloud two times. Ask him or her how you improved the second time you read the section and ask for his or her signature. (check all that apply)

   ❏ Did I read more smoothly?

   ❏ Did I read more words?

   ❏ Did I read with more expression? **Signature** _____

6. Write one comment about the book. _____

   _____

   _____

Source: White, T. G., & Kim, J. S. (2008). "Teacher and Parent Scaffolding of Voluntary Summer Reading." *The Reading Teacher, 62,* 116–125. Reprinted by permission.

Motivating Struggling Readers

Graphic novels are often very appealing to children and in this way can motivate struggling readers. Former school librarian Elizabeth Haynes (2009) explains that graphic novels, like picture books and chapter books, are a format rather than a genre—graphic novels come in many genres. For those to whom the format is unfamiliar, Haynes shares that graphic novels are combinations of text and art. They tell full stories with beginnings, middles, and ends. School media specialist Allyson Lyga (2006) relates the many benefits of graphic novels. She notes that for readers who have difficulty visualizing events as they read, the art in graphic novels provides images. Furthermore, the successive images in the novels build understanding of plot development. Thus, they increase comprehension. Lyga shares that both boys and girls are interested in graphic novels and that there are many to suit each gender; boys may gravitate toward graphic novels like *Buzzboy* and *Adventures of Tintin*, whereas girls may prefer *Peanutbutter* and *Monkey vs. Robot*. Some graphic novels, Lyga notes, are connected with children's favorite television shows and in this way can spur motivation to read. Two examples she cites are *Lizzie McGuire* and *SpongeBob SquarePants*.

does require some instruction for students to understand the use of the response card.

Ray Reutzel and his colleagues (Reutzel, Jones, Fawson, & Smith, 2008) developed a short reading conference that teachers have with each student. During the conference the teacher takes a 1-minute reading sample and notes students' reading accuracy and reading fluency. She then follows this up with a short comprehension assessment. Students retell what they are reading and answer a few generic comprehension questions. For narrative text students are expected to talk about the characters, setting, problems, and events. Students reading expository text should discuss the main idea, supporting details, procedures, and explanations. At the end of the conference the student decides what he plans to read next, how much he plans to read before the next conference, and establishes a plan for sharing his book.

REFLECT and Apply

1. Think about what you read for entertainment, escape, and insight. How do you choose what to read? What influences your reading habits? Create a concept map of how these influences affect what you read. Take what you have learned and think about how you will shape the reading behavior of your students.

2. Jot down a few reasons why it's important for students to do a lot of out-of-school reading as well as in-school reading. Prepare a pep talk on this subject to give to parents on "Back-to-School" night. Write out your pep talk, or give it orally in front of your classmates.

Assessment

You can assess whether students are responding emotionally to literature by occasionally asking students questions such as "How did it make you feel when . . . ?"

Responding to Literature

Perhaps you recall a time when your teachers asked a series of questions about a story you read. You believed there were "right" answers to those questions, and you tried your best to deliver them. Some of those questions certainly did have "right" answers. For example, if your teacher asked you to name the two main characters in "Gone with the Wiener," and you answered Homer and Gustav when they actually were Tina and Joey, your teacher might assume (rightly) that you either read a different story, didn't comprehend the story, or hadn't read the story (certainly an unlikely eventuality!). However, other kinds of questions leave room for interpretation, that personal transaction that takes place between the reader and the text. One such question is, How do you think Tina felt when Joey sent her roses? *You* might answer the question by saying that Tina felt happy because Joey remembered her birthday. However, a classmate might decide that Tina felt nervous because roses are a symbol of love and Tina was ambivalent about her own feelings for Joey. You are responding to the story one way, and your classmate is responding quite a different way to the very same piece of literature.

As discussed in Chapter 1, reader-response theory—much of which evolved from the extended work of Louise Rosenblatt (1938/1995, 1978)—centers on the belief that the reader is crucial to the construction of the literary experience. The reader doesn't come to the text empty, hoping to be filled, but brings meaning to the text. Reading is a transaction between the reader and the writer. Any particular reading of a text—particularly a literary text such as fiction and poetry—will produce an interpretation that reflects both the meaning intended by the author and the meaning constructed by the reader (Galda & Cullinan, 2006; Mills, Stephens, O'Keefe, & Waugh, 2004).

A number of the postreading activities we discussed in Chapter 10—for example, those involving discussion, writing, art, dance, music, and drama—promote reader response. As you recall, many of these encourage students to make personal responses to literature and give them opportunities to use a variety of modes of expression in doing so, as Galda and Graves (2010), among others, recommend. In the Classroom 12.3 illustrates how a class of third-graders might be encouraged to respond artistically after reading several books about animals.

Three Frameworks That Promote Literature and Reader Response

Literature circles, Book Club and Book Club *Plus,* and the reading workshop are instructional frameworks that center around students' reading and personally responding to literature. Although these programs have literature and reader response at their core, they have other goals and instructional objectives as well. Each seeks to develop an understanding of narrative elements, build vocabulary knowledge, and increase the students' use of strategies. These three instructional frameworks vary in terms of how often students work in groups, how much student choice is encouraged, and how much teachers engage in direct instruction. Each of these three approaches can be combined with what we have already discussed about the development of fluency, vocabulary, and comprehension strategies.

Literature Circles

A host of formats for postreading discussion groups designed to foster reader response emerged during the 1990s. One of those was literature circles (Short & Klassen, 1993). Simply defined, literature circles are groups of students who come together to discuss a text they have all chosen to read. Before meeting in the discussion group, students read silently and develop responses they plan to share with their group (Spiegel, 1998). The response format is typically structured so that each student takes on a specific role during the discussion. For example, one student might be the leader and have the job of asking questions. Another student might focus on making

*A*ssessment

For some additional possibilities for small-group discussions of literature, take a look at the SRE lesson plan for *Because of Winn-Dixie* in Appendix B.

12.3

Instructional Routines

Students' Artistic Responses After Reading About Animals

Imagine your third-grade class has just finished a unit on animals. Over a 4-week period, they have read numerous fiction and nonfiction trade books. As a culminating activity, you read William Jay Smith's book of poems, *Birds and Beasts*, aloud to them.

- Divide the class into three heterogeneous groups and assign each group one of the three nonverbal expressive "languages"—art, drama, or dance.
- Have each group decide which animal it will portray in its appointed "language" and brainstorm about what materials and approaches it might take. For example, the art group might suggest watercolor painting, collages, scratch boards, paper sculpture, clay modeling, or papier-mâché. After the students have brainstormed together and decided on their animal and some possibilities for depicting this animal in a visual way with the resources available, have them work individually, in subgroups, or in pairs to create their animal, using whatever medium they feel will best capture the essence of their animal.
- The drama group's goal is to create a play in which the animal they studied is an important character. The group will need to decide whether the play is fantasy, in which the animal can take on any role, or whether it is realistic and therefore the animal may be central to the problem—for example, the play centers on establishing a sanctuary for endangered chimpanzees in Africa. During the brainstorming session, invite students to develop characters, the setting, a problem, and a plot. Older students might write out all the dialogue in the play and younger students might create an outline and rely on improvisation.
- The dance group's goal is to depict its chosen animal through movement. During a brainstorming session, encourage students to offer suggestions about what body movements represent this animal. Their discussion will involve both showing and telling, using the following sorts of words to describe the characteristics and movements of their chosen animal—*slow, steady, heavy, swinging, head-moving, tail-swishing, clomp-clomp-clomp*. The group might decide to work together to create one dance that represents the animal or to work in pairs or subgroups.
- After their brainstorming sessions, give students an hour or so over 2 or 3 days to come up with nonverbal expressions of their chosen animals. On the fourth day, invite them to present their work. They will make their animals come to life in visual art, music, or dance, and the other students can guess the animals they are depicting.

connections between the text and other texts or other ideas. Other students might discuss new interesting vocabulary, or particularly interesting and poignant passages, or summarize what has been read. It is important to point out that these roles in a literature circle demand the same kind of thinking that we stressed when discussing comprehension strategy instruction. Students should also understand the close parallels between strategy instruction and literature circles. Each time the literature circle meets the students change roles, so all practice multiple ways of responding to a text. Discussions are student led, and when students finish reading and discussing one selection, or one book, new groups are formed.

According to Harvey Daniels (1994), the teacher's role in literature circles is that of a facilitator or monitor, but not a participant. However, while examining "teacher talk" in literature circles, Kathy Short and colleagues (Short, Kaufman, Kaser, Kahn, & Crawford, 1999) noted that, in addition to being a facilitator, the teacher sometimes assumes the role of participant, mediator, or active listener, depending on what students talked about and the topic under discussion.

In the Classroom 12.4 describes how to set up literature circles in a fourth-grade classroom.

Establishing Literature Circles in a Fourth-Grade Classroom

- Preselect a number of books and have students look through them. For example, you might choose books by a single author such as Patricia MacLachlan and make available *Sarah, Plain and Tall; Skylark; Caleb's Story; Journey; Baby; The Facts and Fictions of Minna Pratt; Cassie Binegar;* and *Painting the Wind*, which represent a range of interests and reading skills. After the students have familiarized themselves with the books, they select which book they would like to read, naturally forming groups. Alternatively, you can form students into groups by reading levels and then give them two titles from which to choose.

- Teach the roles students will assume during the discussion, which will require two or three lessons. Daniels (1994) suggests the following roles: Discussion Director/ Questioner, Literary Luminary, Illustrator, Connector, Summarizer, Vocabulary Enricher, and Investigator. You will need to give everyone in the class a short text and then model each role, demonstrating how to ask questions, make connections, or summarize. After you have modeled the role, give students the opportunity to try out the role with a short story and then give them feedback. We suggest starting with four students in a group and four roles.

- Place students in groups where they will be reading their book. Once the groups have been formed, determine (with input from each group) how long will be spent reading the book, how many pages a day group members will read, when the group will meet, and who will assume which role. Remind students when the next meeting of their group will be, how many pages they will need to read, and what type of response will need to be completed before their next meeting.

- Students then need independent time to read their book and complete the role sheet. The Discussion Leader has to develop questions; the Literary Luminary has to find passages that are exciting, funny, moving, or puzzling; and the Investigator has to find background information about topics in the book.

- Meet periodically with each group—as a participant, not as a leader. Help each student complete his assigned role. Thus, if the Vocabulary Enricher hasn't located some words, point them out. If the Literary Luminary neglected a particular rich passage, point it out. Try to sit in with each group each week. Remind them to change roles, read the next chapters, and complete their new role sheets. Periodically evaluate the literature circles, noting what went well and what could use improvement.

- When the group is close to completing the book, encourage them to discuss possible postreading activities, such as those listed in the SRE framework described in Chapter 10.

- Form new groups with new reading material. This allows students the opportunity to work with other students and gain other perspectives.

Although In the Classroom 12.4 illustrates literature circles based on works by a single author, groups might also be organized around certain themes or topics—including topics from content areas such as the Civil War, the civil rights movement, or immigration. Historical fiction enables students to link literature to their content areas of study. An excellent resource for identifying theme-related books to introduce to your students is *The Complete Guide to Thematic Units: Creating the Integrated Curriculum* (Meinbach, Rothlein, & Fredericks, 2000).

Whatever their focus, literature circles put a premium on the element of student choice and on student-led discussions. These result in "critical thinking and self-reflection on the text and higher student engagement" (Galda, Ash, & Cullinan, 2000). Through discussion, students share their own understanding of what they have read,

Student-led literature circles result in high student engagement and a deeper understanding and appreciation of literature.

Tannen Maury/The Image Works

test it against what others have gleaned, and come to new insights and interpretations. As third-grader Chris puts it,

> In literature circles, everyone has a chance to give their opinion and even if you don't agree with that person, you keep on talking because you know that you will get more ideas. You aren't trying to figure out one right answer. In reading groups, when someone gave the right answer, we were done talking. In literature circles, we keep on going. We try to come up with as many different directions as possible. (Short & Klassen, 1993)

Through this synthesizing process, readers come to a deeper understanding and appreciation of the literature they read.

Book Club and Book Club *Plus*

Book Club and later Book Club *Plus* are both the result of a collaborative effort involving university-based and school-based educators (Goatley, Brock, & Raphael, 1995; McMahon, Raphael, & Goatley, 1995; Raphael, Florio-Ruane, & George, 2001; Raphael, Florio-Ruane, George, Hasty, & Highfield, 2004; Raphael & McMahon, 1994). According to Taffy Raphael (2000), one of the creators of the Book Club and Book Club *Plus* programs, in the initial planning of the Book Club program she and her colleagues searched for a theoretical model that would foster a high degree of student engagement and also provide opportunities for literacy instruction. What they discovered was a model called the Vygotsky Space (see Figure 12.2), which consists of two axes—the public/private axis and the social/individual axis. When these two axes intersect, four quadrants are formed.

Differentiating Instruction

for

English Language Learners

Using Translators in Literature Circles

In a review of research related to English language learners, Kris Gutierrez (2005) notes that when English language learners are not allowed to use their first language to explore and learn new content, their classroom experiences are impoverished. To prevent this from happening, a teacher in a St. Paul, Minnesota, fourth-grade classroom with many Hmong- and Spanish-speaking students organized literature circles in the following manner. Within each literature circle, she included multiple speakers of each language. At least one of the Hmong- and Spanish-speaking students in each group was able to speak English fairly well. This child could then translate as needed for peers who could not communicate as well in English. The students could also be paired up to complete their role sheets. In this way, the English language learners who were not able to communicate as well in English could share their thoughts with the group, ask and answer questions, and be privy to their English-speaking classmates' thinking via their better-English-speaking peer(s). Every child in these small groups, then, could enjoy and benefit from talking about the literature selections.

Each of the quadrants provides opportunities for an activity or set of activities in the Book Club program. For example, quadrant 1, the public and social, is the whole-class setting where students learn literacy skills, strategies, and attitudes through teacher instruction and modeling. Quadrant 2, the social and private, represents opportunities for students to use what they have learned in quadrant 1 in the same way and for the same purposes. Working in this quadrant, third-graders might read about Gabrielle in *No Copycats Allowed!* (Graves, 1998) or fifth-graders might read about Angel in *The Same Stuff as Stars* (Paterson, 2002) and then write responses in their reading logs about times they have found themselves in new and challenging situations. Quadrant 3, the private and individual, is where students transform privately what they have learned and practiced. Here students make new discoveries and new interpretations. They are not just practicing the strategies that have been taught, but developing new insights. A student reading *Charlie Anderson* (Abercrombie & Graham, 1995), who realizes that the cat that has two homes is a symbol for the girls' lives after a divorce, has made a new interpretation and thus transformed the story. In quadrant 4, the individual and public, publication of private activity occurs. It is through publication—through student writing, book club discussions, or author's chair—that students' proficiency with conventional knowledge or transformation of that knowledge is revealed.

In addition to providing opportunities for students to work within each of these four quadrants, the Book Club program provides opportunities for students to be involved in four types of activities—reading, writing, book club discussion, and community share.

- *Reading* (10 to 20 minutes). The reading component of the Book Club program encourages students to respond aesthetically to what they read with evaluations, personal responses, comparisons to other texts, and the like. However, attention is also given to such matters as fluency, reading vocabulary, comprehension strategies, and genres of literature.

- *Writing* (10 to 15 minutes). The writing component grows out of the reading students do for the Book Club program and is designed to enhance their understanding of and response to what they read. Additionally, opportunities are provided for the kind of writing that requires planning, revision, and publishing.

- *Book clubs* (5 to 20 minutes). Book clubs are the student-led discussion groups for which the program was named. One of the goals of the Book Club program is for students to develop control over book club discussions and their own ways of preparing for them (Tierney & Readence, 2000). Another goal is for students to really learn to talk about books. In the Book Club program the reading material is teacher-selected high-quality literature based both on student interests and on various instructional objectives.

Figure 12.2 The Vygotsky Space

Source: Gavelek, J. R., & Raphael, T. E. (1996). "Changing Talk About Text: New Roles for Teachers and Students." *Language Arts, 73* (3), 182–192. Copyright 1996 by the National Council of Teachers of English. Reprinted with permission.

*A*ssessment

When reporting student progress to parents, use multiple pieces of evidence. Information on students' oral reading, description of their participation in discussion, and some writing samples are three good options.

- *Community share* (5 to 20 minutes). The community share component is a time for teachers to meet with students as a whole class. Community share time can occur before or after students read a selection. Prior to reading, the teacher engages students in activities that will help prepare them for reading, such as building background knowledge or discussing the structure of the upcoming selection. Following book club discussions, students in different book clubs might share their thoughts on their books, debate issues prompted by their reading, or talk about confusing or disturbing aspects of their book that they have not been able to resolve in their individual book clubs. Community share time might also encompass mini-lessons, which can include any one or a combination of explicit instruction, modeling, and scaffolding.

The teacher's role in any of the four quadrants and during any of the four activities can be that of instructor, modeler, scaffolder, facilitator, or participant, depending on what the students or situation requires. That is, the teacher does whatever is necessary to further students' competence.

Book Club *Plus* adds a skills-and-strategy instruction component to the Book Club program and is built around a theme for the year. For example, MariAnne George used "Our Storied Lives" as a theme for her third-grade class (Raphael, 2001). In George's classroom, the Book Club *Plus* instruction took place within three 3- to 8-week units—Unit 1: "Stories of Self," Unit 2: "Family Stories," and Unit 3: "Stories of Culture." The weekly instruction consisted of 3 consecutive days of Book Club, followed by 2 days of a literacy block. In the literacy block, the focus is on instruction and practice of skills and strategies. During this block, students work in guided reading groups and skills centers where they meet with the teacher. When students are not meeting with the teacher, they work independently to practice skills and work on theme-related writing, doing Internet research, journaling, and so on. See Figure 12.3 for a week's organization. The 2-day literacy block can occur at the beginning, middle, or end of the week.

Figure 12.3   **A Week's Organization for Book Club *Plus* Activities**

MONDAY	TUESDAY	WEDNESDAY	THURSDAY	FRIDAY
Daily Teacher Read-Aloud				
Book Club	Book Club	Book Club	Literacy Block	Literacy Block
• Opening community share (5–15 mins.) • Reading (10–20 mins.) • Writing (10–20 mins.) • Book clubs (5–20 mins.) • Closing community share (5–20 mins.)			Guided reading groups Skills centers Internet searches Journaling Unit work/writers workshop	
Social Studies Connection				

Source: Raphael, T. E. (2001). "Book Club *Plus:* A Conceptual Framework to Organize Literary Instruction." *Language Arts, 79,* 159–169. Copyright 2001 by the National Council of Teachers of English. Reprinted with permission.

The Book Club and Book Club *Plus* programs both put quality literature at their core as well as providing space for teachers to impart conventional knowledge about text processing.

Reading Workshop

Like Book Club and Book Club *Plus,* the reading workshop, first developed by Nancie Atwell (1987, 1998), structures reading time and activities to make reading the primary activity and to give students ownership of their reading. The reading workshop stresses the importance of the teacher's demonstrating and endorsing the value of reading by discussing books that he has read and what reading means to him, teaching strategies that will help students become independent readers, giving students time to read, responding to students' responses to what they read, and giving students opportunities to share their responses to what they read with others.

Since Atwell originally proposed the reading workshop, various authors have critiqued, experimented with, and modified the procedure. Our suggestions have been influenced by these authors and by our experiences. The four main components of the version of the reading workshop that we suggest are formatted as follows:

- Teacher sharing time (5–10 minutes)
- Mini-lessons (5–15 minutes)
- Self-selected reading and response (30–40 minutes)
- Students' sharing time (5–10 minutes)

During the short teacher sharing time that begins each session, the teacher shares some of the selections that have touched and interested him. For example, he might share the poem "Buffalo Dusk" by Carl Sandburg with his fifth-graders who are studying American history.

Next comes a short and tightly focused mini-lesson, a 5- to 15-minute period during which the teacher instructs the class as a whole. Early in the year, mini-lessons are likely to deal with procedural matters about conducting the reading workshop: what materials can be read, how long the reading period is, what sorts of reporting will be required, what to include in a response to a selection, what sorts of conferences will be held, and the like. Later mini-lessons can focus on whatever skill, strategy, text structure convention, or figurative language is particularly relevant to what students are reading. You might teach a mini-lesson on a literary device such as foreshadowing, or you might use a mini-lesson to give students advice on how to choose books they're likely to enjoy. Mini-lessons are often motivated by student needs that the teacher has observed. For example, if quite a few students are writing summaries of what they have read and their summaries lack focus, you might review the strategy of summarizing.

Self-selected reading and response is the core of the reading workshop. On workshop days, most students will spend 30 to 40 minutes silently reading. However,

Sharing a self-selected book with a buddy underscores the fun and value of reading.

iStockPhoto

Part of the assessment process involves collecting information about your students. Observing, discussing and questioning, interviewing, and student work samples are all tools you can use to assess student progress and plan for appropriate instruction.

Assessment

When conferencing with students in reading workshop, try the funnel approach described in Chapter 4. Begin with general questions that focus on a particular problem—expository writing, for example. Then move to more specific queries—supporting a main idea with details, for example.

silent reading is punctuated with several other activities, most frequently journaling. As they are reading their books, students keep a dialogue journal, in which they record their reactions, questions, and musings about what they are reading. These dialogue journals typically go to the teacher, who should periodically give a personal response to each student's thoughts. The teacher's response is critical. If no one is listening, most students stop writing. Dialogue journals can also be addressed to other students, so that there is student-to-student dialogue as well as teacher-to-student and student-to-teacher dialogues.

Another activity that takes place during the self-selected reading and response time is teacher conferencing. Periodically, the teacher meets with each student to discuss his reading accomplishments and upcoming plans for reading, as well as any concerns the student has. Because teachers might have 30 students and conferences are spread out, most teachers try to see two or three students a day. Ray Reutzel and his colleagues (Reutzel, Jones, Fawson, & Smith, 2008) have developed a simple system for conducting a reading conference and learning about students' progress in reading. We have reproduced their form in Figure 12.4.

Another possibility is student meetings. If several students discover that they are reading the same author, book, or genre, they may decide they have some things to discuss. Similarly, if the teacher learns that several students have something to share—or a common need—the teacher might schedule a small-group meeting. Whether the teacher is present will depend on the topic and purpose of the meeting.

Student sharing time is the last component in the reading workshop, a time when the class comes together to share what students have been doing. As in the writing workshop, which we describe in Chapter 13, not every student shares each day. Often it works best to have students sign up in advance to share, usually two to four students per session. The most common activity involves students' talking about what they have been reading and sharing their experiences and suggestions for good reading.

The reading workshop can easily exist alongside the other approaches to reading instruction we have already discussed and it should. In some classrooms a teacher will use half of the reading period, 30 to 40 minutes time, for work on skills and strategies instruction, and during the rest of the time the students are engaged in a reading workshop. The reading skills and strategies time allows the teacher to introduce and model new reading strategies, talk about text structure, and develop vocabulary knowledge. Sometimes the teacher meets with the whole class and they learn a new strategy and other times she meets with groups of students who share a common need. After the skills and strategy time is finished, the class shifts into the workshop mode. In this model the mini-lessons are dropped because what students need to know about skills and strategies has been introduced and scaffolded during the first part of the period. A mini-lesson might still be appropriate to review the procedures of the reading workshop or to plan who will be sharing at the end of the day.

Literature circles, book clubs, and the reading workshop are all instructional frameworks designed to stimulate students' interest in reading, to promote wide reading, and encourage interpretative response to literature. These classroom procedures share much in common. In all of these procedures students are expected to read widely and deeply. They reflect on what they read, write about it, and share it with others. Literature circles concentrate on small-group discussions and can be seen as an extension of comprehension strategy work. Book clubs promote both individual and small-group work, whereas the reading workshop is centered more on individual

Figure 12.4 Tracking Form for Individual Student Reading Conferences

Student Name _____   Date of Reading Conference _____

Title of Book Student Is Reading _____

Part A: Fluency
Teacher Running Record of Student 1-Minute Reading Sample

Number of Words Read _____

Number of Errors _____

Words Read Correctly Per Minute _____

Part B: Comprehension
Student Oral Retelling

Narrative Text:
❑ Setting   ❑ Characters   ❑ Problem   ❑ Goals   ❑ Episode(s)   ❑ Resolution

Expository Text:
❑ Main Idea   ❑ Supporting Detail(s)   ❑ Use of Vocabulary Terms

Questions to Discuss
Narrative: Ask story structure questions about setting, problem, characters, etc.
Expository: Ask about the topic, main idea, supporting details, procedures, explanations, etc.

Part C: Goal Setting
Book Completion Goal Date _____
Goal for Pages to Be Read at the Next Reading Conference _____

Part D: Sharing the Book
Book Response Project Selected and Approved with Teacher _____

Source: Reutzel, D. R., Jones, C. D., Fawson, P. C., & Smith, J. A. (2008). "Scaffolded Silent Reading: A Complement to Guided Repeated Oral Reading That Works!" *The Reading Teacher, 62,* 201. Reprinted by permission.

A Glimpse into a Classroom That Combines Instructional Frameworks

For Leigh Murray's students, each day begins with a whole-group activity that focuses on the important goals for the week. At the beginning of the week the whole-group lesson tends to be long as she uses the time to introduce new vocabulary or comprehension strategies and to model a new way of responding in their journal. Later in the week the whole-group time is brief as she spells out what they will be doing for the day, what groups she will meet with, and what students she will confer with.

The students then move to small groups. Each day Ms. Murray tries to see two groups, meeting with her struggling readers more frequently than the better readers. The small-group format allows the students time to practice reading strategies as she provides support and guidance. The students who are not meeting with Ms. Murray are reading on their own in texts that she has selected and then responding to their reading, journaling, or engaging in other writing activities. Some of the students will use this time to work in a literature circle they have organized themselves, deciding how often their literature circle will meet and how much they need to read. During the independent time, the students will complete the assigned readings and accompanying assignments or prepare for their literature circle. The small-group time typically lasts 30 to 40 minutes.

The class then shifts to a reading workshop. At the beginning of the school year, the lessons center on the organization of the classroom: behavioral expectations, choosing books, checking out books, how to complete dialogue journals, grading, and earning extra points. Ms. Murray frequently introduces books and authors that she thinks the children will like. Once students know her expectations and organization, she devotes more lessons to topics such as narrative voice, point of view, author's purpose, theme, and specific reading strategies, such as focusing on important words.

When she finishes the mini-lesson, students begin reading. A few students choose to sit on the cushions in the reading area. One or two pull their chairs to isolated corners of the room. Students do not use the period to look for books in the library unless they happen to finish a book during class. From time to time, students go to the shelves to get their reading dialogue journals. They add the title of the book they just started to a list of previously read books at the back of the journal. They then turn to the correspondence section of their journal, write the date, and begin a letter to the teacher or another adult. All students have to write a minimum of once every 2 weeks, telling Ms. Murray the title and author, sharing their opinions of their books, and relating the books to their lives in some way. Ms. Murray responds in writing to each letter, expressing her own ideas and encouraging students to try books and authors new to them.

student work. All of these frameworks should be combined with explicit instruction in vocabulary and comprehension. In the Classroom 12.5 takes you into a classroom where both direct instruction and frameworks for response to literature have been combined.

REFLECT *and Apply*

③ List as many advantages as you can for one of the approaches discussed in this chapter—literature circles, Book Club or Book Club *Plus* programs, or the reading workshop. Think also of disadvantages to these methods and then discuss the pros and cons of these ways of organizing reading with a classmate or group of classmates.

④ Identify a grade you would particularly like to teach. Then in writing, describe the approach or approaches you would use to foster independence in reading in that class, explaining your rationale and procedure as you might describe them to parents at your first classroom open house.

As we have repeatedly noted, the present-day literacy curriculum is for all students—more accomplished readers, less accomplished readers, challenged readers, and students who do not speak English as their native language. How can teachers accommodate these needs when it comes to encouraging independent reading and reader response?

In Chapter 8, we talked about using readability formulas and other more subjective measures to determine text difficulty and to help match readers with appropriate texts. Another such subjective measure, called leveling, was first developed in New Zealand by Marie Clay (1991), who, as part of her Reading Recovery Program, needed to find books with closely spaced difficulty levels to use with at-risk first- and second-graders. As Edward Fry (2002) points out, leveling takes into consideration factors that are absent from most readability formulas, such as a text's content, illustrations, length, curriculum it may or may not relate to, language structure, reader's background knowledge, and format. Thinking about these factors as you choose books for your challenged readers can help you locate appropriate material for their independent, literature circle, or book club reading.

To help students select their own books for independent reading, you might try color coding, as did Benchmark School, a school that has been particularly successful in improving the reading performance of less proficient readers. All of the books in its very large library are color coded for difficulty (Gaskins, 1994). Benchmark School requires its students, all of whom are less proficient readers, to read a lot of books. Color coding the books greatly simplifies the task of getting the right books to each student.

High-interest, easy-reading series books, specifically written for students who read below their grade level, can be particularly valuable for less proficient readers (Graves & Philippot, 2001). But well-stocked libraries are sometimes not enough. Less proficient readers usually have to be lured into those libraries and connected with the texts. Finding the right book is still key. Learn about the interests of your students, talk to the school and public librarians about exciting books, and preview as many books as you can. When you confer with

students, have a few titles at hand so they have some choice in what they will read.

You also will want to provide encouragement and support to students at the other end of the spectrum, those who do read well and want to think about and discuss what they read. One way of doing this, suggested to us by Anita Meinbach, a teacher of gifted and talented students, capitalizes on that all-important out-of-school reading time. She recommends encouraging students to participate in the book groups available at many local bookstores. Here are Ms. Meinbach's comments on her school's involvement in a Grand Conversations book group, which takes place in a local bookstore once a month:

> For the past five years, I've conducted Grand Conversations at Borders Books. We invite students from several middle schools, and they all get together to discuss a predetermined book they've all read. Borders supplies the drinks and snacks. The kids run the whole show. I just show up, say "Hello," and introduce next month's selection. The idea's catching on. Two other teachers have begun this in their area of the county.
>
> —Anita Meinbach, Teacher of the Year,
> Miami-Dade County, 2003

Three good resources for selecting books for book group discussion in bookstores or other out-of-school locations are your school media specialist, your local library's children's librarian, and children's bookstore personnel. Say, for instance, your students are interested in reading and discussing books on the topic of family life in various time periods and locales. In a quick call to a local children's librarian, we received the following four recommendations: Eva Ibbotson's novel *The Star of Kazan,* a mystery about an adopted foundling child set in Austria and Germany in the early 20th century; *Little Cricket* by Jackie Brown, about a Hmong family's flight from Laos after the Vietnam War to a refugee camp in Thailand and eventually to Minnesota; Kerry Madden's *Gentle's Holler,* which takes place in rural North Carolina in the early 1960s; and Gennifer Choldenko's *Al Capone Does My Shirts,* set on Alcatraz Island during 1935. The first two books are appropriate for readers in grades 4 through 6; the last two are appropriate for readers in grades 6 through 8.

Concluding *Remarks*

In this chapter, we discussed the importance of providing independent reading time, a rich array of reading materials

and incentives to read them, and an inviting place in which to read. We also suggested ways to help students select material for independent reading and to establish and maintain an independent reading program. As an adjunct to independent reading, we talked about the importance of reader response and of discussion groups that encourage students to make personal connections with the texts they read. We emphasized the need to invite students to express their own ideas and to listen to those of other students. Finally, we presented three frameworks that promote reader response—literature circles, the Book Club and Book Club *Plus* programs, and the reading workshop. Each of these frameworks presents a way to organize reading time that makes reading and student response the focal point, with instruction supporting this main endeavor.

The topics presented in this chapter—encouraging independent reading and reader response—are important components of a well-balanced literacy curriculum; both are vital to helping students meet the challenging literacy demands of the 21st century.

Extending *Learning*

1. Imagine you are a beginning teacher in a new school and your principal tells you that the PTA will purchase 30 books for your classroom library. Select a grade you would most like to teach. Write up a brief description of that class—ages of students, ethnic backgrounds represented, and range of reading ability. Using resources such as *Promoting a Global Community Through Multicultural Children's Literature* (Steiner, 2001) and *The Best of the Best from 60 Years of Notable Children's Books, 1940–99* (Association for Library Service to Children, 2004), select 30 books for your library.

2. Select a grade you would most like to teach. If possible, arrange to visit a classroom to observe independent reading and literature discussion groups in this grade. Take notes on what you observe. What are students reading? Do they appear to be engaged in the reading? How do they respond to their reading (in a journal, through discussion, or merely privately in their minds as they read)? Plan a reading experience for these students that will include group discussion that focuses on reader response. Let them select a book, or assign one yourself. Write your plans for this reading experience from beginning to end, including how the students will be prepared for the experience, how the reading will be done, and how the discussion will be handled. Think about questions like the following as you develop your plan: What will your role be? What will students' roles be? How will the reading be handled? How will the discussion be handled? What will be discussed? Who will lead the discussion? How will it begin and end? How will you ensure student engagement, participation, and success? If possible, try out your plan on a group of students. If this isn't possible, present your ideas to your classmates for feedback.

Children's *Literature*

Abercrombie, B., & Graham, M. (1995). *Charlie Anderson*. New York: Aladdin. The story of a cat who is shared between two homes and two girls who live part of the week with one parent and the other part of the week with another. 32 pages.

Brown, J. (2004). *Little Cricket*. New York: Hyperion. In the aftermath of the Vietnam War, 12-year-old Kia and her Hmong family flee from the mountains of Laos to a refugee camp in Thailand and eventually to Saint Paul, Minnesota. 252 pages.

Choldenko, G. (2004). *Al Capone Does My Shirts*. New York: G. P. Putnam's Sons. In 1935, when 12-year-old Moose's family moves to Alcatraz Island, where guards' families were housed at that time, he has to deal not only with his strange new environment but with an autistic sister as well. 228 pages.

Graves, B. (1998). *No Copycats Allowed!* New York: Hyperion. Wanting desperately to fit in at her new school, Gabrielle tries to copy her classmates, only to learn that the best way to make friends is by being herself. 51 pages.

Ibbotson, E. (2004). *The Star of Kazan*. New York: Dutton. After 12-year-old Annika, a foundling living in late 19th-century Vienna, inherits a trunk of costume jewelry, a woman claiming to be her aristocratic mother arrives and takes her to live in a strangely decrepit mansion in Germany. 405 pages.

MacLachlan, P. (1982). *Cassie Binegar.* New York: Harper & Row. One summer, fourth-grader Cassie learns to accept change and to find her own space. 120 pages.

MacLachlan, P. (1985). *Sarah, Plain and Tall.* New York: HarperCollins. This Newbery Medal–winning novel tells the story of mail-order bride Sarah from Maine and the family who long to have her stay with them on the prairie. Audio CD available. 58 pages.

MacLachlan, P. (1988). *The Facts and Fictions of Minna Pratt.* New York: Harper & Row. Eleven-year-old Minna, a cello student in New York City, learns about life, love, and music through her family, her first boyfriend, and Mozart. 136 pages.

MacLachlan, P. (1991). *Journey.* New York: Delacorte. This novel explores how photographs and a grandfather's love enable young Journey to come to terms with his mother's abandonment and restore a past that he feels has been erased. 83 pages.

MacLachlan, P. (1993). *Baby.* New York: Delacorte. This exquisitely crafted short novel is about a family learning to deal with the death of their own infant son after a baby girl is left on their doorstep for them to care for. 132 pages.

MacLachlan, P. (1994). *Skylark.* New York: HarperCollins. In this sequel to *Sarah, Plain and Tall,* Anna and Caleb worry that a drought on the prairie will send their new mother, Sarah, back to her home in Maine. Audio CD available. 86 pages.

MacLachlan, P. (2001). *Caleb's Story.* New York: Joanna Cotler Books. Caleb narrates this sequel to *Sarah, Plain and Tall* and *Skylark,* in which Jacob is reunited with his father. 128 pages.

MacLachlan, P. (2003). *Painting the Wind.* New York: Joanna Cotler Books. By observing how each of four artists paints the same island, a boy hopes to learn how to paint the wind. 40 pages.

Madden, K. (2005). *Gentle's Holler.* New York: Viking. Twelve-year-old Livy dreams of seeing the world beyond the poverty-stricken North Carolina holler where she lives with her large family in the early 1960s. 237 pages.

Paterson, K. (2002). *The Same Stuff as Stars.* New York: Clarion. When 11-year-old Angel and her younger brother are dumped at their great-grandmother's Vermont backcountry home, Angel struggles to make a new life for herself and her family. 256 pages.

Sandburg, C. (1965). Buffalo Dusk. In *Arrow Book of Poetry,* selected by Ann McGovern. New York: Scholastic. This evocative poem laments a time gone by when the great buffalo herds roamed the prairie. 35 pages.

Smith, W. J. (1990). *Birds and Beasts.* New York: Godine. In poetry and pictures, this volume presents a fun and satisfying, if slightly offbeat, view of 29 animals. Unnumbered.

PEARSON
myeducationlab

Take a look at the Literacy Portraits section in MyEducationLab (www.myeducationlab.com), where you can view video case studies of five students developing as readers and writers.

13

Writing and Reading

Bob Daemmrich Photography

Sixth-grader Derrick sits at his desk, his social studies book propped open in front of him, jotting down words in a notebook.

Bryce glances over Derrick's shoulder. "What are you doing?" he asks.

"Writing stuff."

"Why?" Bryce asks.

"So I remember it. We have a test tomorrow . . . in case you've forgotten."

In the third-grade room down the hall, Jasmine plops into a beanbag chair and starts reading a story her friend Brianna wrote. It's a story featuring the characters in a book the class just read. Next to her, Brianna giggles as she reads Jasmine's story.

Next door, second-grade teacher Maria Chavez writes on the board:

Dear Class,
    We have been talking about gifts lately. I just wanted to tell you that each of you is a special gift to me. Thank you for working so hard and for being so kind to one another.
    Love,
    Mrs. Chavez

Each of these writers is using writing for a different purpose—for learning, for understanding, for communicating, and for just having fun with words—as this chapter will illustrate.

CLASSROOM vignette

The Reading-Writing Connection

As you know, we write for a number of different reasons and audiences, and *how* we do it—the *process*—is different for each. But no matter what the reason, the audience, or the process, what we write is usually meant to be read, either by ourselves or by someone else. And, quite obviously, anything we read has to have been written by someone. Writing and reading, as Bernice Cullinan (1993) has noted, are two sides of the same coin. Like speaking and listening, they are two complementary components of a communications process (Pearson, 1990) and depend on the same cognitive structures and strategies (Langer, 1986).

Although there are similarities between reading and writing, viewed from another perspective they are substantially different, especially in their execution, and each process requires a very different brand of instruction. To understand the differences consider this imaginary dialogue between Margaret Mitchell and an unknowing reader in 1942 at a cocktail party in Atlanta. "I just read the most amazing book, *Gone with the Wind*." "I wrote *Gone with the Wind*." Writing and reading *Gone with the Wind* are starkly different mental activities.

Even though this reading-writing connection might appear obvious, these two language arts have traditionally been taught as separate subjects in U.S. classrooms. Today, however, virtually all educators agree that combining reading and writing in the classroom makes a great deal of sense, both theoretically and practically. Forty years ago, John Carroll (1966) suggested that reading and writing be experienced as parallel and reciprocal processes, in much the same way that their own speaking and listening are parallel and reciprocal to younger children. Today, researchers and practitioners alike continue to recommend that this notion be put into practice in the classroom (Atwell, 1987, 1998b; Farr, 1993; Moore, Moore, Cunningham, & Cunningham, 2003; Olson, 1996; Routman, 2003, 2005).

Throughout this chapter, we explore this reciprocal process of reading and writing, focusing on a variety of writing forms, purposes, and procedures. But before we can begin that discussion, the stage must be set. The writing classroom—what does it look, sound, and feel like?

A Positive Reading-Writing Environment

"I write because I have something important to say, and I think people need to hear it!" says Brandon, a fifth-grader. Brandon's heartfelt, if somewhat boastful, comment succinctly captures in one sentence at least three critical truths about writing that will greatly affect your own thinking about the writing opportunities you provide for students:

- Students should write for important purposes.
- What students write should be valued by themselves, by you, and by the others in your classroom community.
- Writing should function to communicate or to foster the writers' own learning, understanding, or appreciation.

If literacy is to prosper in our classrooms, we need to create an environment in which children view themselves as writers. Writers flourish in an atmosphere in which written words are used and valued and writers are encouraged to take risks while being supported in their attempts. This environment involves both the intellectual climate of the classroom and its physical attributes.

The Intellectual Climate

The intellectual climate of the ideal reading-writing classroom conveys this message: "We are all readers and writers. Together we are all learning to be better readers and writers." The intellectual climate will be reflected in the number of children seen reading and writing at any given moment and their engagement in their writing tasks. It will be reflected in the students' writing displayed throughout the room—student-made books, posters, bulletin boards. It will be reflected in the faces and voices of students meeting to read and respond to each other's writing.

In a positive classroom writing environment students write often and for a variety of purposes and also feel free to take risks. Writing across the curriculum provides extended opportunities for students to write, and when they do so, their comfort level increases (Spandel, 2005). Students need to be given opportunities to write without fear of criticism. One very effective way teachers can help establish this risk-taking atmosphere is to become writers themselves. Doing so helps teachers understand the arduous process involved in transforming thoughts into words and to appreciate what it is like to have those words evaluated. Another important element in the intellectual climate of a classroom is the teacher's role as modeler. Writing in front of students, showing them what you are doing, and talking about what you are doing and why provides students with concrete examples of how writers work (Dyson & Freedman, 1991; Graves, 1991; Routman, 2005; Temple, Nathan, Temple, & Burris, 1993).

Literacy prospers in classrooms in which children view themselves as writers and what they write is valued by the classroom community.

iStockPhoto

The Physical Environment

Students need *time* to write, a *place* to do it, and *materials* to write with. The physical environment of a productive reading-writing classroom will reflect the attitude "This is a great place to read and write!" Joanne Hindley, a teacher at the Manhattan New School, has developed this kind of environment. This is what she had to say about the writing environment of her classroom (Hindley, 1998, reprinted with permission).

> I think carefully about how the room needs to look in order to allow comfortable working space for the whole group, small-group, paired, and individual working situations. Materials need to be clearly labeled and organized so that it is easy for children to use and take care of them. This not only promotes good "housekeeping" in the small space we share, it also ensures that the room belongs to all of *us* and not just to *me*. It is much easier for 30 people to take on the responsibility of caring for our home than for one person to do it for the other 29.
>
> When we as teachers think about ourselves as learners, we are able to envision what our students need in terms of support from us and from the environment. Creating an atmosphere that encourages students to interact, feel independent, and take pride in the upkeep of their classrooms is critical for everything we do throughout the year.
>
> —Joanne Hindley, elementary teacher

Guidelines for Creating a Positive Writing Environment

- Establish a predictable writing time.
- Create a writing center equipped with writing necessities—writing materials, dictionaries, a thesaurus, and books on the writer's craft.
- Provide opportunities to write throughout the day in all the subject areas for a variety of purposes and audiences.
- Become a writer yourself, and share with your students your writing and the struggles you experience in writing.
- Provide students with guidance and constructive feedback.
- Stock the classroom library with texts in a variety of genres—magazines, picture books, biographies, informational books, novels, beginning chapter books—that reflect a wide range of interests and readability levels.
- Read aloud quality literature—fiction, nonfiction, and poetry—that can serve as models of good writing.
- Model writing forms and techniques.
- Guide students to write about topics that are important to them—writing that has a genuine purpose and a real audience.
- Provide opportunities for students to share their writing with their peers and receive constructive feedback from them.
- Provide direct instruction on matters of mechanics—grammar, usage, spelling, and punctuation—and the writer's craft—dialogue, characterization, voice, engaging beginnings, and so on—as the need arises.

The main goal is to provide a place where students feel safe and comfortable exploring ideas on paper. In the Classroom 13.1 gives you suggestions for creating such an environment.

The Process Approach to Writing

In recent years, a particular approach to teaching writing—the process approach—has been widely explored, and evidence indicates that students in classrooms that include more elements of the process approach indeed become better writers than those in less process-oriented classrooms (Persky, Daane, & Ying, 2003). We think this evidence is convincing, and we strongly endorse the process approach as a method of teaching writing. However, a good deal of the writing students do in relation to their reading is less planned, less lengthy, less polished, and less formal than that for which the process approach is appropriate. As Gail Tompkins (1996) has pointed out, effective reading teachers give students plenty of opportunities to do both process writing and informal writing. Thus, after discussing the process approach, we will then consider another approach from Australia called systematic functional linguistics. This approach to writing provides a keen focus on text characteristics, which all good readers and writers need to understand. Finally, we will describe the nature and place of less formal writing.

For some writing projects and in some situations, the writer goes through several stages of writing, particularly when writing formal pieces. However, not too long ago, most writing instruction gave virtually no attention to the process of writing. Fortunately, with the release of Janet Emig's (1971) study of twelfth-graders' composing process and Donald Graves's (1975) observations of 7-year-old writers, educational researchers began focusing on the process involved in writing and its implications for classroom instruction. The result of this research has been a shift of emphasis away from the end product of writing toward the process involved in the writing.

Step into a third-grade classroom for a moment, and witness a reading event:

> Gabbie, wearing gray sweatpants, high-top sneakers, and a wide grin, is sitting in the "author's chair," reading her story "The Noise in the Laundry Chute." You are impressed that a third-grader could write so well. You notice, however, that Gabbie's face, her body language, and her whole demeanor are speaking even more eloquently than her words: "This is good. I like this and am proud of my story."

Gabbie didn't get to this moment of accomplishment and satisfaction in one quick leap but went through several stages before arriving at the author's chair to read her "finished" product. First, she engaged in *prewriting* activities, which helped her generate ideas. With the teacher acting as a recorder, the whole class had brainstormed "scary moments" together on the chalkboard. As a second prewriting activity, Gabbie did a quickwrite to let her own thoughts run free and then capture them on paper, discovering what she knew and how she felt about the frightening moments in her life. Next, her teacher directed her thinking to the audience for her story, her purposes for writing it, and the form she would use. She decided she would write and illustrate a picture book for her younger brother and two older sisters, one that would be funny and scary at the same time.

During the next stage, *drafting,* Gabbie wrote a rough draft of her story, trying to keep her audience and purposes in mind. Gabbie went through three drafts before she felt ready to share her story with classmates to get their feedback. When she did read her story to a small group of classmates, they responded to what she had written, giving her positive feedback on some aspects of her story and suggesting what she might think about for her next revision.

Revising the story—reviewing it in light of the comments she received from her classmates and rewriting it—was the next stage in the process. Here, Gabbie reworked her composition by adding, deleting, changing, and moving words, sentences, and even whole sections. During this stage, Gabbie's main interest was in making the story "work." Did it make sense? Was it scary *and* funny? Would her brother and sisters like it?

After Gabbie was satisfied that she had done what she could to tell the story she wanted in the way she wanted, she began *editing* the piece. Here she focused on mechanical elements such as grammar, punctuation, and spelling. This proofreading process required that Gabbie hunt word by word for errors, a different focus from that of the revising stage, in which she concentrated on the meaning she was creating. Because young writers like Gabbie are not usually critical readers, it can be helpful to provide suggestions for revising and editing. Teacher Marilyn Blackley (Five & Dionisio, 1999) finds an editing list, such as the one shown in Figure 13.1, helpful for her students. Using colored pencils, her third-graders work in pairs to edit their own writing.

Students enjoy reading aloud the stories they have written. Sharing one's work with others helps develop an awareness of audience and its importance in the writing process.

Bob Daemmrich Photography

myeducationlab

Revision and editing are two steps in the writing process that are often confused by students and teachers. The two have distinct purposes and skill sets that should be clearly articulated and differentiated. Learn how to make a clear distinction between the processes and teach students to use skills and strategies by completing the activity "Teaching Students to Revise and Edit Effectively." (To find this activity, go to the topic *Writing* in MyEducationLab and click on Building Teaching Skills and Dispositions.)

Figure 13.1

Form to Help Third-Graders Edit Their Writing

Source: Five, C. L., & Dionisio, M. (1999). "Revisiting the Teaching of Writing," *School Talk*, 4, 3. Copyright 1999 by the National Council of Teachers of English. Reprinted with permission.

NAME: _____   DATE: _____

Steps to Editing

⟵————————————————————⟶

THE TITLE OF MY PIECE IS _____.

MY EDITING PARTNER WAS _____.

I read my story to a friend to see where to **STOP** for

> **periods**   ·   _____
> **question marks   ?**   _____
> **exclamation points   !**   _____

I took out extra words that I didn't need (and, then)   _____.

I checked for capital letters

> at the beginning of each sentence _____
> for the first letter of a name   _____
> for the word I   _____

I circled words that may be misspelled.   ———————————

Example: I (plade) with my dog.

The last stage of the process, *publishing,* involved a sharing or "celebration" of the work. To prepare her story for sharing, Gabbie keyed her story into a word processor, printed it, cut it into sections, and pasted the sections in the pages of a booklet. Then she drew pictures to accompany her text. Other types of publishing possibilities are discussed later in this chapter.

To review, the five major steps in the writing process are as follows:

- Prewriting
- Drafting
- Revising
- Editing
- Publishing

A word of caution is in order here. The preceding description gives merely the highlights of what is in reality a very complex and recursive process. Writers don't simply move lockstep from one stage to another; they repeatedly move back and forth between the processes involved in prewriting, drafting, revising, and editing, as the writing task dictates. Different writers, different topics, different purposes, and myriad other factors will affect the writing process. No two writers approach writing in exactly the same manner, and the same writer writes differently at different times. The scenario describing Gabbie's story presents a general characterization of the writing process. Virtually all formal and polished writing is the product of

Children who struggle with reading often struggle with writing and are reluctant to write. An effective way to interest such children is to have them write about their own lives. If you are able to secure funding through a parent organization or other sponsor, the following writing project can be particularly motivating for students. Provide students with single-use cameras. Send a letter home explaining to parents that you have given their child a single-use camera to take pictures of important people, pets, places, objects, and events in his or her life. Ask parents to help their child to take these pictures and then to return the camera to school with their child. When the cameras come in, have the pictures developed. Children then use the pictures as prompts for writing. Because the pictures are grounded in children's lives and depict people, events, and objects that are important to them, children are motivated to communicate their ideas. The photographs and accompanying writing can be bound together to produce "All about Me" books to read and share. ●

a relatively lengthy and multifaceted process that involves thinking, drafting, and revising.

A Genre Approach to Writing

In a genre approach to writing students and teachers work to develop an explicit understanding of how language works so they can grow as readers and writers. This approach, called systemic functional linguistics, an Australian export, engages the class in a close study of the various forms and characteristics of genres of writing (Derewianka, 2000). When students use language to speak, read, or write they do so for specific purposes and must, therefore, select a text that will help to achieve those purposes. Writing begins by exploring a particular genre such as biography or fantasy by reading and studying its structure. From these reading comprehension lessons the students and teachers move to creating their own texts in the same genre.

Erica William's classroom decided to explore the environment around the school, looking for litter and other pollutants. After collecting their data, they needed to report their findings to the principal and other school authorities. The students decided to write a report to share what they discovered and perhaps mount a campaign to persuade the bordering manufacturing companies to change their ways. Reporting and persuading are specific language functions and each requires a specific text organization and employs specific language features.

The curriculum cycle for using the functional linguistics approach, presented in Figure 13.2, begins with building knowledge of the topic, similar to the prewriting step in the writing process. Ms. William's students did this through direct observation and extensive reading about pollution. Their next step is to learn how to write a strong persuasive argument; they must therefore learn about this specific text type. The class begins by studying other pieces of persuasive writing. The students read several examples and examine the structure and characteristics of persuasive writing. They learn that their writing must begin with a thesis statement. Both logical and emotional language should be used to amplify this statement. Next, the students notice that their thesis statement must be supported with well-defined arguments or

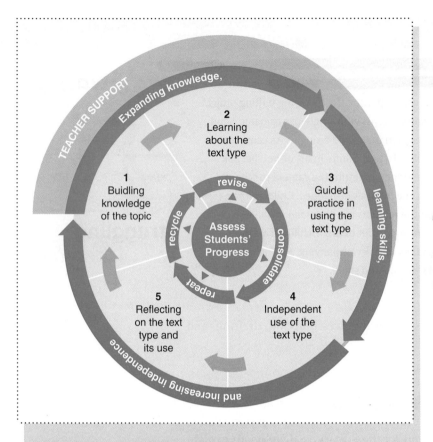

Figure 13.2

Curriculum Cycle for Writing with a Focus on Genre

Courtesy of Bev Derewianka.

reasons. Each argument must have evidence and not just opinion. They also learn that a good piece of writing must conclude with specific recommendations. Beyond structure, they also note that writers use emotional words, they write in the present tense because this is an ongoing problem, and they use signal words to connect their arguments—*first, second, finally.*

Next, the teacher creates a good piece of persuasive writing. This provides the teacher the opportunity to model the process of composing an argument while the students participate. This shared process affords the teacher the opportunity to engage in guided practice. Here the students are taking what they have learned about persuasive writing and putting it into practice. The teacher might start the composing process and then seek ideas from the students. She can accept, modify, and mold the ideas of the students. In the functional linguistics approach students need both models of good writing and demonstrations in which they see the process modeled. These steps are not typically part of the traditional writing process, but they could be.

Once the modeling is completed, the students begin to use the text type on their own. The teacher purposefully leaves a copy of the group's persuasive essay in the room with its parts and language features clearly labeled. The students can use it as a resource to make sure they have included the same elements in their own writing. As the students continue to write, they are engaged in the drafting portion of the writing process. After drafting, the students continue on to revise and consolidate what they have written. Again, the structure of persuasive writing helps to guide the revision process. The students can consult the structure model to see what they might have left out. At the end of the process the students reflect on the text type they have been studying and how its structure helps them compose and comprehend.

By engaging students in a deep study of genre and text characteristics, the functional linguistic approach to writing may provide greater support for reading than does the traditional writing process. As students read models of good writing they learn how texts are organized and the purposes of the various genres. The evidence strongly suggests that knowledge of text structure supports reading comprehension and an understanding of genre helps the reader set a purpose (Armbruster & Anderson, 1984; Duke & Pearson, 2002; Slater, Graves, & Piche, 1985). The second advantage of the functional linguistic approach is the construction of integrated reading and writing units. A teacher who seeks to explore realistic fiction or mystery can do so by both reading stories and writing stories. What students learn through reading stories will support their own compositions. The teacher can take the functional linguistic approach down to an even finer level. For example, to learn to find the main idea it is often a good idea to learn how to construct well-crafted paragraphs. So the strategy of finding the main idea that we developed in Chapter 11 can be paralleled with lessons on writing strong paragraphs. Last, the functional linguistic approach used the same lesson structure that we advocated for teaching reading comprehension—direct instruction, guided practice, and independent practice.

REFLECT and Apply

1 We have discussed reading and writing as being reciprocal and parallel processes, or "two sides of the same coin." Explain what this idea means to you. Think specifically about the functional linguistic approach.

2 Think about your own writing experiences in elementary school. What did you write? For which audiences did you write? Did any of your writing take you through the various processes we talked about in this section? What sorts of informal writing did you do? At this point, jot down the types of writing elementary students might do that illustrate both the process approach and informal kinds of writing.

Informal Writing Forms and Purposes

Typically, a student does informal writing for his own purposes—to learn from his reading, to better understand ideas, and to explore or personally engage with what he is reading. This writing will take the form of notes, lists, diagrams, journals, summaries, and the like. In this section, we take a look at some of the types of writing elementary students are likely to find most useful and talk about when, why, and how each type should take place.

1. Writing to learn and to understand
   - Note taking
   - Brainstorming and quickwriting
   - Semantic mapping
   - Venn diagram
   - Journals

2. Writing to communicate
   - Letters
   - Biographies
   - Reports

3. Imaginative writing
   - Stories
   - Poems

Although we have divided the types into three broad categories, we want to stress that these categories only suggest what is *generally* the purpose or nature of the various types. We by no means intend to suggest a rigid category system or imply that the various types do not overlap in a number of ways. For example, a student could write a story or poem in her journal, a Venn diagram might constitute part of a report, and students could brainstorm topics for poems. These loosely defined categories can, however, serve as a reminder that students can profitably undertake many sorts of writing to enrich and complement reading.

Writing to Learn and to Understand

Often, we use writing as a vehicle to learn about something or to more fully understand it. When students write to learn, they are using written language to help them wrestle with information, ideas, feelings, and intuitions. Reading done in subject matter areas such as science, social studies, and literature offers rich opportunities for this kind of writing, which fosters comprehension and personal response. In this kind of writing, students are actually "thinking on paper" or perhaps on a computer screen. In other words, they are using written language to discover, clarify, refine, expand, or reflect on meaning.

James Britton and his colleagues (1975) have noted that this type of writing is closely related to talk, and Richard Vacca and Wayne Linek (1992) point out that such writing can serve as a catalyst for reading and studying content area material. In fact, many of the writing-to-learn activities we discuss are often accompanied by small-group discussion centered on the topics students are writing about.

What kinds of writing can students do to help them better learn, understand, and personally respond to the information and ideas in the texts they read? To enhance their ability to "think on paper" and actively integrate new knowledge into old? To prepare them for more formal genres such as reports and stories? We discuss note taking, brainstorming, quickwriting, semantic mapping, Venn diagrams, and journals in this section. We described several of these procedures in Chapter 10 when we talked about helping students comprehend the various texts they read. Here, we focus on the writing component of these endeavors.

Note Taking

Although note taking is perhaps the most traditional of all the activities we discuss in this section, students do not pick it up naturally. To help students learn how to take notes, Regie Routman (1995) recommends using demonstration, participation, practice, and sharing in a variety of note-taking situations. These situations include taking notes from texts, oral presentations, films, and videos. To be successful at note taking, students not only need repeated practice in the skill but also need to have it demonstrated to them again and again throughout the school year. In the Classroom 13.2 shows a sample lesson adapted from a procedure Routman and third-grade teacher Julie Beers used with a group of third-graders who were getting ready to begin research reports on animals.

Routman offers the following suggestions for additional work on note taking:

- Have students work in pairs instead of groups, with one acting as scribe and the other giving suggestions and feedback.
- Allow students to take notes on their first reading of the material with their books open.
- Repeat note-taking sessions throughout the year, giving teaching demonstrations and working with various genres and contexts.

Brainstorming and Quickwriting

When brainstorming, students quickly jot down single words or short phrases that come to mind in response to a topic. For example, before a group of third-graders read Steve Parker's *It's a Frog's Life! My Story of Life in a Pond*, they brainstormed words and phrases that the word *pond* brought to mind and came up with this list:

| water | frogs | pollywogs | weeds | woods | forest |
| ducks | green | slime | mud | turtles | |

Sample Lesson on Note Taking

1. Make a transparency of the first page of the selection students will be reading, and leave the other half of the page blank. (For example, Routman and Beers made a transparency of the page on alligators and crocodiles from *Zoo Books 2* [Wildlife Education, 1986].) This transparency will be used on an overhead projector to demonstrate note taking.

2. Slowly read the passage aloud, highlighting key phrases and important information by underlining them with a yellow marker. Verbalize the thought processes you go through in deciding what to highlight. Demonstrate to students how to turn these key phrases into notes by writing them on the right side of the transparency. The process shares much in common with determining importance, which we outlined in Chapter 11.

3. Demonstrate the process several times with additional pages from the text, inviting students to participate in choosing the notes to write down.

4. Have students form small groups. Give each group a photocopied page from the book they will read, a blank transparency, and two pens—a yellow highlighter and a black marking pen for writing on transparencies.

5. Tell students to place the blank transparency over the article and underline key phrases and important points with the yellow marker (as they did earlier as a whole class) and then write their notes on the right side of the page with the black marking pen.

6. Invite each group to come up to the overhead projector with the completed transparency. Ask members to place it over a transparency of the text they have just read, and encourage them to discuss their notes. Give feedback and guidance on their note taking, and invite other students to give feedback as well.

And before sixth-graders read *Sparks Fly Upward*, Carol Matas's historical novel about a Russian immigrant family in 1910 trying to adapt to a new culture and new circumstances, they wrote down words and phrases in response to the word *immigrant*. Brainstorming can be done individually, as a small-group activity, or as a whole-class activity, either before or after reading. However it is done, brainstorming generally leaves students with some raw material that they will employ as they read or write.

In contrast to brainstorming, quickwriting—a technique popularized by Peter Elbow (1973)—is a way of very quickly getting down connected sentences and phrases on a topic without stopping to correct or analyze them. Simply stated, quickwriting is jotting down thoughts on a topic as quickly as they come to mind. Because the students are not worrying about mechanics, structure, or communicating their ideas to someone else, they are free to generate many thoughts and ideas, and they gain confidence and fluency in writing. The following quickwrite was done by a fifth-grade student after reading an excerpt from *Strange Plants* by Howard Halpern and thinking aloud with a partner (Armbruster, McCarthey, & Cummins, 2005).

> I'm writing about stinging nettles. Stinging nettles have sharp needles that have asid in it, and, if you get a needle in you, you will get a read warm rash that stings and hurts very, very, very badly. It will sting for 2 hours or, if its very bad, it will last for a day or even more. I would hate to run into that plant because I've gotton poked by a needle really hard, and it hurts!

Like brainstorming, quickwriting is a strategy students can use as a prereading or postreading activity. Quickwriting before students read a text can help them relate the reading to their lives and activate and build schemata, bringing ideas from the subconscious level to the conscious level. For example, before third- or fourth-graders read any one of Joanna Cole's Magic School Bus books, they might do a quickwrite on

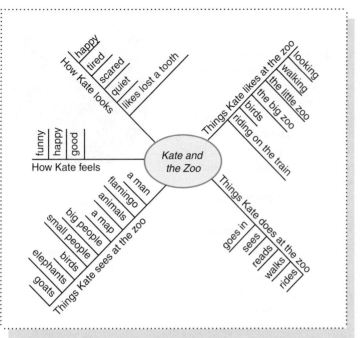

Figure 13.3

Semantic Map Used with First-Graders After Reading "Kate and the Zoo"

Source: Heimlich, Joan E., & Pittelman, Susan D. (1986). *Semantic Mapping: Classroom Applications.* Copyright © 1986 by the International Reading Association (www.reading.org). Reproduced with permission of the International Reading Association via Copyright Clearance Center.

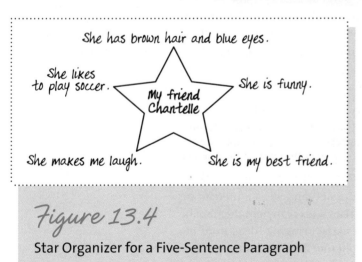

Figure 13.4

Star Organizer for a Five-Sentence Paragraph

what they know about the topic of the book—the human body, for example. Or as a postreading activity after reading Russell Freedman's *Eleanor Roosevelt*, sixth-graders could quickwrite on the most memorable moments in the biography.

Both brainstorming and quickwriting are excellent strategies for generating ideas before or after students read a particular text. Both can also be very effective strategies for gathering thoughts and ideas in the beginning stages of formal writing.

Semantic Mapping and the Venn Diagram

Semantic mapping and Venn diagrams make use of brainstorming to some degree but take it a step or two further by organizing the brainstormed ideas in a specific way. As we discussed in Chapter 9, in semantic mapping (also called clustering or webbing), words generated in brainstorming are linked to a nucleus word, which reflects a main idea. This nucleus word functions in much the same way as the main idea in an outline.

Semantic maps can have one nucleus idea or several and can be used with both narrative and informational texts. Students can develop them individually or as a small- or large-group activity, and they can be used either as a prereading activity to activate prior knowledge, as a postreading activity to recall and organize pertinent information, or as both when students update the map after reading a text (Heimlich & Pittelman, 1986). As a postreading activity, semantic mapping can also serve as a helpful prewriting technique preceding more formal writing such as reports, stories, or biographies. Figure 13.3 shows a semantic map developed by first-graders after reading "Kate and the Zoo," a story from a basal series.

A variation of the semantic map is the star organizer (Poindexter & Oliver, 1998/1999), which can help primary-grade students in the prewriting stages to organize their thoughts when writing a description. The framework can be used as a map for writing a paragraph describing an object. Figure 13.4 shows a star organizer for writing a paragraph about a friend.

Like the semantic map, the Venn diagram is a way to organize ideas and present them graphically. However, in a Venn diagram, two or more topics or ideas are contrasted. Consisting of circles that intersect, the diagram highlights the similarities and differences between topics. The differences are indicated by words or phrases written in the nonoverlapping parts of the circles, whereas

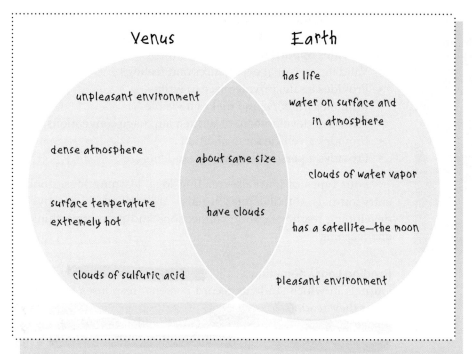

Figure 13.5

Venn Diagram Comparing and Contrasting Venus and Earth

the similarities are written in the space created by the intersection of the circles. Figure 13.5 shows how one group of fifth-graders used a Venn diagram to compare and contrast the planets Earth and Venus after reading *The Planets in Our Solar System* by Franklyn Mansfield Branley.

The Venn diagram is a particularly effective device for students to use when reading informational texts in which two or more topics are being compared and contrasted or when reading narratives and two characters can be compared. It can also be used to compare and contrast books that explore a similar theme or topic, such as Ann Martin's middle-grade novel *Belle Teal*, a fictional account of desegregation, with Ruby Bridges's photobiography *Through My Eyes*, a personal account of the author's own experiences with desegregation. It can also be used with characters in the same story, such as Prince Brat and Jemmy in Sid Fleischman's *The Whipping Boy* or Princess Elizabeth and Iris in Jane Resh Thomas's *The Counterfeit Princess*.

Journals

Perhaps you have used journals yourself, either for personal reasons or as a learning tool in academic classes. If so, you're probably not alone, for journal writing is a widely recommended procedure. Chris Anson and Richard Beach (1995) view the journal as a genre in its own right and a "significant tool for learning." Toby Fulwiler (1987) suggests that journaling engages the writer in a vast range of cognitive activities—observing, questioning, speculating, becoming aware of oneself, digressing, synthesizing, revising, and informing. Routman (1991) describes the journal as a "nonthreatening place to explore learnings, feelings, happenings, and language through writing" and of significant benefit to both teacher and student. The following list shows some of the specific benefits Routman highlights:

*A*ssessment

Model how to use postreading graphic organizers as an organizational tool for writing essays. Student essays can be used to assess reading comprehension as well as essay writing skills.

Journals can be a valuable tool for writers when used for worthwhile purposes that student writers understand and embrace.

Shutterstock

- Promotes fluency in writing
- Encourages risk taking
- Provides opportunity for reflection
- Validates personal experiences and feelings
- Provides a safe, private place to write
- Promotes thinking and makes it visible
- Promotes development of written language conventions
- Provides a vehicle for evaluation
- Provides a personal record for students

Four types of journals—reading logs, learning logs, double-entry journals, and dialogue journals—are particularly effective for developing reading-writing connections and promoting thinking and learning.

Reading Logs. Sometimes called *response journals*, reading logs are journals in which students record personal responses to the literature they read. Before students write in their journals, you will want to talk about some of the topics they might write about and model how you write responses in your own reading journal. In the Classroom 13.3, which shows one way to introduce primary-grade students to response journals, is based on an approach used by first-grade teacher Barbara Werchadlo (Wollman-Bonilla & Werchadlo, 1995).

As good teachers always do, you will want to reflect on the success of the journaling activity and make adjustments if necessary. After Werchadlo's first experiences with response journals, she decided to provide more modeling of varied responses and give prompts that were even more open-ended. She did this in order to help children view journals not as a place to simply retell or predict what might happen in a text, but rather as a place to react personally. The following is a list of possible open-ended questions:

- How does the story make you feel?
- Does anything puzzle you? If so, explain.

In the Classroom

13.3

Instructional Routines

Introducing the Response Journal to Primary-Grade Students

- During the first week of school, read aloud a chapter a day from an engaging book such as *James and the Giant Peach* by Roald Dahl.
- For the first few days, model how to write a response by expressing a few ideas while thinking aloud. Then write a sentence on the board such as *James is very sad because his parents are gone* or *James does not like living with Aunt Sponge and Aunt Spiker.*
- When you think the children are ready, perhaps on the third day, give them their own journals. These can be made by stapling story paper (blank on the top and lined on the bottom) between manilla or cardstock covers that the children can decorate.
- Ask students to write in their journals about the story. Give them writing prompts such as "What did you like about this chapter?" or "What do you think will happen next?"
- Invite students to illustrate their responses when they have finished writing.

- Do the characters seem real to you? Why or why not?
- Are you enjoying the story? Why or why not?
- Are there words that you particularly like? What are they, and why do you like them?
- Does anything in the story remind you of your own life?
- Is anything the author says particularly meaningful to you? Why?

Figure 13.6 provides a sample entry in a fifth-grade student's reading log, written after he had read the first chapter of *Baby* by Patricia MacLachlan.

Learning Logs. In contrast to reading logs or response journals, learning logs are generally oriented to subject matter rather than personal response and are used in content areas such as science, mathematics, and social studies. They can include a variety of entries—questions to the author, summaries of the material, explanations of problems solved, or recording of observations as in an experiment. As Stephen Koziol, Brad Minnick, and Kim Riddell (1996) observe, one important function of learning logs is to enable students to select, connect, and organize knowledge in ways that allow them to better understand what they read. They have suggested three types of questions for learning logs: questions that elicit prior knowledge, questions that encourage students to interact with the text, and questions that ask students to respond retrospectively to what they have learned. Figure 13.7 shows a question and a response for each of these three types, relating to the book *California Condor: Flying Free* by Bonnie Graves.

Double-Entry Journals. Double-entry journals are two-column journals that can be used when reading any type of text. In the left column students might write a

Chapter One: I like the characters, but they are kind of wierd. I mean like there names. The grandmother is called Byrd. The main character is Larkin (a girl) and her friend (a boy) is Lalo.

Grandmother (Byrd!) wears fancy sox (black ones with jewels!) and Larkin's father dances on the coffee table!!

Figure 13.6   Reading Log Entry

Figure 13.7   Three Types of Learning Log Questions and Responses

Anticipatory Question	Reactive Question	Retrospective Question
What do you want to know about the California condor?	What didn't you understand about the California condor?	What information did you learn about the California condor that was the most interesting or important?
I'd like to know why they almost became extinct.	I didn't understand why Topa's parents abandoned him or why he couldn't survive on his own.	I learned that it has taken a long, long time to bring only a few more condors back. It has taken a lot of work. I hope I get to see a condor fly sometime. They're huge!

quotation or a selected passage from the text, and in the right column their comments, questions, or responses to the quotation or passage. Or instead of writing quotations or passages from the text in the left column, the student might write about events, characters, or settings in the left column and then make personal comments on them on the right side, as illustrated in the example in the Classroom Portrait on page 440.

Dialogue Journals. In a dialogue journal, a teacher and a student or two students carry on a written conversation over a designated period of time. As you can see from the following example, the entries in a dialogue journal look very much like informal letters. These entries are written by a fourth-grader and her teacher. They are dialoguing about a book the teacher recommended, *The Tiger Rising* by Kate DiCamillo.

Dear Mrs. G,

I'm on chapter 8 of *The Tiger Rising*. It's a good book so far. I'm not sure if the tiger is real or if Rob just imagined it. I can't imagine finding a caged tiger in my neighborhood!!! I wish Rob could make some friends. But I think he will, probably, I hope. What was your favorite part of the book? So far the tiger is my favorite!!

Dear Andrea,

I'm glad you like *The Tiger Rising*. It's interesting that you think the tiger might be imagined. I'm not going to give away if you are right or not! You'll just have to keep reading to find out, also to find out if Rob does make friends. After you finish reading, I'll tell you my favorite part. I don't want to give anything away!

The dialogue journal can be used to help students become more aware of the power of language (Mode, 1989) and of audience (Wollman-Bonilla, 2001), to help students

Differentiating Instruction

for

English Language Learners

Using Learning Logs

In a study of English language learners' comprehension development, researchers William Saunders and Claude Goldenberg (1999) found that certain kinds of literature log prompts benefited students. For each chunk of a reading selection the teacher assigned, students were given the following kinds of prompts: "write about a personal experience (related to the story); elaborate on something that happened in the story (e.g., assume the role of the character), or analyze/interpret some aspect of the story or theme." These kinds of prompts are open-ended and enable students to express their ideas as they are able. Following writing, students in the study most often shared and elaborated their responses and thinking in small groups with the teacher. Called instructional conversations, students shared their understanding of the story and its theme(s) and their personal experiences related to the story. They used their literature log entries to support their discussion.

To support these learning logs teachers should keep a word wall at the writing center. On this wall teachers place the content words that students need for their writing. For example, when students write about a personal experience that is related to a story, they need words to express the emotions reflected in the narrative. The teacher posts words like *anxious, nervous, elated, cautious,* and so forth. Before students begin to write, these words are reviewed. Sometimes a picture beside the word helps the students remember its meaning.

Guidelines for Journal Writing

- Read and comment on students' journal entries as often as possible. Doing so not only gives you the chance to offer encouragement and feedback but demonstrates to students that you value this activity.
- Make the purposes for journal writing explicit. Students need to know *why* they are writing in their journals and *how* it will benefit them. For example, students might be using their journals to generate ideas for an extended writing project.
- Use journals purposefully and carefully, or, as Regie Routman (2005) advises, "Make sure the writing children do in response to their reading is worth their time." Misuse or overuse could cause students to view journaling as trite, boring, or a waste of time.
- If and when students become bored with the repetitive aspect of journal writing, drop the activity for a while.

In the Classroom

13.4

Instructional Routines

become more comfortable about writing and more willing to write (Britton et al., 1975; Hannon, 1999), to assist students from varied backgrounds in learning to write (Fulwiler, 1987), and as a means for individualizing instruction (Werderich, 2002).

All types of journals—from reading and learning logs to double-entry and dialogue journals—can be used successfully in classrooms from kindergarten through middle school. However, a word of caution: Do not overuse them. All writing forms have a time and a place. Variety is the spice of the student writer's life. To ensure that journals are useful and not viewed by students as busywork, In the Classroom 13.4 offers some worthwhile suggestions by teacher Raymond Philippot.

In this section—Writing to Learn and to Understand—we have highlighted just a few of the many ways writing can be used to help students read, understand, respond to literature, and learn subject matter, as well as prepare them for writing to communicate to an audience what they have learned. Whatever the writing form students use, the primary goal is to get them to think about what they are learning, to try to make sense of the reading experience, and to discover meaning for themselves and their lives. This, of course, is what gives learning its real purpose.

3 Think about the term *writing to learn*. What does it mean to you? Discuss your response with a classmate or classmates.

4 In addition to journal writing, six other writing-to-learn activities were discussed in this section. Give an example of an appropriate reading situation for using each of these six techniques. For example, when might it be appropriate for students to take notes? To quickwrite? To keep a journal?

REFLECT and *Apply*

Writing to Communicate

Although students do some writing primarily to learn and understand, they do other writing in order to communicate. When we talk about writing as communication, four interrelated factors are always involved—audience (who), purpose (why), content (what), and form (how). When students write to communicate, they need to be aware of these factors. Very often, it is the audience, purpose, and content that determines the form the writing will take. Three particularly useful forms to use in conjunction with reading are letters, biographies and autobiographies, and reports, which we discuss here.

Here is the time to bring in the functional approach to writing and follow the curriculum cycle we outlined at the beginning of the chapter. Students need to tackle one genre at a time and learn about its text organization and language features. *Exploring How Texts Work* by Derewianka (2000) is an excellent resource for teaching various text structures. As Courtney Cazden (1991) notes, "Children would not learn to speak a language they do not hear; so how do we expect them to learn the forms they do not read?"

Letters

In assessing students' writing progress, it pays to be organized and focused. Save one sample a week for each writing concept you teach—letter writing, for example. This will help you plan appropriate instruction and give you something concrete to share when conferencing with parents and students.

Letters are a wonderful way to highlight the reading-writing connection. Students can write formal letters to request something, express thanks, issue a complaint, or express a point of view. They might be addressed to businesses, government employees, authors and illustrators, or other adults. Letters actually incorporate many different genres. Letters that inform friends and family about personal experiences are actually personal narratives and require a study of that genre. Other letters require a study of persuasion or argument as in letters to the editor. Before students can write a strong letter they must study the genre essential to their purpose. As we wrote earlier, this requires reading models of good letters. Books that feature letters, such as *Dear Mr. Henshaw* by Beverly Cleary, *The Ballad of Lucy Whipple* by Karen Cushman, *Nettie's Trip South* by Ann Turner, and *Dear Papa* by Anne Ylvisaker can provide good models of this form. Next you must model the process, composing a letter in front of students (either on an overhead transparency or on the board) and explaining the thought processes you go through. Beyond the text structure in the body of the letter, all letters have unique conventions—date, inside address, salutation, body, closing, and signature.

Formal letters are likely to go through several stages—drafting, revising, and editing. Informal letters, however, may or may not require revision and editing. Students who have had plenty of experience writing letters can often pen a friendly letter just once before sending it off. Students can write informal letters to classmates, friends, relatives, and pen pals; in these letters they can deal with reading-related topics such as stories, story characters, and other aspects of stories that they are particularly interested in. Teacher David Carberry has his fifth-graders write letters to first-graders, a writing task his students find particularly appealing. "The kids are very aware of taking their audience and purpose into account," Carberry says.

Students can also write simulated letters to or from fictional characters or to or from real people whom they encounter in reading true narratives or informational books. In the Classroom 13.5 provides some examples.

Biographies and Autobiographies

Students can create a multimedia PowerPoint presentation to illustrate what they have learned. In addition to the traditional writing portfolios in which students' work is archived, students can make electronic portfolios using presentation software.

Biographies and autobiographies are another type of writing in which a primary purpose is to communicate—in this case, communicate some of the events in a person's life. Biographies and autobiographies are a popular genre with children because they enjoy reading about real people and because biographies and autobiographies often represent fairly easy reading, following as they do the basic narrative form children are familiar with. Biographies written expressly for young readers range from picture books such as *Dr. Martin Luther King, Jr.* and *America's Champion Swimmer: Gertrude Ederle,* both by David Adler, or *The Amazing Life of Benjamin Franklin* by James Giblin and *Revolutionary John Adams* by Cheryl Harness to in-depth portraits of noteworthy figures such as *Behind the Mask: The Life of Queen Elizabeth I* by Jane Resh Thomas, *Free*

Writing Letters to or from People Students Read About

- After reading a biography, invite students to write a letter to that person.
- Have students assume the role of a character in a story and write a letter to one of the other characters. For example, in the following letter, a student is assuming the persona of Miata in Gary Soto's *The Skirt* and is writing to Miata's friend Ana:

> Dear Ana,
> What is my mother going to say when she finds out I lost my folklorico skirt? She is going to be so mad! You've got to help me out!
>
> > Your amiga,
> > Miata

- Suggest that two students take on the roles of characters in stories and write letters to each other about novel situations those characters might face. For example, after reading Nancy Carlson's *Arnie and the New Kid,* one student might write a letter from Arnie's perspective and the other student from the perspective of Philip, the new kid in a wheelchair.

> Dear Philip,
> I wish they had given me a wheelchair like yours instead of these dumb crutches. Can you believe I broke my leg falling down some steps?
>
> > Your friend,
> > Arnie

> Dear Arnie,
> Sorry you broke your leg, but now I can do some things faster than you. Ha! Want to come over and play some video games?
>
> > Your friend,
> > Philip

to Dream: The Making of a Poet: Langston Hughes by Audrey Osofsky, and *Pocahontas* by Joseph Bruchac. Biographers take a variety of approaches in presenting their subjects, some focusing on the historical aspects, some on the sociological aspects, and others on the internal conflicts the person faced.

After students have become familiar with the form and content of biographies through ample reading, a good place to start writing them is with a collaborative piece on a familiar subject. This should be someone they all know, perhaps a well-known figure in the school—a secretary, custodian, cafeteria worker, or principal. Once students have had some practice writing about people they know and have built some confidence in their skill with biography, they can write library-researched biographies in conjunction with the reading they do in subject matter areas—for example, biographies of historical figures, scientists, politicians, artists, sports figures, or favorite authors.

Reports

In general, reports represent a more challenging writing and thinking task than do biographies or letters, primarily because they usually do not follow the chronological, narrative structure children are so familiar with and because they often require students to use several sources of information. On the other hand, we are fortunate today that an ever-increasing number of excellent models of informational

Motivating Children with Technology

Children love receiving letters and are therefore motivated to write them. Now, however, we live in an age dominated by email and we want to take advantage of this exciting mode of communication. Email is an informal letter stripped of many of its traditional conventions, but with the addition of new ones. The date is still there, supplied by the computer; the inside address is the email address, and the salutation remains. The subject line is a new feature, but the body may resemble a traditional letter in an informal style. Email still requires concise clear writing with proper spelling, punctuation, and grammar. Email also permits abbreviations such as LOL (laughing out loud) and emoticons (the smiley ☺). Email exchanges between students within the same school or with students in other schools combine the excitement of letters with the power of electronic communication. Just as you would model letter writing, you also need to model the writing of email. Make sure that you monitor this process carefully, because the rapid nature of email does not allow for much reflection and revision.

Teachers might set up email exchanges within the school or across schools among students studying the same topics. Mary Kreul (2005) recommends telecollaborative projects in which teachers and students connect via the Internet to work on specific activities. There are websites where teachers may advertise their specific projects and seek collaborators outside the school or look for existing projects their students might join. Global Schoolhouse (www.globalschoolnet.org) and Scholastic (www.scholastic.com) offer suggestions for Internet collaborative projects. •

writing are becoming readily available. More and more informational books and periodicals—which include everything from why animals have tails to the mechanics of spaceflight—are being written expressly for elementary-level students. Many of these informational materials are intriguing, relevant, and expertly crafted; they provide excellent models for students' own writing of reports. The Reading Corner on page 395 contains a list of a few such authors and titles.

Writing a good report requires many skills, from research and note taking through composing, revising, and editing to publishing. Beverly Derewianka (2000) counsels that reports can refer to several types—from news reports to science reports to weather reports. In school students typically write reports to discuss the classifications of things, to examine the components of systems, or to describe processes. So a report on snakes might begin with looking at their classification in the animal kingdom, move on to a description of their anatomy and habitat, and then look at their life cycle. To write a strong report a student will need training in all of these structures. As we have stressed before, learning about text structure through writing also enhances reading comprehension.

As Shelley Harwayne (1993) so aptly states, in addition to having numerous opportunities to read the sorts of materials they are asked to write, students also need to "develop the same hunger for learning and communicating what they find out"

"Our daily classroom newspaper is a whole-class shared writing activity and one of the best mini-lessons I have for helping children learn about the mechanics of writing. The students are actively engaged in constructing sentences about classroom projects and events in their lives. It's their newspaper and they know it."—Barbara Brunetti

Courtesy of the author

that professional writers demonstrate. Harwayne suggests three lessons we can learn from professional nonfiction writers that we would do well to pass on to our students:

- They take learning about their subject seriously.
- They want to claim the information as their own by offering their own slant or perspective on it.
- They know their options and their audiences.

Spending time communicating these truths to students through the reading-writing opportunities you provide will pay off in their enthusiasm for writing and the quality of their products.

As defined here, reports include a range of informational writing that generally serves two purposes—to learn about a topic and to communicate that information through written language. A report can take any form—a paragraph on table manners, a picture book on penguins (Figure 13.8), a page or two on pandas, or a multimedia research report on natural disasters. We offer the following recommendations for developing students' skill in writing reports:

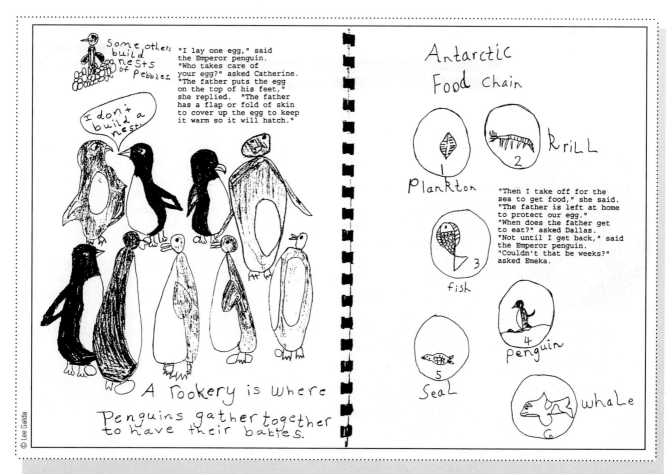

Figure 13.8

Sample Page from a First Grade's Collaboratively Written Book About Penguins

Source: Literature and the Child (7th ed.) by Lee Galda, Bee Cullinan, and Larry Sipe. Copyright © 2010. Reprinted by permission of Lee Galda.

393

Informal Writing Forms and Purposes

- Read informational books and study how they are organized. Make this part of your basic reading curriculum.
- Brainstorm with your students possible topics that they could write about. Encourage students to choose their own topics.
- Model the process of conducting research. Review and share possible resources. Model note taking or double-entry journals.
- Help students develop and outline their report and make connections to what they have learned about the structure of a report. Make sure to consider what text features to include—headings, pictures, captions, and so forth.
- Allow students ample time for drafting, revising, and meeting with you.
- Conduct mini-lessons when common problems occur with students' writing, such as crafting an engaging lead.
- Generally follow the writing process and develop a means for publishing the students' work.

Writing assignments can also be developed to challenge students to think imaginatively. In the Classroom 13.6 illustrates such thinking applied to mathematical problem solving.

Imaginative Writing

In addition to writing to learn and writing to communicate, students deserve and will profit from opportunities to do some imaginative writing in conjunction with the literature and content area texts they read. With imaginative writing, the writ-

In the Classroom

13.6

Instructional Routines

Writing Imaginative Mathematics Scenarios and Questions

1. On a chalkboard or overhead projector, display a mathematical word problem. For example, let's say students have just read the following problem in their math book or found a similar situation described in a trade book they have read:

   > Brad saw a garage sale sign that read: "Baseball cards—cheap!" He fished in his pocket and found two dimes, a nickel, and five pennies. At the garage sale, he discovered cards at two prices: Perfect cards = ten cents. Imperfect cards = five cents.

2. Have students read through the problem and discuss the kinds of questions they might develop out of the situation. As a whole class, work through a variety of examples, including the following:

   > What is the largest number of cards Brad could buy? The largest number of perfect cards? What is the largest number of perfect cards Brad can buy if he also buys imperfect cards? If Brad purchases one perfect card, how many imperfect cards can he buy? What did Brad buy if he spent all his money? What did Brad buy if he had a dime left?

3. As a whole-class shared writing activity, compose another mathematical situation and questions to go with it.

4. When students are ready to work on their own, have them form groups and write similar word problems and imaginative questions about these mathematical situations.

5. Have students exchange their word problems and questions with another group. Make sure students work through their own word problems and questions to confirm that they are doable before giving them to another group of students to read and answer.

Books by Exemplary Nonfiction Children's Book Authors

Science

Aliki. *Wild and Woolly Mammoths.* HarperCollins, 1998. This fascinating delineation of the woolly mammoth and the Ice Age is a "model of interesting factual writing for children" *(Horn Book)*. 32 pages.

Gail Gibbons. *Owls.* Holiday House, 2005. Author-illustrator Gibbons is an expert at depicting complicated subjects in a clear and simple style. In this book, one of many she has written on a variety of science-related topics, she answers questions young readers might have about owls. 32 pages.

Sandra Markle. *Outside and Inside Spiders.* Bradbury/Simon & Schuster, 1994. In a clear and energetic style, the author tells about the life of a spider, its traits, and life processes. Fascinating photos. 40 pages.

Laurence Pringle. *Scorpion Man.* Macmillan, 1994. In a text accompanied by photographs taken by the subject—Gary Polis, the "scorpion man"—Pringle describes the fascinating work of this biologist and the creatures he studies. 42 pages.

Millicent Selsam. *How to Be a Nature Detective.* HarperCollins, 1995. In this text, Selsam shows readers how anyone can be a nature detective by learning to recognize clues, especially footprints, that tell which animals have been around. 32 pages.

Seymour Simon. *Winter Across America.* Hyperion, 1994. The beauty and harshness of winter, from Alaska to the southern United States, is depicted in clear prose and stunning photographs. 32 pages.

Social Studies

David A. Adler. *A Picture Book of Thurgood Marshall.* Holiday House, 1999. One of the books in Adler's Picture Book Biographies series, this title re-creates the life history of the first African American to serve as a judge on the United States Supreme Court. 32 pages.

Russell Freedman. *The Voice That Challenged a Nation: Marian Anderson and the Struggle for Equal Rights.* Clarion Books, 2004. In this chronicle of the acclaimed singer's life—with a special emphasis on the historic 1939 Easter concert at the Lincoln Memorial—Freedman illustrates how a person's life is molded by its historical and cultural context. 128 pages.

Jean Fritz. *Harriet Beecher Stowe and the Beecher Preachers.* Putnam, 1998. This book tells of the life and times of the mid-19th-century woman, born into a celebrated family of preachers, who wrote America's first protest novel, *Uncle Tom's Cabin.* 144 pages.

James Cross Giblin. *Good Brother, Bad Brother: The Story of Edwin Booth and John Wilkes Booth.* Clarion, 2005. In an engaging narrative, Giblin intertwines the tale of the two Booth brothers with accounts of their families, friends, the Civil War, and 19th-century theater. 256 pages.

Patricia C. McKissack and **Frederick McKissack.** *Christmas in the Big House, Christmas in the Quarters.* Scholastic, 1994. The authors depict the last Christmas in Virginia before the Civil War and the fears and dreams of both Blacks and Whites. 80 pages.

Milton Meltzer. *Hear That Train Whistle Blow! How the Railroad Changed the World.* Random House, 2005. In this nonfiction text, illustrated with numerous archival photographs, Meltzer presents the myriad ways in which the railroad affected almost every aspect of modern civilization. 176 pages.

er's intent is more to entertain, evoke feelings, or stimulate imaginative thinking than it is to inform. Imaginative writing—fiction—demands the same attention to structure, organization, and language features as any of the other forms we have discussed. Writing good fiction demands a close attention to narrative structure, and the story map we have already introduced to improve comprehension can be used to guide the writing of a realistic fiction story, a fantasy, or a mystery.

Imaginative writing should include not just stories and poems, but also creative and expressive forms such as play scripts, song lyrics, and riddles.

Fiction

Writing fiction provides opportunities for students to express themselves in creative ways and to explore a topic by giving their imaginations free rein. For example, at Beauvoir, the National Cathedral Elementary School in Washington, D.C., first-graders wrote and recorded their own stories about "If I Was a Sled Dog" as part of their study of the Inuit Indians, and second-graders wrote German folktales after reading and listening to stories by the Brothers Grimm (International Reading Association, 2005). Fifth- and sixth-graders in Anchorage, Alaska, created their own imaginary creatures and wrote about them after a unit on how various species adapt to their environment. Their teacher, Diann Stone, had them select an environment with which they were familiar—in this case, their own neighborhoods—and create a creature who would dwell in that environment. Along with drawing a map of the creature's environment, students wrote a fictional report that included what this creature would look like, what it would eat, and what its habits would be.

Poetry

Poetry can be written in response to anything children read. For example, after reading about the Gold Rush, students could write poetry about some aspect of that particular slice of U.S. history. After reading about the weather, they could write a cloud poem, as second-grader Lucy did (Figure 13.9). Or they could write either jump rope rhymes after reading Afiodelia Scruggs's *Jump Rope Magic* or a variation of the Japanese tanka on the horse, as fourth-grader Julie did (Figure 13.10) after reading several of Marguerite Henry's horse stories. You will find wonderful examples of poetry on almost any subject imaginable to read to your students, which will inspire them to express themselves in this special form as well. In The Classroom 13.7 illustrates one type of poetry writing.

Rachel Weiss, a third-grade teacher, used the three forms of writing in one integrated unit. The students began with a content unit about animals. They read informational books and learned the structure of these books. Next, each student selected one animal to research with the goal of writing his or her own informational book. As

---

PEARSON
myeducationlab

Effective teachers of writing must consider how they present author's craft to their students so that their students will not only understand the strategy, but will also be able to apply it in their own writing. Analyze the effectiveness of teachers' lessons in the activity "Teaching a Mini-Lesson on Author's Craft in Writing." (To find this activity, go to the topic *Writing* in MyEducationLab and click on Building Teaching Skills and Dispositions.)

Nimbostratus
by Lucy Hooper, second grade

Yuckey!
Nasty!
Dismal!
Nimbostratus clouds
are like a witch's huge black
hat with spiders' webs all over it.
Dismal!
Dreary!

Figure 13.9

Second-Grade Student Poetry Sample

HORSES
by Julie Graves, fourth grade

Swift, gallant
great flowing manes
and large flying tales
beautiful!

Figure 13.10

Fourth-Grade Student Poetry Sample

Writing Poems Around a Theme

- Read aloud to students several poems that relate to a theme or unit of study, such as weather.
- Choose a particular poem on which to concentrate, such as "A Week of Weather" by Lee Bennett Hopkins, and talk about the words that the poet has chosen to describe the weather.
- Have students perform the poem as a choral reading.
- Together, as a shared writing activity, write a poem that reflects the week's weather in your town.

the students worked through this process, they learned a great deal about their animals. With that knowledge in hand they next had to write a piece of fiction that featured their animal. Much like Roald Dahl (2007) did in *Fantastic Mr. Fox,* they incorporated all that they learned about their animal's behavior characteristics in the fiction. Finally, they had to feature that animal in a poem, again highlighting its physical characteristics.

An intrinsic feature of each type of writing we have discussed in this and the previous sections is that it is meant to be read. The writer creates a letter, biography, report, story, or poem with an audience and purpose in mind—to inform, entertain, persuade, evoke feelings, or tickle or challenge the imagination. As you read to your students, occasionally ask them to identify the intended audience (Olness, 2005) and purpose. Additionally, as with any writing students do, sufficient scaffolding must be provided before students begin the writing as well as during the writing process. Careful motivation, preparation, modeling, encouragement, coaching, and feedback are crucial to success.

REFLECT *and* **Apply**

5 Think of a piece of writing you have done recently, and briefly answer these four questions about it: Who was the audience? What was your purpose? What was the content? What form did you use?

6 Think of a piece of writing you have done that went through several stages before you finished the piece. Briefly describe the process you went through. Compare your process with the description on pages 376–379.

7 If you wanted to ensure your students' success in writing reports on a topic they had been reading about, what steps would you take to guide them? Be as specific as possible in your explanation.

The Writing Workshop

Simply stated, writing workshop is a designated time during the school day when children write individually or collaboratively on topics of their own choosing, for their own purposes. This writing may take place several times a week or, in some classrooms, every day. As Charles Temple and his colleagues (Temple, Nathan, Temple, & Burris, 1993) point out, the writing workshop provides a setting in which children's "own interest in life, coupled with their desire to express themselves," motivates them to write. Additionally, it provides a predictable structure and routine in which students feel comfortable taking risks, "collaborate with their peers, and take control of their own learning" (Hindley, 1998).

Over the past 25 years, educators have discovered that when students know they will have a chunk of time to write, a time in which they will be actively involved in writing for reasons that are important to them, they really develop as writers. Donald Graves (1991) suggests that it takes at least 3 hours a week for this habit of mind to take hold, and students begin "rehearsing off stage" what they will write about. The writing workshop—a concept developed by Nancie Atwell (1987, 1998b) and a number of other teachers and researchers—is designed to provide your writers with that sort of time.

In the writing workshop, both teacher and student have equally important roles. The teacher's role is that of facilitator, coach, and guide—establishing a community of writers who interact and support one another through all the phases of the writing process. The student's role is to write and encourage and support other writers.

A typical writing workshop has a number of key components and activities, with student writing at the core, as shown in Figure 13.11. Instruction takes place through

Figure 13.11

Key Components of the Writing Workshop

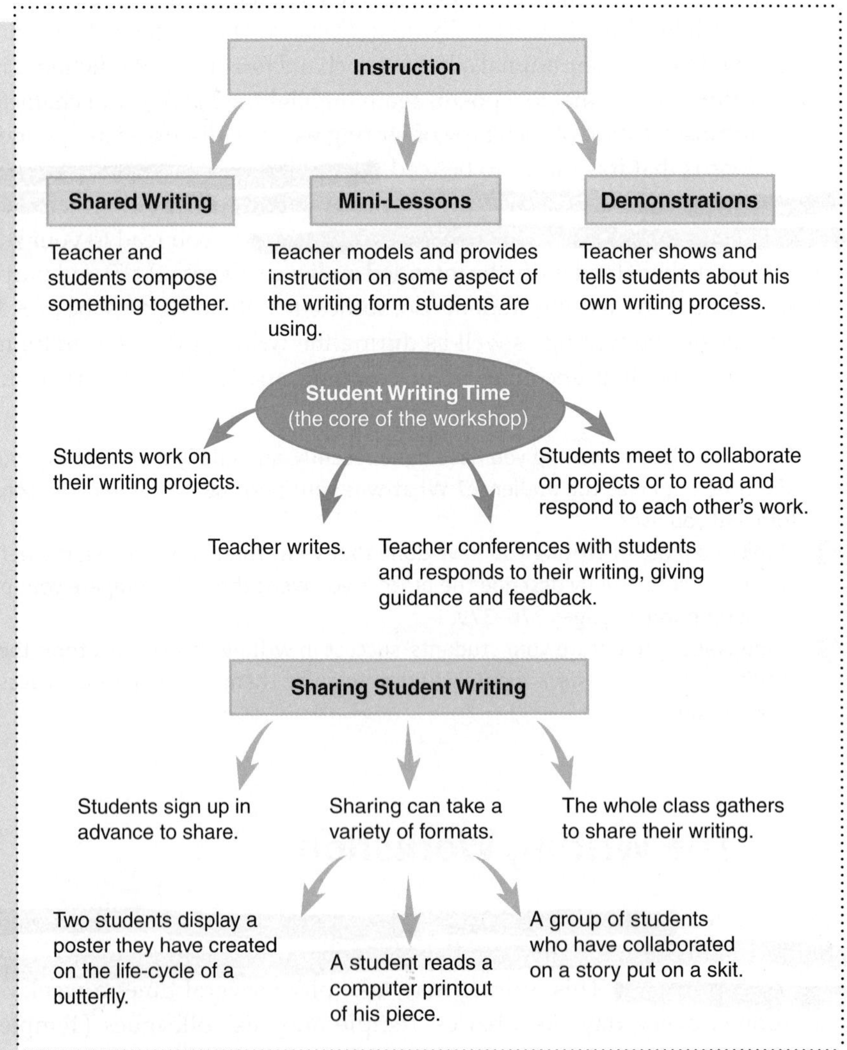

Instruction

Shared Writing
Teacher and students compose something together.

Mini-Lessons
Teacher models and provides instruction on some aspect of the writing form students are using.

Demonstrations
Teacher shows and tells students about his own writing process.

Student Writing Time
(the core of the workshop)

Students work on their writing projects.

Teacher writes.

Teacher conferences with students and responds to their writing, giving guidance and feedback.

Students meet to collaborate on projects or to read and respond to each other's work.

Sharing Student Writing

Students sign up in advance to share.

Sharing can take a variety of formats.

The whole class gathers to share their writing.

Two students display a poster they have created on the life-cycle of a butterfly.

A student reads a computer printout of his piece.

A group of students who have collaborated on a story put on a skit.

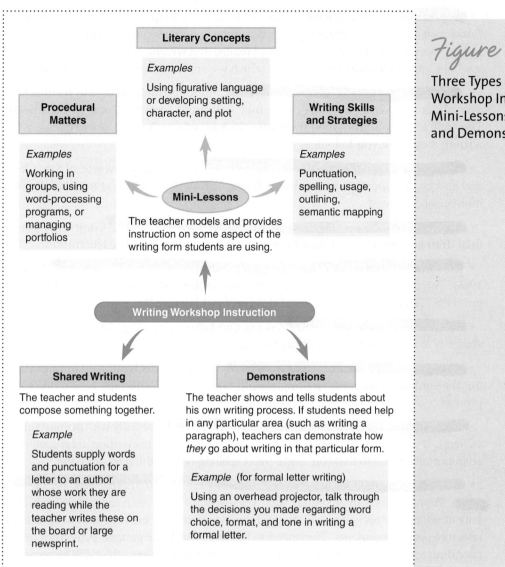

Literary Concepts

Examples

Using figurative language or developing setting, character, and plot

Procedural Matters

Examples

Working in groups, using word-processing programs, or managing portfolios

Mini-Lessons

The teacher models and provides instruction on some aspect of the writing form students are using.

Writing Skills and Strategies

Examples

Punctuation, spelling, usage, outlining, semantic mapping

Writing Workshop Instruction

Shared Writing

The teacher and students compose something together.

Example

Students supply words and punctuation for a letter to an author whose work they are reading while the teacher writes these on the board or large newsprint.

Demonstrations

The teacher shows and tells students about his own writing process. If students need help in any particular area (such as writing a paragraph), teachers can demonstrate how *they* go about writing in that particular form.

Example (for formal letter writing)

Using an overhead projector, talk through the decisions you made regarding word choice, format, and tone in writing a formal letter.

mini-lessons, demonstrations, and shared writing activities, as shown in Figure 13.12. These activities usually occur before students begin their own writing in the workshop setting. The writing workshop, coupled with the wide reading that provides students with both content and form for their writing and frequent opportunities to discuss their reading and their writing, can be one important component of a rich and nurturing literate environment.

Responding to Students' Writing

To grow as readers and writers, students need to receive feedback on their writing and what it reveals about their reading. Here we present a handful of suggestions on how to respond to students' writing in ways that will help them evaluate their own success at achieving their writing goals.

*A*ssessment

Use the read-write cycle assessments in Appendix A to determine the best writing a student can do on any given topic.

- *Be positive.* Emphasize what works in a piece more frequently than what doesn't—"Wow, you really got my attention with that great opening sentence!" Recall the emphasis we placed on success in Chapter 3, and realize that writing is for most of us (authors, teachers, and students alike) an area in which we are very vulnerable to criticism.

- *Respond to only some of what students write.* Students don't need your feedback on everything they write. In many cases, they will profit from feedback by their peers. They will also profit from their own self-criticism, which they can use to decide what writing they want you to look at.

- *Respond to only a few matters at any one time.* It is simply a waste of your time and energy to respond to many things at once. Students will attend to only a limited number of comments.

- *Comment primarily on works in progress rather than final drafts.* Comments after a final draft is completed get very little attention and often produce frustration.

- *Give feedback during brief conferences with students on their works in progress* (Graves, 1996). A typical conference between a teacher-writer and a student-writer might begin with "Tell me about your piece" or "How is it coming?"

- *Observe students as they write.* Asking questions or making statements can lead students to solve their own writing dilemmas.

- *Deal with content first and mechanics later.* It is not that mechanics are unimportant, but the content of students' writing should take priority, especially as it reflects and promotes students' proficiency in reading.

- *Praise correct spelling, but also encourage invented spelling* (especially with primary-grade writers). If your student's goal is to have someone else read his writing, then spelling is an important means to that end, and correct spelling is something to strive for.

- *Make peer response an integral and frequent part of your reading and writing program.* There is probably no better way to learn something than to teach it—which is part of what peer reviewers are doing. However, students must be taught how to be effective peer respondents. They need to be taught both the general principles for responding to a person's writing and the specific writing elements they will be responding to—content, coherence, transitions, form, dialogue, and so on. Having checklists showing the specific criteria is often useful, so that students know what to look for. In his book *Writer to Writer: How to Conference Young Authors,* Tommy Thomason (1998) gives practical suggestions on how to teach students to have peer conferences.

Finally, in addition to following these suggestions for responding to students' writing, like virtually all current writers on writing, we recommend that you have students keep portfolios of their writing—ongoing and cumulative records and examples of their work. Items to be included can be selected by both you and your students. A major strength of these portfolios is that students can use them to evaluate their work and growth as writers. You and the students can use these portfolios as a tool for evaluating their writing and deciding where future efforts might be directed, sharing with parents, and determining and agreeing on grades.

Publishing and Celebrating Writing

There is something universal in the appeal of a book with good-quality paper and a hard cover, something that we hope will continue to live alongside the Kindle and other electronic books. And sometimes good paper and a hard cover will be just the right format for kids' published works. However, charts, posters, articles, and radio or TV scripts can also be "published."

Publishing means making a work available to some "public" audience. This audience might be the writer's classmates, students in another class, the entire school, a broader audience such as readers of a newspaper or magazine, or perhaps even a blog. The Students of the World website (www.studentsoftheworld.info) provides a place for students to create their own blog about a topic or add on to other blogs. Publishing highlights the importance of considering an audience while writing, and writing intended for publication is usually the result of the full writing process—brainstorming, drafting, revising, and editing. Although the larger audiences just mentioned are certainly possibilities, in many cases publishing will be accomplished simply by posting the work in the classroom. Whatever audience it reaches, published work is generally produced with the aid of word processors, spell checkers, computerized dictionaries and thesauruses, and, in some cases, desktop publishing programs.

One such publishing program is Panther Paw Press, with which children's original works can be published as bound books. This is a school-based publishing program that is built on the efforts of students, teachers, parents, and school principals (Chihak, 1999). Another highly successful publishing effort is that of Cheri Cooke's seventh-grade reading classes. Each year, they produce a bound volume of reviews of their favorite books (Cooke & Graves, 1995). Lauretta Beecher's second-graders celebrate their writing in yet another way. They host a party and invite parents and other adults in the school to listen to their stories and poems.

Celebrating students' writing is an important part of the writing process.

Nick White/Photodisc/Getty Images

8 Identify a grade level at which you would like to teach, and consider for a moment the mini-lesson component of the writing workshop. Name some topics you might choose to cover early in the year, some you might choose to cover in the middle of the year, and some you might choose to cover late in the year. Now consider what surprises you might find in your students' writing and how these would affect your plan.

9 We listed nine suggestions for responding to students' writing. Rank these in order from most important to least important, and ask a classmate to do the same. Then get together and discuss the similarities and differences in your rankings, trying particularly to understand any large differences and what those differences suggest about your views of writing instruction.

REFLECT and *Apply*

Strengths *and Challenges* of Diversity

With writing, as with any other curricular area we have discussed, one of the most effective ways to meet the needs of different students is to differentiate the curriculum. For example, let's say that your class of fourth-graders has completed a unit in which they have been reading self-selected books on the theme of courage, and now you want them to respond to what they read by writing on the topic. Students who struggle with writing can enjoy success by dictating "courage stories" to an adult, who then transcribes them. Some students can work together and draft a play about courage. Verbally talented students can be challenged to write a researched biography on a courageous person whom they admire.

Students who find writing a challenge, who speak and write in a dialect other than standard English, or whose native language is not English may profit from extra support and extra time. The following suggestions offer such students help with writing tasks; some were recommended by Robin Scarcella (1996), director of the ESL program at the University of California at Irvine.

- Keep directions simple, and check to be sure students understand them.
- Have a model of the completed writing task available.
- Demonstrate or model the writing activity.
- Guide the students through the activity.
- Have needed writing supplies readily available.
- Provide feedback that is both comprehensible and constructive.
- Show respect for students' home languages and cultures.

A writing activity that shows respect for students' home languages and cultures encourages students to write about stories, songs, or customs from their home cultures or in their own languages (Canney, Kennedy, Schroeder, & Miles, 1999). *Salsa Stories* by Lulu Delacre, in which characters from several South American countries tell stories of their customs and holiday traditions, would be a good read-aloud springboard and model for this writing activity. Should students be allowed to write in their own dialects as well as their home languages?

As educator Lisa Delpit (1988) has eloquently argued, students of color need and deserve to become adept at writing in standard English, and teachers need to assist them in doing so. However, in some situations, such as writing stories that are based on the writer's personal experiences and reflect his cultural heritage, dialect is definitely appropriate, especially if the writer includes dialogue. Three questions can serve to guide both you and your students with regard to whether dialect is appropriate and effective in a piece of writing: What is the purpose for writing? Who is the audience? Who is talking in the story?

Some approaches to writing are especially appropriate for very skillful writers. One activity we have found particularly useful and well received by skillful developing writers is creating narratives or expository pieces related to their reading, such as the following suggestions from Graves & Graves (2003):

- Select a scene from a book, and rewrite it to show what might happen if a character did something differently.
- Write an alternative ending to a story.
- Write a sequel or a prequel to a story.
- Present the events of a text in newspaper format.
- Rewrite a contemporary story as a fairy tale.

Of course, less skilled writers can also profit from some of these activities, but remember that less skilled writers will need sufficient scaffolding to be successful with them.

Another activity particularly suited to gifted writers is participating in writing contests. Submitting writing to contests can be highly motivating, as it provides students with an authentic goal and audience. Magazines, organizations, and state and county fairs all sponsor writing competitions. A listing of writing contests can be found in the *Children's Writer's and Illustrator's Market* (Buening, 2006) in the section titled Young Writers and Illustrators.

Concluding *Remarks*

The value of developing a literate environment and establishing a curriculum to help students grow as writers in concert with their reading has been the overriding theme of this chapter. That means providing a classroom atmosphere, both physical and intellectual, that is safe and nurturing as well as inviting, fun, and challenging. It means providing opportunities to write for real purposes and for real audiences, purposes that include writing to learn for yourself and writing to communicate with someone else. It means providing students with opportunities to improve their writing and thinking skills through all sorts of writing—informal writing, such as brainstorming, quickwriting, and journaling, as well

as formal writing, such as reports and storybooks that require the process approach. It means giving students every benefit possible—providing daily time to write, publishing their works, and giving them constructive feedback. In short, your reading-writing environment and curriculum will help and inspire students to write more often and more effectively. It will encourage them to use writing as a thinking tool to learn more about themselves and their world and as a communicative tool to share their knowledge, feelings, and insights with others, both of which are essential for living successfully in today's world.

Extending Learning

1. Get together with several classmates and develop a set of interview questions that you can use with teachers to learn how they use writing in conjunction with reading in their classrooms. Limit yourselves to five or six questions that can be answered rather briefly. For example, you might ask how often their students write in conjunction with the reading they're doing. Once the questionnaire has been developed, try it out first on one teacher, and modify it as necessary. Then, each person in the group can interview two teachers and record their answers. Finally, get together with your classmates, share the results of your interviews, and discuss to what extent the writing you learned about is consistent with the principles and techniques recommended in this chapter. After your group meeting, you might consider presenting the results of your project to your university class.

2. Observe the reading and language arts periods of an elementary class for at least 1 week (2 weeks, if possible), and keep a detailed record of the writing the students do. Then, as a writing-to-learn activity for yourself, write a description of the class and the teacher, the writing you observed in the 1- or 2-week period, and the extent to which the writing you observed is and is not like that recommended in this chapter. Next, write an evaluative statement on the quality of the writing activities you observed and the extent to which they seem to support and extend the reading experiences students had during the period. Finally, if you believe that what you observed could be modified to better support and extend students' reading, briefly describe the modifications you would suggest.

Children's Literature

Adler, D. A. (2001). *Dr. Martin Luther King, Jr.* New York: Holiday House. This short biography tells the story of Dr. Martin Luther King, Jr.—his life, his accomplishments in the civil rights movement, and his impact on U.S. history. 32 pages.

Adler, D. A. (2005). *America's Champion Swimmer: Gertrude Ederle.* San Diego: Gulliver Books. This picture book biography covers the life of Gertrude Ederle, highlighting her world-record-breaking long-distance swims in the late 1920s, when women were thought to be "the weaker sex." 32 pages.

Branley, F. M. (1998). *The Planets in Our Solar System.* New York: HarperCollins. Part of the Let's Read and Find Out series, this book takes a quick look at the nine planets in our solar system using photographs and color illustrations. 32 pages.

Bridges, R. (1999). *Through My Eyes.* New York: Scholastic. In this photobiography, Ruby Bridges recounts the story of her involvement, as a 6-year-old, in the integration of her school in New Orleans in 1960. 63 pages.

Bruchac, J. (2005). *Pocahontas.* San Diego: Harcourt. Although the book is a historical novel, not a true biography, Bruchac goes to great lengths to present a historically accurate depiction of the relationship between the Virginia colonists and the Powhatans as seen through the eyes of Captain John Smith and the 11-year-old daughter of the Powhatan chief. 192 pages.

Carlson, N. (1990). *Arnie and the New Kid.* New York: Puffin. In this picture book, Arnie begins to better understand the new kid in a wheelchair after he falls and becomes temporarily disabled himself. Unnumbered.

Cleary, B. (1983). *Dear Mr. Henshaw.* New York: Morrow. In this Newbery Medal book, 10-year-old Leigh writes letters to his favorite author that help him to cope with his parents' divorce and a new school and to find his place in the world. Audiotape and filmstrip available. 134 pages.

Cole, J. (1989). *The Magic School Bus Inside the Human Body.* Ms. Frizzle takes her class via the magic bus inside the human body to look at how the body parts work. Spanish CD available. 40 pages.

Cole, J. (1992). *The Magic School Bus on the Ocean Floor.* Ms. Frizzle takes her class to the ocean floor aboard the magic school bus, where they learn firsthand the mysteries of underwater life. Spanish CD available. 40 pages.

Cushman, K. (1996). *The Ballad of Lucy Whipple.* New York: Clarion. While stuck in a California gold-mining town with her adventurous mother and siblings, Lucy pours out her heart and frustrations in a series of letters written to the folks she left behind in Massachusetts, where she longs to return. 195 pages.

Dahl, R. (1961). *James and the Giant Peach*. New York: Scholastic. Young James experiences madcap adventures as he enters a peach as big as a house and encounters new friends. Audio CD available. 128 pages.

Dahl, R. (1970). *Fantastic Mr. Fox*. New York: Puffin. A very resourceful fox saves his family from three disgusting farmers. 90 pages.

Delacre, L. (2000). *Salsa Stories*. New York: Scholastic. In a notebook Carmen Teresa receives as a holiday present, guests fill the pages with their colorful stories from a variety of Latin American countries. 144 pages.

DiCamillo, K. (2001). *The Tiger Rising*. Cambridge, MA: Candlewick. After Rob's mother dies and he and his father move to rural Florida to get their lives back together, Rob finds a way to come to terms with his mother's death through the help of a friend and a tiger. 116 pages.

Fleischman, S. (1986). *The Whipping Boy*. New York: Greenwillow. In this Newbery Medal book, Prince Brat and his whipping boy, Jemmy, run away from the palace, end up trading identities, and have many adventures together. Audio CD available. 90 pages.

Freedman, R. (1993). *Eleanor Roosevelt: A Life of Discovery*. New York: Clarion. This photobiography portrays the first wife of a president to carve out an influential career of her own. 198 pages.

Giblin, J. C. (2006). *The Amazing Life of Benjamin Franklin*. New York: Scholastic. In a concise, readable style, this biography presents a realistic, unsentimental portrait of the famous inventor, statesman, and diplomat, including his contributions and his challenges. 48 pages.

Graves, B. (2002). *California Condor: Flying Free*. Des Moines, IA: Perfection. Through the story of the capture of TopaTopa, the first California condor in the condor recovery program, the reader learns facts about this endangered bird and efforts to save it from extinction. 62 pages.

Halpern, M. (2002). *Strange Plants*. Washington, DC: National Geographic Educational Service. From the Windows on Literacy series, this brief text discusses meat-eating plants. 24 pages.

Harness, C. (2006). *Revolutionary John Adams*. Washington, DC: National Geographic Children's Books. This appealing and informative book is about the life and contributions of the second president of the United States, John Adams, who is often overshadowed by the more colorful Washington and Jefferson. 48 pages.

Hopkins, L. B. (Ed.). (1995). *Weather: Poems for All Seasons*. New York: HarperCollins. This collection of poems by well-known as well as lesser-known poets describes various weather conditions. 64 pages.

MacLachlan, P. (1993). *Baby*. New York: Delacorte. This exquisitely crafted short novel tells of a family learning to deal with the death of their own infant son after a baby girl is left on their doorstep for them to care for. 132 pages.

Martin, A. (2001). *Belle Teal*. New York: Scholastic. In 1962, fifth-grader Belle Teal faces the challenges of sticking up for Black students in her newly desegregated school in Coker Creek, Tennessee, as well as sorting out problems at home. 214 pages.

Matas, C. (2002). *Sparks Fly Upward*. Boston: Houghton Mifflin. In 1910, 12-year-old Rebecca and her Russian immigrant family try to adjust to a new culture while maintaining their traditions and faith. 192 pages.

Osofsky, A. (1996). *Free to Dream: The Making of a Poet: Langston Hughes*. New York: Lothrop, Lee, and Shepard. This is a biography of the Harlem poet who gave a voice to the African American experience in America. 112 pages.

Parker, S. (1999). *It's a Frog's Life! My Story of Life in a Pond*. Pleasantville, NY: Reader's Digest Children's Publishing. This is a look at the busy life of an English pond from a frog's viewpoint. 32 pages.

Scruggs, A. (2000). *Jump Rope Magic*. New York: Blue Sky Press. Shameka and her crew, who love to skip rope to the music of the jump-rope beat, make even Mean Miss Minnie a believer in "jump rope magic." David Diaz's colorful illustrations add to the warmth and fun. 40 pages.

Soto, G. (1992). *The Skirt*. New York: Delacorte. After fourth-grader Miata accidentally leaves her folklorico skirt on the bus, she tries desperately to get it back before her parents find out. 74 pages.

Thomas, J. R. (1998). *Behind the Mask: The Life of Queen Elizabeth I*. Boston: Clarion. This biography of Elizabeth I, daughter of Henry VIII and Anne Boleyn, describes how she takes a personal misfortune and turns it around to make a difference in the world. 196 pages.

Thomas, J. R. (2005). *The Counterfeit Princess*. Boston: Clarion Books. This book is set in 16th-century England, as the young King Edward nears death and various factions vie for control of the throne. Fifteen-year-old Iris, who is trained as a spy for Princess Elizabeth, acts as the princess's double in an effort to save the country from the Duke of Northumberland. 176 pages.

Turner, A. (1987). *Nettie's Trip South*. New York: Macmillan. Based on the actual diary of the author's great-grandmother, this picture book tells about the cruel realities a 10-year-old girl encounters when she visits Richmond, Virginia, and witnesses a slave auction. 32 pages.

Wildlife Education. (1984). *Zoo Books 2: Alligators and Crocodiles*. San Diego: Wildlife Education. This series of books depicts a variety of zoo animals.

Ylvisaker, A. (2002). *Dear Papa*. Cambridge, MA: Candlewick. One year after her father's death in 1942, 9-year-old Isabelle begins writing him letters, which are interspersed with letters to other family members, relating important events in her life and how she feels about them. 184 pages.

myeducationlab

Now go to the topic "Writing" in the MyEducationLab (www.myeducationlab.com) for your course, where you can:

- Find learning outcomes for the topics covered in this chapter along with the IRA standards that connect to these outcomes.

- Complete assignable activities in the Assignments and Activities section that show concepts in action to help you synthesize and apply strategies.

- Explore IRIS Center Resources—training enhancement materials that provide you with research-validated information and interactive materials to develop your skills in working with students.

- Apply and practice your understanding of the teaching skills identified in the chapter with the Building Teaching Skills and Dispositions exercises.

14

Reading Instruction for English Language Learners

Cynthia studied her incoming class of third-graders and once more thought of the increasingly daunting task she faced. She had chosen to teach in a large urban district because she wanted to help the children who most needed her help, and she had never regretted that decision. But each year there seemed to be more challenges, including preparing students for the ever-increasing and ever-more-critical annual state testing and working with more and more students who did not speak English as their first language.

The latter challenge, working with English language learners, was for her the most daunting one. She had completed her teacher education program a decade ago in the Midwest, where no attention had been given to working with children who did not speak English as their first language. This year, almost 30 percent of her students were English language learners. A few of them spoke no English. Two of them had not had any sort of formal schooling. Others had received excellent instruction in their homeland schools and could read and write very well in their native languages.

What could she do? Her task, she knew, was to lead all of her English learners as well as her students who spoke English as their native language toward a level of literacy that would enable them to succeed in school and beyond. She knew a lot about good teaching, and she was convinced that good teaching is effective with all students. But she was constantly on the lookout for approaches that would prove particularly effective for English learners.

CLASSROOM vignette

Learning to Read English as a Second Language in the United States

Before we address approaches to helping English learners, we must first understand the challenges Cynthia and many other teachers face in fostering reading achievement in English language learners. We also need to briefly look at the historical and contemporary U.S. landscape within which English learners learn to read English.

Fostering Reading Achievement in English Language Learners

As Cynthia realizes, addressing the needs of English language learners is a significant challenge. Yet as she and many other educators are increasingly realizing (Vaughan, 2005), good teaching is effective with all students. All students, including English learners, will benefit from both more traditional instructional practices as well as practices motivated by constructivist and sociocultural theories, each of which we summarize in the accompanying features (In the Classroom 14.1 and 14.2). This is not to say that applying effective instructional practices is all that we can do for English learners. There are many more techniques we can use, and later in this chapter's Instructional Principles section, we list several sets of suggestions specific to English learners.

The U.S. Landscape

As noted in the U.S. Department of Education's *The Conditions of Education 2009* (Planty et al., 2009), the number of school-age children speaking a language other than English at home grew from 3.8 million in 1979 to 10.8 million in 2007. During this same period of time, the number of children speaking English with some difficulty increased from 1.3 million to 2.7 million. This huge increase in the number of English language learners has had a tremendous impact on U.S. schools; although the overall number of school-age children increased by 19 percent from 1979 to 2003, the number of children who spoke English with some difficulty increased by 139 percent (Planty et al., 2009).

In the Classroom

14.1

Instructional Routines

Traditional Instructional Principles

- *Focus on academically relevant tasks.* Concentrate on important topics, skills, and strategies that students really need to master.
- *Employ active teaching.* Know your subject well, be the instructional leader in your classroom, and actively convey to students the content to be learned in presentations, discussions, and demonstrations.
- *Foster active learning.* Give students opportunities to manipulate and grapple with the material they are learning.
- *Distinguish between instruction and practice.* Instruction consists of teaching students knowledge, skills, and strategies. Practice consists of asking students to use the knowledge, skills, and strategies that they have already been taught.
- *Provide sufficient and timely feedback.* Whenever possible, respond to students' work with immediate and specific feedback.
- *Teach for transfer.* Transfer seldom occurs automatically. If we want students to take what they have learned in one context and use it in a new context, we need to show them how to do so.

Instructional Principles Motivated by Constructivist and Sociocultural Theories

- *Scaffold students' efforts.* Provide students with the temporary support they need to complete tasks they could not complete independently.
- *Provide instruction in students' zone of proximal development.* Instruct students at a level that challenges them but allows them to achieve with effort and your assistance.
- *Use the gradual release of responsibility model.* Begin instruction on difficult topics by initially doing much of the work yourself; then, over time, give students increasing responsibility for the work until eventually they are doing all of it.
- *Use cognitive modeling.* Think aloud for students, demonstrating the thinking you employ as you complete a task that you are teaching them to do.
- *Use direct explanation.* In teaching strategies, (1) give students a description of the strategy and when, how, and why it should be used; (2) model it; (3) work along with students as they use the strategy; (4) gradually give students increased responsibility for using the strategy; and (5) have students use the strategy independently.
- *Ensure that students contextualize, review, and practice what is learned.* Real learning takes time, effort, and a lot of practice.
- *Teach for understanding.* Teach in such a way that students understand topics fully, remember important information, and actively use what they have learned.

Data cited by Kamil and Bernhardt (2004) indicate that the vast majority of these children—almost three-quarters of them—speak Spanish; no other language is spoken by more than 4 percent of the remainder of the students, including speakers of Vietnamese, Hmong, Cantonese, Cambodian, Korean, and a number of Native American languages. Although English learners can be found in the vast majority of large schools, their distribution across the United States is uneven. The percentages of school-age children who speak a language other than English at home range from 33 percent in the West to 11 percent in the Midwest, with 20 percent in the Northeast and 17 percent in the South (Planty et al., 2005).

The most recent National Association of Educational Progress (NAEP) report (Lee, Grigg, & Donahue, 2007) presents some data comparing performance of English language learners to their English-speaking peers. The NAEP reports students' performance in terms of three achievement levels—basic, proficient, and advanced. The lowest level, the basic level, is defined as denoting "partial mastery of prerequisite knowledge and skills that are fundamental for proficient work at each grade." According to the most recent NAEP report, only 30 percent of ELL fourth-graders scored at or above the basic level, whereas 69 percent of non-ELL fourth-graders scored at or above the basic level. Thus, over twice as many non-ELL students as ELL students succeeded at this level.

Immigrants, many of whom speak languages other than English, have long been a part of the U.S. scene.

Bettmann/Corbis

U.S. schools have always been populated with children from diverse linguistic backgrounds, and teachers have had to confront the challenges of linguistic diversity for many years. One estimate suggests a total of 42 percent of all public school teachers have at least one English language learner in their classes (Olson & Goldstein, 1997). The apparently opposing forces of the home language and English have been at issue since the birth of the United States. Benjamin Franklin, John Adams, and Noah Webster, for example, all argued that a common language was a key element in promoting social unity (Simpson, 1986). Indeed, throughout the development of the U.S. public school system during the 19th and early 20th centuries, the concept of one people/one language was central (Higham, 1988). The world wars, particularly World War I and its aftermath, marked by southern and eastern European immigration, solidified this belief in the minds of many Americans.

Yet other Americans have always viewed ethnic pride as a hallmark of American freedom and the suppression of language and culture as contradicting the American spirit. They argue that the strength of America lies in the diversity of culture, beliefs, and perspectives of persons who flock to the United States seeking a better life (Tollefson, 1995). This tolerance for diversity is certainly reflected in the most recently published large-scale study of reading instruction for English learners, Robert Slavin and Alan Cheung's "A Synthesis of Research on Language of Reading Instruction for English Language Learners" (2005). It is also the position reflected in the report of the National Literacy Panel (August & Shanahan, 2009), an even more comprehensive review of the literature on reading instruction for English learners.

Some Challenges of Learning to Read in a Second Language

Most immigrant families become English-dominant in less than two generations, so why is there anything to be concerned about? We know that the children in our classrooms will more than likely become speakers of English. Isn't it a simple case of waiting until this happens? The answer is no! Research indicates that it takes English language learners at least 5 years to reach the oral skill level of their English-speaking peers (Cummins, 2001). Waiting 5 years to begin reading instruction would mean delaying literacy learning for many ELL children until they are adolescents. This would be educationally and morally absurd. We know that all children need to begin literacy learning as early as possible in order to become effective readers and writers. What then does every teacher need to understand about the relationship of a first oral language to acquiring a second language and then learning to read in that language? We will discuss this question first in terms of the challenges faced by learners, then in terms of the challenges faced by teachers, and finally in terms of the light that research can shed on these challenges.

Before we do so, however, we will introduce some linguistic terms and concepts. Some of these terms and concepts are probably familiar to you and some probably are not, but at this point it is crucial that you become familiar with all of those listed in Figure 14.1.

Challenges Faced by English Language Learners

The oral language that children bring to school is a terrific starting point for literacy learning. English-speaking children have internalized an extraordinary amount of

Figure 14.1   Some Key Linguistic Terms

- **Syntax** refers to the ways in which words combine to form sentences. The syntax of an English sentence is most often a subject followed by a verb followed by an object, as in *I see the man*. An unacceptable combination in English would be *I the man I see* because the syntax of English requires the verb to follow the subject in most cases.
- **Morphology** refers to ways that words are built through adding parts. *Man*, for example, is an individual word and one morpheme. We can add the morpheme *-ly* to form *manly*, a new word that contains two morphemes. Different languages have different morphological systems for word building.
- **Inflections** are special types of morphemes. The addition of *-s* on many words indicates plural in English. We add *-ed* to regular verbs to indicate past tense and *-er* to indicate the comparative. Inflections do not change the type of the word they are attached to (verbs remain verbs and nouns remain nouns).
- The **lexicon** of a language is the body of words that make up the language. There are hundreds of thousands of words in the English lexicon. The English lexicon is made up of a very small set of frequently used words and a very large set of infrequently used words.
- **Orthography** refers to writing systems. English, Spanish, French, German, and Finnish all use Roman letters and hence have Roman orthography. Russian uses a different alphabet, the Cyrillic alphabet, and hence has Cyrillic orthography.

language by the time they come to school—about 75 percent of all the syntax and morphology they will ever acquire. Effective literacy teaching is rooted in understanding how children use what they already know about oral language as they learn to deal with printed language.

Like their English-speaking classmates, English language learners also come to U.S. schools with a considerable amount of language knowledge. They too possess nearly all of the structure and morphology they will need to become fluent speakers. The difference, though, is that they are on the road to becoming fluent speakers of a language that is not typically used for either instruction or assessment in U.S. schools. It is not that English language learners come to school with a language deficit. They come with a lack of knowledge of the particular language that is used in the schools they will be attending—English. This presents several significant challenges.

There is a surface-level mismatch between the child's language and the language of the school. Children who speak a language other than English will approach learning to read with the best strategy they have—matching the oral language they know with the written language they see. This, however, presents them with an enormous challenge: *The oral language they know and the written language they must learn will have differing degrees of overlap.*

In addition to this surface-level mismatch, there are less obvious and in some ways deeper differences between English-speaking children raised in the United States and some non-English-speaking children raised in other settings. As we pointed out in Chapters 6 and 7, most children who have grown up in the United States have internalized a number of concepts relevant to learning to read. These concepts, of course, may or may not be well developed, and some children certainly have more extensive and richer preschool literacy experiences than other children. Nevertheless, regardless of their backgrounds, an English-language print experience surrounds virtually all students who grow up in the United States; they generally know that print signals a relationship to meaning.

The situation is quite different for some students who were not raised in the United States. Some children come from cultures that are not literate. Print, reading, and the many experiences that surround print and reading have never been part of their world. These children must learn what print actually is and how it functions. This brings us to a second challenge: *They have yet to develop the rich and varied knowledge that many children internalize from growing up in a literate culture.*

Quite a different situation exists for other students. Many children come from cultures with rich literacy heritages (children from Arab nations and India, for example), but those literacy heritages may have produced quite different understandings about print and how it functions. This brings us to a third challenge: *The rich and varied knowledge about literacy that they internalized from growing up in their culture may need to be altered.*

Like their English-speaking classmates, English language learners will exhibit different degrees of skills, intelligences, and motivations. As with all children in our classrooms, we see the array of talents that they demonstrate each day. We often assume that the more verbal children are the more able learners and that the very social children are the more cooperative and interested learners. However, English language learners frequently come from cultures that do not value a great deal of verbal behavior from children, perceiving it to be rude. Moreover, and perhaps more important, English language learners frequently cannot express what they do in fact know. This brings us to a fourth challenge—really a pair of them: *The verbal abilities of children may not match what they actually know, and they may be reticent to express themselves verbally in class.*

Challenges Faced by Teachers

Like children who must learn to read in a second language, teachers who strive to assist English language learners in becoming competent readers face significant challenges. How can we bridge the gap between students who have 5 or 6 years of oral language development that is directly relevant to the literacy task at hand and students whose oral language development is only indirectly relevant to the literacy task at hand? Three particularly important challenges confront us here.

First, the extra processing steps needed by English language learners make the instructional task doubly difficult. In many cases, these children have the concepts necessary to understand a text, but they use sounds and words that do not match the print. *We as teachers must prepare students to succeed at this difficult matching task by building their oral English skills.*

Second, as Figure 14.2 illustrates, speakers of different languages will have varying amounts of processing to do as they move from the language they know to the language they are learning. The Spanish-speaking child needs to go from the Spanish *gato* to the English *cat*, two words that show some distinct print overlap. But what of the child who has to go from the Vietnamese *mão* to *cat*? The task for the Vietnamese-speaking child is considerably more difficult because none of the letters overlap with those of the English word. *We as teachers must prepare for success both those students whose language overlaps a lot with English and those whose language overlaps very little with English.*

As daunting as these instructional issues are, they pale in comparison with the third challenge—dealing with the potential mismatch between children's conceptual

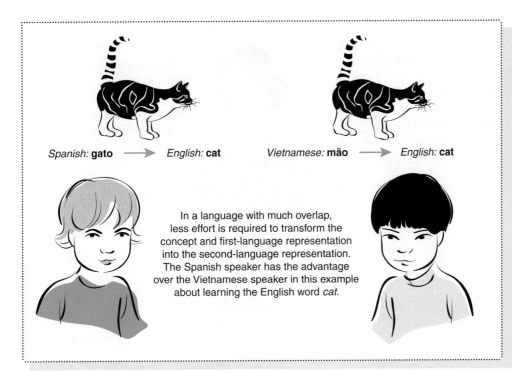

Figure 14.2

Differential Amounts
of Print Overlap
in Languages

Spanish: **gato** → English: **cat**   Vietnamese: **mão** → English: **cat**

In a language with much overlap,
less effort is required to transform the
concept and first-language representation
into the second-language representation.
The Spanish speaker has the advantage
over the Vietnamese speaker in this example
about learning the English word *cat*.

understanding and their verbal abilities in English. Figure 14.3 illustrates this mismatch. As Juan's thoughts reveal, he definitely learned some things from the field trip, but he is unable to verbalize his understanding. As a result, the teacher mistakenly believes that he learned nothing from the trip and thus grossly underestimates his understanding. Most unfortunately, this inaccurate assessment is quite likely to influence the teacher's future work with Juan. If she believes that Juan does not understand, she is very likely to interpret many of Juan's future actions in light of this understanding. *We as teachers must work to build ELL students' conceptual understanding and also realize that they may sometimes be unable to verbalize the conceptual understanding they actually possess.*

What Light Does Research Shed on These Challenges?

Prompted by the huge increase in English learners in U.S. schools, a good deal of research has focused on how to best help nonnative speakers of English develop their English literacy skills. A number of reviews provide excellent summaries of this research. In one of them, Jill Fitzgerald (1995) focuses on instructional issues. In another, Diane August and Kenji Hakuta (1998) review the research located by a national committee investigating instruction for language-minority children. In a third review, Elizabeth Bernhardt (2000) gives a general account of issues in second-language reading for students of various ages. In still another, Georgia Garcia (2000) deals with the problems of young, mostly bilingual students who are learning to read English. In a fifth report, Russell Gersten and Scott Baker (2000) focus on instructional issues. In a sixth report, Robert Slavin and Alan Cheung (2005) concentrate on the effects of the language or languages that are used for instruction. Diane August and Timothy Shanahan (2009) present the result of research reviewed by the National Literacy Panel on Language Minority Children and Youth. Here we focus on several of the most immediate findings: the importance of language knowledge, the importance of literacy in the first language, cross-language influences, and cross-cultural influences.

Figure 14.3

Mismatch Between What a Student Knows and What He Says in Response to a Teacher's Question

The Importance of Language Knowledge

There is no question that, when doing tasks in a second language, the more the learner knows about the structure and vocabulary of the language, the better. Research has indicated that at least 30 percent of the process of second-language reading involves grammatical and lexical knowledge (Bernhardt & Kamil, 1995; Brisbois, 1995; Hulstijn, 1991). This finding suggests that facilitating language development is crucial. Simply put, the more English words ELL students know and the more English sentence structures they learn, the better off they will be.

It is critical, however, to place this finding in the context of the fact that second-language acquisition is developmental in nature. That is, learning a second language is more like learning a first language than different from it. Neither providing direct instruction in grammatical forms before students exhibit developmental readiness nor teaching forms out of context will lead to functional proficiency in a second language, any more than it does in a first language. ESL teacher James Garcia stresses the importance of recognizing this developmental sequence:

> Whenever I am working with English language learners, I remind myself that they will follow certain sequences in their learning of English, regardless of what I do. For example, verbs with -*ing* forms will appear early in their spoken language; inflections, such as the third-person singular -*s*, will appear quite late, if they ever appear. Similarly, learning to deal with forming negatives is a process of first learning the negation words and attaching them externally to sentences; internal negation develops over time. The development of question forms and the creation of relative clauses also proceed over time. They are not "not there" one day and then "there" the next, no matter how much instruction I provide.
>
> —James Garcia, ESL teacher

In order for this developmental growth to occur, the learner must experience many examples of language use. How can the learner know what is more sophisticated unless she hears it or sees it? In like manner, the influence of peers—the desire to be part of the group—is enormous. This desire compels the learner to take on the linguistic characteristics present in the environment. The more rapidly these dynamics take hold, the higher the second-language literacy achievement. Bilingual teacher Margaret Thayer suggests one powerful way to foster interactions between English language learners and native English speakers—establishing a buddy system:

> One of the most successful things we have done in our classroom is to set up a buddy system in which we deliberately pair our native English speakers with our English language learners. We do this at the beginning of the year or whenever an English language learner enters the class, and from that time on, the two students do many things together. They work as a pair doing in-class assignments, talk about what they have read, and work together on homework. Of course, in many cases, the native speaker serves more often as the tutor and the English language learner as the learner. But whenever possible, we try to get the English language learner in the teacher's role. Often, for example, the English language learner teaches his English-speaking buddy some things about his language or culture. And, in many cases, the pairing doesn't end at the school. Buddies often visit each other's homes, share holidays, and pal around together. As I said, the buddy system has been a real success. Also, it does not take up a lot of the teacher's time, always an important consideration when you have lots of kids who need your assistance.
>
> —Margaret Thayer, bilingual teacher

The Importance of Literacy in the First Language

Unquestionably, there is a strong relationship between literacy skills in a first language and literacy skills in a second. Research indicates that about 20 percent of the process of reading in a second language is predictable on the basis of the level of first-language literacy (Bernhardt & Kamil, 1995; Brisbois, 1995; Hulstijn, 1991). In other words, the more knowledge of reading and understanding of literacy a student has in her first language, the better will be her knowledge and understanding of a second. Even when children are literate in a language that has little or no overlap with English, the mere fact that they are already literate really helps them. Why is this the case?

Attaining literacy means having developed a set of strategies for coping with written materials. Literate children understand that print represents meaning and that there are purposes for reading. They have already begun to develop many of the proficiencies described throughout this book.

The most challenged English language learner is one who has no first-language literacy. This type of learner is in double jeopardy—she has to learn the language, and she has to learn what literacy is about.

Cross-Language Influences

How a person processes a second language is influenced by her processing of the first language (Bernhardt, 1991). English, for example, tends toward subject-verb-object word order, as in *The man sees the dog.* Other languages, such as German, have more flexible word order; it is the inflectional system that indicates who is seeing what. While *man* and *dog* in a German-language sentence may be in the same order as in an English sentence, the inflectional system might indicate that the man is being seen by the dog. *Der Mann sieht den Hund, Den Hund sieht der Mann, Der Hund sieht den Mann,* and *Den Mann sieht der Hund* are all possibilities in German. Subject-object-verb languages, such as Chinese, will represent the word order as *The man the dog sees.*

Because of the linguistic transfer from language to language, readers will assume that the word order they are used to will be used in the language they are learning. The comprehension challenges that such cross-language influences present are daunting.

Cross-Cultural Influences

There is no question that second-language readers employ background knowledge. This is consistent with what you have learned throughout this book about all learners. Unfortunately, in some cases the background knowledge an English language learner brings to a text is absolutely irrelevant, and in other cases it is simply inconsistent with the knowledge assumed by the text. Such situations, of course, create serious challenges for English language learners.

One study forcefully demonstrating the influence of background knowledge was conducted by Margaret Steffenson and her colleagues (Steffenson, Joag-Dev, & Anderson, 1979). Readers were asked to read passages about weddings—from their own culture and another culture. Even though they had no language problems, the readers' recollections of the passages were consistent with the way that weddings were conducted in their own culture. They took the language at hand and reconfigured it in a way that made sense within their own framework. This is an absolutely critical issue in the second-language literacy process. Learners both read and write within the framework that is most familiar to them—their linguistic and cultural framework. They need to learn to break with these patterns in order to develop literacy abilities in English. Sixth-grade teacher Susan Chen comments on being alert to cross-cultural differences:

> I'm always on the lookout for concepts and ideas that my Hmong students are likely to interpret somewhat differently than my Anglo students or points at which my Hmong students are likely to have had somewhat different experiences that they can share with other students. For example, whenever we talk about U.S. holidays such as Martin Luther King, Jr., Day or Labor Day, I make it a point to ask my Hmong students to talk about some of their holidays and what they celebrate. Or, if we are talking about farms and most of my students are thinking of the huge farms that exist in California and the Midwest today, I ask my Hmong students to describe the small family farms that they have known or have learned about from their parents and other grown-ups. This leaves both my Anglo students and my Hmong students knowing more than they would have without the other group's contributions. It also avoids confusion, such as that which develops when both groups are considering farms but one group is thinking of huge corporate farms and the other group is thinking of small plots of land.
>
> —Susan Chen, sixth-grade teacher

1. Listen carefully to the radio or television or examine several magazines or newspapers. What kinds of attitudes toward nonnative speakers of English do you find in these media?

2. Imagine a 10-year-old student who has just arrived in the United States after growing up in Iraq. Brainstorm a list of just a few of the myriad topics familiar to virtually all 10-year-olds who grew up in the United States but probably unfamiliar to this student from Iraq. Now brainstorm a list of a few topics you expect are familiar to 10-year-olds who grew up in Iraq but probably unfamiliar to U.S. students.

Instructional Principles

We now turn to practical application of the information we have discussed in the earlier sections of the chapter. Your own situation will, of course, be unique. You may have a class in which only one language other than English is spoken, or you may have a class in which several different languages are spoken. You may have only one or two nonnative speakers in your classroom, or you may have many. Whatever your specific situation, the following guidelines and principles will lead you to ask appropriate questions and work toward effective classroom instruction.

As a cardinal rule, note that it is important that you remember everything you know about first-language reading when you are teaching reading to English language learners. Most of the principles and practices will work as they do for children who speak English as natives. Some of them, of course, will have to be adapted. But very few will have to be discarded altogether. In the next three sections of the chapter, we present three sets of instructional suggestions. The first is from Lisa Delpit, and the second is a version of Michael Kamil and Elizabeth Bernhardt's (2004) recommendations. The third set is from various sources.

Delpit's Principles for Working with Poor Urban Children

Lisa Delpit (1995) has presented a set of principles for working with poor urban children. Although many English language learners are urban and poor, many are not. However, much of what Delpit suggests applies to all children. Here we discuss and interpret those of Delpit's principles that we see as most important for working with English learners.

Demand Critical Thinking

Often, we fall into the trap of thinking that students who speak a different language are not as bright as other students. Consequently, we often reason that they cannot handle critical thinking. No judgment could be more debilitating to students' growth. The goals of a high level of literacy and the literacy curriculum that we discussed throughout this book are just as appropriate for English language learners as they are for any other students. For example, teaching for deep understanding—such as Text Talk and Questioning the Author—are absolutely crucial to second-language learners.

Ensure Access to the Basic Skills, Conventions, and Strategies Essential to Success in U.S. Education

We sometimes begin teaching nonnative speakers with less emphasis on skills than middle-class children typically receive. This will not work! We are not suggesting that you teach only basic skills. As we just noted, a high level of literacy is the goal. But do remember that although not all children come to school with the same skills, all students need to master the building blocks that lead to literacy. As a teacher, you want to be certain that your students acquire whatever skills they need to be successful in school and in later life, something Timothy Hayden, a third-grade teacher, makes a conscious effort to do:

> One thing I really try to work on with my Puerto Rican students is mastery of basic skills, such as standard usage and spelling, while still giving them plenty of chances to do critical thinking. This is a tough decision to make because I know that in many cases my kids know more than their English skills show, and so in some sense I'm slowing them down to work on the basics. Yet I also know that if they can't read when they leave school, or use poor grammar or spelling when they're looking for a job, they won't get very far. That's why I feel that I have to balance attention to basics with attention to higher-level stuff.
>
> —Timothy Hayden, third-grade teacher

Empower Students to Challenge Racist Views of Their Competence and Worthiness

Racism and classism often extend to children who are nonnative speakers of English. You must support your English language learners' egos and help them build the sort of self-worth that will lead them to persevere when they encounter challenges. All students need the support and skills that will enable them to meet challenges, be successful, and realize that success is something under their control. Creating an "I can do it!" attitude in your English language learners and conveying to them that you as their teacher hold an "I can help you do it!" attitude are crucial. In the Classroom 14.3 shows how sixth-grade teacher Ann Beecher provides reading experiences that promote positive attitudes.

Recognize and Build on Strengths

The importance of building on students' strengths is such a truism, repeated so often, that it does not have a great deal of meaning for many of us. How, indeed, does one "build on a strength"? If you do not go beyond what a student already knows and can do, you run the risk of boring that child and losing her for the real tasks of learning that are to follow. Building on strength means that you should *begin* with what she can do best and work toward those things that she does not know or does not do well. Ensure that students take on challenges they can meet and experience a steady diet of success by scaffolding their efforts as they move from the known to the new. Then gradually release responsibility to the students themselves as their competence and confidence grow. For some students, this will mean a lot of scaffolding and a very gradual handing over of responsibility. Others may readily accept challenges and thrive on them.

Creating an "I can do it!" attitude in second-language learners and conveying to them that you as their teacher hold an "I can help you do it!" attitude are crucial.

Michael Newman/PhotoEdit

Use Familiar Metaphors and Experiences from the Children's World

Using metaphors and experiences from the children's world is another technique good teachers use instinctively. We know the importance of background knowledge. As Delpit suggests, instead of insisting

Using the Shared Reading Experience in a Sixth-Grade ESL Class

Ann Beecher teaches sixth grade in a public school in a Los Angeles suburb. The majority of the students in her ESL class speak Spanish as their primary language, with a sprinkling of students speaking a variety of other languages. Ms. Beecher has found that the shared reading experience—students and teacher reading aloud together—is a highly effective technique for developing confidence and building on students' skills in reading and speaking English. "My English language learners are often reticent to risk being wrong or making mistakes when it comes to speaking or reading in English," Ms. Beecher says. "So I need to think of ways to create a safe environment that will support their learning. One of those ways is the shared reading experience. It's a risk-free way for them to use oral language." Here are the steps Ms. Beecher usually follows in preparing a shared reading experience:

- *Choose a selection.* Ms. Beecher most frequently uses poetry, perhaps a poem from Shel Silverstein's *Falling Up* (1996) or a poem from their literature text. "One of the class favorites is 'The Shark' by John Ciardi. They enjoy reciting the colorful words Ciardi uses to describe the shark, such as *gulper, ripper, snatcher, grabber.*" Ms. Beecher occasionally uses a very short piece of prose, also something from their literature text. "The key is choosing something that will engage students, something that they will really enjoy and can relate to," Ms. Beecher says. "One of the values of using the shared reading experience is that the students are reading 'at grade' materials. This is a big boost to their confidence. It gives them a real sense of accomplishment."

- *Set up an overhead projector, and make copies of the selection for each student.*

- *Prepare and motivate students for the selection.* "This usually takes very little effort," Ms. Beecher says. "When the kids see the overhead projector, they know it means we're going to read something together. It's one of their favorite things we do. Like singing or reciting jazz chants, they enjoy the rhythm of the language and the community experience of speaking the same words together."

- *With expression and enthusiasm, read through the selection once or twice, and then invite students to read along in unison.*

- *Focus on a particular reading skill or strategy.* "If we are reading rhyming poetry, usually I will circle the rhyming words on the overhead and have students do the same on their copies. I will talk about certain words and check for students' understanding. Also, sometimes when I first read the piece through, I will stop occasionally and have students predict what will happen next."

- *Follow up the reading with a variety of activities.* Use art (illustrating the shark *gulping, ripping, snatching, grabbing,* for example), writing, or evaluating: "How did we do? Did you like the piece? Why? What did you like about it? Is there anything we should do differently next time? What's your favorite new word you learned?"

that all children have the same background knowledge at the beginning, deal with the knowledge and background students have and use that as the basis of teaching. This means you will need to learn something of their culture, and doing so will ingratiate you to them. For example, if you are teaching about the destructive power of tornadoes and have Vietnamese children in your class, you can use their knowledge of the awesome power of typhoons as a bridge to understanding the power of tornadoes.

Create a Sense of Family and Caring

ESL teacher Lillian Colon-Vila (1997) knows how crucial it is that all students feel that they are a valuable part of the class and will be supported in their efforts by both the teacher and the other students in the class:

To welcome my ESL students, I always begin the semester by telling a story. It's usually a simple one to welcome them to the United States and particularly to my classroom. Because I use the students' names and their native countries, I invent the stories on the spur of the moment. I use puppets, pictures, flash cards, or the chalkboard to draw pictures as I go along.

I make it a point to share my own first day of school, too—how I stuttered, mispronounced the teacher's name, and wished for the floor to swallow me. The students laugh and relate to my experience. The iceberg between us breaks, and I can begin to teach.

—Lillian Colon-Vila, ESL multigrade teacher

In the terminology we used earlier in the book, your classroom must be a literate environment for *all* students.

Monitor and Assess Needs, and Then Address Them with a Wealth of Diverse Strategies

Bring your English language learners into the assessment process early on. At the beginning of the school year, share with students what you expect them to be able to do at the end of the year. Ask them to tell you about their personal literacy goals.

Effective teaching cannot be done without careful assessment and evaluation of what students know and learn. Teachers need to be vigilant and prepared to discontinue teaching techniques that prove inappropriate for some students. Students can often benefit from a different teaching strategy when the one initially attempted did not work. Such choices require careful reasoning based on data gathered in assessing the students. As we emphasized in Chapter 4, assessment does not simply mean formal assessment. You will need to use a wide range of techniques to gauge students' strengths and weaknesses and then create ways to build on their strengths. These techniques are likely to include the use of formal tests, but they will also include talking to students, carefully observing them as they work at school tasks, and seeking insights from parents and others in your students' home communities. Figure 14.4 illustrates how a drawing can show a student's understanding of a story.

Honor and Respect Children's Home Cultures

It would be difficult to imagine anything seemingly easier than honoring and respecting children's home cultures, but unfortunately honor and respect are too often lacking in classrooms. Knowledge that has been gained in children's home cultures constitutes a strength that can be brought into the classroom and used as the basis for learning to read about all manner of ideas and topics. Besides, changing children's

Figure 14.4

Maria's Drawing of *Island of the Blue Dolphins* by Scott O'Dell (1960) Reveals Her Understanding of the Story

cultural orientations and allegiances is not really an option. Children come to school having spent a huge amount of time within their cultures and their families, and once they begin school, they will continue to spend far more time at home than in the classroom. You cannot win against such odds. It is just not possible to instill in children a totally different culture in a few hours a day—it may even be impossible to do so in a lifetime. Your goal must be to support students' attempts to maintain their cultural identities and to support them in becoming successful in the mainstream culture represented by the school. One small step toward doing this might be taken during birthday celebrations. Inviting English language learners to share their birthday traditions with the class gives status to those traditions and adds to other students' store of knowledge about different cultures.

Another and more significant step toward demonstrating and fostering respect for children's home cultures is to provide students with literature that accurately and fairly represents a variety of cultures, as does Hispanic literature such as *Cinco de mayo* by Linda Lowery, *Julio's Magic* by Arthur Dorros, and *Napí* by Antonio Ramírez.

REFLECT
and *Apply*

3 Think about attitudes toward English language learners that you have observed. Have you encountered attitudes that might negatively influence the ways in which teachers interact with students? How might you guard against allowing those attitudes to negatively affect your classroom style?

4 Consider your own family traditions. Can you think of any holiday celebrations you and your family enjoy that are not widely observed? Do you think they are any less valuable because they are not more widely observed? How might you use these holiday celebrations when you are teaching students?

Kamil and Bernhardt's Techniques for Working with English Language Learners in Typical Classrooms

Michael Kamil and Elizabeth Bernhardt (2004) have developed a set of techniques specifically for working with English learners. Here we present a slightly modified and shortened version of their recommendations. Like Kamil and Bernhardt, we have placed these techniques in an order reflecting their utility; thus, you should probably attempt to implement these principles in the order given. You will probably have a good deal more success than if you simply select one or another of the principles from the list.

Take Advantage of the 20 Percent Rule

Remember that, although languages are different, there is considerable transfer between them. As indicated in the first part of this chapter, research suggests that the overlap between languages can be as much as 20 percent. Thus, your task in teaching literacy in a second language is far easier than if there were little or no overlap. You do not have to start at the beginning with English language learners; rather, you can consider yourself as being one-fifth of the way to success.

Figure 14.5 shows the 20 percent rule in action. In this graphic display of generation of electricity, there are 17 Spanish words used. Three of the words—*natural, vapor,* and *magma*—are identical to the equivalent terms in English. Another seven words—*turbina, generador, uso, energía, geotérmica, producir,* and *electricidad*—are almost identical and certainly recognizable. This simple example illustrates the overlap between English and Spanish and reminds us that children do possess substantial information that they can draw on for reading second-language texts.

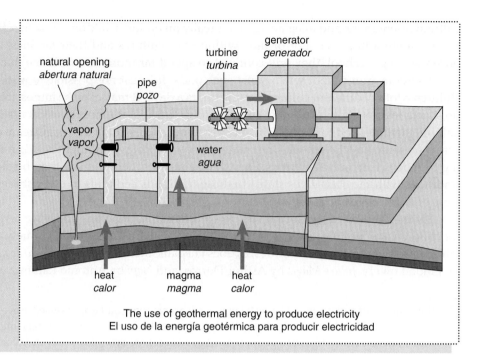

Figure 14.5

Graphic Display of Overlap Between Spanish and English Vocabulary

Source: Ciencias by Mallision, Mallision, Smallwood, & Valentino. Copyright © 1985 by Silver Burdett Ginn, Simon & Schuster Elementary. Used by permission.

natural opening
abertura natural

pipe
pozo

turbine
turbina

generator
generador

vapor
vapor

water
agua

heat
calor

magma
magma

heat
calor

The use of geothermal energy to produce electricity
El uso de la energía geotérmica para producir electricidad

Of course, as we all know, there is never a free lunch, and this rule holds true for the 20 percent dividend. The percentage will be different for each language. In some languages, the overlap may be greater than 20 percent, and in others, less.

When students in your classroom have some native-language literacy and are able to work with content, have them conduct Internet searches on topics you are covering in current events. For example, major new geologic discoveries, such as finding the bones of an ancient mammal, are often reported in *Weekly Reader* or in books that children naturally gravitate to; such findings are almost always discussed in the Internet press. Have your students read something about these findings in their native-language press and report on any differences between reports in English and what they have read. Such an activity reinforces using their first language to support their learning of the second. It also enhances their critical thinking skills by asking them to compare and contrast information presented in an array of sources and boosts their self-esteem by demonstrating to their peers that bilingualism actually provides greater access to information than monolingualism does.

Give English Language Learners and Yourself Plenty of Time

It is important to remember that children who do not speak English as a native language will, in all likelihood, not be as automatic as native speakers at completing any English-language task, including, of course, reading. Figure 14.6 provides an example of the very different amounts of time it would take students reading at three different rates to complete a typical intermediate-grade book, in this case Gary Soto's *The Skirt*. If children are reading a longer book, something like Kazumi Yumoto's *The Spring Tone,* the amounts of time needed vary even more: To complete this book, Maria would need only about an hour, Carlos would need about 2 hours, and Chen would need over 5½ hours. The instructional implication of these illustrations is straightforward: Provide English language learners with extra time to complete the linguistic tasks you ask them to do.

Following this simple suggestion can minimize what is perhaps the greatest difficulty teachers face in multilanguage classrooms. The question, of course, is how you can provide this extra time, and we have several suggestions. Students who need the time can be given opportunities to complete their work as part of free-choice activities. Or they might be allowed to take home work that isn't completed during class. Or you might give students the questions you will ask ahead of time during reading lessons, being sure to give *all* students sufficient time to do the reading and thinking necessary to answer them. Still another option is to shorten some of the selections students are asked to read by summarizing parts of them. In the Classroom 14.4, for example, includes a summary of the first half of Pegi Deiz Shea's *The Whispering Cloth: A Refugee's Story.*

Figure 14.6 **Times Required for Three Students, with Varying Reading Rates, to Read Gary Soto's *The Skirt***

Student	Reading Rate (Words per Minute)	Chapter One (1,000 Words)	Whole Book (8,000 Words)
Maria	250	4 minutes	32 minutes
Carlos	150	7 minutes	53 minutes
Chen	50	20 minutes	2 hours, 40 minutes

In the Classroom

14.4

Instructional Routines

Summarizing Part of a Selection

The Whispering Cloth: A Refugee's Story is a touching story of a young Hmong girl, Mai, who learns to create embroidered tapestries—*pándau* in the Hmong language—while in a refugee camp in Thailand. The book is beautifully illustrated with both watercolors and reproductions of the *pándau* Mai creates. Although the book is not a long read for students who read fluently, for students beginning to read English it constitutes a formidable task. Summarizing the first half of the book would simplify that task considerably, particularly for Hmong students, coming as they do from a culture that does not have a written language.

Introduce the book in a fashion that you and your students will be comfortable with. You might tell children that it is the story of a young Hmong girl in a refugee camp in Thailand, show children the location of the refugee camp and the Hmongs' homeland in northern Laos, and briefly discuss the situation that forced the Hmongs to become refugees. Then explain to children what embroidery or *pándau* is, show a sample of embroidery (actual Hmong *pándau*, if possible), and explain that *pándau* plays an important part in the story. You might also tell children that the main characters in the story are Mai and her grandmother, who is simply called Grandma. Finally, tell children that you are going to summarize the first half of the book for those who would like it summarized and that they can either listen to your summary or begin reading on their own. After children have made their choices, perhaps with some guidance from you, you can gather around you those who want to hear the summary and then read or paraphrase a summary like this one:

> As *The Whispering Cloth* opens, we learn that Mai lives in a refugee camp with her grandmother and that Mai can remember little of her life outside of the camp. She knows, though, that many people leave the refugee camp and some of them go to America, and it seems that she would like to go there too. Partly to give her something to do and partly to provide the family with some income, Grandma teaches Mai to make *pándau*. Mai learns very quickly and is soon very good at making this beautiful "flowery cloth." One day, Mai begins to work on a *pándau* in which she tells a story that is filling her head with thoughts.

Then introduce the reading as follows:

> As you read the rest of the book, you will see pictures of the *pándau* that Mai stitched. Now read the rest of the book to see the *pándau* and what it meant to Mai and her Grandma and what they decided to do with it.

To be an effective teacher of language-minority students, you also need to give yourself extra time, particularly when making day-to-day informal assessments of their progress. You will have to train yourself to perceive their progress in different ways, as that progress will not look or sound the same as progress for native speakers. The extra moments to think through whether you have made the right instructional decision for a second-language child will pay off in the end both for the child and for your self-confidence as a teacher.

Use the Rosetta Stone Technique

We have all heard about the wonder of the Rosetta Stone. This tremendous discovery, shown in Figure 14.7, contains the same text in Egyptian hieroglyphics, Egyptian demotic script, and several ancient Greek languages. The discovery of the Rosetta Stone allowed linguists to decipher Egyptian hieroglyphics, which they did not know how to read, based on their knowledge of ancient Greek, which they could read.

One useful vocabulary technique for working with a class that includes English language learners is based on this approach. If you make a chart of everyday English words in one column, your students who speak other languages can contribute the equivalent words from each of their languages in other columns. Alternatively, your English language learners might periodically put words from their native languages on the chart and solicit the equivalent English word and words in other languages represented in your class. Or as you encounter words in a content lesson, you could use them as the entries in the Rosetta chart and have students add the equivalent words from their languages, creating a multilingual word wall.

Whatever the specific source of words you put on the chart, be certain to practice pronouncing both non-English and English words with the nonnative speakers as well

Figure 14.7

The Rosetta Stone—Showing Greek, Demotic, and Hieroglyphic Scripts as with the entire class. In this way, all students will be able to do well at some parts of the task. Also, not only will your students for whom English is a native language begin to learn some vocabulary in another language; they will also begin to appreciate the difficulties other students are having. And they will be able to see that English language learners know a great deal that native English speakers do not know.

Involve Parents, Siblings, and Other Speakers of the Children's Languages

Often, parents, siblings, or other relatives can help in translating between the native language and English, or vice versa. Sometimes all it takes is a bridge between languages to get children started. Translating the first page or so of a text they have begun to read or making a graphic organizer of what they are going to read, such as the example shown in Figure 14.8, can be extremely helpful for young learners. Moreover, such a bridge can work both ways. As students become more proficient in English, many times they assume the role of translator for parents who are not quite as proficient. This will give students a reason for wanting to learn more English and may encourage the parents to learn more English as well. In addition, as students become increasingly competent in English, they will be motivated to become still more competent.

Parents or other volunteers who speak the English learners' language can be a huge help in your classroom.

Nancy Richmond/The Image Works

Siblings can sometimes be particularly helpful in the classroom. Older brothers or sisters who may be reluctant to participate in their own class because they are not as proficient as their first-language classmates may work extremely well with their younger brothers or sisters. An added bonus here is that, when tutoring these younger students, the older siblings may very well realize that they know more English than

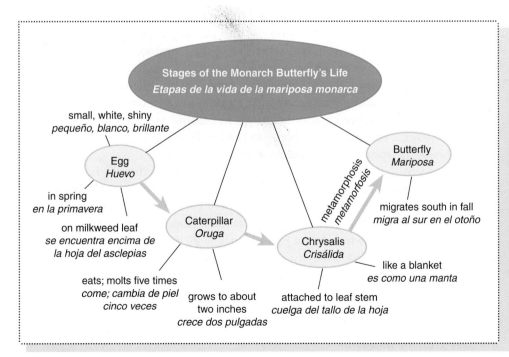

Figure 14.8

Graphic Organizer in English and Spanish for a Section of Lynn Rosenblatt's *Monarch Magic!*

they thought and consequently feel encouraged to attempt to read when they would have otherwise been reluctant to do so.

Use All the Available People Resources

As we have pointed out several times, tutoring can be a useful technique in a host of literacy learning contexts. For learning to read in a second language, it may have particular benefits. Of course, one great benefit will accrue if you are fortunate enough to have older students who speak the same languages as your students and are somewhat more proficient in reading English than your students are. Again, sometimes the older students may realize that they know more English than they thought and be encouraged to attempt more challenging reading tasks themselves. They may also be motivated to learn more because they begin to realize what they do not know yet or because they wish to do a better job in helping the younger students.

Of course, students who are the same age as the tutees but have somewhat more advanced English reading skills can also serve as classroom tutors. And as is the case with cross-age tutors, peer tutors are likely to benefit from the teaching they do. As we have noted before, the research strongly demonstrates that students tutoring other students is a true win-win situation in which both tutor and tutee benefit markedly (Cohen, Kulic, & Kulic, 1982). Finally, students are not the only people resources that may be of help in your classroom. Aides, volunteers, college students preparing to be teachers, and sometimes even administrators and maintenance personnel can perform a variety of helpful tasks with English language learners.

In Assessing Students, Give Them the Freedom to Choose the Language in Which to Respond

Research tells us that students often demonstrate greater abilities when they are given the option of responding in the language in which they feel most comfortable. This is particularly true, of course, when the text is in English and the students are not fluent in English.

Although allowing students to respond in their native languages is a very easy change for you as an instructor to make, it can pay big dividends. In addition to demonstrating better understanding when using the language of their choice, students may also be able to remember more of what they have learned in their native language. Also, students' language preference may vary for different reading materials. For example, a reading passage about a student's native country might be best responded to in the student's native language. In reading a passage about American history, however, a student might choose to use English. The key is to allow the student to choose the appropriate language in which to respond.

One concern some teachers have about this technique is their feeling they may not be able to understand and assess what the students wrote or said. However, even if you cannot understand the language the student chooses, all is not lost. The easiest way to handle the situation is to have the student respond in her native language and then have her do the translation into English. Note the terrific practice this gives the student. She is, in effect, using the language-experience approach—writing down her own words and then translating them. Note also that allowing students to do this is one way of providing the extra time we have recommended. Alternatively, if the student cannot read what she wrote back to you or translate it into English later, you might obtain the assistance of a sibling, parent, or other speaker of the language in the class to do the translating.

Assessment

You don't need to assess your English language learners' language and literacy competencies without assistance. Solicit the help of specialists, colleagues who are familiar with students' culture and language, and students' parents.

Babelfish (http://babelfish.yahoo.com/translate_txt) is a website that translates text from one language into another. You can type in up to 150 words at a time. Gunning (2005) notes that you can use the translator to provide students with short summaries of key concepts under study. Gunning suggests that teachers type the concept summaries into Babelfish and translate them into students' first languages—something we recommend as well—or students who have suf-ficient keyboarding skills can do this also. The languages into which text can be translated on Babelfish are Chinese, English, Dutch, French, German, Greek, Italian, Japanese, Portuguese, Russian, and Spanish. Another idea is to have students create dual-language texts using Babelfish. A brief dual-language text a second-grader created is shown in Figure 14.9.

Quiocho and Ulanoff (2009) call attention to musical resources that can be very motiva-tional and beneficial for English language learners. The first resource they recommend is Carolyn Graham's *Jazz Chants for Children*. According to the website ESL.net (www.esl.net/jazz_chants .html), these are "upbeat chants and poems that use jazz rhythms to illustrate the natural stress and intonation patterns of conversational American English." Quiocho and Ulanoff suggest that teachers have students practice and perform the chants. The second resource Quiocho and Ulanoff highlight is the Schoolhouse Rock series. They note that the music, lyrics, and visuals on these videos and DVDs each serve to scaffold English language learners as they acquire new concepts. ●

Figure 14.9

A Brief Dual-Language Text Created by a Second-Grader

I spotted a tornado last night. In the morning a lot of things were messed up.

Manché un tornado anoche. Por la mañana muchas cosas fueron ensuciadas.

Por Genevieve

Motivating

Struggling
Readers

Some English language learners struggle not with just a new language, but with the task of learning to read in any language. ELL students bring with them the same range of talents for learning to read as do English language students, and therefore some students require additional small-group targeted intervention. The research summarized by many strongly suggests that the same intervention approaches that work for regular education students will work for ELL students (Lovett, De Palma, Frijters, Steinbach, Temple, Benson, & Lacerenza, 2008; Mathes, Pollard-Durodola, Cárdenas-Hagan, Linan-Thompson, & Vaughn, 2007). Intervention for ELL students will require a greater focus on vocabulary and the development of prior knowledge. The following list delineates some basic principles that meet the characteristics outlined by Michael Coyne, Edward Kame'enui, and Deborah Simmons (2001).

- *Conspicuous instruction in strategies.* It is not enough for students to know letter sounds; they must also have a strategy or process to use that knowledge. Teachers must make these strategies clear and model them explicitly

- *Mediated scaffolding.* The student needs support when learning new skills or strategies. Sometimes the program provides that support—easier letters and sounds are introduced before more difficult patterns, and sometimes the teacher provides that support. Through coaching, hints, and modeling the teacher helps the student try out the new strategy. We provided a strong guide for scaffolding the decoding process in Chapter 10.

- *Strategy integration.* Students should always understand that the separate skills of reading are not isolated. Phonemic awareness needs to be taught alongside decoding so students understand that segmenting and blending sounds leads to ease in recognizing words. Phonemic awareness and decoding need to be taught along with reading of connected text. Through this integration the whole process makes sense to the students.

- *Primed background knowledge.* Students with reading problems often have memory deficits. So strong instruction requires that previous knowledge and skills be reviewed before new ideas are introduced. To spell, the student has to first segment the sounds in the word. Priming causes the student to think about segmenting before he begins to spell.

- *Judicious review.* Students with reading problems need considerable review. Coyne and colleagues (2001) remind us that review needs to be distributed over time so that it is cumulative while using varied methods. In a sense we cannot assume mastery, drop a topic or skill, and move on.

- *Well-paced instruction.* Strong intervention is well paced. The teacher is organized so that she and the students complete activities quickly and several activities are completed in a short amount of time. A well-paced lesson promotes students' interest and attention.

In addition to giving students the opportunity to respond in the language they choose, you can sometimes give them the opportunity to read in the language of their choice. Bilingual books, a growing set of children's books in which the same book contains both English and another language, make providing this option very convenient. A small sample of the books in this growing genre is shown in The Reading Corner. If you, aides, parent volunteers, or other volunteers speak the home languages of your students, you have still other opportunities to tap their native-language skills. You can give directions for classroom work and homework in both English and the students' native languages. This can be a huge help to students in doing their class work, and it can be a tremendous help to parents in assisting their children with homework. If you have many Hispanic students, learn some Spanish.

Books Available in Bilingual Formats

Books with text in two languages, usually on facing pages, provide an outstanding opportunity for English learners to practice reading in both their own language and English. Moreover, the text in their stronger language acts as a scaffold for reading the text in their weaker language. The books listed below are a sample of the many books available. Searching sites such as Amazon with the terms *bilingual books* and *dual-language books* will yield hundreds more. Additionally, to locate books for Spanish-speaking students, Isabel Schon's *Recommended Books in Spanish for Children and Young Adults: 1991–1995* (1996), *Recommended Books in Spanish for Children and Young Adults: 1996 through 1999* (2001), and *Recommended Books in Spanish for Children and Young Adults: 2000 through 2004* (2004) as well as Schon and Sarah Berkin's *Introducción a la literatura infantil y juvenil* (1996) are extremely valuable.

George Ancona. *The Piñata Maker/El penatero.* Harcourt, 1994. With full-color photos and text in both Spanish and English, this book provides a glimpse into the art of piñata making. 40 pages. Excerpt:

> When the glue is dry, he pastes metallic paper to the point of each cone, the *pico,* so they will glitter.
>
> Cuando se seca el engrudo, pega papel metalico a la punta de cada cono, o al pico, para que reluzcan.

Rebecca T. Anonuevo. *Ang Mahiyaing Manok (The Shy Rooster).* Pan Asia Publications, 2000. In this English/Filipino book, a shy young rooster who cannot crow as well or as loud as the other roosters proves his worth. 32 pages.

Eileen Browne. *Handa's Surprise* (Somali–English Bilingual Edition). Mantra Publishing, 1999. In this African tale, Handa puts delicious fruits in a basket to take to her friend in another village and passes several animals who find the fruit very inviting. 24 pages.

Fred Burstein. *The Dancer/La bailarina.* Bradbury, 1993. As a father accompanies his daughter to her ballet lesson, the sights they encounter—a horse, a flower, a fish, and more—are given in English, Spanish, and Japanese. 32 pages.

Lois Ehlert. *Moon Rope/Un lazo a la luna.* Harcourt, 1992. In this adaptation of a Peruvian folktale, Fox and Mole try to climb to the moon on a rope woven of grass. 32 pages.

Juan Ramon Jimenez. *Platero y yo/Platero and I.* Clarion, 1994. Short vignettes, evocatively illustrated with woodcuts, tell of the rambles of a man and his donkey around the countryside in Andalusia, Spain. 42 pages.

Robert Kraus and **Debby Chen.** *The Making of Monkey King.* Pan Asian Publications, 1998. This first book in the Adventures of Monkey King series, a fantasy about the adventures of a hero magically born from a rock who sets out to find the secret of immortality, is available as a bilingual text in English and Spanish, Chinese, Vietnamese, or Hmong. 34 pages.

Diana Dávila Martinez and **Gabriela Baeza Ventura (translator).** *A School Named for Someone Like Me/Una escuela con un nombre como el mio* (Bilingual Edition). Piñata Books, 2004. This inspiring biography chronicles the life of Jaime Dávila, a role model and a hero in his Hispanic neighborhood in Houston. 63 pages.

Pat Mora. *Listen to the Desert/Oye al desierto.* Clarion, 1994. In this informational book, author and artist portray the sounds and sights of the desert. 32 pages.

Roser Ros. *Musicians of Bremen/Los músicos de Bremen* (Spanish–English Bilingual Edition). Chronicle Books, 2005. Retold in both Spanish and English, the universally loved story will delight early readers and older learners alike. 32 pages.

Jessica Souhami. *Rama and the Demon King: An Ancient Tale from India* (Punjabi–English Bilingual Edition). Chronicle Books, 2005. This ancient tale of Prince Rama relates his demon-killing adventures in the forest after being exiled for 14 years by his father, the king. 36 pages.

Use Informational Texts as a Significant Part of Instruction

Informational texts are not often used in our schools for reading instruction, and this can have serious consequences (Duke, 2004). We strongly recommend that you use informational texts with English language learners for three reasons. First, students can read informational texts to find out things that they can use in their lives outside of the classroom. This may be a greater motivation to learn to read in English than anything else you can do. It will give students a reason to work as hard as they can to understand texts in English. The task can be as simple as reading a recipe for making chocolate chip cookies or as complex as reading a science article on hibernation. Being able to read informational texts may also contribute to the stature of a child, as the new skill can be taken home and used to help others in her family.

Second, it is possible to find informational texts dealing with topics that English language learners have a lot of background knowledge about and that do not demand background knowledge specific to U.S. culture or to English, such as Taro Gomi's very simple picture book *Spring Is Here = Llegó la primavera* or Gail Gibbons's *Dinosaur Discoveries*. Knowledge of basic facts about common animals, for example, is independent of the language and culture in which those facts were learned. Conversely, in stories written for U.S. children, there is often a good deal of cultural knowledge assumed that some English language learners may not have.

Third, informational text can expand opportunities for home–school connections (Duke & Purcell-Gates, 2003). Some parents, older siblings, and relatives of English learners seldom have the time or interest to read fiction. These same people, however, may welcome opportunities to work with their children in reading and understanding newspapers, magazines, and other nonfiction texts that deal with real-world topics. As we noted earlier in this chapter, involving parents, siblings, and other speakers of students' native languages can be a huge benefit for all parties.

A note of clarification is needed here. We are not advocating the elimination of narrative texts from the reading curriculum. We are, however, recommending that exposition be used as a focus, rather than as a secondary choice, in reading instruction. In one study (Kamil & Lane, 1997), approximately 50 percent of reading instruction in first grade employed expository text, while the remaining 50 percent employed narrative text. This seems like a reasonable balance of these two different and important text types. Of course, some books—for example, Bonnie Graves's *The Whooping Crane*—both tell a story and provide a good deal of information on a topic.

One important concept to keep in mind when giving English learners informational texts is not to require them to learn large bodies of new knowledge in English. Another thing to keep in mind is to be sure to include sufficient instructional assistance when English learners are expected to learn from informational English texts. In other words, provide plenty of scaffolding. Expecting English learners to learn large amounts of new information by reading English texts without sufficient scaffolding is simply an invitation to failure.

In addition to the teaching suggestions and the descriptions of informational books provided throughout this book, Nell Duke and Susan Bennett-Armistead's *Reading and Writing Informational Text in the Primary Grades* (2003), Rosemary Bamford and Janice Kristo's *Making Facts Come Alive* (1998), and Eileen Burke and Susan Glazer's *Using Nonfiction in the Classroom* (1994) provide a number of useful teaching ideas as well as bibliographies of informational books.

Use Alternative Assessment Strategies

Another way to lessen the burden on students who are not yet fully proficient in English is to give them opportunities to use some of the multiple intelligences that Howard Gardner (1993) has outlined and that we briefly described in Chapter 10. For example, drama, which we discussed in some detail in Chapter 10, is often an effective means for getting English language learners to develop oral language skills, and those oral

One assessment tool you can use to determine English language learners' instructional reading level is the IRI (informal reading inventory). The IRI includes graded lists of words and short graded narrative and expository passages for students to read orally.

skills will be useful bridges to comprehending written text. Art and music, which we also considered in Chapter 10, are also useful. Not only will you find that students can develop their literacy skills by using these diverse modes of expression, but you may often be able to better understand their intended meaning when they use them.

For example, if a child is allowed to draw a picture to illustrate a written assignment, as Maria did in Figure 14.4, you may be able to assess informally what the student meant to write, even if it is not clear from her text. This information will help you determine what the child needs to know about the language. You will not have to assume, for example, that the child did not know how to write, read, or understand *any* of the content of the lesson.

Beginning Reading Instruction with English Language Learners

In addition to Delpit (1995) and to Kamil and Bernhardt (2004), a number of other authorities have suggested ways in which teachers and schools can assist English learners. We have addressed many issues in the upper grades and now look at the problem of beginning reading instruction for the English language learner. In this section, we briefly present a way of looking at beginning reading based on our experience in schools with a significant number of ELL students.

The English language learner has to learn to decode written English and acquire the alphabetic principle. In several ways, teaching the young ELL student to read is similar to teaching monolingual students but with some added complications. When a child is learning to read in his or her first language, word recognition problems are a bit simpler. Once the child has decoded a new word, sounded it out, his existing vocabulary provides a point of recognition and lets him know that the task was successful. In many cases the student only has to produce an approximation of the word before the mind completes the task of pulling a known word from the child's oral vocabulary.

When the ELL student decodes a new word, that rich vocabulary is not available. So when the student gets close to the correct pronunciation there is no moment of recognition, there is no "aha" experience. The ELL student often does not know that he has correctly identified the word. Lacking a rich English vocabulary, the ELL student is hampered in both word recognition and comprehension. So word recognition for the ELL must proceed carefully, taking into account another set of problems for ELL students just learning to read English. There is often a mismatch between the phonemes in the student's first language and the sounds of English. While the teacher is diligently trying to get the students to pronounce one sound the students are hearing another. A few common language interference problems are presented in Figure 14.10. Being aware of these potential language interference problems, the astute teacher can minimize language confusions by careful pronunciation and by guiding students in the proper mouth movements (Olguin, 1968).

Given the problems associated with teaching phonics to ELL students, the teacher must craft phonics lessons that ameliorate potential problems for the students. In the Classroom 14.5 (p. 433) presents a phonics lesson you might use with a mixed group of ELL students and English-only students.

The integration of phonics and vocabulary development is essential for the development of decoding skills and vocabulary. Students will fail to benefit from the phonics unless their English vocabulary builds at the same time. For the English-speaking students in the class the extra emphasis on vocabulary helps to ground the decoding work in a meaningful context, making the work much less abstract. The lesson in In the Classroom 14.5 is built on some principles developed by Russell Gersten and Scott

Figure 14.10 Sources of Sound Confusion Between English and Spanish

English		Spanish
Sounds	*Words*	*Problems of Recognition*
"u" schwa	fun	Spanish has no schwa. The closest would be the "aw" in *fawn*.
"a" There are eight basic ways to pronounce *a*.	cat, about, play	Spanish has one sound for "a." The nearest sound to short *a* in Spanish would be the "e" in *hen*.
"i" There are four basic ways to pronounce *i*.	pig, till, bike	It is difficult for the Spanish ear to hear the short sound of *i*. The Spanish speaker will hear "ill" as "eel" or "ell."
"ch" The digraph is pronounced with a high volume of air.	chair, church,	"sh" and "ch" are very similar in Spanish because Spanish is spoken with a low volume of air, making the sounds similar.
"wh"	why, what, where	The "wh" does not occur in Spanish and it will be perceived as "gwai," "gwhat," and "gwear" in Spanish.
"sc," "sp," or "st"	scan, speak, stick	In Spanish the "s" at the beginning of a word is followed only by vowels. So these words will be perceived as "escan," "espeek," or "esteek."

Baker (2000) and also echoed by the work of Robert Jimenez (2000), who has worked extensively with Hispanic students, as shown in the following recommendations.

- *Build and apply vocabulary as a curricular anchor.* Vocabulary is crucial to understanding content and to becoming proficient in English. Increasing English learners' vocabularies should be one of your major goals.
- *Provide visuals to reinforce concepts and vocabulary.* Visuals are helpful to all students, but they are particularly helpful to students who have yet to achieve sophisticated verbal skills in English.
- *Employ cooperative learning and peer tutoring.*
- *Use students' native language strategically.*
- *"Modulate" cognitive and language demands to fit your English language learners.* The principal way to assist learners in meeting the reading demands they face is to scaffold their efforts, which we discussed in detail in Chapter 10 and which one of us and a colleague discuss in even greater detail in *Scaffolding Reading Experiences for English Language Learners* (Fitzgerald & Graves, 2004).
- *Adopt approaches that have proven highly effective for native speakers.* For example, provide explicit instruction, make sure students receive sufficient time on task, foster active engagement, and give frequent and clear feedback.

Phonics Instruction for ELL Students and the Rest of the Class

Phonics instruction for ELL students follows the same general lesson plan that would be used with English-speaking students, but it is best to work with small groups composed of English-speaking and ELL students. The teacher would start by developing phonemic awareness and then move to letter-sound associations and finally decoding practice (lesson based on Beck, 2006). The lesson should weave in words from Spanish, if that is the ELL students' home language, and English words. There should be a heavy focus on vocabulary, so that words are not just decoded but the meanings explained and discussed.

Phonemic Awareness

Develop phonemic awareness by focusing attention on the initial sounds in words. Students might conduct a picture sort and then isolate the initial sound in the word. Use words like *dog* /d/, *perro* /p/, *cat* /c/, *gato* /g/. After each picture is sorted the students name the picture and identify the initial consonant sound. The activity can be repeated to identify the final sound in each word using both English and the child's first language.

Connect Letter to Sound

Show the students a large letter card and explain that this is the letter *m* and it makes the /m/ sound as in *Maria, Michael, Miguel, mother,* and *milk*. Say, "Each time I point to the letter you say the letter sound." Next show the students several words that contain an *m* and have them point to and say /m/ as in *man, ham,* or *jamón*.

Discriminate Sounds

The students will now discriminate among words that contain the /m/ sound and words that do not. "If the word I say begins with the /m/ sound, hold up your *m* card and say /m/. If it doesn't begin with the /m/ sound, shake your head no." Then say words like *milk, leche, money, dinero, mother, madre,* and so forth. After the students respond, discuss and define the word or share a picture. Vocabulary is being developed alongside phonics.

Blending/Decoding

The last step in the lesson is to build words with the letter-sound associations that have been introduced. The students will be decoding English words, but the lesson must stress the meanings of these words. After each word is decoded the teacher should define the word or share a picture. The ELL student is building both decoding ability and vocabulary.

Place the letters *h a m* in a pocket chart and give the students the same letters. Point to the letters one at a time and say the sounds of the letter. Then have the students repeat the process. Slide the letter *a* over to the letter *h* and say /ha/. Slide your finger under the *ha* and pronounce it and hold it until you point at the letter *m* and say /m/. Have the student repeat what you say with their letters. Move the *m* over to the *ha*. Slide your finger under *ham* and say /ham/. Have the students repeat the process. Discuss what *ham* is and when you might eat it. Say it in Spanish: *jamón*. The process would continue as students sound out additional words—*ham, him, hit, hid, had, dad*. With each word make sure the students understand what it means and have them try it out in an oral sentence. You can have the students work together to develop a sentence for each word with an English-speaking student assisting an ELL student.

- *Draw on both languages when and where they are needed.* Use the students' first language, when possible, to explain concepts that might be difficult in English. Directly teach and use English to help students build their English skills.
- *Validate Spanish speakers' language.* Provide students with Spanish-language texts, invite Spanish-speaking volunteers into the classroom, encourage the use of Spanish during cooperative learning, and learn and use Spanish vocabulary.

We conclude this section by looking at the recommendations of Deborah Short and Jana Echevarria (2004–2005) and those developed by the American Educational Research Association. In the Classroom 14.6 and 14.7 show in turn what we consider to be the most compelling and practical suggestions of each.

Short and Echevarria's SIOP Model

This set of recommendations from Deborah Short and Jana Echevarria (2004–2005) was developed over the course of a 7-year research project that produced the Sheltered Instruction Observation Protocol (SIOP) model (Echevarria, Vogt, & Short, 2004). The SIOP model is specifically designed to promote English learners' academic literacy in content areas, as shown in the following brief list of their recommendations.

- Identify the language demands of the content course.
- Plan language objectives for all lessons, and make them explicit to students.
- Emphasize academic vocabulary development.
- Activate and strengthen background knowledge.
- Promote oral interaction and extended academic talk.
- Review vocabulary and content concepts.
- Give students feedback on language use in class.

AERA's Recommendations

The set of recommendations we present here was developed by the American Educational Research Association (AERA, 2004), the major educational research association in the United States. Like several of the other sets we have presented, AERA's recommendations are grouped under several headings.

Word Recognition

- Emphasize decoding skill early. Like other children, English learners can learn to decode words relatively quickly—in two years or so.
- Provide systematic training in phonemic awareness.
- Give students lots of practice reading.
- Provide explicit instruction in phonics.
- Use frequent in-class assessment to find out where students need assistance, and then provide that assistance.

Comprehension

- Allot a substantial period of time to building sophisticated language skills. Comprehending and producing academic language and acquiring a rich and powerful vocabulary is likely to take at least 5 years.
- Engage students in substantive reading, writing, and discussion on academic topics.
- Provide in-depth instruction in both oral and reading vocabulary, and be sure to teach a significant number of words using powerful approaches.
- Provide instruction in learning from text.
- Provide comprehension strategy instruction.

Extensive Learning Time

- Provide more time during each year by means such as extending the school day and school year.
- Provide this extended time over a number of years.

If you compare the six sets of principles we have presented—those of Delpit, Kamil and Bernhardt, Gersten and Baker, Jiménez, Short and Echevarria, and AERA—you will find that there is a good deal of overlap. This is good news. We deliberately included the overlapping recommendations to show how much agreement there is on how to assist English learners. Another piece of good news is that many of these recommendations are easily implemented by typical teachers in typical classrooms. We encourage you to make use of as many of these recommendations as you can in your classroom.

5 Think about reading activities that are not specific to a particular language. For example, the process of using a table of contents in a book is the same, regardless of the language used. What other reading tasks are similar across different languages?

6 Create your own Rosetta Stone chart, with words or phrases that you know in English and in one or two other languages. For example, you might already know that *mesa* is the Spanish word for "table." If you cannot construct much of a chart by yourself, get together with classmates who speak other languages and create a chart together.

Concluding Remarks

In this chapter, we have outlined some of the history of English language learning in the United States, noted some of the linguistic challenges that English language learners and teachers face, and described a number of instructional approaches that can be used with English language learners. In concluding the chapter, we want to emphasize three points.

First, with English language learners, as with all children, it is not merely low-level literacy or the rudiments of literacy that we must assist students in reaching. The goal is full literacy in English—the ability to use the English language as a vehicle for thinking, for problem solving, and for communicating—in other words, the ability to use English in a way that makes possible full and productive participation in our society.

Second, vocabulary instruction was stressed in many of the sets of suggestions we have discussed throughout this chapter. Vocabulary is increasingly recognized as absolutely crucial to English learners (August, 2005). Take advantage of the many techniques for vocabulary instruction described in Chapter 9. Also, you may want to consider the fuller discussion of vocabulary learning and instruction one of us presents in *The Vocabulary Book* (Graves, 2006).

Finally, the task of assisting non-English-speaking children in reaching the goal of English literacy for the 21st century is difficult. Yet it is a task we can accomplish and one we must aim for; the ultimate rewards for our society will be among the greatest we could imagine.

Extending Learning

1. Visit a school with English language learners. You might volunteer to work with some students whose first language is not English. If you cannot find such a school, many social service agencies, religious organizations, and other nonprofit groups have programs that target reading for English language learners. Volunteering to work in these settings, or even simply observing, will allow you to see how the principles in this chapter play out in real life.

2. Study the instructional recommendations made throughout this chapter. There are over 40 of them, many more than you can implement at one time. Identify half a dozen or so that you see as particularly useful and as steps that you definitely could take in your present or future classroom. Explain in writing why you selected each of these recommendations and in what order you are likely to implement them.

Children's *Literature*

Children's Books

Ciardi, J. (1975). "The Shark." In *Fast and Slow: Poems by John Ciardi.* Boston: Houghton Mifflin. This poem provides a colorful and engaging description of a shark. 1 page.

Dorros, A. (2005). *Julio's Magic.* New York: HarperCollins. Julio, a young woodcarver in a rural Mexican village, helps his elderly mentor complete a set of beautiful carvings to enter in a wood-carving competition. 32 pages.

Gibbons, G. (2005). *Dinosaur Discoveries.* New York: Holiday House. In simple language, Gibbons provides details of the most recent theories about the history of dinosaurs, along with amazing facts about dinosaur discoveries. 33 pages.

Gomi, T. (2006). *Spring Is Here = Llegó la primavera.* San Francisco: Chronicle Books. In this colorful dual-language picture book, a winsome calf provides the backdrop for the story line, which follows the cycle of the seasons from one spring to the next. In spare text, the author conveys the underlying themes of renewal and growth. 34 pages.

Graves, B. (1997). *The Whooping Crane.* Des Moines, IA: Perfection Learning. While on an airplane ride from Texas to Maryland, a young girl sits next to a biologist transporting a whooping crane chick to the Patuxent Wildlife Research Center and learns about this endangered species. 64 pages.

Lowery, L. (2005). *Cinco de mayo.* Minneapolis, MN: Lerner. This colorful book honors the joyful holiday that celebrates Mexico's victory over the French army at the Battle of Pueblo in 1862. 48 pages.

O'Dell, S. (1960). *Island of the Blue Dolphins.* Boston: Houghton Mifflin. By using her wits and the resources at hand, a young Indian girl survives alone on an island for several years. Newbery Medal winner. Audio- and videotapes available. Spanish text also available. 154 pages.

Ramírez, A. (2004). *Napí.* Toronto: Groundwood Books. A Mazateca girl, who lives beside a river in Oaxaca, describes her home and village at different times of the day. 32 pages.

Rosenblatt, L. (1998). *Monarch Magic!* Charlotte, VT: Williamson Publishing Co. Simple text and colorful photographs depict the life cycle of a monarch butterfly, from egg to caterpillar to chrysalis to butterfly. Includes 40 butterfly activities. 96 pages.

Shea, P. D. (1995). *The Whispering Cloth: A Refugee's Story.* Honesdale, PA: Boyds Mills Press. A young Hmong girl in a Thai refugee camp creates a *pándau* (embroidered tapestry) that tells her own story. Includes glossary. Illustrated by A. Riggio, with reproductions of *pándau* by Y. Yang. 32 pages.

Silverstein, S. (1996). *Falling Up.* New York: Scholastic. This book includes over 100 poems and drawings by this favorite author. 171 pages.

Soto, G. (1994). *The Skirt.* New York: Bantam-Doubleday. When Miata leaves the skirt she is to wear for the folklorico dance performance on the school bus, she must use all her wits to get it back before her parents find out. Illustrated by Eric Velasquez. Audio CD available. 74 pages.

Yumoto, K. (1999). *The Spring Tone.* New York: Farrar, Straus and Giroux. Resenting the changes in her life and resisting growing up, Tomomi joins her younger brother in taking revenge against the neighbors with whom her family is battling. 166 pages.

Bibliography

Schon, I. (2004). *Recommended books in Spanish for children and young adults: 2000 through 2004.* Lanham, MD: Scarecrow Press. Schon's newest bibliography of books in Spanish presents critical annotations for over 1,300 books.

Schon, I. (2001). *Recommended books in Spanish for children and young adults: 1996 through 1999.* Lanham, MD: Scarecrow Press. This is an excellent bibliography of books in Spanish.

Schon, I. (1996). *Recommended books in Spanish for children and young adults: 1991–1995.* Lanham, MD: Scarecrow Press. This, too, is an excellent bibliography of books in Spanish.

Schon, I., & Berkin, S. C. (1996). *Introducción a la literatura infantil y juvenil.* Newark, DE: International Reading Association. (Available only in Spanish.) This is an excellent resource for Spanish-speaking teachers.

Courtesy of the author

A Day in the Life of David Weiss and His Fifth- and Sixth-Grade Students

David Weiss has been teaching fifth- and sixth-graders at Oak Grove Intermediate School for 10 years. Oak Grove, which includes grades 4 through 6, is located in a southern suburb of Minneapolis. Most of the children at Oak Grove come from middle- to lower-income families; the majority are European Americans, with a sprinkling of Asian Americans, Native Americans, and African Americans.

David works in a team with three other teachers, which is fairly typical of many upper-elementary classrooms. Before the school year begins, the team meets to make program decisions and to discuss matters such as scheduling and curricular responsibilities. The four classrooms in David's team each have approximately 30 students, equally divided between fifth- and sixth-graders. When the sixth-graders move on to junior high school, 15 fifth-grade students take their place, so students are with the same homeroom teacher for 2 years.

When we asked David to describe the literacy program he and his colleagues have developed, he spoke of the diverse range of student abilities.

The literacy program we have developed over the years reflects the unique challenge we face as upper elementary teachers. Differences in reading ability are extreme in students in grades 5 and 6. For example, one of my students, 11-year-old Kelly, reads at an 11th-grade level and devours John Grisham novels during her free reading period. Tommy, also 11 years old, struggles with anything beyond second-grade materials. He finds it difficult to read even short, episodic stories. This disparity presents a critical question for my teammates and me: How do we meet the needs of students, given such a huge range of ability? My team has developed a plan we think best meets the needs of our students.

On the following pages, David describes in his own words his team's plan for organizing the fifth-/sixth-grade curriculum to emphasize reading and writing instruction throughout the school day and to meet the wide range of needs in their classes.

Every district has a list of goals and objectives or learning outcomes. At the beginning of, during, and following the school year, my colleagues and I sit down and figure out what to teach. Our team looks for connections within all the language arts and within broad themes as well. As a starting point, we choose a broad theme that will connect all the students' learning experiences to their knowledge and experiences. The theme we choose is determined by a number of factors, including appropriateness of topic, access to resources, our own talents and failings, and district and state standards. Typically, we choose three themes over the course of the year.

Although each day has a particular focus for instruction, I have found it useful to teach content that will serve the students in a variety of settings throughout the school year. Over the years, I have become more and more convinced that the teaching of comprehension strategies makes for more powerful readers. I choose strategies that are flexible and widely applicable. I will ask the students to use them in their content area classes and when using self-selected materials, as well as in my class. My suggestion to a beginning teacher—or any teacher—is to develop a small number of them (five to six) throughout the year. The students' repertoire of strategies will grow through the year, so by the end they will successfully employ multiple strategies.

At the beginning of the year, I note several strategies I think would be helpful for my students. One of my favorites is teaching students to create advanced story maps (see Chapter 10). Although story maps were introduced to most students by second grade and have been reviewed in subsequent grades, now my students are ready for a more in-depth analysis of narrative structure. My first goal is to review the story mapping strategy in such a way that all students will recall previous concepts. For this reason, I choose content that is familiar to all students and that they do not need to read. For example, I may ask them to recall the story "Little Red Riding Hood" as a text to use in doing their story mapping. I let students know that they will be learning a more sophisticated version of the strategy designed to help them understand the reactions and motives of the characters. Then I model the activity in a large-group setting. I begin by listing the elements of a story map and then ask the students to assist me in identifying the characters, setting, problem, and events:

Story Elements	Little Red Riding Hood
Characters	Little Red Riding Hood, Grandmother, the Big Bad Wolf
Setting	The forest, Grandmother's house
Problem	Little Red Riding Hood wanted to bring food to her grandmother
Events	Red begins her journey to Grandmother's house and encounters a wolf

After creating their first map, we begin to deepen our understanding of narrative structure by considering two new elements in the story grammar or story map, character motives and reactions. I pose the following questions: "Why was Red visiting Grandmother's house? How did she feel when she encountered the wolf?" I want the students to understand that there is more to the narrative than a simple listing of the literal elements in a story. We review the entire fairy tale, discussing the motives and reactions of each character and adding them to the story map. I use a read-aloud for the next one; again, my interest is minimizing the effect of reading ability as a critical factor in acquiring the strategy. I've found picture books to be an excellent vehicle for this, as they are nonthreatening to the listener—short, full of illustrations, and appealing. Following whole-group instruction, the students will use this strategy in small groups and individually later in the day. The students have learned a strategy that may be applied to a variety of texts; have had an opportunity to integrate reading, writing, listening, and speaking; and have created responses to share with the other groups in the class. One student's map for *The True Story of the Three Little Pigs* by Jon Scieszka is shown in the figure on the next page.

Two aspects of our team approach are particularly important to our use of a language arts block. First, the language arts block provides time for focusing on and interrelating all of the language arts. Second, we use both flexible grouping and

Name: <u>Coltrane, B.</u>

Title of book: <u>The True Story of the Three Little Pigs</u>

Author of the book: <u>Jon Scieszka</u>

On the left side of the page, list the important events in the story (choose between 3 and 12 events). On the right side, describe how the main character felt at the end of the event and what caused him to take the actions he did. You may write from the point of view of the wolf or the three little pigs.

1. The wolf was sick and wanted a cup of sugar.	The wolf loved his grandmother and wanted to make her a cake even though he had this rotten cold.
2. The wolf sneezed and blew down the first pig's house.	The wolf thought the pig was stupid for building his house from straw.
3. The wolf ate the first pig.	The wolf's diet is small animals and he didn't want the dead pig to spoil, so he ate it up.
4. The wolf sneezed and blew down the second pig's house.	The wolf's cold is not getting any better and he felt it was stupid to build a house of sticks.
5. The wolf ate the second pig.	Again, ham is part of the wolf's diet and he didn't want the dead pig to spoil.
6. The wolf went to the third pig's house and sneezed, but nothing happened.	The wolf felt the third pig was rude and selfish because he would not loan him a cup of sugar for his cake. The wolf was hurt that the pig insulted his grandmother.
7. The police came and thought the wolf was trying to blow down the pig's house.	The wolf felt framed by the pig and angry that the reporters changed the story to make the wolf look bad.
8. The police took the wolf to jail.	The wolf felt justice went awry and sad that his grandmother did not get her cake.

student self-selection of reading materials. I regularly introduce new books and stress the genre of the books. This encourages students to read widely across many different genres. The students may read individually or in self-selected groups or literature circles. The literature circles are particularly important because they promote independent reading, strategy use, and group responsibility. The students respond to the texts in a variety of ways, sometimes determined by the instructor and sometimes determined by the students.

A literature-based approach is particularly attractive to fifth- and sixth-grade students. Meeting to discuss what they read in literature circles (see Chapter 12) helps students develop rich, engaging schemata. The students really get into a piece of writing when they are sharing the experience with others. I find it easy to model and be enthusiastic about appropriate literature circle behaviors, as I am able to relate my own experiences in a book club. Literature circles and other literature-based approaches encourage deep understanding of texts. The circles have an advantage over whole-group instruction in that participants find it difficult to check out of the discussion. Students who are eye-to-eye and knee-to-knee and responsible for developing meaning have a greater chance of experiencing the "aha" phenomenon—gaining a perspective that they hadn't considered before. An additional advantage to literature-based approaches is that students are able to self-select their groups. The teacher, for example, may select four texts—differing in length, type of characters, and so forth—that all relate to a broad, general theme. Emily may be ready for Lynne Rae Perkins's *Criss Cross*, a complex Newbery Medal–winning story, while James may prefer a book made up of short, easy-to read episodic stories like Donald Sobol's *Encyclopedia Brown and the Case of the Jumping Frogs*. Allowing student choice increases the likelihood that students will read an engaging book at their level of reading competence.

Our approach to reading instruction does not ignore basic skills. As I said at the outset, six of our students are still struggling with basic print skills and they read between a second- and third-grade level. I make it a plan to meet with these six students every day. During our 20-minute small-group lessons we are working on decoding by analogy and oral reading fluency. Each week the students are introduced to four or five key words that contain a common and useful rime. The students then practice using that rime to decode increasingly complex words. The figure shows that today the students worked on words with the spelling patterns in *rain* and *hide*. For oral reading fluency the students are working on a readers theater project that they will present to the whole class. The six students are organized into groups of three and each is learning and practicing a short play.

"Each group checks with me for feedback, and following my okay, groups may exchange their story maps with other groups working through different books."—David Weiss
Courtesy of the author

There are five important features in our organization of time, curriculum content, space, and students. First is the concept of the homeroom, second is scheduling large blocks of time for students to be in one place with one teacher, third is centering instruction around a broad theme, fourth is working with students to acquire some of the decoding and fluency skills they still lack, and fifth is selecting reading comprehension strategies and procedures to teach throughout the year that are flexible and broadly applicable. Here is what our typical schedule looks like:

8:30–11:00	Homeroom—Reading/Language Arts
8:30	Independent silent reading, journal writing, reading conferences
9:00	Whole-group morning meeting, knowledge development, strategy instruction
9:30	Teacher guided small-group instruction, literature circles, process writing
11:00	Mathematics
12:00	Lunch and recess
12:45	Special subjects: Physical education, art, music
1:30	Social studies, science, health
3:00	Homeroom and school logs
3:15	Dismissal

Key Words	rain	hide
Words to Decode	gain	ride
	main	side
	pain	slide
	plain	snide
	slain	tide
	strain	wide
	abstain	bedside
	disdain	confide
	obtain	reside
	remain	provide
	restrain	coincide

As the schedule shows, each homeroom stays intact for over 2 hours in the beginning of each day. For example, fifth- and sixth-grade students in my homeroom stay with me from 8:30 to 11:00 and then move to another teacher for mathematics. Heterogeneous groups made up from each of the four classrooms within our team comprise the classes for instruction in social studies, science, art, and health.

Large blocks of time have a number of advantages. To begin with, the students have less downtime between classes. They spend less time moving from room to room. Lengthier time periods also allow for greater depth and breadth of instruction. We have greater opportunities to go into detail on a given topic, or we can use the extended time to develop connections to other curricular areas. Another advantage of large time blocks is greater flexibility for everyone involved, making it easier to schedule special education services, computer lab time, and guest speakers.

8:30 Independent Silent Reading, Journal Writing, Reading Conferences

Homeroom begins with one of two different activities—independent silent reading or journal writing, which I alternate throughout the school year. Having a structured activity ready for the students helps them warm up for school and establishes a healthy working culture for the classroom.

Independent Silent Reading

Independent silent reading (see Chapter 12) is an important part of any elementary-level reading curriculum. I've found it helpful to ask the students to have their books out and ready to read the moment class begins. I think it is good practice to feature sustained reading of student-selected texts as a primary feature of the classroom, rather than an adjunct to the "real work" of the day. If students are asked to do silent reading only when their other assignments are done, this almost guarantees that the least successful students will get the least amount of time to read independently and the least opportunity to develop fluent, success-oriented reading practice. My students are especially interested in a pre-set quiet reading time, as this gives them time to complete the response log, which is a required part of their independent reading. During independent reading I confer with three or four students every day. During this time we assess their oral reading, comprehension, and vocabulary knowledge, plus we discuss what they might like to read next.

Journal Writing

I have tried all sorts of journal writing, both structured and nonstructured. I have responded at length to students' writing and have enjoyed it, although it is terrifically time-consuming. However, having students write to a real audience is powerfully motivating. Lately, I have found it particularly productive to have students share their writing thoughts with two or three others. I may suggest a topic for a journal entry, or the students may choose their own. The small group that develops as a result of this journaling activity is asked to respond to what each member of the group writes.

As David has noted, by the time students reach fifth and sixth grades, some students can tackle texts written for an adult audience.

Steve Skjold/Alamy

4/14 Kaj—So far I think this book is very interesting, but it is kind of hard to believe that a four year old could read books like Oliver Twist, Kim, & Animal Farm & actually understand what she is reading.

J. R.

I think that your right Justin, because it is amazing that she read books that thick and that fast. It also is amazing that she understands the books that she is reading when she goes to the library every afternoon.

K. L.

4/15 Kaj—I think it is hilarious how Matilda put glue in her Dad's hat, it was also pretty good how she put the parrot up the chimney & her parents thought it was a ghost. I'm surprised when she didn't cry when her father tore the pages out of the library book.

A. B.

Justin—I think that you are right it is pretty hilarious, you were also right that the book is different than the movie that I saw. I like the part where Matilda slams the door on her dad.

K. L.

Some of the students are writing to each other via the school email system. Conversations between students develop in print, similar to what happens in dialogue journals (see Chapter 13). I like to introduce this activity by modeling my own journal writing and students' responses, sharing these on an overhead projector. The figure shows two journal entries by students reading *Matilda* by Roald Dahl.

Working in small groups not only provides students with a real audience but also allows me to give feedback quickly and efficiently. To give this feedback, I ask each group of three or four students to come up to my desk, where I respond orally to their writing.

9:00   Whole-Group Morning Meeting, Knowledge Development, and Strategy Instruction

Morning Meeting

Just about every teacher I know sets aside time during the beginning of the day to do the routine chores that are part of every classroom. Here, we talk about the day's schedule, important dates, current events, and the like. I list on the board which groups I will be meeting with and what tasks they should have finished before small-group time.

The time required for our morning meeting varies day by day. It is common practice in my classroom to use this time to assign ad hoc student committees designed to solve problems. For instance, we may have a party coming up. Following a list of guidelines, a student committee is formed to submit their written recommendations as to treats, activities, and the like. A committee may be responsible for cleaning and putting fresh water in the iguana cage or figuring out a way to get homework to absent students. In almost all cases, students are asked to submit a written plan, which I will review. These authentic language arts experiences allow students to have an impact on their world, and they really work well with fifth- and sixth-graders.

Knowledge Development

I will use for our whole-class lesson a selection in the basal taken from *Call It Courage*, Armstrong Perry's Newbery Medal–winning story about a shipwrecked boy searching for courage. This selection will serve to introduce the theme of the sea, develop prior knowledge, and review some comprehension strategies. Purpose and selection, of course, are two of the three factors of the scaffolded reading experience (discussed in Chapter 10). The third is taking into account the readers. So next, I consider what each of my students will be reading. I have four groups in the classroom with some reading well above grade level, and one group struggling to read the basal story.

I begin developing a reading scaffold by thinking of my prereading activities, asking myself what sort of background knowledge will be required for the students to understand the story. One advantage of using a story out of a basal text (which is usually highly illustrated) is that all students have access to a powerful cue—illustration. Illustrations are one way to tap into the students' existing knowledge. I ask them to look at the pictures and to write predictions of what they expect will happen in the story. The illustration for *Call It Courage* shows the character Mafatu on a beach, apparently making something out of bamboo. He appears to be alone, but for a seagull and a dog. Students might predict that he is alone on an island and that he is intent on building a shelter, which they will later find to be the case. Analyzing illustrations is also a helpful way to introduce semantic mapping to further activate background knowledge. Besides activating background knowledge, mapping serves an additional purpose. Inevitably, important vocabulary will surface; or you, as the instructor, can make it surface. My colleagues and I have found that the key in vocabulary instruction is picking out critical terms or concepts and giving the students repeated exposure to them, using a variety of techniques. Students need to hear and use critical vocabulary in a variety of contexts.

Strategy Instruction

At this point in the instruction I will review the current strategy, story mapping with the focus on character motives and reactions, plus other strategies that the students will be using in their small-group discussions. Some students will be working on self-questioning, others on predicting, summarizing, or comprehension monitoring. I will continue to model these strategies with the basal text from *Call It Courage*. Because the text is difficult for some students, I will read a portion of it aloud. Then, when whole-group instruction ends some of the students, will read the text independently while others might read it with a partner. They have to finish the story so we can discuss it in whole group tomorrow. Next the students will move to small-group instruction. I have already written the assignments for each group on the assignment board so that students know what to do next without having to get my attention.

Teacher Guided Small-Group Instruction, Literature Circles, and Process Writing

Teacher Guided Small-Group Instruction

I meet with my lowest group of students first, so that I have ample time to explain and scaffold their work. In addition to partner reading the basal story, *Call It Courage,* this group will read one of the leveled readers that accompanies the basal story. Because many of the students in this group read 2 years below grade level, we will also review strategies for decoding words focusing on decoding by analogy (see Chapter 7). In our comprehension discussions about *Call It Courage,* we consider characters' motives and reactions, the strategies for the week. While I meet with the struggling readers, the rest of the class will be reading independently or working with their literature circle.

The strongest readers will be meeting with their literature circle discussing *The Great Wide Sea* by M. H. Herlong. The book continues the theme from the basal story and students will be able to apply their newly developed knowledge. The book should also challenge those reading above a sixth-grade level. As they discuss the story the members of the literature circle will focus on summarizing, questioning, clarifying, predicting, and character motives and feelings. After they finish their discussion they will work on their book poster, which includes a short plot outline. Our work on story mapping should help with this task. They are also responsible for finding new vocabulary words and sharing them with the class. After I finish with the lower group I will meet with this group.

The next group will also be working in their literature circle. They had chosen the book *Voyage of the Frog* by Gary Paulson, another survival story but well matched to their reading ability. Like the other groups, my *Voyage of the Frog* people will be focusing on the same comprehension strategies—summarizing, questioning, clarifying, and character motives and feelings. This group will also complete a book poster and search for new vocabulary words.

Notice that the entire class is engaged in parallel activities but at their instructional level and each has an opportunity for teacher feedback. I allocate about 90 minutes for small groups, literature circles, and independent work. It is important to see the below-level readers everyday. After I see the below-level readers, the reading specialist comes into the room and continues with them for another 20 minutes, working on decoding and fluency. Before or after the students meet with me, they work on a number of independent projects. Some will be working in literature circle books, others will be working on their readers theater project, and all will be completing a story map based

David often pairs up English-language learners with a buddy when an assignment, such as developing a story map, proves to be too much of a challenge.

David Grossman/Alamy

on what they have been reading. Again, there is an implicit appeal here for integrating language arts—students are reading, writing, speaking, and listening. Furthermore, now that the students have demonstrated facility in creating story maps, each is able to use this strategy with his or her own content. Students are able to use the procedure to take notes for their posters or generate discussion questions, which they will share when they next meet with me.

At the end of the small-group time I bring the whole class together so they can share what they have accomplished. Each group discusses how story mapping has helped them today. This builds a common purpose and a sense of community among the groups as well as providing a transition to writing.

Writing Instruction

Because we have been reading about survival stories and studying story maps, the students are also working on their own survival stories. We started several days ago and considered how a story is organized and how the plot is developed. I gave the students the task of creating a story map or plot for the story they plan to write. I ask each of the groups to share some interesting points of conflict from the plot of their story. As the students are working I meet with individual students and help them organize their stories. Tomorrow we will focus on leads, or interesting ways to start a story. We are following the writing process and by the end of the week the students will be editing and getting ready to share what they have written.

 ## Mathematics

As I said earlier, our team is made up of four classrooms, each serving two grade levels. My teammates and I are always looking for ways to connect with our theme. For example, I know through team meetings that the science teacher will be using whales to illustrate content in a unit on oceanography. I have an opportunity to illustrate mathematics in an engaging way, which will enrich their understanding of our theme, by having my students make cutout re-creations of whales. In doing so, the students work from a pattern, grid out an image, and convert their numbers, using the concept of scale in creating paper or chalk models. In a variety of ways, my students will develop a better sense of number and demonstrate facility in the use of ratios and estimation, while further developing a rich and engaging schema that will serve them in other content areas.

 ## Lunch and Recess

The themes here are eating and playing!

 ## Special Subjects: Physical Education, Art, Music

Our district uses specialists to teach these three content areas. The students alternate classes on a 3-day rotation. I can't always integrate physical education, art, or music with common themes, as these teachers have their own scope and sequence. Integration requires meeting with these teachers to plan our curricular content together, which, although it is a challenge, I occasionally do with music. For example, a music teacher developed a score for a play that my classroom was working on.

1:30 Themes: Social Studies, Science, and Health

As I mentioned earlier, my team—Nancy Eller, Troy Miller, and Suzy Neet—uses a thematic approach to interrelate our classes. Our goal is to find a way to connect the disciplines of science, social studies, art, and health, given available curricular materials, district outcomes, and teacher expertise. Nancy and Suzy's area of expertise is social studies. Troy's is science. The students attend two of the three classes each day.

Social Studies

Nancy has a pretty good background in ancient civilizations. For the present unit, she's going to focus on the Roman Empire's movement throughout the Mediterranean region. She plans to focus in part on trade routes, commerce, and the transmission of Greco-Roman culture throughout the Mediterranean. Social studies requires a good deal of expository reading by the students, which is particularly difficult. It would be appropriate for all team members to use a comprehension procedure—for instance, K-W-L (discussed in Chapter 10)—in the language arts setting.

Science

Troy has decided to do a unit on oceanography. The content fits with our district outcomes in that he will explore relationships between a marine environment and all sorts of creatures. There are many opportunities to connect with mathematics, including graphing the ocean floor via echo sounding and determining the speed of sound in various environments.

Health

Connecting health to other content areas has always been a stretch for our team. Suzy has agreed to do health the past several years. Sometimes she is able to make connections, but in this case the topic of the sea fails to inspire her. As her colleagues are at a loss to make thematic connections between health and the sea, she will be out of the loop this time around. She will likely have greater success when we pursue other themes—challenges, for example.

In trying to find connections between theme and subject areas, we have learned something that Sean Walmsley (1996, p. 54) stresses: "Don't try to integrate every subject area into every theme." Sometimes there are important connections, and sometimes not. We try to concentrate on connections that really make sense. Walmsley offers some other tips about theme teaching that I'd like to pass along:

- When you teach a theme, tuck the skills inside it.
- Balance teacher-generated and student-generated themes.
- Avoid cutesy treatment of themes.
- Draw themes from a variety of arenas—concepts, content areas, current events, people, the calendar.
- Make sure your themes are the right size.

- Approach year-long and schoolwide themes with caution because you may simply run out of energy.
- Bump up your own knowledge of the themes you're preparing.
- Borrow theme ideas from others.

Although writing thematic units can be hard work and time-consuming, we have found the process of planning together to be fruitful and stimulating and the results rewarding. Resources such as *The Complete Guide to Thematic Units* (Meinbach, Rothlein, & Fredericks, 2000), which provides 20 comprehensive units that can be adapted to fit any classroom, can help you with valuable and time-saving information on teaching strategies and books to use.

Homeroom and School Logs

All of our students have school logs. At the end of each day, I ask students to write down what happened over the course of the day. The purpose of the activity is to give them an opportunity to reflect on learning, to have a written record to communicate to parents, and to note any assignments or other tasks that will be due. This can be difficult unless you really make it a vital part of your everyday activities.

3:15 Dismissal

Appendixes

Appendix A

Assessments

Tile Test

Directions

Grade Level: Kindergarten–Second Grade

The Tile Test is designed to quickly assess students' understanding of letters, sounds, words, and sentences. Metalinguistic questions encourage students to talk about the strategies they use when decoding and spelling words.

General Procedures

1. Start with a collection of letter tiles, not just one card.
2. Allow sufficient time for each response.
3. Provide general positive feedback to encourage students; do not correct mistakes.
4. Write the students' responses to each item:
   a. Correct response is marked + or ✓.
   b. Incorrect responses will be recorded in full.
   c. No response will be recorded as DK (doesn't know).
   d. Self-correction is marked SC and counted as correct.
   e. Segmented words read without blending sounds will be marked with slashes between sounds (e.g., /t/a/p/).
5. Administer all components.
6. Stop rule: If a student is unable to respond to any word of the first four items, use teacher judgment to discontinue this segment and move to the next. If a student is unsuccessful in reading the word tiles at all, do not proceed to sentence reading.

Letters and Sounds

Begin with a collection of letter tiles [m, a, p, i, f, s, t, d, n].

1. Have students point to the letter you name.
2. Ask students to tell you the *name* and *sound* of each letter.

Words

Add the following letters to the collection of letter tiles [h, e, w, c, k, v, u, l, s, o, d, d, b, r, p, g].

1. Manipulate individual letters to build the given words. The teacher builds, and the student reads. Follow-up with the Metalinguistic (ML) and Articulation questions below.
2. Ask the student to use the letter tiles to build the words you read. (ML and Articulation.) Record student responses. Observe and record strategy use (e.g., orally articulating sounds) and behaviors.

3. Use the word tiles provided on page 454 to assess word reading. Leave word tiles on the table for use in the next section.

Metalinguistic (ML) and Articulation Questions

Following the reading of "pat" and "sat" and the building of "tan" and "tad," ask how the student knew to make the change(s) he or she made. After the successful reading or building of the most difficult word, ask the student what his or her mouth did to say the first sound of the word. Then ask how he or she knew to read/build the word that way. Record student responses. Provide and document probing questions as necessary (e.g., "What were you looking at?" "I noticed your mouth moving; how did that help you?"). Score the ML questions using the Tile Test Metalanguage Rubric.

Sentences

Use the collection of tiles to create sentences. Record student responses.

1. Using the word tiles, build each sentence and have the student read.
2. Ask the student to use the word tiles to build sentences you read. Then ask the student to read the sentence he or she built. Record student responses.
3. Hand the student the sentence on a separate sheet and have the student read it. Record student responses.

Metalinguistic Rubric

0	No response; "I don't know."
1	"I know it;" "My mom taught me;" "I'm smart."
2	Recognition of letters: "I looked at the letters."
3	Recognition of sounds: "I sound it out;" "I listen to the sounds."
4	Partial linking of sounds to letters: "It starts with a P /p/, then a /a/. Partial analogy: "Pat is like cat."
5	Explains spelling of each sound. Full analogy: "Pat is like cat, but it starts with a /p/."
6	Explains how sounds are articulated: "It starts with /p/. My lips are together and the air pops out; my tongue is resting in the middle of my mouth. . . . "

Recording Sheet

Student _____ Teacher _____ School _____ Date _____

Letter Identification

Lay out letter tiles [m, a, p, i, f, s, t, d, n].

"Here are some letters. I'll say the name of a letter and ask you to point to the letter. Point to the card that has the letter m." *(Record, continue procedure.)*

"Now, I'll point to a card and you'll tell me two things about the letter. First, the *name* of the letter, and second, the *sound* that it makes." *(Record.)*

	Identification	Name	Sound			Identification	Name	Sound
m					s			
a					t			
p					d			
i					n			
f								

Words

Add these letter tiles to the tiles above: [b, c, d, d, e, h, k, l, o, r, r, s, u, v, w].

"Now let's put some letters together to make words. Some of the words are real words and some are pretend words. I'll go first and make a word, and then I'll ask you to read it for me." *(Manipulate only necessary letters, stop after sat and ask the first ML and articulation questions.)*

↓pat _____	vute _____
*sat _____	flass _____
sam _____	lodded _____
hin _____	wembick _____

ML: "I noticed that you said 'sat' *(or repeat what the student said if different)*. How did you know to change it that way from 'pat' *(or repeat what the student said)*?" _____

_____

_____

Articulation: "Tell me what your mouth did to say the first sound in _____ *(repeat the most difficult word they read correctly)*." *(Record verbal responses and behaviors.)*

ML: "How did you know to say _____ *(use the most difficult word decoded correctly)* that way?"

_____

_____

"Now, I'll say a word, and you make it for me." *(As you dictate, clearly articulate by "stretching" each sound. Example: tan = /t/ /ă/ /n/. Stop after tad and ask the first ML and articulation questions.)*

↓tan _____	plat _____
*tad _____	mape _____
tap _____	pridder _____
leb _____	radmin _____

ML: "How did you know to change [the 'n' to a 'd']?" *(Use the letter changes the student has made.)*

_____

_____

Articulation: "Tell me what my mouth did to help you spell _____ *(repeat the most difficult word they spelled correctly)."* *(Record verbal responses and behaviors.)*

ML: "How did you know to spell _____ *(use the most difficult word spelled correctly)* that way?

_____

_____

Words

Lay out the collection of word tiles on page 454.

"I'll show you some words, and you read each one." *(Record, and if incorrect, say the right word.)*

I _____	me _____	the _____	a _____
is _____	at _____	look _____	dog _____
cat _____	big _____	map _____	can _____
sat _____	fat _____	sit _____	on _____
run _____			

Sentences

"I'll make a sentence with some words, and you read the sentence for me."

I can run. _____

Look at me. _____

I sat on the cat. _____

The map is big. _____

Sit the dog on the fat cat. _____

"Now I'll say a sentence, and you can make it for me." *(Have the student read the sentence after building it. Record sentence made and the student's read of it.)*

I can sit. _____

The dog is fat. _____

Look at the map. _____

A dog can look at me. _____

The big cat sat on the dog. _____

"Now I want you to read one sentence for me." *(Give the student the sheet with the sentence printed on it. Record the student's reading.)*

General Observations: _____

_____

_____

_____

_____

Copy this page. Cut out and laminate each tile for use in word and sentence reading segments.

I	.	at	me
look	the	dog	a
cat	is	big	A
map	on		can
run	sat		Look
fat	Sit	sit	The

Graduated Running Record

The Graduated Running Record is an assessment that allows a teacher to systematically observe what a child does as he or she reads connected text aloud. It brings to the forefront the student's use of the semantic, syntactic, and graphophonemic cueing systems, enabling the teacher to quickly determine areas of strength and weakness.

The Graduated Running Record is formatted in a manner that minimizes the time commitment needed to individually assess an elementary class. Each version offers one paragraph on an interesting social studies, science, or narrative topic. The early reading format assesses young students' reading at the pre-primer/primer level. In the two elementary-level formats each of the seven sentences in the passage increases in difficulty from the previous sentence. Starting the passage at a mid-first-grade level, the sentences advance in difficulty by grade, with the final sentence reflecting a sixth-grade reading level. The average time needed to administer varies with the reading level of the child, but should not exceed 90 seconds. Because comprehension is jeopardized when fluency is poor, the 90-second stop limit is used as one criterion for ending the reading. A second stop limit is based on the number of grade-level words missed in a sentence.

Teachers can evaluate each student's in order employment of the semantic, syntactic, and graphophonemic cueing systems in order to individualize instruction and promote optimal growth in reading. This knowledge is gained by evaluating the total amount of text read in the allotted time for fluency; the types of substitutions, omissions, and self-corrections the child makes; and the level of expression and phrasing employed while reading the passage aloud to the teacher. Comprehension for each version is assessed by having the student retell the story. If the student does not finish the story in 90 seconds, then the test administrator reads the remaining portion of the story aloud to the child. When this occurs, both listening and reading comprehension can be evaluated with the retell.

Administration Guide

The Graduated Running Record assesses accuracy, fluency, expression or prosody, and comprehension for the pre-primer and primer levels in the early reading format, and the mid-first-grade level to the sixth-grade level in the elementary-level formats. In the elementary-level formats the first sentence is a measure of the mid-first-grade level, while the second sentence assesses the reading level for the end of first grade. Each of the following sentences advances a grade, with the third sentence at second grade and the last sentence assessing sixth grade. The early reading format assesses young students' reading at the pre-primer and primer levels.

Directions

Read the title of the passage to the student and direct him or her to read the passage aloud to you. Tell the student

> "The title of this story is _____. Now, I would like you to read this story aloud to me. Think about the story as you read it. After you finish reading, I will ask you to tell me what you remember from the story. As you read I will be making marks on my paper to help me remember what you say. The words in the story will be getting harder with each sentence. I may ask you to stop reading before you have finished the story. If you have not finished reading the story, I will read the rest of it to you."

Use the recording sheet to note everything the child says. Specific notations are used in the following manner.

Assessing Fluency

Accurate reading:	Every word read correctly is denoted with a check mark (✓).
Substitutions:	Substitutions are counted as errors. Write the substituted words above the intended text word.
Omissions:	Omissions are counted as errors. Draw a line through an omitted word. If the student is trying to decode the word, let him continue. If the student gives up on a word, tell him the word.
Insertions:	Insertions are counted as errors. Use a caret (^) to indicate an inserted word. Write the inserted word above the caret.
Self-corrections:	Self-corrections are not counted as errors, but give teacher insight into the students' metacognitive processes. Write the incorrect pronunciation of the word. Then write SC above the word.
Repetitions:	Repetitions are not counted as errors. Underline the repeated word, phrase, or sentence.

Stop rules: Stop the assessment when the child has four or more errors *of underlined words only* in a sentence, *or* if the child has not completed the story in 90 seconds or less. If the student activates one of the stop criteria before reading to the end of the passage, then finish reading the rest of the passage to the child.

Determining the reading grade level: Note the sentence in which the student has made four or more errors, or where he or she was stopped due to the 90-second time limit. If the student is stopped in mid-sentence, then this partial sentence represents the student's frustration level. Reading grade level will be one grade level lower. For example, if frustration level was third grade then the reading level will be second grade.

If the student completes the last sentence read, then that sentence indicates his reading grade level. For example, if the student finishes the last word in the fifth-grade sentence as she reaches the 90-second cut-off point, and she has not misread four or five underlined words, then her reading level is fifth grade.

Calculating accuracy rate: Using only the underlined words on the recording sheet, count the total number of words read correctly. Then, count all of the underlined words to the point the student stopped reading.

Using only underlined words, calculate accuracy rate:

$$\frac{\text{\# of underlined words read correctly}}{\text{total underlined words to the stop point}} \times 100 = \text{\% of words read correctly}$$

EXAMPLE:

$$\frac{63 \text{ underlined words read correctly}}{70 \text{ underlined words to the stop point}} \times 100 = 90\% \text{ accuracy rate}$$

Assessing Expression (Prosody)

Indicate the grade level of the last sentence in which the student has read most of the time with appropriate "flow" and phrasing as well as attended to punctuation with pauses and appropriate inflection. If the child does not read with appropriate expression or prosody, then score expression with a 0. For example, if the student reads through the second-grade sentence with correct expression and continues through the fourth-grade sentence without appropriate expression before reaching the 90-second stop rule, then the score for expression is second grade.

Assessing Comprehension—The Retelling

When the student has finished reading the passage or after you have finished reading the passage to the student, say to him, "Please tell the story to me as if I had never heard it before." On the elementary-level recording sheets, 30 phrases or individual words are in bold to indicate the main concepts of the passage. Twenty words or phrases are in bold on the pre-primer/primer level recording sheet. Listen for those words and phrases; an approximation of the phrases should be considered correct. Do not consider it an error if the retelling is somewhat out of order when comparing it to the actual text. Record the information that the student includes in the retelling on the right side of the recording sheet. You may prompt the student by saying, "Can you tell me more?" or "What else do you remember?" or by reminding her of the title of the passage.

Divide the number of concepts remembered by the student by the total number of concepts in the passage. Then, multiply by 100. That will give you the percentage of correct concepts remembered. The greater the percentage, the higher the comprehension level is. For example:

$$\frac{20 \text{ correct concepts retold}}{30 \text{ total concepts}} \times 100 = 66.7\% \text{ comprehension of the passage}$$

(If the child read some of the passage, and you read the rest of the passage aloud to the child, you can compare the percentage of reading comprehension to the percentage of listening comprehension.)

The Good Dog

That dog is little and red. He is my pal. I call him Spot. Spot likes to play at my house, but then he runs away to his home up the hill.

Every day the children who live around here ask to see Spot. They think the dog is funny when he sprints past them to the plants and drops the stick that they tossed. On most days we all romp in the grass with Spot from sun-up to sunset.

PRE-PRIMER/PRIMER LEVEL RECORDING SHEET

The Good Dog

Student _____   Teacher _____   School _____   Date _____

Underlined Words Correct _____   Underlined Words Total _____   Total Time _____

Self-Corrections _____   Omissions _____   Substitutions _____   End Sentence _____

% Accuracy _____   Prosody _____   Retell Score _____

Pre-Primer

Notes

The Good Dog

$\underline{That}$ $\underline{dog}$ is $\underline{little}$ and $\underline{red}$. $\underline{He_5}$ is $\underline{my}$ $\underline{pal}$.

I $\underline{call}$ $\underline{him}$ $\underline{Spot_{10}}$. Spot $\underline{likes}$ to $\underline{play}$ at my $\underline{house}$,

$\underline{but_{15}}$ $\underline{then}$ he $\underline{runs}$ $\underline{away}$ to $\underline{his}$ $\underline{home_{20}}$ $\underline{up}$ $\underline{the}$ $\underline{hill}$.

Primer

$\underline{Every}$ $\underline{day_{25}}$ the $\underline{children}$ who $\underline{live}$ $\underline{around}$

here $\underline{ask}$ to see Spot. They $\underline{think_{30}}$ the dog is $\underline{funny}$

$\underline{when}$ he $\underline{sprints}$ $\underline{past}$ them to the $\underline{plants_{35}}$ and $\underline{drops}$

the $\underline{stick}$ that they $\underline{tossed}$. On most $\underline{days}$ we all $\underline{romp_{40}}$

in the $\underline{grass}$ $\underline{with}$ Spot $\underline{from}$ $\underline{sun\text{-}up}$ to $\underline{sunset_{45}}$.

Retell

That **dog**   is **little and red.**   1.

He is **my pal.**   2.

I call him **Spot.**   3.

Spot **likes to play**   at my house,   but then he **runs away**   to **his home**   up the hill.   4.

Every day   **the children**   **who live around here**   ask to **see Spot.**   5.

They think the **dog is funny**   when he **sprints past**   6.

them **to the plants**   and **drops the stick** that they tossed.

On **most days**   we all **romp in the grass with Spot**   from **sun-up to sunset.**   7.

Retell Score:

_____ %

First Home

What made this a good place for a mother, father, and children to work and play? Many children who were living on this land a very long time ago slept at night in little huts. These small houses were made with reeds or branches and had places carefully made of stones for cooking the food the family found. Early each morning the hard-working people living together in the tiny village were ready to walk to different places looking for special foods. After gathering a variety of edible acorns and seeds using woven reed baskets, these women and girls of the settlement mashed their mounds of nuts into meal. Several men traveling by particular routes into the wilderness hunted the plentiful small prey such as squirrels, rabbits, and birds with nets, curved throwing sticks, or bows and arrows. Other adults rowed large wooden boats protected with tar to neighboring island settlements to trade for unique and nourishing sources of protein to expand their seafood diet.

ELEMENTARY-LEVEL RECORDING SHEET—FORM A

First Home

Student _____ Teacher _____ School _____ Date _____

Underlined Words Correct _____ Underlined Words Total _____ Total Time _____

Self-Corrections _____ Omissions _____ Substitutions _____ End Sentence _____

% Accuracy _____ Prosody _____ Retell Score _____

First Home

What made this a good place₅ for a mother, father, and children to work₁₀ and play? *Mid 1st*

Many children who were living on this land₁₅ a very long time ago slept at night in little huts₂₀. *End 1st*

These small houses were made with reeds or branches and had places carefully₂₅ made of stones for cooking the food the family found. *End 2nd*

Early₃₀ each morning the hard-working people living together₃₅ in the tiny village were ready to walk to different places looking for special₄₀ foods. *End 3rd*

After gathering a variety of edible acorns and seeds using woven₄₅ reed baskets, these women and girls of the settlement mashed their mounds₅₀ of nuts into meal. *End 4th*

Several men traveling by particular routes₅₅ into the wilderness hunted the plentiful small prey such as squirrels, rabbits, and birds with nets, curved₆₀ throwing sticks, or bows and arrows. *End 5th*

Other adults rowed₆₅ large wooden boats protected with tar to neighboring island settlements to trade for unique₇₀ and nourishing sources of protein to expand their seafood₇₅ diet₇₆. *End 6th*

Student _____ Teacher _____ School _____ Date _____

First Home	Retell
What made this a **good place** for a **mother, father, and children** to **work and play**?	1.
Many children who were living on this land a very **long time ago** **slept** at night **in little huts**.	2.
These small **houses** were **made with reeds or branches** and had places carefully made of **stones for cooking** the food the family found.	3.
Early each morning the **hard-working people** living together **in the tiny village** were ready to **walk** to different places **looking for special foods**.	4.
After gathering a variety of edible **acorns and seeds** using woven reed **baskets,** these **women and girls** of the settlement **mashed their mounds of nuts** into meal.	5.
Several **men** traveling by particular routes **into the wilderness** **hunted** the plentiful small prey such as **squirrels, rabbits, and birds** with **nets, curved throwing sticks, or bows and arrows.**	6.
Other **adults** rowed large wooden boats protected with tar **to neighboring island** settlements **to trade** for unique and nourishing **sources of protein** to expand their **seafood diet.**	7.

Retell Score:

_____ %

Making Work Like Play

That man comes to this place to work and to play with his children. He thinks it's great to swim under the water to find many animals that live there. This morning he quietly noticed some light green fish eating insects that carefully landed on the blue water near the beach. As the seaside became more crowded, he swam to the entrance of another cove because he knew there would be hundreds of limpets covering the rough rocks along the shore. Here on the island's windward side, the ocean waves entered the cove's coral-guarded boundaries without a problem and then fought to escape to the freedom of the open sea again. From all indications, the shoreline explorer was convinced he would be astonished by the impressive number of oysters and other sea creatures living in the cove free from threatening pollution. In his role as a prominent marine biologist, he planned to conduct extensive research on the organisms found in this watery environment while vowing to protect it aggressively from inappropriate use by hostile commercial businesses.

Student _____ Teacher _____ School _____ Date _____

Underlined Words Correct _____ Underlined Words Total _____ Total Time _____

Self-Corrections _____ Omissions _____ Substitutions _____ End Sentence _____

% Accuracy _____ Prosody _____ Retell Score _____

Making Work Like Play

That man comes to this$_5$ place to work and to play with his children.$_{10}$ *Mid 1st*

He thinks it's great to swim under the water$_{15}$ to find many animals that live there$_{20}$. *End 1st*

This morning he quietly noticed some light$_{25}$ green fish eating insects that carefully$_{30}$ landed on the blue water near the beach. *End 2nd*

As the seaside$_{35}$ became more crowded, he swam to the entrance of another$_{40}$ cove because he knew there would be hundreds of limpets$_{45}$ covering the rough rocks along the shore. *End 3rd*

Here on the island's$_{50}$ windward side, the ocean waves entered the cove's coral-guarded$_{55}$ boundaries without a problem and then fought to escape to the freedom$_{60}$ of the open sea again. *End 4th*

From all indications, the shoreline explorer was convinced$_{65}$ he would be astonished by the impressive number of oysters and other sea creatures$_{70}$ living in the cove free from threatening pollution. *End 5th*

In his role as a prominent marine biologist$_{75}$, he planned to conduct extensive research on the organisms$_{80}$ found in this watery environment while vowing to protect$_{85}$ it aggressively from inappropriate use by hostile commercial businesses$_{90}$. *End 6th*

Making Work Like Play

Student _____   Teacher _____   School _____   Date _____

Making Work Like Play		Retell
That **man** comes to this place **to work** and **to play** with his children.		1.
He thinks **it's great** to **swim under the water** to **find many animals** that live there.		2.
This morning he quietly **noticed some light green fish eating insects** that carefully landed on the blue water **near the beach.**		3.
As the seaside became **more crowded,** he swam to the entrance of **another cove** because he knew there would be **hundreds of limpets** covering the rough rocks **along the shore.**		4.
Here on the island's **windward side,** the ocean waves entered **the cove's coral-guarded boundaries** without a problem and then **fought to escape** to the freedom of **the open sea again.**		5.
From all indications, the **shoreline explorer** was convinced he **would be astonished** by the impressive **number of oysters** and **other sea creatures** living in **the cove** free from **threatening pollution.**		6.
In his role as a prominent **marine biologist,** he planned to **conduct extensive research** on the **organisms found** in this watery environment while **vowing to protect** it aggressively from **inappropriate use** by hostile commercial **businesses.**		7.

Retell Score:

_____ %

Interactive Reading Assessment System— Revised

The Interactive Reading Assessment System—Revised (IRAS-R) is an informal reading inventory comprising a set of subtests that are individually administered to determine a student's reading strengths and weaknesses. The skills tested include most of those generally accepted as necessary for success in skilled reading. The rationale for the array of tasks selected for IRAS-R rests on a theory of reading as a set of independent component skills (Calfee & Drum, 1979). By "independent," we mean that a student may have *relative* strengths or weaknesses within the several areas. The primary skill areas reflected in the tasks include decoding, vocabulary, grammar, understanding paragraphs, and understanding longer passages (Calfee & Spector, 1981).

Overview of the System

IRAS-R is particularly suited to students past the initial primer level. The materials in the test are selected to cover a wide range of skills and knowledge in the areas of reading and oral language, from the level expected of a midyear first-grader to that of a junior high school student.

If all subtests of the IRAS-R are selected, IRAS-R can be administered in one session of about 40 to 50 minutes, or in two sessions of approximately 30 minutes each. However, the system is designed to assess one or more skills as needed; a selection of appropriate subtests should be made to address the identified skills in question. If you are planning to administer the sight word and the comprehension tasks, use the word recognition/decoding first. Directions for administration are included at the beginning of each subtest.

Decoding and word knowledge is measured in four ways.

1. The student is asked to read common sight words within the student's reading vocabulary and beyond.
2. The student is asked to define words. Depending on how well he or she performs, the student is moved to lists of easier or more difficult words.
3. Letter-sound correspondence is measured in two ways, using an alphabet recognition task that asks for letter identification and letter-sound relationships and by having the student read lists of synthetic words. The synthetic words are divided into six categories according to the spelling pattern: vowels controlled by a final "e," vowels controlled by single and double consonants, vowel and consonant digraphs, vowel plus "r," segmented polysyllables, and polysyllabic words the student is asked to divide before reading.
4. The student is asked to spell or build a list of phonetically regular synthetic words of increasing difficulty.

The order of administering the decoding and word knowledge tests is up to the discretion of the teacher. If the student is young or has a severe reading problem, you might want to start with the letter and sounds items and then move to the reading of real or synthetic words. Try to estimate the student's level of skill and start testing at the most appropriate level. If the word list you picked is too difficult you can always move down to an easier list or if the list is very easy move up to a harder list.

Oral reading and comprehension is assessed in several ways. The sentence reading and text passages roughly correspond to the sight word reading lists. First, the student is asked to read a graded series of sentences to assess fluency. The next set of tasks includes reading narrative and expository passages to assess comprehension. The materials are designed to give students the opportunity to read orally and silently. Passages above students' reading ability are also included to assess students' listening comprehension. Comprehension is assessed with a retelling of the passage and probe questions.

Interactive Reading Assessment System–Revised Recording Sheet

Student _____ Teacher _____ Grade _____

Administrator _____ School _____ Date _____

Age _____ Gender (circle one):   Male   Female

First Language: English   Spanish   Other (specify): _____

	Raw Score	Grade Level
Alphabet Recognition: # named _____ # sounds known _____		
Word Recognition/Decoding: Last list passed		
Metalinguistic Question: Score		
Vocabulary: Last list passed		
Decoding Synthetic Words: Last list passed		
Word Building (Spelling) **Synthetic Words:** # built _____		
Sentence Reading: Last sentence passed		
Passage Reading: Fluency		
Passage Reading: Comprehension		

Notes:

_____

_____

_____

_____

_____

_____

_____

_____

_____

_____

_____

Directions: Tester points to a letter and says, "What is the name of this letter? What sound does it make?"

a	s	m	u	e	n
c	p	l	o	t	d

A	S	M	U	E	N
C	P	L	O	T	D

Decoding and Vocabulary

RESPONSE SHEET

Directions:

I. Word Recognition / Decoding

Show the first four lists to the student and ask which list is the most difficult one he/she can read. Begin with that list. Proceed through the lists until four or more errors are made on one list. If four errors are made on the first list attempted, have the student try the previous list. If the child reads the word correctly, make a check mark (✓). If the child reads the word incorrectly, write in the best phonetic equivalent of what she said. Continue in this fashion until three or fewer errors are made. Once you have established the word recognition level proceed to Step II, Metalinguistic Question.

II. Metalinguistic Question

Select the last word pronounced correctly. Ask the metalinguistic question:

> "You were right when you said _____ for this word. How did you know to pronounce (say) it that way?"

If the student is reluctant to answer, use probes such as: "Have you seen that word before?" "Did it remind you of another word?" "Do these letters or syllables help you? How?"

Scoring the metalinguistic questions: The metalinguistic question is scored on a 3-point scale. If the student is able to describe one clear strategy for pronouncing the word or two related strategies, she receives 3 points. ("I looked at the first letter, sounded it out, and then added the ending sound.") If the student is able to describe one strategy or partial strategy, she receives 2 points. ("It has a part or ending that I know.") If the student indicates only the vague use of a strategy, she receives 1 point. ("I sounded it out.") If the student cannot describe any strategy or part thereof, he receives no points. If you ask the question multiple times, average the raw scores.

III. Vocabulary

Beginning with the decoding list on which the student failed, tell the student the first underlined word and ask for the definition. If the student is unable to define the word, use the accompanying prompt and place a check on the prompt line. Ask the student, "Does *glad* mean sad, happy, or nervous?" Record the student's responses. Continue asking for the definitions of only the underlined words until the student is unable to define two underlined words on one list. If the student is unable to define the first word set attempted, go back through the lists until the student is able to define at least two words.

Stop rule: Stop the Decoding portion at four or more errors in one list.
Stop the Vocabulary portion at two or more errors in one list.

Word List	Decoding	Prompt	Definition/Alternatives
A. Grade Level: Early 1st			
<u>mud</u>	_____	_____	_____ a large bird/wet dirt/a book
pig	_____		
its	_____		
<u>glad</u>	_____	_____	_____ sad/nervous/happy
sent	_____		
<u>top</u>	_____	_____	_____ a high place/inside a box/bottom
B. Grade Level: Early 1st			
spent	_____		
<u>rub</u>	_____	_____	_____ to wash/to brush together/to bounce
<u>basket</u>	_____	_____	_____ something to hold things/to bounce/to drive
until	_____		
them	_____		
<u>fist</u>	_____	_____	_____ a kind of dance/a way to hold your hand/ a water animal

Metalinguistic question: Use only when you reach the last list in which the student made fewer than four errors.
Select the hardest word to pronounce correctly.

"You were right when you said _____ for this word. How did you know to pronounce (say) it that way?"

_____

_____

_____

Stop rule: Stop the Decoding portion at four or more errors in one list.
Stop the Vocabulary portion at two or more errors in one list.

Word List		Decoding	Prompt	Definition/Alternatives
C. Grade Level: Mid 1st				
<u>end</u>	v.	_____	_____	_____
				to stop/go slow/start
long		_____		
<u>little</u>	a.	_____	_____	_____
				something large/tall/small
time		_____		
<u>house</u>	n.	_____	_____	_____
				animal to ride/place to live/bus stop
same		_____		
D. Grade Level: Late 1st				
<u>food</u>	n.	_____	_____	_____
				something to eat/to wear/to play
city		_____		
<u>best</u>	a.	_____	_____	_____
				something as sweet as can be/as big as can be/as good as can be
paper		_____		
<u>tell</u>	v.	_____	_____	_____
				to cry/say/yell
room		_____		

Metalinguistic question: Use only when you reach the last list in which the student made fewer than four errors. Select the hardest word to pronounce correctly.

"You were right when you said _____ for this word. How did you know to pronounce (say) it that way?"

_____

_____

_____

Stop rule: Stop the Decoding portion at four or more errors in one list.
Stop the Vocabulary portion at two or more errors in one list.

Word List		Decoding	Prompt	Definition/Alternatives
E. Grade Level: Mid 2nd				
fast	a.	_____	_____	_____
				quick/loud/slow
black		_____		
feel	v.	_____	_____	_____
				to tease/taste/touch
table		_____		
birds	n.	_____	_____	_____
				thorns on a bush/animals with feathers/ animals with scales
cold		_____		
F. Grade Level: End 2nd				
music	n.	_____	_____	_____
				sound patterns/loud noises/twinkling lights
watch		_____		
explain	v.	_____	_____	_____
				to tell your name/count to ten/tell meaning
color		_____		
heat	v.	_____	_____	_____
				to burn/warm/go fast
machine		_____		

Metalinguistic question: Use only when you reach the last list in which the student made fewer than four errors. Select the hardest word to pronounce correctly.

"You were right when you said _____ for this word. How did you know to pronounce (say) it that way?"

_____

_____

_____

Stop rule: Stop the Decoding portion at four or more errors in one list.

Stop the Vocabulary portion at two or more errors in one list.

Word List		Decoding	Prompt	Definition/Alternatives
G. Grade Level: Mid 3rd				
<u>skin</u>	n.	_____	_____	outside of a balloon/outside of your body/ inside of a grape
race		_____		
<u>afraid</u>	a.	_____	_____	surprised/frightened/successful
please		_____		
<u>fight</u>	v.	_____	_____	to hit/break/fall
middle		_____		
H. Grade Level: End 3rd				
<u>hungry</u>	a.	_____	_____	in a hurry/going away/wanting food
finger		_____		
<u>visit</u>	v.	_____	_____	to go to see a friend/for a bus ride/to a show
electric		_____		
<u>crowd</u>	n.	_____	_____	kind of party/type of bird/lots of people
kitchen		_____		

Metalinguistic question: Use only when you reach the last list in which the student made fewer than four errors. Select the hardest word to pronounce correctly.

"You were right when you said _____ for this word. How did you know to pronounce (say) it that way?"

_____

_____

_____

Stop rule: Stop the Decoding portion at four or more errors in one list.
Stop the Vocabulary portion at two or more errors in one list.

Word List		Decoding	Prompt	Definition/Alternatives
I. Grade Level: Mid 4th				
<u>lonely</u>	a.	_____	_____	_____
				to want friends/feel sad/wait for dinner
development		_____		
<u>ability</u>	n.	_____	_____	_____
				a kind of test/skill/award
honor		_____		
<u>observe</u>	v.	_____	_____	_____
				to see through/look at/light up
industry		_____		
J. Grade Level: End 4th				
<u>committee</u>	n.	_____	_____	_____
				people who meet/have a party/build a house
atom		_____		
<u>delicate</u>	a.	_____	_____	_____
				breakable/soft/round
judge		_____		
<u>prevent</u>	v.	_____	_____	_____
				to stop/allow/pretend
mission		_____		

Metalinguistic question: Use only when you reach the last list in which the student made fewer than four errors. Select the hardest word to pronounce correctly.

"You were right when you said _____ for this word. How did you know to pronounce (say) it that way?"

_____

_____

_____

Stop rule: Stop the Decoding portion at four or more errors in one list.
Stop the Vocabulary portion at two or more errors in one list.

Word List		Decoding	Prompt	Definition/Alternatives
K. Grade Level: Mid 5th				
issue	v.	_____	_____	_____
				to order/give/refuse
muscle		_____		
annual	a.	_____	_____	_____
				lately/monthly/yearly
curiosity		_____		
literature	v.	_____	_____	_____
				kinds of writing/bag of trash/scratch paper
permanent		_____		
L. Grade Level: End 5th				
decade	n.	_____	_____	_____
				several days/ten years/two weeks
bomb		_____		
promptly	adv.	_____	_____	_____
				helpfully/in a hurry/right away
grease		_____		
demonstrate	v.	_____	_____	_____
				to experiment/demand/show
extensive		_____		

Metalinguistic question: Use only when you reach the last list in which the student made fewer than four errors. Select the hardest word to pronounce correctly.

"You were right when you said _____ for this word. How did you know to pronounce (say) it that way?"

_____

_____

_____

Stop rule: Stop the Decoding portion at four or more errors in one list.
Stop the Vocabulary portion at two or more errors in one list.

Word List		Decoding	Prompt	Definition/Alternatives
M. Grade Level: Mid 6th				
deserve	v.	_____	_____	_____
				to have a need/wish/right
retain		_____		
consequence	n.	_____	_____	_____
				outcome/failure/lie
graduation		_____		
ominous	a.	_____	_____	_____
				threatening/shocking/appealing
skyscraper		_____		
N. Grade Level: End 6th				
proclaim	v.	_____	_____	_____
				to shout/deny/announce
elegance		_____		
controversial	a.	_____	_____	_____
				agreeable/debatable/doubtful
astute		_____		
aroma	n.	_____	_____	_____
				pleasant smell/pretty sunset/spicy taste
implement		_____		

Metalinguistic question: Use only when you reach the last list in which the student made fewer than four errors. Select the hardest word to pronounce correctly.

"You were right when you said _____ for this word. How did you know to pronounce (say) it that way?"

_____

_____

_____

Stop rule: Stop the Decoding portion at four or more errors in one list.

Stop the Vocabulary portion at two or more errors in one list.

Word List		Decoding	Prompt	Definition/Alternatives
O. Grade Level: Mid 7th				
<u>pessimistic</u>	a.	_____	_____	_____
				gloomy/worried/happy
dormant		_____		
<u>boredom</u>	n.	_____	_____	_____
				drowsiness/activity/monotony
prudent		_____		
<u>illuminate</u>	v.	_____	_____	_____
				to burn/light up/destroy
frustration		_____		
P. Grade Level: End 7th				
<u>mandatory</u>	a.	_____	_____	_____
				required/permitted/released
flamboyant		_____		
<u>traverse</u>	v.	_____	_____	_____
				to pass over/move across/make calm
veritable		_____		
<u>anthology</u>	n.	_____	_____	_____
				collection of stories/study of man/humorous saying
tumultuous		_____		

Metalinguistic question: Use only when you reach the last list in which the student made fewer than four errors. Select the hardest word to pronounce correctly.

"You were right when you said _____ for this word. How did you know to pronounce (say) it that way?"

_____

_____

_____

DECODING SYNTHETIC WORDS

Directions: Stop at four or more errors in one list and ask the metalinguistic question at the bottom of the page. (Words in list 5 are read as blended words. Words in list 6 are read first as separate syllables and then blended.)

Word List 1

hin _____

nelp _____

flass _____

scrong _____

pame _____

vute _____

Word List 2

shile _____

throve _____

snay _____

toin _____

spawk _____

spleek _____

Word List 3

clur _____

derb _____

folp _____

sark _____

shald _____

plair _____

Word List 4

worch _____

knop _____

ceft _____

flage _____

wrudge _____

glies _____

Word List 5

lod - ded _____

fen - ing _____

wem - bick _____

lude - ful _____

un - fro - ten _____

im - pen - tive _____

af - fre-mi - a - tion _____

syn - thod _____

an - a - phen - ist _____

Word List 6

jemming _____

saped _____

rimple _____

befade _____

dacture _____

conspartable _____

rhosmic _____

paraplast _____

euchormonium _____

Metalinguistic question:

"You were right when you said _____ for this word. How did you know to pronounce (say) it that way?"

_____

_____

_____

Possible prompts: "Have you seen the word before?" "Did it remind you of another word?"

WORD BUILDING (SPELLING): SYNTHETIC WORDS

If available, lay out the appropriate letter tiles for student word-building activities. If letter tiles are not available, use pencil and paper.

"Now, I'm going to say some funny pretend words and I want you to say the word after me. Then I want you to build the word for me." If the student misspells the word, continue through the set of three until one word is spelled correctly. If none are spelled correctly, stop.

A. **1.** dut (but) _____

      2. mape (cape) _____

      3. leb (web) _____

B. **4.** feening (screening) _____

      5. sidded (bid) _____

      6. javes (caves) _____

C. **7.** broint (joint) _____

      8. glire (fire) _____

      9. grotious (ferocious) _____

D. **10.** frintle (mint) _____

     11. choober (goober) _____

     12. pridder (grid) _____

E. **13.** strandister (stand, sister) _____

     14. closterish (roster, wish) _____

     15. thrinkerlant (thinker, land) _____

Metalinguistic question:

"You were right when you spelled this word _____. How did you know to spell it that way?"

_____

_____

_____

Sentence Reading

Student _____ Teacher _____ School _____ Date _____

Score _____

Directions: Stop when the student fails to read a minimum of one **BOLD** word correctly or when student takes more than 20 seconds to read a set of sentences. Score 1 point for each completed sentence, ½ point for partial success (only one highlighted word read correctly).

A. I **LIKE** to **PLAY.**
I like to eat a **RED** apple.

B. Ann wants Mom to **MAKE** a **CAKE.** Mom cannot do it. She has to go to **WORK.**

C. The man made the light **SHINE.** Right away Ed saw the baby **FOX** on top of its **CAGE.**

D. The kitten was **SCARED** and climbed up the tree. The girl tried to **REACH** it but she had no **LUCK.**

E. Jeff was **AFRAID** that he would miss the first act. As soon as he bought the **POPCORN,** he **HURRIED** to find Rose.

F. About three miles from the **HARBOR,** Ray's boat was **CAUGHT** in an unexpected current. He spotted a tiny **ISLAND** and realized that he was approaching its shore.

G. Harriet made many heroic **ATTEMPTS** to lead other slaves to freedom in the North. Her courage and **DETERMINATION** made her an **IMPORTANT** figure in the nation's history.

H. Slowly the women **ASCENDED** the steep and icy **MOUNTAIN.** There were times when the sheer cliffs and the bitter cold **DISCOURAGED** them, but they would not relent.

After studying the IRAS-R Passage Reading format, teachers are encouraged to create similar grade-level passages with retelling and probe recording sheets from passages in the level book sets typically found in today's classrooms.

First, the student enters the passage reading subtest at the starting point indicated by his Sentence Reading performance. If the student reads the sentence set at Level C with adequate speed and accuracy, but cannot meet these criteria for set D, then he should begin with Oral Reading Comprehension, Narrative C1.

The student begins with either the oral or silent reading task, depending on her entering level. If she cannot read sentence set A, or if she failed word list A, then she should go immediately to Listening Comprehension, Narrative A2.

At each passage level, the student is tested on the narrative passage first, then the expository passage at the same level. Most students will find the narrative structure easier to comprehend than the expository structure.

STOP RULES

For oral reading, the task is ended when the student exceeds 100 seconds to read a passage. Time is the only criterion; comprehension is *not* taken into account.

For silent reading and listening:

1. The student has succeeded at the retelling task if he passes half or more of the designated items.
2. The student has passed an element if he at least mentions it briefly.

The guiding principle in this task, as elsewhere in IRAS-R, is to give the student the benefit of the doubt and move on to a more difficult task whenever possible.

SCORING COMPREHENSION

When the student has finished reading the passage or after you have finished reading the passage to the student, say to him, "Please tell the story to me as if I had never heard it before." On the recording sheet, make a check mark for each idea that the student recalls. Listen for those words and phrases; an approximation of the phrases should be considered correct. After the student has finished retelling ask the probe questions for any idea not recalled. Do not consider it an error if the retelling is somewhat out of order when comparing it to the actual text. Record the information that the student includes in the retelling on the right side of the recording sheet.

Total the number of ideas recalled and divide that total by the number of ideas in the passage. This will produce the percent of recalled ideas in the passage. There will be a different number of ideas in each passage. In some of the passages, the parts of the story are labeled (Setting, Goal, Attempt) and these carry subscripts. The numbers refer to the number or sequence of events in the story, but have little bearing on the scoring. However, do note if students tend to remember the first or last thing that they read.

Record times for reading only.

ORAL READING COMPREHENSION/NAR A1

TIME START

_____

		Response Retell	Probe	Probe Questions
1. Setting Goal$_1$ Attempt$_1$	It is a sunny day. ANN is on her bike. TOM WANTS to PLAY BALL. He ASKS ANN to PLAY with him.	_____	_____	What did Tom want Ann to do?
2. Outcome$_1$ Initiating event$_2$ Reaction$_2$	She will NOT PLAY ball now. She WANTS to RIDE. TOM is SAD.	_____	_____	What did Ann want to do (when Tom asked her to play)?
3. Attempt$_2$	He ASKS Ann, "Can we take a RIDE and THEN PLAY BALL?"	_____	_____	What did Tom say to Ann (when she didn't want to play ball)?
4. Outcome$_2$ Resolution	"YES," SAYS ANN. "That will be fun." So TOM GETS his BIKE and THEY PLAY.	_____	_____	How did the story end?

TIME STOP

_____

		Response Retell	Probe	Probe Questions
1. Setting	JILL HAS a TREE HOUSE.			
Goal$_1$	She WANTS to PAINT IT green.			
Attempt$_1$	She ASKS SAM to HELP.	_____	_____	What did Jill want Sam to do?
2. Outcome$_1$	SAM CANNOT help.			
Initiating event$_2$	He is GOING OUT with Pat.			What was Sam going to do (when
Reaction$_2$	JILL is SAD.	_____	_____	Jill asked him to help)?
3. Attempt$_2$	She ASKS DAD, "CAN YOU come out and HELP me?"	_____	_____	What did Jill ask Dad?
4. Outcome$_2$	"YES," SAYS DAD. "I will help you paint the tree house."			
Resolution	So JILL goes to GET the green PAINT.	_____	_____	How did the story end?

		Response Retell	Probe	Probe Questions
1. Setting	PAM LIVED in a house BY a HILL.			
Initiating event₁	One morning she TOOK her brown BALL to the TOP of the HILL. The GRASS was WET and Pam FELL. The BALL ROLLED DOWN the HILL.			How did the story begin? (What happened when Pam took her ball to the top of the hill?)
Reaction	PAM began to CRY.	_____	_____	
2. Attempt₁	She RAN AFTER IT,	_____	_____	What did Pam do when the ball began to roll?
3. Outcome₁	but she COULD NOT STOP it. She SAW it FALL into a POND.	_____	_____	Where did the ball land?
4. Initiating event₂	Then a BOY WALKED by the POND. He SAW SOMETHING in the WATER.			What happened after the ball fell in pond? (What did Pam ask the boy to do?)
Attempt₂	PAM SAID, "TRY to GET my BALL."	_____	_____	
5. Outcome₂	The BOY JUMPED into the cold WATER. He GOT Pam's BALL.	_____	_____	What did the boy do?
6. Resolution	PAM THANKED him and then WALKED up the hill and PLAYED.	_____	_____	How did the story end?

		Response Retell	Probe	Probe Questions
1.	You should see ANN'S DOG. His name is Ed. He is BIGGER THAN ANN. She thinks he is getting bigger and BIGGER ALL THE TIME.	_____	_____	How big is Ann's dog?
2.	His COAT is RED, but the HAIR on his HEAD is dark BROWN.	_____	_____	What is odd about Ed's hair? (What color is his coat? / his head?)
3.	He has LONG THIN LEGS and BIG FAT FEET. He has a BIG NOSE, too.	_____	_____	What do Ed's legs, feet, and nose look like?
4.	Ann thinks HE is funny. He can RUN like a RABBIT, but he EATS like a PIG.	_____	_____	Why does Ann think Ed is funny? (How does he run?) (How does he eat?)

| | | Response | | |
		Retell	Probe	Probe Questions
1. Setting	ED WORKS AT the ZOO in town.			
Initiating event₁	One night he TOOK some FOOD TO the baby FOX. He went TO its CAGE, but the FOX was NOT THERE.			How did the story begin? (What happened when Ed took food to
Reaction	ED was SURPRISED.	_____	_____	the baby fox?)
2. Attempt₁	He LOOKED AROUND, but he DID NOT SEE it.	_____	_____	What did Ed do when he found that the fox was missing?
3. Outcome₁	The FOX HID in the DARK.	_____	_____	Why did Ed not see the fox?
4. Initiating event₂	Then a MAN WALKED by. He HAD a LIGHT.			
Attempt₂	ED SAID, "SHINE the LIGHT on the CAGE." The MAN made the LIGHT SHINE.	_____	_____	What happened after the fox hid in the dark? (What did Ed ask the man to do?)
5. Outcome₂	Right away Ed SAW the baby FOX on TOP of its CAGE.	_____	_____	Where did they find the fox?
6. Resolution	So he PUT it BACK IN the CAGE and GAVE it some FOOD.	_____	_____	How did the story end?

		Response Retell	Probe	Probe Questions
1.	BILL was DRESSED for WINTER. He had on a ROUND, FUR HAT. It was PULLED down OVER his EARS.	_____	_____	What was Bill's hat like?
2.	His long COAT was BUTTONED up TO his CHIN.	_____	_____	How was his coat buttoned?
3.	The BUTTONS were BIG and RED. They made him look LIKE a CLOWN.	_____	_____	What did his buttons look like?
4.	Yes, Bill was DRESSED FOR the COLD. He had on his fur hat and his long coat. BUT his SHOES were all WET. I laughed when he HOPPED up and down to KEEP his FEET WARM.	_____	_____	Why did Bill have to hop up and down?

		Response Retell	Probe	Probe Questions
1. Setting	Once there was an old MAN who LIVED BY a RIVER. It was WINTER and the RIVER was COVERED with ICE.			
Initiating event₁	One day he looked out his window and SAW a BOY by the river. The boy started to WALK ACROSS the river on the ICE.			
Reaction	The old MAN was AFRAID that the ICE would BREAK.	_____	_____	What were the man and the boy doing at the beginning of story?
2. Attempt₁	He opened the window and CALLED out to the boy.			What happened when the old man saw the boy walk on the ice? (What did the man do? What did the boy do?)
Outcome₁	But the BOY DIDN'T HEAR him, and he just KEPT on GOING.	_____	_____	
3. Initiating event₂	When he got to the middle, the ICE BROKE, and the BOY FELL into the WATER.	_____	_____	What happened when the boy got to the middle of the river?
4. Attempt₂	The old MAN GOT a long LADDER and ran down to the river. He SLID the ladder ACROSS the ICE.	_____	_____	What did the man do when the boy fell in?
5. Outcome₂	The BOY GRABBED the LADDER and the MAN PULLED him OUT.	_____	_____	How was the boy saved?
6. Resolution	The next day the BOY visited the old man and THANKED him for saving his life.	_____	_____	How did the story end?

TIME START

_____

		Response Retell	Probe	Probe Questions
1.	It is easy to MAKE BUTTER. First you NEED a JAR and some heavy CREAM.	_____	_____	What do you need to make butter?
2.	FILL the JAR PART way with CREAM. Then SHAKE it for about <u>20</u> MINUTES.	_____	_____	What is the first thing you do?
3.	SOON the CREAM will start to get LUMPY. STOP WHEN most of the cream turns into LUMPS. You will find that the LUMPS are BUTTER.	_____	_____	When should you stop shaking the cream?
4.	Take the lumps out of the jar and WASH them with COLD WATER.	_____	_____	What do you do with the lumps in the jar?
5.	Mix a little SALT with the lumps of butter and PAT them TOGETHER. Leave the butter in a COOL PLACE over night.	_____	_____	After you wash the butter, what do you do?
6.	In the morning the BUTTER will be HARD and READY to EAT.	_____	_____	How do you know when the butter is ready to eat?

TIME STOP

_____

		Response Retell	Probe	Probe Questions
1. Setting	Once there was a little GIRL who HAD a KITTEN. The KITTEN liked to PLAY in the YARD by a tall tree.			
Initiating event$_1$	Early one morning a dog was walking in front of the house. It was windy and the gate blew open. The DOG RAN INTO the YARD. The KITTEN was SCARED and RAN UP the TREE.	_____	_____	What happened at the beginning of the story?
2. Attempt$_1$	The GIRL TRIED to REACH it, but she had NO LUCK.			What happened when the kitten ran up the tree? (What happened
Outcome$_1$	The KITTEN CLIMBED to the HIGHEST BRANCH.	_____	_____	when the girl tried to reach the kitten?)
3. Initiating event$_2$	The girl's SISTER SAW the kitten FROM her WINDOW.	_____	_____	What did the girl's sister see?
4. Attempt$_2$	She OPENED the window and LEANED OUT. She COULD REACH the BRANCH. "COME INSIDE," she SAID softly.	_____	_____	How did the sister try to save the kitten?
5. Outcome$_2$	She REACHED out when the KITTEN came closer. The she PULLED it INTO the HOUSE.	_____	_____	What happened when the kitten came near the window?
6. Resolution	That night the little GIRL TOLD everyone WHAT HAD HAPPENED. She was GLAD that her SISTER had SAVED the KITTEN.	_____	_____	How did the story end?

		Response Retell	Probe	Probe Questions
1.	One way to MAKE MONEY in the summer is to SELL LEMONADE.	_____	_____	How can you make money in the summer?
2.	It is easy to make. You NEED LEMONS, WATER, SUGAR, and ICE.	_____	_____	What do you need to make lemonade?
3.	PUT the JUICE from TEN LEMONS into TEN CUPS of WATER. ADD TWO CUPS of SUGAR and lots of ICE. Then stir it.	_____	_____	How do you make lemonade?
4.	When you have the lemonade, GET some PAPER CUPS and enough MONEY to make CHANGE. Also get a SMALL TABLE to put things on.	_____	_____	What things do you need to get in addition to lemonade?
5.	The FIND a SPOT to set up. The CORNER of a STREET is GOOD.	_____	_____	Where is a good spot to set up your table?
6.	When it GETS HOT, PEOPLE will stop to BUY a DRINK.	_____	_____	When will people stop to buy a drink?

TIME START _____

		Response Retell	Probe	Probe Questions
1. Setting₁	JOE and his daughter SUE were FISHING at the LAKE.			
Initiating event₁	They were THERE for an HOUR and had NOT CAUGHT any FISH.			
Goal₁ Attempt₁	JOE WANTED to find a BETTER SPOT so he started to WALK AROUND the LAKE.	_____	_____	How did the story begin? (Why did Joe want to find another spot to fish?) (What did he do then?)
2. Outcome₂ Initiating event₂	He PASSED a few FISHERMEN NEAR the DOCK. They TOLD HIM that they were CATCHING LOTS of FISH.			What happened when Joe started to walk around the lake? (What did the fishermen tell him?)
Reaction₂	JOE was EXCITED to hear the news,	_____	_____	
3. Attempt₂	and he STARTED BACK to GET his DAUGHTER.			
Setting₂	Meanwhile, SUE was FISHING by HERSELF.	_____	_____	What did Joe do after he talked to the fishermen?
4. Initiating event₃	She GOT TIRED and FELL ASLEEP with the pole in her hand.	_____	_____	What happened when Sue was fishing by herself?
5. Development₃	She slept until she FELT a strong TUG on her line.			
Reaction₃	She was STARTLED to find that the fishing ROD was being PULLED INTO the WATER.	_____	_____	What woke Sue up?
6. Attempt₃	Sue RUSHED INTO the LAKE just as her FATHER RETURNED.	_____	_____	What did Sue do as her father returned?
7. Outcome₃	Then she GRABBED the fishing POLE and PULLED it OUT of the water.	_____	_____	What did Sue do (when she ran into the lake)?
8. Resolution	BOTH Joe and Sue were AMAZED to discover an enormous FISH hooked ON the LINE.	_____	_____	How did the story end?

TIME STOP _____

TIME START _____

		Response Retell	Probe	Probe Questions
1.	There is a big, old TREE in the yard outside my window. It is STRAIGHT and TALL and looks LIKE a CONE.	_____	_____	What shape is the tree?
2.	The BRANCHES at the BOTTOM are WIDE and FULL.	_____	_____	What are the bottom branches like?
3.	The tree GOES way ABOVE the ROOF of my house.	_____	_____	How high does the tree go?
4.	At the TOP it is NARROW and comes to a POINT.	_____	_____	What is the tree like at the top?
5.	The green LEAVES that cover its branches are NOT REALLY LEAVES at all. They are SHARP and POINTED and make me think of NEEDLES.	_____	_____	What are the leaves like?
6.	The tree in my yard is ALWAYS GREEN. In winter the other trees lose their leaves. But even when snow falls and it is cold, I can look at my tree and think of spring.	_____	_____	What is the tree like in winter?

TIME STOP _____

		Response Retell	Probe	Probe Questions
1. Setting$_1$	KATE and her cousin, JEFF, WENT to the CIRCUS. They arrived a half-hour before the afternoon show.			
Goal$_1$	KATE WANTED to find GOOD SEATS.			
Attempt$_1$	She WALKED inside			
Outcome$_1$	and SAW two empty SEATS in the FIRST ROW,	_____	_____	What did Kate do at the beginning?
2. Initiating event$_2$	but a LADY TOLD her that the SEATS were TAKEN.			
Reaction$_2$	KATE was UNHAPPY because the front rows were already filled.	_____	_____	What happened when she tried to find good seats?
3. Attempt$_2$	She WALKED TO the BACK to FIND two SEATS.			What did Kate do when the lady told her that the seats were taken?
Setting$_2$	Meanwhile, JEFF was WAITING in line AT the CANDY STAND.	_____	_____	
4. Initiating event$_3$	He WANTED to get some POPCORN before the show began.	_____	_____	Why was Jeff waiting in line at the candy stand?
5. Development$_3$	Suddenly he HEARD the BAND begin to PLAY.			
Goal$_3$	He wanted to find Kate.			
Reaction$_3$	He WAS AFRAID that he would MISS the FIRST ACT.	_____	_____	What happened while Jeff was waiting in line?
6. Attempt$_3$	As soon as he BOUGHT the POPCORN, he HURRIED to find Kate.	_____	_____	What did Jeff do when he heard the band begin to play?
7. Outcome$_3$	ON the WAY to his seat, he TRIPPED and SPILLED the POPCORN.	_____	_____	What happened to Jeff on the way to his seat?
8. Resolution	Finally, he FOUND his COUSIN IN the BACK ROW and THEY began to WATCH the SHOW. They DIDN'T HAVE GOOD SEATS and they didn't have any POPCORN, but they ENJOYED the CIRCUS anyway.	_____	_____	How did the story end?

		Response Retell	Probe	Probe Questions
1.	Not far from where I live there is an old CASTLE. It is NOT very BIG. It is made of GRAY STONES and has a TOWER on one SIDE of the MAIN BUILDING.	_____	_____	What does the castle look like?
2.	The TOWER is ROUND and about <u>30</u> FEET TALL.	_____	_____	What does the tower look like?
3.	There is a LONG NARROW WINDOW near the TOP. The GLASS in the window has been BROKEN for many years.	_____	_____	What does the window in the tower look like?
4.	There is a CELLAR HOLE on the OTHER SIDE of the castle.	_____	_____	What is on the other side of the castle?
5.	It is FILLED with ROCKS and WEEDS. Some WOOD also remains FROM the BARN that used to be there.	_____	_____	What is in the cellar hole?
6.	It is EASY to TELL that NO ONE has LIVED there for a long time. Even the ROAD is GROWN OVER with GRASS.	_____	_____	How can you tell that no one has lived there for a long time?

		Response		
		Retell	Probe	Probe Questions
1. Setting	The moon had just risen as JAN looked toward the old deserted house.			
Goal₁	She was WAITING for her FRIEND Ellen. Together they PLANNED to FIND out IF the HOUSE was HAUNTED.	_____	_____	How did the story begin? (Why were Jan and Ellen meeting by the old house?)
2. Initiating event₁	When ELLEN ARRIVED the two friends began to WALK nervously UP the PATH. A strange SHADOW seemed to FALL ACROSS the WINDOW next to the porch.			What did the girls do right after Ellen arrived? (What happened as they walked up the path?)
Reaction₁	Both GIRLS were SCARED, but they pretended not to notice.	_____	_____	
3. Attempt₁	Then as ELLEN HELD the FLASHLIGHT, JAN anxiously pushed OPEN the DOOR.			
Outcome₁ Initiating event₂	Once INSIDE the house they were STARTLED to HEAR a peculiar SCRATCHING SOUND.	_____	_____	What did the girls hear when they entered the house?
4. Attempt₂	ELLEN FLASHED her LIGHT all around,	_____	_____	What did Ellen do when she heard the scratching sound?
5. Outcome₂	but she could NOT FIND where the SOUND was coming from.	_____	_____	Did she find where the sound was coming from?
6. Initiating event₃	But it seemed to be COMING TOWARD THEM. Suddenly JAN felt SOMETHING RUB against her LEG.			
Reaction₃	She TRIED to SCREAM but was too SCARED to make a sound.	_____	_____	What happened to Jan?
7. Attempt₃	She GRABBED ELLEN'S ARM and stared at her in shock. ELLEN FLASHED the LIGHT her way, and then	_____	_____	What did Ellen do when Jan grabbed her arm?
8. Outcome₃	they both REALIZED WHAT was HAUNTING the HOUSE.			
Resolution	It was just an old BLACK CAT who had made the house its home.	_____	_____	What did the girls discover in the end?

		Response		
		Retell	Probe	Probe Questions
1.	An AMUSEMENT PARK is OPENING in town next Saturday.	_____	_____	What is happening on Saturday?
2.	There will be a PARADE, FIREWORKS, and FREE ADMISSION on opening day. More than FIVE THOUSAND PEOPLE are EXPECTED to attend.	_____	_____	What will opening day be like?
3.	WORK first began on the park TWO YEARS ago. At that time the SITE WAS an UNUSED FIELD. It was FILLED with WEEDS and TRASH. Although occasional ATTEMPTS had been made to CLEAN it up, NOTHING had WORKED.	_____	_____	What did the site of the park used to look like?
4.	SINCE then more than FIFTY RIDES, a PLAYHOUSE, and a PICNIC GROUND have been built. Many TREES and BUSHES also have been PLANTED.	_____	_____	What is the park like now?
5.	After opening day, ADMISSION to the park will cost THREE DOLLARS. However, CHILDREN UNDER TWELVE will be let in FREE IF they come WITH an ADULT.	_____	_____	What about admission to the park?
6.	All RIDES will cost FIFTY CENTS, except the ROLLER COASTER, which will cost a DOLLAR.	_____	_____	How much will rides cost?

		Response Retell	Probe	Probe Questions
1. Setting	It was LATE AFTERNOON.			
Initiating event₁	ALICE STOOD by the OPEN BARN DOOR. She had LATCHED the door this MORNING, but NOW it was OPEN and her HORSE, Sam, was MISSING.			
Reaction₁	Alice FEARED that SAM would NOT RETURN before nightfall.	_____	_____	How did the story begin? (Why was it odd that the door was open?)
2. Attempt₁	So she DECIDED to go LOOK for him.	_____	_____	What did Alice do when she found that Sam was missing?
3. Outcome₁	A short way from the barn she SPOTTED Sam GRAZING in a PASTURE, but he was not alone.			
Initiating event₂	ANOTHER HORSE from a neighbor's farm was alongside him.			
Reaction₂	ALICE was SURPRISED to see the other horse.	_____	_____	What did Alice see in the pasture?
4. Attempt₂	She GOT two ROPES and WENT into the pasture AFTER the HORSES.	_____	_____	How did Alice try to catch the horses?
5. Outcome₂	When she finally caught both of them, Alice PUT SAM back IN the BARN.	_____	_____	When she caught him, what did Alice do with Sam?
6. Initiating event₃	Then she TRIED to TIE the OTHER horse TO a nearby POST, BUT he BROKE LOOSE from her grasp.			
Reaction₃	ALICE was beginning to get ANGRY.	_____	_____	What happened after Alice got Sam back in the barn?
7. Attempt₃	She TRIED to CATCH the HORSE again, but before she could reach him, he RAN to the BARN and LIFTED the LATCH WITH his NOSE.	_____	_____	What happened when Alice tried to catch the other horse? (What did the other horse do after he broke away?)
8. Outcome₃ Resolution	Suddenly Alice REALIZED why the DOOR had been OPEN. The neighbor's HORSE had LET SAM OUT.	_____	_____	Why was the barn door open all this time?

		Response Retell	Probe	Probe Questions
1.	A GROUP of students is PLANNING to start a NATURE CLUB.	_____	_____	What are some students planning to do?
2.	Anyone INTERESTED in WILD ANIMALS, BIRDS, PLANTS, or WILDERNESS HIKING is INVITED to join. NO membership FEE will be charged.	_____	_____	What is told about joining the club?
3.	The CLUB is being FORMED in order to COMBINE the INTERESTS of several SMALLER GROUPS.	_____	_____	Why is the club being formed?
4.	In the past, these GROUPS have NOT had ENOUGH MEMBERS to BECOME official SCHOOL CLUBS. At least TWENTY members are NEEDED to MEET school REQUIREMENTS.	_____	_____	What problems have some groups had in forming clubs?
5.	There are several BENEFITS to having an OFFICIAL CLUB. The SCHOOL PROVIDES an adult ADVISOR, MONEY for activities, and HELP in PLANNING FIELD TRIPS. It provides OFFICE space and ALLOWS the club to hold MEETINGS DURING SCHOOL hours.	_____	_____	What are the benefits of having an official club?
6.	Without these BENEFITS it is DIFFICULT for groups to FUNCTION.	_____	_____	Why are the benefits important?

		Response Retell	Probe	Probe Questions
1. Setting	It was the year <u>1849</u> in the small town of BUCKSTOWN, MARYLAND.			
Goal$_1$	A young black SLAVE, named Harriet Tubman, DECIDED to ESCAPE from the SOUTH and SEEK her FREEDOM. Harriet AWAITED a CHANCE to begin the trip NORTHWARD.	_____	_____	What did Harriet want to do at the beginning?
2. Initiating event$_1$	One evening a farmer VOLUNTEERED to HIDE Harriet in his CART underneath a LOAD of VEGETABLES.			
Reaction	Harriet was TERRIFIED that she would be CAUGHT trying to escape, but she was DETERMINED to take the RISK.	_____	_____	How did the farmer help Harriet?
3. Attempt$_1$	Harriet TRAVELED on a ROUTE known as the UNDERGROUND RAILROAD.	_____	_____	What route did Harriet travel?
4. Elaboration (definition)	The underground was not a real railroad, but an ORGANIZATION of people who PROVIDED rides and hiding places for slaves ESCAPING from PLANTATIONS in the South.	_____	_____	What was the underground railroad?
5. Outcome$_1$	Harriet spent several exhausting NIGHTS traveling. Finally she ARRIVED at the PENNSYLVANIA border. She was a FREE citizen for the first time in her life.	_____	_____	Tell about Harriet's trip. (How did it end?)
6. Resolution	AFTERWARD, Harriet made many HEROIC ATTEMPTS to LEAD other SLAVES to FREEDOM in the North. Because of her COURAGE and DETERMINATION she is an important FIGURE in the NATION'S HISTORY.	_____	_____	Why is Harriet an important figure in the nation's history?

		Response Retell	Probe	Probe Questions
1.	You can still FIND GOLD in some California streams. All you NEED is a METAL PAN and a lot of LUCK.	_____	_____	What do you need to pan for gold?
2.	First SELECT a place where the CURRENT is SLOW. GOLD is CARRIED BY moving WATER, but DROPS to the stream bed WHERE the WATER is STILL.	_____	_____	What is the first thing you should do? (Why is it best to pan where the water is still?)
3.	Next SCOOP some GRAVEL from the stream INTO your PAN and gently WASH OUT any DIRT.	_____	_____	What is the first thing you do with your scoop of gravel?
4.	Then PUT a little WATER in the PAN and ROCK it in a circle so that the larger bits of GRAVEL will SPILL OUT.	_____	_____	What do you do when the dirt is washed out?
5.	Soon there should be only a HANDFUL of SAND LEFT. LOOK for SHINY YELLOW PARTICLES.	_____	_____	What is left when the gravel spills out of the pan?
6.	You can DETERMINE if these are GOLD by HITTING them WITH a HAMMER. Real GOLD will FLATTEN BECAUSE it is SOFT.	_____	_____	How can you tell if the shiny particles are gold?

		Response		
		Retell	Probe	Probe Questions
1. Setting	It was WINTER in the town of KITTY HAWK, NORTH CAROLINA.			
Goal	This was the day WILBUR and ORVILLE WRIGHT PLANNED an attempt to BECOME the FIRST men to FLY in an ENGINE-POWERED AIRPLANE.	_____	_____	What did Wilbur and Orville plan to do?
2. Initiating event	When the two men AROSE at DAWN, the WIND was BRISK and a THREAT of RAIN lingered in the air.	_____	_____	What was the weather like the day of the flight?
3. Elaboration (definition)	The DECISION they had to make was DIFFICULT. It might be DANGEROUS to fly in high WINDS, especially IF they ENCOUNTERED a SUDDEN GUST. But if the WIND held steady, it COULD actually HELP them in TAKING OFF.			
Reaction	WILBUR and ORVILLE were NERVOUS as they made the historic decision.	_____	_____	Why was their decision difficult?
4. Attempt	At about NOON, they STARTED the ENGINE. Suspense mounted as the AIRPLANE MOVED forward and gradually LIFTED into the air.	_____	_____	What happened at about noon that day?
5. Outcome	The machine FLEW for a brief TWELVE SECONDS before COMING to a HALT on the ground.	_____	_____	How did the flight turn out? How long did they fly?
6. Resolution	Wilbur and Orville were TRIUMPHANT. They had accomplished their goal. Their achievement that day marked the BEGINNING of man's VENTURE INTO the SKY.	_____	_____	Why was their achievement important?

502

		Response Retell	Probe	Probe Questions
1.	A CATERPILLAR makes a sleeping bag called a COCOON. It USES a kind of STICKY THREAD that comes from its mouth.	_____	_____	What is the cocoon made of?
2.	First the caterpillar GRABS a TWIG with its BACK FEET. This leaves the front part of its body free to move.	_____	_____	What is the first thing the caterpillar does? (How does it grab the twig?)
3.	Then it begins to BEND and TURN and SPIN the THREAD around itself and the twig like a net. But it leaves room inside the net to move around.	_____	_____	What does the caterpillar do after it grabs the twig?
4.	When the net is made, the caterpillar MOVES its HEAD back and forth to PUT in a FLOOR.	_____	_____	What happens after the net is made?
5.	Then it FILLS in all the SPACES in the net and finally CLOSES it all up.	_____	_____	What does it do after it puts in the floor?
6.	After that, the caterpillar goes to SLEEP. When it WAKES up in a few months, it will be a MOTH.	_____	_____	What happens after the net is finally closed?

		Response Retell	Probe	Probe Questions
1. Setting	Hundreds of RACERS were SET at the starting line.			
Elaboration	The most POPULAR BICYCLE RACE in the world was about to begin. It is called the TOUR DE FRANCE.	_____	_____	What is the Tour de France?
2. Initiating event	As the starting gun sounded, the RACERS SET OUT on a GRUELING and DANGEROUS COURSE. For 24 DAYS they would race over 2,500 MILES	_____	_____	Describe the course. How long is the race?
3. Elaboration	of French countryside, through BUSY CITY STREETS and over RUGGED mountain ROADS.			
Reaction$_2$	For the first few miles RACERS were TENSE but EXCITED.	_____	_____	Where does the course go?
4. Elaboration	The CROWDS that lined every small town and village along the route CHEERED encouragement.	_____	_____	What were the first few miles like?
5. Attempt	Several days into the race a FEW cyclists had BROKEN away from the PACK. Each in turn CHALLENGED for the LEAD as they headed UP a steep MOUNTAIN pass.	_____	_____	What happened several days into the race? Who challenged for the lead?
6. Elaboration	DETERMINATION, SKILL, and LUCK became critical FACTORS.	_____	_____	What were the critical factors in getting the lead?
7. Outcome	SOME QUIT when they became too TIRED to keep pedaling up the mountain. OTHERS lost control on the way down the other side, SKIDDING OFF the ROAD and slamming into rocky ditches at speeds approaching 60 miles an hour. SEVERAL DROPPED OUT when their EQUIPMENT FAILED.	_____	_____	What events knocked some of the leaders out of the race?
8. Resolution	In the end THREE racers headed out, seemingly ALONE, across the level plains TOWARD a still distant FINISH line. Only ONE would WIN the MONEY and FAME that goes to the champion.	_____	_____	How did the story end?

		Response		
		Retell	Probe	Probe Questions
1.	The SEAHORSE is an ODD kind of FISH. It is THREE INCHES tall and looks LIKE a MATCHSTICK frame COVERED with fine CLOTH.	_____	_____	What does the seahorse look like? Describe its body.
2.	Its SKIN is BROWN, it has a SNOUT like a TUBE, and has long HAIRS on its HEAD.	_____	_____	Describe its head.
3.	If you watched a seahorse you might notice that it SWIMS UPRIGHT but spends most of the time with its TAIL HOOKED around SEAPLANTS.	_____	_____	How does a seahorse swim? How does it spend its time?
4.	Since these PLANTS are also BROWN, the SEAHORSE is often DIFFICULT to FIND.	_____	_____	Why is a seahorse hard to find?
5.	When it is hungry the seahorse EATS small WORMS and SHELLFISH, which it SUCKS OFF PLANTS with its long SNOUT.	_____	_____	What does a seahorse eat? How does it get its food?
6.	When it is time to reproduce, the FEMALE LAYS EGGS LIKE all other FISH.	_____	_____	When it is time to reproduce, what does the female do?
7.	But it is the MALE that TAKES CARE of them. He BABYSITS the eggs by KEEPING them in a POUCH UNTIL they HATCH.	_____	_____	What does the male do? How?
8.	Thus, although the SEAHORSE is a FISH, the way it LOOKS, SWIMS, and HATCHES its EGGS makes it a very UNUSUAL fish, indeed!	_____	_____	What makes the seahorse an unusual fish?

a   s   m   u   e   n

c   p   l   o   t   d

A   S   M   U   E   N

C   P   L   O   T   D

A

mud
pig
its
glad
sent
top

B

spent
rub
basket
until
them
fist

C

end
long
little
time
house
same

D

food
city
best
paper
tell
room

E

fast
black
feel
table
birds
cold

F

music
watch
explain
color
heat
machine

G

skin
race
afraid
please
fight
middle

H

hungry
finger
visit
electric
crowd
kitchen

I

lonely
development
ability
honor
observe
industry

J

committee
atom
delicate
judge
prevent
mission

K

issue
muscle
annual
curiosity
literature
permanent

L

decade
bomb
promptly
grease
demonstrate
extensive

M

deserve
retain
consequence
graduation
ominous
skyscraper

N

proclaim
elegance
controversial
astute
aroma
implement

O

pessimistic
dormant
boredom
prudent
illuminate
frustration

P

mandatory
flamboyant
traverse
veritable
anthology
tumultuous

List 1

hin
nelp
flass
scrong
pame
vute

List 2

shile
throve
snay
toin
spawk
spleek

List 3

clur
derb
folp
sark
shald
plair

List 4

worch
knop
ceft
flage
wrudge
glies

List 5

lod - ded
fen - ing
wem - bick
lude - ful
un - fro - ten
im - pen - tive
af - fre - mi - a - tion
syn - thod
an - a - phen - ist

List 6

jemming
saped
rimple
befade
dacture
conspartable
rhosmic
paraplast
euchormonium

A.   I like to play.

      I like to eat a red apple.

B.   Ann wants Mom to make a cake. Mom cannot do it.
      She has to go to work.

C.   The man made the light shine. Right away Ed saw the baby
      fox on top of its cage.

D.   The kitten was scared and climbed up the tree. The girl tried
      to reach it but she had no luck.

E.   Jeff was afraid that he would miss the first act. As soon
      as he bought the popcorn, he hurried to find Rose.

F.   About three miles from the harbor, Ray's boat was caught in
      an unexpected current. He spotted a tiny island and realized
      that he was approaching its shore.

G.   Harriet made many heroic attempts to lead other slaves to
      freedom in the North. Her courage and determination made
      her an important figure in the nation's history.

H.   Slowly the women ascended the steep and icy mountain.
      There were times when the sheer cliffs and the bitter cold
      discouraged them, but they would not relent.

It is a sunny day. Ann is on her bike.

Tom wants to play ball. He asks Ann to play with him. She will not play ball now. She wants to ride.

Tom is sad. He asks Ann, "Can we take a ride and then play ball?"

"Yes," says Ann. "That will be fun."

So Tom gets his bike and they play.

LISTENING COMPREHENSION/NAR A2

Jill has a tree house. She wants to paint it green.

She asks Sam to help.

Sam cannot help. He is going out with Pat.

Jill is sad. She asks Dad, "Can you come out and help me?"

"Yes," says Dad. "I will help you paint the tree house."

So Jill goes to get the green paint.

Pam lived in a house by a hill.

One morning she took her brown ball to the top of the hill.

The grass was wet and Pam fell. The ball rolled down the hill.

Pam began to cry. She ran after it, but she could not stop it.

She saw it fall into a pond.

Then a boy walked by the pond. He saw something in the water.

Pam said, "Try to get my ball."

The boy jumped into the cold water. He got Pam's ball.

Pam thanked him and then walked up the hill and played.

You should see Ann's dog. His name is Ed. He is bigger than Ann. She thinks he is getting bigger and bigger all the time.

His coat is red, but the hair on his head is dark brown. He has long thin legs and big fat feet. He has a big nose, too.

Ann thinks he is funny. He can run like a rabbit, but he eats like a pig.

Ed works at the zoo in town. One night he took some food to the baby fox. He went to its cage, but the fox was not there.

Ed was surprised. He looked around, but he did not see it. The fox hid in the dark.

Then a man walked by. He had a light. Ed said, "Shine the light on the cage." The man made the light shine.

Right away Ed saw the baby fox on top of its cage. So he put it back in the cage and gave it some food.

Bill was dressed for winter. He had on a round, fur hat. It was pulled down over his ears. His long coat was buttoned up to his chin. The buttons were big and red. They made him look like a clown.

Yes, Bill was dressed for the cold. He had on his fur hat and his long coat. But his shoes were all wet. I laughed when he hopped up and down to keep his feet warm.

Once there was an old man who lived by a river. It was winter and the river was covered with ice. One day he looked out his window and saw a boy by the river. The boy started to walk across the river on the ice.

The old man was afraid that the ice would break. He opened the window and called out to the boy. But the boy didn't hear him, and he just kept on going. When he got to the middle, the ice broke, and the boy fell into the water.

The old man got a long ladder and ran down to the river. He slid the ladder across the ice. The boy grabbed the ladder and the man pulled him out.

The next day the boy visited the old man and thanked him for saving his life.

It is easy to make butter. First you need a jar and some heavy cream. Fill the jar part way with cream. Then shake it for about 20 minutes. Soon the cream will start to get lumpy. Stop when most of the cream turns into lumps. You will find that the lumps are butter.

Take the lumps out of the jar and wash them with cold water. Mix a little salt with the lumps and pat them together. Leave the butter in a cool place over night. In the morning the butter will be hard and ready to eat.

Once there was a little girl who had a kitten. The kitten liked to play in the yard by a tall tree.

Early one morning a dog was walking in front of the house. It was windy and the gate blew open. The dog ran into the yard. The kitten was scared and ran up the tree.

The girl tried to reach it, but she had no luck. The kitten climbed to the highest branch. The girl's sister saw the kitten from her window. She opened the window and leaned out. She could reach the branch. "Come inside," she said softly. She reached out when the kitten came closer. Then she pulled it into the house.

That night the little girl told everyone what had happened. She was glad that her sister had saved the kitten.

One way to make money in the summer is to sell lemonade. It is easy to make. You need lemons, water, sugar, and ice.

Put the juice from ten lemons into ten cups of water. Add two cups of sugar and lots of ice. Then stir it.

When you have the lemonade, get some paper cups and enough money to make change. Also get a small table to put things on. Then find a spot to set up. The corner of a street is good.

When it gets hot, people will stop to buy a drink.

Joe and his daughter Sue were fishing at the lake. They were there for an hour and had not caught any fish.

Joe wanted to find a better spot so he started to walk around the lake. He passed a few fishermen near the dock. They told him that they were catching lots of fish.

Joe was excited to hear the news, and he started back to get his daughter.

Meanwhile, Sue was fishing by herself. She got tired and fell asleep with the pole in her hand. She slept until she felt a strong tug on her line. She was startled to find that the fishing rod was being pulled into the water.

Sue rushed into the lake just as her father returned. Then she grabbed the fishing pole and pulled it out of the water.

Both Joe and Sue were amazed to discover an enormous fish hooked on the line.

ORAL READING COMPREHENSION/EXP D1

There is a big, old tree in the yard outside my window. It is straight and tall and looks like a cone. The branches at the bottom are wide and full. The tree goes way above the roof of my house. At the top it is narrow and comes to a point. The green leaves that cover its branches are not really leaves at all. They are sharp and pointed and make me think of needles.

The tree in my yard is always green. In winter the other trees lose their leaves. But even when snow falls and it is cold, I can look at my tree and think of spring.

Kate and her cousin, Jeff, went to the circus. They arrived a half-hour before the afternoon show.

Kate wanted to find good seats. She walked inside and saw two empty seats in the first row, but a lady told her that the seats were taken. Kate was unhappy because the front rows were already filled. She walked to the back to find two seats.

Meanwhile, Jeff was waiting in line at the candy stand. He wanted to get some popcorn before the show began. Suddenly he heard the band begin to play. He wanted to find Kate. He was afraid that he would miss the first act. As soon as he bought the popcorn, he hurried to find Kate. On the way to his seat, he tripped and spilled the popcorn.

Finally, he found his cousin in the back row and they began to watch the show. They didn't have good seats and they didn't have any popcorn, but they enjoyed the circus anyway.

Not far from where I live there is an old castle. It is not very big. It is made of gray stones and has a tower on one side of the main building. The tower is round and about 30 feet tall. There is a long narrow window near the top. The glass in the window has been broken for many years.

There is a cellar hole on the other side of the castle. It is filled with rocks and weeds. Some wood also remains from the barn that used to be there.

It is easy to tell that no one has lived there for a long time. Even the road is grown over with grass.

The moon had just risen as Jan looked toward the old deserted house. She was waiting for her friend Ellen. Together they planned to find out if the house was haunted.

When Ellen arrived the two friends began to walk nervously up the path. A strange shadow seemed to fall across the window next to the porch. Both girls were scared, but they pretended not to notice. Then as Ellen held the flashlight, Jan anxiously pushed open the door.

Once inside the house they were startled to hear a peculiar scratching sound. Ellen flashed her light all around, but she could not find where the sound was coming from. But it seemed to be coming toward them.

Suddenly Jan felt something rub against her leg. She tried to scream but was too scared to make a sound. She grabbed Ellen's arm and stared at her in shock.

Ellen flashed the light her way, and then they both realized what was haunting the house. It was just an old black cat who had made the house its home.

An amusement park is opening in town next Saturday. There will be a parade, fireworks, and free admission on opening day. More than five thousand people are expected to attend.

Work first began on the park two years ago. At that time the site was an unused field. It was filled with weeds and trash. Although occasional attempts had been made to clean it up, nothing had worked. Since then, more than fifty rides, a playhouse, and a picnic ground have been built. Many trees and bushes also have been planted.

After opening day, admission to the park will cost three dollars. However, children under twelve will be let in free if they come with an adult. All rides will cost fifty cents, except the roller coaster, which will cost a dollar.

It was late afternoon. Alice stood by the open barn door. She had latched the door this morning, but now it was open and her horse, Sam, was missing. Alice feared that Sam would not return before nightfall. So she decided to go look for him.

A short way from the barn she spotted Sam grazing in a pasture, but he was not alone. Another horse from a neighbor's farm was alongside him. Alice was surprised to see the other horse.

She got two ropes and went into the pasture after the horses. When she finally caught both of them, Alice put Sam back in the barn. Then she tried to tie the other horse to a nearby post, but he broke loose from her grasp. Alice was beginning to get angry. She tried to catch the horse again, but before she could reach him, he ran to the barn and lifted the latch with his nose.

Suddenly Alice realized why the door had been open. The neighbor's horse had let Sam out.

A group of students is planning to start a nature club. Anyone interested in wild animals, birds, plants, or wilderness hiking is invited to join. No membership fee will be charged.

The club is being formed in order to combine the interests of several smaller groups. In the past, these groups have not had enough members to become official school clubs. At least twenty members are needed to meet school requirements.

There are several benefits to having an official club. The school provides an adult advisor, money for activities, and help in planning field trips. It also provides office space and allows the club to hold meetings during school hours. Without these benefits it is difficult for groups to function.

It was the year 1849 in the small town of Buckstown, Maryland. A young black slave, named Harriet Tubman, decided to escape from the South and seek her freedom. Harriet awaited a chance to begin the trip northward.

One evening a farmer volunteered to hide Harriet in his cart underneath a load of vegetables. Harriet was terrified that she would be caught trying to escape, but she was determined to take the risk.

Harriet traveled on a route known as the underground railroad. The underground was not a real railroad, but an organization of people who provided rides and hiding places for slaves escaping from plantations in the South.

Harriet spent several exhausting nights traveling. Finally she arrived at the Pennsylvania border. She was a free citizen for the first time in her life.

Afterward, Harriet made many heroic attempts to lead other slaves to freedom in the North. Because of her courage and determination she is an important figure in the nation's history.

You can still find gold in some California streams. All you need is a metal pan and a lot of luck.

First select a place where the current is slow. Gold is carried by moving water, but drops to the stream bed where the water is still. Next scoop some gravel from the stream into your pan and gently wash out any dirt. Then put a little water in the pan and rock it in a circle so that the larger bits of gravel will spill out. Soon there should be only a handful of sand left. Look for shiny yellow particles. You can determine if these are gold by hitting them with a hammer. Real gold will flatten because it is soft.

It was winter in the town of Kitty Hawk, North Carolina. This was the day Wilbur and Orville Wright planned an attempt to become the first men to fly in an engine-powered airplane.

When the two men arose at dawn, the wind was brisk and a threat of rain lingered in the air. The decision they had to make was difficult. It might be dangerous to fly in high winds, especially if they encountered a sudden gust. But if the wind held steady, it could actually help them in taking off. Wilbur and Orville were nervous as they made the historic decision.

At about noon, they started the engine. Suspense mounted as the airplane moved forward and gradually lifted into the air. The machine flew for a brief twelve seconds before coming to a halt on the ground.

Wilbur and Orville were triumphant. They had accomplished their goal. Their achievement that day marked the beginning of man's venture into the sky.

A caterpillar makes a sleeping bag called a cocoon. It uses a kind of sticky thread that comes from its mouth.

First the caterpillar grabs a twig with its back feet. This leaves the front part of its body free to move. Then it begins to bend and turn and spin the thread around itself and the twig like a net. But it leaves room inside the net to move around.

When the net is made, the caterpillar moves its head back and forth to put in a floor. Then it fills in all the spaces in the net and finally closes it all up.

After that, the caterpillar goes to sleep. When it wakes up in a few months, it will be a moth.

Hundreds of racers were set at the starting line. The most popular bicycle race in the world was about to begin. It is called the Tour de France.

As the starting gun sounded, the racers set out on a grueling and dangerous course. For 24 days they would race over 2,500 miles of French countryside, through busy city streets and over rugged mountain roads.

For the first few miles racers were tense but excited. The crowds that lined every small town and village along the route cheered encouragement. Several days into the race a few cyclists had broken away from the pack. Each in turn challenged for the lead as they headed up a steep mountain pass. Determination, skill, and luck became critical factors.

Some quit when they became too tired to keep pedaling up the mountain. Others lost control on the way down the other side, skidding off the road and slamming into rocky ditches at speeds approaching 60 miles an hour. Several dropped out when their equipment failed.

In the end three racers headed out, seemingly alone, across the level plains toward a still distant finish line. Only one would win the money and fame that goes to the champion.

The seahorse is an odd kind of fish. It is three inches tall and looks like a matchstick frame covered with fine cloth. Its skin is brown, it has a snout like a tube, and has long hairs on its head.

If you watched a seahorse you might notice that it swims upright but spends most of the time with its tail hooked around seaplants. Since these plants are also brown, the seahorse if often difficult to find.

When it is hungry the seahorse eats small worms and shellfish, which it sucks off plants with its long snout.

When it is time to reproduce, the female lays eggs like all other fish. But it is the male that takes care of them. He babysits the eggs by keeping them in a pouch until they hatch.

Thus, although the seahorse is a fish, the way it looks, swims, and hatches its eggs makes it a very unusual fish, indeed!

Read-Write Cycle Assessments

Introduction

The Read-Write Cycle Assessments are dynamic assessments designed to determine the best writing a student can do on a given topic. The format used with this assessment is grounded in the tenets of social cognitive learning, closely resembles regular classroom instruction, and reflects the reading-writing connection. Included in the design are pre-writing activities that use cooperative/collaborative instructional strategies to scaffold each student's background knowledge. During the pre-writing activities, students work individually, in pairs or small groups, or as a whole class to pool their knowledge and understanding of the topic. These activities work to "level the playing field" so that students are better able to demonstrate their ability to compose text in an academic setting without being hampered by less than adequate topic knowledge. Teachers can get a clearer understanding of their students' skill in expressing ideas coherently and with organization and in using appropriate vocabulary, grammar, and mechanics than they would if administering the more commonly utilized on-demand writing assessments.

The example assessment that follows is appropriate for upper-elementary and middle school students. Ideally, it would be administered over a 2-day block during one class period each day. A rubric for scoring the writing done on the second day is given after the assessment. Finally, an example of a Read-Write portfolio generated by a different Read-Write Cycle Assessment is given to illustrate the thought processes a student uses throughout the experience.

Once teachers have become familiar with the general design of a Read-Write Cycle assessment, they are encouraged to create their own versions to assess writing across the curriculum.

SAMPLE ELEMENTARY AND MIDDLE SCHOOL ASSESSMENT:
WINNING THE LOTTERY

Day 1 Directions

Topic:	What would happen if my family (or I) won the lottery?
Group Organization:	Whole class or partners
Teacher Materials:	Chart paper, markers
Student Materials:	Text, group task sheets
Time:	One class session, two days in a row

Note: Adjust the dialogue as appropriate for you and your students.

Pre-Reading: Introduce the activity. This segment should take 5–7 minutes.

Connect: "What would happen if your family (or you) won the lottery?" (Option: individual quick write, partner brainstorm.)

Brainstorm: "Let's get some of your ideas on the chart paper. What would happen if your family (or you) won the lottery?"

Prompts: "What are some positive things?"
"You've mentioned positives to having money. Any negatives?"

Prompt students with questions regarding

- Behaviors
- Emotions
- Relationships
- Other

Vocabulary to highlight: millionaire, purchase, opinion
(Check and adjust text to meet your students' needs.)

Organize: "Look at our brainstorming list. How might we group some of these ideas together? Let's think of some headings we could use to categorize the items we have on the list. We are going to organize the list by making a web. The web will help us think about our ideas. Now tell me where each item should go and why you think that is the best place for it."

Make a web with "Winning the Lottery" in the center circle. Draw lines to circles surrounding the center circle, placing category titles in the surrounding circles. Place lines radiating out from the category title circles and write the appropriate items from the brainstorm list at the ends of the lines. Be sure to have the student justify the placement.

Students can make their own webs modeled on the class web.

Purpose: "During the next two days you will be talking and reading about what happens to people when they win large amounts of money—positive things and perhaps negative things. You will share your ideas and hear the ideas of others. Tomorrow you will write about how life would be different if you won the lottery. I will be looking at your writing to see the ways that you share your ideas on paper and to find what you like to write about. Later in the year, we will look at this piece of writing to see how you've developed as writers."

Reading: Distribute the text. Students can read independently or with a partner. (Note any additional support provided, for example, teacher reading to a specific student.) "As you read, think about the two questions on the side. Write down some notes either while you are reading or when you are finished." Plan about 5–7 minutes for reading and 5–7 minutes for individual responses to the passage.

Facilitate by drawing attention to the question and providing support/clarification as appropriate. (Because students read at various paces, have a plan for what they will do when finished.)

(Option: Whole-group discussion of student responses to questions.)

Post-Reading: Help students get started by introducing the activity as a whole-class discussion. Recreate the Venn diagram (see p. 531) on chart paper or overhead transparency. Explain the meaning of each section of the diagram (characteristics of having much money, little money, and commonalities).

Organize: "What is life like when you have lots of money?"
"What is life like when you have little money?"
Once students begin generating ideas, move into smaller groups (see below).

Discussion prompts: "Tell us more about that."
"Make connections between the sections."

Divide students into groups of two or four. Have them continue comparing and contrasting life with and without money. Give each group a copy of the Venn diagram on p. 531 to fill in. (Use your judgment for effective arrangements based on your students' experiences with cooperative groups.)

Small-Group Report: The purposes are (1) to add further ideas and vocabulary to the original webbing chart and (2) to focus individual students on the theme or position for the upcoming writing assignment.

> "I'd like each group to share their Venn diagram. Tell us two or three of your items and where you put your items. If you hear something that you didn't think about for your Venn diagram, you can add it to yours."

Each group will have 1–2 minutes to share highlights from their Venn diagrams.

Closure: Recap by adding new information to the web (as appropriate).

> "Tomorrow you will take this information, as well as the ideas you've heard from your classmates, and write about what your life would be like if you and your family won the lottery."

Millionaire Moms and Kids

The dress is the lightest shade of blue: floor-length, fitted on top, and flowing into a full skirt. It costs $139. For 15-year-old Cheyanne Maples, owning this dress would have been impossible in the past.

Today Cheyanne and her brother, John, don't even look at price tags as they shop for the big dance.

Three months ago, their mother, who worked at a company for 25 years, lost her job because the plant was shut down.

But the family got lucky! Just after losing the job, they became millionaires by winning the Lotto. The prize was beyond their wildest dreams! For the next 20 years, their mother will receive $135,000.

Shop till you drop

That money has meant changes for the family. The Maples purchased a satellite dish, a new dishwasher, and two new cars (one a Miata). They are planning to build a new house. Everyone is wearing new clothes.

The family agrees that shopping is the best part of winning the lottery.

Talk of the halls

At West Lake High School, where Cheyanne and John go to school, news of the big win spread fast. Everybody knew about their good luck—and everybody had an opinion about it.

On the first day, Cheyanne received a marriage proposal in the cafeteria ("He was on his knees right in front of my lunch tray!" she groans.)

Soon life got back to normal. Cheyanne still spends one class period working in the school office; John still stays after school to play chess.

It looks the same from the outside, but some things have changed. Cheyanne's friend Annie thinks the money's made Cheyanne forget her real friends. "I'm glad it wasn't me," she says. "Money makes people do stupid things."

And Jason says, "John got a big head. All he talks about is what he's bought and what he's going to buy next."

Cheyanne thinks people notice her more now. She asks, "Why didn't they like me before? It's not like I have any more money. My mom does."

They also know that while money can change what you have, it cannot change who you are or what your parents expect from you. In the end, it's their money.

John might be able to buy expensive clothes, but he still gets in trouble for not putting his clothes in the dryer.

The bottom line?

Money can bring you wonderful things, but you'll still be the same person you always were, coping with the same stuff you always did.

What do you think about how the family decided to spend their money?

They got their money 3 months ago. What do you think their lives will be like in a year?

Name: _____

Date: _____

VENN DIAGRAM

List 5–7 items in each section.

Having a Million Dollars

Having Little Money

Day 2 Directions

Topic:	What would happen if I won the lottery?
Group Organization:	Whole class and individuals
Teacher Materials:	Chart paper, markers
Student Materials:	Pre-writing worksheet, writing paper, previous day's materials
Time:	One class session, immediately following day 1

Note: Adjust the dialogue as appropriate for you and your students.

Pre-Writing: *Whole-class activity.* Review the previous day's session, remind students of the topic, webbing chart, and Venn diagram. Hand out the Pre-Writing Worksheet and instruct students about how to transfer key words from the webbing chart, and how to add their own words to the worksheet. You may also direct the students to include a graphic organizer (e.g., matrix, reorganized web, Venn diagram) as part of their planning.

Writing: *Individual task.* The students will have access to the Pre-Writing Worksheet and the Webbing Chart (Day 1) and other resources allowed by the teacher, including a dictionary and thesaurus. Discuss and ask questions about the directions for the writing task to ensure that all the students understand what they are being asked to do. Remember, the goal is to obtain optimal performance. Students may ask the teacher for clarification about the task, but students may not help one another.

Post-Writing: *Whole-class activity.* Debrief the class after the papers are turned in. "How did you feel about the writing task?" Ask students to describe problems they encountered and allow other students to suggest solutions. Students can briefly assess their performance by thinking to themselves, talking with a neighbor, or providing an appropriate signal (e.g., thumbs up, thumbs down).

Pre-Writing Worksheet

Name: _____   Date: _____

List 5–7 items for each question. Find words from the web and the Venn diagram that will help you when you write. Use words, phrases, pictures, or sentences.

What would I do for <u>myself</u>?	What would my family do for <u>each</u> <u>other</u>?	What would my family and I do for <u>others</u> (friends, neighbors, our community, strangers, etc.)?

Winning the Lottery

Name: _____   Date: _____

Write 1–2 pages in response to one of the prompts below. Use your Pre-Writing Worksheets to get ideas and words for your paper. You can also use new ideas. If you run out of space, please attach additional sheets of paper to this page.

When you finish, read your paper again.

- Will the reader understand what you are thinking?
- Check for spelling and grammar (periods, capitalization, etc.).

1. **If my family and I won the lottery, . . .**
2. **I think that my family and I should win the lottery because . . .**

_____

_____

_____

_____

_____

_____

_____

_____

_____

_____

_____

_____

_____

_____

_____

_____

_____

_____

_____

Scoring Rubric

Score	Length*	Coherence	Grammar/Mechanics
6	3–5 pages or 176 or more words	• Provides overall links/transitions; examples and descriptions presented logically • States main topic and supports with details and examples • Topic shifts easy to follow and logical	• Few, if any, errors in grammar and punctuation • Utilizes appropriate variety of sentence structures, including phrases and clauses
5	1–2 pages or 86–175 words	• Ease and facility in expressing ideas • Writing flows smoothly and naturally, and is understandable • Generally focused on topic • Provides description, elaboration, evidence, and support • Writer provides overall links, but transitions may not always be smooth; ideas/reasons are clear and logical	• Some variation in sentence structure, including phrases and clauses • Minimal errors may be present as students explore complex structures • Few run-ons or fragmented sentences
4	3/4 page or 61–85 words	• Provides descriptions, elaboration, evidence, and support • Information or examples may be in a list-like form (no tying together of ideas) • Addresses the topic without wavering • Writing is generally understandable and coherent, but lacks complete control • Focus may shift and be somewhat difficult to follow	• Clear sentence sense • May display variety in sentences • Minimal or no errors in punctuation • Few, if any, run-ons or fragmented sentences
3	4 sentences/ 1/2 page or 36–60 words	• Addresses the topic • Little description, elaboration, evidence, or support • May construct rambling sentences or lists with no elaboration • Vague and/or confusing	• Simple repetitive sentences • May include fragments and run-ons • Some errors in punctuation and grammar that do not impede reading
2	2–3 sentences/ 1/4 page or 11–35 words	• Addresses the topic minimally • May wander off topic • Fragmented expression of ideas	• Simple sentence structure or phrases with many fragments and/or run-ons • Errors are highly evident and interfere with reading
1	1 sentence or less or 0–10 words	• Generally unintelligible or unrelated • Copied from the board or another student	• Unintelligible due to grammar or punctuation • Copied from the board or another student

*Grade-level appropriate paper, margins, and penmanship; no skipping lines

(continued)

Scoring Rubric (continued)

Score	Vocabulary	Spelling
6	• Substantial use of complex Romance words • Lexical variety • Precision in dealing with topic • Latin and Greek roots and affixes	**Complex Conventional** • Substantial evidence of attempting complex words with few errors (polysyllabic words, prefixes and suffixes, Latin and Greek roots and affixes) • Command of vowels in polysyllabic words • Mastery of conventional spellings for familiar 1–2 syllable words
5	• Some evidence of complex but familiar Romance words • Limited variety and reliance on relatively common words (national) • Latin (and Greek) roots and affixes • Precise and rich language (no ordinary friend, compassionate)	**Conventional** • Command of long/short vowel contrast • Few errors • Polysyllabic words are present and have few or no errors
4	• Substantial number of familiar polysyllabic words (interesting, understand), including compounds • Noticeable increased precision ("friendly" for "nice")	**Phonetic Appropriate** • Beginning to show long/short vowel contrast • Short vowels accurate • May have other vowel errors (e.g., digraphs) • Reversals may be present (especially in blends and r/l patterns) • Polysyllabic words (including compounds), if present, include vowels
3	• 1–2 syllable words, but mostly frequent and little variety or precision • May include compounds and Anglo-Saxon affixation* (prepositions, comparatives: under-, -er, -est) • May include descriptive words	**Phonological** • Short vowels accurate • Represents each sound—very few omissions • Reversals may be present (especially in blends or r/l patterns) • Easily readable
2	• Frequent one-syllable (CVC) and basic sight words • Short, "safe" words commonplace • Simplistic and imprecise language	**Beginning Phonological** • Identification of consonants • Vowels are included, but frequently incorrect selection • Omission of sounds (sitr = sister) • Readable with minimal effort
1	• Most words difficult to interpret • Few words and/or limited to words provided by the teacher • Incorrect and ineffective language use	**Alphabetic, Pre-Phonetic** • Uses letters • Consonants may represent some sounds • Omission of most vowels • Sight words may or may not be spelled conventionally • Unreadable or readable with considerable effort

*Most Anglo-Saxon words can stand alone and be affixed. Affixes are often prepositional: over-, under-, in-, for-.
Common suffixes include -ed, -er, -ing, -ly, -hood, -ness.

Portfolio Entries

The following series of portfolio entries illustrates a fifth-grader's efforts as she and her classmates work on a read-write cycle task. Portfolio entries, such as those that follow, can help the teacher understand the thinking processes their students use as they work through a read-write cycle assessment. The teacher can also use the data gathered to inform future writing instruction. By comparing the prewriting graphic organizers, the writing sample, and the portfolio entries from a series of read-write cycle assessments at the beginning, middle, and end of the school year, it is possible for teachers, students, and students' parents to gain a clear picture of students' growth in writing skills across the academic year.

DEVELOP: The big problem for us fifth-graders is that our school has decided to replace all the desserts in the cafeteria with fruit. We think that we should have a choice of fruit or a dessert. When we talked to our teacher about it, she suggested that we write a letter to the principal and the school board about this decision. We brainstormed what things we might put in our letter. Our teacher even brought in an article from the newspaper for all of us to read. It was about how the Los Angeles Unified School District has decided to cut back on sugar available in their schools. They are replacing their high-sugar desserts with different kinds of fruit. We even went to the library and the Internet to find out more about how much sugar is in different fruits and desserts. We were able to add to our brainstorm and then organized all of that information into a matrix, so we could think about it better.

[Portfolio includes brainstorming results]

DRAFT: Fifth-graders are old enough to make good choices about their health. The school really needs to offer a selection of foods that we could eat as a dessert. We made a list of desserts and fruit so we can compare the sugar in them. Our class would like to meet with you to talk about possible choices that the cafeteria could have for us.

[This is a synopsis of a two-page draft, all of which is included in the portfolio.]

REVIEW: I asked other students about the letter, and they suggested a couple of things. One was to find out how much each dessert choice would cost. Another was that it will take a while to do anything. Are we expecting changes before we go on to middle school?

[Evidence that the student has consulted with peers and learned something from the experience.]

REVISE: Some of us have talked with our parents, and they are willing to help. Three of them have written letters promising to meet with you and with our group. We also know that changing the cafeteria menu will take a while. It's May, and we will soon be leaving for middle school. But we think that a choice of foods will be good for everyone, and so we are willing to help solve the dessert problem even if it won't make things better for us.

[This is one of several notes on revising that are in the portfolio.]

POLISH: We looked over the revision for spelling and grammar errors and other ways to improve the final version.

[The portfolio contains several drafts, making it possible to see how successful students were in revising.]

PUBLISH: [The letter, prepared on a computer and signed by all of the students, was delivered to the principal's office by a delegation. The portfolio includes a photograph of the principal receiving the letter from the students.]

Dear Ms. S,

Our fifth-grade class is worried about the changes in cafeteria food available at our school. We all have different likes and dislikes. We enjoy having the opportunity to choose from a variety of foods. We also like it better when we know if the food we eat is good for us or not.

Having a larger choice of desserts will cost more money for the school. We did some research about the amount of sugar in different kinds of desserts and fruits. We made a list of the foods that had the lowest amount of sugar to help you compare the sugar content and the number of calories. We also estimated how much a serving of each fruit or dessert would cost.

We have talked with our parents, and three of them have promised to meet with you and us to talk about how to fix the food choice problem. It will take a while to make changes in the lunch menu, and since we are graduating in May, it won't help us. But delicious, healthy choices in the cafeteria will help everyone. We have talked with the fourth-graders, and they agree. Will you meet with our class and our parents to see what we can do?

Sincerely,

The 2005 Fifth-Grade Class

Appendix B
Lesson Plans

Introduction to the Lesson Plans

In this appendix, we have included five lesson plans illustrating several different sorts of instruction. Each lesson plan is related to a chapter, and you can learn more about the types of instruction illustrated in each lesson plan by consulting the appropriate chapter in the book.

The first lesson plan is a detailed description of an in-depth procedure for teaching students to infer the meanings of unknown words they come across as they read. Teaching students to use context clues is both very important and something that takes a good deal of time and effort on your part and on the part of your students. More information on teaching context clues can be found in Chapter 9, Vocabulary Development.

The second lesson plan is a detailed description of an in-depth procedure for teaching students to unlock the meanings of unknown words using their knowledge of prefixes. Teaching students to use prefixes to unlock the meanings of words they do not know is another important word learning strategy, and it too requires in-depth instruction. A list of the most frequent prefixes, those that are most worthy of instruction, is included in Chapter 7, Word Recognition. More information on teaching students to use prefixes and information on teaching them to use other word parts is included in Chapter 9, Vocabulary Development.

The third lesson plan is a Scaffolded Reading Experience (SRE) for teaching Kate DiCamillo's award-winning novel *Because of Winn-Dixie*. In addition to helping students learn strategies such as using context and using prefixes, it is important to help students read, understand, learn from, and enjoy the books and other materials they read for your class. SREs are research based, powerful, and flexible ways to do that. More information on SREs can be found in Chapter 10, Scaffolding Students' Comprehension of Text.

The fourth lesson plan is a description of the first three days of instruction on making inferences designed for third- through fifth-graders. Comprehension is, of course, the ultimate goal of reading, and one of the most vital things that readers do is infer knowledge and connections that the authors imply. More information on comprehension strategies and how to teach them can be found in Chapter 11, Teaching Comprehension Strategies.

The fifth and final lesson plan is a fairly detailed description of Questioning the Author (QtA), a type of comprehension instruction developed by Isabel Beck and Margaret McKeown. QtA is a whole-group questioning and discussion strategy designed to help students clarify any misunderstandings they have and construct significant meaning for what they read. It is one of several procedures for assisting students in building rich and lasting understanding of important topics, which we discuss in Chapter 10, Scaffolding Students' Comprehension of Text.

DAY 1	DAY 2	DAY 3	DAY 4	DAY 5
Introduction and motivation to using context to infer meaning using a videotape	Introduction to using context clues to infer word meanings and to the four-step strategy	Detailed instruction in the first two steps of the strategy: Play and Question and Slow Advance	Detailed instruction in the second two steps of the strategy: Stop and Rewind and Play and Question	Game in which students earn points for using the four-step strategy to infer word meanings
DAY 6	**DAY 7**	**DAY 8**	**DAY 9**	**DAY 10**
Review of using context clues and the four-step strategy Renaming of the four steps without the VCR terminology	Guided practice—and further instruction if necessary—in using the four-step process with teacher provided narrative texts	Guided practice—and further instruction if necessary—in using the four-step process with teacher provided expository texts	Guided practice—and further instruction if necessary—in using the four-step process with authentic texts currently being used in the class	Review of using context clues and the four-step strategy Student–teacher planning on strategically using and learning more about context clues

Vocabulary Lesson: Using Context Clues to Infer the Meanings of Unknown Words

Using context clues to infer the meanings of unknown words is the first word-learning strategy to consider because it is the most important one. Most words are learned from context, and if we can increase students' proficiency in learning from context even a small amount, we will greatly increase the number of words they learn. It is therefore vital that we provide students with rich, robust, and effective instruction on using context clues. Providing such instruction takes a good deal of time and effort on the part of both teachers and students. The instruction outlined here takes place over ten 30–45 minute sessions. A sample schedule is shown in Figure B.1. In what follows, we describe the first two days of instruction in some detail and then much more briefly describe the rest of the unit. The instruction is described as it would be presented to students in the upper elementary grades. With younger or older students, the language and examples would be adjusted accordingly.

Day 1: Introduction and Motivation

Because learning to use context clues is a demanding and challenging task, the teacher introduces the unit with a substantial motivational activity designed to both gain students' interest and enable them to relate the task of using context clues to infer word meanings to an activity they are familiar with—using a VCR/DVD or the Internet.

She begins by telling students that over the next few weeks the class is going to be working on using context clues to figure out the meanings of unknown words they come across while reading. Using clues to figure out things they don't know, she tells them, is something they do all the time, something they're good at, and something that is fun. Then, she tells them that they'll begin their study of context clues by viewing a brief video showing a place they might know and that their job is to look for clues to what the place is.

Just before showing the video, the teacher passes out the Clue Web shown in Figure B.2, puts a copy of the Clue Web on the overhead or document camera, and tells students that they will use the Clue Web today as they watch the video and over the next few weeks as they learn to use context clues. She goes on to tell them that they probably won't be able to answer all of these questions and should jot down brief answers while trying to figure out as much as possible about the place described in the video.

At this point, the teacher shows the video, gives students a few minutes to fill in clues on their Clue Webs, and then begins a dialogue with them.

"Was everyone able to get all of the information they needed to answer the questions after watching the video once? Did you catch all that the tour guide said? What would help you figure out even more of the answers?"

Figure B.2 Clue Web

Where is it?	What does it look, smell, sound, taste, and/or feel like?	What does it do?
_____	_____	_____
_____	_____	_____
_____	_____	_____
_____		_____

Unknown word/object: _____

What's another word for it?	When does it happen?	What is the opposite of it?
_____	_____	_____
_____	_____	_____
_____	_____	_____
_____	_____	_____

Other Notes

_____

_____

_____

_____

Students will almost certainly say that they could learn more if they could watch the video again. If they don't, the teacher points this out and then replays the video.

After this, she asks for a volunteer to identify the place described in the video, which is Hawaii.

Next, the teacher asks students what clues suggested it was Hawaii. Likely responses include "Hawaiian music," "palm trees," "the beach," and "tropical fruits." The teacher writes these clues on the Clue Web and compliments students on their efforts. Then, she challenges them to identify more clues that this is Hawaii and replays the video as many times as students request.

The teacher concludes the introductory lesson by noting that finding all of the clues and figuring out that the place shown in the video was Hawaii required hard work and persistence, that each time they viewed the video again they found more clues, and that this same sort of sleuthing is what they need to do when they are trying to figure out unknown words they meet while reading. She goes on to say that beginning tomorrow they will learn a particular strategy for figuring out the meanings of unknown words they come across. And, she notes, they will find that the strategy is a lot like the approach they used to figure out that the place shown in the video was Hawaii.

Day 2: Introduction to Using Context Clues and the Four-Step Strategy

The teacher begins Day 2 with a brief review of what the class did on Day 1, and then moves quickly to the topic for the day, learning a strategy for figuring out the meanings of unknown words they meet while reading.

> "Today, we're going to learn a strategy for using clues to figure something out. But this strategy will not be for figuring out what place is shown in a video. Instead, it will be for figuring out the meanings of unknown words that we meet when we're reading.
>
> "Actually, we won't exactly be 'figuring out' meanings. Instead, we'll be 'inferring meanings.' The strategy is called 'inferring word meanings from context.' When we infer something, we make an educated guess about it. And when we infer word meanings from context, we are making educated guesses about the meanings of the words. The context in which we find a word doesn't usually tell us the exact meaning of a word, but it often gives us a good idea of the word's meaning, and that is often enough to understand what we are reading."

At this point, the teacher puts up a large and colorful poster with the name of the strategy and the four steps and begins discussing the strategy. A sample poster is shown in Figure B.3.

> "Do you recognize this strategy?"

A number of students note that they do recognize it, that it is the VCR/DVD strategy they worked with the day before.

> "Right. This is the same strategy we used yesterday, but now we are applying it to figuring out unknown words we meet in reading rather than to figuring out an unknown place we see in a video. Here's how it works.
>
> "As you can see, the first step in the strategy is Play and Question. That means you read carefully, always asking yourself if you are understanding what you are reading. Also ask yourself, 'What is this paragraph about?'
>
> "Then, when you come to a word you don't know, you move to the second step—Slow Advance. At this point, you slow down, read the sentence at least

and ?   **Play and Question**

- Read carefully.
- Frequently ask yourself, "Does this make sense?"

Slow Advance

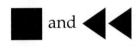

- Notice when you don't know the meaning of a word and slow down.
- Read that sentence at least once more, looking for clues.
- Ask yourself, "What is this paragraph about?"

Stop and Rewind or Fast Forward

 and ◀◀

- If necessary, go back and reread, looking for clues that help you figure out what the word might mean. Read ahead to look for clues.

Play and Question

▶ **and ?**

- When you figure out what the word might mean, substitute your guess for the difficult word and see if the sentence makes sense.
- If it does, keep reading.
- If it doesn't, stop, rewind, and try again.

once more looking for clues to the meaning of the word, and see if you can infer its meaning.

"If you can infer the word's meaning from just rereading the sentence, that's great. You continue to read. But if you can't infer the word's meaning from rereading the sentence, it's time to move to the third step of the strategy—Stop and Rewind or Fast Forward. At this point you stop, go back, and read the sentence or two that comes before the one with the unknown word, again looking for clues to the meaning of the word.

"If you can now infer its meaning, excellent! You can move on to the fourth step of the strategy, which is also called Play and Question. But this time, Play and Question means to try out the word you inferred. Substitute your educated guess for the word you didn't know and see if that works. If it does, keep on reading. If it doesn't, you'll need to Stop and Rewind again, ask someone about the word, look it up in the dictionary, or simply continue to read, understanding the passage as well as you can without knowing the meaning of the word.

"I know that all of this sounds pretty complicated. And using context clues to infer the meanings of unknown words is going to take some work. But the work is well worth it because learning to use context clues helps to make you an independent and powerful reader, a reader who can read anything because you know what to do when unknown words come up."

Sample Teacher–Student Dialogue

Shown below is a sample dialogue in which the teacher and the class work together to infer the meaning of a difficult word.

Teacher: Much like we did with the video, we are going to take a small section of a book and make sure we understand it before moving on. I will read a paragraph aloud *(give students a copy)* and then stop and check to make sure everyone understood the words and ideas. The book is *The Phantom Tollbooth* by Norton Jester. As you will see, the story is set in a very strange place. Here is the paragraph we're going to work with.

"A-H-H-H-R-R-E-M-M," roared the gateman, clearing his throat and snapping smartly to attention. "This is Dictionopolis, a happy kingdom, advantageously located in the Foothills of Confusion. The breezes come right off the Sea of Knowledge and cool the foothills gently. In this kingdom we don't have the cold temperatures like at the top of the mountains, nor the rain that the other side of the mountain gets."

Teacher: This gateman is welcoming the main character, Milo, into his city of Dictionopolis. Notice that Foothills of Confusion and Sea of Knowledge are capitalized. What does that tell you?
Students: They're proper nouns. They're names of places.
Teacher: Exactly. Knowing what sorts of words are capitalized will help you understand this section.

Did everyone understand the paragraph completely? If we don't understand everything, what could we do?
Students: Reread it. Read it again. Read it slower. Ask ourselves questions as we are reading it.
Teacher: Good thinking. You came up with two of the steps to our strategy, Slow Advance and Stop and Rewind. Let's use those two steps now. As I reread the sentence, listen for words that you don't know.

The teacher again reads the paragraph aloud.

Teacher: Were there any difficult words in that sentence? If so, what were they?
Students: *Advantageously.*
Teacher: Let's highlight that one. Now, let's reread just the sentence that *advantageously* is in and the one after it. We don't need to reread the whole thing every time, just the section we're focusing on.

The teacher rereads just the one sentence.

Teacher: Does *advantageously* sound like a positive thing?
Students: It does to me. It says that it is a happy kingdom. I think that it has a positive meaning.
Teacher: What are some of the things the paragraph tells us about this kingdom?
Students: That it gets nice breezes off the sea. It's not as cold as the mountain peaks and it's not as rainy as the other side of the mountain.
Teacher: Would that make it a pleasant place to live?
Students. Yes. It's nice to have a breeze. It's also good that it's not too cold. And being not so rainy is a good thing too.
Teacher: What is the word *advantageously* describing?
Students: Where this city is located.
Teacher: That's right. The city is located in an advantageous place. What do you think that *advantageous* could mean?

Students: Nice?

Teacher: Let's add an -ly to that because our unknown word had an -ly. Then, let's write *nicely* above the word *advantageously*. Now, we should reread the paragraph with our replacement word to see if it makes sense. This time, while I'm reading, ask yourself if you understand what sort of place the story takes place in.

The teacher crosses out *advantageously* on the overhead and replaces it with *nicely*.

Teacher: What do you think? Did *nicely* fit in the sentence OK? Does the sentence make sense now?

Students: Yes. It does make sense. Dictionopolis sounds like a good place to live.

Teacher: I agree. I think that we now have a better understanding of the whole paragraph because we understand the word *advantageously* better. That's what learning to use context to infer word meanings can do. It can help us learn words, and it can help us better understand what we read.

Independent Practice

In addition to the guided practice illustrated in the teacher–student dialogue, each session from the second day of instruction includes independent practice. This first independent practice activity is brief and does not require the students to do a lot on their own. The teacher gives them a brief paragraph with some difficult words, asks them to read it several times and mark any words they don't know or are uncertain of, and tells them they will discuss using the context clue strategy with this paragraph the next day. As the instruction continues, the guided practice portions of the lessons will become much shorter, and the independent practice sessions will become longer and more challenging.

Review and Question Session

Each session ends with a review and question session. The teacher reviews what students have learned that day and throughout the unit, primarily by calling on students to recap what they have learned. Each ending session also gives students an opportunity to ask questions and get clarification on anything they are uncertain of.

The Remaining Eight Days of Initial Instruction

As shown in Figure B.1, over the next 8 days, the class receives detailed instruction on the four-step strategy, interrupts the hard work with a game using the strategy, does guided practice with both narrative text and expository text, uses the strategy with authentic text, and makes plans for using the strategy in the future. There are also several important things that the figure cannot show: Increasingly, the students talk more and the teacher talks less. The students do more of the work. They take more responsibility for the strategy, and they increasingly self-monitor and self-regulate their use of the strategy. At the same time, the teacher is always there to support students' efforts, providing encouragement, scaffolding, and feedback as needed.

Transfer, Review, and Integration Activities

It is vital to realize that this initial unit of using context clues, substantial as it has been, is only the first step in assisting students in becoming competent and confident users of this important strategy. In the weeks, months, and years after the initial instruction, students need lots of independent practice, feedback, brief reviews and mini-lessons, opportunities to use the strategy, reminders to use it, and motivation to do so. It is only with such a long-term effort that students will fully learn the strategy, internalize it, and make it a part of their approach to building their vocabularies.

Vocabulary Lesson: Using Prefixes to Unlock the Meanings of Unknown Words

Teaching students to use context clues is the most important word-learning strategy to teach, but teaching them to use word parts is a close second. In fact, about half of the new words that students meet in their reading are related to familiar words. Once students can break words into parts, they can use their knowledge of word parts to attempt to deduce their meaning—if, of course, they understand word parts and how they function. Of the three types of word parts to consider teaching—prefixes, suffixes, and roots—prefixes are the most powerful elements to teach for the reasons shown below.

- There are relatively few prefixes to teach.
- They are used in a large number of words.
- They are consistently spelled.
- They appear at the beginnings of words, where they are easy for students to spot.

Here, we describe a procedure for teaching prefixes in detail.

Day 1: Introduction, Clarification, Motivation, and Overview

On Day 1, the teacher introduces the concept of prefixes and the strategy of using prefixes to unlock the meanings of unknown words, attempts to motivate students by stressing the value of prefixes, and gives students an overview of the unit. It is particularly important to be sure that students understand exactly what prefixes and prefixed words are.

The teacher might say something like this: "Over the next few days, we're going to be looking at how you can use prefixes to help you figure out the meanings of words you don't know. If you learn some common prefixes and how to use your knowledge of these prefixes to understand words that contain those prefixes, you're going to be able to figure out the meanings of a lot of new words. And, as you know, figuring out the meanings of words you don't know in a passage is an important step in understanding the passage."

Next, the teacher asks students what they already know about prefixes, reinforcing correct information students provide and gently suggesting that any incorrect information they give is not quite on target. It is critical that students have a clear understanding of prefixes, and for this reason, the teacher follows the discussion with a presentation supported by an overhead transparency. Figure B.4 is the transparency that the teacher shares with the students.

This is a lot for students to remember—too much in fact. For this reason, the teacher constructs a shortened version of these points and writes them on a "Basic Facts About Prefixes" poster (see Figure B.5 on p. 548). As the unit progresses, the prefixes, their meanings, and example words can be added to the poster.

Lesson adapted from "Teaching Prefixes: As Good as It Gets?" by Michael F. Graves. In J. F. Baumann and E. B. Kame'enui, *Vocabulary Instruction: Research to Practice* (pp. 81–99). New York: Guilford Press. Copyright © 2003 Guilford Press. Reprinted with permission of the Guilford Press.

BASIC FACTS ABOUT PREFIXES

- A prefix is a group of letters that goes in front of a word. *Un-* is one prefix you have probably seen. It often means "not."

- Although you can list prefixes by themselves, as with *un-*, in stories or other things that we read, prefixes are attached to words. They don't appear by themselves. In *unhappy*, for example, the prefix *un-* is attached to the word *happy*.

- When a prefix is attached to a word, it changes the meaning of the word. For example, when the prefix *un-* is attached to the word *happy*, it makes the word *unhappy*, which means "not happy."

- It's important to remember that, for a group of letters to really be a prefix, when you remove them from the word, you should still have a real word left. Removing the prefix *un-* from the word *unhappy* still leaves the word *happy*. That means it's a prefix. But if you remove the letters *un* from the word *uncle*, you are left with *cle*, which is not a word. This means that the *un* in *uncle* is not a prefix.

At this point, the teacher asks students if they know any additional prefixes, being generally accepting of their answers, but (assuming that some responses are incorrect) noting afterwards that some of the elements given are not actually prefixes and that the class will continue to work on what is and what is not a prefix as the unit progresses.

Finally, the teacher introduces the three prefixes for study the next day—*un-* (not), *re-* (again), and *in-* (not)—putting them on the poster, asking students to copy them down, and asking each student to bring in a word beginning with one of the prefixes the next day.

Day 2: Instruction to the First Three Prefixes

At the beginning of the session, the teacher refers to the "Basic Facts" poster, briefly reminding students what prefixes are, where they appear, and why it is important to know about them. Then, the teacher calls on some students to give the prefixed

Basic Facts About Prefixes

1. A prefix is a group of letters that goes in the front of the word.

2. In *unhappy*, the prefix is *un-* and the root word is *happy*.

3. A prefix changes the meaning of a word. If you remove a prefix, you still have a real word.

4. Knowing about prefixes can help you determine the meaning of a new word.

Some Important Prefixes

Prefix	Meaning	Example
un-	not	unhappy
re-	again	review
in-	not	incomplete

words they have located, jotting those that are indeed prefixed words on the board, and gently noting that the others are not actually prefixed words and that they will discuss them later.

After this, the teacher begins the standard instructional routine for teaching prefixes and prefix removal. We suggest this standardized routine for three reasons. First, there is experimental evidence that it works. Second, using the same routine for teaching all prefixes means that students can soon learn the procedure itself and then concentrate on learning the prefixes and how to work with them. Third, the routine suggested can serve as a model teachers can use in creating a complete set of materials for teaching prefixes and the strategy of prefix removal and replacement.

Next, the teacher tells students that today they will be working with the three prefixes introduced the day before and how to use them in unlocking the meanings of unknown words. The three prefixes are *un-*, meaning "not"; *re-*, meaning "again"; and *in-*, also meaning "not." In teaching these three prefixes, the teacher will use several types of materials—transparencies introducing each prefix, worksheets with brief exercises requiring use of the prefix just taught, transparencies of these worksheets, exercise sheets requiring additional use and manipulation of each prefix, and

THE PREFIX RE-

1. Tom was asked to <u>rewrite</u> his spelling test a second time.

    rewrite—to write again

2. Carmen had to <u>repeat</u> her joke because her grandfather did not hear it.

    repeat—to say again

3. After the heavy doors were battered by the enemy, the soldiers rushed to <u>refortify</u> their stronghold.

    refortify—to make strong again

4. The original movie had been a big hit, so they decided to <u>remake</u> it with some current stars.

    remake—to make again

5. If <u>commence</u> means "begin," then <u>recommence</u> means _____.

review sheets on which students manipulate the three prefixes and the words that were used in illustrating the prefixes for the day. On the back of the worksheets, exercise sheets, and review sheets are answer keys so that students can immediately check their efforts.

Each introductory transparency presents one prefix, illustrates its use with two familiar words and two unfamiliar words, and uses each of the four words in a context-rich sentence. Below each sentence, the word and its definition are shown. And below these sample sentences is a fifth sentence, which gives students a root word and requires them to generate the prefixed form of the word. The introductory transparency for the prefix *re-* is shown in Figure B.6.

Instruction begins with the teacher displaying the first sentence on the introductory transparency and leading students from the meaning of the familiar prefixed word to the meaning of the prefix itself as illustrated in the following dialogue.

Teacher: If Tom were asked to rewrite a test, what must he do?

Students: He has to take it over. He has to take it again.

Teacher: That's correct. Using your understanding of the word *rewrite,* what is the meaning of the prefix *re-?*

Students: Again. A second time. Over again.

The process is repeated with the next three sentences on the transparency. With some prefixes, students are likely to be able to volunteer the response without difficulty. With others, they may need further prompting, in which case the teacher rephrases the sentence to add more clues. If students are still unable to respond after the prompting, the teacher gives the definition. After going through the first four sentences on the *re-* introductory transparency, the teacher presents the fifth sentence, which defines the unknown root word and asks students to define the prefixed word.

After completing introductory instruction on the first prefix, students individually complete their check sheets while a student volunteer completes the check sheet on a transparency. Part of a check sheet is shown in Figure B.7. As soon as students complete their check sheets, the volunteer puts the transparency on the overhead so that all students receive immediate feedback on their work. If the volunteer has made an error, the teacher corrects it at this time.

These same procedures are then completed with the two remaining prefixes for the day—*un-* and *in-.* Following initial instruction on the three prefixes, the students complete a review sheet and immediately receive feedback by checking the answers on the back of the sheet. Part of a review sheet is shown in Figure B.8 (p. 552). While students are completing the review sheet, the teacher monitors their work and provides assistance when requested. This concludes the second day of the unit.

Day 3: Review the Prefix Strategy and the Remaining Three Prefixes

Day 3 begins with the teacher reviewing the basic facts about prefixes on the poster. Then students complete a review sheet on the three prefixes taught the previous day and immediately correct their work.

Next comes another crucial part of the instruction—instruction in the prefix strategy. The teacher introduces the strategy by telling students that now that they have worked some with the strategy and understand how useful prefixes can be in figuring out the meanings of unknown words, the teacher is going to teach a specific strategy for working with unknown words. The teacher titles the procedure "Prefix Removal and Replacement," emphasizing that they are using a big name for an important idea.

The teacher then puts up the "Prefix Removal and Replacement" transparency, which is reproduced on a prominently displayed "Prefix Removal and Replacement Strategy" poster (shown in Figure B.9 on p. 553), and talks students through the procedure with one or two sample prefixed words.

Following this explicit description of the strategy and modeling of its use, the teacher tells students that they will continue to work on learning the meanings of prefixes and learning to use the strategy today, tomorrow, and in future review sessions. The teacher then points out to students that they now have two posters to refer to when they come to an unknown word that may contain a prefix—the "Basic Facts" poster and the "Prefix Strategy" poster. Finally, the teacher teaches and reviews the remaining three prefixes (*dis-, en-,* and *non-*) using procedures and ma-

CAN YOU FIND IT?

A word or prefix is hidden in each line of letters below. Read the definition of the word or prefix. Then circle the word or prefix when you find it.

1. Find the prefix meaning "under" or "below"

    antidissubplegohnobitto

2. Find the word in each line that means:

    a. "underground railroad"

        shelaunomessubwaywathoning

    b. "to put under water"

        lasubmergersinthergerows

    c. "a plot beneath the main plot"

        thisenroutelesubplotrudiw

    d. "underwater boat"

        mopeitaqksubmarinetshowl

terials that exactly parallel those used on Day 2. This concludes the third day of the unit.

Day 4: Review of the Information About Prefixes, the Prefix Strategy, and the Prefixes Taught

Day 4 begins with the teacher reviewing the four facts about prefixes, again using the "Basic Facts" poster in doing so. As part of the review, the teacher asks students a few questions about these facts to be sure they understand them and answers any questions students have.

Next, the teacher reviews the prefix removal and replacement strategy using the "Prefix Strategy" poster. After this, the teacher continues with the explicit instruction model, first modeling use of the strategy with two of the six prefixes taught and then collaboratively using the strategy in a whole-class session with two more of the

REVIEW SHEET ON *UN-*, *RE-*, AND *IN-*

A. Match the prefix in the first column to its meaning in the second column.

  a. *re-* _____ not

  b. *in-* _____ again

  c. *un-* _____ not

B. Complete the following sentences with a word from the list below.
You will not use every word.

   rewrite   inaudible   incomplete

   reconnect   unhappy   ungrateful

  1. Because Feng-Yi was in such a hurry to finish her test before the bell
rang, her last answer was _____ .

  2. A nearly _____ cry escaped her as she hid behind the
curtain.

six prefixes. After this, the teacher divides students into small groups and provides guided practice by having the groups use the strategy with the final pair of prefixes. The teacher also has some of the groups share their work and their findings, thus providing guided practice.

As the final activity of the initial instruction, small groups of students work together on a quiz. The quiz requires them to state the four facts about prefixes, state the steps of the prefix removal and replacement strategy, and give the meanings of the six prefixes taught. As soon as students complete the quiz, they correct the quiz in class so that they get immediate feedback on their performance and hand the corrected quizzes in so that the teacher has this information to plan reviews.

Reviewing, Prompting, and Guiding Students to Independence

At this point, the instruction is far from complete. If we really want students to remember what a prefix is, recognize and know the meanings of some prefixes, and use the prefix removal and replacement strategy when they come to unknown words

THE PREFIX REMOVAL AND REPLACEMENT STRATEGY

When you come to an unknown word that may contain a prefix:

- Remove the "prefix."

- Check that you have a real word remaining. If you do, you've found a prefix.

- Think about the meaning of the prefix and the meaning of the root word.

- Combine the meanings of the prefix and the root word, and infer the meaning of the unknown word.

- Try out the meaning of the "unknown" word in the sentence, and see if it makes sense. If it does, read on. If it doesn't, you'll need to use another strategy for discovering the unknown word's meaning.

in their reading, reviewing what has been taught and prompting students to use the strategy while reading is crucial.

By reviewing, we mean formal reviews. Have the first review about a month after the initial instruction, a second review two months after that, and a third review, if it seems necessary, several months after that. Each review might last 30–45 minutes. Two somewhat conflicting considerations are important in undertaking these reviews. The first is that it does no good and in all probability does some harm to spend time "teaching" students things they already know. Thus, if at the beginning of a review, it is apparent that students already know the material, the review should be very brief or should be conducted for that small group of students who still need additional instruction.

By prompting, we simply mean reminding students about prefixes and the prefix strategy at appropriate points when they are reading. Thus, when students are about to read a selection that contains some unknown prefixed words, the teacher might say something like, "In looking through today's reading, I noticed some pretty hard words that begin with prefixes. Be on the lookout for these, and if you don't know them, try using the prefix strategy to figure out their meanings." This sort of prompting should probably be fairly frequent, as it can do a lot to move students toward independent use of the strategy.

Comprehension Lesson: A Scaffolded Reading Experience for Teaching the Novel *Because of Winn-Dixie*

Introduction

> Take one disarmingly engaging protagonist and put her in the company of a tenderly rendered canine, and you've got yourself a recipe for the best kind of down-home literary treat. Kate DiCamillo's voice in *Because of Winn-Dixie* should carry from the steamy, sultry pockets of Florida clear across the miles to enchant young readers everywhere.
>
> —Karen Hesse

With the support of the 1998 McKnight Artist Fellowship for Writers and a local writing group, author Kate DiCamillo wove an engaging story for children starring a thoughtful 10-year-old, India Opal, and her beloved friend and pet dog, Winn-Dixie. The resulting book, *Because of Winn-Dixie,* has received much praise, including being named as a 2001 Newbery Honor book and a 2001 Riverbank Review Children's Book of Distinction.

The well-developed characters, universal themes of friendships and grief, and the lyrical prose of the novel have helped make it very popular with children in the intermediate grades. The protagonist, Opal, is a lonely child and searches for friends in the new town to which she and her father have recently moved. The diversity of the friends she gradually makes—from an elderly librarian to a guitar-playing ex-felon who works in the local pet store—and the way she brings them together as a community make for an entertaining tale.

This Scaffolded Reading Experience focuses on these strengths of the novel, making use of DiCamillo's rich and memorable cast of characters. The SRE is designed to help students develop the skills of identifying character traits and distinguishing between personal attributes and physical traits, and to see clearly how authors develop the personality of their characters. Students are asked to use textual quotes as "evidence" of certain traits of individual characters. The SRE was developed particularly for fifth- and sixth-graders and uses instructional routines such as partner and group work, repeated trials at various tasks, and practice at reading skills such as making predictions.

Objectives

- To introduce students to two types of character traits: personal attributes and physical traits
- To give students experience using textual quotes to support an opinion or judgment
- To give students experience making predictions in fiction stories
- To help develop students' awareness of character development in novels

Higher-Order Thinking Skills

- Understanding—Constructing meaning from instructional messages, including oral, written, and graphic communications
- Analyzing—Breaking material into its constituent parts and determining how the parts relate to one another and to an overall structure or purpose
- Evaluating—Making judgments based on criteria and standards

Lesson adapted from Lauren A. Liang, University of Minnesota. Copyright © 2003 Seward Learning Systems, Inc. Available at OnLine Reading Resources, http://onlinereadingresources.com.

Detailed Description of Activities

Day 1

Prereading Activity

Relating the Reading to Students' Lives (20 minutes). Hand out the story preview to students and read it aloud together (see Student Materials). Then have students write for 5 minutes about a time they experienced moving or being the newcomer in a situation at camp, school, etc. After 5 minutes of writing, have students share their writing with a partner in a 2-minute pair-share (In a 2-minute pair-share, each student has 2 minutes to talk without any interruptions about what he or she wrote. After each partner has had 2 minutes, allow 2 minutes for students to ask one another questions or offer comments.) Then ask students to share with the whole group if they so desire.

Next, brainstorm as a whole class ways to make new friends when you are new to a place. After generating a short list of possibilities, tell students the book they are about to read is about a 10-year-old girl who moves to a new town in Florida and the experiences she has as she gets used to her new surroundings and makes friends, as well as dealing with some of the past experiences she has had in her life.

During Reading Activity

Reading to Students (20–25 minutes). Have students open their books and follow along as you read aloud the first two chapters. Discuss the definition of "missionary" when you come across the word. You may also need to describe "Winn-Dixie" if students are unfamiliar with the store.

During Reading Activity (as homework)

Silent Reading. Have students read Chapters 3 and 4 for homework but allow time for them to begin reading at school.

Day 2

Postreading Activity

Questioning (5 minutes). On the board or overhead, have students help write the list of 10 things Opal finds out about her mother.

Prereading Activities

Preteaching Concepts (20 minutes). Ask students which of the items are physical traits; that is, things that describe Mama's physical appearance. Label these items "P. T." Then have students look at the remaining items. Explain that these items describe Mama in a different way: They are all examples of personal attributes Mama has. Tell students that when we describe a person, we often use both physical traits and personal attributes. For example, Brian is tall with brown hair and very patient with younger children. Then ask students, "How does an author let the reader get to know a character?" Brainstorm ideas, ultimately leading students to see that authors, most of the time, develop characters through physical descriptions, dialogue with others, inner thoughts, and actions. Through these ways, we get a picture of that character and his or her personality. Tell students that while they read this book, they are going to be looking and talking about the "character traits" of the characters. They'll be finding quotes in the story that show physical traits and personal attributes each character has.

Have students practice this idea of using physical traits and personal attributes for description by choosing a person they know well (their mom or dad, brother or sister, or best friend) and making a list of five physical traits and five personal attributes of that person. Circle the room and check students' work to see if they have the right idea. Have students share some of the personal attributes they came up with. Then pass out the list of possible personal attributes (see Student Materials). Explain that this is only a partial list and that they should add more ideas to the list.

Now ask students to think about the character of Opal. Based on what they have read so far, what personal attributes does Opal have? As students suggest ideas, ask them to explain why they think that attribute fits and back up their reason with a specific quote from the book. You will likely need to guide students to find quotes. For example, if a student suggests Opal is brave because she saved Winn-Dixie from the pound, have students look at pages 9 and 10 and find the quote that supports this idea: " 'Wait a minute!' I hollered. 'That's my dog. Don't call the pound.' All the Winn-Dixie employees turned around and looked at me, and I knew I had done something big. And maybe stupid, too. But I couldn't help it. I couldn't let that dog go to the pound."

Direction Setting (15 minutes). Pass out the double-entry journal guide (see Student Materials) to students. Read through the guide with students and explain they will be responsible for doing an entry for each chapter assigned for homework. They must do personal attributes and not physical traits, and should do two for each chapter. (These do not have to be for the same character.) Demonstrate an example on the board or overhead using a personal attribute for Opal that was just suggested.

During Reading Activity (as homework)

Silent Reading. Have students read Chapters 5 and 6 for homework but allow time for them to begin reading at school.

Postreading Activity

Writing. Students should write in their double-entry journals for each chapter (two personal attributes with textual evidence per chapter).

Day 3
Postreading Activity

Discussion (10 minutes). Begin by having students briefly share their double-entry journal assignments, either with partners or in small groups. Ask a few students to volunteer examples to the whole class.

Then as a whole class, briefly discuss Opal's adaptation to her new town so far. Does it seem like she has made any new friends?

Prereading Activity

Predicting (10 minutes). Give students 3 or 4 minutes to write down their predictions of what Miss Fanny's story might be. Share a few of these ideas as a whole class

During Reading Activity

Reading to Students (15 minutes). Read aloud Chapter 7 to the students while they follow along.

Prereading Activity

Predicting (5 minutes). Have students make predictions about Amanda and the role she will play in the book.

During Reading Activity (as homework)

Silent Reading. Have students read Chapters 8, 9, and 10 for homework.

Postreading Activity (as homework)

Writing. Students should write in their double-entry journals for each chapter (two personal attributes with textual evidence for each chapter).

Day 4
Postreading Activity

Graphic Activity (45 minutes). Have students in partner groups create a list of all the characters in the book so far. For each character, they should list two personal attributes next to the character's name. Next to these two traits, have the students draw the character, showing two physical traits in the picture.

Have students share their work with each other.

Prereading Activity

Building Background Knowledge (5 minutes). Discuss briefly with students how animals often react to storms.

During Reading Activity (as homework)

Silent Reading. Have students read Chapters 11, 12, and 13 for homework but allow time for them to begin reading at school.

Postreading Activity (as homework)

Writing. Students should write in their double-entry journals for each chapter (two personal attributes with textual evidence for each chapter).

Day 5
Postreading Activity

Discussion (5 minutes). Ask students to share one of the personal attributes they discovered in the previous night's reading, and the textual evidence they wrote down as the supportive quote.

During Reading Activity

Reading to Students (15 minutes). Read aloud Chapter 14 to students as they follow along.

Postreading Activity

Discussion (20 minutes). Have students reread the lines on page 96 that say, "Judge them by what they are doing now." Then ask students if they would rather be judged by what they are doing right now or by what they were like in the past. Have students debate this idea in small groups and then as a whole class.

During Reading Activity (as homework)

Silent Reading. Have students read Chapters 15, 16, and 17 for homework but provide time for them to begin reading at school.

Postreading Activity (as homework)

Writing. Students should write in their double-entry journals for each chapter (two personal attributes with textual evidence for each chapter).

Day 6
Postreading Activities

Writing and Drama (40 minutes). On the board or overhead, write the word "bittersweet." Give students 10 to 15 minutes to write about an experience in their lives that they would call "bittersweet." After the writing time is over, have students share their stories with small groups. Then have each small group of students choose one story to act out in a brief skit for the class. Allow a few of the groups to act out their stories for the class.

Discussion (5 minutes). As a whole class, briefly discuss why India Opal's life is "bittersweet."

Prereading Activity

Predicting (5 minutes). Have students predict what they think will happen next in the story.

During Reading Activity (as homework)

Silent Reading. Have students read Chapters 18, 19, and 20 for homework.

Postreading Activity (as homework)

Writing. Students should write in their double-entry journals for each chapter (two personal attributes with textual evidence for each chapter).

Day 7
Postreading Activity

Discussion (10 minutes). Have students pull out their double-entry journal assignments. Looking at what they have written, does it look like any of the characters have changed and may show different personal attributes than they did before? Have students give examples from the text that show how characters may have changed.

Prereading Activity

Predicting (5 minutes). Have students predict what will happen at the party.

During Reading Activity

Reading to Students (25 minutes). Read aloud Chapters 21 and 22 to your students.

During Reading Activity (as homework)

Silent Reading. Have students read Chapters 23, 24, and 25 for homework.

Postreading Activity (as homework)

Writing. Students should write in their double-entry journals for each chapter (two personal attributes with textual evidence for each chapter).

Day 8
Postreading Activity

Discussion (10 minutes). Have students share with partners their favorite parts of the last four chapters in the book. Share a few of these as a whole class.

During Reading Activity

Reading to Students (15 minutes). Read aloud Chapter 26 to students.

Postreading Activity

Questioning (20 minutes). Have students respond in writing to two questions:

1. Why is 10 things not enough?
2. Do you think the ending is positive or negative? Why?

If time allows, you may want to discuss these questions orally.

Days 9–10
Postreading Activities

Graphic and Artistic Activities and Writing (60–120 minutes and as homework). As a final activity for the book, have students work on the following assignment in class and as homework: "Make a poster featuring one of the characters in the story. The poster must contain a picture of the character exhibiting three physical traits that were mentioned in the story. These traits should be labeled and a quote from the text written by the label as evidence. Underneath the picture, list five personal attributes of the character with a quote from the text to support each attribute. At the very bottom of the poster, write what is 'bittersweet' for that character" (see Student Materials).

Discussion (20–30 minutes). Allow students to view one another's posters and make positive comments. One way you can do this is to have students place their posters on their desks and rotate seats every few minutes. A piece of paper left at the desk can be used for the "visiting" students to write a positive comment.

Optional Additional Activities

1. Write an essay about an experience you have had that is bittersweet.
2. Read Kate DiCamillo's book *The Tiger Rising* (Candlewick Press, 2001). How is it bittersweet? Compare India Opal to Rob of *The Tiger Rising*.
3. Draw a picture of one of the scenes in the book that you think is very important to revealing one of the character's personality traits. Explain in writing why you think this scene is important for that reason.
4. Write a song (lyrics only, to a tune you know) that Oliver might sing to his pets in the store. Explain why you think Oliver would sing this song.

Student Materials

Student materials for *Because of Winn-Dixie* include a preview, a possible personal attributes (character traits) handout, a double-entry journal handout, and a final project prompt and checklist.

- Preview for *Because of Winn-Dixie*. A preview (Graves, Prenn, & Cooke, 1985) is a well-crafted introduction to a text that is read to students prior to their reading the text itself. Previews include an introduction designed to gain students' attention, an overview of the text up to a suitable stopping place, and brief directions for reading.
- *Because of Winn-Dixie* Possible Personal Attributes (Character Traits) Handout. This handout lists attributes that characters might have.
- *Because of Winn-Dixie* Double-Entry Journal Assignment. A form for listing character traits and quotes indicating those traits.
- *Because of Winn-Dixie* Final Project. Instructions for creating the final project, a poster with specific characteristics.

Preview for *Because of Winn-Dixie*

Have you ever moved to a new town? Or transferred to a new school with very few people you know? Or maybe gone to a summer camp away from home? Most people at one point or another have experienced what it is like to be new to a place. Perhaps the biggest challenge of being the newcomer is making friends. Think back to a time when you were the new person. How did it feel not to know anyone? Did you try to start conversations with others? Did you watch people closely? Can you remember what it felt like when you first met someone who might be a friend?

In *Because of Winn-Dixie,* you will meet India Opal, a 10-year-old girl who has just moved to a new town in Florida. You'll go along with her as she begins to get used to her new home and make friends. You will hear her first impressions of the people she meets, and see if any of those impressions change. You may also see that moving to the new town could change Opal, too.

Because of Winn-Dixie **Possible Personal Attributes (Character Traits) Handout**

Aggressive	Enthusiastic	Kind	Self-conscious
Agreeable	Fearless	Lazy	Selfish
Ambitious	Flexible	Loyal	Self-sacrificing
Angry	Foolish	Merciful	Sensible
Appreciative	Friendly	Mischievous	Serious
Arrogant	Generous	Modest	Servile
Bashful	Gentle	Narrow-minded	Shy
Boastful	Grouchy	Noble	Stubborn
Brave	Gullible	Obedient	Subservient
Calculating	Hard-working	Observant	Superstitious
Candid	Honest	Overconfident	Suspicious
Cautious	Honorable	Patient	Thoughtful
Clever	Humble	Perceptive	Thoughtless
Conceited	Humorous	Persistent	Timid
Confident	Imaginative	Proud	Trusting
Considerate	Impatient	Reasonable	Uncooperative
Cooperative	Impulsive	Reliable	Understanding
Courageous	Inconsiderate	Responsible	Unreasonable
Curious	Independent	Rigid	Unselfish
Deceitful	Industrious	Sarcastic	Wise
Determined	Insecure	Scornful	
Dishonest	Insincere	Self-centered	

Because of Winn-Dixie Double-Entry Journal Assignment

For each chapter of Kate DiCamillo's *Because of Winn-Dixie* you will create a page in your character double-entry journal. Use the format below and the sample entry to help you.

Today's Date: _____

Chapter: _____

Character's Name and Personal Attribute	Quote from Text Showing This Personal Attribute
Name of Character: Personal Attribute:	Page Number of Quote: Quote: Why This Quote Works:
Name of Character: Personal Attribute:	Page Number of Quote: Quote: Why This Quote Works:

Sample Entry for Double-Entry Journal

Today's Date: _April 13_

Chapter: _15_

Character's Name and Personal Attribute	Quote from Text Showing This Personal Attribute
Name of Character: *Opal* Personal Attribute: *considerate*	Page Number of Quote: *p. 100* Quote: *"I worried about him hogging the fan."* Why This Quote Works: *This quote shows that Opal is worried that her dog, Winn–Dixie, is sitting in front of the fan and Miss Fanny might not get any of the cool air from the fan. Since it is Miss Fanny's library and her fan, Opal doesn't want her dog, who is a guest, to hog all the fan.*

Because of Winn-Dixie **Final Project**

    As a culminating activity after reading Kate DiCamillo's *Because of Winn-Dixie,* you are to create a special poster for one character of your choice. The poster must contain a picture of the character exhibiting three physical traits that were mentioned in the story. These traits should be labeled and a quote from the text written by the label as evidence. Underneath the picture, list five personal attributes of the character with a quote from the text to support each attribute. At the very bottom of the poster, write what is "bittersweet" for that character.

Checklist for Final Project

Name of Character:

Put a check mark by each step when you complete it.

    1. Picture of character.

    2. Three physical traits of character labeled on picture.

    3. Quote from text for each physical trait next to label.

    4. List of five personal attributes of character.

    5. Quote from text for each personal attribute labeled.

    6. Paragraph written on bottom of poster explaining what is "bittersweet" for the character.

Sources of the Reading Selections, Additional Readings, and Other Material

Sources of the Reading Selections

DiCamillo, Kate. *Because of Winn-Dixie.* New York: Candlewick Press, 2000. 182 pp.

DiCamillo, Kate. *The Tiger Rising.* New York: Candlewick Press, 2001. 116 pp.

Criticism/Book Reviews

Engberg, Gillian. *Because of Winn-Dixie. Booklist.* May 1, 2000, Volume 96, Number 17, p. 1665.

James, Helen Foster. *Because of Winn-Dixie. School Library Journal.* June 2000, Volume 46, Number 6, p. 143.

Because of Winn-Dixie. The Horn Book Magazine. July 2000, Volume 76, Number 4, p. 455.

Internet Sites

http://childrensbooks.about.com/cs/authorsillustrato/a/katecamillo.htm—Summary of chat with Kate DiCamillo.

www.katedicamillo.com/about.html—Kate DiCamillo's personal website.

Reference

Graves, M. F., Prenn, M. C., & Cooke, C. L. (1985). The coming attraction: Previewing short stories to increase comprehension. *Journal of Reading, 28,* 594–598.

Comprehension Lesson: Teaching Students the Strategy of Making Inferences

Strategies are mental actions we use to understand and remember what we read. Teaching comprehension strategies—such as establishing a purpose for reading, using prior knowledge, asking and answering questions, making inferences, determining what is important, summarizing, dealing with graphic information, imagining and creating graphic representations, and monitoring comprehension—is important at all grade levels. Only when the reader has acquired some word recognition fluency is he able to turn his mental energy to comprehension strategies. Starting in second grade students are able to use comprehension strategies to construct meaning and can begin to do so without continual teacher support. Described below are the first three days of a unit on making inferences as it might be presented to third-, fourth- or fifth-grade students.

Day 1: Making Inferences Introduction

Motivation and Interest Building (about 5 minutes)

Make a small chart on the whiteboard (see Figure B.10). Ask the students what toy or game they would very much like to have. Answers will vary, but Wii or Playstation 4 will most likely be included. Label these as goals. Then ask the students how they plan to acquire a Wii. They might say they will ask for it as a birthday present, do odd jobs, or beg. Explain that these are strategies, actions we can take to achieve a goal.

Now switch the discussion to reading and ask, "What are your goals when you read?" Some possible responses might include finish the assignment, remember new ideas, enjoy a good story, or learn information. If the students leave out any of these ideas, add them to the chart yourself. Once you have established the goals, begin to discuss strategies. "What are some strategies that we use that help us achieve these goals?" The students' responses might include rereading a story, making notes, sounding out words, and so forth. You might add other strategies you have studied, such as making predictions and asking questions. Explain that today the class will learn a new strategy called making inferences.

Figure B.10 Just What Is a Strategy?

	Your Goals	**Your Strategies**
Toys & Games	To have a Wii or a Playstation 4	Ask for it as a birthday present Do odd jobs Save up my allowance
Reading		

Explanation and Modeling (about 20–30 minutes)

Write the following sentence on the board and begin the discussion leading the students to understand what inferences are and how we make them.

> Mary looked at her menu trying to find the cheapest entrée while John gazed lovingly in her eyes.

First ask, "Where are John and Mary?" Almost all students will infer that they are in a restaurant, but your goal is to discover how that inference is made. Ask the students what clues in the sentence tell them that John and Mary are in a restaurant. Most will focus on the words *menu* and a few on the word *entrée.* Now that they have discovered the text information necessary to draw an inference, lead the students to examine their own experiences or knowledge, the second component of an inference. Ask the students, "Have you been to a restaurant?" "Do all restaurants have menus?" "Does your mother hand you a menu before dinner at home?" As these questions are discussed, explain that we make an inference by considering text clues and our prior knowledge to add to a text what the author has left out. Enter the students' responses on the "Making Inferences" chart (Figure B.11).

Briefly discuss why the author does not have to explain everything and why he can leave out the important fact that Mary and John are in a restaurant. He counts on the reader to add his or her knowledge and experiences to the text to complete what the author has omitted. We call this process *making inferences,* or *reading between the lines.* At times, we can infer how a character feels, what kind of person the character is (character traits, see the list in the previous lesson on p. 562), or what causes a character to act or behave in a certain way.

Reveal more about how the strategy works by reading the next paragraph and discussing with the students what inferences they might make. Make sure that the students think about what the author did not explain, what was left out. Next, tell students to look for clues in the text and think about what they know or have experienced in their own lives.

> The team boarded the school bus and started out for the big game. If they won this game, they would be champions! Suddenly, fifteen miles from the site of the game, the bus broke down. There they sat, waiting. Nobody seemed to know what to do, and it was getting closer and closer to game time.

Figure B.11 **Making Inferences Chart**

Clues in the Text	Your Knowledge/Experiences	Inferences/Conclusions
Menu, entrée	All restaurants I have been to have a menu, even McDonalds.	Mary and John must be in a restaurant.

As the discussion about this paragraph develops, point out the salient text clues if the students do not. They should note that the bus has broken down, the students are going to an important game, and nobody knows what to do. If they don't point out these clues, you must. Next, ask the students how they might feel if they were trapped in a similar situation. Update the "Making Inferences" chart with text clues, the students' prior knowledge, and the inferences they have drawn.

Have the students read the next paragraph and then work with a partner to discover what the author left unsaid. The goal is to discover the feelings, goals, or motives of the characters. Use the chart in Figure B.11 to record the text clues and the students' personal experiences.

Mario was smiling. There were cute little puppies lined up in cages and lots of goldfish swimming around in a huge tank. He could hear birds chirping, kittens meowing, and gerbils running on their little wheels. He had a big decision to make. His dad looked at him, smiled, and said, "Well, here we are! Are you ready for your new responsibility?" Mario's heart started beating faster. He was so glad Dad said yes to what he had wanted for so long!

End the lesson by introducing the anchor chart (see Figure B.12). At this time you will review what an inference is and the thinking process that most readers employ. Check to see if students were following you by asking a few students to explain the strategy and tell why it is important when they read.

Day 2: Large-Group Student Guided Practice (20 minutes)

Begin the lesson by asking the students to explain the strategy they were studying yesterday. Ask students to name the strategy, explain how to make an inference, and

---

Figure B.12 Inference Anchor Chart

MAKING INFERENCES

- Think about what the author did not tell us—feelings, character traits, motives.

- Look for clues in the text.

- Think about what you know. Think about similar experiences you have had.

- Relate your experiences to the clues in the story. Make the inferences.

- Do the inferences make sense in the context of the story?

explain the importance of making inferences. Expand on the question of importance by exploring with the students when we make inferences. The discussion should focus on the following ideas.

- We make inferences when we sense that the author has left something out. Often it is a clear statement about a character's feelings, traits, or motives.
- We make inferences when we add something to the text that helps the story make more sense.

Continue the discussion and have the students explain how we go about making inferences, using the inference anchor chart (Figure B.12) as a guide. Remind them that the strategy of making inferences has several different names. At times it will be called "making inferences," others may call the strategy "drawing conclusions" and sometimes "making generalizations." The underlying thinking is the same. You need to read between the lines and think about what the author did not tell you. Next, you need to search for text clues and at the same time relate what you are reading to your own knowledge and experiences.

Then, using the paragraphs below, engage the students in a third round of making inferences. Have the students consider what the author might have left out. What can they infer about the characters, what they are doing, and what they are feeling?

> Billy was crying. His hands were scraped up and his knees were bloody. Grandpa said, "You have tried so hard today and you haven't given up! You know they say, 'Practice makes perfect.' I know you can do this." Billy stood up and let out a big sigh. "I know, Grandpa. But I'm getting tired." "How about two more tries and then we'll go get some ice cream?" "Okay, sounds good," Billy responded.
>
> He grabbed the handles, pulled on the button, and rang the bell. The tinkling sound always made him feel better. He slowly straddled the seat and put his left foot on the pedal. "Take your time," Grandpa warned. As he picked up a little speed, Billy put his right foot on the other pedal. He could sense Grandpa close behind him holding the seat. All of a sudden, he felt the wind blowing into his face. Grandpa let go and started clapping. Billy was doing it! He swallowed the lump in his throat and laughed out loud. Grandpa was right! The more you practice, the better you will get.

Add the students' comments to the "Making Inferences" chart in Figure B.11. Be sure to discuss the clues in the text and the students' prior knowledge or experiences. Several more paragraphs for you to use with your students are included at the end of this lesson.

Day 3: Making Inferences with Real Text (20 minutes)

It is now time to apply the task of making inferences to the reading and comprehending of a real text, not just a few well-formed paragraphs. We can support students' inference generation by asking many inferential questions, but we should also help them discover these inferences on their own. For this next lesson, review all of the information on the inference poster. Students should have a decent understanding of an inference and the thinking process that underlies it. They should think about what the author has omitted, search for text clues, and relate their prior knowledge and experiences to the text.

Planning the Third Day Lesson

Planning is key to the success of helping students make inferences with lengthy texts such as short stories or novels. First, pick a text that demands that the reader make inferences—a text that demands that the reader think along with the writer. Next, read the selection twice, first to gain an overall understanding and second to determine what inferences will be necessary to fully comprehend the selection. Examine the text and determine whether you need to teach any vocabulary words to support the students' comprehension. Consider what prior knowledge you will need to develop before the students read and discuss the selection. Next, pick the points where students will stop reading to discuss portions of the selection. Finally, prepare the questions and prompts you will use to stimulate the inference generation process and encourage discussion.

Introduce the Selection and Develop Prior Knowledge

Begin the lesson by giving the students a brief preview of the reading selection and taking some time to develop their prior knowledge. Remember, if the students are to make inferences, they must draw upon their prior knowledge. So this portion of the lesson is critical to their success in making inferences. If for example, the story is about a boy wishing his father would take him fishing and the father avoiding the idea at all costs, begin with a few simple questions.

1. What do you like to do with your parents?
2. Do your parents always do what you want them to do? How do you feel when they say no?
3. How do you get your parents to do what you want?

This discussion will build the knowledge that the students need to make the necessary inferences. Before reading, it is also important to teach a few of the critical vocabulary words that the students do not know.

Reading the Selection and Making Inferences

Have the students read a portion of the selection and then stop to discuss it. Begin the discussion by asking the students to summarize what they have read. Ask, "What is the story about? What did the author tell us?" Next, begin the inferential thinking by starting with broad questions. "What did we learn about the character?" "What kind of person is he or she?" "What did his words or actions tell us about his feelings or his character?" If these broad questions do not solicit the necessary inferences, then become more specific and focus on particular events and reactions in the story. Remember to ask students to search for important text clues.

When students have difficulty answering these inferential questions, it is important to take them into their own experiences. For example, if in the story the child repeatedly asks about going fishing, but the father has excuses and puts the son off, ask the following question: "How do you think that the son feels?" If the students struggle to construct an answer, remind them of their own experiences. "How do you feel when your parents don't do what you have asked?" Making the questions personal helps the students apply what they know and have experienced to answering the questions.

You will continue discussing the selection in this manner. When you have completed the discussion, review some of the important inferences that your students made. What have you and the students learned about the characters, their feelings, and their motivations? Consider what clues in the text helped you make these inferences and what prior knowledge was necessary to make these inferences. As you and the students continue to read and discuss short stories, picture books, and novels during the year, making inferences will always be an important strategy. Return to the poster whenever students need a review of the strategy.

Sasha licked her bowl clean. She grabbed her bone, jumped up on the chair, and started chewing. When she heard keys jingle in the doorknob, she started wagging her tail. Jermaine was home!

My forehead started sweating as I pumped my arms in the wind. My new sneakers felt great on my feet. I picked up my pace. I could see the finish line in the distance. The crowd was going wild for me!

Mom and Jeffrey raced around the house collecting Jeff's spikes, glove, water bottle, cap, and uniform. His stuff was hard to find because it was still dark outside and they didn't even think to turn the lights on. Jeff yawned as he searched every corner of the house. When they finally gathered everything in Jeff's bag, they ran out the door. This was going to be a long day, but Jeffrey was excited!

Jenny's arms were sore and her legs were tired. She let out a heavy sigh. She was sick of putting her belongings in all the boxes. As she took down pictures of her friends off the wall, she wiped her tears away. Who knew when she would see them again? Her room was almost empty. By tonight her family would be gone.

The boys snuck slowly up the front sidewalk. The sun was almost behind the trees so it was pretty dark. They tiptoed up the creaky stairs of the front porch. The door squealed as David slowly pushed it open. Spider webs hung in the dark corners of the tall ceiling. It looked like no one had lived there for years. There was dust covering everything. All of a sudden, there was a loud BANG upstairs. John screamed! David felt a chill up his spine. It sounded like someone was slowly walking down the stairs! The stories they had heard were true! They ran out the door and never went back again.

Mario was smiling. There were cute little puppies lined up in cages and lots of goldfish swimming around in a huge tank. He could hear birds chirping, kittens meowing, and gerbils running on their little wheels. He had a big decision to make. His dad looked at him, smiled, and said, "Well, here we are! Are you ready for your new responsibility?" Mario's heart started beating faster. He was so glad Dad said yes to what he had wanted for so long!

Comprehension Lesson: A Description of Questioning the Author (QtA)

Questioning the Author is a large- and small-group questioning and discussion procedure developed and validated by Isabel Beck and Margaret McKeown (Beck, McKeown, Hamilton, & Kucan, 1997, 1998; Beck, McKeown, Worthy, Sandora, & Kucan, 1996; McKeown, Beck, & Sandora, 1996). It is, as Beck and McKeown explain, "an approach to text-based instruction that was designed to facilitate building understanding of text ideas" (Beck et al., 1997). Beck and McKeown developed the procedures after several years of research on textbooks (Beck, McKeown, & Gromoll, 1989). They found that textbooks were often difficult for students to understand because they often assumed that students had more prior knowledge of the topics being dealt with than they actually did. As a result, the explanations of ideas and events given in the text were often insufficient to allow students to construct much meaning. This shortcoming of the textbooks was further compounded by the fact that students assumed the texts to be absolute authorities and thus beyond question. When students read a text and did not understand what they had read, they repeatedly saw themselves as totally responsible for their lack of understanding and failed to even consider the possibility that the text itself might be less than perfect.

Prompted by these findings, Beck and McKeown developed QtA with two ideas in mind: (1) to encourage and assist young readers in getting under the surface of the material they were reading, dig into it, and engage with the ideas the texts presented and (2) to assist students in realizing that textbooks are simply someone's ideas written down and that readers frequently need to work hard to figure out what the author is trying to say.

Their procedure for doing this is simple and straightforward. First, the teacher explains to children that texts are in fact written by ordinary people who are not perfect and who create texts that are not perfect. Consequently, readers need to continually work hard to figure out what the authors are trying to say. QtA proceeds by having the class read a text together, with the teacher stopping at critical points to pose queries that invite students to explore and grapple with the meaning of the text. The queries include initiating prompts such as "What's the author trying to say?" to get students started in grappling with the text, follow-ups such as "What does the author mean by that?" to encourage them to dig for deeper meaning, and follow-ups such as "How does that connect with what the author told you?" to encourage them to put ideas together. However, queries are not scripted, and teachers are encouraged to modify those suggested and make up their own to fit the students and texts they are working with.

The key purpose of QtA is building understanding from text. As Beck and McKeown note, understanding does not come from a casual reading of the text and the assumption that the author's meaning will somehow be absorbed by the reader. Instead, understanding comes when the reader considers, manipulates, grapples with, and integrates information gleaned from the text with his existing knowledge. QtA involves students as they read the text for the first time rather than after they have read or during a second reading. This is a very important characteristic of QtA and one that distinguishes it from many other questioning and discussion techniques. The goal of QtA is that students will actually have the experience of constructing meaning for text as they are reading, not that they will be told about what they might have experienced after the fact.

Another very important characteristic of QtA that distinguishes it from many other questioning and discussion techniques is that QtA discussions focus specifically on the text. QtA discussions are not wide-ranging conversations in which students are encouraged to engage in sharing a wide range of opinions and ideas. Instead, the discussion focuses on clarifying, collaboratively constructing meaning for, and ultimately understanding the ideas in the text they are reading. The QtA queries are strategically used by the teacher to direct the discussion to that end. They are general probes that have a very specific purpose—engaging students in grappling with and constructing meaning for the ideas in a text.

In the remainder of our discussion of QtA, we present a segment of a QtA session, consider queries in a bit more detail, explain the process of planning a QtA session, characterize the sorts of discussion you are trying to prompt with QtA, and suggest how you might introduce QtA into a class.

A Sample Questioning the Author Segment

The following classroom scenario, taken from Beck and colleagues (1996, 1997), shows a fifth-grade social studies class studying Pennsylvania history. The class has been working with QtA for some time and is quite skilled in grappling with text ideas. The class is discussing a text segment about the presidency of James Buchanan, a Pennsylvania native. The text indicates that many people believed that Buchanan liked the South better than the North because he believed that it was a person's choice whether or not to have slaves. Following is the class discussion (McKeown, Beck, & Sandora, 1996, pp. 112–113).

Fifth Graders Questioning the Author

Teacher: All right. This paragraph that Tracy just read is really full of important information. What has the author told us in this important paragraph?

Laura: Um, they um think that Buchanan liked the South better because they, he said that it is a person's choice if they want to have slaves or not, so they thought um that he liked the South better than the North.

Teacher: Okay. And what kind of problem then did this cause President Buchanan when they thought that he liked the South better? What kind of problem did that cause?

Next, Janet gives her interpretation of how Buchanan's position on slavery might have affected the voters in Pennsylvania.

Janet: Well, maybe um like less people would vote for him because like if he ran for President again, maybe less people would vote for him because like in Pennsylvania we were against slavery and we might have voted for him because he was in Pennsylvania, because he was from Pennsylvania. That may be why they voted for him, but now since we knew that he was for the South, we might not vote for him again.

At this point, the teacher summarizes Janet's remarks.

Teacher: Okay, a little bit of knowledge, then, might change people's minds.

Then, another student acknowledges Janet's explanation and offers some of his own thoughts.

Jamie: I have something to add on to Janet's 'cause I completely agree with her, but I just want to add something on. Um, we might have voted for him because he was from Pennsylvania so we might have thought that since he was from Pennsylvania and Pennsylvania was an antislavery state, that he was also against slavery. But it turns out he wasn't.

Finally, a third student acknowledges her classmates' thoughts and contributes her ideas to the developing interpretation.

> *Angelica:* I agree with the rest of them, except for one that um, like all of a sudden, like someone who would be in Pennsylvania you want to vote for them but then they wouldn't, they be going for the South and then you wouldn't want to vote for them after that.

The scenario illustrates several key attributes of a QtA discussion. The students are indeed grappling with text meaning; they are really trying to understand the author's meaning. The teacher adroitly directs the discussion, but she does not dominate it. She leaves plenty of room for student input because the purpose is for the students to understand the text; if they're the ones who are going to understand the text, they're the ones who must do most of the talking and thinking. The students respond at some length. Finally, they listen to each other and build on each other's responses as they jointly construct meaning for the text.

Queries

One way to begin to understand queries is to contrast them to traditional questions, which we are more familiar with. Beck and McKeown suggest three dimensions on which the two differ. First, traditional questions assess comprehension with the goal of finding out whether the students understand what they have read. Queries assist students in grappling with text ideas, with the goal of helping them put ideas together. Second, traditional questions serve to evaluate individual student responses and foster teacher-to-student exchanges. Queries "facilitate group discussion about an author's ideas and prompt student-to-student interactions." Finally, traditional questions are generally used either before reading or after reading. Queries "are used on-line during initial reading" of the text.

As we have already pointed out, queries are not scripted and teachers are encouraged to adjust their queries to fit their students, the text, and the purposes in reading the text. Nevertheless, Beck and McKeown have identified a set of queries that are quite useful and serve to illustrate the nature of successful queries. These are shown in Figure B.13.

These, of course, are general queries. In posing queries for a specific text, they become more specific. We have already seen specific examples of initiating and follow-up queries in the QtA segment on President Buchanan. Here, the teacher's initiating query and its lead-in were "All right. This paragraph that Tracy just read is really full of important information. What has the author told us in this important paragraph?" In this same segment, one of the teacher's follow-up queries was "Okay. And what kind of problem then did this cause President Buchanan when they thought that he liked the South better? What kind of problem did that cause?"

Narrative queries, a type we haven't yet discussed, are uniquely suited to narratives. They are used with narratives in addition to initiating and follow-up queries. A representative example of a narrative query comes from a teacher whose class was using QtA as they read George Seldon's *The Cricket in Times Square* (1970). In the part of the story students have just read, Mario Bellini's pet cricket, Chester, ate half of a two-dollar bill. This is a problem because two dollars is a lot of money to the Bellinis. Here is the next paragraph of the story.

> Chester Cricket sat frozen on the spot. He was caught red handed, holding the chewed-up two dollars in his front legs. Muttering with rage, Mama Bellini picked him up by his antennae, tossed him into the cricket cage and clicked the gate behind him. He half

Figure B.13 Some Questioning the Author Queries

INITIATING QUERIES

- What is the author trying to say here?
- What is the author's message?
- What is the author talking about?

FOLLOW-UP QUERIES

- So what does the author mean right here?
- Did the author explain that clearly?
- Does that make sense with what the author told us before?
- How does that connect with what the author has told us here?
- But does the author tell us why?
- Why do you think the author tells us that now?

NARRATIVE QUERIES

- How do things look for this character now?
- How does the author let you know that something has changed?
- How has the author settled that?
- Given what the author has already told us about this character, what do you think he (the character) is up to?

Source: Beck, I. L., McKeown, M. G., Hamilton, R., & Kucan, L. (1997). *Questioning the Author*, p. 45. Newark, DE: International Reading Association.

expected that she would pick him up, cage and all, and throw him onto the shuttle tracks.

After students have read the paragraph the teacher poses this narrative query: "How do things look for Chester?"

As you can see from the sample queries and these examples, the purposes of initiating queries are to make the text information public in the classroom and to get the discussion underway, and the purposes of follow-up queries are to keep the discussion focused and to assist students in elaborating and integrating ideas. The purposes of narrative queries are to focus students' attention on characters and the roles they are playing in the story and on the way the author is crafting the plot.

Planning

There are three steps in planning a QtA lesson. The first step is to read and study the text thoroughly in order to identify the major understandings that you want students to achieve and the potential problems that they may have in achieving those understandings. For example, in reading the text on President Buchanan mentioned above, the teacher might determine that one thing she wants students to understand is that President Buchanan was supported and influenced by people representing diverse views and had to somehow deal with these diverse views. She might further infer that students are unlikely to appreciate the very different views on slavery advanced by different states.

The second step is to segment the text, to divide it into short sections that are read and discussed before students go on to the next section. Sometimes a segment will be quite lengthy, perhaps a page or so. At other times, a segment will be relatively short; for example, the sample discussion we presented for the Buchanan text dealt with a single paragraph—"All right. This paragraph that Tracy just read is really full of important information. What has the author told us in this important paragraph?" At still other times, a segment might be even shorter, dealing with a single sentence, as fifth-grade teacher Rona Greene tells us.

> My fifth-graders are familiar with the Questioning the Author procedure, so when I come up with just a single sentence for them to analyze, they're not surprised. Recently, while reading R. Lawson's *Ben and Me* (1939), I ran across a sentence that was challenging enough and important enough to constitute a Questioning the Author segment. In the story, in which Benjamin Franklin has a mouse companion named Amos, who narrates the story, there comes a point at which Franklin is about to send Amos up in a kite to examine lightning. The text reads, "This question of the nature of lightning so preyed upon his mind that he was finally driven to an act of deceit that caused the first and only rift in our long friendship." I decided that this particular sentence, which indirectly reveals the depth of the friendship between Amos and Franklin but does not directly describe it, was worth serious consideration.

Finally, in addition to deciding what is important in a text, what the likely stumbling blocks are, and how the text will be segmented for the discussion, you need to write down the queries. Although many queries will be modified or even discarded as the discussion proceeds, queries such as "What has the author told us in this important paragraph?" and "How do things look for Chester?" are planned in advance.

Discussion

We have already given one fairly lengthy example of a QtA discussion and described the sort of discussions that QtA is designed to foster. Here, we give another example of a QtA discussion, also from Beck and colleagues (1997), and conclude with a quotation emphasizing that students need to be the principal participants in QtA discussions.

This discussion deals with the sentence from *Ben and Me* just given—"This question of the nature of lightning so preyed upon his mind that he was finally driven to an act of deceit that caused the first and only rift in our long friendship"—and begins with the initiating query shown in the dialogue on the next page (McKeown, Beck, & Sandora, 1996, pp. 110–111).

> *Teacher:* What's the author trying to tell us about Ben and Amos?
>
> *Temika:* That their friendship was breaking up.
>
> *Teacher:* Their friendship was breaking up? OK, let's hang on to that. What do you think, April?
>
> *April:* I agree with the part that their friendship did break up, but um, I think that they got back together because when you were reading um, further, it said that he was enjoying the mouse.
>
> *Teacher:* OK, so let me make sure. You say that he knows that they're friends, and something happened that made them almost not be friends? But they're still friends?

Alvis: I think that um, Amos is just, I think Amos is just lying because in the story it said if they weren't good friends, why would um, um, Ben build a um, kite for, build a kite for him so he could have fun.

Teacher: OK, so Alvis is telling us that, why would Ben go to all that trouble and build that beautiful kite if they weren't friends? A lot of people agreed that their friendship was broken up. Alvis doesn't think their friendship is broken up. Can somebody help me out? What's the author want us to figure out here?

(The teacher sees that April and Alvis are making sense of this sentence by bringing in supporting information from other parts of the text, and she attempts to rephrase their statements to better clarify the nature of the friendship.)

The discussion continues, with two more students grappling with the meaning of the sentence.

Tammy: Um, um, deceit was an act of lying so that means, that means um, sometimes a lie broke up a friendship and, because it made a rift and um, so, and deceit was an act of lying, so their friendship must've broke up because of somebody told um, some kind of lie.

Teacher: Oh, that's interesting. Tammy said that if there were some lying going on, something to break up their friendship, because that's what Amos said, "the first and only rift in our friendship," something must've happened. How many of you agree that something had to happen?

Jamal: I disagree, cause a break in their friendship don't mean they gotta break their friendship.

Teacher: OK, so Jamal thinks that they might still be friends, even though something happened. OK? We're gonna continue 'cause the only way we're gonna find out is if we read some more.

In addition to illustrating how a teacher rephrases and clarifies ideas and keeps the discussion focused as she guides students toward full understanding of this important sentence, this excerpt shows how QtA discussions are dominated by students rather than by teachers. "Students do the work. They construct the meaning, wrestle with the ideas, and consider the ways information connects to construct meaning." Thus, "the discussion becomes an opportunity for students to formulate complete thoughts, respond to the text, react to each other's ideas, and consider new notions" (Beck et al., 1997).

Introducing QtA

Introducing QtA is a straightforward matter, but it is important to include several points in your introduction. First, tell students that the way they are going to be reading and discussing text is probably different from they way they have typically dealt with it. Next, tell them that you and they are going to be reading and discussing short sections of text at some length. That is, they will read a segment of text and then stop and discuss what it means with their classmates. Explain that the reason they need to do this is that a text is simply somebody else's words written down and that sometimes, in fact in quite a few cases, understanding what the author is saying requires close attention to and a good deal of discussion of the text. Finally, note that the discussions you are going to have will deal with the text and the meaning the author is trying to convey rather than with more wide-ranging matters.

That's it. With this ground work laid, and after thoroughly familiarizing yourself with the QtA procedure, you are ready to begin QtA sessions.

Questioning the Author's Impact

Beck and McKeown and their colleagues have worked with QtA for several years and have gathered several sorts of data on its efficacy. First, they implemented QtA with two teachers who showed the traditional pattern of teacher-initiated questions aimed mainly at retrieving information directly from the text and brief student responses that were quickly acknowledged before the next question was asked. A more recent study indicated that QtA helped students achieve greater comprehension than did a more strategy-focused discussion (McKeown, Beck, & Blake, 2009).

But with QtA, their lessons began to change. Typically, a QtA lesson showed collaborative construction of meaning. A student would offer an idea in response to a query, and the teacher and other students would build on and elaborate that idea. As an example, here is a brief excerpt from a QtA social studies lesson on "international cooperation." The class had just read a text segment about countries cooperating to share resources through world trade.

> *Teacher:* What's the author reminding us of here? Reggy?
>
> *Reggy:* That we, um, that we trade resources out of their countries and they trade us out of our resources and we cooperate, by helping each other.

Notice in the above excerpt that Reggy's response is in his own words, strongly suggesting that he is presenting his ideas rather than simply parroting text information. Now notice in the following excerpt how the teacher handles Reggy's response by summarizing part of it and then extending the discussion by forming a question from another piece of what Reggy said.

> *Teacher:* OK, Reggy said we help each other, and that's how we cooperate. When you cooperate, you're working together to get something done. What does Reggy mean by, "we trade resources out of their countries?" What's he talking about? Darleen?

Darleen responds with an explanation about how trade works.

> *Darleen:* He's talking about, when he says we're trading resources out of our country, he means that other countries, like Britain and Japan and China, we get our cotton and our resources that we have that are really popular, and we trade them for money sometimes.

Darleen's response is a fitting conclusion to our discussion of QtA because it indicates the amount of listening, thinking, and connecting that a QtA lesson can elicit. This is the sort of active engagement students need to demonstrate if they are to fully understand a text.

References

Abramson, M. (2002). Lunch special. *Book, 24,* 34–35.

Adams, M. J. (1990). *Beginning to read: Thinking and learning about print.* Cambridge, MA: MIT Press.

Adams, M. J., Foorman, B. R., Lundberg, I., & Beeler, T. (1998). *Phonemic awareness in young children.* Baltimore: Paul H. Brookes.

Afflerbach, P. (2007). *Understanding and using reading assessment, K–12.* Newark, DE: International Reading Association.

Afflerbach, P., Pearson, P. D., & Paris, S. G. (2008). Clarifying differences between reading skills and strategies. *The Reading Teacher, 61*(5), 364–373.

Airasian, P. (1994). *Classroom assessment.* New York: McGraw-Hill.

Allington, R., Guice, S., Michelson, N., Baker, K., & Li, S. (1996). Literature-based curricula in high-poverty schools. In M. F. Graves, P. van den Broek, & B. M. Taylor (Eds.), *The first R: Every child's right to read* (pp. 73–96). New York: Teachers College Press.

Allington, R. L. (1977). If they don't read much, how they ever gonna get good? *Journal of Reading, 21,* 57–61.

Allington, R. L. (1983). The reading instruction provided readers of different abilities. *Elementary School Journal, 83,* 548–559.

Allington, R. L. (1984). Oral reading. In P. D. Pearson, R. Barr, M. L. Kamil, & P. B. Mosenthal (Eds.), *Handbook of reading research* (Vol. 1, pp. 829–864). New York: Longman.

Allington, R. L. (2001). *What really matters for struggling readers: Designing research-based programs.* New York: Longman.

Allington, R. L. (2002). *Big brother and the national reading curriculum: How ideology trumped evidence.* Portsmouth, NH: Heinemann.

Allington, R. L. (2005). The other five "pillars" of effective reading instruction. *Reading Today, 22*(5), 3.

Alvermann, D. (1991). The discussion web: A graphic aid for learning across the curriculum. *The Reading Teacher, 45,* 92–99.

American Educational Research Association. (2004). English language learners: Boosting academic achievement. *Research Points: Essential Information for Educational Policy, 2*(1), 1–4. Washington, DC: Author. Available at www.aera.net/publications/?id=314.

American Educational Research Association (AERA), American Psychological Association (APA), & National Education Association (NEA). (1985). *Standards for educational and psychological testing.* Washington, DC: Author.

American Educator. (1995, Summer). *Learning to read: Schooling's first mission* (Special Issue). Washington, DC: American Federation of Teachers.

American Educator. (1998, Spring/Summer). *The unique power of reading and how to unleash it* (Special Issue). Washington, DC: American Federation of Teachers.

American Federation of Teachers. (1999). *Teaching reading **is** rocket science: What expert teachers of reading should know and be able to do.* Washington, DC: Author.

American Federation of Teachers (AFT), National Council on Measurement in Education (NCME), & National Education Association (NEA). (1990). Standards for teacher competence in educational assessment of students. *Educational Measurement: Issues and Practice, 9*(4), 30–32.

American Guidance Service. (1987). *Woodcock-Johnson reading mastery test.* Cinole Pines, MN: Author.

Ames, C. (1992). Classroom: Goal, structures, and student motivation. *Journal of Educational Psychology, 84,* 261–271.

Anderson, L. W., & Krathwohl, D. R. (2001). *A taxonomy for learning, teaching, and assessing: A revision of Bloom's Taxonomy of Educational Objectives.* New York: Longman.

Anderson, R. C. (1996). Research foundations to support wide reading. In V. Greaney (Ed.), *Promoting reading in developing countries* (pp. 55–77). Newark, DE: International Reading Association.

Anderson, R. C., Hiebert, E. F., Scott, J. A., & Wilkinson, I. A. G. (1985). *Becoming a nation of readers.* Washington, DC: National Institute of Education.

Anderson, R. C., & Nagy, W. E. (1992). The vocabulary conundrum. *American Educator,* Winter, 14–18, 44–47.

Anderson, R. C., & Pearson, P. D. (1984). A schema-theoretic view of basic processes in reading. In P. D. Pearson (Ed.), *Handbook of reading research* (pp. 255–291). White Plains, NY: Longman.

Anderson, R. C., Wilson, P., & Fielding, L. (1988). Growth in reading and how children spend their time outside of school. *Reading Research Quarterly, 23,* 285–303.

Anderson, T. H., & Armbruster, B. B. (1984). Content area textbooks. In R. C. Anderson, J. Osborn, & R. J. Tierney (Eds.), *Learning to read in American schools* (pp. 193–226). Mahwah, NJ: Erlbaum.

Anglin, J. M. (1993). Vocabulary development: A morphological analysis. *Monographs of the Society for Research in Child Development, 58* (10, Serial No. 238).

Anson, C. M., & Beach, R. (1995). *Journals in the classroom: Writing to learn.* Norwood, MA: Christopher-Gordon.

Applegate, A. J., Applegate, M., McGeehan, C. M., Pinto, C. M., & Kong, A. (2009, February). The assessment of thoughtful literacy in NAEP: Why the states aren't measuring up. *The Reading Teacher, 62*(5), 372–381.

Armbruster, B. B., McCarthey, S. J., & Cummins, S. (2005). Writing to learn in elementary classrooms. In R. Indrisano & J. R. Paratore (Eds.), *Learning to write, writing to learn: Theory and research in practice* (pp. 71–96). Newark, DE: International Reading Association.

Aronson, E., Blaney, N., Stephan, C., Sikes, J., & Snapp, M. (1978). *The jigsaw classroom.* Newbury Park, CA: Sage.

Aronson, E., & Patnoe, S. (1997). *The jigsaw classroom: Building cooperation in the classroom.* New York: Longman.

Asfeld, S. T., Schwab, J., Gagliardi, S., & Henke, M. A. (1994). *Nutrition: The good way to health.* Unpublished manuscript.

Association for Library Service to Children. (2004). *The best of the best from 60 years of notable children's books, 1940–99.* Chicago: American Library Association.

Atwell, N. (1987). *In the middle: Writing, reading, and learning with adolescents.* Portsmouth, NH: Heinemann.

Atwell, N. (1998a). *In the middle: New understandings about writing, reading, and learning* (2nd ed.). Portsmouth, NH: Boyton/Cook.

Atwell, N. (1998b). *In the middle: Writing, reading, and learning with adolescents* (2nd ed.). Portsmouth, NH: Heinemann.

Au, K. H. (1993). *Literacy instruction in multicultural settings.* New York: Harcourt, Brace, Jovanovich.

Au, K. H. (1999). Foreword. In J. T. Guthrie & D. E. Alvermann (Eds.), *Engaged reading: Processes, practices, and policy implications* (pp. 17–45). New York: Teachers College Press.

Au, K. H., & Mason, J. M. (1983). Cultural congruence in classroom participation structures: Achieving a balance of rights. *Discourse Processes, 6,* 145–167.

August, D. (2005, October). *Building vocabulary in English-language learners.* Paper presented at the 3rd Guy Bond Memorial Conference on Reading, Minneapolis, MN.

August, D., Carlo, M., Dressler, C., & Snow, C. (2005). The critical role of vocabulary development for English language learners. *Learning Disabilities Research & Practice, 20*(1), 50–57.

August, D., & Hakuta, K. (1998). *Educating language-minority children.* Washington, DC: National Academies Press.

August, D., & Shanahan, J. (Eds.). (in press). *Report of the National Literacy Panel on Language Minority Children and Youth: Acquiring literacy in a second language.* Mahwah, NJ: Erlbaum.

Avery, P. G., & Graves, M. F. (1997). Scaffolding young learners' reading of social studies texts. *Social Studies and the Young Learner, 9*(4), 10–14.

Bamford, R. A., & Kristo, J. V. (1998). *Making facts come alive: Choosing quality nonfiction literature K–8.* Norwood, MA: Christopher-Gordon.

Barnes, B. L. (1996/1997). But teacher you went right on: A perspective on Reading Recovery. *The Reading Teacher, 50,* 284–292.

Barr, C. (Ed.). (1998). *From biography to history.* New Providence, NJ: R. R. Bowker.

Baum, S., Viens, J., & Slatin, B. (2005). *Multiple intelligences in the elementary classroom: A teacher's toolkit.* New York: Teachers College Press.

Baumann, J. F. (1986). The direct instruction of main idea comprehension ability. In J. F. Baumann (Ed.), *Teaching main idea comprehension* (pp. 133–178). Newark, DE: International Reading Association.

Baumann, J. F. (1988). *Reading assessment: An instructional decision-making perspective.* Columbus, OH: Merrill.

Baumann, J. F., Font, G., Edwards, E. C., & Boland, E. (2005). In E. H. Hiebert & M. Kamil (Eds.), *Teaching and learning vocabulary: Bringing research to practice* (pp. 179–205). Mahwah, NJ: Erlbaum.

Baumann, J. F., Kame'enui, E. J., & Ash, G. E. (2003). Research on vocabulary instruction: Voltaire redux. In J. Flood, D. Lapp, J. R. Squire, & J. M. Jensen (Eds.), *Handbook on research on teaching the English language arts* (2nd ed., pp. 752–785). Mahwah, NJ: Erlbaum.

Beach, R. W. (1993). *A teacher's introduction to reader-response theories.* Urbana, IL: National Council of Teachers of English.

Bear, D. R., Invernizzi, M., Templeton, S., & Johnston, F. (2004). *Words their way: Word study for phonics, vocabulary, and spelling instruction* (3rd ed.). Upper Saddle River, NJ: Merrill.

Beaver, J. (1997). *Developmental reading assessment.* Parsippany, NJ: Pearson Learning Group.

Beck, I. L., & McKeown, M. G. (1981). Developing questions that promote comprehension: The story map. *Language Arts, 58,* 913–918.

Beck, I. L., & McKeown, M. G. (1983). Learning words well: A program to enhance vocabulary and comprehension. *The Reading Teacher, 36,* 622–625.

Beck, I. L., & McKeown, M. G. (2001). Text talk: Capturing the benefits of read-aloud experiences for young children. *The Reading Teacher, 55,* 10–20.

Beck, I. L., & McKeown, M. G. (2004). *Increasing young children's oral vocabulary repertoires through rich and focused instruction.* Unpublished paper. University of Pittsburgh, Learning Research and Development Center.

Beck, I. L., McKeown, M. G., & Gromoll, E. W. (1989). Learning from social studies text. *Cognition and Instruction, 6,* 99–158.

Beck, I. L., McKeown, M. G., Hamilton, R., & Kucan, L. (1997). *Questioning the author: An approach for enhancing student engagement with text.* Newark, DE: International Reading Association.

Beck, I. L., McKeown, M. G., Hamilton, R., & Kucan, L. (1998). Getting at the meaning: How to help students unpack difficult text. *American Educator, 22*(1–2), 66–71, 85.

Beck, I. L., McKeown, M. G., & Kucan, L. (2002). *Bringing words to life: Robust vocabulary instruction.* New York: Guilford Press

Beck, I. L., McKeown, M. G., & Omanson, R. C. (1987). The effects and uses of diverse vocabulary instructional techniques. In M. G. McKeown & M. E. Curtis (Eds.), *The nature of vocabulary acquisition* (pp. 147–163). Hillsdale, NJ: Sage.

Beck, I. L., McKeown, M. G., Worthy, J., Sandora, C. A., & Kucan, L. (1996). Questioning the author: A year-long classroom implementation to engage students with text. *Elementary School Journal, 96,* 385–414.

Becker, W. (1977). Teaching reading and language to the disadvantaged: What we have learned from field research. *Harvard Educational Review, 47,* 518–543.

Berliner, D., & Biddle, B. (1995). *The manufactured crisis.* White Plains, NY: Longman.

Berliner, D. C. (1979). Tempus educare. In P. L. Peterson & H. J. Walberg (Eds.), *Research on teaching: Concepts, findings, and implications* (pp. 120- 135). Berkeley, CA: McCutchan.

Bernhardt, E. (1991). *Reading development in a second language.* Norwood, NJ: Ablex.

Bernhardt, E. (2000). Second language reading as a case study of reading scholarship in the twentieth century. In M. Kamil, P. Mosenthal, P. Pearson, & R. Barr (Eds.), *Hand-*

book of reading research (Vol. 3, pp. 791–812). Mahwah, NJ: Erlbaum.

Bernhardt, E. B., & Kamil, M. (1995). Interpreting relationships between L1 and L2 reading: Consolidating the linguistic threshold and the linguistic interdependence hypotheses. *Applied Linguistics, 16,* 15–34.

Berninger, V. W. (1995). Has the phonological recoding model of reading acquisition and reading disability led us astray? *Issues in Education: Contributions from Education and Psychology, 1,* 59–63.

Berninger, V. W., Yates, C., & Lester, R. (1991). Multiple orthographic codes in reading and writing acquisition. *Reading and Writing Quarterly: An Interdisciplinary Journal, 3,* 115–149.

Betts, E. A. (1946). *Foundations of reading instruction.* New York: American Book.

Biemiller, A. (2001). Teaching vocabulary: Early, direct, and sequential. *American Educator, 25*(1), 24–28, 47.

Biemiller, A. (2003, April). *Teaching vocabulary to kindergarten to grade two children.* Paper presented at the annual meeting of the American Educational Research Association, Chicago.

Biemiller, A. (2010). *Words worth teaching.* Columbus, OH: McGraw-Hill SRA.

Bissex, G. L. (1980). *Gnys at wrk: A child learns to read and write.* Cambridge, MA: Harvard University Press.

Blachowicz, C. L. Z., & Fisher, P. (2000). Vocabulary instruction. In M. Kamil, P. Mosenthal, P. D. Pearson, & R. Barr (Eds.), *Handbook of reading research* (Vol. 3, pp. 503–523). New York: Longman.

Block, C. C., & Pressley, M. (Eds.). (2002). *Comprehension instruction: Research-based best practices.* New York: Guilford Press.

Bloodgood, J. R. (1999). What's in a name? The role of name writing in children's literacy acquisition. *Reading Research Quarterly, 34,* 342–367.

Bloom, B. S., Englehart, M. D., Furst, E. J., Hill, W. H., & Krathwohl, D. R. (1956). *The taxonomy of educational objectives. Handbook I: Cognitive domain.* New York: David McKay.

Bloom, B. S., Hastings, J. T., & Madaus, G. F. (1971). *Handbook of formative and summative evaluation of student learning.* New York: McGraw-Hill.

Bloom, B. S., Madaus, G. F., & Hastings, J. T. (1981). *Evaluation to improve learning.* New York: McGraw-Hill.

Blythe, T. (1998). *The teaching for understanding guide.* San Francisco: Jossey-Bass.

Boaler, J. (2002). *Experiencing school mathematics.* Mahwah, NJ: Erlbaum.

Bogner, K., Raphael, L., & Pressley, M. (2002). How grade 1 teachers motivate literate activity by their students. *Scientific Studies in Reading, 6,* 135–165.

Bond, G. L., & Dykstra, R. (1967/1997). The cooperative research program in first-grade reading instruction. *Reading Research Quarterly, 2*(4), 1–142. (Reprinted in *Reading Research Quarterly, 32*(4)).

Bransford, J. D., Brown, A. L., & Cocking, R. R. (Eds.). (2000). *How people learn: Brain, mind, experience, and school* (Expanded ed.). Washington, DC: National Academies Press.

Bransford, J. D., & Schwartz, D. L. (1999). Rethinking transfer: A simple proposal with multiple implications. *Review of Research in Education, 3*(24), 61–100.

Brisbois, J. (1995). Connections between first- and second-language reading. *Journal of Reading Behavior, 27,* 565–584.

Britton, J. N., Burgess, T., Martin, N., McLeod, A., & Rosen, H. (1975). *The development of writing abilities.* New York: Macmillan.

Brophy, J. (1986). Teacher influences on student achievement. *American Psychologist, 41,* 1069–1077.

Brophy, J. (1987). Socializing students' motivation to learn. In M. L. Maehr & D. A. Kleiber (Eds.), *Advances in motivation and achievement: Enhancing motivation* (Vol. 5, pp. 181–210). Greenwich, CT: JAI Press.

Brophy, J. (2000). Beyond balance: Goal awareness, developmental progressions, tailoring to the context, and supports for teachers in ideal reading and literacy programs. In B. M. Taylor, M. F. Graves, & P. van den Broek (Eds.), *Reading for meaning: Fostering comprehension in the middle grades* (pp. 170–192). New York: Teachers College Press.

Brophy, J. (2004). *Motivating students to learn* (2nd ed.). Mahwah, NJ: Erlbaum.

Brown, A. L., & Campione, J. C. (1990). Interactive learning environments and the teaching of mathematics and science. In M. Gardner, J. G. Greeno, F. Reif, A. H. Schoenfeld, A. diSessa, & E. Stage (Eds.), *Toward a scientific practice of science education.* Mahwah, NJ: Erlbaum.

Brown, A. L., & Day, J. D. (1983). Macrorules for summarizing text: The development of expertise. *Journal of Verbal Learning and Verbal Behavior, 22,* 1–14.

Brown, A. L., & Palincsar, A. M. (1989). Guided cooperative learning in individual knowledge acquisition. In L. B. Resnick (Ed.), *Knowing, learning, and instruction.* Mahwah, NJ: Erlbaum.

Brown, J. S., Collins, A., & Duguid, P. (1989). Situated cognition and the culture of learning. *Educational Researcher, 18*(1), 32–42.

Brown, R., Pressley, M., Van Meter, P., & Schuder, T. (1996). A quasi-experimental validation of transactional strategies instruction with low-achieving second-grade readers. *Journal of Educational Psychology, 88,* 18–37.

Brozo, W. G. (2002). *To be a boy, to be a reader.* Newark, DE: International Reading Association.

Bruck, M., & Treiman, R. (1992). Learning to pronounce words: The limitations of analogies. *Reading Research Quarterly, 27,* 375–388.

Buening, A. P. (2006). *Children's writer's and illustrator's market.* Cincinnati, OH: Writer's Digest Books.

Burke, E. M., & Glazer, S. M. (1994). *Using nonfiction in the classroom.* New York: Scholastic.

Burns, M. S., Griffin, P., & Snow, C. E. (1999). *Starting out right: A guide to promoting children's reading success.* Washington, DC: National Academies Press.

Calfee, R. C. (1999). *Interactive reading assessment system-revised* (IRAS-R). Unpublished.

Calfee, R. C. (2000). Writing portfolios: Activity, assessment, authenticity. In R. Indrisano & J. R. Squire (Eds.), *Theoretical models and processes of writing* (pp. 278–304). Newark, DE: International Reading Association.

Calfee, R. C., & Calfee, K. H. (1976). Reading and mathematics observation system (RAMOS/II) (rev.). Unpublished manuscript, Stanford, CA.

Calfee, R. C., & Drum, P. A. (1986). Research on teaching reading. In M. C. Wittrock (Ed.), *Handbook of research on teaching* (3rd ed., pp. 804–849). New York: Macmillan.

Calfee, R. C., & Hiebert, E. H. (1991). Classroom assessment of reading. In R. Barr, M. Kamil, P. Mosenthal, & P. D. Pearson (Eds.), *Handbook of research on reading* (2nd ed., pp. 281–309). New York: Longman.

Calfee, R. C., & Hoover, K. (2004). The interactive reading assessment system–revised. In K. Wilson, R. C. Calfee, M. F. Graves, & G. Trainin, *Assessments and lesson plans for Teaching Reading in the 21st Century* (3rd ed.). Boston: Allyn & Bacon.

Calfee, R. C., & Patrick, C. L. (1995). *Teach our children well.* Stanford, CA: Stanford Alumni Association.

Calfee, R. C., & Perfumo, P. (1993). Student portfolios: Opportunities for a revolution in assessment. *Journal of Reading, 36,* 532–537.

Calfee, R. C., & Wilson, K. M. (2004). Assessment frameworks for composition. In B. Ehren & K. Apel (Eds.), *Handbook of language and literacy development and disorders.* New York: Guilford Press.

California Test Bureau. (1996). *Terra Nova.* Monterey, CA: Author.

Calkins, L. M., Montgomery, K., Santman, D., & Falk, B. (1998). *A teacher's guide to standardized achievement tests: Knowledge is power.* Portsmouth, NH: Heinemann.

Campbell, J. R., Hombo, C. M., & Mazzeo, J. (2000). *NAEP 1999 trends in academic progress: Three decades of student performance.* Washington, DC: U.S. Department of Education.

Canney, G. F., Kennedy, T. R., Schroeder, M., & Miles, S. (1999). Instructional strategies for K–12 limited English proficiency (LEP) students in the regular classroom. *The Reading Teacher, 52*(5), 540–544.

Carey, S. (1978). Child as word learner. In M. Halle, J. Bresnan, & G. Miller (Eds.), *Linguistic theory and psychological reality* (pp. 347–389). Cambridge, UK: Cambridge University Press.

Carroll, J. B. (1966). Some neglected relationships in reading and language. *Elementary English, 43,* 577–582.

Cazden, C. (2001). *Classroom discourse* (2nd ed.). Portsmouth, NH: Heinemann.

Cazden, C. B. (1991). Contemporary issues and future directions: Active learners and active teachers. In J. Flood, J. M. Jensen, D. Lapp, & J. R. Squire (Eds.), *Handbook of research on teaching the English language arts* (pp. 418–422). New York: Guilford Press.

Center for Educational Policy. (2005). *From the capital to the classroom: Year 3 of the No Child Left Behind Act.* Washington, DC: Author. Available at www.cep-dc.org.

Chall, J. S. (1967). *Learning to read: The great debate.* New York: McGraw-Hill.

Chall, J. S. (1996). *Stages of reading development* (2nd ed.). Fort Worth, TX: Harcourt-Brace.

Chambliss, M. J., & Calfee, R. C. (1998). *Textbooks for learning: Nurturing children's minds.* Oxford, UK: Blackwell.

Chen, H-C., & Graves, M. F. (1996). Effects of previewing and providing background knowledge on Taiwanese college students' comprehension of American short stories. *TESOL Quarterly, 29,* 663–686.

Chihak, J. (1999). Success is in the details: Publishing to validate elementary school authors. *Language Arts, 96*(6), 491–498.

Chomsky, C. (1978). When you still can't read in third grade: After decoding, what? In S. J. Samuels (Ed.), *What research has to say about reading instruction* (pp. 13–30). Newark, DE: International Reading Association.

Clark, K. F., & Graves, M. F. (2005). Scaffolding students' comprehension of text. *The Reading Teacher, 56,* 570–580.

Clay, M. (1991). *Becoming literate: The construction of inner control.* Portsmouth, NH: Heinemann.

Clay, M. (1993). *An observation study of early literacy achievement.* Portsmouth, NH: Heinemann.

Clay, M. M. (1979). *The early detection of reading difficulties.* Portsmouth, NH: Heinemann.

Clay, M. M. (1994). *Reading Recovery: A guidebook for teachers in training.* Portsmouth, NH: Heinemann.

Cobb, L. (1835). *The North American reader.* New York: B and S Collins.

Cohen, E. (1994). *Designing group work: Strategies for heterogeneous classrooms.* New York: Teachers College Press.

Cohen, P., Kulic, J., & Kulic, C. L. (1982). Educational outcomes of tutoring: A meta-analysis of findings. *American Educational Research Journal, 19,* 237–248.

Collier, C. C., & Redmond, L. A. (1974). Are you teaching kids to read mathematics? *The Reading Teacher, 5,* 804–808.

Colon-Vila, L. (1997, February). Storytelling in an ESL classroom. *Teaching K–8,* 48.

Connor, C. M., Jakobsons, L. J., Crowe, E., & Meadows, J. G. (2009). Instruction, student engagement, and reading skill growth in reading first classrooms. *The Elementary School Journal, 109,* 221–250.

Connor, C. M., Morrison, F., & Petrella, J. N. (2004). Effective reading comprehension instruction: Examining child instruction interactions. *Journal of Educational Psychology, 96*(4), 682–698.

Connor, C. M., Morrison, F. J., Schatschneider, C., & Underwood, P. (2007). Algorithm-guided individualized reading instruction. *Science, 315,* 464–465.

Connor, C. M., Morrison, F. J., & Underwood, P. S. (2007). A second chance in second grade: The independent and cumulative impact of first- and second-grade reading instruction and student's letter-word reading skill growth. *Scientific Studies of Reading, 11,* 199–234.

Cooke, C. L., & Graves, M. F. (1995). Writing for an audience—for fun. *Middle School Journal, 26*(3), 31–37.

Costa, A. L. (2001). *Developing minds: A resource book for teaching thinking.* Washington, DC: Association for Supervision and Curriculum Development.

Costa, A. L., & Kallick, B. (2004). Launching self-directed learners. *Educational Leadership, 62*(1), 51–55.

Cremin, L. A. (1990). *Popular education and its discontents.* New York: Harper & Row.

Cronbach, L. J. (1960). *Essentials of psychological testing* (3rd ed.). New York: Harper & Row.

Csikszentmihalyi, M. (1990). *Flow: The psychology of optimal experience.* New York: Harper & Row.

CTB/McGraw-Hill. (2001). *Terra Nova* (2nd ed.). Monterey, CA: Author.

Cullinan, B. (1993). *Pen in hand: Children become writers.* Newark, DE: International Reading Association.

Cummins, C., Stewart, M. T., & Block, C. C. (2005). Teaching several metacognitive strategies together increases students' independent metacognition. In S. E. Israel, C. C. Block, K. L. Bauserman, & K. Kinnucan-Welsch (Eds.), *Metacognition in literacy learning* (pp. 277–298). Mahwah, NJ: Erlbaum.

Cummins, J. (2001). *Negotiating identities: Education for empowerment in a diverse society* (2nd ed.). Los Angeles: California Association for Bilingual Education.

Cunningham, A., & Stanovich, K. (2003). Reading matters: How reading English influences cognition. In J. Flood, D. Lapp, J. R. Squire, & J. M. Jensen (Eds.), *Handbook of research on teaching the English language arts* (pp. 666–675). Mahwah, NJ: Erlbaum.

Cunningham, A. E. (2005). Vocabulary growth through independent reading and reading aloud to children. In E. H. Hiebert & M. L. Kamil (Eds.), *Teaching and learning vocabulary: Bringing research to practice* (pp. 45–68). Mahwah, NJ: Erlbaum.

Cunningham, P. (2005, June). *What good is phonics if they don't use it?* Paper presented at the 2005 Minnesota Reading First Summer Literacy Institute, Minneapolis.

Cunningham, P. M., & Allington, R. L. (1999). *Classrooms that work: They can* all *learn to read and write* (2nd ed.). New York: Longman.

Cunningham, P. M., & Cunningham, J. W. (1992). Making words: Enhancing the invented spelling-decoding connection. *The Reading Teacher, 46,* 106–115.

Cunningham, P. M., Hall, D. P., & Defee, M. (1991). Nonability-grouped, multilevel instruction: A year in a first-grade classroom. *The Reading Teacher, 44,* 566–571.

Cunningham, P. M., Hall, D. P., & Defee, M. (1998). Nonability-grouped, multilevel instruction: Eight years later. *The Reading Teacher, 51,* 652–664.

Daniels, H. (1994). *Literature circles: Voice and choice in the student-centered classroom.* New York: Stenhouse.

Deeney, T. A. (2010). One-minute fluency measures mixed message in assessment and instruction. *The Reading Teacher, 63*(6), 440–451.

Delpit, L. D. (1988). The second dialogue: Power and pedagogy in educating other people's children. *Harvard Educational Review, 58,* 280–298.

Delpit, L. D. (1995). *Other people's children: Cultural conflict in the classroom.* New York: The New Press.

Deno, S. (1985). Curriculum-based measurement: The emerging alternative. *Exceptional Children, 52,* 219–232.

Deno, S. (1991). Curriculum-based measurement: The emerging alternative. In J. Kramer (Ed.), *Curriculum-based assessment: Examining old problems, evaluating new solutions.* Mahwah, NJ: Erlbaum.

Derewianka, B. (1990*). Exploring how texts work.* Sydney, NSW: Primary English Teaching Association.

Deshler, D. D., & Schumaker, J. B. (1993). Skills mastery by at-risk students: Not a simple matter. *Elementary School Journal, 94,* 153–167.

De Temple, J., & Snow, C. E. (2003). Learning words from books. In A. van Kleeck, S. A. Stahl, & E. B. Bauer (Eds.), *On reading books to children* (pp. 16–36). Mahwah, NJ: Erlbaum.

Developmental Studies Center. (2004–2005). *Making meaning.* Berkeley, CA: Author.

Dewitz, P., Carr, E., & Patberg, J. (1987). Effects of inference training on comprehension and comprehension monitoring. *Reading Research Quarterly, 22*(1), 99–121.

Dewitz, P., Jones, J., & Leahy, S. (2009). Comprehension strategy instruction in core reading programs. *Reading Research Quarterly, 44*(2), 102–126.

Dewitz, P., Leahy, S., Jones, J., & Sullivan, P. M. (2010). *The essential guide to selecting and using core reading programs.* Newark, DE: International Reading Association.

Diller, D. (1999). Opening the dialogue: Using culture as a tool in teaching young African American children. *The Reading Teacher, 52,* 820–828.

Dillon, J. T. (1988). *Questioning and teaching: A manual of practice.* New York: Teachers College Press.

Dole, J. A., Brown, K. J., & Trathen, W. (1996). The effects of strategy instruction on the comprehension performance of at-risk students. *Reading Research Quarterly, 31,* 62–88.

Dole, J. A., Valencia, S. W., Greer, E. A., & Wardrop, J. L. (1991). Effects of two types of prereading instruction on the comprehension of narrative and expository text. *Reading Research Quarterly, 26,* 142–159.

Dolezal, S. E., Welsh, L. M., Pressley, M., & Vincent, M. (2003). How do grade 3 teachers motivate their students? *Elementary School Journal, 103,* 239–267.

Donovan, M. S., Bransford, J. D., & Pellegrino, J. W. (Eds.). (1999). *How people learn: Bridging research and practice.* Washington, DC: National Academies Press.

Duffy, G. G. (2002). The case for direct explanation of strategies. In C. C. Block & M. Pressley (Eds.), *Comprehension instruction: Research-based best practices* (pp. 28–41). New York: Guilford Press.

Duffy, G. G., & Roehler, L. R. (1982). Commentary: The illusion of instruction. *Reading Research Quarterly, 17,* 438–445.

Duffy, G. G., Roehler, L. R., Meloth, M., Vavrus, L., Book, C., Putnam, J., & Wesselman, R. (1986). The relationship between explicit verbal explanation during reading skill instruction and student awareness and achievement: A story of reading teacher effects. *Reading Research Quarterly, 21,* 237–252.

Duffy, G. G., Roehler, L. R., Sivan, E., Rackliffe, G., Book, C., Meloth, M., Vavrus, L. G., Wesselman, R., Putnam, J., & Bassiri, D. (1987). Effects of explaining the reasoning associated with using reading strategies. *Reading Research Quarterly, 22,* 347–368.

Duin, A. H., & Graves, M. F. (1988). Teaching vocabulary as a writing prompt. *Journal of Reading, 22,* 204–212.

Duke, N., & Pearson, P. D. (2002). Effective practices for developing reading comprehension. In A. E. Farstrup & S. J. Samuels (Eds.), *What research has to say about reading instruction* (pp. 205–242). Newark, DE: International Reading Association

Duke, N. K. (2004). The case for informational text. *Educational Leadership, 61*(6), 40–44.

Duke, N. K., & Bennett-Armistead, V. S. (2003). *Reading and writing informational text in the primary grades: Research-based practices.* New York: Scholastic.

Duke, N. K., & Pearson, P. D. (2002). Effective practices for developing reading comprehension. In A. E. Farstrup &

S. J. Samuels (Eds.), *What research has to say about reading instruction* (3rd ed., pp. 205–242). Newark, DE: International Reading Association.

Duke, N. K., & Purcell-Gates, V. (2003). Genres at home and at school: Bridging the known to the new. *The Reading Teacher, 57,* 30–37.

Dyson, A. H., & Freedman, S. W. (1991). Writing. In J. Flood, J. M. Jensen, D. Lapp, & J. R. Squire (Eds.), *Handbook of research on teaching the English language arts* (pp. 754–774). New York: Guilford Press.

Echevarria, J., Vogt, M. E., & Short, D. (2004). *Making content comprehensible to English learners: The SIOP model.* Boston: Allyn & Bacon.

Ehri, L. C., & Robbins, C. (1992). Beginners need some decoding skill to read words by analogy. *Reading Research Quarterly, 27,* 13–26.

Elbow, P. (1973). *Writing without teachers.* Oxford, England: Oxford University Press.

Emig, J. (1971). *The composing process of twelfth graders.* Urbana, IL: National Council of Teachers of English.

Ennis, R. (1985). A logical basis for measuring critical thinking skills. *Educational Leadership, 43*(2), 44–48.

Estes, C. (1995). Musical links: Part I. *Book Links, 4,* 48–52.

Farr, R. (1993). Writing in response to reading: A process approach to literary assessment. In B. E. Cullinan (Ed.), *Pen in hand: Children become writers* (pp. 64–79). Newark, DE: International Reading Association.

Farr, R., & Carey, R. F. (1986). *Reading: What can be measured?* (2nd ed.). Newark, DE: International Reading Association.

Farr, R., & Tone, B. (1994). *Portfolios and performance assessment.* San Antonio, TX: Harcourt Brace.

Fetterman, D. M. (1998). *Ethnography step by step* (2nd ed.). Newbury Park, CA: Sage.

Fielding, L. G., Wilson, P. D., & Anderson, R. C. (1986). A new focus on free reading: The role of trade books in reading instruction. In T. E. Raphael (Ed.), *The contexts of school-based literacy* (pp. 149–160). New York: Random House.

Fillenworth, L. I. (1995). *Using reciprocal teaching to help at-risk college freshmen study.* Unpublished doctoral dissertation, University of Minnesota.

Fitzgerald, J. (1995). English-as-a-second-language reading instruction in the United States: A research review. *Journal of Reading Behavior, 27,* 115–152.

Fitzgerald, J., & Graves, M. F. (2004). *Scaffolding reading experiences for English-language learners.* Norwood, MA: Christopher-Gordon.

Five, C. L., & Dionisio, M. (1999). Revisiting the teaching of writing. *School Talk, 4*(4), 5.

Flavel, J. (1976). Metacognitive aspects of problem solving. In L. B. Resnick (Ed.), *The nature of intelligence* (pp. 231–235). Mahwah, NJ: Erlbaum.

Flesch, R. (1955). *Why Johnny can't read—and what you can do about it.* New York: Harper.

Flynn, R. M. (2004/2005). Curriculum-based readers theatre: Setting the stage for reading and retention. *The Reading Teacher, 58*(4), 361.

Forsythe, S. J. (1995). It worked! Readers theatre in second grade. *The Reading Teacher, 49*(3), 264–265.

Fountas, I. C., & Pinnell, G. S. (1996). *Guided reading: Good first teaching for all children.* Portsmouth, NH: Heinemann.

Fountas, I. C., & Pinnell, G. S. (1999). *Matching books to readers.* Portsmouth, NH: Heinemann.

Fountas, I. C., & Pinnnell, G. S. (2006). *Leveled books, K–8: Matching texts to readers for effective teaching.* Portsmouth, NH: Heinemann.

Frayer, D. A., Frederick, W. D., & Klausmeier, H. J. (1969). *A schema for testing the level of concept mastery* (Working Paper No. 16). Madison: Wisconsin Research and Development Center for Cognitive Learning.

Freeman, J. (1995). *More books kids will sit still for: A read-aloud guide.* New Providence, NJ: R. R. Bowker.

Friedland, E. S., & Truesdell, K. S. (2004). Kids reading together: Ensuring the success of a buddy reading program. *The Reading Teacher, 58*(1), 76–79.

Fry, E. (1977). Fry's readability graph: Clarifications, validity, and extension to level 17. *Journal of Reading, 21,* 242–252.

Fry, E. (2002). Readability versus leveling. *The Reading Teacher, 56,* 286–291.

Fry, E. B. (2004). *The vocabulary teacher's book of lists.* San Francisco: Jossey-Bass.

Fry, E. B., Polk, J. K., & Fountoukidis, D. (2000). *The reading teacher's book of lists.* Upper Saddle River, NJ: Prentice Hall.

Fry, E. F. (1998). *Phonics patterns: Onset and rhyme word lists* (4th ed.). Laguna Beach, CA: Laguna Beach Educational Books.

Fuchs, D., Fuchs, L. S., & Vaughn, S. (2008). *Response to intervention.* Newark, DE: International Reading Association.

Fuchs, L. S., & Fuchs, D. (2000). Building students' capacity to work productively during peer-assisted reading activities. In B. M. Taylor, M. F. Graves, & P. van den Broek (Eds.), *Reading for meaning: Fostering comprehension in the middle grades* (pp. 95–114). New York: Teachers College Press.

Fukkink, R. G., & de Glopper, K. (1998). Effects of instruction in deriving word meanings from context: A meta-analysis. *Review of Educational Research, 68,* 450–469.

Fulwiler, T. (Ed.). (1987). *The journal book.* Portsmouth, NH: Boyton/Cook.

Galda, L. (1998). Mirrors and windows: Reading as transformation. In T. Raphael & K. Au (Eds.), *Literature-based instruction: Reshaping the curriculum.* Norwood, NJ: Christopher-Gordon.

Galda, L., Ash, G. E., & Cullinan, B. E. (2000). Children's literature. In M. Kamil, P. Mosenthal, P. D. Pearson, & R. Barr (Eds.), *Handbook of reading research* (Vol. 3, pp. 361–379). Mahwah, NJ: Erlbaum.

Galda, L., & Cullinan, B. E. (2009). *Literature and the child* (7th ed.). Belmont, CA: Wadsworth.

Galda, L., & Graves, M. F. (2007). *Reading and responding in the middle grades: Approaches for all classrooms.* Boston: Allyn & Bacon.

Gambrell, L. B. (1996). What research reveals about discussion. In L. B. Gambrell & J. F. Almasi (Eds.), *Lively discussions! Fostering engaged reading* (pp. 25–38). Newark, DE: International Reading Association.

Gambrell, L. B., & Mazzoni, S. A. (1999). Principles of best practice: Finding the common ground. In L. B. Gambrell, L. M. Morrow, S. B. Neuman, & M. Pressley (Eds.), *Best practices in literacy instruction* (pp. 11–21). New York: Guilford Press.

Garcia, G. (2000). Bilingual children's reading. In M. Kamil, P. Mosenthal, P. Pearson, & R. Barr (Eds.), *Handbook of reading research* (Vol. 3, pp. 813–834). Mahwah, NJ: Erlbaum.

Gardner, H. (1985). *The mind's new science.* New York: Basic Books.

Gardner, H. (1993). *Multiple intelligences: The theory in practice.* New York: Basic Books.

Gardner, H. (1999). *Intelligence reframed: Multiple intelligences for the 21st century.* New York: Basic Books.

Gardner, H. (2005). *Development and education of the mind: The selected works of Howard Gardner.* London: Routledge.

Gaskins, I. W. (1994). Creating optimum learning environments. Is membership in the whole language community necessary? In F. Lehr & J. Osborn (Eds.), *Reading, language, and literacy: Instruction for the twenty-first century* (pp. 115–130). Mahwah, NJ: Erlbaum.

Gaskins, I. W. (2005). *Success with struggling readers: The Benchmark School approach.* New York: Guilford Press.

Gaskins, I. W., Ehri, L. C., Cress, C., O'Hara, C., & Donnelly, K. (1997). Procedures for word learning: Making discoveries about words. *The Reading Teacher, 50,* 312–327.

Gavelek, J. R., & Raphael, T. E. (1996). Changing talk about text: New roles for teachers and students. *Language Arts, 73*(3), 182–192.

Gergen, K. J. (1985). The social constructionist movement in modern psychology. *American Psychologist, 40,* 266–275.

Gersten, R., & Baker, S. (2000). What we know about effective instructional practices for English-language learners. *Exceptional Children, 66,* 454–470.

Gillespie, J. T. (2002). *Best books for children: Preschool through grade 6.* Westport, CT: Bowker-Greenwood.

Goatley, V. J., Brock, C. H., & Raphael, T. E. (1995). Diverse learners participating in regular education "Book Clubs." *Reading Research Quarterly, 30,* 352–380.

Good, R. H., & Kaminski, R. A. (Eds.). (2002). *Dynamic indicators of basic early literacy skills* (6th ed.). Eugene, OR: Institute for the Development of Educational Achievement. Available at http://dibels.uoregon.edu.

Good, T., & Brophy, J. (2003). *Looking into classrooms* (9th ed.). Boston: Allyn & Bacon.

Goodman, K. (1970). Behind the eye: What happens in reading. In K. S. Goodman & O. S. Niles (Eds.), *Reading: Process and program* (pp. 1–38). Urbana, IL: National Council of Teachers of English.

Goodman, K. (1986). *What's whole in whole language?* Portsmouth, NH: Heinemann.

Goodman, K. (2005). Making sense of written language: A lifelong journey. *Journal of Literacy Research, 37,* 1–24.

Goodman, K. S., Goodman, Y. M., & Hood, W. J. (1989). *The whole language evaluation book.* Portsmouth, NH: Heinemann.

Goodman, Y. (1978). Kidwatching: An alternative to testing. *Journal of National Elementary School Principals, 57*(4), 22–27.

Gordon, E. W. (2004). Closing the gap: High achievement for students of color. *Research Points, 2*(3), 1–4. Available at www.aera.net/publications/?id=314.

Goswami, U., & Bryant, P. (1992). Rhyme, analogy, and children's reading. In P. B. Gough, L. C. Ehri, & R. Treiman (Eds.), *Reading acquisition* (pp. 49–63). Mahwah, NJ: Erlbaum.

Goswami, U., & Mead, F. (1992). Onset and rime awareness and analogies in reading. *Reading Research Quarterly, 27,* 153–162.

Graves, D. H. (1975). An examination of the writing processes of seven-year-old children. *Research in the Teaching of English, 9,* 227–241.

Graves, D. H. (1991). *Writing: Teachers and children at work.* Portsmouth, NH: Heinemann.

Graves, D. H. (1996, April). Spot the lifetime writers. *Instructor, 105*(7), 26–27.

Graves, M. F. (1998, October/November). Beyond balance. *Reading Today,* 16.

Graves, M. F. (2000). A vocabulary program to complement and bolster a middle-grade comprehension program. In B. M. Taylor, M. F. Graves, & P. van den Broek (Eds.), *Reading for meaning: Fostering comprehension in the middle grades* (pp. 116–135). New York: Teachers College Press.

Graves, M. F. (2004a). Teaching prefixes: As good as it gets? In J. F. Baumann & E. B. Kame'enui (Eds.), *Vocabulary instruction: Research to practice* (pp. 81–99). New York: Guilford Press.

Graves, M. F. (2004b). Theories and constructs that have made a significant difference in adolescent literacy—but that have the potential to produce still more positive benefits. In T. Jetton & J. A. Dole (Eds.), *Adolescent literacy research and practice* (pp. 433–452). New York: Guilford Press.

Graves, M. F. (2006). *The vocabulary book: Learning and instruction.* New York: Teachers College Press.

Graves, M. F. (Ed.). (2009a). *Essential readings on vocabulary instruction.* Newark, DE: International Reading Association.

Graves, M. F. (2009b). *Teaching individual words: One size does not fit all.* New York: Teachers College Press and International Reading Association.

Graves, M. F., & Dykstra, R. (1997). Contextualizing the first-grade studies: What is the best way to teach children to read? *Reading Research Quarterly, 32,* 342–344.

Graves, M. F., & Graves, B. B. (2003). *Scaffolding reading experiences: Designs for student success* (2nd ed.). Norwood, MA: Christopher-Gordon.

Graves, M. F., Graves, B. B., & Braaten, S. (1996). Scaffolded reading experiences: Bridges to reading success. *Educational Leadership, 53,* 14–16.

Graves, M. F., & Philippot, R. A. (2001). High interest-easy reading book series. In B. E. Cullinan & D. G. Person (Eds.), *The encyclopedia of children's literature.* New York: Continuum.

Graves, M. F., Prenn, M. C., & Cooke, C. L. (1985). The coming attraction: Previewing short stories to increase comprehension. *Journal of Reading, 28,* 594–598.

Graves, M. F., & Slater, W. H. (in press). Vocabulary instruction in content areas. In D. Lapp, J. Flood, & N. Farnan (Eds.), *Content area reading and learning: Instructional strategies* (3rd ed.). Mahwah, NJ: Erlbaum.

Graves, M. F., & Watts, S. M. (2002). The place of word consciousness in a research-based vocabulary program. In S. J. Samuels & A. E. Farstrup (Eds.), *What research has to say about reading instruction* (3rd ed., pp. 140–165). Newark, DE: International Reading Association.

Graves, M. F., & Watts-Taffe, S. W. (2008). For the love of words: Fostering word consciousness in young readers. *The Reading Teacher, 62,* 185–193.

Greene, F. (1979). Radio reading. In C. Pennock (Ed.), *Reading comprehension at four linguistic levels* (pp. 104–107). Newark, DE: International Reading Association.

Guthrie, J. T., & Anderson, E. (1999). Engagement in reading: Processes of motivated, strategic, knowledgeable, social readers. In J. T. Guthrie & D. E. Alvermann (Eds.), *Engaged reading: Processes, practices, and policy implications* (pp. 17–45). New York: Teachers College Press.

Guthrie, J. T., Van Meter, P., Hancock, G. R., Alao, S., Anderson, E., & McCann, A. (1998). Does concept-oriented reading instruction increase strategy use and conceptual learning from text? *Journal of Educational Psychology, 90*(2), 261–278.

Guthrie, J., & Wigfield, A. (2000). Engagement and motivation in reading. In M. Kamil, P. Mosenthal, P. D. Pearson, & R. Barr (Eds.), *Handbook of reading research* (Vol. 3, pp. 403–424). Mahwah, NJ: Erlbaum.

Gutierrez, K. D. (2005). The persistence of inequality: English-language learners and educational reform. In J. Flood & P. L. Anders (Eds.), *Literacy development of students in urban schools: Research and policy* (pp. 288–304). Newark, DE: International Reading Association.

Hannon, J. (1999). Talking back: Kindergarten dialogue journals. *The Reading Teacher, 53*(3), 200–203.

Hansen, J. (1981). The effects of inference training and practice on young children's reading comprehension. *Reading Research Quarterly, 16*(3), 391–417.

Hansen-Krening, N., Aoki, E. M., & Mizokawa, D. T. (Eds.). (2003). *Kaleidoscope: A multicultural booklist for grades K–8* (4th ed.). Urbana, IL: National Council of Teachers of English.

Harcourt Educational Measurement. (2001). *Stanford Achievement Test Series* (10th ed.). San Antonio, TX: Author.

Harlen, W. (Ed.). (1994). *Enhancing quality in assessment.* London: Paul Chapman.

Harp, B. (1991). *Assessment and evaluation in whole language programs.* Norwood, MA: Christopher-Gordon.

Hart, B., & Risley, T. R. (1995). *Meaningful differences in the everyday experiences of young American children.* Baltimore: Paul H. Brookes.

Hart, B., & Risley, T. R. (2003, Spring). The early catastrophe: The 30 million word gap. *American Educator, 27*(1), 4–9.

Hart, D. (1994). *Authentic assessment: A handbook for educators.* Menlo Park, CA: Addison-Wesley.

Harwayne, S. (1993). Chutzpah and the nonfiction writer. In B. E. Cullinan (Ed.), *Pen in hand: Children become writers* (pp. 19–35). Newark, DE: International Reading Association.

Hasbrouck, J., & Tindal, G. (2005). *Oral reading fluency: 90 years of measurement* (Tech. Rep. No. 33). Eugene: University of Oregon, College of Education, Behavioral Research and Teaching. Available at http://brt.uoregon.edu/tech_reports.htm.

Heath, S. B. (1983). *Ways with words: Language, life, and work in communities and classrooms.* Cambridge, MA: Cambridge University Press.

Heckelman, R. G. (1969). A neurological-impress method of remedial-reading instruction. *Academic Therapy Quarterly, 4,* 277–282.

Heimlich, J. E., & Pittelman, S. D. (1986). *Semantic mapping: Classroom applications.* Newark, DE: International Reading Association.

Helman, L. (2008). English words needed: Creating research-based vocabulary instruction for English learners. In A. E. Farstrup & S. J. Samuels (Eds.), *What research has to say about vocabulary instruction* (pp. 211–237). Newark, DE: International Reading Association.

Henderson, E. (1981). *Learning to read and spell: The child's knowledge of words.* DeKalb: Northern Illinois Press.

Henderson, E. H. (1990). *Teaching spelling* (2nd ed.). Boston: Houghton Mifflin.

Herman, J. L., Aschbacher, P. R., & Winters, L. (1992). *A practical guide to alternative assessment.* Alexandria, VA: Association for Supervision and Curriculum Development.

Hiebert, E. H. (1994). Reading Recovery in the United States: What difference does it make to an age cohort? *Educational Researcher, 23*(9), 15–25.

Hiebert, E. H. (1996). Creating and sustaining a love of literature and the ability to read it. In M. F. Graves, P. van den Broek, & B. M. Taylor (Eds.), *The first R: Every child's right to read* (pp. 15–36). New York: Teachers College Press.

Hiebert, E. H. (2002). *QuickReads: A research-based fluency program.* Parsippany, NJ: Modern Curriculum.

Hiebert, E. H. (2005). In pursuit of an effective, efficient vocabulary program. In E. H. Hiebert & M. Kamil (Eds.), *Teaching and learning vocabulary: Bringing research to practice* (pp. 243–263). Mahwah, NJ: Erlbaum.

Hiebert, E. H., & Calfee, R. C. (1992). Assessment of literacy: From standardized tests to performances and portfolios. In A. E. Farstrup & S. J. Samuels (Eds.), *What research says about reading instruction* (pp. 70–100). Newark, DE: International Reading Association.

Hiebert, E. H., Pearson, P. D., Taylor, B. M., Richardson, V., & Paris, S. G. (1998). *Every child a reader: Applying reading research in the classroom.* Ann Arbor, MI: Center for the Improvement of Early Reading Achievement.

Hiebert, E. H., & Taylor, B. M. (Eds.). (1994). *Getting reading right from the start: Effective early literacy interventions.* Boston: Allyn & Bacon.

Higham, J. (1988). *Strangers in the land: Patterns of American nativism, 1860–1925.* New Brunswick, NJ: Rutgers University Press.

Hindley, J. (1998). The workshop environment. *School Talk, 3*(4), 4.

Hoffman, J. V., McCarthey, S. J., Abbott, J., Christian, C., Corman, L., & Curry, C. (1994). So what's new in the new basal? A focus on first grade. *Journal of Reading Behavior, 26,* 47–73.

Hoffman, J. V., McCarthey, S. J., Elliot, B., Bayles, D. L., Price, D. P., Ferree, A., & Abbott, J. A. (1998). The literature-based basal in first-grade classrooms: Savior, Satan or same-old, same-old. *Reading Research Quarterly, 33,* 168–197.

Hoffman, J. V., Sailors, M., Duffy, G. R., & Beretvas, S. N. (2004). Effective elementary classroom literacy environment: Examining the validity of the TEX-IN3 observation system. *Journal of Literacy Research, 36,* 303–334.

Hoover, H. D., Hieronymus, A. N., Frisbie, D. A., & Dunbar, S. B. (1996). *Iowa test of basic skills, form M.* Itasca, IL: Riverside.

Horn Book guide to children's and young adult books. (2002). Boston, MA: Horn Book.

Horowitz, R., & Freeman, S. H. (1995). Robots versus spaceships: The role of discussion in kindergartners' and second graders' preferences for science text. *The Reading Teacher, 49,* 30–40.

Hulstijn, J. (1991). How is reading in a second language related to reading in a first language? *AILA Review, 8,* 5–15.

Ihnot, C. (2001). *Read naturally* (Masters ed.). Saint Paul, MN: Read Naturally.

Ihnot, C. (2002). *Read naturally rationale and research.* Saint Paul, MN: Read Naturally.

Ihnot, C. (2004). *Read naturally* (Software ed., version 2.0). Saint Paul, MN: Read Naturally.

International Reading Association. (1997a, February/March). Program gets parents, students to love reading "beary" much. *Reading Today.*

International Reading Association. (1997b). *The role of phonics in reading instruction.* Newark, DE: Author.

International Reading Association. (2005, April/May). Wordsmiths: Helping students develop as writers. *Reading Today.*

Invernizzi, M., Juel, C., & Rosemary, C. A. (1996/1997). A community volunteer tutorial that works. *The Reading Teacher, 50,* 304–311.

Jacobi-Karna, K. (1996). Music and children's books. *The Reading Teacher, 49*(3), 265–269.

Jiménez, R. T. (2000). Literacy lessons derived from the instruction of six Latina/Latino teachers. In B. M. Taylor, M. F. Graves, & P. van den Broek (Eds.), *Reading for meaning: Fostering comprehension in the middle grades* (pp. 152–169). New York: Teachers College Press.

Johnson, D. D., & Pearson, P. D. (1984). *Teaching reading vocabulary* (2nd ed.). New York: Holt, Rinehart & Winston.

Johnson, D. W., & Johnson, R. T. (1989). *Cooperation and competition: Theory and research.* Edina, MN: Interaction Book Company.

Johnson, D. W., & Johnson, R. T. (1996). Conflict resolution and peer mediation programs in elementary and secondary schools: A review of the research. *Review of Educational Research, 66,* 459–506.

Johnson, D. W., & Johnson, R. T. (2002). Teaching students to resolve their own and their schoolmates' conflicts. *Counseling and Human Development, 34*(6), 1–12.

Johnson, D. W., Johnson, R. T., & Holubec, E. J. (1987). *Structuring cooperative learning: Lesson plans for teachers.* Edina, MN: Interaction Book Company.

Johnson, D. W., Johnson, R. T., & Holubec, E. J. (1994). *The new circles of learning: Cooperation in the classroom.* Alexandria, VA: Association for Supervision and Curriculum Development.

Johnson, F. R., Invernizzi, M., & Juel, C. (1998). *Book buddies: Guidelines for volunteer tutors of emergent and early readers.* New York: Guilford Press.

Johnson, M. S., Kress, R. A., & Pikulski, J. J. (1987). *Informal reading inventories.* Newark, DE: International Reading Association.

Johnston, P. H. (1990). Steps toward a more naturalistic approach to the assessment of the reading process. In J. Algina & S. Legg (Eds.), *Cognitive assessment of language and mathematics outcomes* (pp. 92–143). Norwood, NJ: Ablex.

Johnston, P. H. (1992). *Constructive evaluation of literate activity.* New York: Longman.

Johnston, P. H., & Winograd, P. N. (1985). Passive failure in reading. *Journal of Reading Behavior, 17,* 279–301.

Juel, C. (1988). Learning to read and write: A longitudinal study of fifty-four children from first through fourth grade. *Journal of Educational Psychology, 80,* 437–447.

Juel, C. (1990). Effects of reading group assignment on reading development in first and second grade. *Journal of Reading Behavior, 22,* 223–254.

Juel, C. (1994). *Learning to read and write in one elementary school.* New York: Springer-Verlag.

Juel, C. (2005). The impact of early school experiences on initial reading. In D. K. Dickinson & S. B. Neuman (Eds.), *Handbook of early literacy research* (Vol. 2, pp. 410–426). New York: Guilford Press.

Juel, C., Griffith, P. L., & Gough, P. B. (1986). Acquisition of literacy: A longitudinal study of children in first and second grade. *Journal of Educational Psychology, 78,* 243–255.

Juel, C., & Minden-Cupp, C. (2000). Learning to read words: Linguistic units and instructional strategies. *Reading Research Quarterly, 35*(4), 458–492.

Juel, C., & Roper/Schneider, D. (1985) The influence of basal readers on first grade reading. *Reading Research Quarterly, 18,* 306–327.

Just, M. A., & Carpenter, P. H. (1980). A theory of reading: From eye fixations to comprehension. *Psychological Review, 87,* 329–354.

Kame'enui, E., Simmons, D., & Cornachione, C. (2001). *A practical guide to reading assessments.* Eugene: University of Oregon, National Center to Improve the Tools of Educators.

Kamil, M. L., & Bernhardt, E. B. (2004). Reading instruction for English-language learners. In M. F. Graves, C. Juel, & B. B. Graves, *Teaching reading in the 21st century* (3rd ed., pp. 496–541). Boston: Allyn & Bacon.

Kamil, M. L., & Lane, D. (1997). *Using informational text for first-grade reading instruction.* Paper presented at the annual meeting of the National Reading Conference.

Kintsch, W. (1998). *Comprehension: A paradigm for cognition.* Cambridge, UK: Cambridge University Press.

Kirsch, I., & Jungeblut, A. (1986). *Literacy: Profiles of America's young adults.* Princeton, NJ: National Assessment of Educational Progress and Educational Testing Service.

Knapp, M. S., et al. (1995). *Teaching for meaning in high-poverty classrooms.* New York: Teachers College Press.

Koziol, S. M., Minnick, J. B., & Riddell, K. (1996). *Journals for active learning: A two-day workshop module for primary teachers in Bosnia.* Pittsburgh, PA: University of Pittsburgh, International Institute for Studies in Education.

Krashen, S. (2004). False claims about literacy development. *Educational Leadership, 61*(6), 18–21.

Kuhn, M. (2004/2005). Helping students become accurate, expressive readers: Fluency instruction for small groups. *The Reading Teacher, 58,* 338–344.

Kuhn, M. R., & Stahl, S. A. (2003). Fluency: A review of developmental and remedial practices. *Journal of Educational Psychology, 95,* 3–21. An earlier version is available at www.ciera.org/library/reports/inquiry-2.

Kurlansky, M. (1997). *Cod: A biography of the fish that changed the world.* New York: Walker and Company.

Kurlansky, M. (2002). *Salt: A world history.* New York: Walker and Company.

LaBerge, D., & Samuels, S. J. (1974). Toward a theory of automatic information processing in reading. *Cognitive Psychology, 6,* 293–323.

Langer, J. (1986). *Children reading and writing.* Norwood, NJ: Ablex.

Lee, J., Grigg, W., & Donahue, P. (2007). *The nation's report card: Reading 2007* (NCES 2007-496). Washington, DC: U.S. Department of Education, National Center for Educational Statistics, Institute of Educational Sciences.

Leslie, L., & Caldwell, J. (2006). *Qualitative reading inventory-4.* New York: Longman.

Lovett, M. W., De Palma, M., Frijters, J., Steinbach, K., Temple, M., Benson, N., & Lacerenza, L. (2008). Interventions for reading difficulties: A comparison of response to intervention by ELL and EFL struggling readers. *Journal of Learning Disabilities, 41*(4) 333–352.

Lovett, M. W., Lacerenza, L., Borden, S. L., Frijters, J. C., Steinbach, K. A., & De Palma, M. (2000). Components of effective remediation for developmental reading disabilities: Combining phonological and strategy-based instruction to improve outcomes. *Journal of Educational Psychology, 92*(2), 263–283.

Lukens, R. J. (1990). *A critical handbook of children's literature* (4th ed.). Oxford, OH: Scott Foresman.

Lundberg, I. (1984, August). Learning to read. *School Research Newsletter.* Sweden: National Board of Education.

Maclean, M., Bryant, P., & Bradley, L. (1988). Rhymes, nursery rhymes, and reading in early childhood. In K. E. Stanovich (Ed.), *Children's reading and the development of phonological awareness* (pp. 11–37). Detroit, MI: Wayne State University Press.

Maehr, M., & Midgley, C. (1996). *Transforming school cultures.* Boulder, CO: Westview Press.

Mandler, J., & Johnson, N. (1977). Remembrance of things parsed: Story structure and recall. *Cognitive Psychology, 9,* 111–151.

Mann, H. (1965). Method of teaching young children on their first entering school. In N. B. Smith (Ed.), *American reading instruction* (2nd ed., p. 117). Newark, DE: International Reading Association. (Original work published in 1884.)

Manning, J. M. (1999, September 15). Remarks made in an interview on the Minneapolis Public Radio *Midmorning* program. Minneapolis, MN: MPR.

Mansukhani, P. (2002). The explorers' club: The sky is no limit for learning. *Language Arts, 80,* 31–39.

Marshall, J. (2000). Response to literature. In M. Kamil, P. Mosenthal, P. D. Pearson, & R. Barr (Eds.), *Handbook of reading research* (Vol. 3, pp. 381–402). Mahwah, NJ: Erlbaum.

Marzano, R. J. (2000). *Transforming classroom grading.* Alexandria, VA: Association for Supervision and Curriculum Development.

Mathes, P. G., Denton, C. A., Fletcher, J. M., Anthony, J. L., Francis, D. J., & Schatschneider, C. (2005). The effects of theoretically different instruction and student characteristics on the skills of struggling readers. *Reading Research Quarterly, 40*(2), 148–182.

Mathes, P. G., Pollard-Durodola, S. D., Cárdenas-Hagan, E., Linan-Thompson, S., & Vaughn, S. (2007). Teaching struggling readers who are native Spanish speakers: What do we know? *Language, Speech, and Hearing Services in Schools, 38,* 260–271.

McClure, A. A., Harrison, P., & Reed, S. (1990). *Sunrises and songs: Reading and writing poetry in an elementary classroom.* Portsmouth, NH: Heinemann.

McClure, A. A., & Kristo, J. V. (Eds.). (2002). *Adventuring with books: A booklist for pre-K-grade 6* (13th ed.). Urbana, IL: National Council of Teachers of English.

McConkie, G. W., & Zola, D. (1981). Language constraints and the functional stimulus in reading. In A. M. Lesgold & C. A. Perfetti (Eds.), *Interactive processes in reading* (pp. 155–175). Mahwah, NJ: Erlbaum.

McCracken, R. A., & McCracken, M. J. (1978). Modeling is the key to sustained reading. *The Reading Teacher, 31,* 406–408.

McKeown, M. G., & Beck, I. L. (2003). Taking advantage of read-alouds to help children make sense of decontextualized language. In A. van Kleeck, S. A. Stahl, & E. B. Bauer (Eds.), *On reading books to young children* (pp. 159–176). Mahwah, NJ: Erlbaum.

McKeown, M. G., Beck, I. L., & Blake, R. G. K. (2009). Rethinking reading comprehension instruction: A comparison of instruction for strategies and content approaches. *Reading Research Quarterly, 44*(3), 218–253.

McKeown, M. G., Beck, I. L., & Sandora, C. A. (1996). Questioning the author: An approach to developing meaningful classroom discourse. In M. F. Graves, P. van den Broek, & B. M. Taylor (Eds.), *The first R: Every child's right to read* (pp. 97–119). New York: Teachers College Press.

McMahon, M. M., & McCormack, B. B. (1998). To think and act like a scientist: Learning disciplinary knowledge. In C. R. Hynd (Ed.), *Learning from text across conceptual domains* (pp. 227–262). Mahwah, NJ: Erlbaum.

McMahon, S. I., Raphael, T. E., & Goatley, V. J. (1995). Changing the context for classroom reading instruction: The Book Club project. In J. Brophy (Ed.), *Advances in research on teaching* (Vol. 5, pp. 123–166). Greenwich, CT: JAI Press.

McNamara, D. S., Kintsch, E., Songer, N. B., & Kintsch, W. (1996). Are good texts always better? Interactions of text coherence, background knowledge, and levels of understanding in learning from text. *Cognition and Instruction, 14*(1) 1–43.

McTighe, J., Seif, E., & Wiggins, G. (2004). You can teach for meaning. *Educational Leadership, 62*(1), 26–30.

Meinbach, A. M., Rothlein, L., & Fredericks, A. D. (2000). *The complete guide to thematic units: Creating the integrated curriculum* (2nd ed.). Norwood, MA: Christopher-Gordon.

Miller, G. A., & Gildea, P. M. (1987). How children learn words. *Scientific American, 257*(3), 94–99.

Mills, H., Stephens, D., O'Keefe, T., & Waugh, J. R. (2004). Theory in practice: The legacy of Louise Rosenblatt. *Language Arts, 82,* 47–55.

Mitchell, R. (1992). *Testing for learning: How new approaches to evaluation can improve American schools.* New York: Free Press.

Mode, B. A. (1989). Dialogue journal writing. *The Reading Teacher, 42,* 568–571.

Mokhtari, K., & Reichard, C. A. (2002) Assessing students' metacognitive awareness of reading strategies. *Journal of Educational Psychology, 94*(2), 249–259.

Moll, L. C. (1992). Literacy research in community classrooms: A socio-cultural approach. In R. Beach, J. L. Green, M. S. Kamil, & T. Shanahan (Eds.), *Multidisciplinary perspectives on literacy research* (pp. 211–244). Urbana, IL: National Council of Teachers of English.

Moore, D. W., Moore, S. A., Cunningham, P. M., & Cunningham, J. W. (2003). *Developing readers and writers in the content areas K–12.* Boston: Allyn & Bacon.

Mullis, I. V. S., Martin, M. O., Gonzales, E. J., & Kennedy, A. M. (2003). *PIRLS 2001 international report.* Boston: International Study Center, Boston College.

Mullis, I. V. S., Martin, M. O., Kennedy, A. M., & Foy, P. (2007). *IAE progress in international reading literacy study in primary school in 40 countries.* Boston: TIMSS and PIRLS International Study Center, Boston College.

Nagy, W. E., & Anderson, R. C. (1984). How many words are there in printed school English? *Reading Research Quarterly, 19,* 304–330.

Nagy, W. E., & Scott, J. A. (2000). Vocabulary processes. In M. Kamil, P. Mosenthal, P. D. Pearson, & R. Barr (Eds.), *Handbook of reading research* (Vol. 3, pp. 269–284). Mahwah, NJ: Erlbaum.

Nation, I. S. P. (2001). *Learning vocabulary in another language.* Cambridge, England: Cambridge University Press.

National Center on Education and the Economy. (1997). *New standards: Performance standards. Volume 1: Elementary schools.* Pittsburgh, PA: University of Pittsburgh.

National Council of Teachers of English (NCTE) Commission on Reading. (2004). *On reading, learning to read, and effective reading instruction.* Retrieved December 2005 from www.ncte.org/about/over/positions/category/read/118620.htm.

National Council of Teachers of English and International Reading Association. (1996). *Standards for the English language arts.* Urbana, IL: Authors.

National Reading Panel. (2000). *Report of the National Reading Panel: Teaching children to read.* Bethesda, MD: National Institute of Child Health and Human Development.

National Research Council. (2004). *Engaging schools: Fostering high school students' motivation to learn.* Washington, DC: National Academies Press.

New Standards Primary Literacy Committee. (1999). *Reading and writing grade by grade.* Pittsburgh, PA: National Center on Education and the University of Pittsburgh. Available at www.ncee.org.

Newmann, F. N. (1996). *Authentic achievement: Restructuring schools for intellectual quality.* San Francisco: Jossey-Bass.

Newmann, F. N. (2000). Authentic intellectual work: What and why? *Research/Practice, 8*(1), 15–20.

Nitko, A. J. (1996). *Educational assessment of students* (2nd ed.). Englewood Cliffs, NJ: Merrill.

No Child Left Behind Act of 2001. Public Law No. 107-110. 115 Stat. 1425 (2002).

Noddings, N. (2003). *Happiness and education.* Cambridge, UK: Cambridge University Press.

O'Connor, R. E., Bell, K. M., Harty, K. R., Larkin, L. K., Sackor, S. M., & Zigmond, N. (2002). Teaching reading to poor readers in the intermediate grades: A comparison of text difficulty. *Journal of Educational Psychology, 94*(3), 474–485.

Ogle, D. (1986). K-W-L: A teaching model that develops active reading of expository text. *The Reading Teacher, 39,* 564–570.

Olness, R. (2005). *Using literature to enhance writing instruction: A guide for K–5 teachers.* Newark, DE: International Reading Association.

Olson, C. B. (1996). Strategies for interacting with text. In C. B. Olson (Ed.), *Practical ideas for teaching writing as a process at the elementary and middle school levels* (Rev. ed., pp. 231–235). Sacramento: California Department of Education.

Olson, J. F., & Goldstein, A. A. (1997). *The inclusion of students with disabilities and limited English proficient students in large-scale assessments: A summary of recent progress.* Washington, DC: National Center for Education Statistics.

O'Malley, J. M., & Pierce, L. V. (1996). *Authentic assessment for English language learners: Practical approaches for teachers.* New York: Addison-Wesley.

Orehovec, B., & Alley, M. (2003). *Revisiting the reading workshop: Management, mini-lessons, and strategies.* New York: Scholastic.

Osborn, J., Lehr, F., & Hiebert, E. H. (2003). *A focus on fluency.* Honolulu, HI: Pacific Resources for Education and Learning.

Owocki, G., & Goodman, Y. M. (2002). *Kidwatching: Documenting children's literacy development.* Portsmouth, NH: Heinemann.

Palincsar, A. M., & Brown, A. L. (1984). Reciprocal teaching of comprehension and monitoring activities. *Cognition and Instruction, 1*(2), 117–175.

Palincsar, A. M., & Brown, A. L. (1985). Reciprocal teaching: A means to a meaningful end. In J. Osborn, P. T. Wilson, & R. C. Anderson (Eds.), *Reading education: Foundations for a literate America* (pp. 299–310). Lexington, MA: DC Heath.

Palincsar, A. M., & Brown, A. L. (1986). Interactive teaching to promote independent learning from text. *The Reading Teacher, 39,* 771–777.

Palincsar, A. M., & David, Y. M. (1991). Promoting literacy through classroom dialogue. In E. Hiebert (Ed.), *Literacy for a diverse society: Perspectives, programs, and policies.* New York: Teachers College Press.

Paris, S. G., Calfee, R. C., Filby, N., Hiebert, E. H., Pearson, P. D., Valencia, S. W., & Wolf, K. P. (1992). A framework for authentic literacy assessment. *The Reading Teacher, 46,* 88–98.

Patterson, L., Santa, C. M., & Smith, K. (1993). *Teachers as researchers: Reflection and action.* Newark, DE: International Reading Association.

Pearson, P. D. (1990). Foreword. In T. Shanahan (Ed.), *Reading and writing together: New perspectives for the classroom* (pp. v–vi). Norwood, MA: Christopher-Gordon.

Pearson, P. D. (2000). Reading in the twentieth century. In T. L. Good (Ed.), *American education: Yesterday, today, and tomorrow* (pp. 152–208). Chicago: National Society for the Study of Education.

Pearson, P. D., & Duke, N. K. (2002). Comprehension instruction in the primary grades. In C. C. Block & M. Pressley (Eds.), *Comprehension instruction: Research-based practices* (pp. 247–258). New York: Guilford Press.

Pearson, P. D., & Gallagher, M. C. (1983). The instruction of reading comprehension. *Contemporary Educational Psychology, 8,* 317–344.

Pearson, P. D., Roehler, L. R., Dole, J. A., & Duffy, G. G. (1992). Developing expertise in reading comprehension. In S. J. Samuels & A. E. Farstrup (Eds.), *What research has to say about reading instruction* (2nd ed., pp. 145–199). Newark, DE: International Reading Association.

Perie, M., Grigg, W., & Donahue, P. (2005). *The nation's report card: Reading 2005.* Washington, DC: U.S. Department of Education.

Perie, M., Moran, R., Lutkus, A. D., & Tirre, W. (2005). *NAEP 2004 trends in academic progress: Three decades of student performance in reading and mathematics.* Washington, DC: U.S. Department of Education.

Perkins, D. (1992). *Smart schools: From training memories to educating minds.* New York: The Free Press.

Perkins, D. (1993). Making education relevant: Teaching and learning for understanding. *New Jersey Educational Association Review,* October, 10–18.

Perkins, D. (1994). *Knowledge as design: A handbook for critical and creative discussion across the curriculum.* Pacific Grove, CA: Critical Thinking Press.

Perkins, D. (2004). Knowledge alive. *Educational Leadership, 62*(1), 14–18.

Perkins, D., & Blythe, T. (1994). Putting understanding up front. *Educational Leadership, 51*(5), 4–7.

Persky, H. R., Daane, M. C., & Ying, J. (2003). *The nation's report card: Writing 2002.* Washington, DC: U.S. Department of Education.

Phillips, D. C. (Ed.). (2000). *Constructivism in education.* Chicago: National Society for the Study of Education.

Phye, G. D. (Ed.). (1996). *Handbook of classroom assessment.* Orlando, FL: Academic Press.

Piasta, S. B., Connor, C. M., Fishman, B. J., & Morrison, F. J. (2009). Teachers' knowledge of literacy concepts, classroom practices, and student reading growth. *Scientific Studies of Reading, 13*(3), 224–248.

Pierce, K. M. (Ed.). (2000). *Adventuring with books: A booklist for pre-K–grade 6.* Urbana, IL: National Council of Teachers of English.

Pikulski, J. J., & Chard, D. J. (2005). Fluency: Bridge between decoding and reading comprehension. *The Reading Teacher, 58,* 510–519.

Pinnell, G. S., Fried, M. D., & Eustice, R. M. (1990). Reading Recovery: Learning how to make a difference. *The Reading Teacher, 43,* 282–295.

Pittelman, S. D., Heimlich, J. E., Berglund, R. L., & French, M. P. (1991). *Semantic feature analysis: Classroom applications.* Newark, DE: International Reading Association.

Poindexter, C., & Oliver, I. (1998/1999). Navigating the writing process: Strategies for young children. *The Reading Teacher, 52*(4), 420–423.

Popham, W. J. (1999). *Classroom assessment: What teachers need to know* (2nd ed.). Boston: Allyn & Bacon.

Prawat, R. S. (1989). Teaching for understanding: Three key attributes. *Teaching and Teacher Education, 5,* 315–328.

Press, F. (1984, May 30). Address given at the annual commencement convocation, School of Graduate Studies, Case Western Reserve University, Cleveland, OH.

Pressley, M. (2000). What should comprehension instruction be the instruction of? In M. Kamil, P. Mosenthal, P. D. Pear-son, & R. Barr (Eds.), *Handbook of reading research* (Vol. 3, pp. 545–561). Mahwah, NJ: Erlbaum.

Pressley, M. (2002). Comprehension strategies instruction: A turn-of-the-century status report. In C. C. Block & M. Pressley (Eds.), *Comprehension instruction: Research-based best practices* (pp. 11–27). New York: Guilford Press.

Pressley, M. (2005). Final reflections—Metacognition in literacy learning: Then, now, and in the future. In S. E. Israel, C. C. Block, K. L. Bauserman, & K. Kinnucan-Welsch (Eds.), *Metacognition in literacy learning* (pp. 391–411). Mahwah, NJ: Erlbaum.

Pressley, M. (2006). *Reading instruction that works: The case for balanced teaching* (3rd ed.). New York: Guilford.

Pressley, M., & Afflerbach, P. (1995). *Verbal protocols of reading: The nature of constructively responsive reading.* Mahwah, NJ: Erlbaum.

Pressley, M., Allington, R. L., Wharton-McDonald, R., Block, C. C., & Morrow, L. M. (2001). *Learning to read: Lessons from exemplary first-grade classrooms.* New York: Guilford Press.

Pressley, M., Dolezal, S. E., Raphael, L., Mohan, L., Bogner, K., & Roehrig, A. (2003). *Motivating primary grade students.* New York: Guilford Press.

Pressley, M., El-Dinary, P. B., Wharton-McDonald, R., & Brown, R. (1998). Transactional instruction of comprehension strategies in the elementary grades. In D. H. Schunk & B. J. Zimmerman (Eds.), *Self-regulated learning: From teaching to self-reflective practice* (pp. 42–56). New York: Guilford Press.

Pressley, M., Harris, K. R., & Marks, M. B. (1992). But good strategy instructors are constructivists! *Educational Psychology Review, 4,* 3–31.

Pritchard, A., & Cartwright, V. (2004). Transforming what they read: Helping eleven-year-olds engage with internet information. *Literacy, 38*(1), 26.

Purcell-Gates, V. (1989). What oral/written language differences can tell us about beginning instruction. *The Reading Teacher, 42,* 290–294.

Rahne, D. S. (1997). *Beyond the case for cooperative learning: Comparing the jigsaw and peer-response methods.* Unpublished master's thesis, University of Minnesota.

RAND Reading Study Group. (2002). *Reading for understanding: Toward an R&D program in reading comprehension.* Santa Monica, CA: Rand Education. Also available at www.rand.org/multi/achievement-forall/reading.

Raphael, T. E. (2000). Balancing literature and instruction: Lessons from the Book Club project. In B. M. Taylor, M. F. Graves, & P. van den Broek (Eds.), *Reading for meaning: Fostering comprehension in the middle grades* (pp. 70–94). New York: Teachers College Press.

Raphael, T. E., Florio-Ruane, S., & George, M. (2001). Book Club Plus: A conceptual framework to organize literacy instruction. *Language Arts, 79,* 159–169.

Raphael, T. E., Florio-Ruane, S., George, M. A., Hasty, N. L., & Highfield, K. (2004). *Book Club Plus! A literacy framework for the primary grades.* Laurence, MA: Small Planet Communications.

Raphael, T. E., & McMahon, S. I. (1994). Book Club: An alternative framework for reading instruction. *The Reading Teacher, 48,* 102–116.

Rasinski, T., Blachowicz, C. L. Z., & Lems, K. (Eds.). (in press). *Teaching reading fluency: Meeting the needs of all readers.* New York: Guilford Press.

Rasinski, T. V. (2003). *The fluent reader: Oral reading strategies for building word recognition, fluency, and comprehension.* New York: Scholastic.

Renaissance Learning. (2005). *Fluent reader.* Wisconsin Rapids, WI: Author.

Resnick, L. B. (1987). *Education and learning to think.* Washington, DC: National Academies Press.

Reutzel, D. R., & Cooter, R. B. (1991). Organizing for effective instruction: The reading workshop. *The Reading Teacher, 44,* 548–554.

Reutzel, D. R., Fawson, P. C., & Smith, J. A. (2003, December). *Teaching comprehension strategies using information texts.* Paper presented at the annual meeting of the National Reading Conference, Scottsdale, AZ.

Reutzel, D. R., Jones, C. D., Fawson, P. C., & Smith, J. A. (2008). Scaffolded silent reading: A complement to guided repeated oral reading that works! *The Reading Teacher, 62,* 194–209.

Rinsky, L. A. (1993). *Teaching word recognition skills.* Scottsdale, AZ: Gorsuch Scarisbrick.

Rosenblatt, L. (1978). *The reader, the text, the poem: The transactional theory of the literary work.* Carbondale: Southern Illinois Press.

Rosenblatt, L. M. (1938/1995). *Literature as exploration.* New York: Modern Language Association.

Routman, R. (1995). *Invitations: Changing as teachers and learners K–12.* Portsmouth, NH: Heinemann.

Routman, R. (2003). *Reading essentials: The specifics you need to teach reading well.* Portsmouth, NH: Heinemann.

Routman, R. (2005). *Writing essentials: Raising expectations and results while simplifying teaching.* Portsmouth, NH: Heinemann.

Rumelhart, D. E. (1977). Toward an interactive model of reading. In S. Dornic (Ed.), *Attention and performance* (Vol. 6, pp. 573–603). Mahwah, NJ: Erlbaum.

Rumelhart, D. E. (1980). Schemata: The building blocks of cognition. In R. J. Spiro, B. C. Bruce, & W. F. Brewer (Eds.), *Theoretical issues in reading comprehension* (pp. 33–58). Mahwah, NJ: Erlbaum.

Sales, G. H., & Graves, M. F. (2005). *Teaching comprehension strategies.* Minneapolis, MN: Seward Incorporated.

Sampson, M. B., Sampson, M. R., & Linek, W. (1994/1995). Circle of questions. *The Reading Teacher, 48,* 364–365.

Samuels, S. J. (1979). The method of repeated reading. *The Reading Teacher, 32,* 403–408.

Samuels, S. J. (2002a). *Building reading fluency.* Retrieved 2003 from http://education.umn.edu/CI/MREA/Fluency/fluencyMODtoc.html.

Samuels, S. J. (2002b). Reading fluency: Its development and assessment. In S. J. Samuels & A. E. Farstrup (Eds.), *What research has to say about reading instruction* (3rd ed., pp. 166–183). Newark, DE: International Reading Association.

Samuels, S. J. (in press). Reading fluency: Its past, present, and future. In T. Rasinski, C. L. Z. Blachowicz, & K. Lems (Eds.), *Teaching reading fluency: Meeting the needs of all readers.* New York: Guilford Press.

Samuels, S. J., & Farstrup, A. E. (Eds.) (2006). *What research has to say about fluency instruction.* Newark, DE: International Reading Association.

Scarcella, R. C. (1996). English learners and writing: Responding to linguistic diversity. In C. B. Olson (Ed.), *Practical ideas for teaching writing as a process at the elementary school and middle school levels* (pp. 97–103). Sacramento: California State Department of Education.

Schlesinger, A. M., Jr. (1986). *The cycles of American history.* Boston: Houghton Mifflin.

Schmitt, N. (2000). *Vocabulary in language teaching.* Cambridge, England: Cambridge University Press.

Schon, I., & Berkin, S. C. (1996). *Introducción a la literatura infantil y juvenil.* Newark, DE: International Reading Association. (Available only in Spanish.)

Schumaker, J. B., & Deshler, D. D. (2003). Can students with LD become competent writers? *Learning Disability Quarterly, 26,* 129–141.

Schunk, D. H., & Zimmerman, B. J. (Eds.). (1998). *Self-regulated learning: From teaching to self-reflective practice.* New York: Guilford Press.

Scott, J. A., & Nagy, W. E. (2004). Developing word consciousness. In J. F. Baumann & E. J. Kame'enui (Eds.), *Vocabulary instruction: Research to practice* (pp. 201–217). New York: Guilford Press.

Searle, J. R. (1993). Rationality and realism: What is at stake? *Daedalus, 122*(4), 55–83.

Serafini, F. (2004). *Lessons in comprehension: Explicit instruction in the reading workshop.* Portsmouth, NH: Heinemann.

Shany, M. T., & Biemiller, A. (1995). Assisted reading practice: Effects on performance of poor readers in grades 3 and 4. *Reading Research Quarterly, 30,* 382–395.

Share, D. L., Jorm, A. F., Maclean, R., & Matthews, R. (1984). Sources of individual differences in reading achievement. *Journal of Educational Psychology, 76,* 1309–1324.

Shaywitz, S. (2003). *Overcoming dyslexia: A new and complete science based program for reading problems at any level.* New York: Knopf.

Shea, M., Murray, R., & Harlin, R. (2005). *Drowning in data: How to collect, organize, and document student performance.* Portsmouth, NH: Heinemann.

Shinn, M. R., & Shinn, M. M. (2002). *Aimsweb training workbook.* Eden Prairie, MN: Edformation.

Short, D., & Echevarria, J. (2004–2005). Teacher skills to support English language learners. *Educational Leadership, 62*(4), 8–13.

Short, K., Kaufman, G., Kaser, L. H., Kahn, L. H., & Crawford, K. M. (1999). "Teacher-watching": Examining teacher talk in literature circles. *Language Arts, 76,* 377–385.

Short, K. G., & Klassen, C. (1993). Literature circles: Hearing children's voices. In B. E. Cullinan (Ed.), *Children's voices: Talk in the classroom* (pp. 66–85). Newark, DE: International Reading Association.

Simmons, D. C., & Kame'enui, E. J. (2003). *Early reading intervention.* Glenview, IL: Pearson, Scott Foresman.

Simpson, D. (1986). *The politics of American English, 1776–1850.* New York: Oxford University Press.

Slater, W. H., Graves, M. F., & Piche, G. L. (1985). Effects of structural organizers on ninth-grade students' comprehension and recall of four patterns of expository text. *Reading Research Quarterly, 20,* 25–32.

Slavin, R. E. (1987). *Cooperative learning: Student teams* (2nd ed.). Washington, DC: National Education Association.

Slavin, R. E., & Cheung, A. (2005). A synthesis of research on language of reading instruction for English language learners. *Review of Educational Research, 75,* 247–284.

Smith, F. (1971). *Understanding reading: A psycholinguistic analysis of reading and learning to read.* New York: Holt, Rinehart & Winston.

Smith, L.E., Borkowski, J. G., & Whitman, T. L. (2008). From reading readiness to reading competence: The role of self-regulation in at-risk children. *Scientific Studies of Reading, 12*(2), 131–152.

Smith, N. B. (2002). *American reading instruction* (Special ed.). Newark, DE: International Reading Association.

Smolkin, L. B., & Donovan, C. A. (2002). "Oh excellent, excellent question!": Developmental differences and comprehension acquisition. In C. C. Block & M. Pressley (Eds.), *Comprehension instruction: Research-based best practice* (pp. 140–157). New York: Guilford.

Snow, C. E. (Ed.). (2004, Winter). English language learners: Boosting academic achievement. *Research Points: Essential Information for Educational Policy, 2,* 1–4. Available at www.aera.net.

Snow, C. E., Burns, M. S., & Griffin, P. (1998). *Preventing reading difficulties in young children.* Washington, DC: National Academies Press.

Spandel, V. (2005). *The 9 rights of every writer: A guide for teachers.* Portsmouth, NH: Heinemann.

Spiegel, D. L. (1981). *Reading for pleasure: Guidelines.* Newark, DE: International Reading Association.

Spiegel, D. L. (1998). Reader response approaches and the growth of readers. *Language Arts, 76,* 41–56.

Stahl, S. A. (1998). Four questions about vocabulary knowledge and reading and some answers. In C. R. Hynd (Ed.), *Learning from text across conceptual domains* (pp. 73–94). Mahwah, NJ: Erlbaum.

Stanovich, K. E. (1991a). Changing models of reading and reading acquisition. In L. Rieben & C. A. Perfetti (Eds.), *Learning to read* (pp. 19–31). Mahwah, NJ: Erlbaum.

Stanovich, K. E. (1991b). Word recognition: Changing perspectives. In R. Barr, M. L. Kamil, P. B. Mosenthal, & P. D. Pearson (Eds.), *Handbook of reading research* (Vol. 2, pp. 418–452). New York: Longman.

Stanovich, K. E. (1992). Speculations on the causes and consequences of individual differences in early reading acquisition. In P. B. Gough, L. C. Ehri, & R. Treiman (Eds.), *Reading acquisition* (pp. 307–342). Mahwah, NJ: Erlbaum.

Stanovich, K. E. (1994). Constructivism in reading education. *Journal of Special Education, 28,* 259–274.

Stauffer, R. G. (1969). *Directing reading maturity as a cognitive process.* New York: Harper & Row.

Steffenson, M. S., Joag-Dev, C., & Anderson, R. C. (1979). A cross-cultural perspective on reading comprehension. *Reading Research Quarterly, 15,* 10–29.

Steiner, S. F. (2001). *Promoting a global community through multicultural children's literature.* Portsmouth, NH: Teacher Ideas Press.

Stephens, D., & Story, J. (2000). *Assessment as inquiry: Learning the hypothesis-test process.* Urbana, IL: National Council of Teachers of English.

Sternberg, R. J. (1987). Most vocabulary is learned from context. In M. G. McKeown & M. E. Curtis (Eds.), *The nature of vocabulary acquisition* (pp. 89–105). Mahwah, NJ: Erlbaum.

Sternberg, R. J., & Grigorenko, E. L. (2004). Intelligence in the classroom. *Theory Into Practice, 43,* 274–280.

Sternberg, R. J., & Spear-Sperling, L. S. (1996). *Teaching for thinking.* Washington, DC: American Psychological Association.

Stiggins, R. J. (1994). *Student-centered classroom assessment.* New York: Merrill.

Stipek, D. (2002). *Motivation to learn: Integrating theory and practice* (4th ed.). Boston: Allyn & Bacon.

Strickland, K., & Strickland, J. (2000). *Making assessment elementary.* Portsmouth, NH: Heinemann.

Sulzby, E., & Teale, W. (1996). Emergent literacy. In R. Barr, M. Kamil, P. B. Mosenthal, & P. D. Pearson (Eds.), *Handbook of reading research* (Vol. 2, pp. 727–758). New York: Longman.

Sum, A., Kirsch, I., & Taggart, R. (2002). *The twin challenges of mediocrity and inequality: Literacy in the U.S. from an international perspective.* Princeton, NJ: Educational Testing Service.

Swift, K. (1993). Try reading workshop in your classroom. *The Reading Teacher, 46,* 366–371.

Taylor, B. M., Hanson, B. E., Justice-Swanson, K., & Watts, S. M. (1997). Helping struggling readers: Linking small-group intervention with cross-age tutoring. *The Reading Teacher, 51,* 196–209.

Taylor, B. M., Pearson, P. D., Clark, K., & Walpole, S. (2000). Effective schools and accomplished teachers: Lessons about primary-grade reading instruction in low-income schools. *Elementary School Journal, 101,* 121–165.

Taylor, B. M., Pearson, P. D., Peterson, D. S., & Rodriguez, M. C. (2003). Reading growth in high-poverty classrooms. *Elementary School Journal, 104,* 3–28.

Taylor, B. M., Pressley, M., & Pearson, P. D. (2002). Research-supported characteristics of schools and teachers that promote reading achievement. In B. M. Taylor & P. D. Pearson (Eds.), *Teaching reading: Effective schools, accomplished teachers* (pp. 361–373). Mahwah, NJ: Erlbaum.

Taylor, B. M., Short, R. A., Frye, B. J., & Shearer, B. A. (1992). Classroom teachers prevent reading failure among low-achieving first-grade children. *The Reading Teacher, 45,* 592–597.

Taylor, B. T., Pearson, P. D., Peterson, D. S., & Rodriguez, M. C. (2003). Reading growth in high-poverty classrooms. *Elementary School Journal, 104,* 3–28.

Taylor, B. T., Pearson, P. D., Peterson, D. S., & Rodriguez, M. C. (2005). The CIERA school change framework. *Reading Research Quarterly, 40,* 40–69.

Temple, C., Nathan, R., Temple, F., & Burris, N. A. (1993). *The beginnings of writing* (3rd ed.). Boston: Allyn & Bacon.

Thomason, T. (1998). *Writer to writer: How to conference young authors.* Norwood, MA: Christopher-Gordon.

Thorndyke, P. (1977). Cognitive structures in comprehension and memory of narrative discourse. *Cognitive Psychology, 9,* 97–110.

Tierney R. J., Carter, M. A., & Desai, L. E. (1991). *Portfolio assessment in the reading-writing classroom.* Norwood, MA: Christopher-Gordon.

Tierney, R. J., & Readence, J. E. (2005). *Reading strategies and practices: A compendium* (6th ed.). Boston: Allyn & Bacon.

Tierney, R. J., & Readence, J. E. (2000). *Reading strategies: A compendium* (5th ed.). Boston: Allyn & Bacon.

Tollefson, J. W. (1995). Introduction: Language policy, power, and inequality. In J. W. Tollefson (Ed.), *Power and inequality in language education.* Cambridge, England: Cambridge University Press.

Tomlinson, C. A. (1999). *The differentiated classroom.* Alexandria, VA: Association for Supervision and Curriculum Development.

Tompkins, G. E. (1996). Becoming an effective teacher of reading. *WSRA Journal, 13*(2), 1–7.

Torgesen, J. K. (1998). Catch them before they fall. *American Educator, 22*(1–2), 32–39.

Treiman, R. (1992). The role of intrasyllabic units in learning to read and spell. In P. B. Gough, L. C. Ehri, & R. Treiman (Eds.), *Reading acquisition* (pp. 65–106). Mahwah, NJ: Erlbaum.

Trelease, J. (1995). *The new read-aloud handbook* (4th ed.). New York: Penguin Books.

U.S. Department of Education. (1995). *Listening to children read aloud.* Washington, DC: Author. Available at http://nces.ed.gov/pubs95/web/95762.asp.

Vacca, R., & Linek, W. M. (1992). Writing to learn. In J. W. Irwin & M. A. Doyle (Eds.), *Reading/writing connections: Learning from research* (pp. 145–159). Newark, DE: International Reading Association.

Vandervelden, M. C., & Siegel, L. S. (1995). Phonological recoding and phoneme awareness in early literacy: A developmental approach. *Reading Research Quarterly, 30,* 854–875.

Vaughan, S. (2005, October). *A three-tier model for preventing and remediating reading difficulties: Response to intervention.* Paper presented at the 3rd Guy Bond Memorial Conference on Reading, Minneapolis, MN.

Vellutino, F. R., Scanlon, D. M. Sipay, E. R., Small, S. G., Pratt, A., Chen, R., & Denckla, M. B. (1996). Cognitive profiles of difficult to remediate and readily remediated poor readers: Early intervention as a vehicle for distinguishing between cognitive and experiential deficits as basic causes of specific reading disability. *Journal of Educational Psychology, 88*(4), 601–638.

von Glaserfeld, E. (1984). An introduction to radical constructivism. In P. Watzlawick (Ed.), *The invented reality* (pp. 17–40). New York: W. W. Norton.

Vygotsky, L. S. (1978). *Mind in society: The development of higher psychological processes.* Cambridge, MA: Harvard University Press.

Walmsley, S. A. (1996, August). Ten ways to improve your theme teaching. *The Instructor,* 54–60.

Walpole, S., & McKenna, M. C. (2007). *Differentiated reading instruction: Strategies for the primary grades.* New York: Guilford Press.

Wanzek, J., & Vaughn, S. (2007). Research-based implications from extensive early reading interventions. *School Psychology Review, 36*(4), 541–561.

Watts, S. M., & Graves, M. F. (1997). Fostering middle school students' understanding of challenging texts. *Middle School Journal, 29*(1), 45–51.

Werderich, D. E. (2002). Individualized responses: Using journal letters as a vehicle for differentiated reading instruction. *Journal of Adolescent and Adult Literacy, 45*(8), 746–754.

Wertsch, J. V. (1998). *Mind as action.* New York: Oxford University Press.

Wharton-McDonald, R., Pressley, M., & Hampston, J. M. (1998). Literacy instruction in nine first-grade classrooms: Teacher characteristics and student achievement. *Elementary School Journal, 99,* 101–128.

White, T. G., Graves, M. F., & Slater, W. H. (1990). Growth of reading vocabulary in diverse elementary schools: Decoding and word meaning. *Journal of Educational Psychology, 82*(2), 281–290.

White, T. G., & Kim, J. S. (2008). Teacher and parent scaffolding of voluntary summer reading. *The Reading Teacher, 62,* 116–125.

White, T. G., Slater, W. H., & Graves, M. F. (1989). Yes/no method of vocabulary assessment: Valid for whom and useful for what? In S. McCormick & V. Zutel (Eds.), *Cognitive and social perspectives for literacy research and instruction.* Chicago: National Reading Conference.

White, T. G., Sowell, J., & Yanagihara, A. (1989). Teaching elementary students to use word-part clues. *The Reading Teacher, 44,* 302–307.

Whitehead, A. N. (1929). *The aims of education and other essays.* New York: Macmillan.

Whitehurst, G. J., Arnold, D. S., Epstein, J. N., Angell, A. L., Smith, M., & Fischel, J. E. (1994). A picture book reading intervention in day care and home for children from low-income families. *Developmental Psychology, 30,* 697–699.

Wiencek, J. E. (1996). Planning, initiating, and sustaining literature discussion groups: The teacher's role. In L. B. Gambrell & J. F. Almasi (Eds.), *Lively discussions! Fostering engaged reading* (pp. 208–223). Newark, DE: International Reading Association.

Wigfield, A., & Eccles, J. S. (2002). *Development of achievement motivation.* San Diego, CA: Academic Press.

Wiggins, G., & McTighe, J. (1998). *The understanding by design handbook.* Alexandria, VA: Association for Supervision and Curriculum Development.

Wiggins, G. P. (1993). *Assessing student performance.* San Francisco: Jossey-Bass.

Wilkinson, G. S. (1995). *Wide-range achievement test 3.* Wilmington, DE: Jastak.

Willingham, D. T. (2006a). How knowledge helps: It speeds and strengthens reading comprehension, learning and thinking. *American Educator, 30*(1), 30–37.

Willingham, D. T. (2006b). The usefulness of brief instruction in reading comprehension strategies. *American Educator, 31*(Winter), 39–45.

Winebrenner, S. (1992, September). Meeting the needs of your high-ability students. *Instructor,* 60–63.

Wirt, J., Choy, S., Rooney, P., Hussar, W., Kridl, B., & Livingston, A. (2005). *The conditions of education 2005.* Washington, DC: U.S. Department of Education.

Wise, B. W. (1992). Whole words and decoding for short-term learning: Comparisons on a "talking-computer" system. *Child Psychology, 54,* 147–167.

Wise, B. W., Olson, R. K., & Trieman, R. (1990). Subsyllabic units in computerized reading instruction: Onset-rime versus postvowel segmentation. *Journal of Experimental Child Psychology, 49,* 1–19.

Wiske, M. S. (Ed.). (1998). *Teaching for understanding: Linking research with practice.* San Francisco: Jossey-Bass.

Wittrock, M. (1986). Students' thought processes. In M. C. Wittrock (Ed.), *Handbook of research on teaching* (3rd ed., pp. 297–314). New York: Macmillan.

Wollman-Bonilla, J. E. (2001). Can first-grade writers demonstrate audience awareness? *Reading Research Quarterly, 36*(2), 184–201

Wollman-Bonilla, J. E., & Werchadlo, B. (1995). Literature response journals in a first-grade classroom. *Language Arts, 72*(8), 562–570.

Wood, D. J., Bruner, J. S., & Ross, G. (1976). The role of tutoring in problem-solving. *Journal of Child Psychology and Psychiatry, 17*(2), 89–100.

Wood, K. D., Lapp, D., & Flood, J. (1992). *Guiding readers through text: A review of study guides.* Newark, DE: International Reading Association.

Wood, K. D., & Mateja, J. A. (1983). Adapting secondary-level strategies for use in elementary classrooms. *The Reading Teacher, 36,* 492–496.

Woodcock, R. W., McGrew, K. S., & Mather, N. (2001). *Woodcock-Johnson III tests of achievement.* Itasca, IL: Riverside Publishing.

Wylie, R. E., & Durrell, D. D. (1970). Teaching vowels through phonograms. *Elementary English, 47,* 787–791.

Yokota, J. (Ed.). (2001). *Kaleidoscope: A multicultural booklist for grades K–8* (2nd ed.). Urbana, IL: National Council of Teachers of English.

Yopp, H. (1995). A test for assessing phonemic awareness in young children. *The Reading Teacher, 49*(1), 20–29.

Young, T. A., & Vardell, S. (1993). Weaving readers theatre and nonfiction into the curriculum. *The Reading Teacher, 46,* 396–406.

Zevenbergen, A. A., & Whitehurst, G. J. (2004). Dialogic reading: A shared picture book reading intervention for preschoolers. In A. V. Kleeck, S. A. Stahl, & E. B. Bauer (Eds.), *On reading books to children: Parents and teachers* (pp. 177–200). Mahwah, NJ: Erlbaum.

Author and Title Index

Subject Index

reader response approaches, 19, 358–369

reading comprehension strategies, 324–348

responding to literature, 358–359

rich array of reading material, 353–354

silent reading, 442

time management and, 56

Individual differences, 122–124

environmental causes, 122–123

learning disabilities, 122

Matthew Effect and, 123–124

Individually guided instruction, 124–125

Individual words, 260–266

basic vocabulary, 258, 260–261

Inert knowledge, 39

Inference, in reading comprehension strategy, 329–330

Inflection, for struggling readers, 241

Inflectional suffixes, 190, 191, 269

Inflections, defined, 411

Informal reading inventory (IRI), 92, 244, 245

Informal writing, 381–397

imaginative writing, 394–397

writing to communicate, 389–394

writing to learn and understand, 382–389

Informational texts, 30, 429–430

Initial blending, 210

Inquiry, assessment as, 79, 85–109

collecting evidence, 93–103

framing problems, 86–88

interpretation, 106–107

plan of action, 88–93

reporting and decision making, 107–109

Inspiration, 263

Instruction, practice versus, 31–32

Instructional charts, 54, 62

Instructional design of interventions, 139–141

Instructional principles, 26–40

constructivist perspective, 33–40, 409

for English language learners (ELLs), 417–435

highly effective teachers and schools, 27–28

sociocultural perspective, 33–40

traditional, 28–33

Instructional routines

balanced strategies instruction model, 267

constructivist and sociocultural theories in, 409

directed reading-thinking activity (DR-TA), 287

fluency-oriented reading instruction (FORI), 236

Fry Readability Formula, 247

high-frequency words, 201

informal reading inventory, 245

interactive oral reading, 256

letter puppets, 161

literature circles, 361

making inferences, 330

measuring reading rate and accuracy, 239

new words representing known concepts, 262

new words representing new concepts, 263

note taking, 383

partner reading, 232

prereading activity, 288

questioning ability of students, 345–346

repeated reading, 228

response journals, 386

semantic feature analysis, 264–265

semantic mapping, 264

shared reading experience in sixth grade ESL class, 419

summarizing part of a selection, 423

tape-assisted repeated reading, 231

traditional instructional principles, 408

vowel patterns, 208

writing imaginative mathematics scenarios and questions, 394

writing poems around a theme, 397

Integrative approach, 81

cognitive-constructivist, 5–6

strategy, 140

Intensive instruction, 274–275

Interactive oral reading, 255–257

Interactive read-alouds, 164

Interactive Reading Assessment System (IRAS), 90

Interactive Reading Assessment System–Revised (IRAS-R), 92, 244–245, 466–525

Interest building, in teaching strategy, 337–339

Interests, assessing student, 53

International Association for the Evaluation of Educational Achievement (IEA), 13, 14

International Reading Association (IRA), 16, 212

Internet, 176

Interpretation, in assessment process, 106–107

Interviewing, 95–96

Intonation, for struggling readers, 241

Invented spelling, 158–159, 161–162

Iowa Test of Basic Skills (ITBS), 89

Joke books, 241

Journals, 172–173, 179–180, 310, 385–389, 442–443

dialogue, 366, 388–389

double-entry, 387–388

guidelines for writing, 389

learning logs, 387, 388

reading logs, 386–387

response journal, 386

Judicious review, 140–141

Key words, 214

Kidspiration, 263

Kindergarten, 91, 132–133, 156, 166, 176–180, 230, 256

Knowledge

background, 3, 186, 249–250, 288

gained in home culture, 420–421

inert, 39

language, 414–415

about print, 159–161, 188–193

prior, 21–22, 329

text-specific, 288–289

about text structure, 164–165

about word structure, 154–156

Knowledge development, 444

Known concepts, 258, 262

Known words

clarifying and enriching meanings of, 259, 262–266

learning to read, 258, 261–262

K-W-L, 180, 302, 303

Language, diversity in, 249

Language-experience approach, 173

Language-rich classroom, 165–166

Large-group participation, 70

in teaching strategy, 338–339

Learned helplessness, 60

Learning centers, 149–151, 172

Learning disabilities, 122

Learning logs, 387, 388

LeBlanc, Jenna (teacher), 146–151

Lesson plans, 539–579

comprehension lessons, 554–579

introduction, 539–540

vocabulary lessons, 540–553

Letter cards, 204, 211

Letter puppets, 161

Letters, writing, 390, 391, 392

Letter-sound correspondences

blending, 209

common grammatical endings, 203

consonant blends, 202, 203

consonant digraphs, 202, 203, 204

consonants, 202–205

diphthongs, 203, 208

emergent literacy, 171

long vowels, 203, 207–209

multisyllable words, 192

Reader
    matching purpose with text, 284–285
    matching with text, 18, 243–249
    in scaffolding, 280–281
Reader response approaches, 358–369
    book clubs and book clubs *plus*,
        362–365, 366–368
    independent reading and, 19,
        358–369
    literature circles, 37–38, 359–362,
        366–368
    postreading activities, 359
    reader-response theory, 10–11,
        358–369
    reading workshop, 365–368
    responding to literature, 358–359
Reader-response theory, 10–11, 358–369
Readers theater, 232–233, 291
Reading
    aloud, 175, 257, 290–291, 319
    choral, 232, 291
    classroom opportunities for, 167–169
    in content areas, 319–323
    guided comprehension, 291–292
    known words, 258, 261–262
    listening versus, 186–187
    oral, 102, 109–110, 128, 238–240,
        255–257, 291
    positive reading-writing
        environment, 374–376
    readers theater, 232–233, 291
    reading–writing connection, 374
    shared, 149, 173
    silent, 56, 290–291, 314, 442
Reading aloud, 175, 257, 290–291, 319
Reading center, 149
Reading comprehension. *See also*
        Reading comprehension
        strategies
    AERA recommendations for, 434
    in differentiated instruction, 129–130
    for emergent readers, 163–164
    as goal of word study instruction,
        197
    procedures for expository texts,
        302–304
    and responding to narratives,
        300–302
    suggesting strategies for, 290
Reading comprehension strategies,
        324–348
    for all types of text, 304–306
    characteristics, 326–328
    determining what is important,
        330–332
    for expository texts, 302–304
    graphic information, 332
    inferences, 329–330
    key strategies, 328–335
    lesson plans, 554–579

in literacy curriculum, 19
metacognition, 6–7, 216, 333–334
for narratives, 300–302
powerful approach to teaching,
    336–342
as prereading activity, 290
purpose for reading, 328
questions, 329
summarizing, 332
teaching, 19
using prior knowledge, 329
Reading Corner, 392
Reading Counts, 67
Reading First, 16–17, 44, 78, 81, 225
Reading guides, 302–304
Reading instruction, 24–45
    basal readers, 41–43
    brief history of, 40–44
    fostering achievement in English
        language learners, 408
    grouping students for, 70–72
    second-language. *See* Second-
        language reading instruction
    traditional instructional principles,
        408
Reading logs, 386–387
Reading process
    cognitive-constructivist view of
        reading, 2–11
    cognitive psychology and, 2–3, 195
    constructivism in, 5–6
    developmental phases, 194, 224, 227,
        250
    processes involved in reading
        words, 195–196
    stages of reading development, 194,
        224, 227, 250
    subprocesses, 10
    and writing, 374–376
Reading proficiency, 11–16
    assessment of, 244–245
    diversity in, 250
    literacy for today and tomorrow,
        15–16
    response to current criticisms, 12–15
Reading purpose, 284–285
    establishing, 328
    function of, 284
    improving fluency, 248–249
    matching selection with reader,
        284–285
    matching with text and reader,
        284–285
Reading Recovery, 141, 220, 369
Reading to children/students, 290–291
Reading workshop, 365–368
Reading–writing connection, 374
Reading-writing environment, 374–376
    intellectual climate, 375
    physical environment, 375–376

Read Naturally, 212
Read Naturally Masters Edition,
    237–238
Read-write cycle model, 96, 100–101,
    526–538
ReadWriteThink website, 334
Reciprocal teaching, 333, 342–346
    development of, 342–343
    formal studies, 343–344
    stages of, 344
Recordings, 175–176
Reliability, 113
Repeated reading, 226–229
    automaticity in, 226–227
    original method, 226–228, 229
    simultaneous, 228–229
    tape-assisted, 230–231
Report cards, 107–108
Reports, writing, 391–394
Response journals, 386
Response to Intervention (RTI), 78, 81,
    124, 126–127, 138–139
Reteaching, as postreading activity,
    298
Reviewing
    in assessment process, 96
    constructivism and, 37–38
Revising, 377, 380
Rewards, 67
Rimes
    in decoding by analogy, 215
    defined, 210
    letter-sound correspondences,
        210–213, 219
    onset/rime practice, 214, 219
Roots Project, 81–85, 104
Root words, 190
Rosetta Stone technique, 424–425
Rubric systems, 97–99
    read-write-cycle model, 96, 100–101

Scaffolded reading experience (SRE),
    286–299
    background and rationale, 286–287
    during-reading activities, 290–293
    for English language learners
        (ELLs), 298
    framework, 287
    postreading activities, 293–299,
        384
    prereading activities, 287–290
Scaffolding, 36–37, 83, 278–307
    in assessment process, 87–88
    comprehension of text, 19
    directed reading activity (DRA),
        285–286
    directed reading-thinking activity
        (DR-TA), 286, 287
    diversity and, 307
    guided reading, 39, 299

books about words and word games, 272
"chunking," 211, 213, 216
established, 254
high-frequency, 200, 201
key, 214
known, 258, 261–262
multisyllabic, 192, 213
new. *See* New words
target, 266
teaching individual, 257–266
unknown, 254, 258–259, 262
Word analysis, 266
Word banks, 199
Word building activities, letter-sound correspondences, 209–210, 211, 214
Word consciousness, 271–275
expressive instruction, 274–275
intensive instruction, 274–275
modeling adept diction, 272–274
Word detectives, 215
Word families, 190
Word games, 272
Word identification, 159–162
Word knowledge
acquainted level, 254
established level, 254
unknown level, 254, 262, 263
Word-learning tasks and strategies, 258–259, 266–271
context clues, 267, 268
dictionary and, 269–271
word parts, 268–269
Word parts, 268–269
Word recognition, 184–220
AERA recommendations for, 434

alphabetic principle, 161–162
automatic, 187–188
coaching, 216–218
emergent literacy, 172
errors in, 228
learning to read words, 193–196
in listening, 186–187
makeup of spoken/written English, 188–190
phonics instruction, 18, 193, 202
printed words in, 186–188, 192–193
reading a lot for, 213–216, 218–219
in reading process, 4, 9
skills in, 18
structure of spoken and printed words, 188–193
word study instruction, 196–218
Words correct per minute (WCPM), 238
Word sorts
long vowel sounds, 207–209
short vowel sounds, 206–207
Word structure, emergent knowledge about, 154–156
Word study instruction, 196–218
basic reading vocabulary, 197–202
contextual reading in, 213–218
diversity and, 219–220
general principles, 196–197
larger units in words, 210–213
letter-sound correspondences, 202–210
technology in, 212
word study, defined, 196
Word walls, 200–202
Work samples, in assessment process, 96–97

Writing, 376–402, 446. *See also* Journals
alphabetic principle in, 161–162
classroom opportunities for, 172–175
to communicate, 389–394
diversity and, 401–402
emergent literacy, 172–175
functional linguistics approach to, 379–381
genre approach to, 379–381
imaginative, 394–397
informal, 381–397
positive reading-writing environment, 374–376
as postreading activity, 295
process approach to, 376–379
and reading process, 374–376
reading–writing connection, 374
responding to student, 399–400
shared, 173
stages of, 377–378
writing workshop, 397–399
Writing center, 149, 205
Writing for Sounds activity, 205
Writing system, 197
Writing workshop, 397–399
key components, 398
mini-lessons, 399

Yopp-Singer Test of Phoneme Segmentation, 92–93

Zone of proximal development, 38–39